CW01033551

THE CROSS GOES N   ...11

Processes of Conversion in Northern Europe, AD 300–1300

Rune stone U 489, Morby, Lagga parish, Uppland, raised by
the mother Gullög who had a bridge made for her daughter
Gillög's soul (after *Upplands runinskrifter*)

THE CROSS GOES NORTH

Processes of Conversion in Northern Europe, AD 300-1300

Edited by
Martin Carver

THE BOYDELL PRESS

First published 2003
York Medieval Press
Reprinted in hardback 2004

Reprinted in paperback 2005
The Boydell Press, Woodbridge

Transferred to digital printing

ISBN 978-1-90315-311-6 hardback
ISBN 978-1-84383-125-9 paperback

The Boydell Press is an imprint of Boydell & Brewer Ltd
PO Box 9, Woodbridge, Suffolk IP12 3DF, UK
and of Boydell & Brewer Inc.
668 Mt Hope Avenue, Rochester, NY 14620, USA
website: www.boydellandbrewer.com

*The first printing of this book was made possible by a gift to the University of
Cambridge in memory of Dorothea Coke, Skjaeret, 1951*

A catalogue record for this book is available
from the British Library

This publication is printed on acid-free paper

Contents

Plates

Figures

Part I

Processes of Conversion

1

Introduction: Northern Europeans Negotiate their Future

MARTIN CARVER

This book was born from a conference held in July 2000 to mark the beginning of the third Christian millennium, opened by David Hope, Archbishop of York. In accordance with the spirit and energy of early church councils, 55 papers were heard in five days and each evening our indefatigable delegates also attended a party and a public lecture on 'Heritage and the Holy Land today'.[1] It was an occasion of incomparable enrichment, which brought to light the art and culture of early people of every degree and condition and their preoccupation with fundamental questions about what life is for, and how it should be lived.

Given the venue, the City of York, and the interests of its Department of Archaeology, it is not surprising that in the event a majority of the papers focussed on the experience of northern Europe in the first millennium AD, and this has been the basis of their selection for publication. This book surveys episodes of conversion from the Dingle Peninsula to Estonia and from the Alps to Lapland, and ranges in time from Roman Britain and Gaul in the third and fourth centuries to the conversion of peoples in the Baltic area a thousand years later. In Europe, the cross went north, and also east, as the centuries unrolled and this basic narrative provides the structure of the book. We begin in the Celtic lands, proceed to England and then to the Rhineland and Scandinavia, ending in Estonia where the principal conversion initiative took place in the thirteenth century.

However, to read the conversion story as a narrative does no justice to the complexity of the process, as our authors show. History is written by those who have won power and represent what is orthodox, so the surviving documents

---

[1] The four public lectures were held in the Tempest Anderson Hall and attended each night by up to 300 people. They were: *Excavations on the Herodian Temple Mount 1994–6* (Dr Ronny Reich, Haifa University), *The Church of the Holy Sepulchre in Jerusalem: recent investigations and new discoveries* (Prof. Martin Biddle, Hertford College, Oxford); *The Conservation of the Al-Aqsa Mosque and the Dome of the Rock* (Dr Isam Awwad, Restoration Committee of the Dome of the Rock); *Byzantine Churches and Monasteries of Jordan* (Dr Konstantinos Politis, British Museum).

extol the achievements of individual missionaries, and emphasise their success. They can also encourage us to believe that the adoption of Christianity, with a hierarchy of bishops and a network of monasteries and churches was somehow irresistible. This perspective paints a picture in which some of the converted got the message early, some later; others did not wholly understand it and mixed it with previous beliefs, but all eventually entered the fold and became as one.

But, as the later history of Christianity shows, wherever the human mind is active diversity is endemic. In the conversion period it seems highly probable that the mood was experimental and that the adaptation of practice if not of doctrine was regularly exercised.[2] Our authors show us the under-side of the process, more secret and more subtle, and ultimately more significant, by turning the spotlight from the missionaries onto the converted, and exploring their local situations and motives. What were the reactions of northern peoples to the Christian message? Why would they wish to adopt its structures and its strictures for the sake of its alliances? In what way did they adapt the Christian ethos and infrastructure to suit the social structure and natural environment of their own community? How did conversion effect the status of farmers, of smiths, of princes and of women? Was society wholly changed, or only in marginal matters of devotion and superstition?

These are the questions we address in this book, using the techniques of different disciplines and the experience of different parts of Europe. Some answers come from astute re-readings of the texts alone, but most are owed to a combination of history, art history and archaeology working together. Material culture, like texts, is way of expressing ideas, but unlike early texts, early material culture occurs in a hierarchy of investment from the casual to the monumental. Material culture makes use of allusion to earlier times and other peoples; it sometimes proclaims these earlier messages, sometimes imitates them, sometimes opposes them, sometimes conceals them. The interpretation of material culture is therefore no more straightforward than that of texts. However, even if it is not clear exactly what a burial or a standing stone stela might mean, we can be sure that it meant something, and that it is through material culture that the local, the unorthodox, the marginalised and the disempowered could find their voice. Our task is to interpret these signs of individual ideology, and our book is thus concerned less with the narrative of conversion than with its processes. Many of our chapters lift the blanket of 'Christianisation' to reveal an exciting, querulous world of independent thinking and dissent.

---

[2] Cf Patrick Wormald 'Bede, Beowulf and the conversion of the Anglo-Saxon aristocracy' in R.T. Farrell (ed.) *Bede and Anglo-Saxon England* (Oxford 1978): 68: 'There have been about as many 'conversions of Christianity' as there have been societies in receipt of the faith.' For recent general reviews of the Christian conversion of Europe, see Peter Brown *The Rise of Western Christendom* (Blackwell 1996); Richard Fletcher *The Conversion of Europe. From Paganism to Christianity 371–1386 AD* (Harper Collins 1997); Pluskowski, A.G. (ed.) *Early Medieval Religion: Archaeological Review from Cambridge 17: 2.* (Bar Hill: Victoire Press 2000). For a stimulating and wide-ranging essay on the processes of conversion in England, see N.J. Higham *The Convert Kings. Power and religious affiliation in early Anglo-Saxon England* (Manchester UP 1997), especially Chapter 1.

The two first papers set out the new agenda. Urbanczyk, speaking with an anthropological voice, tabulates the incentives and consequences of conversion, stressing the variety of prescriptions needed to match the improvements in social control that could be achieved when Christianisation had taken hold. Pluskowski and Patrick then comprehensively review the evidence for this variety, ranging across Europe and through the whole millennium that gives us our frame. The variety of documented thinking which was provoked in the target communities was formidable, and was not confined to a supposed inaugural period of confusion. It could even survive the establishment of the institutionalised religion itself, among the Christian Franks, for example, where 'pagan culture lived on in the habits and lifestyle of the Frankish monarchy and aristocracy'. These variations do not necessarily indicate deviant doctrines, or heresies; and heresy is not necessarily reflected in material culture.[3] Provided orthodoxy is not successfully enforced, never an easy thing to do, it should be legitimate to regard local variations of practice as real variations in thinking and belief. Pluskowski and Patrick's paper gives increased confidence that it is local ideological experiments of this kind that are being signalled by the parade of diverse and intriguing archaeological cultures collected by our authors.

In the other three parts of the book we travel through Europe, noting how texts, art and archaeology illuminate the political and philosophical debates that were taking place in public or private, in the hall or at the grave-side, in this most intellectually vivid of times. Three aspects of the research collected in this volume seem to point the way to new horizons and make it especially worthy of the reader's attention: the ideological variety that was possible within communities, the role of women in the management of ideology, before, during and after conversion, and the way that ideology and its infrastructure were expressed by the landscape itself. These new aspects of the conversion process are offered in the main by archaeological reasoning which, if it has no special claim to the truth, is no less entitled to an opinion. The diverse material culture that we shall see in burial, shrines, brooches and landscapes represents deliberate investment. It rarely falls into easily labelled orders, such as 'pagan', 'monastic', 'episcopal' or 'secular', but that does not mean that people meant nothing by it – only that it is often nothing that we immediately recognise.

Mapping Ideological Variety

At one level the northward journey of the symbol of the cross on brooches and sculpture can be read as the track of conversion led by missionaries (Müller-Wille), who came only from the south and west, as opposed to the eastern church (Beskow). But at another, the diverse character of the symbols and their

---

[3] However, see pioneering work by William H.C. Frend *The Archaeology of Early Christianity* (Chapman 1996), e.g. 230.

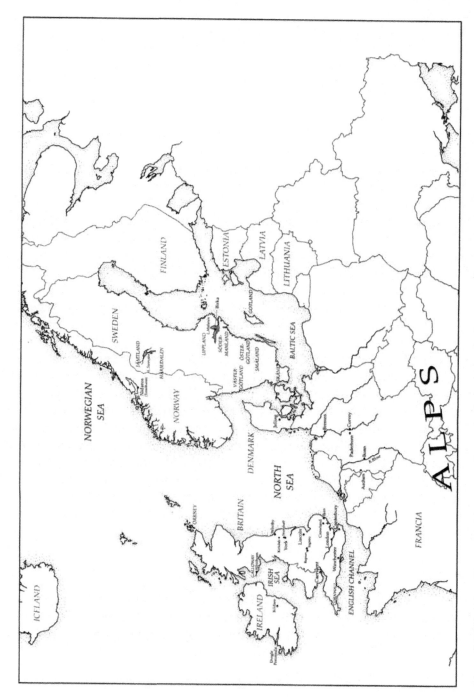

Figure 1.1 Northern Europe in the Conversion period, showing the location of some of the places mentioned in the book

context of use shows that creative decisions were being made: 'As all the Christian visual motifs, whether as crosses or on bracteates, originate from the Mediterranean area, we are observing without doubt a very conscious choice on the part of peoples living north of the Alps' (Bierbrauer). If material culture signifies ideology, the ideological map of Europe in the conversion period is one of extraordinary variety. Here we find examples of contemporary groups living side by side, but proclaiming their difference. We also find examples of consecutive generations living in the same place who experienced a sequence of re-conversions, each with a different political alignment.

Pagans lived alongside Christians in Roman Britain (Frend), but the Christians were not homogenous in their practice. Some were signalled by their gypsum burials (Sparey-Green), others by votive deposits, and others by their investment in villas (Petts). In north Roman Gaul it was the use of relics that created a new religious landscape and a local identity. The origins and source of relics were selected local graves which had an iconic value for the new breakaway ideological groups: 'Family bodies in their graves signify the ultimate family heirloom and martyrs' graves and bodies serve the same role at community level, representing the collective memory of the self-defining group' (Pearce). Further north in the fifth and sixth centuries, Germanic peoples not immediately threatened by the Christian empire, but acutely aware of it, expressed their view on the future of Europe on their brooches. Ideological difference was proclaimed in animal art, the one narrative (and imperial), the other anti-narrative (and anti-imperial) (Wicker).

As the conversion process took hold, the sub-kingdoms and estates of post-imperial Europe signalled their diverse aspirations inside their communities and between them. Ó Carragáin presents an example from western Ireland, where many early Christian territories in Ireland were monastic, marked by stone crosses, while others were indicated rather by a distribution of shrines. These different kinds of ecclesiastical territories were negotiating for space with each other throughout the seventh–ninth centuries. A primary weapon in the competition was appeal to Rome, 'the ultimate authority', which had what Neuman de Vegvar calls the 'validating power of the past'. In the case of Kildare this appeal was in the form of allusions to Rome in the architecture of its seventh-century church.

In fifth-sixth-century England, pagan Saxon and Christian British communities seem to have co-existed either side of the vale of Pickering in Yorkshire, and it was the British side of the valley that largely acquired the monasteries of the converted English in the seventh century (Rahtz and Watts). Richards gives us a fine example of ideological diversity for a later period: in late ninth century Derbyshire, two factions of the same Viking army raised their mortuary banners 4km apart; at Repton the men of Halfdan seem to have appropriated the Mercian royal burial ground; while at Heath Wood, followers of Guthrum 'preferred traditional pagan values', memorialising their companions as cremations under mounds. Likewise, Barrett offers us a vivid and convincing glimpse of the lively

archipelago of Orkney in the tenth century; a small world this, but not too small
for divisions, with rival potentates camped under opposing ideological banners
in temporary equilibrium.

Some of these divisions were explicitly ethnic. In Jämtland, central Sweden, the
pre-Christian Germanic and Saami peoples at first shared a common spiritual
system using the hall (*hov*) as the ritual centre. By the eleventh century, coincident
with an unprecedented economic expansion, the Germanic sector had separated
or redefined itself as Christian, and aligned with Christian nations to the west
and south, while the Saami redefined themselves as pagan and independent. But
they did not thereby become marginal, as their excavated hoards show: 'The
Saami élite were members of extensive exchange-networks during the Early
Middle Ages. But for them, there were advantages in not becoming Christian'
(Welinder). In Estonia, following enforced Christianisation by German aristocrats
in the thirteenth century, three different ideological groups co-existed: Christian,
local non-Christian and semi-Christian. The Christian later fragmented into
Catholic and Lutheran. The basic division was between Germanic aristocracy and
Estonian serfs: 'This system of apartheid and ethnosocial segregation lasted until
the early nineteenth century when serfdom was abolished.' Cremation continued
in Estonia until the sixteenth century and graveyard feasts continue today. This
late survival of a confronted system provides a source of unusual value, showing
us something of the complex relations with the other world that were experienced by individual pagans. Where Christianity was merely the concomitant
of an invading power, only the most important of the local gods was deemed
to have been toppled at the same time as the indigenous human lords. Minor
deities and their functions survived, just as the less important people had survived. Christianity could not bring sustenance to these people until they had been
set free; until then lakes, trees and rocks provided spiritual support and seemed
nearer to life's ultimate purpose (Valk).

In many places conversion happened several times, each representing not
only an updated spiritual model but a different political alignment. Britain was
visited by Christianity from the continent in the third century and again in the
fifth century without any apparent continuity between them (Frend). During
the seventh century England was evangelised from Rome and Ireland, and for
all the modern tendency to play down the political differences of the western
and southern churches,[4] it would be surprising if there were no differences
in thinking; the Synod of Whitby, convened to consider them, should have had
a pivotal role in the political alignment of England (Barnwell, Butler and
Dunn). Scotland received Christian prescriptions from north Britain in the fifth
century, Ireland in the sixth century and England in the eighth. The Viking

---

[4] Martin Carver 'Why that, why there, why then? The politics of early medieval monumentality',
in A. Macgregor and H. Hamerow (eds) *Image and Power in Early Medieval British Archaeology:
Essays in honour of Rosemary Cramp* (Oxbow: Oxford): 1–22.

incursions provoked further Christian adaptations (Rahtz and Watts; Barrett, Richards).[5]

This was not merely traditional insular non-conformity, for the conversion process was no more homogenous on the Continent. At Bonn Cathedral, Roman imperial Christianity made an appearance in the third–fourth century and then disappeared for 150 years, to be reborn and re-branded under Frankish authority (Keller). The establishment of dated sequences at sites like the cathedral excavations in Bonn is notoriously difficult;[6] but Keller shows that Christian investment at Bonn was not continuously maintained, but was enhanced or re-invented at intervals from its beginnings in the third, sixth, eighth, and eleventh centuries. These operations of renewal are not necessarily due to the demands of building repair; more decisive would be the impetus of a new power or a new people that revises and reconfigures the ideology. 'Continuity' of Christian worship is thus only applicable in a general sense: the detail shows a discontinuous sequence of restless change.

These examples show that different reactions to the Christian idea were endemic and were practised on the ground. This is not to dismiss the intellectual impact of the gospel message, but serves to emphasise how people struggled to adapt it to their world-view. Important factors would have been the pre-existing behavioural ethos of the area, the attitude of the aristocracy to tax and centralisation, and the diplomatic exigencies of the day. As more control was achieved in Europe, variety could be less easily expressed and tolerated. Thus later conversions may have been more stringent in their application. Alcuin of York was involved with the missions which accompanied Charlemagne's conquests, where political absorption left little room for religious manoeuvre (Rambridge).

The Spiritual Authority of Women

The role of women in adapting and managing conversion emerges as a major theme in this book. In the fifth century, native Roman women living in the pre-Alps were among the first people to signal Christian affiliation, using dove and peacock brooches (Bierbrauer). Their Scandinavian contemporaries further north used bracteates to signal pagan affiliation in the face of Christian missions (Wicker). In England, Anglo-Saxon 'cunning women' had control of burial, a responsibility which is likely to have survived conversion (Geake). After conversion, Anglo-Saxon women wore objects of Christian instead of pagan symbolism, suggesting to Yorke 'that the custom was considered to be sufficiently important

---

[5] See Martin Carver 'Conversion and politics on the eastern seaboard of Britain: some archaeological indicators', in B.E. Crawford (ed.) *Conversion and Christianity in the North Sea World* (St Andrews, 1998): 1–40.

[6] For two pivotal examples see C. Bonnet *Les fouilles de l'ancien groupe épiscopal de Genève (1976–1993)* (Genève, 1993) and A.D. Philips and B. Heywood *From Roman Basilica to Norman Minster. Excavations at York Minster* Vol. 1 (Royal Commission on Historical Monuments, London, 1996).

to be adapted to the new religion'. The political acumen of Raedwald's queen recorded by Bede shows that England had a tradition of female guidance in matters of policy and belief which was active in early seventh century East Anglia.[7] By the end of the seventh century, 'widowed queens and princesses became the religious specialists of the royal houses' (Yorke). Women continued to influence the ideological posture of the English kingdom up to the 10th century reform, mainly through their sex-appeal according to Karkov. Women were seen as primary religious authorities in tenth-century Denmark, a status celebrated in wagon burial, and in eleventh-century Sweden, where they were important sponsors of runestones (Staeker). The spiritual authority of women is advanced here as an ancestral role which survived conversion and only turned sour after the church became institutionalised in the twelfth century (Gräslund).

Converting the Landscape

The runestones carried their own message both in the form of their inscriptions and iconography, and in the way they were distributed on the ground. The landscape, composed of monuments, burial grounds and settlements, is itself a document expressive of the deployment of power and organisation of ideological space. Some of the earliest Christian geographies made use of prehistoric burial mounds (Knight, Meaney), referring to or claiming the existing ritual spaces.[8] In Lincolnshire, a stretch of the River Witham used for votive deposits since the Bronze Age was given into the keeping of early monasteries which presided over continued votive deposition until the fourteenth century. 'Rather than destroying individual artefacts and structures belonging to the indigenous ideologies, the success of the Christian church in the seventh century lay in its concern to appropriate and 'convert' them to serve the causes of the new religion' (Stocker and Everson). In Cornwall, areas of early arable (now mapped through the new technique of Historic Landscape Characterisation) were laid out as part of Christianisation in the fifth–seventh century, each with its central monastery. In a later phase, ninth–tenth century, numerous churches of lesser status were founded in association with small lordships (Turner). In Ireland, the ecclesiastical estates mapped on the ground also seem to belong to a second phase of Christianisation in the eighth–ninth century, and denote institutional competition: 'The hundred years from AD 750 to 850 was the major period of territorial demarcation between various churches.' By the later ninth century this process was complete and a period of relative stability for the Irish church began (Ó Carragáin).

---

[7] Bede, *A History of the English Church and People*. Raedwald's unnamed queen was a source for his decision to mitigate the commitment of his conversion by worshipping Christ with other gods in his temple at Rendlesham (II, 15). On another occasion she advised him against the murder of Edwin, the refugee prince of Northumbria, as unworthy and dishonourable (II, 12).

[8] The conversion of individual holy places is a process that was still better documented in the conversion to Islam. See Martin Carver 'Transitions to Islam', in N. Christie and S. Loseby (eds) *Towns in Transition* (Scolar 1996): 184–212.

In the ninth–tenth century stone monuments were used as the boundary markers of the ecclesiastical estates in western Ireland (Ó Carragáin), in south-west Scotland (Crowe) and Cornwall (Turner). Sculpture thus provides one of the most powerful markers of the changing landscape. In early Britain the inscribed stones of the fifth–seventh centuries may already have marked earlier territories or vistas yet to be defined. The stones were splendid with gilded letters and coloured backgrounds, the inscriptions more iconic than literal (Okasha). Highlighting personal names of the famous dead, they were analogous to monumental tombs (Higgitt). In the seventh–ninth century, the new generation of ornamental stelae, 'many brightly coloured with paint and inset with paste glass and metal', carried iconographical scenes which were rich in metaphor and learned allusions – 'sacraments in stone' celebrating a privileged link with God (Hawkes).

Trajectories of Conversion

Several authors can discern distinct stages in the conversion process. Birkeli's three phases, *infiltration, mission* and *institution*, are developed by Lager, who notes that different phases can be in progress in contemporary parts of the same land. Mission and institution are certainly key stages, but it may be that between them lies an even more interesting stage of *adaptation*, where Christianity is being mapped on to the pre-existing social structure. The distribution of rune-stones seems to signal this stage in Sweden (Lager), except in Svealand where the number of runestones increases after institutionalised Christianity has arrived (in the eleventh century). Lager attributes this to influence from Britain: 'It seems reasonable to assume that the Christians that came to Sweden were aware of the Anglo-Scandinavian stone-crosses in the British Isles and that they recognised that the runestones were comparable with these as expressions of Christian faith.' But the Anglo-Scandinavian crosses can be interpreted as indicating a switch from an institutionalised to a privatised ecclesiastical infrastructure; according to this model, the Vikings 'converted the English' by dissolving the monastic network and replacing it with a deregulated secular Christianity, enabling the aristocracy to retain economic and social control of their communities.[9] It may be that this was the preferred option in Svealand too. The English link is also exemplified by the extraordinary story of St Botulph, a seventh century East Anglian saint who was adopted in Scandinavia in the eleventh century (Toy), symbol of an enduring spiritual alliance between like-minded peoples.

Negotiating the Future

In Christian conversion, the missionary is an instrument of diffusion, but need not be the inevitable agent of the faith. The missionary model needs now to be

[9]   Carver 1998 op.cit. in note 5: 24–6.

tempered by a picture in which people, with a full knowledge and understanding of the options, make choices and devise their own ideological structures – so long as they have the political power to do so. The secular power, the kings, were in a state of continual negotiation with the church, with their aristocracy and with each other. In early seventh century England, the kings took sides, and at various times seem to have favoured one of three different programmes, roughly equivalent to those of Rome (Kent), Ireland (Northumbria) and Scandinavia (East Anglia), which may crudely be equated in turn with episcopal, monastic and secular infrastructures. By the mid seventh century some were adopting and legitimising the political instrument of Christianity by going into religious houses, associating the new religion with ancient notions of sacred kingship and enduring as saints (Yorke). The kings could use material benefits to persuade the aristocracy to convert, in a way that missionaries could not (Sanmark), but their power did not always prevail – particularly if they were advancing a policy of European unity and the perceived sharing of sovereignty.

The Age of Conversion was thus an age of ideological diversity and political experiment, in which north Europeans were debating fundamental questions about their future. Central to this debate, then as now, was the question of whether Europe itself was to have the principal identity and authority, or whether each of the new kingdoms should be left to follow its own independent path. Since interaction between neighbours is inevitable, this was a matter for continual negotiation. The larger power blocks were able to claim the moral and the economic high ground and the overall conversion of Europe eventually succeeded. Christianity had at its disposal the material language of thousands of years of prehistory, the aspirations of Empire, the scrapyard of imperial technology and the ethos of the Northerners' heroic soul. From this was forged by the twelfth century a nearly homogenous branding. But during the first centuries of the encounter northern Europeans experimented with Christianity's implications and created their own agenda for the future. In their graves, their monuments and their landscapes they gave expression to an intellectual debate many elements of which remain relevant for us today.

ACKNOWLEDGEMENTS

The York 2000 conference was supported by the Department of Archaeology, University of York, the Centre for Medieval Studies at the University of York, York Archaeological Trust, English Heritage (Northern Region), the Society for Medieval Archaeology and the City of York Museums.

The York City Art Gallery mounted the exhibition *Ruins reviewed: Yorkshire's Abbeys through the eyes of William Richardson and Peter Heaton,* and the Palestine Exploration Fund mounted the exhibition *The Church of the Nativity, Bethlehem: shrine and scandal.*

We were particularly grateful for grants from the Millennium Churches Fund and the British Academy.

I would like to record my personal thanks to David Hope Archbishop of York for opening the conference, to Simon Trafford, Jane Grenville and Kate Giles who managed the conference programme and events, to Anne-Sofie Gräslund for help with attracting speakers, Michael Müller-Wille for convening the papers which have given our book its title and to Greville Freeman-Grenville who was a constant source of inspiration.

We are most grateful to the Trustees of the Dorothea Coke Fund for a contribution towards the publication of this book.

2

The Politics of Conversion in North Central Europe

PRZEMYSŁAW URBAŃCZYK

Christianity had a profound impact on many spheres of early medieval life. It legitimised the centralisation of power relations, helped to develop the idea of unquestioned dynastic succession, and facilitated the integration of large and culturally differentiated territories. Elites could find support for their rule in trans-regional and trans-ethnic norms. Christianity pacified social tensions making the extraction of surplus easier, and it regulated the daily life of all people with new prescriptions on diet, labour and rites of transition.

Considering the fundamental transformation of ideology, social structure, power organisation and geopolitical relations that resulted from the conversion it is necessary to ask why Christianity expanded so rapidly with relative ease over vast areas of Central and North Europe around the year 1000. To answer such a question one has to look at Christianity with the eyes of the pagans or, rather, the pagan élites who played a decisive role in the process of conversion. A change of the religion itself was not their priority because their strategy was directed, first of all, at political and economic goals. Estimating short-term advantages they chose various strategies when faced with expanding Christianity. Some tried to actively oppose the 'inevitable', others remained indifferent, while others eagerly welcomed the new 'civilisation'. Usually, it is the last group only that was well recorded and memorised.

Written sources are not of much help to understand these attitudes because they were usually composed by people who represented the viewpoint of expanding Christianity. For them the conversion was an obvious process of accepting the Revealed Truth by uncivilised barbarians. Archaeological evidence is less useful than it might be because the chronology of the transition period is underdeveloped and the interpretation of data causes serious methodological problems.

One strategy open to us is a theoretical analysis whereby anthropological concepts of social power and the role of ideology in attaining, sustaining and reinforcing privileged positions are applied to early medieval societies.

Religious beliefs belong to the most private sphere of every human being. At the same time, however, they have important social meaning as an element of group identity and the main constituent of ideological systems. There are many ways of looking at past and contemporary religions, many systems for classifying and studying them. Here I want to compare pagan and Christian ideologies at the level of their political implications, because historiography has rarely viewed the conversion of early medieval pagan societies as a political process.

Christianity originated in different cultural traditions, including the legacy of the Roman Empire. Although Christ did not formulate any political doctrine, ages of coexistence with state structures formed the attitudes of Christianity towards centralised territorial organisations. Therefore, during the phase of early medieval state-building, Christianity appeared to be the most important ally of centralised power, because it provided ideological foundations for its legality. The Church offered a symbolic and factual connection with pan-continental politico-cultural norms.

Pagan and Christian Systems in Contrast

Although paganism and Christianity in early medieval Europe showed many similarities, there were also many important differences that should be stressed to understand the final success of the new faith.

(1) Pagan beliefs were **naturally acquired** in the informal process of gradual education that prepared individuals for functioning in their society. If there were initiations, they led to a higher level of participation in the religious life of the society, rather than to a higher level of knowledge. Such religion took shape as a multigenerational tradition, being an inseparable element of the ideological system (including the laws) that regulated the life of the whole of society (Łowmiański 1979: 242; cf. also the different opinion of Dušan Třeštik 1994: 446f). One may suppose then, that individual and collective religious behaviour showed a high level of conformity, causing no conflicts between the daily practice of individuals and the norms of group loyalty. It was formulated literally by John Canaparius reporting the reaction of the Prussians who, rejecting the new religion offered to them in 997 by St. Voitech-Adalbert, claimed that: 'We and the whole of this country . . . are bound by the common law and the single way of life' (*Vita I*, 28).

Christianity, similarly to other world religions (Judaism, Islam and Buddhism), is a system which legitimates its doctrine by the revealed truth recorded in writing. Thus, like any other 'religion of the book', it must be **formally taught** by prepared specialists. And authoritative enforcement of imposed views usually causes conflicts between individual experience and forced universal norms.

(2) Pre-Christian religions were characterised by **territoriality and collectivity** because they were shaped by the group consciousness of local populations and not by the objectified interpretation of the extra-sensual world that would be universal. For the early medieval pagans it was obvious that other territorial communities may have had another set or another hierarchy of deities. Therefore, it was an inwardly determined ideology that was not inclined to expand. Tolerant,

non-aggressive, and devoid of any sense of superiority in relation to the other's heterodoxy, it was an important component of group self-identity.

Christianity was concentrated on **universal and individual** salvation: relief from earthly suffering through a systematic plan of moral life, which was available to anybody. Neither social criteria or esoteric knowledge, nor extraordinary experience were required. Baptism purified the initiate and led to membership of the inter-territorial/catholic community. Through observance of a set of clear rules, anybody could await a reward in his/her after-life, with no regard to the ethnic affiliation or the place of habitation. At least such could have been a literary understanding of the Christian doctrine that sounded simple, egalitarian and universal.

(3) The mythical-symbolical world of pagans was not clearly separated from nature or the people. It was a sacral unity full of sacred objects, sacred sites, sacred gestures and sacred moments. Time, space and people were all elements of cosmic unity. Stability of that unity was guaranteed by the cyclic character of changes occurring in nature and by the **sustaining of the status quo**, i.e. of 'the world originating from the ancient mythical times and unchanged since then' (Třeštik 1994: 449; cf. also 450f). Any change could distort the natural cycle that was life-giving for agricultural populations. Therefore, the Prussians expelled St. Voitech-Adalbert, being afraid that because of his mission their '. . . soil will not yield crops, trees will not bear fruits, new animals will not be born and the old ones will become extinct' (*Vita II*, 25). Similarly, a pagan priest in the West-Slavic Wolgast persuaded his people that only the old faith might 'cover meadows with grass and trees with leafs; it ensures harvest in the fields . . . [and] fertility of animals' (Herbord III, 4).

Christianity with its aim of regulating all spheres of human activity 'encouraged a drive for moral and social improvement even against wordly authority' (Mann 1986: 398). Thus, it promoted **correction of the imperfect world** showing what this world should be like (Tilley 1995: 63) and became the main driving force of the cultural dynamism of the early Middle Ages.

(4) Traditional concepts of time, conceived as a coincidence of the past, present and future, gave people a comfortable feeling of social and individual safety. It was a **cyclic time** reduced to the necessary minimum that allowed people to survive and prevented radical changes. Repetition and not development, persistence and not change, 'today' and not 'yesterday' or 'tomorrow' were the foundations of the pagan world that consisted of societies whose live, dead and mythical members composed a timeless unity that was based on tradition and was not subject to any changes.

In addition to that 'natural' cyclic perception of time, Christianity introduced (after Judaism) a concept of **linear time** that was also irreversible, finite and purposeful. Such a concept of time had important cosmological consequences, forming a basis for a way of thinking that ordered visible reality in causal chains. Accepting the teleology of time leading unavoidably from the day of Creation to the day of the Final Judgement formed a particular way of thinking. It forced the

NUMINOUS
strong spiritual/religious quality
SACRAL relating to rites or symbols

people of the Middle Ages to think perspectively and not only within the dimension of the individual worldly life.

(5) In pagan society, the rules of social cooperation were seen as elements of the final cosmic order. Gods discerned within that order were rather 'domesticated' because they were bounded by privileged relations to the kin and territory. They formed a rather **'socialised' divinity** that was commonly understood, felt and accepted. Gods and divine ancestors of the neighbouring populations did not substantially differ one from another, forming a loose pantheon of changeable hierarchy, reflecting the changeability of inter-group relations.

Christianity impinged on that sacred pagan time-space, with its rather 'secular' concept of the terrestrial world. Many elements of visible reality lost their sacral dimension. **Deity** became **invisible and inaccessible**, and contact with it tended to be reduced to a narrowly defined liturgy and verbal sphere. The sensed sacrality of the pagan world was to be replaced by the unilateral verbal transmission controlled by specially educated people – the priests. It was the revealed Word controlled by priests that determined the subjective shape of the world. One may say that the medieval Christian world was as numinous as the pagan one, but its sacral dimension was less material. However, human need of close contact with the divine did not disappear. And it was mitigated with the help of the expanding cult of the saints and holy relics.

(6) The development of relatively stable pagan political units, aiming at superiority over larger and larger territories, was supported by the creation of regional **periodic cult centres** serving bigger and bigger populations. Even though most of these centres were activated only periodically, control over the converging political, religious, legislative and economic functions of such sites could serve as a magnificent tool for manipulating people's philosophy of life, steering assembly decisions and capturing surplus products. These localities functioned as focal points offering the persons/groups controlling them a very attractive means of information surveillance, and attracted many political leaders who sought reinforcement of their power position (Urbańczyk 1992: 208). The most important rituals were usually performed on the border of 'this' and 'another' world represented by mountains and large waters. Thus, the most famous cult sites among the Slavs were placed on holy mountains enclosed with impressive stone-walls (e.g. Ślęża in Polish Silesia) or peninsulas (e.g. Arkona in North-East Germany). During the late pagan period West Slavs had cult centres with elaborate temples where councils, law courts, public meetings and divinations took place. They could, also, be used as potential treasuries where large quantities of valuable items were stored (for Redars see Thietmar VI, 25; for Rugians – Helmold I, 51; for Szczecin – Herbord II, 32; for Arkona – Saxo Grammaticus XIV, 39).

Assembly

Sites

To perform Christian rituals it was necessary to construct sacral buildings that became **permanent religious centres**. These also were socio-topographic focal points and nodes for information-exchange, but the range was extended and specialised. Everybody who wanted to be informed on both the 'official' interpretation of the material world and the extra-sensual sphere, those who wanted to participate in common rituals and those who wanted to bury their dead properly, all had to come to a church, which thereupon defined a socially important centre.

(7) In pre-Christian societies progressive **hierarchisation** of the social structure was paralleled by the hierarchisation of the pagan pantheons. Attempts at establishing a paramount power centre needed ideological support, which often led to religious henotheism like that imposed c.986 by Vladimir in Kiev.

Christianity offered an effective ideological alternative to support the political-military struggle for establishing a paramount power centre. Hierarchical Church organisation clearly defined religious and social hierarchy and introduced divine legitimacy for **monopolistic political power**.

(8) In pre-Christian societies individuals who aspired to dominating social positions could strengthen their power by **combining the functions of military-political leadership with religious leadership**. Control over the religious sphere furnished an effective 'means to reproduce the structures of [social] domination by ideological support for maintaining the relations of dependence' (Urbańczyk 1992: 206). The chief-priest did not lead any institutionalised organisation responsible for supervising ideological order but his sacral function offered him a dominant position during many meetings.

Written sources rarely point directly to the priestly functions of pagan chiefs, 'princes' and 'kings'. In Icelandic sagas some of the famous Viking chiefs are called 'great sacrificers' (*blotmadr mikil*) (cf. Urbańczyk 1992: 205f). Similarly, the author of the earliest history of Iceland claimed that 'Earl Hákon [Grjotgardsson] was holding sacrifices' (*Landnámabók*, S149). Thus, some historians have suggested that there was 'a close relation between religious leadership . . . and political leadership' in pre-Christian Scandinavian societies (Bagge 1986: 151). It was a tradition derived from Odin who as a worldly king was to collect tributes. In return he 'should have defended the country against the war and made oblations for good yields' (*Ynglinga saga* 8). Reference to the religious function of a king may also be found in Ynglingatal (11) where the king is called 'the warden of a sanctuary'. A similar combination of the two functions among the Prussians is suggested by the story of St. Adalbert's mission where Sicco, the missionary's killer, is called 'priest of the idols [sacerdos idolorum] and the leader of the band' (*Vita I*, 30).

We cannot judge the reliability of these references but the repetition of such information in various sources suggests that the combination of political and religious functions was observed by some pagan societies. In such ways larger territorial populations were bound in an organisational frame of interpenetrating lay and sacral structures. The controlling position, located at the point joining both spheres, was occupied by the chief/monarch who was responsible for the prosperity of those who entrusted him with power. 'The ruler who personally made offerings for plentiful yields or military victories was a charismatic mediator between his people and the god. When the king was left by his "good luck", i.e. gods, he could be overturned or even sentenced to death' (Eliade 1995: 63) because his dominant position was conditional and subject to permanent control. Combination of political and priestly functions may be traced in Europe directly to the Roman Empire where emperors held the title of *pontifex maximus*. Christianised barbarians like Theodoric the Great made direct use of that tradition.

Missionaries were aware that in pagan societies political power was combined with control over the religious sphere. Therefore, they usually headed straight to the main political centres, aiming at initial Christianisation of the leading élites, for in those societies religious attitude was not so much a question of individual choice but of political loyalty. St. Otto's mission in Pomerania in 1124 may confirm that pagans were conscious of some kind of *cuius regio eius religio*. For when he tried to start his mission in Wolin, he was told by the locals that he 'should rather go and convert those who are thought to be the leaders of the tribe. When they convert there will be nothing else to do with regard to the others' (*Vita from Prüfening II*, 7). This led him to Szczecin that was called by Herbord *civitatem antiquissimam et nobilissimam in terra Pomeranorum matremque civitatum* (MPH VII, 3: 111; cf. also von Padberg 1995: 263f). The decisive role of political centres in the sphere of religion was clearly shown during the processes of converting pagan societies. We have numerous examples of conscious decisions to change religion taken by political leaders who carefully considered their geopolitical situations. Rostislav of Great Moravia, Venceslas of Bohemia, Mieszko I of Poland, Vladimir of Rus', St. Stephen of Hungary, Emund the Old of Sweden (c.1050–c.1060) judged several options before they decided when and how to convert.

In Christian states, **royal and priestly functions** were formally, though not always practically, **separated**. Christian rulers lost the prerogative to conduct important religious rituals. Priestly activities were now reserved for functionaries of the Church. It was, however, a loss that was not quite obvious, for Christian monarchs who were formally released from the responsibility for failure in contacts with the supernatural powers, at the same time, controlled the appointments of the bishops and the loyalty of the ecclesiastical hierarchy. Like Charlemagne, they could convene the synods and participate in doctrinal discussions. They were also divinely anointed, just like all bishops.

(9) The natural maleability of pagan religions was enhanced by the illiteracy of their followers: doctrines and even traditions were impossible to stabilise 'objectively'. Therefore they were **eclectic and adaptable** systems reflecting changing power-relations in equally unstable pre-state political organisations called chiefdoms. They were characterised by long-term periodicity because the tendency to centralise dominance over all spheres of social activity was counter-acted by the mechanisms of collective control, preventing the stabilisation of such domination. Breaking this barrier was possible only by the use of force that could raise the leader above the rules controlling the countrymen/tribesmen. The success of such 'attempts' against a relatively egalitarian society depended very much on the skilful ideological justification of such action (cf. Urbańczyk 1996).

Christianity stabilised in written form kept its original content even after crossing long distances. This resulted in a relatively **stable and uniform** interpretation of the universal aspects of human existence, and in a consciousness of some inter-territorial unity. This enabled the mobilisation even of dispersed populations into a normative community. With the expansion of Christianity a continental geopolitical order could appear that was based on ideologically legitimised common standards of manifestation and execution of political power.

(10) Pagan religions were **polytheistic and decentralised**, locally changing and difficult to control. They took shape during the evolution of societies that were comprised of relatively autonomous rural populations. They were part of a system of keeping the balance between unavoidable centralising tendencies and the tradition of relatively egalitarian organisation in these societies. Serving as the ideology of pagan societies they fulfilled real social needs but they did not promote 'more effective', i.e. hierarchical, organisation which was the aim of ambitious leaders who wanted to stabilise their advantageous positions (Urbańczyk 1996). Sacral legitimation of this domination was based on declarations of divine origins of their kin. Good examples are the Swedish *Ynglings* who derived their ancestry from the god Frøj and the giant Gerd Gymesdotter. Norwegian jarls of Lade considered themselves descendants of the god Njord and the giant Skade (Ynglinga saga 8 and 9). However, the polytheistic character of pagan religion prevented establishment of an unchallengeable political hierarchy with one paramount authority.

It was only during the late pagan period that attempts to create such authority by appointing a paramount leader of the pantheon, connected by kin relations to the ruling dynasty, could be seen in some regions. Genealogy connected to theogony was constructed already by the Amals, and some other Germanic dynasties copied these examples, deriving their roots from Votan/Odin. Such a pattern survived in seven out of eight genealogies of English royal houses (Dumville 1977). Although officially Christian, they did not reject tribal/pagan tradition and symbolism. A similar tendency was observed among the Polabian Slavs in the second half of the twelfth century. Helmold (I, 84) wrote that they believed 'that they descend from his blood and that people are the higher the closer they are to this god of gods'. These situations were all attempts to adapt traditional ideology to the needs of the centralising power structure. Some rulers sought divine legitimation for their dominant political position by creating ideological support for their leadership.

Similarly, among the Slavs the original polydoxy was transformed into polytheism, where the dominant position was occupied by Perun – 'the highest Slavonic god, the lord of the thunders', 'the guarantor of the world's order' (Gieysztor 1982: 87 and 257). I do not think that there was any uniform Slavic pantheon even though the process of hierarchisation was common because of applying similar geopolitical strategies. Helmold (I, 84) wrote in the second half of the twelfth century that the Polabian Slavs worship many gods but 'they believe that there is one God who rules in the heaven over all other gods; that he surpasses the others by his might'. This hierarchisation of the Polabian pantheon should be considered as an attempt to keep pace with the needs of the centralising power structure. It was probably influenced by the state-creative role of Christianity that surrounded the West-Slavic pagan enclave.The opinion of many historians that the concept of henotheism appeared rather late among the Slavs seems to be undermined by the Procopius of Caesarea (III, 14). He wrote in the mid-sixth century that *Sclavins* believed that 'only one god, the creator of the lightning is the lord of the whole world'. However, this note relates to Slavs that were then already under strong Byzantine influence. A need to reorganise their social structure to face a hierarchically organised neighbour might have also caused parallel reorganisation of the pantheon of those Slavs. Similar attempts are reported for Kiev, where Perun was established as the main god shortly before Christianisation in 988, and for Garz on Rugia where missionaries met a princely pantheon led by the main god Rugievit in 1168. Such examples may support Lotte Hedeager's (1992: 289) observation that 'the establishment of a divine lord has to be looked at in the light of the worldly kings' attempts to underpin their power by transferring their own political ideals to the religious field'.

Christianity, as a **monotheistic** religion, established one absolute point of reference for the whole cosmic order, making possible a parallel organisation of society. A long experience of coexistence with the centralised Roman Empire turned it into a system that was perfectly fitted for the needs of a centrally ruled state.

The Political Implications of Conversion

We do not know how far the social élites of pagan societies were aware of the political advantages offered by Christianity. We may imagine, however, that they admired the concrete results of its influence and realised its socio-technical potential. This facilitated, or perhaps even conditioned, the difficult operation of transforming the chiefdom-tribal system into the dynastic kingdom. In practice, the effects of Christianisation, if not its goals, were to introduce new rigour and force into social control.

(1) Pagan tradition, based on collective memory and verbal transmission, was difficult to manipulate, but behaviour taught by a formal didactic process based on a book offered the possibility of the conscious shaping of the philosophy of life. The matter of cult, and especially liturgy became the domain of properly prepared specialists who had a monopoly of the interpretation of reality. This made **control of socially vital information** much easier.

(2) Conviction of the intellectual and moral weakness of a man left by himself justified the tendency to change the earthly world by **force**. This made easier the introduction into the ideological sphere of changes that legitimised alterations imposed on the political sphere.

(3) Being a universalistic religion, Christianity could not accept that some societies might have had their own 'truths'. Acceptance of the basic canons

defined and limited the concept of humanity, and encouraged intolerance, as exemplified by Bruno of Querfurt calling the Polabian god Svarog a 'devil' (Letter to King Henry II: 255). Such a feeling of cultural superiority promoted an aggressive attitude towards pagan neighbours, **justifying political and territorial expansion**.

(4) Conversion, voluntary or coerced, was supervised by the Church. Often particular dioceses were given responsibility, e.g. the Hamburg archbishopric supervised missionary work 'in the North' (including Slavs living west of Peene river) according to the papal decision of 1053. The Church was steadily developing a pan-continental network of social interactions centred in Rome. The Church was, also, repository for Roman traditions and knowledge (organisational, legal, agricultural, architectural etc.). In this way an **institution** was slowly created with a system for circulating, collecting and recording information, based on a common language (Latin). On the political level the Church was more and more bound to the state organisational structures. During the Ottonian period it became not only the ideological but also the bureaucratic guarantor of the effective functioning of the state. Priests with their valuable skill of literacy formed the frame of a system of centralised bureaucracy. This enabled a shift from oral culture, dependent on human memory, to literature which offered a much more effective means of information storage and control. However, this also meant that a small but skilled group could manipulate the interpretation of information, indispensable for maintaining the relations of power and for legitimising the structure of dominance (Urbańczyk 1992: 208f).

(5) Churches were the main sources of the interpretation of surrounding reality for peasant masses. A church itself, being the result of conscious creation of an **information centre** required those who wanted to be informed to move over long distances and to gather within definite time periods (at least once a year at Easter) offering effective means of information control and/or manipulation.

(6) The ideological influence of Christianity worked to **relieve social tensions** emerging between privileged élites and agricultural masses. On the ethical level it taught patience, honesty and Christian solidarity. In this way the Church promoted not coercive but normative pacification because the main sanction was not physical compulsion but exclusion from the community (Mann 1986: 381). All this persuaded people to show each other (at least at some minimal level) an additional trust that did not depend on kin, territory, language or sex.

(7) The fundamental condition for participation in this 'God's peace' was acceptance of Christian doctrine and the fulfilment of some conditions that were not very severe. Already in the seventh and eighth centuries 'the Church began to put less stress on introducing people into the secrets of the faith', thus reducing to the minimum preparation for the baptism (Riché 1995: 485f). From later times we have precise information in the Polish chronicle of Jan Długosz (Johannes Dlugossi X, a.a. 1387) who noted that converted Lithuanians only needed to know three main principles and two prayers. Thus, it was an **offer open to everybody** but excluded those who did not accept it.

(8) When confronted with the daily aspects of individual and social life early medieval Christianity showed substantial **syncretic flexibility**. 'Old customs were accepted, redressed in the clothes of the new faith. Its dogmas, attributes and rituals were imposed on old forms during civil as well as sacral celebrations' (Samsonowicz 1991: 41). Therefore, although 'conversion to Christianity caused many new interpretations and revaluations of ancestral traditions it never managed to erase the pagan legacy' (Eliade 1995: 64) that survived over centuries as superstitions .

In many places Christian and pagan communities lived side by side for a long time, as has been suggested by studies of medieval Gotland (Thunmark-Nylen 1989: 223). It was a period of ideology 'in action', i.e. used to support competing socio-economic interests. It resulted in interweaving separate symbolic systems into an 'intertext' which eased the tensions between the two. Such coexistence may survive centuries when some elements of the old beliefs are dropped abruptly, some slowly fade away, but others are retained in various forms.

(10) Also important was the **legitimisation of social inequality**. Already at the turn of the first millennium the Church accepted, as far as one can judge, the division of society into different 'classes'. At the end of the tenth century Ælfric the English abbot of Eynsham mentioned main components of the society: 'Sive sis sacerdos, sive monachus, seu laicus, seu miles . . .' (*Aelfric's Colloquy*: 240). It is even better supported by the letter of bishop Adalbéron of Laon written to King Robert the Pious in 1027 which says that the state comprises three inseparable and cooperating groups: these who pray (*oratores*), these who fight (*bellatores*), and these who work (*laboratores*) (LeGoff 1996: 240). While the functions of the priestly and monk class were already institutionalised, at the opposite end the peasants had no extensive group self-consciousness at all. In between these two the ethos of the knightly class took shape. It bound the lay social élites of Europe by the links of exclusiveness and solidarity manifested in the developing norms of behaviour and class ideology that could 'justify and legitimize the differential accumulation and use of resources' (Hirth 1996: 224). Thus, around the year 1000 the formal division of society into three classes took shape, with its Christian explanation (Anderson 1974: 157). 'This classification expresses the opinion that in feudal society the clergy gets ahead of the laymen, among whom the lords stand above their subjects' (Vauchez 1996: 27). This way, in contradiction to its original idea, the Church legitimized not only the unequal distribution of material resources, but also the qualitative differentiation of people. For bishop Adalbéron this inequality was obvious, for he thought that 'no free man could live without subjects' (after Baszkiewicz 1978: 58). Especially advantageous was the lack of a clear social cosmology that allowed contradictions between doctrine and social reality to be disguised. Thus, women had full rights of participation but they could not take official functions, which reinforced the patriarchal structure of the society. Slavery was regrettable but it was considered unavoidable because of primordial sin.

(11) The Old Testament tradition of the king being *Christos Dei* (anointed by God) established the **sacral immunity of authority**. Recognition of the sanctity of the kings spreading and defending the faith in the countries of 'new Christianity' (Venceslas and Ludmila, Stephen, Vladimir, Olav Haraldson, Kanut) strengthened this concept giving many ruling dynasties the sacral legitimation for their domination in the power structure. Already Charlemagne included in his imperial *intitulatio* the clear formula 'a Deo coronatus' with the declarative invocation 'in nomine patris et filii et spiritus sancti' which was later commonly copied. Such deliberate combination of Italian and Byzantine traditions (cf. Wolfram 1995: 46) aimed at placing Christian rulers above the human law. Still earlier in Western Europe the ceremony of anointing Christian kings by bishops had appeared. The Visigothic King Wamba was anointed in Toledo in 672. Pippin the Short sanctioned his usurpation by anointment in 751. The English prince Egfrid did the same in 787. Later this became more and more popular, tending to be the rule by the turn of the millennium. Such sacral legitimation of the royal power was made actual with each anointment and replaced reference to distant ancestors who had personal relations with pagan gods. One way or another the 'religious basis of central authority . . . emphasizes the general nature of the leadership' (Earle 1987: 286f). But Christianity was a much more powerful instrument in legitimating and expanding royal power. Transcendent support legitimised a king's claims to superiority over secular spheres, furnishing a kingdom with an 'ideological platform for promoting the change from a kin-centred society to a state society' (Steinsland 1989: 207).

(12) Christianity offered **normative pacification** of contacts between individuals and of relations between groups in a way that did not exist before. Social pressure strengthened the expectation that a Christian should behave correctly. This offered a basis for the gradual creation of a universal community based on a consciousness of identity that surpassed kin- and locality-relations. This meant that every more-or-less isolated population was potentially open, because it might consider itself as a part of the larger whole. Hence, it was potentially expansive. As a model 'the identity of Christendom was transnational, based not on territory or locality as anyone could actually experience them but on something wider, something more abstract and transcendent' (Mann 1986: 380). At least such was to be the ideological legitimisation for Emperor Otto III's *renovatio imperii Romanorum*.

Thus, 'the framework of paganism, inseparably connected to the old patriarchal type of the kin-tribal culture, and thus ethnically closed within the limits of the separate tribes', became too tight for the early state organizations being formed (Joannisjan 1995: 21). The variety of forms and the changeability of pagan religious systems made the creation of larger organizational structures difficult. Christianity introduced some impersonal elements that meant that in public situations people showed some basic confidence. Hence, the limit of hostile distrust could be moved from kin and/or local groups with 'strangers' to the contacts of Christians with 'pagans'.

Even if the distinction 'Christian/pagan' was not as clear as some theologians thought it ought to have been, at the end of the first millennium, Europe was divided into two different parts. One consisted of the South and West, united by Christian universalism and referring to the Roman-Carolingian or Roman-Byzantine traditions (with exception of Islamic Spain), while the other was the pagan North and East. This picture changed very fast and by the year 1000 Denmark, Norway and Iceland in the North and Bohemia, Poland, Rus' and Hungary in the Central-East joined the Christian world, which determined their further development.

Although the conversion of the North and Central Europe happened rather quickly, it was a very uneven process with locally differentiated outcomes. There were areas subject to slow infiltration of the new faith (e.g. Sweden) but also countries where radical transformations were introduced by local rulers (e.g. Poland). There were examples of easy acceptance of Christianity (e.g. Hungary) but also vigorous opposition that resulted in counter-Christian religions (Polabian Slavs). There were conversions imposed by outer powers (e.g. Bohemia) and complex power-games played by local political leaders (e.g. Rus'). There were 'national' churches dominated by foreigners who promoted classic (Latin or Greek) rituals but also 'ethnic' versions of Christianity preached and written in vernacular (Great Moravia and Iceland). There were bishops who cooperated with political power centres and some who opposed profane power holders (e.g. St Voitech-Adalbert).

All this makes North and Central Europe a very interesting field for studying the whole complexity of the conversion process that resulted in formation of the zone of civilisation, which was nominally uniform ideologically but, in fact, consisted of many differentiated local versions of Christianity.

References

Original sources

Aelfric's Colloquy, G.N. Garmonsway (ed.) London, 1938.
Helmold [The Chronicle of the Slavs], J. Matuszewski (trans.) Warszawa, 1974.
Herbord, *Dialogus de Vita s. Ottonis episcopi Babenbergensis*, J. Wikarjak (ed.) MPH s.n. 8, Warszawa, 1974.
Johannes Dlugossi, *Johannes Dlugossi Opera Omnia*, vol. 12, Kraków, 1876.
Landnámabók [The Book of Settlement], H. Pálsson and P. Edwards (eds) University of Manitoba, 1972.
Letter to King Henry II, K. Abgarowicz (trans.) Warszawa, 1966.
Procopius of Caesarea, *De bello Gothico*, J. Haury (ed.) vol. 2, Leipzig, 1905.
Saxo Grammaticus, *Gesta Danorum*, J. Olrik and H. Raeder (eds) Kopenhagen, 1931.
Thietmar, Chronicon, M.Z. Jedlicki (ed.) Poznań, 1953.
Vita I, K. Abgarowicz (trans.) Warszawa, 1966.
Vita II, K. Abgarowicz (trans.) Warszawa, 1966.
Vita from Prüfening, J. Wikarjak (trans.) Warszawa, 1979.

Literature

Anderson E.A. 1974 Social idealism in Ælfrics Colloquy, *Anglo-Saxon England*, 3.

Bagge S. 1986 Borgerkrig og stasutvikling I Norge I middelalderen, *Historisk Tidsskrift*, vol. 67: 45–97.

Dumville D.N. 1977 Kingship, genealogies and regal lists, in *Early Medieval Kingship*, P. H. Sawyer, I. N. Wood (eds), Leeds.

Earle T.K. 1987 Chiefdoms in an archaeological and ethnohistorical perspective, *Annual Review of Anthropology*, 16: 279–308.

Gieysztor A. 1982 *Mitologia Słowian* [Mythology of the Slavs], Warszawa.

Hedeager L. 1992 Kingdoms, ethnicity and material culture: Denmark in a European perspective, in M.O.H. Carver (ed.) *The Age of Sutton Hoo. The seventh century in North-Western Europe*, Woodbridge: 279–300.

Hirth K.G. 1996 Political economy and archaeology: perspectives on exchange and production, *Journal of Archaeological Research*, 4.3: 203–39.

Joannisjan O.M. 1995 Kreščenie Rusi i drevnerusskaja chudožestvennaja kultura, in *Cerkovnaja archeologia. Čast 1*, Sankt-Petersburg: 21–7.

LeGoff J. 1996 Człowiek średniowiecza, in J. LeGoff (ed.) *Człowiek średniowiecza*, Warszawa: 7–50.

Łowmiański H. 1979 *Religia Słowian i jej upadek* [Slavic religion and its end], Warszawa.

Mann M. 1986 *The sources of social power*, vol. 1, Cambridge.

Padberg L.E. von 1995 Odin oder Christus? Loyalitäts- und Orientierungskonflikte in der frühmittelalterlichen Christianisierungsepoche, *Archiv für Kulturgeschichte*, vol. 77, z. 2: 249–78.

Riché P. 1995 *Edukacja i kultura w Europie Zachodniej. VI-VIII w.*, Warszawa (first pub. 1973).

Samsonowicz H. 1991 *Dziedzictwo średniowiecza. Mity i rzeczywistość* [The legacy of the Middle Ages. Myths and reality], Wrocław.

Steinsland G. 1989 Religionsskiftet i Norden – et dramatisk ideologiskifte, in A. Andrén (ed.) *Medeltidens fødelse*, Lund: 203–12.

Thunmark-Nylen L. 1989 Samfunn och tro på religionsskftets Gotland, in A. Andrén (ed.) *Meddeltidens fødelse*, Lund: 213–32.

Tilley C. 1995 *Plots of time. An inquiry into history, myth and meaning*, Gainesville.

Třeštik D. 1994 Křest českých knížat roku 845 a chrystianizace Slovanů [The baptism of Bohemian princes in 845 and Christianisation of the Slavs], *Česky časopis historický*, 92.3: 423–59.

Urbańczyk P. 1992 *Medieval Arctic Norway*, Warszawa.

—— 1996 Religia pogańska jako ideologia społeczności plemiennych, *Światowit*, 49: 168–73.

Vauchez A. 1996 *Duchowość średniowiecza*, Warszawa (first pub. 1975).

Wolfram H. 1995 Political theory and narrative in charters, *Viator. Medieval and Renaissance Studies*, 26: 39–51.

3

'How do you pray to God?' Fragmentation and Variety in Early Medieval Christianity

ALEKSANDER PLUSKOWSKI AND PHILIPPA PATRICK

Introduction

In his statement to the Inquisition court at Pamiers, Arnaud Sicre distinguished his religious beliefs and practices from that of the Cathar perfect, Bélibaste. Both considered themselves to be good Christians.

> And you, how do you pray to God? Bélibaste asked Arnaud Sicre, son of a notary of Tarascon and of a lady of Ax. I cross myself, answered Sicre, I commend myself to God who died for us on the cross, and to the Virgin Mary, I say the Pater Noster and the Ave Maria, I fast on the vigil of the Virgin.
>
> (Ladurie 1978: 306)

Bélibaste's reply is noted as (predictably) sarcastic and cuts straight to the point:

> The sheep bleats because it does not know how to speak. Let me tell you that the Ave Maria is worthless. It is an invention of the priests. As for your fasting, it might as well be the fasting of a wolf! (ibid.)

As a heretic and murderer, passionate in his opposition to a single Christian doctrine broadcast from Rome, Bélibaste was eventually consigned to the stake in 1321, the last Cathar perfect in Languedoc (O'Shea 2000: 246). From a generalised perspective, definitions of 'orthodoxy' and 'heresy' were polarised and finally expressed in the persistent elimination of the Cathars at the hands of the Dominican Inquisition. Yet documented heretical ideas and sects continued to harass the Church, before and beyond the schism of the Reformation. These were only a few strands within the web of shifting theological amendments and clarifications of doctrine, political fluctuations between Church and State and the filtering of effective influence and communication with distance from the great centres of religious administration in medieval Europe: Rome, Byzantium and later Avignon. This dynamic web was itself set against a rich tapestry of local saints' cults, feast days and regional customs whose variations owed something to the differential and often staggered pace of religious conversion from pagan to Christian, or from Christian to Christian.

During the conversion period, Christianity encountered a variety of different cultures and mentalities as it moved north and changed what it could with varied success. Subsequent modifications took place through further Christianisation, pagan reintroductions, localised ideological mutations and social upheavals. Ultimately, on one level, it is possible to see a stable religious infrastructure, Wulfstan's *ecclesia* (Swanton 1975: 137–8), based upon the episcopal system and characterised by the distribution of churches, cathedrals, shrines and monasteries, and later, medieval hospitals and seminaries. Yet in many ways this is a convenient, generalised mask obscuring a variety of 'Christianities' and confounding us with its internal inconsistencies. Christianity, as much as paganism, infiltrated life in medieval Europe, influencing burial rites, iconography, architecture, social organisation and status, diet, sexual preferences, marital and martial practices. Some have attempted to draw clear lines between the *functions* of Christianity and paganism (Dowden 2000), for example, in terms of promoting 'belief' or 'faith'; although this may seem plausible and clear when considering a select core of evidence, there is too much apparent variation in both religious systems and gaps in our existing knowledge, especially regarding European paganism, to suggest such clear polarity.

This chapter will set out to question the predominantly simplistic reconstructions of early medieval Christianity in northern Europe, focussing on the conversion period. Unfortunately there are no clear alternatives to the traditional approaches, but we will attempt to suggest potential directions for future research. This discussion involves highly selective examples and does not claim the coverage provided by Fletcher (1998) or the focussed detail given by Geake (1997). The ideas presented in this chapter are partly inspired by the work of Carver (1998a) and his illumination of the complexity of Christian diversity in eastern Scotland and its effect upon the lives, material investments and politics of early medieval north European communities.

Narratives and analyses of the conversion period tend to begin with a definition of paganism, how it can be recognised from written and archaeological evidence, and following on from this how Christianity can be identified, in some cases as a direct contradiction of the materialised elements of the defined 'paganism'. Typically this categorisation is followed by considerations of intermediate shifts from pagan to Christian: through syncretism and transitional forms. Before proceeding further, it is necessary to consider the problematic definitions associated with these terms. Kilbride (2000: 8) has attacked the validity of the entire concept of 'syncretism' on the basis that its definition suggests a compromise between two static, pristine states (Christian and pagan) and denies the fluidity in both. However, the term can be used effectively to refer to any mingling of the two contrasting paradigms; this of course assumes that there is sufficient difference between the varieties of 'pagan' and 'Christian' paradigms which enable us to identify material culture associated with each. The recognition of syncretic form is through a mixture of aspects of both paradigms, clearly recognisable in monuments such as the St Andrews Cross on the Isle of Man (cf. Hultgård 1992). Thus our use of 'syncretism' will not assume any religious stasis, and the recognition of dynamic fluidity in both Christian and pagan paradigms remains a central issue. Below is a summary of the variations to be explored in this paper.

There are several potential scenarios relating to religious change during the conversion period:

- complete change from pagan practices to Christian;
- partial change followed by relapse or de-conversion, followed by partial or complete change;
- syncretic fusion of practices and beliefs. This can be extremely variable and should include both pagan and Christian paradigms as potentially dominant influences;
- acceptance of a Christian paradigm whilst retaining a pagan paradigm;
- changing aspects of an existing Christian paradigm: Christians converting Christians;
- complete rejection of a Christian paradigm (including acceptance of paganism, Islam or Judaism).

When considering any conversion period context, we should bear in mind the following factors regarding pagan-Christian interaction:

- the character of pre-existing religions;
- the character of pre-existing magical systems, stories and customs;
- pre-existing social structure and hierarchy;
- relationships with the environment; specifically with the land/seascape and its associated flora and fauna;
- artistic conventions, materials and links to existing religious/magical systems;
- investment in the new religion;
- politics;
- variable concepts and uses of 'time' and 'space';
- the situation in neighbouring areas; spheres of influence and interaction;
- changes over time: all the above factors several decades/centuries later.

In the case of Christian-Christian interaction, aside from above, the following should also be considered, particularly as a framework for any 'archaeology of heresy'. As always, one must beware of confusing 'heresy' with 'variety':

- the differential use and emphasis of symbolism with regard to variation, especially rare or unique examples. this includes considerations such as audience types, distribution, media of transmission etc;
- the differential use of space, bearing in mind the notion that religious perceptions can be mapped onto geographical space;
- documented variety in similar temporal and spatial contexts;

- similarity in different temporal and spatial contexts;
- variable treatment of both christian and pagan monuments;
- consideration of the 'life history' of material culture representing variability or potential heresy. This should include the persistence of particular icon-ographic or architectural forms as well as any *renaissance* of these up to and including the present day. Each context should be examined in its own right, and reasons for continuity or re-invention should be addressed;
- the removal or reshuffling of elements of the Christian paradigm into a secular context.

Juggling the properties of the established formula, we will begin with a consideration of the potential variability present in early Christianity and why it is essential to consider medieval Christianity as being in a state of variable flux. The interactions between groups of Christians, and between Christians and pagans produced an enormous range of material traces in both the written and archaeological records. Distinctions between pagans and Christians have often used generalised assumptions using documentary evidence, burial evidence and place names (for example, Mayr-Harting 1977). Singular events in the documentary record are taken as typical of the religion, such as the priest Coifi flinging a spear into the temple (*ibid*. 26, Bede 2: 8). However here we emphasise rather the variety *within* Christianity and between newly converted Christians. Interactions between Christianity, Judaism and Islam, although important to bear in mind, are not central to this discussion. Having established some loose possibilities for religious mutation from orthodox through to heterodox forms, we will attempt to paint a general picture of how Christianity adapted to its new and variable environment during the conversion period with appropriate reference to later periods. We will conclude with a suggested framework for approaching conversion period contexts. The time scale of the conversion is vast: from the gradual establishment of Christianity in Gaul by the end of the fifth century (Loseby 1992: 144), through to 1505 when the last northern crusading bull was sent to the Russian frontier from Rome (Christiansen 1997: 1). Ironically, by this time, the fragmentation of the Reformation had already begun.

From Magician to Pantokrator: the Changing Faces of 'Orthodox' Christianity

Christianity is, in theory, a definable religion with recognisable tenets. As Russell (1996: 35) observed regarding relativist definitions of Christianity, 'if the essence of Christianity is always in a state of flux, how can any particular form of belief or observance be deemed "non-Christian"?' Christianity can be recognised from a variety of material and textual indicators; both suggest a vast spatial and temporal range for expressing various aspects of religious belief and practice. Schmitt (1998a) has criticised the general term 'religion' as anachronistic for the Middle Ages in that this definition included:

... participation in rituals and even more generally participation in an entire social organization and in the sum of symbolic practices and of relationships of meaning among men, between men and nature, and between men and the divine. (Schmitt 1998a: 384)

Although it is clear that religion, both Christian and pagan, infiltrated virtually every aspect of daily life in the Middle Ages including language and metaphors (Lager 2000: 125), it is possible and necessary to identify the primary indicators of religious practices and extrapolate from there, whilst acknowledging the wider picture and its variables. One of the problems relating to definitions seems to appear when 'Church' is used synonymously with 'Christianity'. This leads *ipso facto* to positing the existence of 'One Christianity' and by extension 'one religion' (Milis 1998: 5). In complete contrast, Tyson (1973: 334) has suggested that one cannot talk about 'Christian' ideas, only refer to Johannine, Pauline, Gnostic etc. The defining characteristic of Christianity was its adaptability. It is important to bear this trait in mind when examining and analysing seemingly contradictory evidence for Christian practices over a wide geographical space. Much has been written on this variety; in fact the dynamism of Christian culture is often referred to in the same breath as changes in art, architecture, literacy, medicine, astronomy etc. Campbell warned against taking a 'striking or moving instance as a guide to the whole' and that we should always be ready for surprises (Campbell 1986: 84). We will use some selected examples from the range of 'Christian material culture' to illustrate this; a full study incorporating and tracking the changes and the detail of variety, in a holistic form, is yet to be written.

The Roman Empire in the fourth century was the arena for a crucial battle of iconography: Christ, a new god on the scene, set against the pantheon of popular deities, primarily Jupiter (Mathews 1993) but also a host of important female deities. Yet, here we are faced with a polymorphous rather than a single Christ: he was presented as a powerful magician, a god who interacted with and comforted ordinary people with occasional hints of androgyny in order to reach out to both men and women. The Bible had left no account of the physical appearance of Christ and in any event its claims far exceeded all visual symbols; thus artisans invented without inhibition. The multiple qualities of Christ documented in the Gospels were represented in as many iconographic facets of his person as possible, so as to somehow encompass the totality of the unimaginable mystery (Matthews 1993: 180). In his detailed study of the iconographic variability, Mathews distances himself from the traditional 'imperialist' interpretation of depictions of Christ and attempts to answer questions relating to the interaction between different groups of people and their newly chosen god. How did people grasp him? How did they feel about him? How did they relate to him? In effect, how did people imagine Christ? The answers are clearly visible in the variable iconography of this crucial time, when Christianity was rooting itself conceptually and winning popular support, and the questions are pertinent to every subsequent introduction of Christian iconography into non-Christian cultures.

This will be discussed in more detail later; for now it is important to reaffirm the idea that the shifting image of Christ was interpreted differently by people in various places. This initial flexibility, present from the genesis of organised Christianity, would continue to drive the dynamic framework of Christian material culture and theology throughout the Middle Ages. The differences between variable audiences described above should be maintained within the context of the conversion period and beyond. As Schmitt has concisely stated, there are many levels within the Christian community of any given country:

> It is necessary to keep in mind the specific positions of the urban and rural clergy, the *ordinario* (the hierarchy of secular clerics) and the monks and friars, as well as the strategic positions of the parish priests and of the various social classes that formed the core of the laity. This allows us to imagine far more complex relationships among distinct and multiple poles.
>
> (Schmitt, 1998a: 382)

During the progress of the conversion, coherent and *updated* understanding of different segments of the Christian paradigm, particularly in terms of theological variants, was primarily held by specific groups: urban clergy and then filtered down to the country clergy and finally the laity. Levels of education, foreign contact and the availability of resources worked in the favour of the ecclesiastical hierarchy; to put it another way: 'The simple do not often know much about doctrine' (Eco 1998).

We shall use the example of early medieval England to illustrate the changing and variable face of the Christian paradigm. Christianity had to be introduced afresh to the Anglo-Saxons who were 'pagan' when they first came to England, although a separate strand of British Christianity had survived or been reintroduced into western Britain by the end of the fifth century. The interaction between groups of Christians with divergent perspectives was not particularly peaceful; Bede wrote about Augustine's confrontation with the Celtic Christians. Pope Gregory told Augustine to instruct the unlearned, strengthen the weak and correct the perverse (Bede *HE* 1: 27). But the British bishops did not agree with Augustine's arguments of unity with Rome and so he threatened them with vengeance. Eventually his threat was fulfilled by King Ethelfrith at the battle of Caerlegion or Chester, where according to Bede (*HE* 2: 2) 1,200 monks and priests praying for 'that nation of heretics' were slaughtered (Duggan 1997: 58–9). Indeed, Augustine seems to have started from scratch in his efforts to evangelise the English (Frend, Chapter 5 in this volume), although this is not the whole story (see below). The decision regarding the future direction of 'English Christianity' was finally resolved at the synod of Whitby in 664 (Barnwell *et al.*, Chapter 19 in this volume), where the teachings of the Roman rather than the Celtic Church were chosen as the orthodox line subsequently reinforced by Abbot Hadrian of Naples. Many monasteries of British foundation were simply assimilated into the Anglo-Saxon Church, although those in Cornwall were not finally granted recognition until the tenth century (Hooke 1998: 52; Turner, Chapter 11 in this volume). The survival of Christianity in Britain following the removal of direct Roman influence has been demonstrated by Thomas (1981: 274) and Watts (1991: 226). Sites displaying continuity include Cannington cemetery, St Paul-in-the-Bail, St Pancras and St Albans. The search for remains of British Christian objects and funerary practices continues, primarily focussing on overlaps between modes of burial and continuity in the location of churches, such as the disputed presence of an early church under the crypt of Canterbury Cathedral (Brooks 2000).

Identifying Christian burials should, in theory, be relatively easy. They are largely unfurnished, regimented, oriented in a singular direction and inhumed rather than cremated. Furthermore, as with the commonly used 'vacuum left by paganism filled with Christianity' notion, the absence of any explicitly non-Christian forms of disposal leads to the assumption that burials are Christian (Morton 1992: 72). In practice of course, there are many spatial and temporal variations, not just in the individual grave compositions themselves, but also in the changing structure and location of cemeteries. Burials from Anglo-Saxon Hamwic with grave goods dated post-700 were interpreted as having been buried in a 'broadly Christian context' (ibid., 75). At Cross Close cemetery, north-south orientation and reported presence of grave goods in at least one of the graves suggested that the Christian community respected the pre-existing pagan alignment and this peculiar continuity may have been linked to the political status of Hartlepool as a royal centre (Daniels 1999: 110). Through the late sixth and early seventh century, there was a transformation in the stratification of English society: the grave goods of conversion-period England were used to construct and express a pan-English neo-classical national identity, drawing heavily on Roman prototypes and visible in architecture, sculpture, manuscript art and coins. This identity was promoted by the Church and State to legitimise the power of their hierarchies (Geake 1997: 136). In a similar vein, Hadley (2000) has suggested how burials in barrows and churchyards in the seventh and early eighth centuries signified a concern with monumentality, reflecting different expressions of a similar social need (cf. Carver 1986: 98). The end to furnished burial remains enigmatic, although long-term mechanisms related to changes in the use of material wealth have been proposed (Duby 1973: 66–67; Carver 1989: 157; Geake 1997: 134). Furnished burials continued into the first half of the eighth century when there was a favourable climate for imposing taxes; churches had become an accepted channel for alternative ideological and fiscal investment (Geake 1997: 135). The graves are not noticeably anti-Christian; they are in essence a transitional stage where localised groups were interpreting and adapting Christianity within the variably regulated confines of the episcopal system. This transitional period lasted until the late tenth century. The variability within individual burial structures is something to take into consideration (Hadley 2000: 164). Despite the problems of a small sample, there is potential for recognising certain groups at various scales: from the local to the national. From stone coffins, through to stone linings, pillow stones, clothed or shrouded bodies and the presence of charcoal or additional artefacts, the range and distribution of

'Christian' grave types demonstrates variability ultimately bound within the common denominator of consecrated ground.

Continental shifts in Christian organisation and thinking did not always resonate in every corner of Britain. According to Ó Carragáin's (1999: 200) hypothesis, the Ruthwell community would have been remote from the religious upheavals on the Continent and, in their isolation, used their iconography on the Ruthwell cross for new contemplative purposes.

With the Viking settlement of England came a new injection of Scandinavian motifs into Anglo-Saxon art. Before this time, stone sculpture was primarily found in monastic art. After the tenth century, sculptors turned to a lay market for patronage and new workshops were created. The Scandinavian settlement introduced a secular element to English sculpture, notably in figures of armed warriors and depictions of legendary heroes (Bailey 1981: 86). There was also a proliferation of syncretic art, such as the sculptures found at Gosforth, in Cumbria, and St Andrews on the Isle of Man. This cultural injection is equally as important as the historically documented raids on monasteries, the seizure of land in the Danelaw and its associated political, economic and religious upheavals. Although one can say that the Vikings accelerated the secularisation of certain forms of Anglo-Saxon Christianity (Cramp 1980: 18), there was no overturning conversion from Christian to pagan. Instead, the Vikings adhered to the pre-existing generalised religious viewpoint and privatised it, introducing what has been called a ninth century 'dissolution of the monasteries' (Carver 1998a: 26). The fragmentation of estates at the hands of the Vikings contributed to the creation of rural parishes and parish churches in the tenth and eleventh centuries. The acquisition of monastic estates in the Danelaw itself may have directly facilitated this process: new secular landowners sought to demonstrate their power and wealth by the construction of private churches (Richards 1991: 99–101). In some cases, pagan practices were injected back into local religious custom, for example at Chapel Hill, Balladoole on the Isle of Man, a Viking ship burial deliberately cut through Christian cist graves (ibid. 104). The overall result was a likely modification of both Anglo-Saxon and Scandinavian religious systems with gradual assimilation; we should expect to find further variety with Scandinavian contact with Ireland, Scotland and Wales. It is quite likely that Scandinavian settlers took advantage of existing Christian power structures by incorporating Christian elements into their hybridised lifestyles (Hadley 2000: 169). In the case of Hiberno-Norse Ireland, the powerful monastic structure was severely shaken by the Viking incursions and a wider secularising effect can be seen, especially with the growth of towns such as Dublin (Marsden 1996: 115). However, in terms of religious assimilation the pattern is similar for all the Scandinavian colonies in that there was no concerted effort to evangelise the Vikings. This is an area demanding further research but frustratingly lacking in detailed material evidence.

English Christianity changed its face again after 1066. The Normans brought across new concepts of architecture and materialised their secular power and wealth in the oppressive castle, their religious power in vast new constructions;

stamping a similar mark of brand new authority and control in places such as Canterbury Cathedral, levelled and rebuilt by Lanfranc from the 1060s through to the 1080s (Calkins 1998: 160; Tatton-Brown 1994: 25), as Bernard of Castanet was to do with the construction of the Cathedral of St. Cécile in Albi in the 1280s (Barber 2000: 192; O'Shea, 2000: 3). This is perhaps not something to be removed from its specific context since changes in ecclesiastical architecture did not necessarily reflect upheavals in the social fabric. They were, however, frequently associated with varying emphasis on the Christian paradigm, as for example, with the architecture of the Cistercian order (Calkins 1998: 134). In fact, it has been argued that the changes brought about through Anglo-Norman Christianity were inevitable, following continental trends, although it is clear that the replacement of English abbots and bishops was undertaken primarily for political motives (Golding 1994: 155). By 1120, the English Church was truly an amalgamation of English and Norman culture (*ibid*. 176).

Variability can be found throughout the spatial and temporal extent of the conversion. In Scandinavia, local expressions of Christianity can be found in the runestones of the Mälar valley. It is possible that the Frankish church, dominating southern Scandinavia in the Viking era was not as tolerant towards this local-ised expression of religious independence since the erection of runestones was curtailed (Lager 2000: 130; Chapter 31 in this volume). Further south, Christian communities in the towns of eastern Illyricum may have permitted some degree of symbiosis between the local representatives of the Greek and Latin Churches, owing as they did political allegiance to Byzantium and ecclesiastical obedience to Rome. It seems possible to speak of a bridge between Greek and Latin Christianity in a few cities of the central area of the Balkans between 600 and 750. By 800, with the Iconoclast policies of Byzantium, these dioceses fell under the jurisdiction of the Orthodox Patriarch by Imperial decree (Oblensky 1988: 51). The potential impact upon regional interpretations of Christianity, of the split between the Eastern and Western Churches, has already been briefly dismissed in relation to certain parts of England, but it clearly had an impact on many subsequent religious, artistic and political developments. The Iconoclasm was initiated by Leo II in the 730s and died down at the death of Constantine V in 755, only to rear its head again in 815. 'Orthodoxy' was finally restored in 843 (Hussey 1986: 43–63). The split with Rome primarily concerned disagreements on issues such as the *Filioque* clause in the creed (the idea that the Holy Spirit proceeds from both the Father and the Son) and Papal primacy (Oblensky 1988: 63; Fletcher 1998: 329). In 867, the Byzantine Patriarch Photius declared the Pope deposed and excommunicate over the doctrinal error of the Filioque. Relations were restored by the new Emperor Basil I but religious tensions would have at least been reflected in the Balkan missionary activities at this time.

The basic tenets of Christianity as expressed in iconography, architecture and symbolism played a vital role in transmitting personal information. Each image fitted the viewer's ideal (Morgan 1999: 32), whether this was a comforting Christ, a scene of severe judgement or the *Mater Dolorosa* of the later Middle Ages.

Christ *Pantokrator*, the iconographic all-powerful ruler placed at the symbolic centre of creation in the Byzantine dome, was a figure of wonder and intimacy rather than terror or severity (Mathews 1995: 212, 215). Moving the focus away from the material sphere where temporal and spatial differences have been stretched to a wider Christian phenomenon, the saints, it is clear that there are deeper levels of variability to consider.

Shifting Emphases and Further Variety: the Role of Saints

Regional and national cults of individual saints encapsulate in many ways the breadth of variety within the Christian paradigm. Here the figures of God or Christ are pushed into the background, though omnipresent as the authority from which the saints derive their inspiration and power. As with the polymorphous Christ, saints offered an additional range of personalities and attributes for the wider, converted audience, in many cases displacing existing polytheistic characters (Wilson 1983: 2). Saints were not simply worshipped deities but also lesser supernatural beings which people turned to in times of minor crises. Saints' cults met basic needs and provided reassurance in daily matters (Williams 1980: 110). The power of the saints, particularly the martyr cults associated with relics, became the magical catalysts within the Christian paradigm. 'Magic' in Hutton's sense of the term, as will be discussed later, co-existed independently of religion (Hutton 2000). In this context we are referring to peoples' personal experience of Christianity, with varying emphasis placed on Christ and the saints. This emphasis is reflected in the relative distribution of iconography, church dedications, inscriptions, statues, pilgrimage routes and offerings. This is true for both eastern and western Churches, although in the East, prayers before icons were enjoined by the clergy and parallelled in public liturgy. In the West, images and pilgrimage 'souvenirs' became material foci of attention. Particularly interesting is the use of 'ex-votos' or votive offerings, often models of body parts, deposited at saints' shrines. Emphasis on different saints was related to a whole host of factors: local history, audience types, monastic relic monopolies and degrees of regulation from the episcopal level. At Hovingham, repeated iconographic use of the Virgin Mary on a sarcophagus implies that the body may have been that of a woman, and/or those worshipping at the shrine included a strong female presence (Hawkes 1999: 213). In late Anglo-Saxon England, the cult of the Virgin, manifested through liturgy, prayer and art, initially based in Northumbria and Mercia, and later in the southern centres of Benedictine reform, was purely devotional (Clayton 1990: 142, 272). In France and Britain, Mary Magdalene was a particularly potent symbol in Christian practices and continues to dominate aspects of religious life in some regions today (Haskins 1993; Saxer 1959).

Let us briefly consider the various manifestations of the Virgin Mary, particularly the Black Madonna. Birnbaum suggests that the selective emphasis on this aspect, prevalent in many parts of Europe, related to continuities from a pre-Christian Earth Goddess (Birnbaum 1993). Gharib has demonstrated the prominence of Mary at the centre of the apostolic church (Gharib 1987). Birnbaum attempts to reconcile this dominating figure with the phenomenon of the Black Madonna; like the prehistoric goddess, the Madonna has many names and many manifestations (Birnbaum 1993: 40). Mainly drawing her source material from nineteenth-century Italy, Birnbaum suggests that the various Black Madonnas embodied vernacular beliefs in justice and equality (*ibid.* 171; Begg 1985); the political dimension is ever present and inextricably bound up with daily life. The continuity in the image of the Madonna from pagan to Christian is described further by Hani, with the maintenance of the division between local, popular belief and the clerical (Hani 1995). The Black Madonna is one of the most fascinating and varied Christian cults to study and track from the Middle Ages up to the present day and regrettably there is only space to refer to it briefly by example. She is one aspect of the Virgin Mary, manifested in countless ways throughout Europe (and today, the world). Harris describes the general devotion attached to the Virgin Mary during the nineteenth century:

> The Children of Mary, congregations of pious girls and women devoted to emulating the Virgin in all her guises, was [*sic*] founded in parishes across France. They took a special role in the activities of the Month of Mary in May, when the contemplation of the mysteries of the rosary was a duty, and the processions in honour of the Virgin an often dramatic demonstration of devotion. Massive churches were built in her honour at Puy, at Fourvière in Lyon, at Notre-Dame de Lorette in Paris, while bishops across the land promoted sumptuous ceremonies to crown existing and new statues. Catholic houses – from the richest to the poorest – were adorned with porcelain images of the Virgin, while, in later years, pious families displayed reproductions of Our Lady of Lourdes. (Harris 1999: 15)

Inevitably, cults devoted to saints threatened to rival the worship of God. In the third and fourth centuries, distinctions are prevalent in the literature between *latria* or the worship owed to Christ, *hyperdulia*, veneration attached to the Virgin Mary and the *dulia* or veneration of the saints (Wilson 1983: 4). This was plausible enough in the abstract, but was often difficult to maintain in practice (Woodward 1991: 58). Saints, as objects of popular devotion, were accessible and easy to identify with. In some cases, veneration of the saint could be moved from the sphere of the Church into the 'folk' or domestic sphere. This was invariably influenced by personal politics as much as anything else. The inevitable outcome, as with private veneration of any supernatural power, was potential for subtle divergence of beliefs (Birnbaum 1993: 68–9). The transference of relics from tombs to churches and the 'discovery' of previously unrecognised saintly remains led to the acceleration in the dismemberment and distribution of relics, each one charged with the saint's power (*ibid.* 63; Rollason 1986: 32). Despite the incorporation of saints' cults into the liturgy, the preoccupation with relics confirmed the triumph of the saint as a 'source of miraculous power' over the saint as an 'example of the imitation of Christ' (*ibid.* 64). On a wider level, saints proved useful for their unfailing support for national causes, such as St Denis, who became the principal protector of the French realm under the Capetians (Spiegal 1983: 141). Shrines of varying manifestations of the Virgin or Christ were regarded as belonging to distinct divine beings and may be treated as a form of saintly shrine (Wilson 1983: 12). Clearly much investment went into maintaining the presence of a saint. After the demolishing of the Old Minster at Winchester, St Swithun's presence was preserved by a stone coffin representing his tomb. This resulted in a dual focus cult; one based around the feretory within the Norman Cathedral and the other around the empty tomb outside the north door of the nave (Biddle 1986: 28). Popular devotion to individual saints was by definition difficult to regulate:

> As saints are persons possessed of a charisma that is potentially dangerous and anarchic, and which the authorities seek to control by channelling it via monasticism, canonization procedures, formal liturgies and the emphasis on the post-mortem cult, so pilgrimage cuts across geographical and social boundaries, takes people out of their established places, mixes social strata and the sexes, allows individuals to wander like vagabonds, and focuses not on the Church's formal rituals though these may be present, but on a whole range of para-liturgical and unorthodox practices (such as touching tombs, kissing relics, making circuits and processions, bathing, imbibing, feasting) which the clergy could only partially control.
>
> (Wilson 1983: 14)

Whilst it is important to remember that pilgrimage routes were marked out and local religious centres had a certain amount of regulatory control (*ibid.*), Rollason's (1986: 36) study of relationships between the distribution of relics, their shrines and translations in Anglo-Saxon England, suggests that the seats of episcopal power, cathedrals, did not have exclusive rights to this distribution. Instead, relics were concentrated in churches with particular 'ambitions and traditions', and caution against generalised models of religious vertical control.

In some cases, public and private devotion towards saints verged on direct heretical conflict with the Church's desire for doctrinal stability. The *idea* of heresy is particularly illuminating in its explicit demonstration of variability and the potential for extreme variability within the Christian paradigm. It is important to bear in mind the spectrum of the definition here: the Roman Church, creator of the Inquisition and persistent in its attempts to crush all visible forms of heresy, was itself declared heretical by the Byzantine Church during the Iconoclasm.

Extreme Variability: the Establishment and Use of a Definition of Medieval Heresy

The word 'heresy' derives from the Greek *harens* – the act of choosing or leading to the choice of philosophical principles (O'Grady 1985: 4). Heresies arose from the very start of Christianity and were almost immediately condemned (*Corinthians* XI, 18–19, *Epistle to Titus*, II, 10). However, the meaning of heresy as 'doctrine maintained within the church but disruptive of its unity' was not fixed until the fourth century. The definition became elaborated with time:

fundamentally mistaken theological opinion or doctrine held *in opposition* to the orthodox doctrine of the Church and adhered to with obstinacy (*ibid*. 6). The earliest heresies were primarily concerned with doctrine and prompted the re-formulation and clarification of the orthodox line. In the later Middle Ages, most heresies centred on ecclesiastical and practical controversies or on the individual conscience against the established order. It is sometimes difficult to isolate orthodox dogma from heretical trends: Montanism worked within the Christian paradigm with heavy emphasis on martyrdom and millennianism. Donatism threatened to split the Church with its rejection of the spiritually impure. The Gnostic and Manichaean doctrine of 'pure spirit escaping from hostile matter' no doubt influenced fourth century asceticism whilst the Arian heresy, which attacked the concept of Trinitarianism (the acceptance of a unified holy Trinity) established as the official religion of the Empire by Theodosius, was at one time the mainstream version of Christianity in the Roman and the Gothic kingdoms. Manichaeism went underground from the end of the fifth until the eleventh century, appearing in southern France and Spain among the Cathars. In the east, a resurgence in Manichaeism was encouraged by the Bogomils. The Arian kingdoms had been absorbed into Catholicism by the seventh century and by the eighth century Arianism as an organised heretical form had disappeared although its ideas probably survived (*ibid*. 96; Barnes and Williams 1993). In the early fifth century, Pelagius came to Rome from Britain with his doctrine of human freedom of choice and the denial of original sin. The Council of Carthage condemned these ideas in 416; Pope Zosimus retracted the attack whilst the Emperor Honorius confirmed the council's condemnation in 418. Although Pelagius died, his ideas continued to spread and finally the Council of Ephesus condemned Pelagianism as heretical in 431. However, most historians agree that from the seventh to the eleventh century, the structure of society and the primarily monastic character of Christianity did not foster widespread dissenting beliefs with a popular, lay base, nor did it allow for the range of inquiry that later led to the growth of intellectual, philosophical heresy (Peters 1980: 3). The first official execution of heretics en masse (the first individual execution was in 385, Moore 1995: 21) took place in Orléans in 1022 (*ibid*. 15) and conveniently marked the beginning of the acceleration towards the collision between mainstream, popular heretical traditions and the orthodox line generated at Rome.

The Cathar heresy was perhaps the final episode in the polarisation of orthodox and heretical beliefs and arguably the greatest heretical challenge to the Church in the eleventh and twelfth centuries with a lasting legacy (Barber 2000: 1, 5). In November 1215, the Ecumenical Council held in Rome was attended by three patriarchs, 400 bishops and 800 abbots and priors, together with various repre-sentatives of the secular powers. Their purpose was to reaffirm through defini-tions and resolutions, the stability, continuity and orthodoxy of the reformed Church; aiming at a universal system headed by the Pope. The cumulative result of the Albigensian crusade was a more centralised, authoritarian Church sanctioning the use of force and no longer tolerating radical reform. Notions of

'Christendom' and 'Christian identity' began to cohere at this time. Finally, in the eyes of the Papacy, members of the Christian Church were 'orthodox or they were nothing' (Frayling 1995: 98).

However, it is important to put things into perspective. Whilst the first inquisitors were pursuing their investigations in southern France, Lithuanians were actively worshipping pagan deities. Relations between the papacy and Lithuania were not as simple as a choice between full acceptance of Roman Catholicism and extermination. Lithuania's pagan rulers maintained economic and diplomatic ties with their Christian neighbours. Treaties and negotiations delaying the Christianising brand of baptism enabled Lithuania to maintain its independence by being able to deal politically with both Catholic and Eastern Orthodox Churches, as well as other parties such as the Hansa, Rus and the Teutonic Order (Mazeika 1997: 131). The teachings of the Eastern Orthodox Church were also frayed by heretical strains, notably the *Strigoniki* and the *Judaizer* heresy in the fourteenth and fifteenth centuries (Orchard 1992: 48–50), as well as the dualist heresies which turned up in widely separated regions of the Byzantine Empire and of which probably only a small proportion were detected (Hussey 1986: 161). If one adds to the religious equation the repeated waves of Mongol incursions throughout the medieval period, the result is further diversity and variability of localised religious systems.

The paradigm of the early Christian Church was modified on one level by ideas which were later condemned as heretical with a resulting acceleration towards a stable orthodox line. Heresy forced the Church to progressively define its doctrines and anathematise deviant theological opinions (Lambert 1999: 3; O'Grady 1985: 7) It is difficult to estimate the extent to which heretical ideas contributed to stimulating and modifying local variations of Christianity. There is very little evidence that it did, but the possibility should not be altogether dismissed. For example, an excavated cathedral at Vegesala, Algeria was identified as Donatist from its inscriptions (Frend 1996: 238). The search for material evidence for heretical ideas tends to revolve around identifiable strains described in the literature and as such is sparse: after all, heretics did not design cathedrals, although some schools of thought on the academic fringe attach heretical symbolism to certain types of ecclesiastical decoration in specific contexts. In theory, architectural images as symbols of ideas could contain complete ideological programmes (Heitz 1986: 90). On more certain grounds, one might label as 'heretical material culture' the late medieval works of Bosch (produced between the 1480s and mid 1490s) containing Manichaean symbolism (Harris 1995), or the apparent Arian crosses on a sarcophagus lid in southwest France, dismissed by James (1977: 69). Physical evidence of heresy can also be found in the thirteenth-century stone memorials in Bosnia, at a time when Catharism was the state religion. Over seven thousand of these are decorated using a clear heretical as opposed to orthodox iconography (Harris 1995: 184). A sarcophagus lid from late tenth, early eleventh-century Macedonia is carved with stylistically Byzantine symbols, which are unique and impossible to explain within the known paradigm of the Eastern Church yet which crop up in Bosch's paintings and on Bosnian tombstones and are suggested as heretical (*ibid.* 221–3). This general topic requires further, detailed research, although one instant hurdle which springs to mind is separating 'heresy' from 'variation'. It is even doubtful whether the term 'heresy' is useful when describing anything except what was branded as such by the Church.

The idea of heresy seems to have been a simple contradiction of the status quo and did not necessarily include all deviations or modifications to a singular Christian doctrine. In this light it would be senseless to ascribe the label 'heretical' to local variations of Christianity, particularly visible in the archaeological record, including ones which borrowed ideas and images from pagan culture. Clearly the Christian paradigm held together as a whole and there was plenty of scope for deviation within the established European episcopal systems, without the tendency for what the later Inquisition would deem as 'aberration'. This is particularly important in any conversion-period context, where one is likely to find the highest range of variation.

Mutual Assimilation and Mutation: the Merging of Pagan and Christian Elements

The conversion did not bring about any instant, overnight changes. There was a gulf between those who expressed the Church's doctrinal position and the everyday religious practices of those who had only recently, and only very superficially, come into contact with Christianity (Dierkens 1998: 54). As with all other speculations about the continuity of pagan customs, relatively recent folklore is often cited at great length, but projecting this back into the past is dangerous because it may reflect potential re-inventions within the framework of the Christian paradigm (Ryan 1999: 14). Christianity incorporated many elements of ancient paganism, for example, festivals were fixed upon dates already associated with major pagan celebrations (Hutton 2000: 285). The fluidity of both pagan and Christian paradigms has already been emphasised, and given our lack of detailed knowledge of European pagan religious systems, speculation on the survival of pagan elements can be difficult to substantiate without physical evidence. In the past, the most popular approach has been a basic polarity: anything obviously 'un-Christian' within our generalised summaries defining religion in the Middle Ages must be a remnant of pre-Christian practices; medieval Christianity was (and in many cases still is) treated as 'paganism given a thin layer of Scripture' (*ibid.* 286). Naturally this is far too simplistic; there is no general approach for every possible context and scenario, although there are patterns relating to the continuity of pagan practices visible in the archaeo-logical record, for example the changes in the distribution and range of grave goods. We are unlikely to find that Le Goff's (1967) division between the clerical culture and the 'folklorique', or Ginzburg's (1979) similar opposition between hegemonic and popular religion, was so clear or even prevalent in all areas, at all times. Duffy (1992: 3) has even rejected the label 'popular religion' in favour of the relatively less problematic 'traditional religion'. But first it is necessary to define some of the mechanisms of religious assimilation during the conversion period.

The problem of syncretism has already been mentioned. This should simply refer to any 'fusion' visible in the archaeological and textual record. Syncretism is also likely to have wider spatial and temporal variation; target audiences differed immensely. In studies of the conversion of Greece, there is a general assumption for pagan continuity throughout this period, with specific references to syncretism at the local, 'street' level (Gregory 1986: 242). However, there may be subtle variations present in any fusion, in the form of 'religious acculturation' where modifications do not affect the central elements of a religion (Gräslund 2000: 94). In order for both paradigms to co-exist simultaneously there must be evidence for pagan worship, rather than the use of pagan motifs in iconographic or literary variants within a Christian framework. Hutton (2000) has consistently argued for the treatment of seemingly 'pagan' practices such as fertility rites, Green men and spells as variants of Christianity, since there is no evidence for any devotion to a pagan deities:

> When looking for 'pagan survivals' in the medieval Church, it is not enough for historians to detect parallels, relics or imitations of paganism. It is necessary to demonstrate that certain things, although now existing within a Christian structure, kept alive a memory of, and reverence for, the old deities. Otherwise they were part of Christianity. (Hutton 2000: 289)

Although Hutton shows that it is largely absent in Britain, there are repeated claims of pagan survival through what has been labelled as 'submerged beliefs' (Birnbaum 1993: 29). In the case of the Italian Black Madonna, many cultures were superimposed on the original goddess who appears to have retained her power into the Christian period (*ibid.* 44).

Gräslund (2000) has summarised the situation relating to the loss of memory associated with pagan connotations coupled with the retention, and adaptation of the form:

> The question of continuity versus change has often been discussed in archaeology, and in many cases it is obvious that there is continuity within the change, so that remaining elements from the past, even if they lose their meaning, still remain. (Gräslund 2000: 91)

When Christianity encountered paganism, the adoption of semiotics was mutual, with differential dominant influences. In the case of Scandinavian runestones bearing both crosses and traditional symbols such as snakes, the existing religious system had incorporated Christian symbolism into its existing repertoire (Lager 2000: 126; Chapter 31 in this volume) and *vice versa*. A later example of this, visible in northern European Romanesque art, can be found in the shared semiotics associated with the wolf, and goes further to explain the inconsistencies within any generalised view of medieval Christianity (Pluskowski 2001).

The brand of Christianity transmitted to Germanic people had to override existing religious responses to fundamental military, agricultural and personal matters. An unintended result of implementing missionary policy accommodating these concerns was the 'Germanization' of early medieval Christianity (Russell 1996: 4). It is likely that Clovis believed in the Christian God as 'the giver of victories' (Wallace-Hadrill 1962: 70). Despite his acceptance of the Christian paradigm, Clovis was still a barbarian chieftain in essence; his lawcode, *Patus Legis Salicae*, continued to protect pagan graves and sacrifices, whilst polygamy was maintained within family units (Cusack 1998: 76). Even when Christianity was firmly established as the religion of the Franks, pagan culture lived on in the habits and lifestyle of the Frankish monarchy and aristocracy (*ibid.* 80). Poems like the *Heiland* portrayed God as a Germanic warrior leader, retelling the Gospel story in the cultural mode of the Germanic peoples (*ibid.* 129). While the new faith was apparently very successful in providing alternative and parallel functions to the former cults, it was much less effective in preventing recourse to magic, at all levels of society. After all it was a religion, and no more able to satisfy the impulses which drove people to use spells than any other. Thus magic cannot, strictly speaking, be described as 'pagan'. It was separate from the worship of the old deities, could flourish within a Christian culture (Duffy 1992: 285), and was a constant factor before and after the Christian conversion. Evidence of animal sacrifice and other seemingly pagan activities had been detached from any previous religious context. Hildegard of Bingen's use of herbs for various ailments incorporated knowledge from the pre-Christian, Germanic magical system, simultaneously incorporating the power of God as the ultimate activator of the healing properties (Charon 1998). Likewise, nine iron masks discovered in the 1930s within the Great Palace of Constantinople complement textual evidence of masquerades at the Byzantine palace, clearly resonating with pagan practices within a Christian context where even the clergy joined in (Franceschini 1995: 132).

An interesting example of the survival and Christian utilisation of a pagan folktale is cited by Lebbe (1998: 75) in his analysis of the wild hunt and changing ideas about the dead in the Middle Ages following the conversion. Petrus Venerabilis, the twelfth-century Abbot of Cluny, related a story about a priest called Stephen from the Bishop of Vienne in *De miraculis libri duo*, essentially utilising a variant of the wild hunt: the ghostly rider, as a way of attacking the heretical sect of Petrus of Brys. The Petrobrusians did not believe that the living could intervene in the fate of the dead, and thus opposed orthodox funerary practices, particularly the provision of alms and prayers for the deceased. Lebbe notes how Petrus Venerabilis resorted to a popular tale of the ghostly hunt to combat heresy, suggesting that there was a certain amount of attachment to old, atavistic ideas rather than purely to the Church's vision (*ibid.*).

Overall, the transition from pagan to Christian in Britain and Scandinavia was gradual and multi-faceted (Brink 2000; Gräslund 2000). The term 'Conversion' simply referred to the adoption of a creed and submission to the authority of the

Church (Thomas 1935: 38). In Britain and Scandinavia, this term covers a multitude of small and often stressful negotiations as shown by many examples in this book. The process in these countries in most cases began with political conversion, followed by the filtering of the Christian paradigm through the lower strata of society, through vertical transmission (Wes 1992: 252; but see Chapter 31 by Lager in this volume). This is an alternative model to the transmission of the Christian paradigm *en masse*: a group matter rather than an individual one (Addison 1936: 21). In Poland, the conversion has been described as a state cult gradually replacing former tribal cults (Kloczowski 2000: 21). As the Church's dealings with the Wends in the eleventh and twelfth centuries demonstrate, a grasping desire to extend political control and increase the revenues of the Church was characteristic of much so-called missionary activity and largely accounted for its failure (*ibid.* 20). Yet it seems hardly plausible to suggest that a whole country and region was instantly converted overnight after the acceptance of a missionary by the controlling ruler or court. The historical record for both Britain, and central and eastern Europe, for example, is riddled with pagan relapses following apparent 'conversions', some of which were politically motivated revolts as in the case of Saxony. Several examples will illustrate the variety of pagan-Christian interactions preserved in archaeological and textual records.

The evidence of burials during and after the conversion period can throw some light on the issue of religious fusion and localised interpretations of both pagan and Christian paradigms. As we have already emphasised, one cannot simply attach sweeping religious labels to categories of graves and their contents (Dierkens 1998: 43; Halsall 1995: 62). There is no necessary connection between the burial rite and specific beliefs regarding the afterlife (Ucko 1969) and the Church clearly never had a blanket anti-grave goods policy or anything against lavish burials. There is little evidence for overriding orthodox concerns over grave orientation; more significant was the change of location of aristocratic burials to within or around churches (Lucy 2000: 184). Christians did not routinely continue to place objects in graves in the manner of many earlier pagan practices, although there are several examples from clear Christian contexts in England and Frankia where they did (Abrams 1998: 116). Carver (1998a: 15) has suggested that the decrease in grave goods reflects the rise of a centralised taxation system and therefore a shift in the mechanism of wealth distribution, in which the newly established Church was the beneficiary. In relation to Christianity, paganism may have had little in the way of structuring in the funerary domain (Young 1999: 83), in that pagan graves were not always associated with shrines or sacred places; but this assumes a generalised paganism throughout Europe. In Northern England, for example, the diversity in pre-churchyard burial practices cautions against monocausal explanations (Hadley 2000: 159). Clear indicators of pagan burial rites such as cremation, mound, ship (Carver 1998a: 14) and horse burials (although the latter could reflect status as much as religious affiliation; Dierkens 1998: 53) disappear with the conversion to Christianity at different times in different areas. In East Anglia, it has been argued that specific pagan burial rites were re-emphasised as a response to the political threat of Christianity (Carver 1998b: 136).

Moving east, the conversion of Scandinavia is generally perceived as a multi-faceted process, expressed differently in different areas, with mutual influence between Christian and pagan ideas estimated over a period of at least three centuries (Andersson 1997: 353; Chapter 31 by Lager, Chapter 32 by Welinder in this volume). Scandinavia was exposed to several different varieties of Continental European Christianity in the conversion period (Andersson 2000: 143) including the possibility of Byzantine missions and material culture (Staecker 1997: 442, 447; disputed in Chapter 35 by Beskow in this volume). The varying pace of the conversion is particularly interesting to track through the evidence of changing burials in Scandinavia. Andersson's case study of the small settlement of Valsta contrasted with the ecclesiastical centre of Sigtuna provides a clear example of this variation and how Christianity was interpreted in different ways at the microscale. At Valsta, and also Skälby (the latter used from the mid-tenth century), cremation and inhumation were present simultaneously (Andersson 2000: 137). These instances are not unique, for similar patterns can be observed at Väster Arninge, Ärvinge and Kymlinge containing a mixture of grave goods and orientations (ibid. 140). Mixtures of typical pagan and Christian traits also occur; clearly Christianity was not segregated in the funerary space nor, following Andersson's supposition, within the social groupings reflected by this (Andersson 1997: 363). In the year 1100, new graves appeared retaining their old forms and Barrow A1 constructed in the mid-ninth century had its centre removed and replaced with three cist graves forming the shape of a cross. Careful treatment of the remains and the shell of the barrow suggest that there was a general desire for continuity and stability (ibid. 366); the sudden change may reflect the filtering down of episcopal authority from Sigtuna, where regimented graves, seemingly devoid of localised social groupings, characterise the funerary space. The general pattern seems to be an increase in variation in the countryside as opposed to the urban centres where the episcopal system was strong. This does not imply that people in the countryside were any less Christian (Andersson 2000: 142). Evidence of the incorporation of pre-Christian elements into the later medieval Christian culture can be seen in the belief in prehistoric flint objects as thunderbolts. This was prevalent throughout Europe, but particularly densely distributed throughout medieval contexts at Lund in contrast with the sparse distribution across the rest of Sweden (Carelli 1997: 393). Together with the re-use of pre-Christian monuments such as runestones, this is another example of the blending of material culture, although neither example suggests a continuation of pagan devotion.

Further east, Byzantine Christianity in Russia was (and still is) in many ways a world apart from that of typical western Catholics. In rural parishes, the community selected its own clergy, appointing the necessary sacristans and cantors; before taking up his office, the parish priest had to first present the bishop with a document embodying the agreement between him and his parishioners

(Orchard 1992: 41). Russian historians frequently characterise popular religion in Russia as part of the *dvoeverie* or culture of 'double-belief' (Ryan 1999: 14; Valk, Chapter 37 in this volume). Sometimes this is defined as the coexistence of two separate belief systems, Christian and pagan, a situation disputed on theoretical grounds by Schmitt (1998a: 384), sometimes as syncretism and sometimes as simultaneous acceptance of both. Pagan cult artefacts dominate over Christian ones in the archaeological record from the first two or three centuries of Christianity in Russia (Ryan, 1999: 14). One study of burial practices and grave goods in Kievan Rus' between the tenth and thirteenth centuries demonstrates the continuity of pre-Christian amulets in graves also containing amulets bearing Christian motifs (*ibid*. 219). Christianity clearly took over many elements of pagan 'magical' functions despite officially condemning such practices. Christianity introduced its own set of amulets and talismans with thaumaturgical properties: a ninth-century apocryphal letter of the Oriental Patriarchs to the Emperor Theophilus includes a list of the twelve most potent miracle-working icons, essentially loaded with the same magical function as pagan devices (*ibid*. 233). Of course the difference lay in the source of power: Christian 'magic' as in the case of Hildegard's healing herbs, ultimately derived from God, whilst pagan magic claimed its origin from other supernatural forces (Hutton 2000: 255–6). It is likely that in most cases, the original spiritual associations of those talismans and amulets attached to specifics within the pagan system were replaced and Christianised, in some cases shifting from amulet to relic (Fletcher 1998: 251).

Further claims of a double faith, coexisting during the Middle Ages, come from the writings of Jacobus of Serugh, Buchard of Worms and Petrus Venerabilis which demonstrate the existence of two cults of the dead, one emanating from the Church, the other independent of it (Lebbe 1998: 79–80). Whilst deliberately ignoring the syncretisms and pagan inspirations for medieval attitudes towards the dead, Schmitt has demonstrated how these were re-worked and repeatedly modified during the Middle Ages by various social groups, particularly monastic orders (Schmitt 1998b).

The official conversion of Bulgaria in 865 followed intensive questioning of the Roman Curia by Khan Boris, regarding the definitions and understanding of the Christian paradigm. Ultimately Byzantine Christianity was chosen with related political connotations (Hussey 1986: 99), although the presence of Christian symbols such as the cross, ship, tree and serpent appear overlapped or surrounded by pagan images; primarily animals and hunting scenes. 'Amateur' depictions of Christian symbols suggest that Christianity was spread throughout the lower social levels before its official adoption, however there are many problems with attempting a clear analysis of the co-existence of pagan and Christian imagery. The tree, for example, recalled passages from the Bible but was also part of the pagan shamanistic complex of images (Minaeva 1996: 95).

The formal Christianisation of Estonia occurred in 1208–1277 through a series of crusades, although it is difficult to ascertain the point of a full conversion, since this saw the conclusion of the crusades leading to a period of double-faith and syncretism. According to Valk (Chapter 37 in this volume), the long persistence of local traditional beliefs was favoured by a strong ethno-social polarisation of society between the Estonian-speaking lower classes and the German-speaking nobility, including the clergy. Estonian syncretism was clearly reflected in sacred places: semi-pagan cultic practices continued until the late seventeenth and early eighteenth century; offerings were made to trees, groves, stones and springs until the mid or late nineteenth century. This almost never merged with the cult of saints. The inhabitants of the Baltic were baptised and re-baptised many times: first by the Russians, then by the Germans who re-baptised them into the Latin Church. The Russians tried re-conversion to the Byzantine creed and this was followed by subsequent re-baptism at the hands of the Danes and Swedes (Olins 1928: 34). Although there is a political dimension present in all of this, in that baptism was considered a legal title for possession of the country, it must have confused and distorted religious belief and practice on the ground. This is perhaps particularly well summed up by the Count de Bray regarding the impact of the Reformation in converted Livonia:

> As to the people . . . they hardly noticed that a change of religion had taken place. Under Catholicism they automatically attended the ceremonies which were not explained and the prayers that were recited in an unknown language. (Olins 1928: 76)

The interplay between religion and politics is not central to this discussion, although it is clearly an important aspect of the conversion process. The episcopal system brought with it new forms of administration and territorial identification. In England, the Church contributed to the introduction of bookland (land held by charter (Campbell 1986: 82)). There is quite a strong possibility that the development of monasticism brought about major changes in the pattern of settlement (Turner, Chapter 11 in this volume).

Sacred Landscapes: the Conversion of Topography

The conversion in northern Europe changed conceptual and physical landscapes. It arguably led to the wholesale reinterpretation of geography; religious traditions mediate perceptions of the numinous in the landscape. The translation of saints' cults in the West created coherent patterns of sacred geography, a process codified by canon laws regulating the distribution of relics (Howe 1997: 65). The end result was a fully articulated parish structure. Beneath and beyond the sacred grid of saints, their churches and shrines, intersected by pilgrimage routes, existed a sacred geography based upon nature. Springs, wells, forests and mountains were reclaimed for Christ during the conversion although their pagan resonance remained. There is a connection between many important pagan and Christian sites in terms of continuity, for example at Tavigny in the Ardennes, excavations of a small Gallo-Roman temple dating to the second or third century revealed that it had been later abandoned, become a cemetery in the eighth or ninth centuries and finally a chapel dedicated to St. Martin was raised on its ruins. This is not an existing structure being converted, but proof of the persistence of a sacral tradition (Dierkens 1998: 42). There was no simple substitution of a pagan for a Christian religious topography (Markus 1990: 155) – instead there was a slow attrition of the un-holiness of pagan sacred places and the emergence of a new holiness attached to particular spots. To convert the landscape completely in any one country took centuries (Howe 1997: 66–8). Various considerations must be included when mapping religious landscapes. Churches took a variety of forms and were the product of the interaction between foreign influences and local traditions, between stone and wood and between liturgical demand and construction techniques (Stoepker 1990: 216). But they were also a means of advertising function and newly constructed identity. Similarly, stone crosses and later Viking monuments in Britain proclaimed different orders. The distribution of relics cannot be excluded from a study of the geography of power and influence (Rollason 1986: 42; Pearce, Chapter 4 in this volume), as well as local religious traditions.

Christian attitudes towards woodland provide a particularly interesting example. The documentary evidence does not reveal any desire for the wholesale clearance of woodland on account of broader pagan associations; there are individual accounts of sacred groves and trees being felled but nothing to justify the popular link in the minds of medieval Christians between pagans and woodland. There is also nothing in the pollen record to suggest a sudden acceleration of woodland clearance at the time of the conversion. The wilderness became populated with hermits, and wild animals described in simplistic terms by popular dictionaries of symbols, as 'evil' or representing a random sin, often had conceptual, aesthetic and economic status. The detailed and multiple relationships between humans and their physical and conceptual landscapes is an area which demands further research and will invariably provide further evidence of spatial and temporal variation within medieval religious paradigms.

Conclusion: Conversion and the Mosaic of Medieval Christianities

When Ulryk von Jungingen, Grandmaster of the Teutonic Knights, declared his intention to invade Poland in 1409, his ambitions were driven by politics rather than religion (Christiansen 1997: 127). There was not even the excuse of smiting the heathen that had worked so well for Charlemagne's campaigns against the Germans and the Teutonic Order's crusades against the pagan Slavs. It is easy to exaggerate the importance of 'politics' out of context. Were the heresies which had a profound effect upon the daily life of people in Languedoc and Bohemia unique episodes? How widespread were undocumented heretical ideas throughout the history of the Church? Although the adoption of Byzantine Christianity in Bulgaria resulted in the reorientation of relations and the political system with Constantinople, did this have a dramatic impact on the attitudes of people in the lower social strata? Of course, religious beliefs may themselves influence political behaviour on more than one level. There is plenty of evidence for the frequent incorporation and occasional survival of pagan elements into new forms of Christianity as official religious frontiers were breached in the north. In some cases Christ may have been added to a list of existing deities, and saints may have come to present the equivalent of a polytheistic pantheon in popular belief, despite the dogmatic supremacy of the Trinity and its imposition by the episcopal system, an issue which, incidentally, was challenged and modified to and fro across a vast geographical space by Arianism, itself see-sawing from heretical heterodoxy to imperial orthodoxy. Yet by the time Lithuania had been converted 'in name' at least, and the religious frontier shifted to Russia, the Reformation was beginning to flower in central Europe, and to shock the system with the declared split from Rome and subsequent dissolution of monastic houses in England in the 1530s. But even here, historians have argued convincingly that Henry VIII remained a good Catholic till the last (Duffy 1992: 449). The shift was yet another re-interpretation and physical re-working of the Christian paradigm, explained recently in a more novel way as a pattern recurring throughout the history of the Church by Fernandez-Ármesto and Wilson (1996).

It is difficult to generalise about countries or even cultures. Scholars speak of 'The Anglo-Saxon Church' (Butler and Morris 1986) or 'The Frankish Church' (Wallace-Hadrill 1983) recognising the fluidity of the early Christian paradigm, yet even these categories can be further subdivided both temporally and spatially. Clearly, within the framework of medieval Christianity, there were differences related to how life should be organised and God worshipped, how much empha-sis to place on specific aspects of religious practice such as the liturgy or a saint's cult. In the case of Britain, Carver (1998a: 21) has suggested that there were, potentially at least, three different infrastructures for Christianity on offer in the seventh to ninth centuries, characterised by episcopal, monastic and secular organisations, each recognisable by their different material investments and supported by different economic systems; conversion could take place to, and between, any one of them. Dierkens (1998: 50) stated that: 'It is impossible to draw any general or direct conclusions from a Christian symbol or scene: each case has to be looked at and interpreted individually and set in its proper geographical and chronological context.' Since both pagan and Christian religions remained integral to all other aspects of life, it should not be surprising to find variation governed by factors such as local politics, aesthetic conventions, social relations and the specific needs of a particular audience. According to Campbell (1986: 84), this is one of the 'safe' generalisations we can make about England and its Church and by extension about the whole of medieval Christianity. We should be cautious, but not dismissive, about mapping potentially anachronistic scenarios from the Renaissance era or from ethnographic analogies back onto the early Middle Ages. For example, Ginzburg's (1983) popular religious beliefs continuing from pre-Christian traditions, prevalent among the lower classes, modified and ultimately attacked by the Inquisition, were inevitably re-interpreted within a Christian framework and affected by the political, social, religious and economic variables of the time. Calculation, hesitation, diplomatic nicety, *Realpolitik*, greed and self-promotion cannot be ignored in our study of the conversion period (Fletcher 1998: 521). But we should also beware of reducing our explanations for religious variation to solely non-religious factors (Hadley 2000: 161; Kilbride 2000: 12; Patrick 2000: 50; Pluskowski 2000: 75). The ultimate questions that we should ask when examining and analysing a specific conversion period context are these: How did *they* imagine Christ? How did *they* pray to God? How did *they* interpret Christianity?

ACKNOWLEDGEMENTS

We would like to thank Professor Martin Carver for the inspiration and opportunity to present this response to the Conversion Conference at York, 2000. We would also like to thank Dr Catherine Hills and Paul Bibire for their invaluable comments and Professor Rev. William Frend for his advice on medieval heresy.

References

Abrams, L. 1998. 'History and Archaeology: The Conversion of Scandinavia.' In Crawford, B.E. (ed.) *Conversion and Christianity in the North Sea World. The Proceedings of a Day Conference held on 21st February 1998*. St Andrews. 11–40.

Addison, J.T. 1936. *The Medieval Missionary. A Study of the Conversion of Northern Europe AD 500–1300*. New York: International Missionary Council.

Andersson, G. 1997. 'A Struggle for Control: Reflections on the Change of Religion in a Rural Context in the Eastern Mälaren Valley.' In Andersson, H., Carelli, P., and Ersgård, L. (eds) *Visions of the Past: trends and traditions in Swedish medieval archaeology*. Lund Studies in Medieval Archaeology 19. Stockholm: Central Board of National Antiquities. 353–72.

—— 2000. 'West and East: Two sides of the Same Coin? On Variation and Their Significance in Inhumation Burials in Eastern Central Sweden c 950–1150 AD.' In Pluskowski, A.G. (ed.) *Early Medieval Religion: Archaeological Review from Cambridge 17: 2*. Bar Hill: Victoire Press. 133–47.

Bailey, R.N. 1981. 'The Hammer and the Cross.' In *The Vikings in England*. Exhibition Catalogue of 'The Vikings in England and their Danish Homeland', Yorkshire Museum, York, April 3rd – September 30th 1982. London: Anglo-Danish Project.

Barber, M. 2000. *The Cathars: Dualist Heretics in Languedoc in the High Middle Ages*. Harlow: Longman / Pearson Education Ltd.

Barnes, M.R. and Williams, D.H (eds). 1993. *Arianism after Arius: essays on the development of the fourth century trinitarian Conflicts*. Edinburgh: T&T Clark.

Bede. *Historia ecclesiastica (Ecclesiastical History) (HE)*. Colgrave, B. and Mynors, R.A.B. (eds) Oxford: Clarendon Press. 1969: 1991 Printing.

Begg, E. 1985. *The Cult of the Black Virgin*. London: Arkana.

Biddle, M. 1986. 'Archaeology, Architecture and the Cult of Saints in Anglo-Saxon England.' In Butler, L.A.S. and Morris, R.K. (eds) *The Anglo-Saxon Church: Papers on History, Architecture and Archaeology in Honour of Dr. H.M .Taylor*. London: Council for British Archaeology. 1–31.

Birnbaum, L.C. 1993. *Black Madonnas: feminism, religion and politics in Italy*. Boston: Northeastern University Press.

Brink, S. 2000. 'The Christianization of Scandinavia – the Philological Evidence.' Lecture given at the Age of Conversion in Northern Europe, Friday 21 July 2000.

Butler, L.A.S., and Morris, R.K. (eds) 1986. *The Anglo-Saxon Church: papers on history, architecture and archaeology in honour of Dr. H.M. Taylor*. London: Council for British Archaeology.

Brooks, N.P. 2000. 'From British to English Christianity: Deconstructing Bede's Interpretation of the Conversion'. Abstract from *York 2000: The Age of Conversion in Northern Europe. 17th-22nd July*. The University of York.

Calkins, R.G. 1998. *Medieval Architecture in Western Europe: from AD 300 to 1500*. Oxford: Oxford University Press.

Campbell, J. 1986. *Essays in Anglo-Saxon History*. London: Hambledon Press.

Carelli, P. 1997. 'Thunder and Lightning, Magical Miracles: on the popular myth of Thunderbolts and the presence of Stone Age Artefacts in Medieval Deposits.' In Andersson, H., Carelli, P. and Ersgard, L. (eds) *Visions of the Past: trends and traditions in Swedish medieval archaeology*. Lund Studies in Medieval Archaeology, 19. Stockholm: Central Board of National Antiquities. 393–417.

Carver M.O.H. 1986. 'Sutton Hoo in context.' *Settimane di Studio del Centro Italiano di Studi sull'Alto medioevo* 32. 77–117.

—— 1989. 'Kingship and material culture in early Anglo-Saxon East Anglia.' In S. Bassett (ed.) *The Origins of Anglo-Saxon Kingdoms*. Leicester: Leicester University Press. 141–58.

—— 1998a. 'Conversion and Politics on the Eastern Seaboard of Britain: Some Archaeological Indicators.' In Crawford, B.E. (ed.) *Conversion and Christianity in the North Sea World. The Proceedings of a Day Conference held on 21st February 1998*. St Andrews. 11–40.

—— 1998b. *Sutton Hoo: burial ground of kings?* London: British Museum Press.

Charon, V. 1998. 'The Knowledge of Herbs.' In Milis, L.J.R. (ed.) *The Pagan Middle Ages*. Woodbridge: Boydell Press. 109–28.

Christiansen, E. 1997. *The Northern Crusades*. London: Penguin.

Clayton, M. 1990. *The Cult of the Virgin Mary in Anglo-Saxon England*. Cambridge: Cambridge University Press.

Cramp, R. 1980. 'The Viking Image'. In Farrell, R. (ed.) *The Vikings*. London: Phillimore. 8–19.

Cusack, C.M. 1998. *Conversion Among the Germanic Peoples*. London: Cassell.

Dierkens, A. 1998. 'The Evidence of Archaeology.' In Milis, L.J.R. (ed.) *The Pagan Middle Ages*. Woodbridge: Boydell Press. 39–64.

Dowden, K. 2000. *European Paganism: The Realities of Cult from Antiquity to the Middle Ages*. London: Routledge.

Duffy, E. 1992. *The Stripping of the Altars: traditional religion in England, c1400 – c1580*. New Haven and London: Yale University Press.

Duggan, G. 1997. 'For Force is Not of God? Compulsion and Conversion from Yahweh to Charlemagne.' In Muldoon, J. (ed.) *Varieties of Religious Conversion in the Middle Ages*. Gainesville: University of Florida Press.

Eco, U. 1998. *The Name of the Rose*. London: Vintage. First published in English, in 1983, by Secker & Warburg.

Fernandez-Ármesto, F. and Wilson, D. 1996. *Reformations: A Radical Interpretation of Christianity and the World (1500–2000)*. New York: Scribner.

Fletcher, R. 1998. *The Conversion of Europe: From Paganism to Christianity 371–1386 AD*. London: HarperCollins.

Franceschini, E.B.R. 1995. 'Winter in the Great Palace: The Persistence of Pagan Festivals in Christian Byzantium.' In Effthymiadis, S., Rapp, C. and Tsougarakis, D. (eds) *Bosphorus: Esays in Honour of Cyril Mango*. Byzantinische Forschungen Band XXI. Amsterdam: Adolf M. Hakhert.

Frayling, C. 1995. *Strange Landscape: A Journey Through the Middle Ages*. London: Penguin.

Frend, W. 1996. *The Archaeology of Early Christianity: a History*. London: Geoffrey Chapman.

Geake, H. 1997. *The Use of Grave-Goods in Conversion-Period England, c.600–c.850*. BAR British Series 261.

Gharib, G. 1987. *Le icone Mariane: Storia e culto*. Rome: Città Editrice.

Ginzburg, C. 1983. *The Night Battles: Witchcraft and Agrarian cults in the Sixteenth and Seventeenth Centuries*. Tedeschi, A. and Tedeschi, J. (trans.) London: Routledge and Kegan Paul. First published in 1966.

—— 1979. 'Introduction.' *Quaderni Storici* 41.

Golding, B. 1994. *Conquest and Colonisation: The Normans in Britain, 1066–1100*. Basingstoke: Macmillan.

Gräslund, A-S. 2000. 'The Conversion of Scandinavia: a sudden event or a gradual process?' In Pluskowski, A.G. (ed.) *Early Medieval Religion: Archaeological Review from Cambridge 17: 2*. Bar Hill: Victoire Press. 83–98.

Gregory, T.E. 1986. 'The Survival of Paganism in Christian Greece: A Critical Essay.' *American Journal of Philology, Vol. 107, No. 2*. 229–42.

Hadley, D. 2000. 'Equality, Humility and Non-Materialism? Christianity and Anglo-Saxon burial practices.' In Pluskowski, A.G. (ed.) *Early Medieval Religion: Archaeological Review from Cambridge 17: 2*. Bar Hill: Victoire Press. 149–78.

Halsall, G. 1995. *Early Medieval Cemeteries: An Introduction to Burial Archaeology in the Post-Roman West*. Skelmorlie: Cruithne Press.

Hani, J. 1995. *La Vierge Noire et le Mystère marial*. Paris: Guy Trédaniel Éditeur.

Harris, L. 1995. *The Secret Heresy of Hieronymous Bosch*. Edinbugh: Floris Books.

Harris, R. 1999. *Lourdes: Body and Spirit in the Secular Age*. London: Penguin.

Haskins, S. 1993. *Mary Magdalen: Myth and Metaphor*. London: Harper Collins.

Hawkes, J. 1999. 'Anglo-Saxon Sculpture: Questions of Context.' In Hawkes, J. and Mills, S. (eds) *Northumbria's Golden Age*. Stroud: Sutton.

Heitz, C. 1986. 'The Iconography of Architectural Form.' In Butler, L.A.S. and Morris, R.K. (eds) *The Anglo-Saxon Church: Papers on History, Architecture and Archaeology in Honour of Dr. H.M. Taylor*. London: Council for British Archaeology. 90–104.

Howe, J.M. 1997. 'The Conversion of the Physical World: The Creation of A Christian Landscape.' In Muldoon, J. (ed.) *Varieties of Religious Conversion in the Middle Ages*. Gainesville: University of Florida Press.

Hultgård, A. 1992. 'Religiös förändring, kontinuitet och acculturation/syncretism i vikingtidens och medeltidens Skandinaviska religion.' In Nilsson, B. (ed.) *Kontinuitet i kult och fro från vikingatid till medeltid*. Projektet Sveriges Kristnande, Publikation 1. Uppsala.

Hussey, J.M. 1986. *The Orthodox Church in the Byzantine Empire*. Oxford: Clarendon Press.

Hutton, R. 2000. *The Pagan Religions of the Ancient British Isles: their nature and legacy*. First edition printed in 1991. Oxford: Blackwell.

James, E. 1977. *The Merovingian Archaeology of South-West Gaul*. Oxford: British Archaeological Reports 25.

Kilbride, W. 2000. 'Why I Feel Cheated by the Term Christianisation.' In Pluskowski, A.G. (ed.) *Early Medieval Religion: Archaeological Review from Cambridge 17: 2*. Bar Hill: Victoire Press.1–17.

Kloczowski, J. 2000. *A History of Polish Christianity*. Cambridge: Cambridge University Press.

Ladurie, E.L.R. 1978. *Montaillou*. Scolar Press. Reprinted in London: Penguin 1990.

Lager, L. 2000. 'Art as a Reflection of Religious Change: the process of Christianisation as shown in the ornamentation on the runestones.' In Pluskowski, A.G. (ed.) *Early Medieval Religion: Archaeological Review from Cambridge 17: 2*. Bar Hill: Victoire Press. 115–32.

Lambert, M. 1999. *Medieval Heresy. Popular Movements from the Gregorian Reform to the Reformation*. Second edition: 1992. Oxford: Blackwell.

Lebbe, C. 1998. 'The Shadow Realm Between Life and Death.' In Milis, L.J.R. (ed.) *The Pagan Middle Ages*. Woodbridge: Boydell Press. 65–82.

Le Goff, J. 1967. 'Culture cléricale et traditions folkloriques dans la civilisation mérovingienne.' *Annales economies, sociétés, cultures* 22. 780–91.

Loseby, S.T. 1992. 'Bishops and Cathedrals: order and diversity in the 5th century urban landscape of southern Gaul.' In Drinkwater, J. and Elton, H. (eds) *Fifth-century Gaul: a crisis of identity?* Cambridge: Cambridge University Press.

Lucy, S. 2000. *The Anglo-Saxon Way of Death*. London: Sutton.

Markus, R.A. 1990. *The End of Ancient Christianity*. Cambridge: Cambridge University Press.

Marsden, J. 1996. *The Fury of the Northmen: Saints, Shrines and Sea-Raiders in the Viking Age*. London: Kyle Cathie. Originally published in 1994.

Mathews, T.F. 1993. *A Clash of Gods: A Reinterpretation of Early Christian Art*. Princeton: Princeton University Press.

—— 1995. 'The transformation symbolism in Byzantine architecture and the meaning of the Pantokrator in the dome.' In Mathews, T.F. *Art and Architecture in Byzantium and Armenia: liturgical and exegetical approaches*. Aldershot: Variorum. 191–214.

Mayr-Harting, H. 1977. *The Coming of Christianity to Anglo-Saxon England*. London: Batsford.

Mazeika, R. 1997. 'Bargaining for Baptism: Lithuanian Negotiations for Conversion, 1250–1358.' In Muldoon, J. (ed.) *Varieties of Religious Conversion in the Middle Ages*. University Press of Florida. 131–45.

Milis, L.J.R.. 1998. 'Introduction: The Pagan Middle Ages – a contradiction in terms?' In Milis, L.J.R. (ed.) *The Pagan Middle Ages*. Woodbridge: Boydell Press. 1–11.

Minaeva, O. 1996. *From Paganism to Christianity: Formation of Medieval Bulgarian Art (691–972)*. New York: P. Lang.

Moore, R.I. 1995. *The Birth of Popular Heresy*. Toronto: University of Toronto Press.

Morgan, D. 1999. *Visual Piety: A History and Theory of Popular Religious Images*. First published in 1998. Berkeley: University of California Press.

Morton, A. 1992. 'Burial in Middle Saxon Southampton.' In Bassett, S. (ed.) *Death in Towns: urban responses to the dying and the dead 100–1600*. Leicester: Leicester University Press.

Ó Carragáin, É. 1999. 'The Necessary Distance: Imitation Romae and the Ruthwell Cross.' In Hawkes, J. and Mills, S. (eds) *Northumbria's Golden Age*. Stroud: Sutton.

O'Grady, J. 1985. *Heresy: heretical truth or orthodox error? A study of early Christian heresies*. Shaftesbury: Element.

O'Shea, S. 2000. *The Perfect Heresy: The Life and Death of the Cathars*. London: Profile Books.

Oblensky, D. 1988. 'The Balkans in the 9th century: Bridge or Barrier?' In Howard-Johnston, J.D. (ed.) *Byzantium and the West, c850-c1200. Proceedings of the XVIII Spring Symposium of Byzantine Studies. Oxford 30th March-1st April 1984.* Byzantische Roschungen Band XIII. Amsterdam: Verlag Adolf M. Hakkert. 47–66.

Olins, P.Z. 1928. *The Teutonic Knights in Latvia*. Riga.

Orchard, G.E. 1992. 'Monasticism in fifteenth-century Russia.' In Greenshields, M.R. and Robinson, T.A. (eds) *Orthodozy and Heresy in Religious Movements: Discipline and Dissent*. Lampeter: Edward Mellen Press. 36–59.

Patrick, P.J. 2000. 'Bloodlust, Salvation or Fertile Imagination? Human Sacrifice in Early Medieval Northern Europe.' In Pluskowski, A.G. (ed.) *Early Medieval Religion: Archaeological Review from Cambridge 17: 2.* Bar Hill: Victoire Press. 19–54.

Peters, E. (ed.) 1980. *Heresy and Authority in Medieval Europe: documents in translation*. London: Scolar Press.

Pluskowski, A.G. 2000. 'The Sacred Gallows: Sacrificial Hanging to Ó#inn.' In Pluskowski, A.G. (ed.) *Early Medieval Religion: Archaeological Review from Cambridge 17: 2.* Bar Hill: Victoire Press. 55–81.

—— 2001. 'En mørk finde? – om truende villdyr i nordeuropeisk middelalder'. (Dark Enemy? The threatening wild in medieval northern Europe) *Spór*, 1/2001. 14–6.

Richards, J. 1991. *Viking Age England*. London: Batsford/English Heritage.

Rollason, D. 1986. 'The Shrines of Saints in Later Anglo-Saxon England: Distribution and Significance.' In Butler, L.A.S. and Morris, R.K. (eds) *The Anglo-Saxon Church: Papers on History, Architecture and Archaeology in Honour of Dr. H.M. Taylor*. London: Council for British Archaeology. 32–43.

Russell, J.C. 1996. *The Germanization of Early Medieval Christianity: a sociohistorical approach to religious transformation*. Oxford: Oxford University Press. First published 1994.

Ryan, W.F. 1999. *The Bathhouse at Midnight: An Historical Survey of Magic and Divination in Russia*. Stroud: Sutton.

Saxer, V. 1959. *Le culte de Marie Madeleine en Occident des origines à la fin du moyen âge*. Auxerre: Publications de la Société des Fouilles Archaeologique et des Monuments Historiques de l'Yonne.

Schmitt, J-C. 1998a. 'Religion, Folklore and Society in the Medieval West.' In Little, L.K. and Rosenwein, B.H. (eds) *Debating the Middle Ages: Issues and Readings*. Oxford: Blackwell. 376–87.

—— 1998b. *Ghosts in the Middle Ages: The Living and the Dead in Medieval Society*. Chicago: University of Chicago Press. Originally published as *Les revenants: les vivants et les morts dans la société médiévale*. 1994, Éditions Gallimard.

Spiegal, G.M. 1983. 'The Cult of St. Denis and Capetian Kingship.' In Wilson, S. (ed.) *Saints and Their Cults: Studies in Religious Sociology, Folklore and History*. Cambridge: Cambridge University Press. 141–68.

Staecker, J. 1997. 'Legends and Mysteries: Reflections on the Evidence for the Early Mission in Scandinavia.' In Andersson, H., Carelli, P. and Ersgård, L. (eds) *Visions of the Past: trends and traditions in Swedish medieval archaeology*. Lund Studies in Medieval Archaeology, 19. Stockholm: Central Board of National Antiquities.

Stoepker, H. 1990. 'Church Archaeology in the Netherlands: problems, prospects, proposals.' In Besteman, J.C., Bos, J.M. and Heidinga, H.A. (eds) *Medieval Archaeology in the Netherlands*. Assen/Maastricht: Van Gorcum.

Swanton, M. (ed. and trans.) 1975. *Anglo-Saxon Prose*. London: Dent.

Tatton-Brown, T. 1994. *Canterbury: History and Guide*. Stroud: Alan Sutton.

Thomas, C. 1981. *Christianity in Roman Britain to AD 500*. London: Batsford.

Thomas, W.B. 1935. *The Psychology of Conversion, with special reference to St. Augustine*. London: Allenson & Co.

Tyson, J.B. 1973. *A Study of Early Christianity*. London: Collier-Macmillan.

Ucko, P. 1969. 'Ethnography and Archaeological Interpretations of Funerary Remains.' *World Archaeology 1*. 262–80.

Wallace-Hadrill, J.M. 1962. *The Long-Haired Kings*. London: Methuen.

Watts, D. 1991. *Christians and Pagans in Roman Britain*. London: Routledge.

Wes, M.A. 1992. 'Crisis and conversion in fifth-century Gaul: aristocrats and ascetics between "horizontality" and "verticality".' In Drinkwater, J. and Elton, H. (eds) *Fifth-century Gaul: a crisis of identity?* Cambridge: Cambridge University Press.

Wilson, S. 1983. 'Introduction'. In Wilson, S. (ed.) *Saints and Their Cults: Studies in Religious Sociology, Folklore and History*. Cambridge: Cambridge University Press. 1–53

Williams, C. 1980. *Saints: their Cults and Origins*. London: Bergstrom and Boyle Books.

Woodward, K. 1991. *Making saints: inside the Vatican: who became saints, who did not and why*. London: Chatto & Windus.

Young, B.K. 1999. 'The Myth of the Pagan Cemetery.' In Karkov, C.E., Wickham-Crowley, K.M. and Young, B.K. (eds) *Spaces of the Living and the Dead: An Archaeological Dialogue*. American Early Medieval Studies 3. 61–85.

Part II

Into Celtic Lands

4

Processes of Conversion in North-west Roman Gaul

SUSAN M. PEARCE

Introduction

There is a range of ways of approaching the meaning of 'conversion' both broadly, and within the context of Late Antiquity. These might include baptismal figures (if we had them), attendance figures at the principal ecclesiastical events, or, less directly but perhaps more accessibly, the spread of church organisation and related buildings. Equally, there is a number of approaches through which analysis of the processes of conversion can be undertaken: through imperial, papal and royal policy; through episcopal history as Humphries (1999) has done for northern Italy; through the sociology of health care and exponential growth as Stark has shown (1994); through analysis of trade and contact patterns; and through the study of the transmission of estates. But one of the most interesting and fruitful, because it offers some chance of accounting for the phenomena of conversion rather than recounting its progress, is to view religious experience as a field of social practice in which identities are constructed and cultural meanings signalled.

Here, I wish to investigate three particular components of the mechanisms of conversion: firstly, the ways in which human bodies were used, with their associated graves, containers and related objects, which together constitute a very special class of material culture; secondly, the creation of focal *loci* in time and space; and thirdly, the character of the networks which bound together crucial actors in the story. I shall do this by looking in detail at a limited area in northern Gaul, comprising the late imperial provinces of Belgica Secunda, Lugdunensis Senonia, Lugdunensis Tertia and Lugdunensis Secunda (although I shall largely leave aside the area which became Brittany), during the period from roughly 350, when the movement towards a general Christian society began to take shape, to *c.*550 when it is clear from the works of Gregory of Tours that such a society had come into being. The success of the Christian enterprise in this area during these two centuries or so should not blind us to the struggle for hearts and minds which conversion involved; during the early period, particularly, things might perhaps have taken several different turns.

The Manipulation of Body Parts: Holy Remains

By the time of Gregory of Tours' death in 594 we have a fairly clear picture of what the saintly cults were in the cities of our area, where they were, how and why contemporaries between *c*.350 and *c*.600 believed they had come into being, what they meant to them, and why they were important (Figure 4.1). All, without exception, involved the ritual recognition of human remains or objects associated with them, such as pieces of cloth which had touched the holy body, or dust from the tomb (McCulloh 1963). All the cults also arose within precise and detailed contexts which involved deliberate choices and initiatives, in which the city-based bishops, and perhaps some other individuals, were crucially involved. Although central and southern Gaul had some substantial histories of local martyrs, some of them, like those at Lyons, reflecting genuine events, the north-west lacked many such well-grounded traditions. At Nantes two local martyrs, Rogatianus and Donatus, and a confessor Similinus, manifested themselves dramatically during a siege of the city in the reign of Clovis (481–511) by an army commander called Chillo; Gregory seemed uncertain of the exact status of the two, calling all three of the saints 'confessors' in his chapter heading, but his story suggests that they all had a reputation which pre-dated *c*.480 (*G. Mart.* 59) Their churches were where we would expect, in fourth/fifth-century extra-mural cemeteries, with the two martyrs sharing a church.

At Sens the locally acclaimed martyrs were Savinian and Potentian, who may originally have rested together, possibly with others named as Serotimus, Alpinus and Eodalus, in a church on the Troyes road which had decayed by 847 when Bishop Wenilo of Sens found their confused remains. The early church dedicated *ad martyres*, apparently referring to Sanctianus, Beata and Augustinus, destroyed in 731, may be the same church, although its site is unknown (Picard 1992). According to Gregory, 'Timotheus and Apollinaris consummated their martyr-dom at Rheims' and 'after building a church in their honour, a pious man sought relics of these martyrs' (*G. Mart.* 54). The story suggests that the relics were available in another place, and had to be conveyed to the new church, so evidently the new building was intended to operate as a form of moral pressure to extract the martyr's relics.

At Troyes the supposed martyr Patroculus seems initially to have achieved only the early stages in the classic pattern: 'Over his tomb was a small oratory where only one cleric served' (*G. Mart.* 63). When, however, a legitimate *Passio* of his sufferings was available, a church was constructed and his festival cele-brated every year. However, there seems to have been confusion over whether the church was on the site of his tomb or his 'cell', which might suggest a certain re-working along monastic lines. Quentinus was recognised as a martyr in St Quentin, the town which now bears his name. Ecclesiastical history at Paris is complex, but the churches of St Denis at *Montmartyre* and St Julien on the Left Bank were believed to house the remains of martyrs, and that of St Julien is in an appropriate position. Orléans possessed the martyrs Baudelius and Scubilius,

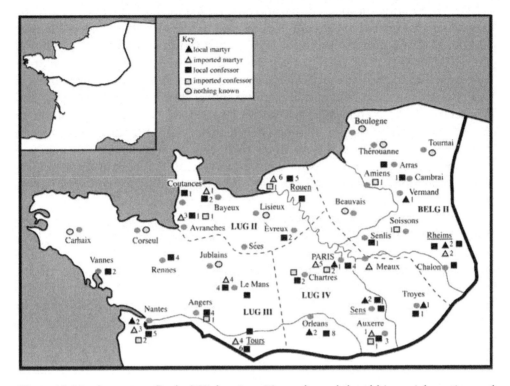

Figure 4.1 North-western Gaul *c.*550 showing cities, cults and the old imperial provinces of Belgica II, Lugdunensis II, Lugdunensis III and Lugdunensis IV Senonia (provincial capitals are underlined)

apparently associated with Anianus, an early bishop, and from 1029 venerated as minor saints within his extra-mural church (Head 1990: 6–12, 20–6).

All these martyrs are in historical or hagiographical terms extremely obscure, and generally their cults do not seem to have taken deep root even in their own localities. Where a city lacked local martyrs, the failure had to be made good by the acquisition of relics from elsewhere (see below). It is noticeable that the cities with their own martyrial traditions form a rough half-circle in the area running from near Rouen to Nantes through the country away from the coast: these are presumably the cities where Christian communities were believed to have been established by *c.*300, while in those to the north and west the local fourth-century bishops had to kindle enthusiasm by acquiring and doing the appropriate things. Tours is a notable gap in the sequence of martyrs. Perhaps its traditions were obscured by those of Martin, or perhaps Martin chose the city because it lacked an ancient focus; we know that he was a very active local evangelist.

'Confessors' were kept separate from martyrs, in that they had not been executed for their faith, but qualified as holy through the sanctity, strenuous effort and severe ascetic practices which had characterised their lives. A substantial number of these confessors were those same bishops who had been active in promoting the local church and developing the martyr cults. At Auxerre, Germanus was buried in the church dedicated to the imported martyrs Maurice and the Thebans, and its dedication was transferred to him. Lupus had a burial church at Troyes; Felix, bishop from 549–582, one at Nantes; Julian one at Le Mans; Victorinus the same at Rouen; and two early but very obscure bishops at Orléans, Anianus and Evurtius, lay in intra-mural churches at Saint-Aignan and South Euverte, both abbeys (Head 1990: 7). Gregory himself in due course joined the roll-call of holy bishops at Tours. Monks, especially founding abbots, were also frequently reckoned as holy. In the sixth century Maximus at the abbey of Micy and Lifordus at Meung-sur-Loire, both founding abbots of these monas-teries, joined the saints of the see of Tours. The paradigm of a confessor in many ways was, of course, Martin of Tours, who was both monk and bishop.

How did contemporaries recognise a holy man's remains? Gregory and the other writers give us a very clear idea of the criteria of authentication. A holy man might reveal the place of his burial to a churchman in a dream or vision, as Gervasius and Protasius did to Ambrose, as Gregory tells us the two virgins Maura and Britta did at Sainte-Maure (G. Conf. 18), and the indignant Bishop Benignus at Saint Branches did to the man who took his sarcophagus lid to cover his dead son (G. Conf. 17). It is interesting that Benignus' tomb is said to have been overgrown with thorn bushes and brambles. Relics might reveal themselves directly, as the martyr Benignus of Dijon did to Bishop Gregorius (G. Mart. 54). The account of Patroclus of Troyes makes it plain that a *Passio* or *Vitae* which carried general acceptance was important, although this meant of course that the heard reading of the written word of the martyr's sufferings gave an emotional authentification to his status, not that all concerned found a sudden interest in historiographical discrimination. Indeed, the actual book of a saint's *Vitae* could operate as holy in its own right and be saved from burning, so that the holy story was not lost (G. Mart. 38). The significance of a newly discovered body was often signalled by its physical condition. Holy remains were intact and had not suffered the normal process of decay and corruption. They were sweet smelling, with 'the fragrance of lilies and roses' (G. Conf. 40) and often their bodily fluids, crucially blood, were still liquid. Holy bodies were fresh and good to look at and be near; they looked like a living body asleep. Gregory describes a body which appeared in the church of St Veneradus at Clermont when a sarcophagus lid was shattered:

> A girl was visible, lying in the sarcophagus; all her limbs were as intact as if she had been recently taken from this world. Her face, her hands, and her remaining limbs were without blemish; her hair was very long; I believe that she had been buried in spices. The robe that covered her lifeless limbs was as [white as] a lamb and intact, neither mutilated by any decay or discoloured by any blackness. Why say more? She appeared to be so robust that she was thought to be sleeping rather than dead. (G. Conf. 47)

Above all, holy remains revealed themselves by their capacity to work miracles, especially miracles of healing.

All this must be put within a cultural context where, over the long period of the past, interference with graves or the manipulation of body parts had both been regarded with abhorrence as a particularly vile kind of magic and as an impious, anti-social, unnatural, perverted act, and had been forbidden by law (Harries 1992). Now the special dead were more alive than the living, and what had been seen as objectified remains appeared as powerful subjects in their own right, capable of treating living humans as objects upon whom miracles could be worked. Late Antiquity sees a detectable shift in the perceived relationship of humans to objects, which came to develop a profound symbolic capacity, related to the inherent powers they were felt to possess. Of course, the classical world had never lacked symbolic objects, but by 300 we see a new range of belts and brooches relating to status, pearl diadems for the imperial family, court dress for bishops and silver plate for important men, which are not just marks of rank but act in their own right as embodiments of identity. Gregory tells us of a crystal chalice at Milan which was smashed and re-made itself, and of a 'good' chalice, pattern and gospel cover at Lyons which prevented an attempt at fake (*G. Conf.* 62; *G. Mart.* 45). The development by the highest levels of society of charismatic objects, conceived of as having an intrinsic, essential, positivist nature signifies the collapse of old values and growth of new ones which privilege the notion of emotional experience through hand and eye over that of mental reasoning. In terms of the martyrs, this shift is expressed by the shocking, but solidly physical, contrasts between stinking corruption and the smell of lilies, or slimy decay and the appearance of sweet sleep.

Emotional and ritual concentration upon relics of the dead, which cross the great divide between dead and alive, objective and subjective, has the effect of focusing the imagination on the fact of death. Profound knowledge of the horror of this dissolution rests within the psyches of us all (Abraham and Toruk 1986; Kristeva 1982) and yet the holy dead serve to soothe this fear by giving access to themselves who have overcome death, and can therefore enable others to do so. It offers a 'win each way' situation in which death is contemplated with all the complex and ambivalent relationships to pain and annihilation which this entails, but also opens up a solution, a state of mind which probably lies behind much of the historical processes of human body fragmentation, and deposition (Chapman 2000), and is, of course, also, at the heart of the Christian message and a fundamental reason why it is so powerful.

In reviewing the broad sweep of funerary practices, Woodward (1993) suggests that separating and handling dead human fragments – 'relic manipulation' – tends to occur in times of social stress and population pressure, and may be linked with the emergence of regionality, defended centres and war. All of these factors clearly come together in north-west Gaul in the period 300–600, although the population pressure was probably felt east, rather than west, of the Rhine. But the context of Christian relic manipulation during these centuries should probably be linked to the fundamental and widespread change in funerary practice which had gathered momentum slowly during the third century across society inside and outside the western Empire, and this is the broad change from cremation to inhumation as the standard funerary rite. There is a fundamental difference of emotional poetic between the two rites. Cremation turns a soft, liquescent, recognizable body into a hard, dry, anonymous heap of ash; its desolation is that of a home where the fire has burnt out, but the transformation achieved is that by flame into a new substance, akin to the change from soft clay to hard, dry pot, or dull ore to shining metal. The imagery is of the cleansing fire which burns away dross leaving the purified spirit. Inhumation, in stark contrast, sees the dead body of a known person put in a damp, dark pit, and the emotional understanding of the transformations which it will undergo opens up in the imagination a can of worms indeed. Ash is not horrible; putrefying flesh is, yet a person buried in the ground remains present in a quite different way. His or her availability is very physical; exhumation in whole or part is always possible no matter how emotionally wrenching, and this arouses its own desires and tensions, which are quite different from those generated by ashes in an urn. Moreover, the dead body occupies his or her own home, which newly dead kin may well join. A grave is a permanent mark on the landscape.

We sense here perhaps the conscious desire to balance the acceptance of horror with the comfort of the grave plot firmly tied to family individuality in time and space, and the developing social practices which created a story around them. The practice was often very jolly, as Augustine's strictures against family parties in cemeteries show, but the whole practice can be related to second/third century cultural upheavals, east, as well as west, of the Rhine which pre-date anything which can be called a Christian society. Within the Empire it encouraged the erosion of the classical ideal of the good life lived here and now collectively in the just city by emphasising the private family, its physical continuity of past, present and future, and the emotional support which a physical grave can offer. It is not difficult to see how, in times of acute stress, precious bones below the surface could become precious bones in the hand, an impulse the more powerful because it caught up the excitement of the forbidden now given a Christian colour. In this sense, family bodies in their graves signify the ultimate family heirloom, and martyrs' graves and bodies serve the same role at community level, representing the collective memory of the self-defining group.

Another facet of the same experiental reality is something close to an obsessive interest in the physical sufferings to which martyrs were subjected. The *Acts* and *Passions* of the martyrs make uneasy reading. Consider this extract from Prudentius' account of the martyrs of Sargossa:

> Thou didst not quit hold of thy flesh though they cut it and would have robbed thee of it, and thou didst tell how grievous were the gashes of thy hideous wounds. The barbarous tormentor tore all thy side, thy blood was shed, thy limbs mangled, thy breast cut off and thy bosom laid open down to the very heart. We saw a part of thy inwards torn away by the grip of the claws and lie far off; wan death possessed something of thine even in thy lifetime.
> (Prudentius *Crowns of Martyrdom* I in Thomson 1961, I: 165)

Victricius of Rouen makes the same point:

> Let not a day pass, brethren, when we do not dwell on these tales. 'This martyr did not blanch under the torturer; this martyr hurried up the slow work of the executioner; this one eagerly swallowed the flames; this one was cut about, yet stood up still.'
>
> (Victricius, *De Laude Sanctorum* in Herval 1966: 130–1)

The sado-masochist satisfaction is obvious, as is the associated necrophiliac element in the concentration on graves, and both march with the growth of, and acclaim given to, ascetic practices. We can link this, perhaps, with a newly increased consciousness of suffering and death brought by the visitations of various plagues which seem to have been endemic in the later Empire, and with events like the invasion of north Gaul by Attila, until he was finally defeated near Troyes in 451. It is also true that late imperial custom permitted the use of torture on the *humiliores* who made up the great bulk of the population, but life for these people was always hard, and this does not seem sufficient reason for the cultural change. It can be linked with the fragmentation of classical certainties, which produced a life-view featuring insecurity and confusion here on earth, and also the transferral of significance to objects and with it any distinction to be made between subjective and objective being in a world where dead objects were more alive and more powerful than living subjects. 'Transference' suggests the abrogation of responsibility, and this recognizes the strain of renunciation and passivity in evidence from the origins of the Church in a culture in which holy people have things done to them, by God, by other people and by themselves, a stance which has, of course, its own potential political leverage. This connects with a certain evident feminisation of culture, in which the stress on the liquid nature of holy bodies, which flow in fresh blood and milk, and in the sexually negating emphasis on continence play a part. Indeed, as Sam Riches (pers. comm.) has suggested, sanctity becomes virtually a form of, or an additional, gender, in which a-sexual bodies become sites of salvation through the deliberate courting of suffering.

The recognition of an existing martyr's grave, the creation of a martyrial site through the acquisition of relics, or the cult burial of a confessor, and the regular readings of his (or sometimes her) sufferings, crystallized profound feelings about a loved one's death, the material world which had become increasingly invasive, and the desire for higher-strung excitement. Just how effectively such sites could deliver highly wrought and, from the point of view of a local population in the process of conversion, not-to-be missed events, Gregory shows us in his account of sensational happenings in St Victor's church at Marseille.

> For not only are ill people often healed after approaching his tomb, but the other possessed people, who are often bruising themselves and shouting out the martyr's name, are freed after their demons have been expelled. The servant of the patrician Aurilianus was possessed by a demon and suffered a terrible calamity, with the result that often he bit himself with his own teeth. He was brought to the church of the saint. After he announced that he

was burning because of the saint's power, he danced through the entire
church. (*G. Mart*, 64)

Appetites for this kind of experience grow by feeding, and through the period of
local conversion in the later fourth and fifth centuries, the church proved able to
continue to generate powerful spectaculars of this kind.

Foci in Time and Space: Holy Places

The real presence of holy persons and its characteristic manifestations could only
happen in the very specific place where their actual remains were at rest. To
put in another way, *locus* – a typical and deeply significant word of the time
meaning exactly these things – was all-important, and we are now coming to a
better understanding of how 'place' works in the construction of experience
(Tilley 1994; Nash 1997). The late Roman cities of north-west Gaul were scattered
relatively evenly across the landscape, and were connected by a network of
Roman roads and navigable rivers in the normal imperial way (for this and what
follows, see Figures 4.2 and 4.3). This pattern invested the landscape with a sense
of purposeful solidity in which the particular style of life we observe as provincial
Roman could be lived bodily and perceptually. But around 300, to take a very
loose figure, most of the cities had experienced a fundamental shift: walls were
built which invariably enclosed a much smaller area than the occupation area of
the city. At Orléans, the area between the theatre and the wall was as large as that
enclosed by the wall; at Paris the Ile de la Cité was fortified leaving the main
settlement open, and, perhaps a little later, the old Forum was separately enclosed;
at Rheims the pattern is similar to Orléans, and it is broadly repeated at sites like
Meaux, Avranches, Evreux and Bayeux (Picard 1992; Pietri and Biarni 1987).

   These mural projects sometimes involved the demolition of well-loved, impressive public buildings like the public baths at Sens, the colonnaded, monumental
complex at Beavais and the fish market at Rouen (Knight 1999: 31; Christie and
Kipling 2000), and they must altogether have aroused the kind of mixed but
passionate local feeling we associate with major planning and motorway schemes.
The visible inclusion of *spolia* within the build up of the new walls has often been
associated with an effort to mitigate the psychological damage and to associate old
securities with the new defences, but the damage was fundamental. What had
been a citizenship, theoretically equal and with equal access to all facilities, now
became two populations, one safely housed within the walls, the other exposed
beyond them. The old landscape, with its deep sedimented meanings embodied
in personal and collective experience through which people, things and places
were brought together to produce and reproduce local society was disrupted, and
the new constructions of gates, towers, stretches of the wall and parts of the city
had to be built into a new story of time, memory and movement.

   The political rift is acute. Within the walls were the local imperial and post-
imperial government, whatever the city may have possessed in the way of a

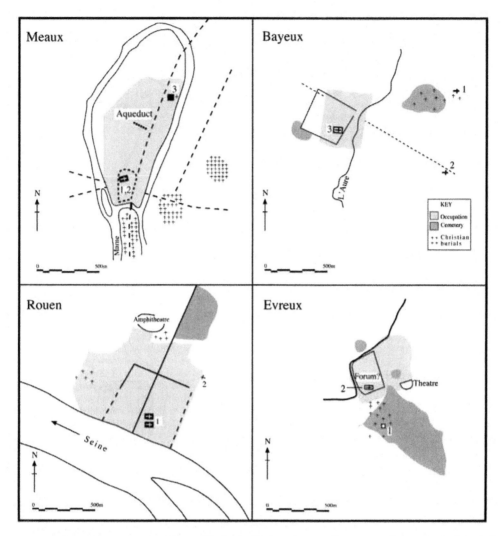

Figure 4.2 Cities of north-western Gaul *c.*500, showing walls, occupation, cemeteries and known potential early ecclesiastical sites. Meaux: 1 cathedral, 2 baptistry, 3 church; Bayeux: 1 monastery church of St Peter, 2 Oratory of St John, 3 cathedral; Rouen: 1 first cathedral, and that constructed by Victricius, 2 basilica of St Peter; Evreux: 1 church, eventually dedicated to St Aquilin, 2 cathedral (Various sources)

garrison with its commanders, and the city bishop with his staff of clerics and perhaps their wives and families. Outside were the workers and beyond them were the rural peasantry, perhaps through the later part of the fourth century beginning to be touched by the Christian practices which the cities now offered, but also, apparently, frequently in the state of 'unrest' associated with the *bacaudae* brigands. Outside, also, were various hostile units like Attila's Huns (up to 451 and possibly somewhat beyond). The civic and social division corresponded to the late imperial status and legal division between *honestiores* and *humiliores*. This

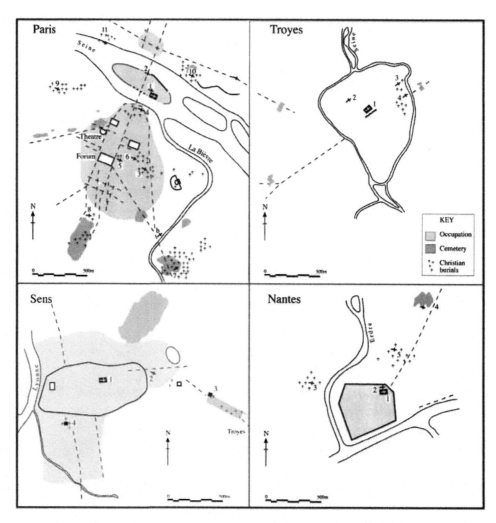

Figure 4.3 Cities of north-western Gaul c.500, showing walls, occupation, cemeteries, and known potential early ecclesiastical sites: Paris: 1 cathedral, 2 Oratory of St Martin, 3 Oratory over the tomb of St Geneviève, 4 Basilica of Blessed Julian the Martyr, 5 Basilica of St Stephen, 6 Basilica of St Symphorien, 7 Tomb/church of St Marcel, 8 Basilica (?of St Mary), 9 Basilica of St Vincent, 10 Basilica of St Columba Virgin, 11 Basilica of St Germanus; Troyes: 1 cathedral, 2 monastery of St Quintinius, 3 Basilica of St Lupus, 4 church of St Aventinus; Sens: 1 church of St Stephen, 2 Basilica of St Leo, 3 monastery of Sts Peter and Paul, 4 Basilica of St Remigius; Nantes: 1 church of Apostles Peter and Paul, 2 church of St John the Baptist, 3 Basilica of Bishop Similinus, 4 Basilica of martyrs Rogatianus and Donatus, 5 church of St Andrew

has a bearing on the accumulating prominence of the religious sites which were also outside the circle of the walls. It was in the ancient cemeteries beside the main roads leading from the settled area that the martyrs' tombs were situated, where many of the later confessors were buried, and where their churches were built, like that of Geneviève at Meaux, or perhaps that of Aquilia at Evreux, or, most powerful of all, that of St Martin outside Tours. By the late Empire the size of these cemeteries lining the main approach roads to the city must have been very large and emotionally impressive, and they must have been disturbed by new works, particularly perhaps in the clearance for defensive ditches outside the new walls. The processes of development and change were subtly different in each case, and our knowledge of detail is generally very poor, but some changes in civic settlement patterns over the period between, say, 180 and 320 are likely to have overtaken what had once been city-edge cemeteries, so that known grave plots or suddenly appearing graves must have sometimes become intermingled with houses and work-shops. Old cemeteries may have been occupied by a variety of squatters, who will have included both the destitute and the disabled, and in any case the upheavals of the third century in Gaul must have created a great deal of localised damage in which stone-work was smashed and ashes and bones exposed.

Equally the building of the big cemetery basilicas must have had a profoundly disruptive effect. Around 515 the church built in honour of the martyr Antolianus, buried in an old civic cemetery at Clermont, meant that:

> . . . while laying the foundations [the builders] removed the bodies of many saints; for they did not know the merits of the people whose tombs they found. Because of the large number of other tombs that had filled the area from long ago, they were unable to rebury these bodies in separate graves. So they threw the bones they had collected in one pile and covered the trench with dirt.

In a vision a man learned that this was not acceptable to God or to the holy martyr. It had evidently caused local problems and so, when the church eventually collapsed later in the century, the earlier disturbance of the tombs was given as the cause (G. Mart. 64). All this suggests that the boundaries between occupation by the dead and by the living in the extra-mural areas may have been much messier and more confused than classical sources and ideals suppose. This, coupled with general insecurity and the impact of a divisive wall, gives context to the emotional explosions of vision and miracle which produced the discoveries of obscure martyrial remains, and probably the sudden appearance of a well-preserved body or grave slab with a legible name was often the inspiration behind an *inventio*.

At an emotional level, the martyr's or confessor's grave offered spiritual security to a poor population which seemed to lack physical security: it is as if the city acquired a second spiritual ring of defences, larger and all-embracing. At a socio-political level, the holy tomb offered an alternative cult centre which might rival, or eclipse, that of the bishop's cathedral. Brown has cogently argued that the position of bishops, depending as it did upon popular acclamation and, for its smooth running, upon a degree of popular support, was always, at least potentially, insecure (Brown 1998: 33–40). An acute and energetic bishop would naturally have been at pains to associate himself with the emergence and validation of what looked like becoming a significant cult. The negotiation of such validation, with its commitment of belief in associated miracles, the impressive ceremonies of translation of the remains, and the investment of capital in a church building over the tomb, must always have been complicated and difficult. Venantius Fortunatus, in his *Life of St. Martin*, tells us about the false martyr of Marmoutier who could not tolerate Martin's prayers, and confessed to being an executed thief. Venantius says firmly: 'By this [Martin's] intervention the false cult was brought to an end' (Venantius Fortunatus, *Vie de Saint Martin* in Quesnel 1966: 16). Similarly, Gregory mentions 'the blessed martyr Liminius' buried in the church of St. Venerandus at Clermont, but 'although the inhabitants possess a history of his [life's] struggle, no ritual of veneration is offered to him' (*G. Conf.* 35). We do not know how many 'failed martyrs' there were in the north Gaulish cities whose extra-mural supporters did not succeed in impressing people enough, but we can be sure that every bishop had to pick his way through social, political and emotional complexities in the recognition and celebration of extra-mural cult sites.

The conjunction of a bishop who could ride the religious politics of his generation and a population whose experiential expectations had been raised could unite to create a powerful *locus*. When Victricius received his second set of relic fragments from Milan in 396 he organised a major reception for them, and this involved a deeply impressive procession of monks emaciated by their privations, young and innocent children, a choir of pious virgins carrying the sign of the Cross, and numbers of widows and others living a continent life (Victricius: 114–115; Clarke 2001). It gave Victricius and the church in Rouen a chance to demonstrate its emotional power by a public and collective show of how many had dedicated so much to Christ. In his sermon on the occasion Victricius was able to draw a cosmological unity between the people, the place and the martyrs who had 'formerly penetrated our hearts; today it is the church of the city which welcomes them' (Victricius: 112–113). The ceremony drew on the well-established ceremonies of the imperial Adventus, and so linked together profoundly significant notions of heavenly splendour, imperial power and human response (Holum and Vicam 1978).

The climax to the formal recognition or reception of new sacred body parts was the creation of a new *locus* through their translation into either an existing church or, as Victricius did at Rouen, the building of a new church in which they could be fittingly housed. The emotional effect was enhanced by the ecclesiastical aesthetic which, like much of the most effective Christian imagery, drew heavily on the imperial cult. The classical aesthetic had certainly produced a mysterious inner space where important things happened, but it also offered an external openness of stone colonnade and sculptured (often coloured) façade. The new aesthetic produced huge brick buildings, blank and dark outside, brilliant with mosaic in rich colour and gold within, and to the generation of church builders, the effect was overwhelming. The style deliberately created a conjunction of feeling and function which stressed controlled access, magnificence and mystery, and which sometimes specifically directed the imaginations of the worshippers, as at St

Martin's at Tours which had a series of moral examinations expressed as monumental statements along the walls. Prudentius describes the church of Eulalia in Merida in glowing terms: 'Overhead the gleaming roof flashes light from its gilded panels and shaped stones diversify the floor so that it seems like a rose-covered meadow blushing with varied blooms' (Prudentius, 155 in Thomson 1961, Vol. II: 37). Fortunatus could describe the church built by Felix at Nantes by saying: 'You will imagine that the paintings depicted in animate colours were alive; the art made the figures breathe again' (Venantius Fortunatus, *Carm.* in Reydellet 1994: 35–36). For many, faith must have been reified in the overwhelming physical presence of the churches. All of this formed part of the direct understanding of the power of the saint through the capacity of his presence in his church to stimulate the kinds of emotion that all concerned had come to anticipate.

This *locus* of the martyrs created a synthesised story in which the practice of particular rituals and the experience of particular emotions at a special place and in a recurring pattern through time brought a new founding narrative for the church, the city, the bishop and the people, and in which past, present, future and eternity were fused. This was one reason why the *Passio* of a martyr like Patroculus was so important, and why *Vitae* of men like Martin and Germanus of Auxerre were written so quickly: the annual celebration of their heavenly birthdays, crucial to the enactment of place and all that went with it, needed the renewing experience of narrative so that the story of what had happened became the story of what always happens. It was also why people's devotion was always tuned to their local saint and his place. The yearly enactment of practice which created the power of the story also tied it to a specific location and a specific group, and this produced the desire to have an eventual part in the narrative by being buried as close as possible to the saint.

Recent work has stressed the creative effects of repeated spectacle and performance (Abercrombie and Longhurst 1998). Specialisation of place, like the range of inter-mural and extra-mural churches most cities developed during the course of the fourth/early fifth centuries, and of people, like the clerical hierarchy, monks, dedicated widows, those hoping for a miracle, together with the general congregation, created the repeated spectacle in which everybody watches everybody else perform. Imagination is the key social practice, embodied in repeated actions and visions linked to the ability of sites to engender feelings of 'the real'. These then became part of individual, family and community cultural memories and biographies, and structured life trajectories, giving men and women ambitions, aspirations and occupations, all of which were deemed significant. Mental images and physical stimuli came together when Victricius' little drops of martyr's blood were adored or a healing miracle happened at Tours. The consumption of experience in and around the great churches became a dynamic process, linking place, past, present and future, as emotions were acted out.

By 600, the new religious and cultural impulses had themselves altered the character of the landscape and people's experience of it. North-west Gaul was now dotted with intra-mural churches, extra-mural martyrial and confessional cult centres, many fully fledged with major churches, and abbeys with tomb-shrine churches. These sites all had new names, generally formed upon a holy individual who was usually still present in the body. The new sites were the focus of much coming and going, both official and popular, they were the *locus* of thrilling events like miracles, and they were the places where a cycle of re-enactments daily, weekly and yearly, wrote the new story into the paths, fields and stones, which then became remembrances and actors in the new cosmology. Martin's tomb at Tours became the centre of a very substantial complex outside Tours which constituted a rival centre to the walled city which held the cathedral. Other churches and abbeys needed additional buildings and perhaps began to enclose themselves in ways which offered some defensive capability. Political conditions post *c*.600 were still, and were to remain, very uncertain, but perhaps the terrors of the fourth/early fifth centuries were in abeyance until the Scandinavian raids began in the ninth century, and this may help to explain why emotional and socio-political pressures did not operate to create many new saints between *c*.600 and 900.

Personal Relationships: Holy Networking

In this cultural scenario the acquisition of relics assumed a fundamental signifi-cance. The tombs of bishops and confessors were likely, of course, to be well known. Emotional pressures could result in what was perceived as the self-manifestation of holy bodies through visions and miracles for which the word *inventio* was used. Other relics were frankly stolen: Fleury near Orléans possessed the body of Benedict at an early point, and could not explain satisfactorily how it had come by it. But the great volume of relics, particularly of martyrs, moved along human networks bound together by the giving and receiving of sacred gifts.

As the fourth century unfolded, the gift networks between bishops them-selves, and bishops and influential lay people, including women, became an important mechanism through which the Church itself established its pattern of urban and rural presence. Knitted into this were the prestigious pilgrimages to the holy sites in and around Jerusalem, begun by the Empress Helena's discovery of the True Cross, and continuing with the pious activities of Egeria, both the Melanias, Silvia, and others of whom we know less. Around 390 for example, Gaudentius returned from the East to take up the see of Brescia, and brought with him relics of Saints John the Baptist, Andrew, Thomas and Luke and the renowned Forty Martyrs of Sebaste (Hunt 1972). The relics of John, Andrew, Thomas and Luke became widespread in northern Italy. When Gaudentius built a new basilica to house these, Ambrose gave him some more from the collection at Milan and the acquisition of relics stimulated the building of new churches at Concordia, Aquileia, Lodi, Florence and Milan itself (Hunt 1972; Humphries 1999). We should remember, too, that the networks were kept alive by a constant flow of letters and similar works, and that all the major figures were accompanied by, or visited by, large households of less senior men who only emerge from anonymity occasionally.

We can pinpoint some significant sequences. Under the emotional pressure generated by Arian opposition, Ambrose had made the dramatic discovery of the relics of Gervasius and Protasius. Ambrose formed an important node in a major web of relationships which included Augustine at Hippo, Paulinus at Nola, Jerome in Jerusalem, Melania, Honoratus of Lerins, and Martin of Tours. Martin stayed for a time at Vienne; by a fortunate find, this is marked for us by the inscription on a slab from the church of Saints Protasius and Gervasius at Vienne, which records how Feodula was baptised by St Martin and buried 'at the seat of the martyrs' (Le Blant 1856:412). This shows, among other details, that Vienne had relics of Gervasius and Protasius, and by the mid-fifth century similar relics had been disseminated to Le Mans, Paris, Rouen and Avranches. These represented and consolidated a gift network which brought together and ratified the Catholic hierarchy, whose patron saints Gervasius and Protasius might be said to be, within difficult contemporary politics. Perhaps also the relics confirmed a significant link to the imperial capital at Milan, just as those of the True Cross, and later of St Stephen, produced a relationship with Constantinople, and so to the imperial ideal of the Empire and Christ. A similar network was, in the years after Martin's death in 397, to distribute his relics relatively widely to Nantes, Auxerre, Amiens, Paris, Cambrai and Avranches, providing a similar recognition of the monastic ideal for which he had stood.

While Martin was at Vienne, he met Paulinus and Victricius, for how long we do not know, nor whether or not Victricius was already bishop of Rouen; in any case it was this meeting which extended the network into north-west Gaul, and subsequently Paulinus wrote Victricius two letters from Nola, in which we hear details of his earlier life as a soldier who had had a difficult time during his coming-out as a Christian. This group of people were at the cutting edge of contemporary Christian style, and we catch a close view of their tone from Paulinus' surviving letters, which can be matched by, for example, those of Augustine. Paulinus writes to Victricius:

> So I looked in the mirror of the spirit and thought of your regard for me and, in turn, of my intimacy with you because of the love my heart bears you; so in keeping our brother here, I have claimed your affection as being kindly disposed to me. The grace of the Lord, which has been given to you in abundance, has ensured that you are loved in the limbs of your body and in the hem of your garment. (Paulinus of Nola, *Letter 18*, in Walsh 1967: 167)

This is in line with tears frequently shed at dramatic occasions, and reminds us of the gushes of sentiment often experienced by all who participated. The overwrought, clearly erotic, charge within this male, and generally celibate, group reminds us of the 'special saintly friend' cultivated by many of them, as Paulinus did Felix, and of the desire to be buried as close as possible to the friend, as Paulinus was. It was mirrored by the frequent pairing of martyrs: Gervasius and

Protasius, Vitalis and Agricola, Timotheus and Apollinaris. Feverish and highly scented as this might well seem, it supplied much of the emotional force which ran along the networks and provided the supporting fervour which fuelled bishops and their clergy in the efforts they were making to sustain and encourage the prevailing religious culture, efforts which surely must have been personally very demanding.

When Victricius became bishop of Rouen around 380 – in circumstances of which we are ignorant – he evidently had with him some tiny fragments of relics (*minutiae*) which seem to have come from Milan. Rouen perhaps did not at that time have a major church; it was not until 396, when Aelianus, a priest of Milan, brought a second set to Rouen, that an impressive church in which to install them all was built. The second batch included the newly found relics of St Nazaire, and those of Saints Andrew, Antoninus, Saturninus, and Gervasius and Protasius (Victricius: 112–13; 138–9). The network of relic-gifting gave Victricius access to the special kind of power and confidence which the ability to control holy objects conferred, and which he could not have had without this support. It gave him opportunities for negotiation which could result in the provision of funds and materials for a major building project which, in its turn, witnessed to the stable presence of the Church in Rouen. Rouen was the metropolitan church of Lugdunensis Secunda, and therefore Victricius was the senior bishop to the cities of Bayeaux, Evreux, Lisieux, Coutances, Avranches and Exmes, later Sées. The early history of all these bishoprics is obscure, but it is possible that Victricius was involved in the nurturing and organizing of the episcopal presence in at least some of these cities. Certainly, the patrons of the diocesan churches show the, probably early, link with Rouen. The city church of Exmes was dedicated to Gervasius and Protasius, and their dedication passed with the see to Sées. Bayeux, similarly, had a cult of St Antonin, another saint whose relics Victricius received from Milan. Victricius was eventually buried in the Rouen church which he had built, as was Evodius, his most illustrious successor: as the recipient of relics he himself became a relic, all together working their wonders in the same sacred *locus*, and so the shaping of a particular kind of religious future emerges.

Some Concluding Thoughts

We can, through all of this, pinpoint some of the significant elements in the complexity of the contemporary Christian life and the operation of conversion in northern Gaul during the fourth and fifth centuries. The generation of drama was important: new discoveries of powerful relics, new miracles, new buildings, all stimulated the sense of movement and possibility and heightened the imagination with expectation. Older boundaries between the living and the dead were redrawn as newly released feelings contemplated death and those whose sufferings had conquered it. The strength of emotion which could be experienced near the relic shrines generated its own justification for the explanatory system which the relics sustained. The opportunity to feel these emotional tides for oneself seems to have been one of the most important benefits the church had to offer, and it was maintained through the promotion of sacred places which defined and were defined by time, space and social action, and sustained by the personal networks along which the crucial relics were transmitted.

Behind this we sense the fragmentation of classical norms which expected the physical world to take its natural, that is accustomed, course, and men to live collective, public, self-responsible lives. In the new individual frame of mind, anything can, and may well, happen, and the appropriate stance of the Christian is a sensitive watchfulness, passive but eager, in a world now tuned to personal local experience. Throughout the two crucial centuries the spiral was upwards and outwards as the fruitful tensions were maintained. By the sixth century, the emotional potencies on offer had produced a Christian community, with believing men and women who had expended their lives to create a land transformed with churches and abbeys. The fabric of early medieval north-west Gaul manifests the imaginative power which the new styles of experience would unlock.

Bibliography

Abercrombie N. and Longhurst B. 1998 *Audiences: a Sociological Theory of Performance and Imagination*, Sage, London.

Abraham N. and Toruk M. 1986, *The Wolf Man's Magic Word: A Cryptonomy*, trans. N. Rand, University of Minneapolis Press.

Brown P. 1998, *Late Antiquity*, Belnapp Press, Cambridge, Mass.

Carver M. (ed.) 1993, *In Search of Cult: Archaeological Investigations in Honour of Philip Rahtz*, Boydell Press, Woodbridge.

Chapman J. 2000, *Fragmentation in Archaeology*, Routledge, London.

Christie N. and Kipling R. 'Structures of Power or Convenience? Exploiting the material past in Late Antiquity and the Early Middle Ages', in Pearce 2000: 38–53.

Clarke G. 2001, 'Translating relics: Victricius of Rouen and fourth-century debate', *Early Medieval Europe* 10, 2: 161–76.

Gauthier N. and Picard J-Ch. 1986–1992 (eds), *Topographic chrétienne des cîté's de la Gaule des Origines au milieu du VIIIe siècle*, Vols I – VIII. Paris.

G. Conf. Gregory of Tours *Glory of the Confessors* in van Dam 1988a.

G. Mart. Gregory of Tours *Glory of the Martyrs* in van Dam 1988b.

Head T. 1990, *Hagiography and the Cult of the Saints*, Cambridge University Press.

Harries J. 1992, 'Death and the Dead in the Late Roman lives', in Bassett S. (ed), *Death in Towns*, Leicester University Press: 56–67.

Herval R. 1966, *Origines Chrétiennes de la deuxième Lyonnaise gallo-romanie à la Normandie Ducale (IV –XIe siècles)*, Maugard, Rouen.

Holum K. and Vicam G. 1978, 'The Trier Ivory, Adventus Ceremonial and Relics of Stephen', *Dumbarton Oaks Papers*, No. 33.

Humphries M. 1999, *Communities of the Blessed: Social Environment and Religious Change in Northern Italy, AD 200–400*, Oxford University Press.

Hunt E. 1972, 'St Silvia of Aquitaine: the role of a Theodosian Pilgrim in the Society of East and West' *J. Theological Studies*, NS XXIII, Part 2: 351–73.

Knight J. 1999, *The End of Antiquity: Archaeology, Society and Religion AD 235–700*, Tempus, Stroud.

Kristeva J. 1982, *The Powers of Horror*, Columbia University Press, New York.

Le Blant E. 1856, *Inscriptions Chrétiennes de la Gaul Antérieures au VIII Siècle*, Vol 1, *Provinces Gallicones*, Paris.

McCulloh J. 1963, 'The Cult of Relics in the Letters and Dialogues of Pope Gregory the Great: A Lexiographical Study', *Traditio* 32, 19: 158–84.

Nash G. 1997, (ed.) *Semiotics of Landscape: Archaeology of Mind*, British Archaeological Reports International Series 661, Oxford.

Pearce S. 2000, *Researching Material Culture*, Leicester Archaeological Monograph No 8, Leicester.

Picard J-Ch. 1992, *Province ecclesiastique de Sens (Lugdunensis Senonia)*, in Gauthier and Picard 1986–92, Vol. VIII.

Pietri L. and Biarni J. 1987, *Province ecclesiastique de Tours (Lugdunensis Tertia)*, in Gauthier and Picard 1986–92, Vol. V.

Quesnel S. 1966, *Venance Fortunat: Vie de Saint Martin*, Les Belles Lettres, Paris.

Reydellet M. 1994, *Venance Fortunat. Poèmes I, Livres I-IV*, Les Belles Lettres, Paris.

Stark R. 1994, *The Rise of Christianity. A Sociologist Reconsiders History*, Princeton University Press.

Thomson H. 1961, *Prudentius* Vols I and II, Heinemann, London.

Tilley C. 1994, *A Phenomenology of Landscape Places, Paths and Monuments*, Berg, Oxford.

van Dam R. 1988a *Gregory of Tours. The Glory of the Confessors*, Liverpool University Press.

van Dam R. 1988b *Gregory of Tours. The Glory of the Martyrs*, Liverpool University Press.

Victricius *De Laude Sanctorum*, in Herval 1966.

Walsh P. 1967, *Letters of St Paulinus of Nola*, Longmans, Green, London.

Woodward A. 1993, 'Cults of Relics in Prehistoric Britain', in Carver 1993: 1–8.

5

Roman Britain, a Failed Promise[1]

WILLIAM H.C. FREND

It is strange that the conversion of Britain, one of the major provinces of the Roman Empire, appears in the present state of evidence to have been a failure. How was it that St. Augustine found so few traces of Christianity in Britain, even in the kingdom ruled by Ethelbert in Kent which was closely allied to the Catholic kingdom of the Franks? For with the notable exception of the shrine of St. Alban on the hill above Verulamium, no trace of an organised Church remained in the areas of Britain ruled by the Angles and Saxons.[2] There were no bishoprics, not even London or York, no churches, except ruins, no parishes or monasteries, such as were flourishing on the near-Continent. There was no representative of a British Church to greet St. Augustine when he landed with his monks on Thanet in 597. In the century and a half since the last 'groan of the Britons',[3] i.e. their last recorded appeal for aid to the Patrician Aetius in Gaul in 446/7 the Church in eastern and central Britain had declined to a point near extinction. Why?

The literary evidence for Christianity in Britain in the first three centuries is not large but comparable with that of other outlying provinces of the empire in the west. Bede (c.731) retains the tradition of the martyrdom of Aaron and Julius at Caerleon. The *vicus* attached to a legionary fortress might be expected to contain Christians, for the military and merchants from the eastern provinces would be among the likely carriers of the new eastern religion to the west. Bede also gives a long extract from the *Acta* of the martyrdom of Alban. But whether either of these martyrdoms took place in the early third century, during the Decian persecution in 250, or the Great Persecution of 303–304 is uncertain.[4]

---

[1] This chapter is an update of my article published in *Britannia* xxiii (1992), 121–33 and contribution to the 13th Congress of International Christian Archaeology at Split in 1994. Published in Vol. iii of the *Acta*, Vaticano-Split (1998), 287–300.

[2] Bede, *Ecclesiastical History of the English People* (ed. Moberly, 1869) 1.7. Bede's account is taken from accounts in Constantius' of Lyons *Vita Germani* (c.475) 16 and 18 and Gildas *De Excidio* 10. See W. Levison, 'St Alban and St. Albans', *Antiquity* xvi (1942), 337ff.

[3] Bede, 1.13. The historical evidence for Romano-British Christianity is discussed by Charles Thomas, *Christianity in Roman Britain to A.D. 500* London, Batsford 1981, Ch. 2.

[4] Thomas, *op. cit.* 48–50, considers with Levison that the middle of the third century is still 'the least improbable period' for Alban's martyrdom.

Ten years after the end of the Great Persecution in the west, Britain was represented by three bishops at the Council of Arles on 1 August 314. This was the first
major Council including all the western province and convoked by the emperor
Constantine. It was designed initially to settle the dispute between Caecilian,
bishop of Carthage and his Donatist opponents. However, the Council quickly
turned to other business, such as the date of Easter, the non-admission of actors
and charioteers to the Church, and the sacramental authority of the diaconate.
The African dispute was relegated to Canon 9.[5]

Britain was represented by three bishops, from London, York, and either
Lincoln or Colchester. This was a better representation than that managed by
Christians in northern Gaul, where only Rouen sent a bishop, Avitianus. There
was no bishop even of Paris. The Church in Britain is shown to have been
organised on episcopal lines, with a hierarchy established in at least three of its
major towns, and able to play its part in deliberating important ecclesiastical
issues.[6]

For long periods in the fourth century the Church in east and west was
dominated by the Arian controversy. Constantine and his son, Constantine II
(337–61), were involved in an increasingly bitter dispute with Athanasius of
Alexandria. The Church in Britain followed its Gallic neighbour in siding with
Athanasius. Its bishops joined with the other westerners at the Council of Serdica[7]
in 343 in his support, and writing from exile in Phrygia in 358, Hilary Bishop of
Poitiers numbers the British bishops along with other westerners among
Athanasius' friends[8] against the threats of the emperor Constantius. Next year,
British bishops took part in the council convoked by the emperor at Ariminum
in north-east Italy. There, confined to one of the large churches in the town in the
stifling heat of the Italian summer and early autumn, the bishops gave way
and assented to a creed that cut out the concept of Christ being of the 'substance'
of the Father. He was, simply, 'like' Him.[9] Three of the British bishops (we do not
know how many attended) accepted the costs of their travel from the emperor
on the grounds of poverty,[10] an act which was remembered with implied criticism
a generation later. It was evident, however, that the British Church, though an
effective body, was not known for its wealth.

The scanty information that exists for the second half of the fourth century and
later shows the Church in a position of some subordination to the Church in Gaul.
Dedicated Christians from Britain visited the monastery at Marmoutier near
Tours and became disciples of Martin there. One Nynia (Ninian) apparently after

[5] J. Gaudemet, *Conciles gaulois du IVe siècle*, Sources chrétiennes 241 (Paris 1977), Canon 1 (Easter,
    which delegates regarded as the most important issue to be discussed) 3, 5 and 6.
[6] J.C. Mann, 'The Administration of Roman Britain', *Antiquity* 35 (1961), 316–20.
[7] Recorded by Athanasius, *Historia Arianorum* 28 (*Patrologia Greco-Latina* 25, col. 728).
[8] Hilary, *De Synodis* i (*Patrologia Latina* 10, col. 479).
[9] Not even, 'like *in all things*'. See for a description of the proceedings B.J. Kidd, *History of the Church
    to A.D. 461* Oxford 1922, Vol. ii, 171–2.
[10] Sulpicius Severus, *Chronicon* (ed. Halm, *CSEL* i) ii. 41.

a visit to Rome returned to Britain north of Hadrian's Wall in c.390 and undertook a mission in south-west Scotland. The 'stone church' which he built at Whithorn inland from the south-eastern point of Wigtonshire was recorded by Bede as having been built 'a long time before',[11] leaving it open to the reader of the *Ecclesiastical History* to decide whether the Christianity of the southern Picts had survived until the coming of Columba in 563.[12] In 396, however, Victricius, the influential bishop of Rouen came to Britain to participate in a council of British bishops at odds over some unstated disciplinary matter, possibly connected with the cult of martyrs and their relics which was becoming increasingly popular in Gaul.[13] In the final stages of recorded Christianity in Roman Britain, many educated Christians espoused Pelagianism and it was the Gallic bishops, Germanus of Auxerre and Lupus of Rheims' who led the orthodox response to the spread of the heresy in 429.[14] It would seem that so long as there was an organised Church in Roman and early sub-Roman Britain it was in the shadow (whether also as regards organisation and liturgy is unknown) of its Gallic neighbour.

The literary evidence for Romano-British Christianity is therefore scanty. In contrast to its neighbours on the Continent, the Church there does not emerge from obscurity in the second half of the fourth century. Though Valentinian I affected a policy of neutrality in religious matters in the west,[15] the Church in the western provinces flourished during his 11 years as emperor (364–375). On his return from exile Hilary of Poitiers observed: 'Every day the number of believing people increases and professions of faith are multiplied. Pagan super-stitions are abandoned together with the impious fables of idolatry and the vanities of idols. Everyone is moving along the road to salvation.'[16] This was not untrue. The number of bishoprics in Gaul had increased from 9 in 314 to 34 at the Council of Serdica.[17] Perhaps more significantly even, the usurper Magnentius (350–353), a reputed pagan who permitted nocturnal sacrifices once again, issued a large bronze coin from his mint at Amiens (Ambianum) whose reverse side was entirely filled with the Christian monogram,[18] as though to prove to his Gallic subjects that he was a better Christian than his Arianising rival, Constantius.

---

[11] Bede, 3.4.

[12] See Charles Thomas' discussion of the evidence in *op. cit.* Ch.11 and, for the excavations at Whithorn, C.A.R. Radford, 'Excavations at Whithorn', *Transactions of the Dumfriesshire and Galloway Nat. Hist. and Antiq. Soc.* 34 (1957), 131–94 (Final Report).

[13] Victricius, *De laude Sanctorum* 1 (*PL* 20, 443–4). All we know is that he visited Britain to 'carry out the instructions' of the Gallic Churches, indicating an element of subordination of the British Churches to those of their Gallic neighbour.

[14] Bede, 1.20. Germanus made a final visit to Britain c.447.

[15] Ammianus Marcellinus, *Res Gestae* xxx.9.5. 'He remained neutral in religious matters and never troubled anyone' (except the Manichees).

[16] Hilary, *Comment. in Ps. 67*, 20 (ed. A. Zingerle, CSEL 22, 215).

[17] Listed by Athanasius as being loyal to him. *Hist. Arianorum* 28 (*PG* 25, col. 728).

[18] Illustrated in Harold Mattingly, *Roman Coins* (1928) Plate LVI, No. 14.

In Spain, North Italy and the Rhineland the story is the same. In Spain, the period 370–380 marks the rise of Priscillian and his ascetic movement. This was an important step towards the perception in the west that a dedicated Christian must be an ascetic. In North Italy, though the see of Milan was occupied from 355–373/4 by the Arianising bishop Auxentius, new bishoprics such as Vercelli were coming into being. The Church was emerging from a small minority to a position of influence in some towns, including Verona and Aquileia.[19] In the Germanies the present-day cathedrals of Trier,[20] Mainz[21] and Bonn[22] were built over the sites of small churches erected at this time.

In Britain our sources give no hint of any forward-looking activity at this period. That there were Christians in sufficiently large numbers to be noticed is clear from the inscription scratched on a tablet found during the excavations of the great bath complex at Bath. Individuals were addressed as 'Whether Pagan or Christian whatever . . .' as though Christians were well known and to be contrasted to Pagans.[23] In the 430s Patrick's family living in a community prob-ably in the north-west of the province had been Christian for three generations,[24] but there was no effective spiritual movement such as the monasticism centred on Lérins, which provided the Church in Gaul with so many of its leaders during the Germanic invasions. The impression in Britain is one of decline alleviated by the presence of Pelagian heresy among educated Christians in the first decade of the fifth century. After 446/7, the date of the final appeal for aid from Aetius and Germanus' last visit, the records are silent, until the first half of the sixth century and the successful propagation of monastic Christianity in the Celtic west, the age of the Celtic saints.

Can one fill any gaps in this account from the material remains of Romano-British Christianity? Broadly speaking, they tell much the same story as the literary record. Down to the end of Constantius II's reign (361) the Church appears to have been growing ever more prosperous. One surprising feature is that, though bishops seem to have been poor compared with their continental colleagues, evidence points to some very wealthy communities and individual Christians at this period.

One of these communities was in the town and industrial centre of Durobrivae (Water Newton) on the Cambridgeshire–Northamptonshire border. A hoard of one gold and 27 silver objects were discovered with a metal detector by the perceptive amateur archaeologist, A.J. Holmes, lying bundled together in a

---

[19] See R. Lizzi, 'Ambrose's contemporaries and the christianisation of North Italy', *JRS* 80 (1990), 156–73.

[20] See S. Loeschke, *Frühchristliche Denkmäler aus Trier* (1936), *Rheinische Nerein für Denkmalpflege*, 91–145.

[21] J. Sauer, 'Frühchristliche Funde in Deutschland aus den letzten 25 Jahre', *Acta iii Congres. arch. christ. 1932* (Roma, Vaticano 1934) 170–1.

[22] See H. Leclercq under 'Xanten', *Dictionnaire d'Archéologie chrétienne et de liturgie* xv.2, 3272–3.

[23] Lead tablets from Bath No. 98. Discussed by Joyce Reynolds, *Britannia* xxi (1990), 382; and compare *Si ser(v)us si liber . . .'* in J.N. Adams, *Britannia* xxiii (1992), 8.

[24] Patrick, *Confession* i.

shallow hole.[25] The dating of the objects is not clear,[26] but would seem to belong to the first rather than the second half of the fourth century. The *pièce de resistance* was a beautiful plain two-handled silver chalice, the first ever found in the western provinces of the empire. It was discovered with a large silver paten, the remains of a silver hanging lamp, once decorated on its exterior with round escutcheons, several bowls donated by individuals, presumably members of the congregation, a strainer, and no less than nineteen silver feather shaped leaves, some but not all stamped with a chi-rho.[27] The collection probably formed a large part of an altar set, supplemented by the silver leaves, used for a votive purpose, which had been fixed to the walls of the church. One of the bowls was particularly interesting. A text inscribed round its side under the rim read after the name of the donor, Publianus, 'sanctum altare tuum D(omi)ne subnixus adoro' (I, Publianus, prostrating myself (or leaning on you) venerate your sacred altar, O Lord).[28] The hexameter is interesting in itself, indicating a fair level of Latin education among members of the congregation. There is also evidence of a sophisticated liturgy, either the act of prostrating before the altar at the Introit or, using the word 'subnixus' as concerned with relics housed below the altar, suggested by inscriptions with the same term in North Africa.[29] The Christian usage of the feather-shaped plaques found on some Romano-Celtic temple sites suggests a Christianity that was tending to absorb current pagan custom rather than confront and destroy it.

One finds a similar outlook when one considers Christian evidence from a number of villas belonging to wealthy owners in south-central Britain. At Hinton St. Mary in Dorset, the central figure on the mosaic covering the largest room in the house is a bust of a youthful Christ behind whom is a chi-rho.[30] The figures round the edges of the ornamental design of the mosaic include the Four Seasons, and a hunting scene, which notably lacks the ferocity frequently displayed on pagan mosaics. In the smaller adjacent room is a mosaic featuring Bellerophon slaying the Chimera.[31]

Two other villas not far from Hinton St. Mary have produced evidence for Christian owners in the middle of the fourth century. At Frampton a chi-rho formed the central feature of a mosaic at the entrance of a small apsed room. Immediately opposite the symbol on an adjoining mosaic was a representative of the god Oceanus, another example of paganism surviving alongside Christianity in what must have been a wealthy household.[32] At Fifehead Neville, some

---

[25] K.S. Painter, *The Water Newton Early Christian Silver*, British Museum Publications 1977, 9: 'just after ploughing by the farmer'.

[26] Dr. Painter now thinks the hoard may be later than c.360–370 (pers. comm.).

[27] Painter, *op. cit.*

[28] *Op. cit.* 15–6.

[29] Frend, *Journal of Theological Studies* N.S. 48 (1997), 125–9.

[30] See J.M.C. Toynbee, 'A new Roman mosaic found in Dorset', *JRS*, liv (1964) 7–14, and K.S. Painter, 'The Roman site at Hinton St. Mary, Dorset', *British Museum Quarterly* 33 (1968), 15–31.

[31] Thus M. Simon, 'Bellérophon chrétien', *Mélanges Jérome Carcopino* Paris, Hachette 1966, 889–904.

3½ miles from Hinton St. Mary, two gold rings inscribed with a chi-rho tell of the religious allegiance of the owner.[33]

The two mosaics appear to come from the same manufactory centred on Roman Dorchester 325–340.[34] Both are stylistically similar and both include the same Christian and pagan symbolism, but the Christian villa owners may have chosen Bellerophon and Oceanus as both were becoming susceptible to a Christian interpretation.[35] The hairstyle of the Christ-figure at Hinton St. Mary is reminiscent of that of the emperor Constans (337–350) on his coinage, and the dating of the mosaic would be similar.

The Christian rooms separated from the rest of the house at Lullingstone are slightly later, post 350 according to Colonel E.W. Meates, the excavator.[36] This quarter lay below the main suite of rooms of the villa. The floor of the principal room was decorated with a representation of Bellerophon and the Four Seasons, though cruder than that at Hinton St. Mary.[37] The discovery of the Christian basement has been a triumph for restorative archaeology. Thousands of fragments of coloured wall-plaster were found in this area sealed by the ruin of the main house above. The laborious task of reconstruction was richly rewarded. Fragments of two chi-rho symbols were found as part of the decoration of the wall of the ante chamber to the chapel.[38] More spectacular were the remains of six standing figures finely clothed in long pearl-lined tunics caught up at the centre by wide red or purple coloured belts. They stood between pillars of a building which appears to have been a church with a shallow penthouse tiled roof. One of these figures standing at the end of the line on the right has a hand raised as if giving a blessing.[39] To the writer these would seem to be either clergy or Apostles, if the latter, survivors from a series of twelve, the remaining six being lost or destroyed.

These are isolated but cumulatively impressive records of the progress of Christianity by the sixth decade of the fourth century. The Lullingstone chapel in particular would seem to have been an estate church. They are supported, especially in eastern Britain, by an array of small finds suggesting the penetration of Christianity to lower ranks of society. Thus, at Lode in Cambridgeshire a farmer

---

[32] See Charles Thomas, *op. cit.* 105.

[33] *Ibid.*, illustrated in British Museum *Guide to Early Christian and Byzantine Antiquities* (1921) 58, Figs. 33 and 34.

[34] D.J. Smith, 'Three fourth-century schools of mosaic in Roman Britain', contributions to La mosaique *Gréco-romaine* (Editions CNRS, Paris 1965).

[35] Oceanus is the central figure on the great dish in the Mildenhall treasure, which would appear to have had a Christian owner. See, in general, D.J. Smith, 'Mythological figures and scenes in Romano-British mosaics', in J. Munby and M. Henig, *Roman Life and Art in Britain* (BAR 41, Oxford 1977).

[36] G.W. Meates, *Lullingstone Roman Villa*, London, Heinemann 1955, 146.

[37] *Ibid.* Plate 3.

[38] *Ibid.* Fig. 13b on 145 and 152.

[39] *Ibid.* 128–34 and Fig. 10 and 11. Chedworth is another villa in which Christian symbols have been found. See Roger Goodburn, *The Roman Villa at Chedworth* (1979), 24.

picked up what may have been the lead base of a candle-stick.[40] The Great Field at Rookery Farm at Great Wilbraham between Cambridge and Newmarket has yielded a small disc (possibly the bezel of a ring) decorated with a chi-rho and what appears to be the flattened remains of a bell decorated with fish symbols.[41] Other finger rings, spoons with Christian symbols and other small objects have come from a wide area, but mainly from southern and eastern Britain; they have been listed by Charles Thomas in his *Christianity in Roman Britain to A.D. 500* (1981).[42]

One particular category of finds would confirm the advance of Christianity in this period, namely the lead tanks used for baptism.[43] These are uniformly large vessels containing up to 40 gallons of water whose original use may possibly have been connected with dyeing clothes. Down to 1991 eighteen of these tanks had been found, with a cluster of eight in an area between Ashton outside Oundle in Northants to Icklingham in east Suffolk. Others have been found since.[44] Seven of these bore the mid-fourth century plain chi-rho symbol and others had symbols such as the St. Andrew's cross that were associated with Christianity.[45] That these tanks were used for baptism is indicated by the frieze on one surviving side of a tank from Walesby in Lincolnshire. This shows below a chi-rho three panels divided by pillar standing figures; the outer two each show three men dressed in tunics and cloaks. The centre panel, though damaged by a gash caused by a plough, shows a naked woman standing, a robe slipping from her right shoulder, flanked by two matrona-like figures 'thickly veiled and draped'. These were perhaps sponsors of a neophyte about to be baptised, with the male figures representing the congregation.[46] Their clothes were those of ordinary provincials.

All this suggests fairly strong evidence for Christianity among many groups of the population especially in the east Midlands, which may at this time have formed part of an imperial estate centred on Castor.[47] The existence of churches

[40] A.J. Rank and W.H.C. Frend, *Antiquaries Journal* lxxii, 1992, 168–70.

[41] Found in 1996 and 1998 by Mr. Peter Rash of Fulbourn, forthcoming.

[42] C. Thomas, *op. cit.* 130–42. For Christian finds from Cambridgeshire to 1999, see Frend Ch. 23 of T. Kirby and S. Oosthaizen (eds), *An Atlas of Cambridgeshire and Huntingdonshire History*, Anglia Polytechnic University 2000, and from the West Country, see G.C. Boon, *Transactions of the Bristol and Gloucestershire Arch. Soc.* Vol. 110 (1992), 37–52. I possess a photo of the Verulamium sherd, whose existence is doubted by Thomas (*op. cit.* 108).

[43] See Dorothy Watts, *Christians and Pagans in Roman Britain* London and New York, Routledge 1991, 158–78 (Distribution map, Fig. 26, 167), and C.J. Guy, 'Roman circular lead tanks in Britain', *Britannia* 12 (1981), 271–6. See also Petts, Chapter7 in this volume.

[44] E.g. near Wellingborough in the ruins of a Roman bath-house. Recorded in NASNEWS (News sheet of the Northamptonshire Archaeological Society) Summer 1999, and from Rushden, published by James Looker in *Northamptonshire Archaeology* 28 (1998), 163–4. It was also damaged.

[45] Dorothy Watts, *op. cit.* 158–66.

[46] Thomas, *op. cit.* 221–4 (illustration, 222). The tank was damaged when found and further damaged by ploughing.

[47] J.P. Wild and G.B. Dannell *Durobrivae* (1984), 22–5 and Fig. 126. The large building showed signs of extensive burning.

such as the large building outside the walls on the south side of Colchester,[48] at Silchester,[49] and possibly at Lincoln,[50] and the 'garrison church' and baptismal font at Richborough[51] confirm the organised character of Christianity already shown from the literary evidence. The evidence of churches is reinforced by that of burial grounds as at Poundbury outside Dorchester[52] (Dorset) and at Lankhills outside Winchester.[53] It was neither predominantly urban nor mainly rural in its distribution, rather unevenly spread, still a minority religion, though stronger in southern Britain than in the north except for York and the Wall.

Why, then, did Christianity fail to follow the same route to ultimate triumph as the Church on the Continent? The story of the church at Silchester provides a warning to those who would believe that churches once built would flourish and become centres of ecclesiastical authority. The small apsed building with a courtyard in front was first found during the excavations in *Calleva Atrebatum* in 1892. This site was never re-occupied after abandonment sometime during the fifth century. The building was regarded then as now as in all probability a church. It was 10 m in length, 8.91 m in width, with transepts on each side of the apse and the remains of a mosaic floor. It had been built *c.*330 on waste land south of the forum. However, it was not destined to remain in its original use for more than about 40 years. By the reign of Valentinian I (364–375) it had been taken over by squatters who left traces of their presence through holes dug roughly through the floor, while the building itself had become half-ruined.[54] Evidently there was at this time neither will nor interest among the inhabitants of Calleva to maintain this symbol of the emperor's religion.

Possible indifference apart, there is some evidence for what may be interpreted as hostility towards Christianity in areas of southern and eastern Britain. Some of the baptismal fonts have been found deliberately mutilated and destroyed. At Ashton, just outside Oundle in Northamptonshire excavators digging a

---

[48] Thomas, *op. cit.* 174–5 lists three 'conceivable extra-mural church sites' at Colchester, two were associated with cemeteries of which the most obvious was a large apsidal building with three aisles, built on a basilical plan just south of the south wall of the Roman town (also observation by author).

[49] S.S. Frere, 'The Silchester Church: the excavations by Sir Ian Richmond 1956–61', *Archaeologia* cv (1976), 277–302.

[50] M.J. Jones, 'Early Christian Archaeology in Europe: Some recent research directions', *Acta* of xiv Congress of Christian Archaeology at Vienna, Sept. 1999 (forthcoming).

[51] P.D.C. Brown, 'The Church at Richborough', *Britannia* 2 (1971), 225–31 and for Thomas' critique, *op. cit.* 216.

[52] C.J. Sparey-Green, 'The cemetery of a Romano-British community at Poundbury, Dorchester, Dorset' in S.M. Pearce (ed.), *The early Church in western Britain and Ireland* (BAR Brit. Series 102; Oxford 1982), 61–76; Thomas, *op. cit.* 237–238.

[53] G. Clarke, 'The Roman cemetery at Lankhills', *Pre-Roman and Roman Winchester Part II* (Winchester Studies 3) OUP 1979.

[54] S.S. Frere, *op. cit.* (n.49). See Fig. 2 for squatters occupation; and perhaps some Eastern (Syrian) influence on the liturgy practised, 293–94. I do not think one can ignore the presence of late-fourth century coins in the squatters' pits, and Frere's suggestion of abandonment to squatters soon after 360 and probably between 360–370 should be accepted (297).

Roman well associated with a small rectangular structure came on the crushed and broken up remains of a lead tank bearing a Christian symbol, beneath which were fragments of a second tank.[55] At Caversham on the Thames in Berkshire a tank found by the Oxford Archaeological Unit had had its base damaged and sides holed (by kicks or missiles?) and had been thrown down a well.[56] At Willingham in Cambridgeshire a paten marked with a chi-rho had been deposited in a hole along with the head of an ox, perhaps some pagan ritual insulting to Christianity.[57]

With these examples in mind one can take a closer look at some of the major hoards of Christian silver. It is noticeable that both in that at Water Newton and Mildenhall, and probably the Corbridge *lanx*, the valuables were found buried in shallow holes, as though deposited in a hurry. The Water Newton treasure raises some questions. The inside of the paten had been burnt; both handles of the chalice had become detached; none of the roundels that had once decorated the outer surface of the silver hanging-lamp had survived.[58] Was this accidental, the result of carelessness by the clergy or bad workmanship by the makers? Or was it the result of robbery, the robbers being in the middle of breaking up and distributing items of the church treasure when they were disturbed and forced to hide their lot in a shallow hole? The great silver treasure from Mildenhall, 40 miles away, was also found in a shallow trench but was deposited intact with no trace of mutilations.[59] It may have belonged to Lupicinus, the *magister militum* despatched by the Caesar, Julian c.360 with a field force to defend Britain against attacks by the Picts and Scots. Later, c.362 he was recalled to Gaul, but the concealment of the treasure in so desolate an area as the Mildenhall heath suggests robbery and concealment by the robbers.[60] Other silver hoards, such as that containing the Corbridge lanx or the Appleshaw pewter[61] may also have been concealed either by robbers or by owners in a time of insecurity, and the same may be said of the Hoxne hoard, though this dates probably to the second or third decade of the fifth century.[62]

The reign of Valentinian I was a period of violence and insecurity in Britain. In a previous article I have remarked on the possible effect of the 'barbarian

---

[55] John Hadman and Stephen Upex with C.J. Guy, 'Ashton 1976', *Durnovaria* 5 (1977), 6–12. Also, Guy, 'Roman circular Tanks in Britain', *Britannia* 12 (1981), 271–6.
[56] Recorded in *Britannia* 20 (1989) and Pl. xxvi.
[57] Briefly recorded by Frend, *Roman Christianity*, 23, in Kirby and Oosthaizen *op. cit.* note 42. Full report by Alison Taylor forthcoming.
[58] Painter, *Water Newton*, Pl. 3, 6 and 4.
[59] Found by a ploughman; 'hurriedly buried' by its owner. See Painter, 'The Mildenhall Treasure, a Reconsideration', *The British Museum Quarterly* xxxvii.3–4 (1973), 154 and 170. The Risley Park lanx was similarly ploughed up. See Catherine Johns, 'The Risley Park Silver Lanx', *Ant. Journ.*, lxi.i (1981), 54–5.
[60] Thus, Painter, 'Mildenhall', 172.
[61] The Appleshaw hoard was found 'in a metre deep pit dug through the cement floor of a villa-house', Thomas, *op. cit.* 110–1.
[62] Catherine Johns and Roger Bland, 'The Hoxne Late Roman Treasure', *Britannia* xxv (1994), 165–73.

conspiracy' of 367–369 on civilised life and not least on the future of Christianity in Roman Britain.[63] Here I would only repeat that while the enemy was an alliance of Picts, Scots, Attacotti and Saxons, the actual fighting took place within striking distance of London. Count Theodosius, sent by Valentinian with four regiments of his field army to restore the situation, had to deliver the city itself from danger. He could not establish his headquarters there before rescuing it from 'the greatest difficulties'.[64]

Thereafter, Theodosius did not advance quickly to York as if to repel invaders from across Hadrian's Wall, but sent out flying columns to round up and destroy parties of invaders.[65] There are reasons why the Saxons and their allies should have aimed at causing destruction in the east Midlands in particular. Much of Cambridgeshire and Northamptonshire may have formed part of an imperial estate administered from a large villa or palace at Castor[66] and bounded on its south side at Titchmarsh where part of a boundary stone was found.[67] This area was studded with agricultural communities, whose grain exports are likely to have filled some of the 600 ships that sailed from Britain yearly to supply the Roman armies on the Rhine frontier.[68] The rivers running into the Wash are sluggish and what went down in the form of exports could come up in the form of raiders. To judge from burnt areas in large aisled storage buildings in the Barnwell-Oundle area of Northamptonshire this is likely to have happened.[69] A deposit of six lead objects carefully cut up with an axe or saw and concealed under part of a milestone at the side of a pond adjacent to storage buildings at Barnwell looks like loot ready for distribution among a gang of robbers. One of the fragments came from a lead tank, others from lead drainage pipes and ingots of lead. The deposit weighed 11½ kg, and we are told by Ammianus Marcellius that government troops caught up with raiders who 'then threw away heavy packs' in order to facilitate their escape.[70] The find at the storage depot at New Lodge Farm, Barnwell, may have been one of these.[71]

In areas where it was strong, Christianity could probably have made an ample recovery from the shock of 3 years of conflict if it were not for other factors. One

---

[63] 'Pagans, Christians and the 'barbarian conspiracy' of A.D. 367 in Roman Britain', *Britannia* 23 (1992), 111–23.

[64] Ammianus Marcellinus, xxvii.8.8.

[65] *Ibid*. 8.7.

[66] For Castor, see J.B.P. Wild and G.B. Dannell, *Britannia* ii (1971), 264, and *Durobrivae* ix (1984), 22–5.

[67] Illustrated in *An Inventory of Archaeological Sites in north-east Northamptonshire* RCHM (1975), Pl. 22.

[68] The emperor Julian, *Letter to the Athenians*, 279–280, puts the figure at 600 ships, Zosimus (fifth century), *Historia Nova* iii.5. says 800.

[69] The aisled building at North Lodge Farm, Barnwell, had been burnt down and later (post 380) rebuilt. A mile away a smaller aisled building excavated by the writer had also been burnt, the fire started on its west side and spread inwards. See Frend, 'A Romano-British Site at Hemington Water tower near Oundle', *Northamptonshire Archaeology* 27 (1997), 157–68.

[70] Ammianus Marcellinus, xxvii.8.7.

[71] See J. Hadman and W.H.C. Frend, *Britannia* 25 (1994), 224–6.

is puzzled why none of the rich Christian villa owners seem to have become bishops like their counterparts in Gaul, or otherwise have led (with the possible exception of Lullingstone) their tenants towards Christianity. Part of the answer to this question may lie in a linguistic as well as a deep social divide between the upper and lower classes in late Roman Britain. The language of the Christian Church in the west was Latin, but it is uncertain how many of the ordinary rural provincials spoke it. The curse tablets from the Roman bath at Bath show that it was used by literate provincials and that a 'British Latin' was emerging in the fourth century,[72] but it never developed into a fully-fledged Romance language as it did in France, Spain, Portugal and Italy. The rural population seem to have remain attached to a Celtic language interspersed with Latin loan words.[73]

With language one may associate other forms of attachment to traditional Celtic society. We may not be able to speak any more with confidence of a 'revival of Romano-Celtic religion'[74] in the late fourth century, but of its survival power in this period there can be no doubt. Romano-Celtic temples often succeeded sacred places in the late Iron Age, Frilford[75] and Harlow[76] being examples. These temples continued to attract worshippers throughout the Roman period, and to judge by the coin-distribution the era of Constantine-Valentinian I (306–375) was the most prosperous. It was in this age that Gaul and the other western provinces were turning increasingly to Christianity. Lydney, where new excavations on the temple of Nodens were undertaken by P.J. Casey and B. Hoffmann in 1980–81, indicated that some of the religious buildings, notably the Long Building ('abaton') and the bath-house, were built in the second half of the third century,[77] the evidence is equally clear that there was a large-scale reconstruction in the reign of Valentinian I.[78] Whether describing the excavation of the Bath-house, the Long Building or the Temple itself Wheeler describes how coins of Valentinian-Gratian were found either below the floor of the final period of building or sunk into the *opus signinum* that covered the floor.[79] Attempts to explain these discoveries away are unconvincing. The temple of Nodens was flourishing

---

[72] See J.N. Adams, 'British Latin, the text, interpretation and language of the Bath Curse Tablets', *Britannia* 23 (1992), 1–26.

[73] K. Jackson, 'The British language during the period of the English Settlements', N.K. Chadwick, *Studies in Early British History*, Cambridge 1954, 61–82.

[74] Thus, P.J. Casey and B. Hoffmann, 'Excavations at the Roman temple in Lydney Park, Gloucestershire 1980 and 1981', *Antiquaries Journal* 79 (1999), 81–143 at 115.

[75] For Frilford, see J.S.P. Bradford and R.G. Goodchild, 'Excavations at Frilford, Berks', *Oxoniensia* iv (1939), 36.

[76] Harlow, *Britannia* x (1980), 378 and xx (1990), 303.

[77] Casey and Hoffmann, *op. cit.* 114.

[78] R.E.M. and T.V. Wheeler, 'Report of the Prehistoric, Roman and Post-Roman site in Lydney Park, Gloucestershire', *Reports of the Research Committee of the Society of Antiquaries* ix (1932), 47 'repairs (to the temple) carried out after the accession of Gratian in A.D. 367'. Wheeler might have accepted a late third-mid fourth century date for the building of the Baths (56). Coins below the floor did not date later than issues of the sons of Constantine (333–337).

[79] *Op. cit.* 47 and 62. I accept Wheeler's evidence for late period dating.

during the reigns of Valentinian-Gratian (367–375). The hoard of bronze coins found in Room xviii of the Bath building, 'deposited against the broken edge of the original mosaic floor before the floor received its final 'repair',[80] suggests long-continued use, extending probably into the fifth century.[81]

At Maiden Castle, the well built Romano-Celtic temple also dates to Valentinian-Valens[82] (the writer himself witnessed coins of that period being excavated from the *cella* in 1934). There is no evidence of a savage destruction of paganism such as undertaken by Martin of Tours in Gaul in the 380s.[83]

The long survival of an organised Romano-Celtic paganism may be combined with the reoccupation of hill-forts, such as Maiden Castle or Lydney itself during the fourth century. Also, equally striking was the revival of specifically Celtic art-forms and the continuation of this movement until the eighth century.[84] Unlike similar reversions to native art-forms in North Africa and Isauria in Asia Minor, the re-emergence of Celtic motifs on enamelled escutcheons decorating hanging bowls seems to owe nothing to Christianity. No crosses were woven into the beautifully coloured enamelled interlaces that characterised the reversion to La Tène types of decoration. Reoccupied hill forts and Celtic art forms fit in well with the little we know of Vortigern's kingdom c.440 whose counsellors were described as 'magi' and not, as one would expect in a Christian realm, 'bishops'.[85]

The evidence does not suggest that Christianity died out in the first decades of the fifth century. Apart from Pelagianism and the forebears of Patrick, we know of the existence of monasticism in the person of the pretender to the empire in the west, Marcus (408) and of the Pelagian bishop Fastidius, referred to by the late-fifth century writer, Gennadius.[86] Christians with very considerable wealth remained in the early fifth century. There are also traces of Christian buildings, at Icklingham in Suffolk and Uley in Gloucestershire, the latter succeeding a Romano-Celtic temple.[87] Recent finds suggest Christian buildings in Wroxeter (Viroconium) and, as mentioned, Lincoln.[88] But when one has added all these

---

[80] *Op. cit.* 127–8.

[81] *Op. cit.* 63.

[82] See R.E.M. Wheeler, *Antiquaries Journal* xv.3 (1935) 271, and in general, P.A. Rahtz and L. Watts, 'The end of Roman temples in the west of Britain', in P.J. Casey (ed.), The End of Roman Britain', *BAR* 79 (1979), 183–201.

[83] Sulpicius Severus, *Vita Sancti Martini*, 13.7; his strong-arm methods resulted in 'crowds of pagan rustics believing in Christ'.

[84] E.T. Leeds, *Celtic Ornament*, Oxford 1933, Ch. vi, The revival finely illustrated; How and why the beautifully decorated hanging bowls should have found their way into sixth-century Anglo-Saxon burials remains to be researched fully. See also Helen Geake 'When were hanging bowls deposited in Anglo-Saxon graves?' *Medieval Archaeology* 43 (1999), 1–18. She would place the deposits mainly in the seventh century.

[85] Nennius, *Historia Brittonum* 40 (M.G.H.. Chron, Minora, iii, 180) and see H.M. Chadwick, 'Vortigern' in Nora K. Chadwick (ed.), *Studies in Early British History*, Cambridge, 1954, 21–46.

[86] Gennadius, *De Scriptoribus Ecclesiasticis* 57 (PL 58, col. 1091).

[87] See Thomas, *op. cit.* 133 and 136: 'Icklingham supposed church'.

[88] M.J. Jones in correspondence with the writer, and see Jones' review of recent discoveries in 'Recent Research in Britain', a paper delivered at xiv Congress of Christian Archaeology at Vienna, Sept. 1999 (forthcoming).

together the total does not stand comparison with the Christian remains elsewhere in the west, not least in neighbouring Gaul.[89] Late-Roman Britain has nothing to compare with the beginnings of the great cathedral complex at Geneva, the churches at Arles and Narbonne, the estate churches at Primulacium, churches built in ruined bath-houses such as at Cimiez, and the seedbed of the Gallic monasticism provided by Lérins.

This survey has attempted to show something of the extent of Christianity in Roman Britain and some of the reasons for its decline. In the writer's view, the 'barbarian conspiracy' of 367–369 was a heavy, perhaps even decisive blow against its continued advance. There were, however, other factors. The upshot was that it needed the emergence of the Celtic saints (c.500–600) before it flourished again in the Celtic west, and Columba's mission from 563 onwards to enable it to take a firm hold of western and central Scotland. It fell to Augustine of Canterbury to replant it even in the Kingdom of Kent, the Anglo-Saxon kingdom most under Continental influence. In Roman Britain Christianity was a failed promise.[90]

[89] For Late-Roman and Merovingian Gaul, see the finely written and beautifully illustrated (ed. Ministère de la Culture et de la Communication, 1991) *Naissances des Arts chrétiens*, especially the chapters on 'Les textes' (including inscriptions) and 'L'architecture culturelle'.

[90] Christianity was never 'in the ascendent' in the 'private sphere of life' as claimed by Casey and Hoffman (*op. cit.* note 75, 115). Nor could its history have been continuous between 447 and 597 as asserted by Martin Henig (in *Antiquaries Journal* 80 (2000), 351). Bede could be expected to have made the connections if any had existed.

6

Where are the Christians?
Late Roman Cemeteries in Britain

CHRISTOPHER SPAREY-GREEN

It was in his study of late Roman cemeteries at York that Herman Ramm first raised the possibility that some distinctive burials, particularly gypsum burials, could be identified as those of early Christians.[1] This research then highlighted Poundbury, Dorchester, Dorset as the other major findspot for such burials in Britain and prompted my initiation of the excavations of that site in 1966.[2]

Since then the wider issue of the characterisation of religious belief from funerary remains has seen much debate, including some on the specific issue of *gypsum* (or plaster) burial as a Christian rite. The latter topic was covered by Philpott in his survey of Romano-British burial customs, and has most recently been touched on by Professor Martin Millett in his review of the Butt Road cemetery, Colchester.[3]

In recent discussion, stress has been laid on aspects of burial-ritual other than religion, including the status of the deceased, the psychological reaction of the relatives and environmental factors. Interpretation also depends on methods of inquiry – the need for an interdisciplinary approach and the use of statistical, locational and graphic analysis – and these have been the subject of theoretical debate.[4] In this paper, however, I will concentrate on the religious context of late Roman cemeteries in Britain and discuss how far it is possible to identify Christians.

---

[1] Ramm, Hermann M., 'The End of Roman York' in *Soldier and civilian in Roman Yorkshire*, ed. R.M. Butler (Leicester University Press, 1971), 179–99 at 188–90.

[2] Green, C.J.S., 'The Cemetery of a Romano-British Christian Community at Poundbury, Dorchester, Dorset', *The Early Church in Western Britain and Ireland*, ed. S.M. Pearce, BAR British Series 102 (Oxford: British Archaeological Reports, 1982), 61–76.

[3] Millett, Martin, 'An Early Christian Community at Colchester?' in *Archaeological Journal* 152 (1995), 451–4; Philpott, Robert, *Burial Practices in Roman Britain, a Survey of Grave Treatment and Furnishing AD 43–410*, BAR British Series 219 (Oxford: Tempus Reparatum, 1991).

[4] Morris, Ian, *Death-Ritual and Social Structure in Classical Antiquity* (Cambridge: Cambridge University Press, 1992); Chapman, Robert and Randsborg, Klaus, 'Approaches to the archaeology of death' in *The archaeology of death*, ed. Robert Chapman, Ian Kinnes and Klaus Randsborg (Cambridge University Press, 1981), 1–24.

In the publication of the Poundbury cemetery, Woodward compared the site to other Romano-British graveyards and pointed up the characteristics that would mark that site as a Christian cemetery without developing a full discussion of the topic; much of the most significant evidence still awaits full publication.[5] In his wider survey of Roman burial customs Philpott saw the features of such a cemetery as no more than those of a well organised burial ground under the control of an urban authority.[6] Bruno Barber and Dave Bowsher have now reviewed the evidence from the East London cemeteries and, following Philpott, dismissed the possibility of identifying religious belief from burial customs.[7] On the other side of the argument Dr Dorothy Watts has set out much detailed documentary evidence for the prescribed form of Christian burial and the nature of the archaeological evidence.[8]

This paper will attempt to summarise the documentary and archaeological evidence supporting the characterisation of Christian cemeteries and, in particular, to answer some of the objections to the feasibility of identifying such sites. First the documentary evidence for Christian burial customs is summarised and then an outline of the relevant archaeological evidence is given.

The treatment of the dead human body in the Roman world firstly entailed a choice between cremation, inhumation or embalmment – the latter would have been rare but it is noteworthy that Lucretius mentions these three as alternatives when discussing attitudes to death and burial in the late Republican period.[9] For the earliest Christians inhumation and, at least, a certain measure of embalmment had the force of precedent as the Jewish rite employed for the burial of Christ. The earliest textual evidence is ambivalent, perhaps reflecting different attitudes to a literal or spiritual resurrection. The treatment of the martyrs at Lyon in AD 177 shows that, in second-century Gaul, the persecutors thought that Christian belief required the preservation of the body for burial.[10] Minucius Felix, however, writing in early third-century Italy, implies a carelessness for the physical remains both on the part of the pagan Caecilius and of the Christian Octavius, but the latter still advocates the old custom of inhumation and alludes to a physical resurrection.[11]

[5] Woodward, Ann, 'Discussion' in Farwell, D.E. and Molleson, T.L., *Excavations at Poundbury 1966–80, Vol. II, The Cemeteries*, Dorset Natural History and Archaeological Society Monograph 11 (Dorchester: Dorset Natural History and Archaeological Society, 1993), 216–39.

[6] Philpott, 'Burial Practices', 226–7.

[7] Barber, Bruno and Bowsher, David, *The Eastern Cemetery of Roman London, Excavations 1983–90*, Molas Monograph 4 (London, 2000), 322.

[8] Watts, Dorothy, *Christians and Pagans in Roman Britain* (London: Batsford, 1991), 38–78.

[9] Lucretius, *De Rerum Naturae*, III, 915.

[10] Tertullian, *Apologeticus*, XLVIII, 2–6, ed. and trans. Glover, T.R., *Tertullian, Apologeticus*, with *De Spectaculis* and *Minucius Felix, Octavius*, ed. and trans. by Gerald H. Rendall, Loeb Classical Library (London: Heinemann, and Cambridge, Mass: Harvard University Press, 1966), 212–5; Eusebius, *Historia Ecclesiastica*, 5,1, 61–3, ed. and trans. Lake, Kirsopp, *Eusebius, Historia Ecclesiastica*, 2 vols, Loeb Classical Library (Cambridge, Mass. and London, 1926–32), 436–7.

[11] *Minucius Felix, Octavius*, XI, 4 and XXXIV, 8–11, ed. and trans. Rendall, Gerald H., *Minucius Felix, Octavius, with Tertullian, Apologeticus and De Spectaculis*, ed. and trans. by T.R. Glover, Loeb

The widespread movement towards inhumation during the second and third centuries cannot be ascribed simply to religious scruples and seems likely to have been a widespread change of fashion originating in the eastern Empire.[12] It may also have been influenced by practical considerations such as shortages in the supply of wood needed for cremation as compared with that required for a bier or coffin.[13] In post-Roman Britain inhumation appears to be firmly established as the standard rite, cremation re-appearing only as the distinctive custom of recently arrived Germanic settlers during the fifth century.[14]

The Christian religion above all was concerned with the re-birth of the dead, an emphasis that distinguished it from other cults of the late Roman Empire. Some mystery-religions might have involved the sacrifice, death and re-birth of the cult-figure in their mythology but few, if any, made specific claims as to the immortality or resurrection after death of their adherents' and none is known to have consequently laid down precepts as to the method and place of burial of the physical remains.[15] It is only the Jewish and Christian believers who appear to have had any interest in a prescribed form of burial. But antagonism between Christians and Jews following the persecution of Christ ensured that in worship and burial the Christians were exclusive, just as there was a desire to avoid mixing with the worshippers of idols and the Graeco-Roman gods. The pagans shunned Christians as having some morbid interest in death and engaging in too close contact with the unclean dead. These factors must have encouraged the development of discrete burial areas set aside exclusively for Christians.

Some account should be given of the development of a specifically Christian funerary rite during the first four centuries of our era.[16] Texts referring specifically

Classical Library (London: Heinemann, and Cambridge, Mass: Harvard University Press, 1966), 342–3 and 420–1.

[12] Ian Morris has recently highlighted the Hellenic origin of the eventually Empire-wide rite, Morris, 'Death Ritual', 67–8.

[13] The practical constraints on the form of burial have been discussed by Patterson, John, 'Patronage, collegia and burial in Imperial Rome', in *Death in Towns: Urban Responses to the Dying and the Dead, 100–1600*, ed. Steven Bassett (Leicester: Leicester University Press, 1992), 15–27 at 16–7, citing Meiggs, Russell, *Trees and Timber in the Ancient Mediterranean World* (Oxford: Clarendon, 1982), 237, on the question of wood-supplies. Although deforestation may not have yet been a serious threat the ready supply of fuel-wood may have been a problem in the major urban centres; *ibid.* 257–7 and 379–82.

[14] Arnold, Christopher J., *An Archaeology of the Early Anglo-Saxon Kingdoms* (London: Routledge, 1988) 130–1.

[15] Roman burial customs have been described by Toynbee, Jocelyn, *Death and Burial in the Roman World* (London: Thames and Hudson, 1971), 33–64. Hopkins, Keith, *Death and Renewal: Sociological Studies in Roman History*, vol. 2 (Cambridge: Cambridge University Press, 1983), 230–2, compares the differing attitudes of Christianity and the pagan cults to the after-life.

[16] The evidence for Britain has been summarised by Thomas, Charles, *Christianity in Roman Britain to AD 500* (London: Batsford, 1981), 228–39. More recently, the matter has been given further detailed consideration by Watts, 'Christians and Pagans', 38–89. The desire for the preservation of the body in the Christian rite has been summarised by Green, C.J.S., 'The significance of plaster burials for the recognition of Christian cemeteries', in *Burial in the Roman World*, ed. Richard Reece, CBA Research Report no. 22 (London: Council for British Archaeology, 1977), 46–53 at 46–7.

to the current burial practices of the early Church are rare. In the first two centuries there is no certainty that a distinctive rite was adhered to; there may have been a tension between those following a generally ascetic view of the religion and others who took a more liberal approach, and this could be reflected in burial customs.[17] The ascetic attitude was represented by Tertullian who, in the third century, contrasted the form of Christian burial with pagan custom and stipulated that the body be anointed with spices and placed in a mausoleum or tomb.[18] In the following century Athanasius explained Christian burial practice as the Jewish custom hallowed by the example of Jesus, that is that the body should be anointed with myrrh and aloes and bound up in linen cloths in the Jewish manner, before deposition in a tomb which had not previously been used.[19] Factors such as the avoidance of elaborate burial furniture and the preference for orientation were not stipulated but the former, at least, is again exemplified by Christ's burial. Orientation is more difficult to ascribe to a specific origin, but a biblical authority can be found in the allusions to Christ as the light of the world, a particularly potent image for Constantine with his family-background of sun-worship reinforced by his observations of solar phenomena.[20]

The Church Fathers established the main features of treatment of the individual, but Tertullian had also directed that, although it was allowed that Christian and pagan should mix in life, in death they should be separate.[21] This established the custom of burial in areas separate from pagans, a practice encouraged by the process of patronage in which rich adherents to the faith allowed burial by other members of the community in their private cemetery-plots. This is most apparent in the early burial areas at Rome, named after the patrons and landowners who had established them, first as surface-cemeteries, but later as underground catacombs when space became limited.[22] The Christian catacombs are strictly skeuomorphs of the surface or 'flat' cemeteries, the *loculi* being equivalent to rows of dug graves, and the *hypogea* to the built mausolea, chapels or roofed covers over surface-sarcophagi.

[17] Morris, Richard, *The Church in British Archaeology*, CBA Research Report 47 (London: Council for British Archaeology, 1983), 18.

[18] Tertullian, *Apologeticum* XLII, 7, ed. and trans. by Glover, pp 192–3; *De Resurrectione Mortuorum*, XXVII, ed. Borleffs, J.G.Ph., Tertullian, *De Resurrectione Mortuorum*, in *Tertulliani Opera II*, ed. Gerlus, A. CCSL II (Turnhout: Brepols, 1954), 956.

[19] Athanasius, *Vita S. Antonii*, 90, ed. Migne, *Patrologia Latina*, XXVI, col. 967–971. John XIX, 39–42, Matthew XXVII, 59–60 and Mark XV, 46–47 also describe the form of the tomb and its closure by a large stone. This may have some significance for the form of tomb and the container of the body in the Christian ritual.

[20] Jones, A.H.M., *Constantine and the Conversion of Europe*, Teach Yourself History (1949, repr. Harmondsworth: Penguin, 1972), 97–101.

[21] Tertullian, *De Idololatria*, XIV, 5, ed. Reifferscheid A. and G. Wissowa, in *Tertulliani Opera II*, ed. Gerlus, A. CCSL II (Turnhout: Brepols, 1954), 114.

[22] Testini, Pasquale, *Le Catecombe e gli Antichi Cimiteri Cristiani in Roma* (Bologna: Cappelli, 1966) for surface cemeteries, 85–92 and the subterranean burial areas, 123–39.

By the time of Tertullian the Church in some Mediterranean cities was well enough established to organise and manage cemeteries on lines similar to the pagan *collegia funeratica*.[23] Eusebius refers to the emperor Valerian as forbidding entry to the cemeteries – a term in origin specific to Christian burial grounds – and then to Gallienus returning control of Christian cemeteries to the Church. Other accounts of the persecutions include mention of grave-diggers working in cemeteries owned by the Church.[24] Outside Rome and other Mediterranean centres, however, a specific burial rite may not have been rigidly enforced at this date, and there is also the possibility that sects emanating from different regions of the Empire might have introduced varying customs to areas such as the north-western provinces.

With the growth of the Church during the fourth century, burial customs and organised cemeteries undoubtedly became more formalised and the pre-occupation with the dead and the care taken by the Christians of their graves is one factor commented on by the Emperor Julian. From his own reading of biblical texts he saw the worship of graves as abhorrent and a cause of criticism of the religion.[25]

In Romano-British cemeteries, archaeological evidence for special respect accorded to individual graves or attempts to preserve the body is rare. No cemetery has yielded epigraphic evidence or has been identified beneath a recorded early focus of Christian activity. In the neighbouring north-western provinces of the Empire such cemeteries have been identified dating back to the pre-Constantinian period. The geographically closest sites are those beneath some churches in the Rhenish cities where the early dedications and epigraphic evidence identify the burials as both late Roman in date and Christian in their context. As evidence by analogy, these sites are of great interest and some have been extensively investigated, as far as overlying structures allow.[26]

No pre-Constantinian Christian cemeteries can be proposed in Britain even though the presence of four bishops from Britain at the Council of Arles in 314 may indicate the existence already of a metropolitan organisation in the civil diocese and thus a likelihood of standardised practices.[27] In the course of the fourth century it would be expected that cemeteries should begin to reflect this

[23] Tertullian, *Apologeticus* XXXIX, 6, ed. and trans. by Glover, *op. cit.* 174–7. The relationship of the *collegia* and the early Church was briefly discussed by Waltzing, Jean-Pierre, *Etude Historique sur les Corporations Professionelles chez les Romains*, 4 vols (Louvain: Peeters, 1895–1900) I, 150–1 and 314. For a recent study of *collegia* in early Imperial Rome see Patterson, 'Patronage', 20–4.

[24] Eusebius, *The History of the Church*, VII, 11 and 13, ed. and trans. Oulton and Lawlor, 168–71; for grave-diggers in the Church see Jones, A.H.M., *The Later Roman Empire 284–602: A Social, Economic and Administrative Survey*, 4 vols (Oxford: Blackwell, 1964), 118.

[25] Julian, *Ad Arsacium* 429D; Against the Galilaeans 335c.

[26] Most recently summarised by Esmonde-Cleary, A.S., *The Ending of Roman Britain* (London: Batsford, 1989), 36–8, but cf. Wightman, Edith M., *Gallia Belgica* (London: Batsford, 1985) 292–96. See Keller, Chapter 26 in this volume.

[27] Haddan, Arthur West and Stubbs, William, eds, *Councils and Ecclesiastical Documents relating to Great Britain and Ireland*, 3 vols (Oxford: Clarendon Press, 1869–78) I, 5.

development, with some increase in the level of organisation and the regulation of funerary activity to conform to a Christian pattern. Cemeteries with a
particularly rigid layout and standard burial rite conforming to the Christian
norm have indeed been identified at this date and some of these have consequently been identified as dedicated to the followers of this religion. The most
notable are the urban burial grounds at Poundbury, Dorchester, Dorset and at Butt
Road, Colchester.[28]

Identification dependent largely on burial rite and cemetery-organisation
is, however, fraught with problems, as Charles Thomas and others have pointed
out.[29] Factors other than Christian belief can be cited to explain the choice of
inhumation, the orientation of graves, or the absence or rare provision of grave-
goods; non-Christian burials may accordingly have been wrongly included or
Christian burials overlooked. Ordered cemeteries with standardised burial rites
have been interpreted by Robert Philpott and others as having no religious
overtones and marking no more than the efficent use of land owned and run by
the urban administration – merely an extension of Late Roman bureaucracy to
the management of cemeteries.[30] Harries has similarly stated that 'the distinc-
tively Christian belief in the resurrection of the body and the power of the saints
. . . did not spill over into a separate concept of burial'. While conceding that there
may have been separate cemeteries run by the Church for charitable purposes,
she declared that 'in general Christians were buried in cemeteries alongside
pagans'.[31]

These objections do not withstand scrutiny. In the latter case, where no ancient
authority is quoted, the statements of Tertullian and others, such as St John
Chrysostom, establish that dedicated Christian cemeteries did exist. In the case
of Philpott's argument that bureaucracy and the economical use of valuable
ground space were the main priorities, then repeated re-use of the burial plot,
without respect for earlier burial, would be the most efficent use – as in recent
cemeteries. This is indeed the characteristic of many standard Romano-British
cemeteries where the ground was densely covered in cremations and inhumations, the burials overlapping and intersecting, the inhumations following no

---

[28] Green, 'The significance', 50–2; Watts, 'Christians and Pagans', 78–89. For Poundbury cemetery 3,
see Green, 'The cemetery', and Farwell and Molleson,'Poundbury', 14–81. For Butt Road see
Crummy, Nina, Crummy, Philip and Crossan, Carl, *Excavations of Roman and later cemeteries,
churches and monastic sites in Colchester, 1971–88*, Colchester Archaeological Report 9, Colchester
1993.

[29] Thomas, 'Christianity', 232–34; Morris, 'The Church', 17–8; Philpott, Robert, 'Late Roman
Cemetery organisation' in Struck, M., ed., *Römerzeitliche Gräber als Quellen zu Religion,
Bevölkerungsstruktur und Sozialgeschichte*, Archäologische Schriften des Instituts für Vor- und
Frühgeschichte der Johannes Gutenburg-Universität Mainz (Mainz: 1993).

[30] The idea has been accepted by Thomas, 'Christianity', 232 ; Esmonde-Cleary, 'The Ending', 80.

[31] Harries, Jill, 'Death and the dead in the late Roman West', in Steven Bassett, ed., *Death in Towns:
Urban Responses to the Dying and the Dead, 100–1600* (Leicester: Leicester University Press, 1992),
56–67 at 61.

set orientation.[32] The standardised orientation of inhumations would have no implications for practical considerations of land-use.

It is also hardly credible that the burial rite adopted in a cemetery such as that at Poundbury is the result merely of an over-eager bureaucracy. The documentary evidence for the management or regulation of burial grounds provides no support for local administrations or the imperial authorities taking any interest in such matters. The legal texts concerning civic duties make no mention of such responsibilities and, at this date, the cities of the Western Empire had other priorities, mainly the raising of taxation and the maintenance of services demanded by the state.[33] At an earlier date in Rome, the administration was concerned only with the enforcement of regulations governing the sanctity of burial places or their position beyond the city limits.[34] These laws controlled the location of burials beyond the city-boundaries, as laid down in the Twelve Tables or in, for instance, the laws of Colonia Genetiva Iulia, the city of Urso, Baetica, Spain, established in the first century BC.[35] At Ostia, where a range of cemeteries dating from republican to late imperial times is known, containing numerous mausolea and *columbaria* furnished with inscriptions, there is no evidence that the plots were other than privately owned and administered. Fines for the misuse or alienation of burial grounds might be paid to the municipality or to Rome but the land was private. Indeed Meiggs states 'One of the most striking features of the cemeteries that we can now see is the apparent absence of public control in their development'.[36]

There is no record that attitudes changed later; even if there was a growth in bureaucracy it was directed towards practical matters of the supply of human and material resources to the state. Official legislation in the fourth and fifth centuries was, it is true, concerned with the violation of monuments and the remains of the dead, but these enactments in the Theodosian Code, later re-enacted by Valentinian III, were prompted by the increasing cult of the martyrs and the consequent disturbance of their graves. They still do not constitute directions as to the municipal management of cemeteries but rather provide further evidence of the Christian interest in burial places.[37]

With the smaller private burial plots the form of interment and structures was left to the next-of-kin and the landowners providing the burial plot, the character

---

[32] As, for example, at York and London: Wenham, Leslie P., *The Romano-British Cemetery at Trentholme Drive, York* (London: HMSO, 1968), and the inhumation and cremation burials on sites F and K, Barber and Bowsher 'The Eastern cemeteries', 17–25.

[33] Jones, A.H.M, *The Later Roman Empire 284–602. A Social, Economic and Administrative Survey*, 4 vols. (Oxford: Blackwell 1964), 725, 734–7; Abbott, Frank F., and Allan C. Johnson, *Municipal Administration in the Roman Empire* (New York: Russell and Russell, 1926), 95–7.

[34] Robinson, O.F., *Ancient Rome: City Planning and Administration* (London: Routledge, 1992), 124–6.

[35] Dessau, *Inscriptiones Latinae Selectae*, no. 6087; Abbott and Johnson, 'Municipal Administration', 300–17.

[36] Meiggs, Russell, *Roman Ostia* (2nd edn) (Oxford: Clarendon, 1973), 456.

[37] Harries, 'Death and the dead', 62–4.

of the site equally reflecting their beliefs. Personal choice and religious belief would be major influences, leading to a wide variety of customs. Larger cemeteries might be owned and regulated communally by burial clubs but, here again, personal preference would have dictated the rite, except in the case of those administered by the Church where the requirements of the religion would have taken precedence. This issue is important since, if the apparent order of these sites cannot be ascribed to direction from local or imperial authority, then the manner of burial and regulation of the cemetery must have been dictated by the community using it and the rite of burial must thus be taken as a true reflection of their social composition and religious attitudes.

Turning to specific burial rites, biblical authority exists for the use of aromatics and preservative materials in Jewish and Christian funerary ritual. Embalmment originated in the pre-Christian eastern Mediterranean but its occurrence in higher status burials of Roman date may have been underestimated. There were some instances of its use in early Imperial Rome, most notably in the case of Nero's wife Poppaea whose body was recorded as being preserved in this way.[38] Embalmment would have been expensive and therefore only employed by the elite including, perhaps, priests of Isis and other eastern cults. In a Christian context it should be noted that depictions of the raising of Lazarus on catacomb wall paintings and carved coffins show the body as tightly wrapped in the manner of a mummy, implying the iconic perception of a body that had been embalmed.[39] Occasionally bodies prepared in this manner have survived in cemeteries from the northern provinces, one child at the St Matthias cemetery in Trier being wrapped in bandages and placed in a lime or plaster-packed stone coffin.[40]

In the later persecutions a judge used denial of embalming and burial as a threat to a recalcitrant Christian.[41] It was also mentioned by Saint Augustine of Hippo when he reported that, before the death of his mother, Monica, she professed that she had no desire for an elaborate burial including this rite.[42] The later record of preserved cadavers, smelling of aromatics when translated, is particularly associated with the cult of the saints.[43] This might be taken as a quasi-miraculous record but, from more recent observations, could be a true record of the deliberate embalming of holy and significant ecclesiastics at the time

---

[38] Tacitus, *Annales*, 16, 6. Poppaea, interestingly, showed some support for the Jewish community in Rome.

[39] Gerke, F., *Die Christliche Sarkophage der Vor-Konstantinischen Zeit. Studien zur Spätantiken Kunstgeschichte* (Berlin, 1940), 41, Fig. 1.1–2 shows an example of a sarcophagus with a scene of the raising of Lazarus, the body wrapped as if mummified.

[40] *Trier: Kaiserresidenz und Bischofssitz. Die Stadt in spätantiker und frühchristlicher Zeit.* Mainz 1984, 212, 97C.

[41] Byeus, Cornelius, *et al.*, *Acta SS Tarachi, Probi et Andronici, in Acta Sanctorum Octobris, V* (Brussels: Greuse, 1852), 576–7.

[42] Augustine, *Confessiones*, IX, 13, ed. Verheijen, Lucas, *Augustine, Confessiones*, CCSL 27 (Turnhout: Brepols, 1981), 153. Evidence for embalming is strong in Augustine's North African homeland.

[43] Rollason, David, *Saints and Relics in Anglo-Saxon England* (Oxford: Blackwell, 1989), 34–41.

of their initial burial, the efficacy of this process then being seen as confirmation of the individual's sanctity. Again, Saint Augustine records an early example in the mention of Saints Protasius and Gervasius at Milan, whose bodies were described as incorrupt when uncovered in AD 386.[44] In Anglo-Saxon England, Bede's specific reference to the Christian precedent for the use of myrrh and aloes in preserving the dead implies that embalming was used at least for high-status ecclesiastical burials.[45] And, of course, the *Historia Ecclesiastica Gentis Anglorum* contains numerous examples where the corpses of the holy were reportedly found to be sweet-smelling and uncorrupt.[46]

In archaeological contexts, the issue is complicated by the poor survival of the organic remains, but the survival of mineral substances which accompanied embalming may indicate its practice. Dorothy Watts played down the significance of 'plaster-packed' burials in general because the rite occurs in conjunction with a variety of other not obviously Christian features.[47] But a distinction should perhaps here be drawn between gypsum, a slightly acid but relatively benign mineral, and lime which was more aggressive and destructive of flesh.[48] While lime, surviving as carbonate, occurs in a far greater variety of grave-types, gypsum is rarer and confined to burials which conform to a rite which could be considered Christian. Gypsum, once kilned to the anhydrous, powdered form, could have acted as a protective and water-absorbent packing for a preserved body, lime serving a different purpose to destroy the body in the manner of the sarcophagus which, as its name implied, was originally intended to consume the body.[49] That gypsum could have a use as a form of preservative or drying agent, similar to silica gel, is borne out by its re-introduction for the packing of embalmed bodies by William Hunter in the eighteenth century.[50]

In Britain gypsum is not readily available and has no use in the Roman period other than for these rare burials, significant numbers of which are known only at York and Dorchester, Dorset. At the latter town the Poundbury cemetery is the larger of the two known cemeteries containing gypsum burials. Elsewhere the rite has been identified at certain centres in the Rhineland and North Africa, most commonly in early Christian cemeteries.[51] For such a seemingly exotic rite to occur at a major city such as York, with proven links to the Rhineland and the

---

[44] Augustine, *Confessiones*, IX, 7, ed. Verheijen, 142. The translation of these bodies may have provoked re-enactment of legislation against the violation of tombs: Harries, 'Death and the dead', 63.

[45] Bede, in *Cantica Canticorum*, III, 4, 14, ed. Hurst, D., *Bede, In Cantica Canticorum in Bedae Venerabilis Opera Exegetica*, CCSL 119B (Turnhout: Brepols, 1983), 165–375, 266–7.

[46] For example, the translation of Aethelthryth at Ely, Bede, Historia Ecclesiastica, IV, 19, ed. and trans. Colgrave, B. and Mynors, R.A.B., *Bede's Ecclesiastical History of the English People* (Oxford, 1969), 390–7.

[47] Watts, 'Christians and Pagans', 59–61.

[48] Sparey-Green, 'The rite of plaster-burial', 429–30.

[49] *Ibid.* 429

[50] Litten, James, *The English Way of Death; the Common Funeral since 1450* (London, 1991), 48.

[51] The major finds in North Africa are summarised in Green 'The Significance', 48–9.

Plate 6.1 Interior of lead-lined coffin in burial 513 at Poundbury. Lumps of gypsum lie around the degraded skeleton (Sparey-Green)

elevation of Constantine to power, is not suprising but why a small cantonal capital such as Dorchester should rival it in this one respect is unexplained. There is, however, other evidence that, in the fourth century, the Dorchester area was unusual in the wealth and culture of at least part of the population and in the extent of Christian belief.[52]

At both York and Dorchester the mineral had to be brought some distance, the burial rite occurring in more than one cemetery. At the latter town the cemeteries were, significantly, set on chalk bedrock; if simply a white mineral was required to surround the body then such was readily available. Gypsum plaster was something special and, moreover, required technical knowledge that could only come from Mediterranean countries where the material was in more common use.

[52] For a summary of the main sites see Thomas 'Christianity', 175, Fig. 24 and 181–3; Sparey-Green, 'Poundbury', 144, summarises the evidence from Dorchester including the important cluster of Christian artefacts from Somerleigh Court in the south-west corner of the town.

A precedent for the form of grave or burial monument was set by Christ's burial. The most important feature was that a new tomb should be used, this manifest in the cutting of a new grave and the creation of large, ordered inhumation cemeteries. Each new cut would, perhaps, have been added to a row of earlier interments, avoiding intersection and super-imposition. From this it would follow that the place of burial was not polluted by a previous body and, equally, that interment would not entail the disturbance of an earlier grave. However, no specific text can be adduced, other than the citation from Tertullian already quoted, and the main support for this is circumstantial and based on comparison with known Christian burial places. In pagan law, preservation of the body follows from scruples concerning violation of property, in this case burial structures, and the pollution of the living which arose from the desecration of graves.[53] For the Christian, respect for the grave, like the preference for inhumation and embalming, where this could be afforded, can be seen as more related to belief in a bodily resurrection.

Adherence to inhumation with the body extended in an oriented alignment would seem to be an entirely separate issue from the mere orderliness of a cemetery and was presumably derived from biblical texts associating Christ with the rising sun and belief in His reappearance in the east at the resurrection.[54] Tertullian alludes to the Christian facing east in prayer, as also did pagans worshipping the sun, the association with sun-worship contributing to Constantine's adoption of the Christian God.[55] From the fourth century identifiably Christian graves do indeed adhere to this custom although, for obvious reasons, catacomb graves are not oriented.

For the avoidance of gravegoods there is no specific textual authority but it may reflect concepts of asceticism in life and the expectation of an afterlife in which material goods were unnecessary. Specifically, Christian belief did not require provision of equipment for a journey whereas many gravegoods in provincial cemeteries, from the provision of coin-payment for the ferryman Charon to interment wearing clothing and hob-nailed footwear, are relevant only to pagan ideas of travelling to the underworld. However, the pagan jurist Ulpian directed that neither ornaments nor any other goods should be put in graves as common people did.[56] Gravegoods are rarely attested in burials which in other ways appear Christian, their inclusion perhaps a sign of respect. These accompanying objects are, however, of particular types, normally items of jewellery set beside the bodies of young women, perhaps as a symbolic dowry honouring the unmarried dead.[57]

---

[53] Summarised by Harries, 'Death and the dead', 61–2, quoting, in particular Ulpian, *Digest* 47.12.3, 5–7 and *Codex Theodosianus* IX, 17.2.

[54] For Christ's advent as like lightning from east to west, see Matthew XXIV, 27.

[55] Tertullian, *Apologeticus*, XVI, 9–10, ed. and trans. Glover, *op. cit.* 84–5.

[56] Ulpian, *Digest*, 11.7.14.5.

[57] The most famous example is perhaps the female inhumation from Sycamore Terrace, York, illustrated in RCHM(E), *Eburacum*, 73, III, b, (v).

Plain, undecorated stone coffins have commonly been found in late Roman Christian cemeteries both in Britain and the Continent. The Railway Station cemetery in York has produced 50 such coffins. Even in the rich cemeteries of the Rhineland cities, at Arles or in the catacombs at Rome, finely decorated marble sarcophagi were rare and confined to those containers originally intended to be set above ground.[58] This may indicate the utilitarian nature of these containers but the rusticated tooling found at Poundbury, York and in the Rhineland might allude to the original rock-cut Christian tomb and its stone door.

Architecturally elaborate mausolea are perhaps unusual, except in the context of Christian Imperial burials, but simple structures with richly decorated interiors were constructed. The better preserved burial chambers in the Roman catacombs are the subterranean equivalent of these lost structures.[59] Other significant survivals exist in the Danubian provinces at, for instance, Sopianae Pecs, the walls decorated with scenes of Adam and Eve in Paradise, Daniel in the lion's den, Christ's resurrection and the chi-rho.[60] Two of the surface mausolea at Poundbury had their walls and ceilings decorated with elaborate paintings, the better preserved including scenes of robed figures on one side wall and the ceiling, nude figures on the east wall (?Adam and Eve) and scenes of a cityscape with gates near the west door.[61]

Surface structures of rectangular plan, perhaps with an apsidal end, occur in known Christian cemeteries, the burials placed beneath the floor or, in the richest examples, placed in decorated coffins ranged around the walls. The internal wall and ceiling decoration of these perhaps served a didactic purpose and provided suitable surroundings for funerary ceremonies, graveside meals and the annual commemoration of the dead. In northern Europe, mausolea have been identifed beneath later churches dedicated to martyrs or significant figures in the early church. At St Maximin's Church, Trier, for example, simple rectangles enclosed stone coffins containing gypsum plaster burials, the rusticated tooling of the ridged coffin lids being paralleled at Poundbury.[62] The mausolea at the latter site are the most significant of this type to have been identified in Britain because of their similarity to these continental mausolea or *memoriae* and because of their internal decoration. Other groups of burials within the Poundbury cemetery were

---

[58] For plainly decorated coffins and simple mausolea in a Christian context, see the cemetery beneath St Matthias church in Trier; Reusch, Wilhelm, *Frühchristliche Zeugnisse im Einzugsgebiet von Rhein und Mosel* (Trier: Paulinus, 1965),165–74. The site also produced one coffin decorated with scenes of Noah; *ibid.* 18–9 and Pl. 1.

[59] Testini, 'Le Catacombe'; for an example of a subterranean 'road' lined with mausolea, see area I in the catacomb of S. Callisto, 130.

[60] Ferenc Levardy, *Early Christian Mausoleum*, Okeresztzeny Mauzoleum, Pecs, n.d.

[61] The description in Sparey-Green, C.J., 'The mausolea painted plaster' in Farwell and Molleson 1993, 135–40 at 137–9 is now in need of revision and development following the identification of new comparative material from Pecs and the Madaba pavement from Israel.

[62] Cuppers, Hans, 'Das Graberfeld von St. Matthias', in Reusch, Wilhelm, *Frühchristliche Zeugnisse im Einzugsgebiet von Rhein und Mosel* (Trier: Paulinus, 1965), 165–74.

not surrounded by continuous foundations but the disposition of the graves suggested that stone bases supporting a structure similar to those in the St Matthias cemetery had surrounded one group of stone and lead coffins.

The anthropological structure of the cemetery population may be important as an unconscious reflection of its make-up and of the community's attitude to the dead. At its most obvious this could be represented by the presence of members of only one sex or by separation of the sexes into discrete areas, suggesting use by a monastic foundation or by a Christian community which emphasised the extended group rather than separate nuclear families. The inclusion of groups of infant burials in a mixed cemetery may be a particularly significant factor since, in the Roman period at least, the pagan custom was for the neo-nates to be casually disposed of within settlement areas. Their presence in significant numbers, and treatment with ceremony equal to that accorded adults, has been interpreted by Dorothy Watts as a criterion for identifying such cemeteries as Christian.[63] No text relates specifically to the Christian attitude to the burial of infants, but since catechumens of any age could be buried alongside the baptised and since infants were shown particular regard in life it has been suggested that this same care was extended to them in death. This may not have been an attitude common to all Christians in the Late Roman period, however, as, for instance, Augustine viewed the unbaptised infants of Christian parents as damned by original sin, but some Pelagian writers saw these infants as having eternal life, even without baptism.[64] Pelagians might, therefore, be willing to accept even the youngest, unbaptised children for Christian burial, unlike the followers of Augustine. The careful interment of so many infants at Poundbury may be of some interest and a hint of beliefs within the community similar to those held by the Pelagians.

Revering the dead who had suffered persecution or who had been important figures in the Church caused their burial places to serve as a focus for worship and for the burial of the faithful, a feature distinctive of Christianity and distinct from mere display of respect for a patron's burial or the monument to a pagan hero. It is therefore a characteristic feature of Christian cemeteries that particular graves of individuals – or occasionally groups of two or three persons – became the focus of particular attention.[65] This may be shown in three ways: by the clustering of burial around the spot, by the erection of a special structure to allow worship over or close to the grave, and by the later veneration of the spot, often marked by the erection of a sequence of later churches which commemorated, or were dedicated to, the saint or saints. In archaeological terms this evidence is unlikely to be confused with any form of pagan monument, but may now be inaccessible beneath later buildings or seriously disturbed by the concentration of later building activity.

[63] Watts, 'Christians and Pagans', 40–51.
[64] Romans, V, 12 on Adam's original sin. Augustine, *De Peccatorum Meritis et Remissione et de Baptismo Paruulorum*, I, 16, ed. Migne, *Patrologia Latina*, XLIV, col. 120–21.
[65] The British evidence is described by Rollason, 'Saints and Relics', 4–18.

Allusion to a desire to be buried close to a holy person comes on an inscription from Trier where the deceased is described as deserving to be buried nearer the sacred spot than was physically possible, so many having already been interred there.[66] Numerous examples exist on the Continent of burials focussed on a recorded holy grave and from sub-Roman Britain we have the accounts of Gildas and Bede, describing the reverence shown the tomb and shrine of Alban, although they make specific reference only to worship on the site; it must be assumed, on the Continental analogies, that the martyrial burial was the focus of later interment.

At Poundbury, in the absence of local traditions or extant Christian dedications referring to specific holy interments, the only possibility is the identification of particular burials that, within the structure of the cemetery, appear unusual and to have acted as foci. Certain burials stand out as distinct from the groups of plaster-packed special graves, these graves seemingly lying at the centre of major clusters of burials. The most significant and unusual of these was the burial of a man accompanied by two infants, the bodies laid in a single grave beneath a partially burnt wooden structure.[67] The association of a man with infant bodies in this way invites comparison with texts alluding to Christ as protector of children. There can be no certainty but the burial had attracted a particularly dense grouping of burial within the centre of the main cemetery enclosure; this was someone of significance.

Identification of early Christian cemeteries in Britain may well have to depend on archaeological evidence alone, posing difficulties and leaving many uncertainties, but at present the Poundbury, Dorchester and York cemeteries can claim identification as such along with other probable cases such as Butt Road, Colchester and Icklingham, Suffolk, sites notable for their burial and monument type.[68] The eastern cemetery in Winchester is another possible case where a cemetery conforming to many of the characteristics outlined here overlies a possible baptistry, adjoining the existing St John Baptist Church.[69]

The definition of Christian burial sites is very difficult without specific textual or epigraphic reference. However, if, as I propose, the character of cemeteries and the aggregate of their component burial customs is a reflection of a community's beliefs and not something imposed by outside secular authority, then the distinctive features of certain cemetery types may be true reflections of Christian attitudes to their dead. The norms of treatment apparent in the remains may then be true indicators of custom, ethnic tradition and religious belief. In particular

---

[66] Gose, E., *Katalog der frühchristliche Inschriften aus Trier* (1958), no. 466.

[67] Grave 243A-C, Farwell and Molleson, 'Poundbury', 66, Fig. 52.

[68] Crummy *et al.* 'Excavations'; West, Stanley E. and Plouviez, Judith, 'The Romano-British site at Icklingham', *East Anglian Archaeology* 3 (Ipswich, 1976), 63–125.

[69] Morris, Michael, 'A Lead-lined Coffin Burial from Winchester' in *Britannia* 17 (1986), 343–6; Collis, John, 'The Eastern Suburb' in *Excavations in the Suburbs and Western part of the Town, Winchester Excavations Vol 2 1949–60* (1978), 40–60 at 43–6.

there may have been customs based on biblical precedent which were distinctive of Christian groups and which may allow us to identify those cemeteries reserved for their use.

One feature of the British sites of the Roman period is the relative rarity of sites with traditional associations with martyrs or recorded figures in the Church. We only know of St Alban, Aaron and Julius at Caerleon and the enigmatic reference to a Saint Sixtus in Kent.[70] There is also an oblique reference to a dedication to St Probus in North Dorset.[71] In no case does any epigraphic evidence survive from the site of an apparent Christian cemetery, unlike on the continent. It is as if all memory was expunged, unless Britain was unusually barren of eminent figures or of those who suffered persecution. It is possible that in the early post-Roman period the Augustinian mission to the Anglo-Saxon kingdoms was particularly efficent in not only converting the English but obliterating any traces of the sub-Roman Church and the memory of its major figures.

The lack of recorded Christian cemeteries in Roman Britain could lead one to conclude that there were few if any such sites and thus few converts to the faith. But if we allow for their identification using analogies drawn from the textual evidence and archaeological evidence from Continental sites, it is possible to point to a few rare examples such as those at Poundbury and York. These examples would serve to indicate the existence of Christian communities in particular regions, clarify the source of missions to the province and the routes by which the faith spread, bringing with it particular teaching, liturgy and burial practices.

---

[70] Rollason, 'Saints and Relics'; Stancliffe, Clare, 'The British Church and the Mission of Augustine', in Richard Gameson, ed., St Augustine and the Conversion of England (Stroud: Sutton, 1999), 107–51 at 121–2.

[71] Barker, Catherine, 'The topography of Sherborne/Lanprobi – A reply', Proceedings of the Dorset Natural History and Archaeological Society, 104 (1982), 197–8.

7

Votive Deposits and Christian Practice
in Late Roman Britain

DAVID PETTS

Conversion and Material Culture

The study of conversion through archaeology has seldom theorised the relation-ship between material culture and religious practice. Often the relationship between the two is assumed to be simple, with different religions having distinct cultural practices. The process of tracking conversion then becomes a process of mapping the changing distribution of these diagnostic elements over time and space. However, the relationship between belief and practice is never so clear. The creation of models for early Christianity derived from textual evidence or archaeological material from a much later period means that there is a danger of forcing the evidence into an interpretative straight-jacket; any religious practice which is not attested textually or found in another period is relegated to a 'pagan' status. This creates an essentialist and abstract model of Christian practice, which fails to take account of local variation.

While Christian belief may be seen as mapping onto a set of archaeologically diagnostic criteria (Thomas 1981; Watts 1988, 1991, 1998; Mawer 1995), the basic concept that there is discrete set of Christian ritual practices that are recognisable in the archaeological record has recently been challenged (Cookson 1987, Kilbride 1996; Millett 1995a, b). In his *Christianity in Roman Britain to AD 500* (1981) Charles Thomas argues for the continuity of Christianity into the fifth century, calling on a wide range of evidence: historical, linguistic and material. Dorothy Watts in her *Christians and Pagans in Roman Britain* (1991) further studies criteria for identifying buildings, artefacts, symbols and inscriptions as Christian, a project continued by Frances Mawer (1995). In this line of reasoning, objects or attributes identified as signifying Christianity are given an appropriate weighting and plotted on a map, and the distribution taken to indicate the relative intensity of Christian practice (Thomas 1981: 96–101, Fig. 16; Watts 1991: Fig. 28). I would like to use this work as a point of departure for examining how far these distributions are owed to variations in depositional practice, or in the way that religion was expressed, as opposed to a variation in the distribution of Christianity itself. The principal example I will use is that of the lead tanks, an accepted Christian signifier.

Roman Lead Baptismal Tanks

These circular containers are unique to Roman Britain. At least twenty examples have been found, many of which carry either a single or multiple decorative motifs, often in panels divided by vertical banding. They vary slightly in size; the largest is 0.97 metre in diameter and the smallest 0.46 metre. It is clear from these motifs that many of the tanks had some form of Christian meaning. Eight are decorated with the *chi-rho* symbol, one has an *alpha-omega* (Icklingham 2; West 1976: Fig. 36) and one has a circular symbol that may be a cross pattée (Oxbrough; Frere 1989: 403).

The function of these tanks has been widely discussed, and the consensus is that they were involved in some manner in the rite of baptism. This is most clearly demonstrated by the small figural frieze on the tank from Walesby (Lincs.) which consists of three panels each containing three figures (Petch 1961). In the left and right-hand panels stand three male figures in short cloaks and tunics. In the central panel stands a naked woman flanked by two clothed women. Charles Thomas has convincingly argued that these tanks were probably used for baptism, probably by affusion (the pouring of the baptismal water over the head of an unclothed candidate) (Thomas 1981: 221–5). Watts has however suggested that they may instead be related to the rite of *pedilavium*, a ritual washing of the feet (Watts 1991: 171).

The tanks are mainly found in Eastern England, especially the East Midlands and East Anglia with only a few outliers: Ireby (Cumbria) (Richmond 1945), Kenilworth (Warks.) (Looker 2000) and Bourton-on-the-Water (Gloc.) (Donovan 1934: 116–7). A traditional approach would simply equate the greatest focus of lead baptismal tanks with the focus of Christianity. However, a consideration of the *context* of their deposition (*sensu* Hodder 1986: 118–46) might allow this interpretation to be enlarged and modified. It is argued that the deposition of the lead tanks may itself have been a ritual practice favoured in East Anglia, thus skewing the distribution of Christian attributes.

Tank-finds as Votive Deposits

Some of the lead tanks have been found in buildings, such as those from Bourton-on-the-Water (Donovan 1934), and some have unrecorded contexts as they were metal-detector finds (e.g. Brough, Notts, Watts 1998: 147–53) or were found by ploughing (Walesby, Lincs.; Petch 1961). But a significant number have been found in pits, wells and other and watery contexts which relate to the European and native British tradition of ritual deposition (cf. Bradley 1998; Brunaux 1988). The use of such contexts was clearly common in Roman Britain (Clarke 1998; Ross 1968). The examples from Ashton were found in a well (Guy 1977; Hadman and

Upex 1977: 8), as was that from Caversham (Frere 1989: 319). The tank found at Heathrow was located in the top of a waterhole, in an area with a long tradition of ritual deposition in such contexts from the late Bronze Age. Others had a riverine context: the Oxborough tank was found by the River Wissey (Guy 1989), the Pulborough tank, near the River Arun (Curwen 1943), the Huntingdon tank from the River Ouse (Donovan 1934) and the Willingham tank from a Fen context. These locations are exactly the sort where ritual deposits occur. The importance of these lead tanks may have been as much in their deposition as in their use. It is clear that whatever their primary use the deposition of the fonts is part of a wider phenomenon of ritual deposition in late Roman Britain. The hoarding and deposition of pewter vessels and tableware is widespread in Roman Britain, the vessels themselves mostly dating from after c.AD 250. Although some writers have argued for a functional reason for their deposition, such as hiding them in times of crisis (e.g. Brown 1973: 201–4), the wider consensus is that they were buried for religious reasons (Beagrie 1989: 179; Poulton and Scott 1993). Pewter plates have been found in riverine contexts at Shepperton (Poulton and Scott 1993) and Verulamium (Frere 1984: 65), whilst similar hoards have been found in pits or wells at several sites, such as at Stanwick (Northants.) (Neal 1989: 165) and Brislington (Avon) (Branigan 1972). In a more clearly religious context a wide range of pewter pieces were found in the spring at the centre of the temple complex at Bath (Henig et al. 1988). Some of these carried inscriptions dedicating them to deities.

It might be argued that the deposition of such pewter hoards was essentially a pagan practice, and that such a practice would not be followed by Christians. The damaged nature of some of the fonts might even be put forward as an argument for the deposition of the tanks by pagans in the process of destroying a Christian site, possibly during a postulated late fourth century pagan revival (e.g. Guy 1981: 275; Watts 1998: 49). However, such an interpretation ignores the clear evidence for the deposition of sets of Christian pewter ware, in exactly the same type of contexts as the non-Christian pewter ware hoards, with no evidence that they had been destroyed or damaged in any way. In these hoards the Christian vessels were treated with as much respect as the putative pagan hoards.

At Appleshaw (Hants.) excavations in the nineteenth century uncovered 32 pewter vessels placed in a pit inserted through the floor of a villa. One of the vessels had a large Constantinian *chi-rho* on the base, and another dish was engraved with a fish symbol (Read 1898). From the Roman small town at Heybridge (Essex) a large hoard of pewter was found in a well of late Roman date; Nina Crummy has noted that one of the objects was decorated with a *chi-rho* symbol (Crummy in Atkinson and Preston, *forthcoming*). Another pewter hoard with probable Christian associations comes from Sutton, Isle of Ely. A pewter bowl from Sutton, almost certainly part of the hoard, also had a Constantinian *chi-rho* between A and Ω (Clarke 1931). A *chi-rho* was also found inscribed on the deliberately buried pewter vessel at Caerwent (Boon 1962: 338–9). A possible ritual riverine find was a pewter bowl or dish found on the bed of the Old Welney River (Cambs.) bearing a *chi-rho* (Thomas 1981: 123).

A more ambiguously Christian pewter hoard is from Appleford (Oxon.) (Brown 1973). Twenty-four pewter vessels were found in a deep well or shaft. A Christian identity for the collection of vessels has not been put forward before. However, there are two elements of the decoration which may be overtly Christian. The first is a possible *iota-chi* cut into the base of a cast fluted bowl (*ibid.* 189, 3). More convincingly, a flat plate is decorated with an incised cross pattée. A similar cross was found carved on the back of a pewter dish from Boltisham Lode (Peal 1967: 28–9). The Appleford hoard is also important for the graffiti inscribed on another large plate, which reads as EMITA PARTA SVA LOVERNIANVS DONAVIT, which has been translated as 'Lovernianus presented the things he had bought'. This inscription is clearly significant if the hoard is interpreted as votive.

It also brings to mind the inscription from the Christian silver hoard from Water Newton. One votive plaque decorated with a *chi-rho* had an inscription in relief reading AMCILLA VOTUM QUO(d) PROMISIT CONPLEVIT. Inscriptions were also found on two silver cups and a strainer (Painter 1977a, 1999). The Water Newton hoard, consisting of a gold disc and 27 silver objects, including sixteen plaques and eight vessels and strainer, raises the wider issue of the deposition of Christian precious metal hoards in Britain. The exact context of the Water Newton hoard is unclear, though its location, in Cambridgeshire, is in the heartland of the distribution of both pewter hoards and lead tanks. Again this area is where most of the precious metal hoards from late Roman Britain are found, especially if the clearly different *hacksilber* hoards found just outside the province, such as Balline (Co. Limerick), Ballinrees (Co. Derry) and Traprain Law (Curle 1923; Henig 1995: 163–4) are ignored. The presence of *chi-rho* symbols on the spoons from the Mildenhall hoard supply a Christian identity to at least an element of the group (Painter 1977b), and it has been argued that the Thetford Hoard also had significant Christian element (Watts 1991: 146–58). The massive Hoxne hoard, deposited in the early fifth century, also contained a Christian component, a group of ten spoons decorated with the *chi-rho* symbol (Bland and Johns 1995). Historically contingent reasons have been produced for the burial of some of these hoards. Johns, arguing for a pagan origin for the Thetford treasure, related the deposition to the anti-pagan decrees of the 390s (Johns 1986a), whilst Painter argued that the Water Newton hoard was hidden to keep it from Roman robbers or by the robbers themselves (Painter 1999: 5–6). However, it is surely more than coincidental that these hoards were found in the very areas where pewter hoards predominate.

A final similarity between the deposition of pewter hoards and the deposition of Christian lead tanks can be seen in the presence of accompanying hoards of iron objects found with both types of deposit (see Manning 1972 for iron-work hoards in Roman Britain). At Icklingham the lead tank found in 1971 was accompanied by a large quantity of iron objects, and an iron object was found with a pewter hoard from nearby. Large quantities of iron objects were also found with the possible Christian pewter hoard from Appleford (Brown 1973: 193–9), including 1.4 m of iron chain, an iron steelyard and a scythe blade. At Stanwick (Northants.) the hoard of four pewter vessels in a pit was found just to the north of a hoard of iron objects. The deposition of iron hoards clearly overlapped with the deposition of pewter hoards and Christian lead tanks. This relationship between lead tanks and iron hoards is curiously found again in the Middle/Later Saxon period, and large hoards of iron objects and a lead tank have been found at a number of sites including Westley Waterless (Cambs.) (Anon 1879) and Flixborough (Loveluck 1998).

A consideration of these hoards and the inscriptions found in the Water Newton hoard make it clear that the deposition of hoards for votive purposes and the ritual dedication of vessels, whether made of pewter or silver, was not incompatible with Christianity. Indeed, the votive plaques from Water Newton are merely Christian examples of the pagan tradition of using such plaques known from a number of sites in Britain (Henig 1984: 145–8). In late Roman Britain the rite of making votive offerings of vessels in watery and other contexts was an expression of religious belief common to both pagans and Christians. In this context the deposition of Christian lead tanks in such contexts takes on a new level of meaning.

Icklingham: a Votive Landscape

The broad similarity in the geographical distribution of Christian lead tanks and pewter hoards can also be seen at a very local level in the area surrounding the small Romano-British site at Icklingham (Suffolk) (West 1976). This site is best known for its possible Christian church (Building B) and a tile-built baptistery or font base 10 metres to its east. These were adjacent to 41 inhumations, of which only one had evidence for any grave-goods. The Christian identity of the site rests primarily on the presence of the remains of at least four lead tanks from the imme-diate area, of which three had *chi-rho* inscriptions. There was also undoubtedly domestic activity in the area, with scatters of pottery in the field adjacent to the 'church' site, and occupation scatters on the opposite bank of the River Lark, and a building with a hypocaust was found about 200 metres to the north-west.

The earliest recorded lead tank from Icklingham was found in 1726/7 (Salmon 1730, 1: 161). It is now lost so the decoration cannot be examined, but 'ornamental work' was recorded on the outside and a mark 'A' was also recorded on one side. This may possibly have been an 'A' from an 'A and Ω' flanking a *chi-rho* symbol. A second tank found in 1932 probably came from the north-east side of Horsland Field, 200–300 yards north-east of the excavated site. This was decorated with *Chi-rho* symbols between a reversed A and Ω. The third tank was found in 1971 probably near the site of the baptistery. This tank was filled with a large deposit of iron objects including hinges, nails and two saws, as well as cakes of lead and the lug of a fourth lead tank. This hoard of iron objects immediately brings to mind the iron-work hoard found with the Appleford pewter hoard.

The tanks and the iron-work hoard are however not the only unusual deposits to be found at Icklingham; no less than four pewter hoards are known from the parish. The earliest found in 1839 at an unknown site contained nine vessels. In 1853 the British Museum purchased a further eighteen vessels from a second hoard, with the four vessels from the same hoard being bought by the Ipswich museum. In 1956 a third hoard of nine pewter vessels and a saw-blade was found on high land to the north of the site (Liversidge 1959: 6–10). One of the objects from this hoard was decorated with a fish, similar to that found on the pewter dish from Sutton (Cambs.) a common symbol of Christianity (e.g. Thomas 1981: 92–3). A fourth small hoard was found on the western edge of the parish in 1962, consisting of a bronze bowl, a pewter platter and a pottery bowl (Liversidge 1962).

There is also evidence for a third form of deliberate deposition, the placement of coin hoards. At least five such hoards are known from Icklingham (West 1976: 64). The earliest recorded came from the villa site in 1877 on the northern corner of a wall in Room 3. It consisted of 33 bronze coins. The only dated coin from this group is a *Magna Urbica*. In 1877 a second hoard was found to the north of the site in a small vase; it consisted of around 400 silver coins dating from Constantius II to Honorius. The next three come from unrecorded contexts. One found in 1902 in an earthenware bowl comprised 1,064 coins dating up to Honorius, a fourth consisted of twelve radiate *minimi* and a fifth found in 1906 contained coins from Claudius II to Valentinian. Other scatters of coins have been found in the same field as the church site, and the fields to the north and south. Another example of deliberate deposition comes from a large pit (F.32) close to the area where the church was later built (West 1976:, 68–70, Fig. 34). This feature was 3.8 metres in diameter and 2.45 metres deep. It seems to have been backfilled in a single event. The contents of this pit are extremely unusual. Most striking was a group of six skulls, including one child. Unusual architectural fragments were also found in it: a complete limestone pillar (1.17 metres long) and fragments of unusual indented and grooved decorative roof-tiles. A final less-understood example of probably deliberate deposition from Icklingham takes the form of an assemblage of masks and statuettes, known as the 'Icklingham Bronzes' found in the area. Unfortunately, these were metal-detector founds looted from the site and thought to have been illegally exported to the USA. Their precise context is unknown, but they appear to be a clear indication of an early Roman votive hoard. Interestingly, the similar Willingham Fen hoard of early Roman bronze figures and cult equipment was also found close to a Late Roman lead font (Wilkes and Elrington 1978: 84–50).

Icklingham is thus the centre of a large number deposits, including lead tanks, iron-work, pewter vessels and coin hoards which appear to be deliberately composed or structured. The focus also appears to extend beyond the parish of Icklingham itself. Three pewter hoards were found in the parish of Hockwold-cum-Wilton around 10 miles to the north, with others in the surrounding area (Gurney 1986: 149–53). Hockwold is the also the site of an important hoard of early Roman vessels (Johns 1986b). Mildenhall is only 4 miles to the north-west of Icklingham and Thetford is 10 miles to the north-east. Other hoards of early

Roman vessels are found at Brandon (10 miles away) and possibly Santon Downham (12 miles away). A set of Iron Age religious equipment was found just across the River Lark at Cavenham, only around a mile distance.

Whilst, individually, the deposits which focus on Icklingham are not unusual, their content and quantity invite a ritual explanation. The unusual architectural fragments in pit F.32 may relate to a focal pre-Christian religious structure, but the wider distribution of the deposits around the parish suggest that such votive activities were carried out throughout the surrounding landscape. At first it might appear that the pagan practice of ritual deposition throughout the landscape was replaced by a specific Christian focus of activity. Apart from the 'Icklingham Bronzes' (which can probably be dated to the first/second centuries AD), the other deposits fit better in a late Roman, indeed a later fourth century context. The most easily datable deposits, the coin hoards, mostly belong to the later fourth century, with coin series extending up to Theodosius and Honorius. Although the only datable coin from the 1877 hoard was early, the context of the find in the ruins of the stone 'villa' structure suggest a later Roman date. It is harder to date the pewter hoards, but such hoards elsewhere mainly date to the fourth century, and are common in the late fourth century (Beagrie 1989: 175). Finally, the lead tanks themselves all date to the second half of the fourth century, as does the construction of the church and baptistery (Phase III) with which they are probably contemporary.

This suggests that the high-point of deposition of ritual objects, especially lead and pewter vessels and tanks, should belong to the period *after* the construction of the church and baptistery and the destruction of any putative temple. Although there was a clear pre-fourth century tradition of votive deposition the peak of such deposits comes after the introduction of Christianity into the area. The deposition of the lead tanks, the Christian element to the Mildenhall and Thetford hoards and the presence of a Christian fish-symbol on one of the pewter hoards might suggest that these deposits were not being placed by pagans in reaction to Christians, but by Christians themselves. For fourth-century Christians in Roman Britain the placement of ritual hoards was as natural as celebrating mass or carrying out baptisms; it was merely one of the options open to them as a means of expressing their beliefs.

Conclusions

The deposition of Roman Christian lead tanks can be seen to be one aspect of a widely practised late Roman tradition of votive deposition, including the placement of hoards of pewter vessels, many decorated with *chi-rho* symbols, and precious metal hoards, again many with a Christian element. It is possible that the placement of lead tanks in such contexts was carried out by pagans as a form of symbolic destruction. However, the presence of *chi-rho* symbols on pewter hoards and on precious metal deposits would indicate that these hoards are as likely to be placed *by* Christians themselves. The lead tanks are perhaps best seen merely as a specialist form of pewter vessel, part of a range of such objects used for hoarding practices.

By appreciating that the lead tanks were objects worthy of votive deposition, we are adding another layer of understanding to their role. This is not to argue that they were not used in a liturgical context, but that they had a more complex biography. In the same way that it has been suggested that some of the pewter hoards were never intended to be used, but merely to be placed in ritual deposits, the ritual deposition of the lead tank may have been inscribed into their cultural life. This may explain why some sites, such as Bourton-on-the-Water, Ashton and Icklingham have produced several tanks. They may have not been used simultaneously, but in series, each never having been intended to be used more than once or twice. In Roman military contexts altars were ritually disposed of through burial in the ground, and it may have been the correct way of disposing of sacred objects (Henig 1984: 89–90).

It is wrong to suggest that the deposition of Christian objects in such a manner is an example of syncretism, or that those who carried out were consciously behaving in a pagan manner. The issue of deposition of objects in votive contexts is more likely to be such a basic way of expressing religious belief that it was seen neither as pagan or Christian. After all, just because pre-Christian religious believers prayed means not that the act of prayer in Christianity is syncretic, but merely an established mode of religious practice.

The consequences for the archaeological study of conversion are clear. Firstly, basic modes of religious practice may show continuity over the period of conversion without indicating syncretism or a hybrid or mongrel religion. Secondly, religious practices can have very practical implications for the survival of certain classes of objects. The fact that lead tanks are found primarily in East Anglia and the East Midlands does not mean that this was the main area in which they were used. It is just that in these areas they were disposed of in such a manner – burial in pits or watery contexts – that they were more likely to survive in the long-term. Other areas of the country may have disposed of tanks in other ways which have left no archaeological trace.

Quantitative maps of evidence cannot easily take account of variations in deposition practice. Using another example, the evidence of Christianity from Roman villas appears mainly in the south-west, which is also the main area of late Roman pagan temples. Both are rare in rural contexts in East Anglia and the East Midlands. This implies that in the south-west religious belief and power was articulated through architectural elaboration rather than hoarding. The way Christianity manifests itself in the material record is, in consequence, very different in the south-west of Britain than in the east. Distribution maps may show not so much the distribution of Christianity, as the variation in the way that Christianity was signalled. It is only by placing specified Christian practices against their wider religious and socio-political contexts that a true archaeological understanding of the process of conversion can be attained.

References

Anon. 1879. *Report of the Cambridgeshire Antiquarian Society*.

Atkinson, M. and Preston, S.J. (forthcoming) *The Late Iron Age and Roman Settlement at Elms Farm, Heybridge, Essex, Excavations 1993–5*.

Beagrie, N. 1989. 'The Romano-British Pewter Industry' *Britannia* 20, 169–91.

Bland, R. and Johns, C. 1995. *The Hoxne Treasure: An Illustrated Introduction* London.

Boon, G.C. 1962. 'A Christian Monogram at Caerwent' *Bull. Board Celtic Stud.* 19, 338–44.

Bradley, R. 1998. *The Passage of Arms: An Archaeological Analysis of Prehistoric Hoards and Votive Deposits* Oxford (2nd edn).

Branigan, K. 1972. 'The Romano-British Villa at Brislington' *Proc. Somerset Archaeol. Nat. Hist. Soc.* 116, 78–85.

Brown. D. 1973. 'A Romano Pewter Hoard from Appleford, Berkshire' *Oxoniensis* 38, 184–206.

Brunaux, J-L. 1988. *The Celtic Gauls – Gods, Rites and Sanctuaries* London.

Clarke, L.G.C. 1931. 'Roman Pewter Bowl from the Isle of Ely' *Proc. Cambridge Antiq. Soc.* 31, 66–72.

Clarke, S. 1998. 'Abandonment, Rubbish Disposal and "Special" Deposits at Newstead' in K. Meadows, C. Lemke and J. Heron (eds) *TRAC 96, Proceedings of the 6th Theoretical Roman Archeology Conference* Oxford, 73–81.

Cookson, N. 1987. 'The Christian church in Roman Britain: a synthesis of archaeology' *World Archaeology* 18, 426–33.

Cottam, S. (ed.) 1995. *Theoretical Roman Archaeology Conference Proceedings 1994* Oxford.

Curle, A.O. 1923. *The Treasure of Traprain. A Scottish hoard of Roman Silver Plate* Glasgow.

Curwen, E.C. 1943. 'Roman Lead Cistern from Pulborough, Sussex' *Antiq. Journal* 23, 155–7.

Donovan, H.E. 1934. 'Excavations of a Romano-British building at Bourton on the Water' *Trans Bristol Gloucester Archaeol. Soc.* 55, 98–128.

Frere, S.S. 1984. *Verulamium Excavations* 3 Oxford; Oxford University Committee for Archaeology.

—— 1989. 'Roman Britain in 1989: sites explored' *Britannia* 20, 258–326.

Gurney, D. 1986. *Settlement, Religion and Industry on the Roman Fen Edge, Norfolk* East Anglian Archaeology 31, Gressenhall.

Guy, C.J. 1977. 'The lead tank from Ashton' *Durobrivae* 5, 6–9.

—— 1981. 'Roman Circular Lead Tanks in Britain' *Britannia* 12, 271–6.

—— 1989. 'The Oxborough Lead Tank' *Britannia* 20, 234–7.

Hadman, J. and Upex, S. 1977. 'Ashton, 1976' *Durobrivae* 5 6–9.

Henig, M. 1984. *Religion in Roman Britain* London.

—— 1995. *The Art of Roman Britain* London.

Henig, M., Brown, D, Sunter, N., Allason-Jones, L. and Baatz, D. 1988. 'The small objects' in Cunliffe, B. (ed.) *The Temple of Sulis Minerva at Bath: Vol.2. The Finds from the Sacred Spring* Oxford; Oxford Committee for Archaeology.

Hodder, I. 1986. *Reading the Past* Cambridge.

Johns, C.M. 1986a. 'Faunus at Thetford: an early Latin deity in late Roman Britain' in M. Henig and A. King (eds) *Pagan Gods and Shrines of the Roman Empire* Oxford; Oxford University Committee for Archaeology, 93–104.

—— 1986b. 'The Roman Silver Cups from Hockwold, Norfolk' *Archaeologia* 108, 1–13.

Kilbride, W. 1996. *Orthodoxy and Liturgy in Late Roman Britain* http://www.gla.ac.uk/
archaeology/staff/wgk/papers/metaphor.html.

Liversidge, J. 1959. 'A New Hoard of Romano-British Pewter at Icklingham, Suffolk' *Proc.
Cambridge Antiq. Soc.* 52, 6–10.

—— 1962. 'A Bronze Bowl and other Vessels from Icklingham, Suffolk' *Proc. Cambridge
Antiq. Soc.* 55, 6–7.

Looker, J. 2000. 'Another Early Christian Font/Tank from Northamptonshire'
Northamptonshire Archaeological Journal 28, 163–4.

Loveluck, C.P. 1998. 'A high-status Anglo-Saxon settlement at Flixborough, Lincolnshire'
Antiquity 72, 146–61.

Manning, W.H. 1972. 'Ironwork Hoards in Iron Age and Roman Britain' *Britannia* 3,
224–50.

Mawer, C.F. 1995. *Evidence for Christianity in Roman Britain: The Small Finds* British
Archaeological Report 243, Oxford.

Millett, M. 1995a. 'An Early Christian cemetery at Colchester' *Archaeological Journal* 152,
451–5.

—— 1995b. 'Treasure: Interpreting Roman Hoards' in Cottam, S. (1995), 99–1–6.

Neal, D.S. 1989. 'The Stanwick Villa, Northants: Interim report of excavations 1984–88'
Britannia 20, 149–68.

Painter, K.S. 1977a. *The Water Newton Early Christian Silver* London.

—— 1977b. *The Mildenhall Treasure Roman Treasure from East Anglia* London.

—— 1999. 'The Water Newton Silver: Votive or Liturgical?' *Journ. Brit. Archaeol. Assoc.* 152,
1–23.

Peal, C.A. 1967. 'Romano-British pewter plates and dishes' *Proc. Cambridge Antiq. Soc.* 60,
19–37.

Petch, D.F. 1961. 'A Roman lead tank, Walesby' *Lincolnshire Archit. Archaeol. Soc. Rep.* 9,
13–15.

Poulton, R. and Scott, E. 1993. 'The Hoarding, Deposition and Use of Pewter in Roman
Britain' *Theoretical Roman Archaeology: First Conference Proceedings* Aldershot, 115–32.

Read, C.H. 1898. 'List of pewter dishes and vessels found at Appleshaw and now in the
British Museum' *Archaeologia* 56, 7–12.

Richmond, I.A. 1945. 'A Roman vat of lead from Ireby, Cumberland' *Trans Cumberland
Westmorland Arch. Assoc.* 45, 163–71.

Ross, A. 1968. 'Shafts, pits, wells – sanctuaries of the Belgic Britons?' in J.M. Coles and
D.D.A. Simpson (eds) *Studies in Ancient Europe: Essays Presented to Stuart Piggot* London.

Salmon, N. 1730. *A New Survey of England* London.

Thomas, C. 1981. *Christianity in Roman Britain to AD 500* London.

VCH Cambs. Victoria County History Cambridgeshire.

Watts, D.J. 1988. 'Circular lead tanks and their significance for Romano-British
Christianity' *Antiq. J.* 68, 210–22.

—— 1991. *Christianity and Pagans in Roman Britain* London.

—— 1998. *Religion and Roman Britain: Forces of Change* London.

West, S. 1976. 'The Romano-British site at Icklingham' *East Anglian Archaeol.* 3, 63–126.

Wilkes, J.J and Elrington, C.R. 1978. *Victoria County History: Cambridgeshire*, Vol. 7: *Roman
Cambridgeshire* London.

8

Basilicas and Barrows: Christian Origins in Wales and Western Britain

JEREMY KNIGHT

In his autobiography, Edward Gibbon described how the idea first came to him of writing *The Decline and Fall of the Roman Empire*:

> It was in Rome, on the 15th of October 1764, as I sat musing amid the ruins of the Capitol whilst the barefoot Friars were singing Vespers in the Temple of Jupiter that the idea of writing the decline and fall of the city first started to my mind'.[1]

By the 'Temple of Jupiter', Gibbon meant the church of Santa Maria in Aracoeli on the Capitoline, which antiquaries of the time thought stood directly on the site of the temple of Jupiter Capitolinus, seat of the Roman state religion. The image of the authority of the Christian Church replacing that of the Roman Empire is a striking and memorable one but, had he known it, Gibbon, instead of going to Rome, could have come to the scene of our conference at York, or to its sister legionary fortress at Caerleon in south Wales, the Roman *Isca*, for both York Minster and the church of St Cadoc at Caerleon overlie the Principia of their Roman Fortress, where the legionary standards were displayed, and the images of the Roman Emperors venerated.

Christianity in Late Roman Wales

It is of course something of an anachronism to speak of 'Roman Wales', for that can only be shorthand for something like 'the mountainous western parts of the province of Britannia Prima'. Yet it was in the immediate post-Roman period that a geographical entity which was to become recognizably Welsh was to develop. It was Christian and literate, first in Latin and in time in Welsh. We can now see that the beginnings of that process were already in place in late Roman times, at least in the two urban centres (in the very broadest sense) of Caerleon (*Isca*) and Caerwent (*Venta Silurum*) in the lowland area of south-east Wales.

---

[1] E. Gibbon. *Memoirs of my Life* ed. G.A. Bonnard (London 1966), 136. There are several manuscript versions of the passage by Gibbon. The one quoted above (Everyman's Library, London 1911, 124) is given by Bonnard as a variant.

Isca, the fortress of Legio II Augusta, stands at the highest convieniently navigable point on the River Usk.[2] From the Roman bridge, whose timber successors remained on the same site until 1806, a road ran eastwards to Caerwent and ultimately to Gloucester below a steep wooded ridge which was the site of one of the major cemeteries of the fortress. After about half a mile, the road divided, one branch climbing the ridge diagonally en-route to Caerwent, the other continuing up the valley bottom. After a further half mile, the latter reached a small Roman civilian or veteran settlement at Bulmore. It was on the ridge above Bulmore that the Martyrium of the Christian martyrs Julius and Aaron stood, sited on the edge of the extra-mural cemetery in the classic location for such martyria throughout the Roman Empire.

The *Territorium Sanctorum Martyrium Julii et Aaron* or *Merthir* (Martyrium) *Jun et Aaron* is attested in charter evidence from the late ninth century onwards, though the primary source for the martyrs is Gildas, writing in the early to mid-sixth century, probably across the Bristol Channel in south-west England.[3] Historians have often been cautious in accepting the reliability of the evidence for Julius and Aaron due to the complications of the documentary evidence. There is firstly the problem of the source of Gildas' information, for *Isca* was largely abandoned under Carausius or Allectus (287–86) and the fortress had been an empty shell for 250 years when Gildas wrote. There is also the possibility, bearing in mind Gildas' reputation for muddling information from documentary sources (as with his notorious misdating of Hadrian's Wall), that he could have mistaken an entry in a martyrology or a liturgical calendar,[4] whilst the Llandaff charters were often regarded, until Wendy Davies' fresh study of them, as twelfth-century forgeries.[5] Most seriously, Geoffrey of Monmouth muddied the historical waters and threw the topographical evidence into confusion by inventing two non-existent abbeys, including a cathedral and a university of Caerleon on Usk, as part of his Arthurian Hollywood epic. To add to the confusion, a relic of St Alban, introduced to the martyrium shortly before 1143, in circumstances which Levison explained, transformed it into the church of Julius, Aaron and Alban and ultimately into the church of St Alban, the other two cults having migrated to other local sites under the influence of Geoffrey of Monmouth.[6]

[2] The best account remains George Boon's *Isca: The Roman Legionary Fortress at Caerleon* (3rd revised edn Cardiff 1972).

[3] *The Text of the Book of Llandav* ed. J.G. Evans and J. Rhys (Oxford 1893), 225. W. Davies *The Llandaff Charters* (Aberystwyth 1979), 121. Gildas *De Excidio* c.10. W. Levison 'St Alban and St Albans' *Antiquity* 16 (1941), 337–59.

[4] E.g. possible confusion with a martyr of Leon (Spain) or the Moesian martyr Julius Veterani (misread as Julii et Aaroni). The writer has searched available sources without success for an entry which might have led to such confusion.

[5] Wendy Davies *An early Welsh microcosm: Studies in the Llandaff Charters* (London, Royal Historical Society, 1978) and *The Llandaff Charters* (Aberystwyth 1979).

[6] Levison *op. cit.*

I have tried to unravel some of this muddle elsewhere,[7] but here my main concern is the archaeological and topographical evidence. Nineteenth-century finds from 'Bulmore', i.e. the valley bottom site of Lower Bulmore and the hillside farm of Upper Bulmore adjacent to the martyrium, include a glass bead with sixth-century Anglo-Saxon parallels[8] and a ninth-century sculptured cross-slab re-used as paving in one of the Bulmore farms. The latter is one of a small group of 'Gwent Group' cross-slabs, all from major church sites with charter or documentary evidence and/or finds of early metalwork and coins suggesting high status.[9] Within the immediate area, the only possible candidate for such a church is the martyrium of Julius and Aaron. The chapel was probably suppressed under Edward VI, and by the early eighteenth century was an archaeological site marked by two fields called Cae'r Fynwent 'the field of the graveyard' and Cae'r Scubor 'the field of the barn'. Like many lesser Gwent churches at this time, the martyrium chapel had become a barn.

The martyrium lay on the Roman road from Caerleon to Caerwent, 9 miles away to the east. Though *Isca* had long been abandoned as a legionary fortress by the time of Gildas, the survival of the Roman name of Caerwent *Venta Silurum* both in that of the present village and that of the sub-Roman successor state of Gwent suggests some measure of political continuity, and there is now archaeological evidence to support continued occupation of Caerwent, and burial in its cemeteries, in post-Roman times. It is possible that information about the cult of Julius and Aaron could have been transmitted from Caerwent across the Bristol Channel to Gildas in south-west England, whose coast is clearly visible from the ridge on which the martyrium stood. Indeed in the twelfth century, Gildas' relics – his bell and Gospel book – were preserved on Steepholm Island in the Bristol Channel, midway between the two.[10]

The most relevant Caerwent find for our immediate purpose is the late fourth-century table service of pottery and pewter ware, hidden in a large jar sealed with an inverted mortarium, and carefully buried in a pit, found in 1907 in House IX, 7N. One pewter bowl has a scratched Christian *chi-rho* monogram on its base. The associated pottery comprises local grey wares, late Oxfordshire colour-coated

---

7   J.K. Knight 'Britain's other martyrs: Julius, Aaron and Alban at Caerleon' in M. Henig and P. Lindley (eds) *Alban and St Albans: Roman and Medieval Art and Archaeology* (Trans. Brit. Arch. Ass. xxiv), 2001, 38–44.

8   M. Guido *The Glass Beads of Anglo-Saxon England c.A.D. 400–700* ed. M Welch (Woodbridge 1999), 27, 188 (type 2 xi ' Caerleon'). For the Bulmore provenance see J.E. Lee *Isca Silurum: An Illustrated Catalogue of the Museum of Antiquities at Caerleon* (London 1862), 54.

9   V.E. Nash-Williams *The Early Christian Monuments of Wales* (Cardiff 1950), no. 290. Others of the group are from St Cadoc's church Caerleon (E.C.M.W. no. 291.); St Arvans (E.C.M.W. no. 292) and St Tatheus's church, Caerwent: M. Redknap 'A pre-Norman cross from Caerwent and its context' *Monmouthshire Antiquary* X (1994), 1–6.

10 A.W. Wade-Evans *Vitae Sanctorum Britanniae et Genealogiae* (Cardiff 1944), *Vita Cadoci* c. 40 (110–13) and c. 56 (126–7). See also *Vita Cadoci* cc. 27 and 34 (Wade Evans, 85–7, 96–7). J.K. Knight 'Late Roman and post-Roman Caerwent: some evidence from metalwork' *Archeologia Cambrensis* 145 (1996), 35–66.

bowls and a jar of East Midlands shell tempered ware, the latter indicating a date not before 360 or 370.[11] George Boon and myself have both suggested that the deposit could have been connected with the Christian *agape* ceremony, a sort of church supper held in the house of a wealthy believer. This implies the existence of an organized Christian community at Caerwent in the final quarter of the fourth century, presumably headed by a bishop. This, and the recent recognition of a possible fourth-century Christian church at Wroxeter on the central borders of Wales, have fundamental implications for Welsh Christian origins. Indeed, it might not be going too far to think in terms of possible late Roman sees of the Silures and Cornovii, or in later terms of Gwent/Glamorgan and Powys, though how many Christians there were outside the two cantonal capitals is quite another matter.

Caerwent has also produced two sub-Roman cemeteries of the kind that Philip Rahtz has made familiar to us in Somerset. One of these is extra-mural outside the East Gate, originally containing several hundred burials, the other intra-mural around the later church. Both have produced radio-carbon determinations spanning the sixth and seventh centuries.[12] There is also a good range of late Roman and early medieval metalwork covering the period from the late fourth to the eleventh centuries. There was still a community of canons there in the twelfth century, sufficiently wealthy to commission a written life of their patron St Tatheus, then said to have been an Irish *peregrinus*.[13]

From Town to Country: Christian Origins in Rural Wales

More problematic are the mechanisms by which the new faith spread from centres like Caerleon, Caerwent and Wroxeter into rural areas. Professor Emrys Bowen produced, many years ago now, a very influential model of the 'Welsh saints' travelling along the Roman roads founding pioneer churches in rural areas[14] (and showing such geographical acumen in doing so that someone suggested that they must all have had degrees in geography from Aberystwyth). Though it is now realised that the church dedications on which Bowen relied for his evidence are mostly much later than the presumed period of the 'Welsh saints',

---

[11] G.C. Boon 'A Christian monogram at Caerwent' *Bull. Board Celtic Studs.* 19 (1960–62), 338–44 and 'The early Church in Gwent. 1: The Romano British Church' *Monmouthshire Antiquary* 8 (1992), 11–24.

[12] Eastgate cemetery: E. Campbell and P. Macdonald 'Excavations at Caerwent Vicarage Orchard 1973: an extra mural post-Roman cemetery' *Archaeologia Cambrensis* 142 (1993), 74–98. Intra mural cemetery: M. Farley 'A six hundred metre long section through Caerwent' *Bull. Board Celtic Studs* 31 (1984), 209–50.

[13] J.K. Knight 'Late Roman and post-Roman Caerwent: some evidence from metalwork' *Archaeologia Cambrensis* 145 (1996), 35–66. *Idem* 'St Tatheus, an analysis of the Vespasian life' *Monmouthshire Antiquary* 3, part 1 (1970–71), 29–36.

[14] E. Bowen *The Settlements of the Celtic Saints in Wales* (Cardiff 1954). See also his earlier articles in *Antiquity* 18 (1944), 16–28 and 19 (1945), 175–86.

the Bowen model is still very useful as a conceptual starting point. The primary archaeological evidence, however, comprises the 140 latin or ogam inscribed memorial stones from Wales, and the sites from which they come. The only other potentially useful sources are two villa sites in the south-eastern coastal plain of Glamorgan which show a sequence from Roman villa to early medieval cemetery to medieval church.

This sequence, relatively commonplace in some areas of continental Europe, is less common in Britain than is sometimes thought. I hope to consider the British evidence more fully elsewhere.[15] Here, we need only note the Glamorganshire examples at Llantwit Major and Llandough. The forthcoming publication of the Llandough cemetery, on the site of the monastery of St Oudoceus, will include a range of radiocarbon dates, still lacking from the equivalent cemetery at the Roman villa at Llanilltud Fawr (Llantwit Major).[16] The monastery at Llandough is attested in charter and other documentary sources from the seventh century onwards, and a late tenth or eleventh-century sculptured cross stands in the adjacent churchyard. At Llantwit, the villa, with its post-Roman cemetery, is some 1.5 kilometres from the church of St Illtyd, which has a range of sculptured crosses from the ninth century onwards, some mentioning abbots of the monastery and kings of Glamorgan.[17] The significance of the juxtaposition of villa and church is emphasised by evidence that the huge medieval parish of Llantwit was a royal estate or *Villa regalis* of the pre-Norman kings of Glamorgan, with its secular centre at Llysworney, the llys or court of the cantref of Gorfynydd, and its religious centre at Llantwit Major.[18] A possible Roman villa has also now been identified close to Bassaleg, a major early church discussed below, but at present archaeological evidence for any intermediate early cemetery is lacking.[19] The circumstantial evidence from these sites may at least indicate the possible role of villas and villa estates as intermediaries between urban and rural Christianity, a role better attested in parts of Gaul.[20]

The main archaeological evidence for this process, however, are the Latin inscribed memorial stones. These use the formulae *Hic Iacet*, in the late Roman vulgar Latin spelling *Iacit*; *Filius*; or a compound form, e.g. *Catacus Hic Iacit Filius Tegernacus* 'Catacus lies here, son of Tegernacus'. These are sometimes accompanied by parallel Irish ogam inscriptions, though these are not our direct concern here. To put the Latin inscriptions into a wider perspective, it is neces- sary to look briefly at their French counterparts. Unlike Britain, France has late

---

[15] In discussion section of Neil Holbrook, excavations at Llandough (forthcoming).
[16] V.E. Nash-Williams 'The Roman villa at Llantwit Major' *Archaeologia Cambrensis* 102 (1953), 89–163; A.H.A. Hogg 'The Llantwit Major villa: a reconsideration' *Britannia* 5 (1974), 225–50.
[17] V.E. Nash-Williams *The Early Christian Monuments of Wales* (Cardiff 1950), nos 220–6.
[18] M. Richards 'Gwrinydd, Gorfynydd and Llyswyrny' *Bull. Board Celtic Studs* 18 (1960), 383–8.
[19] I am indebted to Christopher Musson for information about the possible Bassaleg villa.
[20] J.K. Knight *The End of Antiquity: Archaeology, Society and Religion in Western Europe, A.D. 235–700* (1999), 126–7.

Roman Christian tombstones, some with fourth-century consular dates. These are followed in the early fifth century by stones using the same *Hic Iacet* formula as the insular series, a few, from Lyon, with consular dates in the range 425–50. From about 450 they are replaced by inscriptions using a longer initial formula *Hic Requiescit In Pace*.[21]

The church of Llanerfyl in western Montgomeryshire is a late medieval building. Until it was moved within the church in the nineteenth century, there stood in its churchyard what can either be regarded as the last inscription of Roman Britain or the first early medieval inscription of Wales. It is the memorial of a 13-year-old girl named Rosteece:

> HIC IN
> TVMVLO IA
> CIT. ROSTE
> ECE. FILIA. PA
> TERNINI.
> ANI XIII. IN
> PA (CE)

'Here in the tomb lies Rosteece, daughter of Paterninus, aged 13. In Peace'

The inscription retains many features normal in Gallic memorial stones, but which quickly drop out of use in the insular series. It is a horizontal inscription, not vertical like most of the insular series, and includes punctuation, the age at death and a final *In Pace*. The initial formula is a variant on the *Hic Requiescit in Pace* type and, if Gallic parallels are any guide, it should date to around 450–480.[22]

Llanerfyl was in the tribal territory of the Cornovii, whose capital was at Wroxeter. Wroxeter has produced a fifth-century memorial stone, and now possibly a late Roman church.[23] Llanerfyl is 50 kilometres (22 miles) due west, at a point where the Roman road from the auxiliary fort of Caersws crosses the river Banwy. A late medieval wooden shrine and reliquary within the church show the continuing cult of its patron, a female saint called Erfyl.[24]

Though the area around Caerleon and Caerwent lies outside the distributional range of early medieval memorial stones, the church at Bassaleg west of Caerleon shows many similarities with Llanerfyl. It is the only British example of the place name element *Basilica*, used both in Merovingian Gaul (for example by Gregory of Tours) and in early Ireland for major churches possessing important relics.[25] Its patron was the obscure female saint Gwladys, whose bones lay in a detached grave chapel or *Eglwys Y Bedd*, demolished in the nineteenth century.[26] The major

---

[21] For a more detailed discussion of the Gallic Christian series see *End of Antiquity* 104–11.

[22] *Early Christian Monuments of Wales* no. 294.

[23] R.P. Wright and K. Jackson 'A late inscription from Wroxeter' *Antiq. J.* 48 (1968), 269–300.

[24] *Archaeologia Cambrensis* 70, 1915, 438–40; 87, 1932, 350–8.

[25] C. Doherty 'The basilica in early Ireland' *Peritia* 3 (1984), 303–15.

[26] There is a good mid-nineteenth century drawing of the Eglwys Y Bedd at Bassaleg in the library of the Society of Antiquaries of London: *Gwentia: Ecclesiastical Antiquities* Vol 1, f.10.

early minster of St Gwynllwy, now Newport cathedral, is 2 miles away, but in medieval times it was Bassaleg, not St Gwynllwy's that was the mother church of the cantref of Gwynlliog and of the churches in its uplands. Llanerfyl and Bassaleg may provide a faint clue towards the recognition of possible primary centres of Christian pastoral care in the Welsh countryside, rather like the rural churches in the vici of Touraine which Gregory of Tours records being built by the bishops of Tours.[27]

The archaeological contexts of Welsh memorial stones vary a great deal. Often, they are no more than 'built into a barn' or 're-used as the lintel of a beast house'. Many stand in churchyards, or are built into the church fabric. In some cases, these churches are the Welsh equivalent of an English hundredal minster, a portionary church with a community of canons or secular priests, and a territory much wider than a later parish, equivalent in some cases to a cantref (equivalent to an English hundred) or its subdivision, a *Commote*. Twelfth-century sources refer to something called 'The Seven Cantrefi of Glywysing' (Glamorgan), an early kingdom whose subdivisions are named after the sons of an early eponymous king, Glywys.[28] His name could simply be a back formation from that of the kingdom, but three of the cantrefs, Cydweli, Gwyr and Margan, have major churches with early Latin memorial stones at Llansaint, Llanmadoc and Merthyr Mawr (more properly Merthyr Mymor – the martyrium of Mymor) and an Anglo-Norman document records how a series of parishes were carved out of the *territorium* of Merthyr Mawr, occupying the eastern half of Margan cantref, in the early twelfth century.[29] The western half of Margan probably had its ecclesiastical centre near the later Cistercian Abbey of Margam, which has a cluster of early memorial stones in its vicinity.

Such stones present no real problem, for they are Christian tombstones in Christian churchyards. However, they show that by the sixth or early seventh century, a series of churches with dependant territories was in place, at least in lowland areas (though the cemetery, and perhaps the memorial stone, might have preceded any church). Others however, particularly in upland areas, stand on high moorland, beside a Roman road or a track-way where there has clearly never been a church. Some six even stand on or alongside Bronze age barrows.[30]

Four of these are from upland Glamorgan, but the most significant example is at Clocaenog in Denbighshire, which shows that these were not cases of 'pagan survival' or 'continuity'. Three small farms, Maes Tyddin Uchaf, Isaf and Canol (Upper, Lower and Middle) occupy a sheltered and well watered valley. At its

[27] Gregory of Tours *Historia Francorum* X, 31.
[28] For the seven cantrefs see J.K. Knight in P.F. Wilkinson 'Excavations at Hen Gastell, Briton Ferry, West Glamorgan' *Medieval Archaeology* 29 (1995), 36–50.
[29] F.G. Cowley *Glamorgan County History Vol 3: Medieval Glamorgan* (Cardiff 1971) ed. T.B. Pugh, 116–7.
[30] For a map of early medieval inscriptions from north Welsh churches and from upland sites without churches, see Knight *The End of Antiquity* Fig. 46, 138.

head, a track leads up to a ridge called Bryn Y Beddau ('Hill of the Graves'), where two natural mounds were evidently taken for prehistoric barrows in early medieval times. Edward Lhywd saw here in 1693 'two stones at the head of a grave, four foot asunder'. One, inscribed *Similinus Tovisacus* 'Similinus the Prince' is now in the National Museum of Wales. The other, uninscribed, lies on site. The two natural mounds were evidently taken for ancient monuments, seen as in some way validating the ownership and occupation of the land by Similinus as successor in title. A similar process is known in Dark Age Greece, where Mycenean *tholos* tombs were identified as the graves of heroes like Achilles, or the Seven Against Thebes, and became centres of religious cult, and of burial.[31]

These upland open-country memorial stones can also be explained in terms of the processes of conversion. The Church was reliant on the aristocracy for the resources necessary to establish a framework of rural pastoral care. Both resources and clerical manpower may have been in short supply for a long time after the initial conversion. Even in eighth-century England, Bede complained that many upland communities rarely saw a bishop, and describes a Northumbrian landowner building an estate church on his property.[32] In the later Middle Ages, the huge upland parishes of western Britain and of Wales created problems, and petitions describe the difficulties of parishoners in reaching upland churches for burials and other sacraments, particularly in winter.[33] Two sculptured cross slabs of eighth or ninth-century date from moorland sites in Llangyfelach (Glamorgan) show Christ in the orante position of the Mass, in one case robed in Mass vestments.[34] These could mark secondary centres of pastoral work within this very large upland parish, centres where priest and people might meet together.

---

[31] W Camden *Britannia* ed. Gough (1789), 111, and 'Letter of Edward Llwyd' *Archaeologia Cambrensis* 3 (1848), 310. A.M. Snodgrass *The Dark Ages of Greece: an archaeological survey from the eleventh to the eighth century* (Edinburgh, 1971), 192–5. R. van de Noort 'The context of early medieval barrows in western Europe' *Antiquity* 67 (1993), 66–73.

[32] Bede *Historia Ecclesiastica Gentis Anglorum* V, 2.

[33] For a typical example see the petition of the inhabitants of Bedwellty in Gwent in 1441. It was a daughter church of Mynyddislwyn, but owing to the great distance between the two places, the breaking of bridges and other hinderances, especially in winter, they could not go there, nor could the chaplain of Mynyddislwyn come to them. The bishop of Llandaff agreed that they could have their own priest. (E.T. Davies *An Ecclesiastical History of Monmouthshire Part 1* (Risca 1953), 111, quoting *Calendar of Papal Registers (Letters)*, IX, 203–4.

[34] V.E. Nash-Williams *Early Christian Monuments of Wales* nos. 256, 268. Both stones are now in Swansea Museum.

9

A Landscape Converted: Archaeology and Early Church Organisation on Iveragh and Dingle, Ireland

TOMÁS Ó CARRAGÁIN

Introduction

The process of conversion in Ireland was initiated in the late fourth or fifth century but probably continued until the eighth (cf. O'Brien 1993, 133-6), and the story of the maturation of the Irish Church in this period is one in which the alternative of paganism recedes gradually. The present study concentrates on the period of ecclesiastical consolidation rather than the initial stages of the Church's establishment, essentially because the archaeological data from the later period are currently more intelligible.[1] A model is proposed for the development of the Church and its reshaping of the cultural landscape at the western ends of the Iveragh and Dingle peninsulas, Co. Kerry (Fig. 9.1).

Iveragh and Dingle are poorly served by the early documentary sources but are rich in above-ground archaeological remains. Their eastern and middle sections are dominated by the highest mountains in Ireland – the Slieve Mish and Mt. Brandon Massifs on Dingle and the Macgillycuddy's Reeks on Iveragh (Fig. 9.1) – and there is a strong case for treating the relatively low-lying areas to the west of these as a distinct region, somewhat removed from the eastern sections but united culturally as well as politically[2] by close maritime contacts. The distribution of corbelled, dry-stone churches serves to illustrate the point. This distinctive church type is ubiquitous at the western ends of Iveragh and Dingle, but in contrast definite examples occur at just one site east of the mountains (at Illauntannig on Dingle), and only a handful occur elsewhere in Ireland (Ó Carragáin forthcoming). Broadly speaking the ecclesiastical archaeology of

---

[1] Full publication of excavations at the ecclesiastical site at Caherlehillan on Iveragh will be a significant step forward in addressing the fifth/sixth-century period. The site has produced significant assemblages of B and E ware in contexts which sealed even earlier occupation (Doyle 1996, 106–7; Sheehan 2001).

[2] Large portions of both peninsulas were part of the *Corca Dhuibhne* territory.

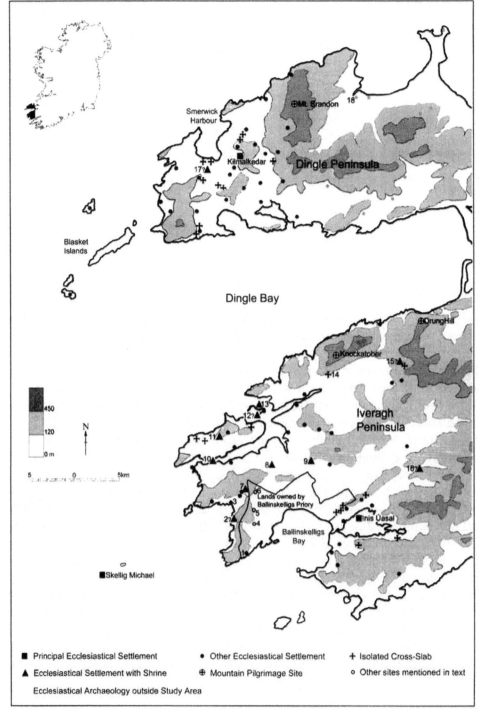

Figure 9.1 The early ecclesiastical archaeology of western Iveragh and Dingle, Co. Kerry:
1 Kildreelig; 2 Killonacaha; 3 Killemlagh; 4 Kinard West; 5 Killurly; 6 Cools; 7 Killabuonia;
8 Killoluaig; 9 Aghatubrid; 10 Illaunloughan; 11 Cool East; 12 Beginish; 13 Church Island;
14 Ballydarrig; 15 Caherlehillan; 16 Cappanagroun; 17 Reask; 18 Drom West

the western sections is well-defined: of the 66 substantial sites the majority are delimited by a bank averaging 37 metres across, within which are a number of domestic buildings, and a cross-slab, burial ground and dry-stone church at the east end. This general coherence lends validity to the present study, which seeks to identify and analyse significant variations within this data set.

Our chronology for these sites is still quite rudimentary. Reask and Caherlehillan have produced late fifth- to sixth-century Mediterranean pottery, which seems to relate to phases characterised mainly by wooden buildings (Fanning 1981, 154–5; Sheehan 2001). There has been considerable uncertainty as to the predominant date-range of the stone structures which replaced these, and until recently an unlikely scenario prevailed in which stone shrines dating to 'as early as c.600' (Thomas 1971, 144) stood next to dry-stone churches dating 'as late as the twelfth [century]' (Harbison 1970, 57). The excavation of Illaunloughan (White Marshall and Walsh 1998) has had an important moderating effect on this dating; it confirms what was already hinted at by recurring association and to some extent art-history: that a significant proportion of these remains are from roughly the same cultural horizon, one which on current evidence centres on the eighth and ninth centuries.

Models of Organisation

In 1957 Françoise Henry published a survey which introduced modern scholars to the richness of the area and this, combined with O'Kelly's (1958) landmark excavation of Church Island, made Iveragh/Dingle something of a battleground for the opposing models of organisation proposed for the early Irish Church. Henry herself presumed that these sites were eremitic monasteries, though she did remark that such a concentration of eremitic sites 'makes a strange picture' (1957, 157). Charles Thomas (1971, 80; 1986, 124) was the first to seriously challenge this orthodoxy, arguing convincingly that by the eighth century many of these sites were 'subservient to popular needs'. He also used a number of examples from Iveragh/Dingle to support his argument that many ecclesiastical sites developed from pre-existing lay cemeteries, with a church and domestic buildings being added later (1971, 69, 82).[3] But excavations suggest that, in this region at least, ecclesiastical sites were, from the outset, primarily *settlements* rather than *cemeteries*, with quite modest areas being set aside for burial (O'Kelly

---

[3] Thomas (1971, 82) interpreted the internal division of the enclosure at Loher as one which divided a clerics' burial area at the east from a larger lay cemetery, but by comparison with Reask, burial was probably confined to the former area, with most of the enclosure being used for domestic and craft activities. He also tentatively suggested (1971, 69) that Church Island in northern Iveragh was originally a lay cemetery to which a hut, oratory and special grave were added in the seventh century. However it seems unlikely that any of the burials at the site pre-date the wooden oratory (O'Kelly 1958, 61) and indeed in a later article Thomas (1995, 68) proposed that the site began as an eremitical establishment, with the cemetery constituting a secondary development.

1959, 61; Fanning 1981, 79–84; White Marshall and Walsh 1998, 106; Sheehan 2001). More recently Richard Sharpe (1992, 90–91) used the ubiquity of sites on Dingle to support his argument that a proto-parochial system was in operation in Ireland from the eighth century. In fact the density of sites is such that only a minority are likely to have been primarily concerned with the provision of pastoral care.[4] Many were probably proprietary churches, i.e. privately owned and transmitted from one generation of non-celibate clergy to the next. Ó Corráin (1981, 339) suggested that Church Island on Iveragh was a proprietary church, and Mytum (1992, 63) has convincingly reinterpreted Reask on Dingle along similar lines.[5]

Notwithstanding this long tradition of fruitful research, only one study has looked in depth at the interrelationships between the sites (Harbison 1991, 71–90), and none has set out to define the ecclesiastical hierarchy of the area. The present attempt to do so is feasible, first because of the excellent surveys now published for the area (Cuppage 1986; O'Sullivan and Sheehan 1996), and second because of recent developments in historical research. Many historians now argue that the fifth/sixth century church resulted from disorganised growth *in situ*, rather than an episcopally organised mission (Sharpe 1984, 241–2), a proposition which is supported by the ambivalent nature of the archaeological evidence for this period. The church from the mid-seventh to early eleventh century is now seen as characterised by organisational continuity and perhaps a degree of regional diversity, and the idea (e.g. Hughes 1966) that it comprised numerous widely dispersed and overlapping monastic federations, or *paruchiae* has been undermined. Etchingham (e.g. 1993, 152), Mac Samhráin (1996) and others have realised that in fact it was organised along territorial lines, much as it was elsewhere in Europe, with principal churches controlling considerable territories in their immediate vicinity, and being affiliated mainly with churches in the same secular kingdom as themselves. This new model of spatial organisation, with its emphasis on relatively small, well defined territories has obvious attractions for the archaeologist.

---

[4] For criticisms of Sharpe's ideas on pastoral care see Etchingham (1991, 106) and Ó Cróinín (1996, 167). From an archaeological perspective the fact that in some areas, most notably western Iveragh, church sites are as numerous as secular sites is against the idea that the former were primarily founded to serve the pastoral needs of the latter. Also, at an average of under 12 m² internally, most of the dry-stone churches of the area were clearly not congregational. While this by no means precludes the possibility that these sites had pastoral functions (see Ryan 1931, 288; Henry 1940, 25–7; O'Kelly 1975, 21; Sharpe 1995, 219), it does bring the usefulness of the term proto-parochial into question. Finally, in contrast to areas such as North Clare (Ní Ghabhláin 1995, 134), the church in Iveragh/Dingle seems to lack the degree of early to late medieval continuity implied by Sharpe's (1992, 86) model. For example, on current evidence, it appears that as many as nine of the eleven medieval parish churches on Iveragh were founded on virgin sites.

[5] Poor osteological preservation at Reask and Caherlehillan make it impossible to establish the sex ratio for these sites (Fanning 1981, 81; Sheehan 2001). The bones from Church Island were not studied systematically, though at least one of the early burials was female (O'Kelly 1958, 61). Work on the Illaunloughan material is ongoing, but preliminary publication suggests the cemetery was predominantly male and therefore, one might argue, monastic (see White Marshall and Walsh 1998, 106).

The archaeological evidence strongly suggests that there were three principal churches in the study area, and it is no coincidence that these are also the only three mentioned in early documentary sources. They are Kilmalkedar on Dingle, and *Inis Úasal* and Skellig Michael on Iveragh.

Kilmalkedar

The archaeological remains at Kilmalkedar are the most impressive in Iveragh/ Dingle, but will be discussed only briefly here. They extend over 10 acres and include a stone-roofed Romanesque church (the only one on Dingle), two earlier dry-stone churches, one of which is dedicated to St Brendan, and several early carvings including an ogham stone, sun-dial and a pillar inscribed with the alphabet (Cuppage 1986, 308–23). There is also a notable clustering of ecclesiastical archaeology in the vicinity of the site with Kilmalkedar parish boasting about three times the average instance of early church archaeology for parishes on Dingle (Fig. 9.2).

Kilmalkedar's influence almost certainly extended well beyond the present boundaries of its parish, with many of the other church sites west of Mt Brandon also being affiliated to it. In the later medieval period Kilmalkedar was the prebend of the chancellor of the Diocese of Ardfert, a sure sign it was a church of regional importance.[6] Its name derives from a local saint, *Maolchéadar*, but it also became the main centre on Dingle for the cult of Brendan the Navigator. The principal expression of this cult was a pilgrimage from Kilmalkedar to St Brendan's Oratory on the summit of Mt Brandon, one of the three great pilgrimage mountains of Ireland (Harbison 1991, 71). This practice may represent a Christianisation of the pagan festival of *Lughnasa* (MacNeill 1962, 102), and was probably already associated with Brendan when his connection to the mountain is alluded to in the *Navigatio Brendani*, which dates to *c*.AD 800 (*ibid*. 80; Wooding 2001). The pilgrim-path, known as *Casán na Naomh* ('The Saints' Road'), still stretches across the west end of the peninsula (ibid. 71–86) and the close association between Kilmalkedar and the Mt Brandon pilgrimage is further emphasised by the fact that a narrow extension of Kilmalkedar parish follows the line of *Casán na Naomh* westwards for over a kilometre, thereby dividing the parish of Marhin into two parts (see Fig. 9.2).[7] The relative importance of Kilmalkedar is also indicated by the nature of the other church sites west of Mt Brandon; archaeology and history indicate that none was of more than local significance.

---

[6] On the tendency of major early sites to become prebends in the later medieval period see for example Blair (1985, 125–6) and Morris (1989, 138).

[7] This association is also strengthened by the archaeological evidence: at the point where the Casán na Naomh reaches the edge of the Kilmalkedar complex there is a north-south oriented platform over 12 m × 5 m in area and approximately 0.8 m high. It is known locally as *An Altóir* ('the Altar'), but may more accurately be described as a *predella* surmounted by an altar, for located centrally on its upper surface are the footings of a modest north-south oriented rectangular structure on which is a small stone cross. This upper structure is now virtually destroyed, but a recent description of

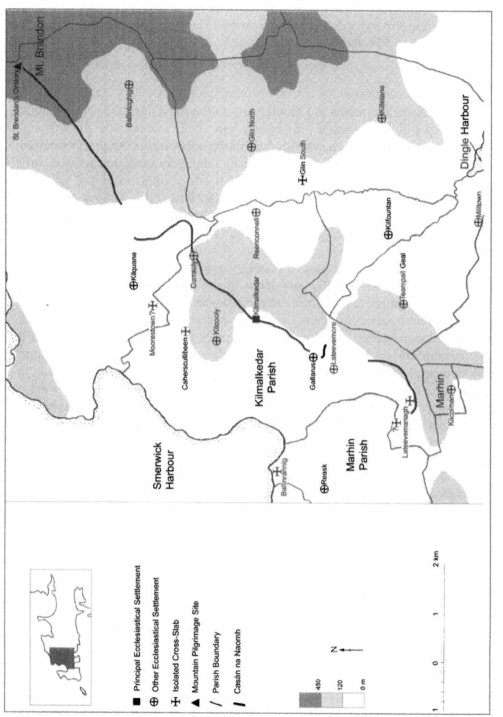

Figure 9.2 Early ecclesiastical archaeology in the vicinity of Kilmalkedar, Dingle

Mountain Pilgrimages on Iveragh

A somewhat more complex network of ecclesiastical territories and affiliations appears to have developed at the western end of Iveragh. The area features not one but two mountain pilgrimages – Drung Hill and Knockatober – but neither was of major regional significance. Both are situated near the north coast, far from the two principal church sites on the peninsula (Fig 9.1). Drung Hill is dedicated to St *Fínán*, patron of *Inis Úasal*, but the two sites do not seem to have been closely associated in the manner of Kilmalkedar and Mt Brandon. Knockatober is dedicated to St Fursey (traditionally a pupil of St. Brendan), and in Ballydarrig townland near a now disused route to its summit is a massive, flat-topped, cross-inscribed boulder, which is best interpreted as an outdoor altar. The design on its upper surface is simple but meaningful (Fig. 9.3). In particular the line dividing the lower left-hand quadrant of the main cross-head into two segments may be a reference to the Eucharist, for the Stowe Missal specifies that before breaking the host for communion the priest must first break a piece from its lower left-hand quadrant in order to recall the wounding of Christ's side with a lance on Calvary. A more sophisticated sculptural representation of this particularly insular method of fraction has been identified on the cross-slab at Nigg, Easter Ross (É. Ó Carragáin 1988, 8–9; Henderson 2001, 125–6). The Nigg host surmounts a chalice whose cup has been de-emphasised in a manner even more accentuated in other paten/host and chalice representations, such as the fifth-century example at Santa Sabina in Rome (see Stalley 1999, Fig. 2), hinting that the stem and triangular base of the Ballydarrig design may also have been intended to signify a chalice. Finally the four small crosslets surrounding the main cross may have been meant to recall those inscribed at the corners of consecrated altar *mensae* (see Thomas 1971, 170).[8]

it (Cuppage 1986, 321) supports the possibility that it was a dry-stone altar. It may have been designed as an outdoor liturgical focus at which pilgrims could congregate before climbing Mt Brandon (Ó Carragáin 1998, 43–4), for certainly no pre-Romanesque church in the region was large enough to accommodate significant numbers. It might be argued that the nearby dry-stone building known as *Poll Jo* (Cuppage 1986, 321) was used in conjunction with *An Altóir*, perhaps serving as a *secretarium*, the early medieval equivalent of a sacristy (see Sternberg 1991, 54–9).

[8] A parallel for the Ballydarrig boulder occurs in Drom West on the Dingle Peninsula (Fig. 9.1, no 18; Fig. 9.5a). This massive boulder is (like Ballydarrig) not directly associated with a church settlement but it may have had a role in the Mt Brandon pilgrimage, for it is quite near Cloghane church where the eastern pilgrimage route to the mountain's summit began. The rather crude design that occurs on one of its broad sides may represent an altar inscribed with the requisite central crosslet surrounded by four corner crosslets. A larger ringed cross seems to surmount the altar proper and its design is similar to that of the processional cross depicted on the base of the north cross at Ahenny (see Harbison 1992, Fig. 11). It is tempting to see the seven small irregular shapes at the base of this cross and the eleven at the base of the design as representing particles of the host after fraction. While this interpretation is not certain, it is worth noting that in the Stowe Missal it is specified that the host should be broken into a number of symbolically significant groups including one group of seven and one of eleven (see O'Loughlin 2000, 135). A cross-slab at Cloonlaur, Co. Mayo also combines many of the motifs found at Ballydarrig: a Chi Rho which, as Henry (1947, 37) points out, is a symbol of the host, surmounts a chalice and is surrounded by four crosslets.

Figure 9.3 Inscribed area on upper surface of a boulder in Ballydarrig townland, Iveragh

Inis Úasal

Several kilometres to the south on Lough Currane is *Inis Úasal* ('Noble Island') (Pl. 9.1), which is dedicated to St. *Fínán*.[9] (Fig. 9.1, Fig. 9.4). That *Inis Úasal* was a centre for monasticism in its primary sense is suggested by the reference in the *Annals of Inishfallen* to the burial there of Amchad, 'anchorite of God' in 1058.[10]

---

[9] The site is now usually known as Church Island, but should not be confused with the Church Island excavated by O'Kelly some kilometres to the north. *Úasal* is the Irish for 'high' or 'noble' and significantly DIL cites examples of the term being used as an adjectival prefix for the words deacon, priest, bishop and church. Gwynn and Hadcock (1970, 31) identify the founder as St *Fínán Cam* of Kinnitty, Co. Offaly, a saint who was reputedly born in *Corca Dhuibhne*, and was a pupil of St Brendan; and certainly the authors of this saint's Latin and Irish Lives claimed such a connection (Plummer 1910, vol.I, 1xix; vol. II 94–5; Ní Ghrifín 1996, 78). However, on *Inis Úasal* the feast of the patron was celebrated not on 7 April, the feast day of *Fínán Cam*, but on 16 March, the feast of St. *Fínán Lobhar*, who was also 'educated by a senior named Brendan' (O'Hanlon 1875 vil. 3, 384), but later took charge of the Columban monastery of Swords, Co. Dublin. The likelihood is that both *Fínáns* ultimately derive from a single cult (see Ó Riain 1997). A local seventeenth-century poem implies that *Fínán* of *Inis Úasal* was a separate individual altogether (O'Donoghue 1893, 61), and this suggests that the cult of St *Fínán* became thoroughly localised on Iveragh, something which is confirmed by the well-attested tradition that he is buried on *Inis Úasal*.

[10] Sheehan (1990, 173) has identified the grave-slab of this individual on *Inis Úasal*. The inscription on it reads *Bennacht F[or] Anmain Anmchad* 'A Blessing on the Soul of Anmchad' (see Fig. 5c). On the relationship between ceonobitic monasticism and eremitism in Ireland see Etchingham (1999, 335–40).

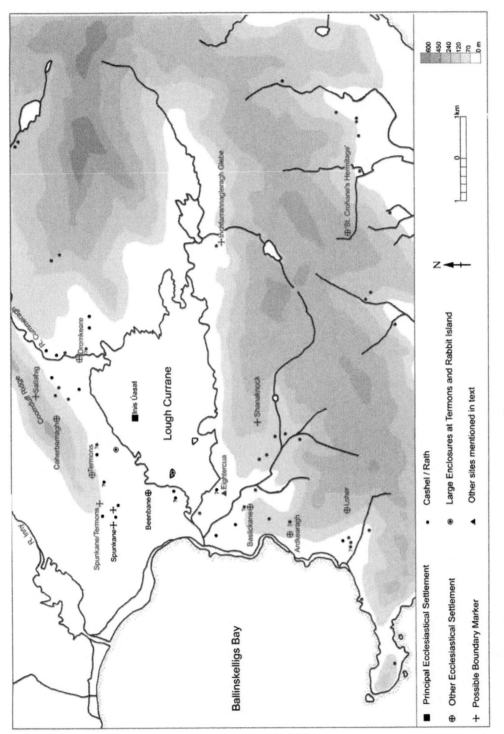

Figure 9.4 Early medieval settlement in the vicinity of *Inis Úasal*, Iveragh

Principal Ecclesiastical Settlement

Other Ecclesiastical Settlement

Possible Boundary Marker

Cashel / Rath

Large Enclosures at Termons and Rabbit Island

Other sites mentioned in text

N

1km

0

Ballinskelligs Bay

Lough Currane

R. Inny

R. Cummeragh

Coastal Ridge

Caherbarnagh

Dromkeare

Saltaing

Spunkane/Termons

Spunkane

Termons

Inis Úasal

Beenbane

Eightercua

Inchfarrannagleragh Glebe

Basickane

Ardkearagh

Loher

Shanaknock

'St. Crohane's Hermitage'

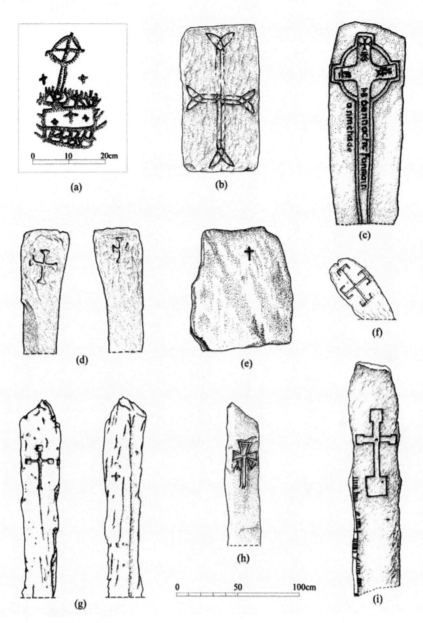

Figure 9.5 Cross-slabs: (a) Inscribed area of boulder at Drom West, Dingle (see footnote 8); (b) and (c) cross-slabs on Inis Úasal; (d) cross-slab on boundary between Termons and Spunkane townlands; (e) cross-inscribed standing stone in Spunkane townland; (f) cross-slab in Shanaknock townland; (g) cross-slab in Inchfarrannagleragh Glebe townland; (h) cross-slab with Alpha and Omega motif at Kildreenagh in Loher townland; (i) cross-inscribed ogham stone at Dromkeare ((a) adapted from Cuppage (1986, Fig. 163); (b)–(i) after O'Sullivan and Sheehan 1996)

Plate 9.1 View of *Inis Úasal*, Iveragh looking south-west in the direction of *Inis Fhearainn na gCléireach*

The early features on the island include a massive dry-stone domestic building connected to the graveyard by a causeway, and a number of ninth- or tenth-century cross-slabs (e.g. Fig. 9.5b; O'Sullivan and Sheehan 1996 Figs. 208a, 208b, 210).[11] More impressive than these are its collection of large eleventh-century cross-slabs (e.g. Fig. 9.5c), and its Romanesque church. Fig. 9.4 illustrates how *Inis Úasal* was capable of sustaining this resource investment. The site is the focal point of a natural amphitheatre defined on most sides by hills and mountains, within which is quite a concentration of modest ecclesiastical sites which are best interpreted as daughter houses or out-farms, sited within its *termon* lands.

The word *termon* was sometimes used to designate the area of sanctuary defined by an ecclesiastical enclosure (about 30 m to 300 m in diameter), but in other instances it designated the lands over which a church claimed direct juris-diction (e.g. Lucas 1967, 206; Kelly 1998, 404; Etchingham 1999, 158). An example of the latter meaning occurs in the Book of Fermoy Life of *Molagga*, a relatively minor Co. Cork saint, in which he is given the 'freedom of his *Termon* from the king and men of Munster, with its boundaries north, south, east and west from *Daire Mochua* to *Inis Gubin* at the River Funcheon on the west, to *Feirnn Leabháin* on the east, and from *Áth na Lee* to *Dairmhagh'* (O'Hanlon 1875 Vol. 1, 351). Not all of these places are now identifiable but it is clear that Molagga's *termon* was a few kilometres across, an area comparable to that proposed here for the *termon* of St Fínán, centred on *Inis Úasal*.

---

[11] Two of the examples cited have Stafford knot terminals, a motif otherwise only encountered once on Iveragh/Dingle sculpture, in debased form on Stone L from Reask (Fanning 1981, 148). Also on the island are the foundations of several rectilinear buildings, some of which are traversed by later field boundaries (O'Sullivan and Sheehan 1996, 321–2).

In the thirteenth century the McCarthy overlords of Iveragh apparently moved their centre of power south from Ballycarbery to Eightercua near the south-west shore of Lough Currane, and remained there until the end of the fourteenth century (Barrington 1976, 265).[12] This may have happened at the expense of *Inis Úasal*, and certainly in the seventeenth century the rectory of *Inis Úasal* was confined to the area adjoining the north-west shore of the lake (Nicholls 1971, 84).[13] By the sixteenth century when it was first surveyed in detail the area had been divided between a number of parties (including a few of the McCarthy septs), but it is likely that the entire catchment area of Lough Currane once constituted a single territory. This is supported by the fact that the three main land-holdings south of the lake – Balline, Baslickane and Eightercua – each controlled a separate portion of the upland territory to the south-east (Keller n.d.). This phenomenon usually results from the need to provide areas of upland for each portion of a sub-divided territory in order to facilitate transhumance (Butler 1925, 58; Blair 1991, 14; Ní Ghabhláin 1995, 258). Archaeological and toponymic evidence suggest that this primary territory constituted the *termon* of *Inis Úasal*.

Inis Úasal itself is located in a townland called Termons, and this also incorporates a band of land to the north of Lough Currane within which is an overgrown early church site (Henry 1957, 133–5). About half a kilometre away on the Coomduff ridge at the boundary of Termons and Spunkane townlands stands a solitary slab inscribed with a cross on both faces, which has been interpreted as a boundary marker (Sheehan 1990, 158; Fig. 9.5d). About 350 m south-west of this in Spunkane townland is a cross-inscribed boulder and 350 m west of this again is a cross-inscribed standing stone (Fig. 9.5e). These stand a few fields from the townland boundaries, but they do extend the line of the Coomduff ridge westwards and it is proposed here that all three served to delimit the *termon* lands.[14] The use of inscribed standing-stones as boundary markers is well attested in the early laws, and just as 'the ogham in the standing stone is like a witness [of ownership]' (translation in Kelly 1998, 409; see also Handley 1998), an inscribed cross may have signalled specifically ecclesiastical ownership.[15]

---

[12] The ruined non-parochial church (O'Sullivan and Sheehan 1996, 354–5) and submerged foundations of a castle (*ibid.* 380) in Eightercua townland probably represent the remains of this settlement.

[13] In the same text *Inis Úasal* is referred to as 'the one prebend left of the ruined church of Aghadoe' (*ibid.*). Aghadoe, situated near Inishfallen and reputedly a foundation of *St. Fínán Cam*, was an archdeaconry of the diocese of Ardfert in the late medieval period.

[14] Furthermore, in Sallahig townland a rock outcrop located at the summit of the only trackway to traverse the Coomduff ridge is incised with several plain crosses (O'Sullivan and Sheehan 1996, 430). Though unlikely to be of early medieval date, these may nonetheless reflect the role of the Coomduff ridge in delimiting the territory south of it.

[15] Another group of boundary crosses occurs at *Mainistir Chiarán*, Aran, Co. Galway (Waddell 1994, 112) but because these delimit an area only 45 m across, they probably fulfilled the role of an ecclesiastical enclosure (see also Herity 1983, 270–77). In contrast the lone boundary cross at Killinaboy, Co. Clare (Rynne 1967, 161), and the two at Penmon in North Wales (Edwards 1999,

One of the more fertile townlands bordering the southern shore of Lough Currane is called *Inis Fhearainn na gCléireach* or 'River-meadow of the land of the clerics' (Ó Cíobháin 1985, 87), strongly suggesting that the *termon* of *Inis Úasal* encompassed this side of the lake also. Near this townland's eastern boundary is another cross-slab inscribed on two faces, standing in a small, unenclosed burial ground (Fig. 9.5g).[16] It is situated some distance south of the only early medieval settlement enclosure at this relatively poor end of the lake and may have signalled the southern limit of cultivated *termon* lands. Another possible boundary marker is the isolated cross-slab in Shanaknock, a townland which also features three placenames incorporating the name *Fínán* (Fig. 9.5f; *ibid.* 150).

At present Lough Currane is bisected by the boundary separating the barony of Dunkerron South from that of Iveragh. However until the early seventeenth century the barony boundary ran along the mountain ridge to the south of the lake (Butler 1925, Map 1), quite possibly following the line of the early *termon* boundary. If this was so then the ecclesiastical sites of Ardkearagh and that of Loher (Fig. 9.5h) were also under the sway of *Inis Úasal*. This boundary also seems to have doubled as the boundary between the *Corca Dhuibhne* and the *Eoghanacht Loch Léin* (Barrington 1976, 26), thereby allowing *Inis Úasal* to benefit from land-grants and patronage from not one but two secular polities (see Ó Riain 1972; 1995, 150). Neither of the proposed southern boundary markers are located along the mountain ridge, but this is explained by the fact that early medieval boundaries were not usually linear territorial boundaries, but divisions between cultivated land and areas of wilderness which acted as buffer zones between different polities (Ní Ghabhláin 1995, 319; Patterson 1994, 97). While there are one or two St. *Fínán* dedications south of the ridge, the possible early ecclesiastical site and the parish itself are dedicated to another saint, *Cróchán*.

West of Shanaknock is Baslikane (Fig 9.4) an ecclesiastical enclosure and related stone cross, abutted by what is probably a small dry-stone church (O'Sullivan and Sheehan 1996, 260). Of greater significance however is the name of the site: Baslikane is a diminutive form of the Latin *basilica*, a term which occurs very rarely in Irish texts or as an element of Irish placenames. In his discussion of the name, Doherty (1984b, 315) points out that on the Continent the diminutive of basilica signified a subsidiary church and cemetery officiated at by a priest who was attached to the principal church of an area. Thus the name Baslickane may

---

7) are situated considerable distances from their respective church sites and therefore probably delimited church lands.

[16] It may be significant that two of the proposed boundary crosses are inscribed on two faces. Of the approximately 120 crosses and cross-slabs on Iveragh only six feature an inscribed cross on two faces and three of these may well be boundary markers. The others are: one on the main terrace on Skellig Michael, an eleventh-century example on *Inis Úasal*, one at the ecclesiastical site in Termons townland, and one isolated cross near the boundary of Cool West townland in northern Iveragh (O'Sullivan and Sheehan 1996, 275, 289, 315, 317). This latter may have delimited the lands of the minor church site of Kildreenagh situated in Cool East. Two pillars at Cloon West are inscribed on all four faces (*ibid.* 270). A higher proportion of the Dingle cross-slabs are inscribed on two faces, and only a small number of these are likely to be boundary crosses, that at Arraglen (Cuppage 1986, 248) being one likely example.

have been used to distinguish this church from the more independent churches in the region, churches through which *Inis Úasal* would not have administered pastoral care (see Ó Corráin 1981, 334). In this context it is interesting to note that the Latin Life of *Fínán Lobhar* recounts how he built a *basilica* and cemetery near an unnamed lake (AASS, Martii, ii, 446). Anyone who fell asleep in the basilica was miraculously removed to the banks of the lake, even though its doors remained shut. The Life tells us only that the lake was in the south of Ireland, but the rarity of the word basilica in Irish sources, and the proximity of Baslikane to Lough Currane, raises the possibility that this was the site which the author of the Life had in mind.

Of the three remaining satellite sites to the north of Lough Currane – Beenbane, Caherbarnagh and Dromkeare (Fig 9.4) – the latter is the most interesting. It features a tall ogham-stone inscribed with a square-serifed cross (Fig. 9.5i). The site is situated on the banks of the Cummeragh, the largest river flowing into Lough Currane, and just outside its enclosure are the previously unnoticed remains of a probable early medieval mill-race and horizontal mill. Thus Dromkeare may have been a centre for processing crops produced in the *termon* lands.[17]

The frequency of raths and cashels within the proposed *termon* is above the average for Iveragh, and if the argument being forwarded here is accepted, these represent the dwellings of the more affluent lay-tenants [*manaig*] of *Inis Úasal*.[18] Most of the settlement enclosures in the area (for distribution see Fig 9.4) are indistinguishable from those elsewhere in the region, but one in Termons townland (49.60 m × 48.75 m internal diameter) and another on Rabbit Island, Lough Currane (47.6 m × 38.3 m internal diameter) are unusually large. The former features a souterrain, and the foundations of two dry-stone structures of probable early medieval date are discernible in the latter (O'Sullivan and Sheehan 1996, 215, 217). Of the 244 extant non-ecclesiastical enclosures west of the Macgillicuddy's Reeks these two have the second and third largest diameters respectively[19] and are more akin to the ecclesiastical rather than the secular settlements of the area. They may therefore represent relatively large-scale ecclesiastical farms.[20]

While most of the boundary-crosses discussed above are not closely dateable, the square-serifed crosses at Dromkeare and Inchfarrannagleragh are similar to

---

[17] On the particular importance of tillage and milling in the economy of the early Irish church see Stout (1997, 129–30) and Etchingham (1999, 413–14). It is worth noting in passing that apart from the building of a basilica, the only incident related in St *Fínán Lobhar*'s Life about his period of lake habitation in the south of Ireland concerned a dispute regarding the erection of a mill (AASS, Martii, ii, 446).

[18] See Etchingham (1999, Chapter 9) on the varying social status of *manaig*.

[19] The only enclosure larger than these occurs in a cluster of four raths in Carhan Upper townland. Raths and cashels in the area average about 23 m in diameter. Calculated for the area west of longitude 09 degrees 50 minutes using measurements in O'Sullivan and Sheehan (1996).

[20] Ian Cantwell (1999, 40) has come to similar conclusions about large enclosures near the monastic complex at Glendalough, Co. Wicklow.

a number of Greek crosses including that on the ninth-century high cross at Kilnaruane, Co. Cork (see Harbison 1992, 382), the late eighth- or early ninth-century metal and wood cross from Co. Antrim (Harbison 1978; Ryan 1993, 36), two cross-slabs at Inishcealtra, Co. Clare and the high cross at Toureen Peakaun, Co. Tipperary. The latter three have recently been assigned to the eighth century by Okasha and Forsyth (2001, 97–101, 295).[21] It is therefore quite possible that the boundaries of the *termon* were established during the eighth or ninth century.

Skellig Michael

The last of the principal church sites is the famous coenobitic complex and pilgrimage centre of Skellig Michael, situated about 14 km off Bolus Head (Fig. 9.1). It features about 60 crosses and cross-slabs, several domestic buildings, and four churches, including the only pre-Romanesque mortared church in the study area. Most impressive of all are the huge terraces on which the monastery is perched; these are indicative of labour investment on a scale not found elsewhere in Iveragh/Dingle. The status which they intimate is confirmed by the documentary sources. For example *Caithréim Chellacháin Chaisil*, an early twelfth-century historical romance, portrays the *Corca Dhuibhne* kings fighting three Viking leaders in revenge for their attack on Skellig Michael (Ó Corráin 1974, 49). In this text the Skellig is portrayed as an establishment of prime regional impor-tance, equivalent to major monastic sites such as Aran, Co. Galway and even *Inis Cathaigh*, Co. Clare and Ardfert, Co. Kerry, which at the time were establishing themselves as episcopal sees.

Thus, placed in its local context, Skellig Michael emerges, not as an insig-nificant hermitage as it is usually portrayed (e.g. Edwards 1990, 16; Doherty 1998, 308), but rather as a daring experiment in ascetic monasticism, which was sustainable only because of the resources available to it from the mainland. Its late medieval successor, the Priory of St. Michael, situated on the north shore of Ballinskelligs Bay, owned most of the parish of Prior, and this may be roughly equivalent to the area controlled by Skellig Michael in the early medieval period. The boundaries of Prior have changed somewhat since the sixteenth century: it did not extend as far north as it does at present, but to the east the Priory owned lands south of the River Inny (since lost to Dromod parish) which were delimited by the Coomduff ridge (Keller, n.d.). Thus the *termon* lands of Skellig Michael may have abutted those of *Inis Úasal* for about 3.5 km, with the three crosses in Termons and Spunkane delimiting the boundary between them (Fig. 9.1).

Nevertheless the temporal resources of Skellig Michael were apparently quite modest compared to those of Kilmalkedar or even *Inis Úasal*. Prior parish is not very fertile and seems to have been sparsely populated, containing as it does just

---

[21] This cross form also occurs on the Ashmolean Museum and Prosperous crosiers which are usually dated to the ninth century (e.g. Bourke 1987), though Johnson (2000) argues they are tenth-century.

seven ringforts and (assuming that the *termon* boundary followed the ridge south from Bolus Mountain) one definite early church site, Kildreelig. Aspects of Kildreelig's construction support the possibility that it was a daughter house of Skellig Michael. In particular Grellan Rourke (pers. comm.) has found that the masonry of its enclosure is closely comparable to that of recently uncovered walling near an entrance to the main terrace on Skellig Michael.[22] A holy well dedicated to St. Michael and surmounted by a beehive-shaped structure occurs in Dungeagan townland, in Prior parish (Henry 1957, Plate XXVIIIa).

Independent Establishments?

In order to corroborate the arguments forwarded above an attempt is made here to identify and characterise sites that were independent of the three principal churches. Historical evidence suggests that this problem is best approached by investigating the cult of relics in the area. The present author agrees with O'Brien's (1992, 136) suggestion that it was not until the late seventh century that the veneration of corporeal relics of native Irish saints began in earnest. While small house-shaped reliquaries were being produced in Ireland from the early seventh century (e.g. Bourke *et al.* 1991, 17), Ó Floinn (1989/90, 54; 1997, 147) is of the opinion that 'at least in origin [these were] designed specifically as a container for relics of the saints and martyrs of the early Church brought back from Rome . . .' rather than for relics of Irish saints. Indeed, Kildare may have been as atypical of Irish seventh-century practice in its enshrinement of the bodies of Brigit and Conlaed as it was in its style of architecture (see Neuman de Vegvar, Chapter 10 in this volume). MacDonald argues that the relics of Columba himself were not translated until the mid-eighth century (1998, 25). Furthermore, the evidence for enshrinements in the *Annals of Ulster*, be it direct or indirect, is almost entirely post AD 700, and becomes much more plentiful and more explicit from the latter half of the eighth century (Aidan MacDonald, pers. comm.; cf. Petrie 1845, 198–9), and it was not until the eighth century that relics became important in the promulgation of laws (*cánaí*) (Charles-Edwards 2000, 565). Three small churches at major monastic sites, which almost certainly served as reliquary-chapels, have recently produced radiocarbon ranges suggesting they are eighth- or, more likely, ninth-century (Berger 1992; see also Harbison 1991, 150–1; O'Keeffe 1998, 116).

---

[22] A late medieval church in Kinard West may be on the site of another daughter house of Skellig Michael, for its name – Reglaish Church – is probably derived from *Reiclés*, a term used to describe a range of ecclesiastical settlement types in the early Irish sources (DIL). MacDonald (1999, 269–71) suggests that from the second half of the tenth century the term acquired a more specific connotation: that of a church within a major ecclesiastical complex used to house relics other than those of the site's patron. Two other sites within the Priory lands are also worth considering as possible early church sites: the children's burial ground with an associated ogham stone at Killurly, and that with an associated souterrain at Cools (Fig. 9.1, nos 4–6; O'Sullivan and Sheehan 1996, 244, 327, 332).

In the seventh century Armagh, and possibly other major centres, strengthened their links with, and authority over, subsidiary churches by distributing secondary relics of Continental saints to them (Doherty 1984a, 92–93). But as the cults of Irish saints developed in the eighth and ninth centuries the primary relics of a local saint could be used to assert a degree of independence. Indeed, Etchingham (1993, 154) has pointed out that in the *Córus Béscnai*, an eighth-century law tract, the very definition of a principal church was one 'in which there are relics of the founder'. Because of this, it is suggested here that evidence for the cult of relics at a particular site can be interpreted as at least an aspiration towards autonomy on the part of that site.

In Iveragh/Dingle the principal sites may well have had metal reliquaries which have not survived,[23] but at the more modest sites an outdoor stone shrine was the norm.[24] The Iveragh/Dingle shrines can be divided into three groups: gable shrines (4), corner-post shrines (3), and miscellaneous (3). The gable shrine at Illaunloughan, recently excavated by Clare Walsh and Jenny White Marshall (1994; 1998), was found to contain the dissarticulated remains of three adult males. Several radiocarbon dates suggest the shrine itself dates to the latter half of the eighth century (Claire Walsh, pers. comm.), and there is every reason to believe that the other gable shrines in the area – those at Killabuonia (Pl. 9.2), Killoluaig and the likely example at Aghatubrid – are of roughly the same date. It may be no coincidence that the only known stone gable shrine in the better-documented eastern half of the country occurs at Slane, for the relics of St. Erc of Slane are mentioned only twice in AU: in 766 when there is a tour (*commotatio*) of them, and 784 when they are brought to the festival of Tailtiu. Perhaps these relics were especially worthy of note in the latter half of the eighth century because they had recently been translated. Corner-post shrines occur at Kildreenagh (Fig. 9.6)[25] and on Church Island,[26] and there is a possible debased example at

[23] It should be mentioned that the eleventh or twelfth-century relic list, *The Reliquary of Adomnán*, includes a rib from the body of *Finán Cam*.

[24] Charles Thomas (1986, 124) once suggested that oratories should also be seen as manifestations of the cult of relics but excavation strongly suggests that in this region oratories had no significant burial or reliquary function (Ó Carragáin forthcoming). A distinction is also made here between structures which had a reliquary function and the simple grave-plots designed for multiple interments, which occur at a number of sites, including Lateevemore on Dingle and Garranebane and Feaghman West on Iveragh. Julia Smith (1990, 340) may be correct in asserting that local saints' cults in Brittany, Wales and Ireland were usually characterised more by secondary relics and healing springs than by corporeal relics. But this was not the case in Iveragh/Dingle where corporeal relics clearly played a central role in the sort of intensely local, orally rather than textually based cults, which she discusses.

[25] First published by Delap and Delap (1908–12, 192–3), this feature is in fact a corner-*block* shrine as defined by Thomas (1998, 94). It is situated a few metres north of the feature marked 'shrine' in O'Sullivan and Sheehan 1996, Fig. 172. Its closest Irish parallels are the previously unrecognised examples at Monasterboice, Co. Louth where four corner-posts are built into the west wall of the south church (see Dunraven 1877, 13), and at Kiltartan, Co. Galway where one corner-post lies loose in the church and another is built into its west wall.

[26] On excavation this shrine produced no bones and O'Kelly (1958, 89) concluded that this was due partly to acid soil conditions but mainly to disturbance. He saw the corner-posts as re-used late

Plate 9.2 Gable shrine at Killabuonia, Iveragh. Note circular perforation (*fenestella*) which facilitated access to the relics of St. Buonia

Caherlehillan (O'Sullivan and Sheehan 1996, 265). Some of the Scottish corner-post shrines are elaborately carved and these have been dated on art-historical and typological grounds mainly to the mid-eighth to early ninth century (Thomas 1973, 28; 1998, 94–95). One might tentatively conclude therefore that on Iveragh corner-post shrines and gable shrines represent alternative and roughly contemporary ways of enshrining corporeal relics.

The miscellaneous group may represent yet another alternative. The structures at Beginish and Cappanagroun consist of a small rectilinear enclosure surrounding a square dry-stone feature (O'Sullivan and Sheehan 1996, 248), while that at Killonacaha (*ibid.* Fig. 196) bears a remarkable resemblance to the platform element of the Illaunloughan shrine: both consist of a two-tier, upright-delimited platform, covered by a scattering of quartz pebbles, and they have similar entrance features at their west ends (Ó Carragáin 1998, 39–40). There are vestiges of rectilinear foci on the upper surfaces of the Cappanagroun and Killonacaha structures. Finally, at Reask, Fanning (1981, 83–5) excavated an enigmatic and not closely dateable, one metre square paved area which he interpreted as a shrine

medieval drip-stones, an interpretation which is explained by the fact that little had been published about corner-post shrines at the time. The posts are of the same conglomerate stone as the Kildreenagh examples, but their form is more closely paralleled at Kilnaruane, Co. Cork (Hourihane and Hourihane 1979, 72; Herity 1993, Fig. 23.5a).

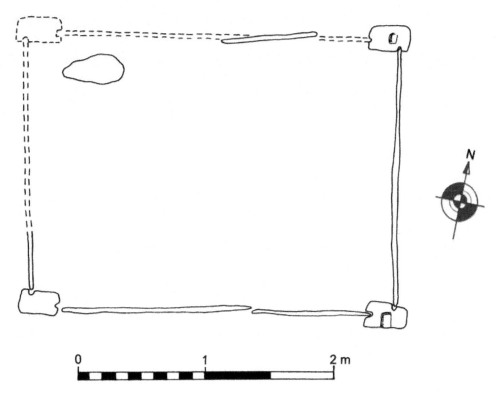

Figure 9.6 Corner-post Shrine at Kildreenagh, Cool East, Iveragh. Dashed lines indicate areas covered by sod. There are c.0.03 m deep rectilinear depressions on the upper surfaces of the north-east and south-east posts. The upright at the north side is unlikely to have formed part of the shrine as it projects much further above the ground surface than the other stones. The irregular stone near the north-west corner-post is white quartzite. A sketch of the shrine was published by Delap and Delap (1908–1912, p.191), and has since been reproduced by Herity (1993, Fig. 23.5b) and O'Sullivan and Sheehan (1996, Fig. 172)

on the grounds that the soil overlying it contained quite high levels of phosphorous. However, high phosphorous readings are not out of the ordinary in a graveyard, and the absence of any diagnostic traits means that this interpretation must be treated with some caution.

Because these outdoor shrines were venerated until recently and because (unlike metal reliquaries) they have no intrinsic economic value they have a high survival rate, and it is suggested here that their distribution offers a unique insight into early church organisation in the area. Fig. 9.1 shows that the questionable example at Reask is the only shrine on Dingle, where other evidence suggests that Kilmalkedar and the cult of St. Brendan were pre-eminent. Four are evenly placed just outside the border of the proposed *termon* lands of Skellig Michael, and there are none in the immediate vicinity of *Inis Úasal*. Indeed almost all of the shrines occur in the northern half of Iveragh, the area most obviously removed from the three principal churches. Thus there is a correlation between the archaeological record on the one hand, and what historical sources say about the status which relics convey on the other. The relative autonomy of these north Iveragh sites is also suggested by the fact that an unusually high number of them, compared to the norm for the region, have names which derive from local saints as at Killabuonia and possibly Illaunloughan, or from family groups, as at Killoluaig, Killonanacaha, Killogrone and Ballycarbery, in which is Church Island.[27]

Conclusions

This concentration of shrines may reflect competition between these minor sites for gravescot and pilgrimage revenues, as well as an assertion of independence from the principal churches. It need not imply that sites in the north of Iveragh were completely free of obligation, for the documentary sources portray a complex system of organisation with several different degrees of independence from or subservience to major establishments (Etchingham 1999).[28] Nor need it imply that on Dingle, where there is a dearth of shrines, the cults of local saints were totally subsumed by that of St. Brendan; place-name and other evidence suggest this was not the case.[29] What it does imply is that in northern Iveragh local identities were more forcefully expressed than elsewhere in the region. If this interpretation is accepted, then the mid-eighth to early ninth century period was a formidable one in the evolution of ecclesiastical organisation in the area. Local churches flourished and, on Iveragh in particular, a significant proportion of them maintained a degree of autonomy. Significantly, it was probably during this same period that the cult of St Brendan was being successfully established at the west end of Dingle (Harbison 1991, 80; Wooding 2001).

---

[27] While an assessment of secular power structures is beyond the scope of this paper, it is interesting to note that for a considerable period secular power in the region appears to have been centred at Ballycarbery (Barrington 1976, 26) suggesting that, as one might expect, independent churches were more common in areas of direct secular rather than ecclesiastical control. Though unlikely, the possibility does exist that some of the shrines were intended for important secular individuals, rather than the relics or putative relics of founder saints (see Ó Floinn 1997, 160). However, in the Irish context, the only recorded instance of this practice occurred in AD 1207 and was part of an attempt to have King Ruaidrí Ua Conchobair, the individual in question, canonised (Manning 1998, 78). In any case the effect, in terms of creating a distinct identity for a church site, may have been much the same.

[28] This is also suggested by evidence for outlying foci of the cult of St *Fínán* outside the proposed termon-lands of *Inis Úasal*. We have already noted that his cult is associated with Drung Hill, and the region around Killemlagh at the extreme western end of Iveragh, is mentioned in the Life of *Fínán Cam* (Ní Ghrifín 1996, 101).

[29] A cross-slab at Kil*fountan* on Dingle bears the name 'Finten', and it has been suggested that an ogham inscription at Kil*colman* in Maumanorig, Dingle includes the name 'Colman' (Fig. 9.2; Macalister 1937, 221–7; *ibid.* 1945, 186–8). The former may well be dedicatory but it probably dates to the seventh century (Swift 1997, 60; Okasha and Forsyth 2001, 37, 163) and is therefore earlier than the likely period of the establishment of St Brendan's cult in the area. McManus (1991, 53, 67, 97) dates the Kilcolman inscription to the early seventh century and finds Macalister's reading of it questionable.

One might even speculate that Viking disruption reinforced this subtle contrast between the two peninsulas, with the well-attested early ninth-century raids on vulnerable Skellig Michael having a decentralising effect.[30] Certainly by the tenth century Vikings had carved a permanent niche for themselves among the plethora of local ecclesiastical and secular interests in northern Iveragh, for the site excavated by O'Kelly (1956) on Beginish is perhaps the most convincing example of that rare thing: a rural Viking settlement in Ireland (Sheehan, Stummann-Hansen and Ó Corráin 2001).

Well-preserved physical remains and unambiguous physical geography make the early church on Iveragh and Dingle more susceptible to archaeological analysis than in most other regions of Ireland. And yet the situation there does seem to mirror the broad pattern of development as reflected in the historical sources. These indicate that, as well as witnessing the continuing decline of paganism in Irish society, the 100 years from AD 750 to 850 was the great period of territorial demarcation between the various churches, with the cessation of inter-church conflicts in the later ninth century reflecting the completion of this process, and the beginning of a period of relative stability for the Irish Church (Ó Corráin 1981, 335–6; Mac Samhráin 1996, 172).

ACKNOWLEDGEMENTS

My thanks are due above all to John Sheehan for encouraging my interest in the early Church on Iveragh. I am also very grateful to Prof. Martin Carver for his encouragement and judicious criticisms; Aidan MacDonald for vital discussions, especially about the cult of relics; Dr. Jonathan Wooding for his insights about relics and the cult of St Brendan; Prof. Pádraig Ó Riain, Prof. Éamonn Ó Carragáin and Maeve Sikora for commenting on early drafts of the paper; Dr Colin Rynne for discussion about the Dromkeare mill; Claire Walsh and Dr. Elisabeth Okasha for pre-publication information about Illaunloughan and Kilfountan respectively; Brendán Ó Cíobháin for toponymic information; Rhoda Cronin for drawing Figs. 9.3 and 9.6; and Eoghan Ó Carragáin for help with the maps. Finally, I would like to thank the Irish Council for the Humanities and Social Sciences for funding my research. Any errors that remain are my own.

---

[30] Raids are recorded on Skellig Michael in the annals for AD 824, and in *Cogad Gáedel re Gallaib* for the period of the late 830s or 840s (Etchingham 1996, 69), suggesting that it was raided more than any other church site in Kerry. There are no recorded raids on Dingle but this does not mean that none occurred (see Etchingham 1996, 31–2). A possible rune stone on Great Blasket island (Bradley 1988, 67) and the placename 'Smerwick' which comes from the Old Norse 'butter bay' (Ó Corráin 1997, 103) suggests more amicable contacts between Scandinavians and people on Dingle in later centuries. A full evaluation of Smyth's (1999, 32) theory that Illaunloughan was abandoned because of Viking raids must await publication of the excavation report, but there is some evidence that the site continued to function into the eleventh century (Claire Walsh, pers. comm.).

Abbreviations

AASS – *Acta Sanctorum* (Antwerp, 1643–1770; Brussels, 1780–1786, 1845–1883, and 1894 ff.; Tongerloo, 1794; and Paris, 1875–1887)
AU – Annals of Ulster
BAR – British Archaeological Reports
DIL – Contributions to a Dictionary of the Irish Language Published by the Royal Irish Academy, Dublin
JIA – Journal of Irish Archaeology
JRSAI – Journal of the Royal Society of Antiquaries of Ireland
JCHAS – Journal of the Cork Historical and Archaeological Society
JKHAS – Journal of the Kerry Historical and Archaeological Society
Med Arch – Medieval Archaeology
NMAJ – North Munster Archaeological Journal
PRIA – Proceedings of the Royal Irish Academy

References

Barrington, T.J. 1976 *Discovering Kerry Its History, Heritage and Topography* (Dublin).
Berger, R. 1992 '14C Dating Mortar in Ireland', *Radiocarbon* 34, No.3, 880–9.
Blair, J. 1985 'Secular minster churches in Domesday Book' in P.H. Sawyer (ed.) *Domesday Book: A Reassessment*, 104–42 (London).
—— 1991 *Early Medieval Surrey Landholding, Church and Settlement before 1300* (Stroud, Gloucestershire).
Bourke, C. 1987 'Irish croziers of the eighth and ninth centuries' in M. Ryan (ed.) *Ireland and Insular Art A.D. 500–1200* (Dublin), 166–73.
Bourke, C., Warner, R. and Ryan, M. 1991 'From Blackwater to Bobbio – a coincidence of shrines', *Archaeology Ireland* 16, 16–17.
Bradley, J. 1988 'The Interpretation of Scandinavian Settlement in Ireland' in J. Bradley (ed.) *Settlement and Society in Medieval Ireland: Studies Presented to F.X. Martin, O.S.A* (Kilkenny), 49–78.
Butler, W.F.T. 1925 *Gleanings from Irish History* (London).
Cantwell, I. 1999 *Society and Settlement in Glendalough and the Vartry before 1650* Unpublished Undergraduate Dissertation, Geography Department, Trinity College Dublin.
Charles-Edwards, T.M. 2000 *Early Christian Ireland* (Cambridge).
Cuppage, J. 1986 *Archaeological Survey of the Dingle Peninsula* (Dublin).
Delap, W.J. and Delap, M.J. 1908–1912 'Three old Kerry burial grounds', *Kerry Archaeological Magazine* 1, 186–94.
Doherty, C. 1984a 'The use of relics in early Ireland' in P. Ní Chatháin and M. Richter (eds) *Ireland and Europe: The Early Church* (Stuttgart), 89–101.
—— 1984b 'The basilica in early Ireland', *Peritia* 3, 303–315.
—— 1998 'The Vikings in Ireland: a review' in H.B. Clarke, M. Ní Mhaonaigh and R. Ó Floinn (eds) *Ireland and Scandinavia in the Early Viking Age* (Dublin), 288–330.
Doyle, I. 1996 *Imported Mediterranean Pottery in Early Medieval Ireland (A and B Wares)* Unpublished MA Thesis, University College Cork.
Dunraven, E. 1877 *Notes on Irish Architecture* Volume 2 (London).

Edwards, N. 1990 *The Archaeology of Early Medieval Ireland* (London).

—— 1999 'Viking-influenced sculpture in North Wales', *Church Archaeology* 3, 5–16.

Etchingham, C. 1991 'The early Irish church: some observations on pastoral care and dues', *Ériu* 42, 99–118.

—— 1993 'The implications of paruchia', *Ériu* 44, 139–162.

—— 1996 *Viking Raids on Irish Church Settlements in the Ninth Century: A Reconsideration of the Annals* Maynooth Monographs Series Minor 1 (Maynooth).

—— 1999 *Church Organisation in Ireland A.D. 650 to 1000* (Naas).

Fanning, T. 1981 'Excavation of an early Christian cemetery and settlement at Reask', *PRIA*, 81c 67–172.

Gwynn, A. 1915 'The reliquary of Adomnán', *Archivium Hibernicum* 4, 199–214.

Gwynn, A. and Hadcock, R.N. 1970 *Medieval Religious Houses in Ireland* (London).

Handley, M. 1998 'The early medieval inscriptions of western Britain: function and sociology' in J. Hill and M. Swan (eds) *The Community, the Family and the Saint: Patterns of Power in Early Medieval Europe* (Belgium), 339–61.

Harbison, P. 1970 'How old is Gallarus oratory? A reappraisal of its role in early Irish architecture', *Med Arch* 14, 34–59.

—— 1978 'The Antrim Cross in the Hunt Museum', *NMAJ* 20, 17–40.

—— 1991 *Pilgrimage in Ireland: The Monuments and the People* (London).

—— 1992 *The High Crosses of Ireland: An Iconographical and Photographical Survey* (Bonn).

Henderson, I. 2001 '"This wonderful monument": the cross-slab at Nigg, Easter Ross, Scotland', in P. Binski and W. Noel (eds) *New Offerings, Ancient Treasures – Studies in Medieval Art for George Henderson* (Gloucestershire), 115–147.

Henry, F. 1940 *Irish Art* (London).

—— 1947 'The antiquities of Caher Island (Co. Mayo)' *JRSAI* 77, 22–38.

—— 1957 'Early monasteries, beehive huts, and dry-stone houses in the neighbourhood of Caherciveen and Waterville (Co. Kerry)', *PRIA* 58, section C, 45–165.

Herity, M. 1983 'The buildings and layout of early Irish monasteries before the year 1000', *Monastic Studies* 14, 247–84.

—— 1993 'The forms of the tomb-shrine of the founder saint in Ireland' in M.D. Spearman and J. Higgitt (eds) *The Age of Migrating Ideas: Early Medieval Art in Northern Britain and Ireland* (Dublin), 188–95.

Hourihane, C.P. and Hourihane, J.J. 1979 'The Kilnaruane pillar stone, Bantry, Co. Cork', *JCHAS* 84, 65–73.

Hughes, K. 1966 *The Church in Early Irish Society* (London).

Johnson, R. 2000 'On the dating of some early-medieval Irish crosiers', *Med Arch* 44, 115–58.

Keller, D.G. n.d. *Iveragh in the Sixteenth Century* Unpublished map in University College Cork Special Collections.

Kelly, F. 1998 *Early Irish Farming* (Dundalk).

Lucas, A.T. 1967 'The plundering and burning of churches in Ireland, seventh to sixteenth century' in E. Rynne (ed.) *North Munster Studies Essays in Commemoration of Monsignor Michael Moloney* (Limerick), 172–229.

McManus, D. 1991 *A Guide to Ogham* Maynooth Monographs 4 (Maynooth).

Macalister, R.A.S. 1937 'The Ogham inscriptions at Kilfountain and Ballymorereigh (St. Manchan's) in the Dingle Peninsula', *JRSAI* 67, 221–8.

—— 1945 *Corpus Inscriptionum Insularum Celticarum* Volume 1 (Dublin).

MacDonald, A. 1998 ' When were St. Columba's corporeal relics enshrined?' *Hallel* 23 (1), 20–30.

—— 1999 '*Reiclés* in the Irish annals to AD 1200', *Peritia* 13, 259–75.

MacNeill, M. 1962 *The Festival of Lughnasa: A Study of the Survival of the Celtic Festival of the Beginning of Harvest* 2 Volumes (Dublin).

Mac Samhráin, A. 1996 *Church and Polity in Pre-Norman Ireland: the case of Glendalough* (Maynooth).

Manning, C. 1998 'Clonmacnoise Cathedral' in H. King (ed.) *Clonmacnoise Studies Vol. 1 Seminar Papers 1994* (Dublin), 56–86.

Morris, R. 1989 *Churches in the Landscape* (London).

Mytum, H. 1992 *The Origins of Early Christian Ireland* (London).

Nicholls, K.W. 1971 'Rectory, vicarage and parish in the western Dioceses', *JRSAI* 101, 53–84.

Ní Ghabhláin, S. 1995 *Church, Parish and Polity: the Medieval Diocese of Kilfenora, Ireland*, Unpublished PhD Dissertation, University of California, Los Angeles.

Ní Ghrifín, S. 1996 *Betha Fhínáin: Edition of the Early Vernacular Life: Textual Transmission and Language Content*, Unpublished MPhil Thesis, Department of Early and Medieval Irish, UCC.

O'Brien, E. 1992 'Pagan and Christian burial in Ireland during the first millennium AD: continuity and change' in N. Edwards and A. Lane (eds) *The Early Church in Wales and the West* (Cardiff), 130–7.

Ó Cíobháin, B. 1985 *Toponomia Hibernia*, Volume 4 (Dublin).

Ó Carragáin, É. 1988 'The meeting of Saint Paul and Saint Anthony: visual and literary uses of a eucharistic motif' in G. Mac Niocaill and P.F. Wallace (eds) *Keimelia: Studies in Medieval Archaeology and History in Memory of Tom Delaney* (Galway), 1–58.

Ó Carragáin, T. 1998 *Leachta as Indicators of Ritual Practice: The Evidence of Iveragh and Dingle, Co. Kerry*, Unpublished MA Dissertation, University of York.

—— (forthcoming) *Pre-Romanesque Churches in Ireland: Interpreting Archaeological Regionalisms*, Unpublished PhD Dissertation, University College Cork.

Ó Corráin, D. 1974 '*Caithréim Chellacháin Chaisil*: history or propaganda?' *Ériu* 25, 1–69.

—— 1981 'The early Irish churches: some aspects of organisation' in D. Ó Corráin (ed.) *Irish Antiquity Essays and Studies presented to Professor M. J. O'Kelly* (Cork), 327–41.

—— 1997 'Ireland, Wales, Man, and the Hebrides' in P. Sawyer (ed.) *The Oxford Illustrated History of the Vikings* (Oxford).

Ó Croinin, D. 1995 *Early Medieval Ireland 400–1200* (New York).

Ó Floinn, R. 1989/90 'A fragmentary house-shaped shrine from Clonard, Co. Meath', *J IA*, 5, 49–55.

—— 1997 'Insignia Columbae I' in C. Bourke (ed.) *Studies in the Cult of Saint Columba* (Dublin), 136–61.

O'Hanlon, J. 1875–1900 *Lives of the Irish Saints* Ten volumes (Dublin).

Okasha, E. and Forsyth, K. 2001 *Early Christian Inscriptions of Munster: A Corpus of the Inscribed Stones* (Cork).

O'Keeffe, T. 1998 'Architectural traditions of the early Medieval Church in Munster' in J. Sheehan and M.A. Monk (eds) *Early Medieval Munster: Archaeology, History and Society* (Cork), 112–24.

O'Kelly, M.J. 1956 'An island settlement at Beginish, Co. Kerry', *PRIA* 57c, 159–94.

—— 1958 'Church Island near Valencia, Co. Kerry', *PRIA*, 59c, 57–135.

—— 1975 *Archaeological Survey and Excavation of St. Vogue's Church, Enclosure and other Monuments at Carnsore, Co. Wexford* (Dublin).

O'Loughlin, T. 2000 Celtic Theology (London).

Ó Riain, P. 1972 'Boundary association in early Irish society', *Studia Celtica* 7, 12–29.

—— 1995 'Pagan example and Christian practice: a reconsideration' in D. Edel (ed.) *Cultural Identity and Cultural Integration: Ireland and Europe in the Early Middle Ages* (Dublin), 144–56.

—— 1997 *The Making of a Saint: Finbarr of Cork 600–1200* (Dublin).

O'Sullivan, A. and Sheehan, J. 1996 *The Iveragh Peninsula: An Archaeological Survey of South Kerry* (Cork).

Patterson, N. 1994 *Cattle-lords and Clansmen: The Social Structure of Early Ireland* (London).

Petrie, G. 1845 *The Ecclesiastical Architecture of Ireland Anterior to the Norman Invasion: An Essay on the origin and uses of The Round Towers of Ireland* (Dublin).

Plummer, C. 1910 *Vitae Sanctorum Hiberniae* Two volumes (Oxford).

Ryan, J. 1931 *Irish Monasticism: Origins and Early Development* (Shannon).

Ryan, M. 1993 *Metal Craftsmanship in Early Ireland* (Dublin).

Rynne, E. 1967 'The tau-cross at Killinaboy: pagan or Christian?' in E. Rynne (ed.) *North Munster Studies: Essays in commemoration of Monsignor M. Moloney* (Limerick), 146–65.

Sharpe, R. 1984 'Some problems concerning the organisation of the church in early medieval Ireland', *Peritia* 3, 230–70.

—— 1992 'Churches and communities in early medieval Ireland: towards a pastoral model' in J. Blair and R. Sharpe (eds) *Pastoral Care before the Parish* (Leicester), 81–109.

—— 1995 *Adomnán of Iona Life of Columba* (London).

Sheehan, J. 1990 'Some early historic cross-forms and related motifs from the Iveragh Peninsula', *JKHAS* 23, 157–74.

—— 2001 *Caherlehillan Early Ecclesiastical Site, Co. Kerry* Unpublished report lodged with *Dúchas*: The Heritage Service.

Sheehan, J. Stummann-Hansen, S. and Ó Corráin, D. 2001 'Beginish – an Island settlement reassessed', *JIA*, 12.

Smith, J.M.H. 1990 'Oral and Written: Saints, Miracles, and Relics in Brittany, *c.*850–1250', *Speculum* 65, 309–43.

Smyth, A.P. 1999 'The effect of Scandinavian raiders on the English and Irish churches: a preliminary reassessment' in B. Smith (ed.) *Britain and Ireland 900–1300 – Insular Responses to Medieval European Change* (Cambridge), 1–39.

Stalley, R. 1999 *Early Medieval Architecture* (Oxford).

Sternberg, T. 1991 *Orientalium More Sectus. Raeume und Institutionen der Caritas des 5. bis 7. Jahrhunderts in Gallien* (Muenster).

Stout, M. 1997 *The Irish Ringfort* (Dublin).

Swift, C. 1997 *Ogham Stones and the Earliest Irish Christians* (Maynooth).

Thomas, C. 1971 *The Early Christian Archaeology of North Britain* (Glasgow).

—— 1973 'Sculptured stones and crosses from St. Ninian's Isle and Papil' in A. Small, C. Thomas and D. Wilson (eds) *St. Ninian's Isle and its Treasures* (London), 8–44.

—— 1986 'Recognising Christian origins: an archaeological and historical dilemma' in L.A.S. Butler and R.K. Morris (eds) *The Anglo-Saxon Church* CBA Research Report (Oxford), 121–5.

—— 1995 'Cellular meanings, monastic beginnings', *Emania* 13, 51–67.

—— 1998 'Form and function' in S.M. Foster (ed.) *The St Andrews Sarcophagus: A Pictish Masterpiece and its International Connections* (Dublin), 84–96.

Waddell, J. 1994 'The Archaeology of Aran' in J. Waddell, J.W. O' Connell and A. Korff (eds) *The Book of Aran* (Galway), 75–136.

White Marshall, J. and Walsh, C. 1994 'Illaunloughan: life and death on a small early monastic site', *Archaeology Ireland*, 30, 25–8.

—— 1998 'Illaunloughan, Co. Kerry: an island hermitage' in M.A. Monk and J. Sheehan (eds) *Early Medieval Munster Archaeology, History and Society* (Cork), 102–11.

—— 2001 'St. Brendan, Clonfert and the Cult of the Navigator' in J. Higgins and C. Cuniffe (eds), *Aspects of Clonfert and its Vicinity* (Crowsrock Press).

10

Romanitas and Realpolitik in Cogitosus' Description of the Church of St Brigit, Kildare

CAROL NEUMAN DE VEGVAR

The description of the monastic church at Kildare in Cogitosus's Latin life of St Brigit has given rise not only to several reconstructions but also to the suggestion that the described church is a literary conceit rather than a lost reality. Based on a close reading of Cogitosus's text, this paper will offer a new reconstruction of this church as a historical reality, exploring its anomalies within the context of contemporaneous Irish ecclesiastical architecture, and suggesting that these anomalies demonstrate the use of *imitatio Romae* as a stratagem of seventh-century ecclesiastical politics.[1]

Cogitosus's *Vitae Sanctae Brigidae* is preserved in numerous manuscripts; but its publication history, first documented by Mario Esposito ([1912] 1988, 307–8), is of primary historiographic importance here since study of the church has relied on printed versions of the text.[2] The first printed edition, an abridged version published before 1480 by Bonino Mombrizio in his *Sanctuarium seu Vitae Sanctorum* ([1910] 1978), does not include the chapter on the church at Kildare. The first complete edition, Heinrich Canisius's *Antiquae Lectiones* (1604, 623–41),

[1] My deepest thanks are owed to Professor Éamonn Ó Carragáin (University College Cork), for encouragement in the preparation of a preliminary version of this paper for the Giornata di studio, *L'immagine di Roma nelle culture insulare fra i seccoli VII e X* at the Università degli Studi Roma Tre on 24 September 1999 and for help with the philology of *clais tarsna*. I am also grateful to Professors Rosemary Cramp (University of Durham), Michael Ryan (Chester Beatty Library) and Richard Sundt (University of Oregon) for critique of earlier editions of this paper, to Mr. Sean Connolly for information on the current edition-in-progress of Cogitosus's *vita*, to Dr Jørgen Jensenius (Norwegian Institute for Cultural Heritage) for his published and unpublished work on the consecration of Norwegian stave churches and for bibliography on the *Leabhar Breac*, and to Dr Edel Bhreathnach (Discovery Programme, Dublin) for a prepublication copy of her paper, 'Abbesses, minor dynasties and kings *in clericatu*: perspectives of Ireland 700–850'. Any errors remaining are the responsibility of the author.

[2] Richard Hayes (1965, 332–34, 617–18) lists 83 manuscripts, of which 36 are abridged, extracted or fragmentary editions; cf. Esposito ([1988] 1912, 308–19, 325–26), with 56 manuscripts.

was based on an anomalous Eichstätt manuscript, now lost (Esposito [1912] 1988, 308). Canisius's edition was used by Thomas Messingham in his *Florilegium insulae sanctorum seu vitae et acta sanctorum Hiberniae* (1624), and revised by Jacques Basnage in his *Thesaurus monumentorum ecclesiasticorum et historicorum* (1725); Basnage in turn was transmitted by Migne (1878) in the *Patriologia Latina* (*PL*), thereby gaining canonical status. John Colgan (1997) produced a somewhat better text in his *Acta Sanctorum Hiberniae: Trias Thaumaturga* in 1647. The most studiously comparative and reliable early edition, produced in 1658 in the Bollandists' *Acta sanctorum Februarii* (1863, vol. 1, 135–41), has not yet been superseded; a new critical edition is anticipated from Sean Connolly and Jean-Michel Picard, who published a preliminary translation in 1987.

Cogitosus was probably a religious at the monastery of Kildare. His *vita* of Brigit is usually dated in the third quarter of the seventh century, given Muirchú's reference to Cogitosus as *pater* in the *Vita Patricii*, which is dated about 680 and certainly before 700 (Esposito [1912] 1988, 321–4; Kenney 1993, 359; Sharpe 1982, 86–7; MacCone 1982, 108; Connolly 1987, 5).[3] Cogitosus's *vita* is variously subdivided; the description of the monastic church at Kildare is in the eighth chapter in the traditional subdivisions and in chapter 32 in Connolly and Picard's translation (1987, 25–6):

> Neither should one pass over in silence the miracle wrought in the repairing of the church in which the glorious bodies of both – namely Archbishop Conleth and our most flourishing virgin Brigit – are laid on the right and left of the ornate altar and rest in tombs adorned with a refined profusion of gold, silver, gems and precious stones with gold and silver chandeliers hanging from above and different images presenting a variety of carvings and colours. Thus, on account of the growing number of the faithful of both sexes, a new reality is born in an age-old setting, that is a church with its spacious [site] and its awesome height towering upwards. It is adorned with painted pictures and inside there are three chapels which are spacious and divided by board walls under the single roof of the cathedral church. The first of these walls, which is painted with pictures and covered with wall hangings, stretches width-wise in the east part of the church from one wall to the other. In it there are two doors, one at either end, and through the door situated on the right, one enters the sanctuary to the altar where the archbishop offers the Lord's sacrifice together with his monastic chapter and those appointed to the sacred mysteries. Through the other door, situated on the left side of the aforesaid cross-wall, only the abbess and her nuns and faithful widows enter to partake of the banquet of the body and blood of Jesus Christ. The second of these walls divides the floor of the building into two equal parts and stretches from the west wall to the wall running across the church. This church contains many windows and one finely wrought portal on the right side through which the priests and the faithful of the male

---

[3] See also Bullough (1965, 18–9) for further discussion of Cogitosus's Latinity and the date of the *vita*.

sex enter the church, and a second portal on the left side through which the nuns and congregation of women faithful are accustomed to enter. And so, in one vast basilica, a congregation of people of varying status, rank, sex and local origin, with partitions placed between them, prays to the omnipotent Master, differing in status, but one in spirit.

Donald Bullough (1964–65, 121, 32–3) found what he considered significant parallelisms of phrasing between this passage and the description of the Anastasis Rotunda in Jerusalem in Adomnán's *De Locis Sanctis* (I: 2–3), and argued that the description of the church at Kildare was a 'pure figment of the imagination' based on Adomnán's text. Since *De Locis Sanctis* is dated about 686, Bullough suggested that the description of the church at Kildare must be an addition to Cogitosus's *vita* by a later writer. However, Bullough's parallelisms are not overwhelmingly convincing, nor do distinctions of style support a difference of authorship between the description of Kildare's church and previous chapters of the *vita* which Bullough leaves to Cogitosus. Further, the passage in *De Locis Sanctis* does not portray the movement of different groups of people, a major component of the Kildare description.[4] Charles Thomas (1971, 206-9) was undoubtedly right in considering Cogitosus's description to refer to an actual church.

The *Vita Sanctae Brigidae* describes the monastic church of Kildare as expanded in the seventh century to accommodate the growing community. Cogitosus's phrasing, 'on account of the growing number of the faithful of both sexes, a new reality is born in an age-old setting', places this reconstruction in the recent past, and the miracle which follows, with the craftsmen's dispute over how to fit an old door formerly used by Brigit into a doorway of the new building, has the freshness of immediate personal experience or of interviews with witnesses. Indeed, the composition of Cogitosus's *vita* may have been part of the same promotion of Kildare as the construction of the new church and the *translatio* of Brigit and Conleth into its sanctuary. If so, then the new church must be estimated to have been consecrated approximately between 640 and 670.

One problem raised by Cogitosus's description of Kildare's church is the location of the longitudinal wall that extends from the north-south transverse wall to one of the end walls of the church. The Bollandists' edition and Connolly and Picard's translation have the wall running to the west, bisecting the nave. In his translation of Cogitosus, Ludwig Bieler (1963, 28) followed the Bollandists, as did R.A.S. MacAlister ([1935] 1978, 182) and Charles Thomas (1971, 145), in their reconstructions of the church (Figs. 10.1 and 10.2).[5] Canisius, followed by Basnage and Migne, has the wall extending from the transverse wall to the 'east wall' of

---

[4] *Periegesis* or description of sequential movement is a standard technique in both classical and Byzantine *ekphrasis*, of which Cogitosus may have been aware through other sources (Webb 1996, 64–8).

[5] This reading has also been accepted by Kathleen Hughes (1972, 268), Roger Stalley (1990, 148 n. 54), and N.B. Aitchison (1994, 263).

the church, bisecting the sanctuary; this text was quoted by Petrie (1845, 197–202), with an unexplained correction to 'west wall' in his translation. C.A. Ralegh Radford (1977, 7), basing his reconstruction on Petrie's Latin text, proposed a dual conventual choir to the east of the transverse wall, bisected by a low screen wall; he placed the altar outside the choir at the east end of the nave, so that the religious of the community would pass through doorways in the transverse wall to receive communion as per Cogitosus (Fig. 10.3).[6] Radford's reconstruction is undermined by reliance on the problematic Canisius tradition, whereas MacAlister's and Thomas's more accurate reconstructions agree with the Bollandist text and the Connolly and Picard translation. Here the longitudinal wall, extending from the west wall to the transverse wall, divides the nave in half, spatially segregating men and women. MacAlister's 1935 ground plan closely follows Cogitosus; Thomas's 1971 reconstruction is more elaborate and more problematic. He reads the transverse wall as solid, suggesting parallels with chancel walls in 'Visigothic Asturias'.[7] He also proposes colonnades paralleling the median wall of the nave; however, aisles separated by colonnades appear in Ireland only in much later stone churches (Hughes and Hamlin 1981, 38). Cogitosus does not mention the medium of construction at Kildare, but Peter Harbison notes that by the eighth century Ireland had only a few stone churches; the earliest certain documented example, at Armagh, is noted in the *Annals of Ulster* for 789 (AU 789.8, 1983, 245; Harbison 1982, 625–6).[8] Had Kildare been an anomalously early aisled stone church, surely Cogitosus would have mentioned this for its potential prestige value. Moreover, annalistic references to Kildare's church from the eighth to the tenth century consistently refer to a *dairthech* or 'oak house,' a technical term for a wooden church (Manning 2000, 38, 42–3).

My reconstruction is based on the Bollandist edition of Cogitosus's text and the Connolly and Picard translation (Fig. 10.4). I have interpreted the transverse wall as a chancel screen. While evidence for the design of early Irish chancel screens or rails is sparse, what does exist suggests a range of practices and terminology.

[6]   Although he adduced no parallels for his dual conventual choir to the east of the transverse wall, Radford (1977, 7) considered the placement of the altar outside the choir probable in an early church, as in seventh-century Winchester, tenth-century Breamore and early Christian North Africa. There is however no reason why this formula should be applied at Kildare; early medieval chancel arrangements were highly variable (De Benedictis 1981, 72–5).

[7]   Thomas refers to Sta. Cristina de Lena as an example of an Asturian chancel screen. However, Sta. Cristina's raised choir, open arcaded chancel screen and low parapet wall are regionally atypical; the screen may have been altered or added in the tenth century (Schlunk 1971, 221–2; Dodds 1990, 54, fig. 19, pl. 48). Several earlier Iberian churches outside Asturias, as at São Gião de Nazaré, São Pedro de Balsemão and Sta. Maria Quintanilla de las Viñas, are closer parallels for Thomas's reconstruction, with solid walls separating nave from choir, pierced by a central opening and sometimes flanking small arched windows or entries from the aisles (Schlunk 1971; Dodds 1990, 22, pls. 9, 11). A variety of chancel barriers, including the solid-wall type, are also found in Britain and Gaul. See notes 14 and 15.

[8]   The place-name Duleek may be a reference to an earlier stone church. Tírechán refers to it in his late-seventh-century *vita* of St. Patrick (Bieler 1979, 146); see Hamlin (1984, 118) for subsequent references in the annals.

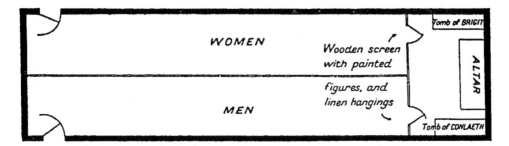

Figure 10.1 Reconstruction of the church at Kildare by R.A.S. MacAlister in his *Ancient Ireland: a Study in the Lessons of Archaeology and History* (1935; repr. 1978 New York: Arno Press) Fig. 29

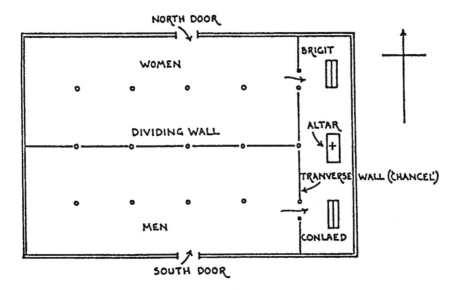

Figure 10.2 Reconstruction of the church at Kildare by Charles Thomas in his *The Early Christian Archaeology of North Britain; The Hunter Marshall Lectures delivered at the University of Glasgow, 1968* (Oxford University Press for the University of Glasgow, 1971) Fig. 65 (By permission of the author, the publisher, and the University of Glasgow.)

The *Leabhar Breac* (Dublin, Royal Irish Academy), a compendium of texts compiled in the fourteenth century, includes a tract on the consecration of a church. Although the compilation itself is late, the consecration tract is probably much earlier because it refers to the bishop marking various structural surfaces with crosses using a knife, anticipating a wooden rather than a stone church (Olden 1900, 98). In describing the liturgical geography of the church the tract refers to a *crand mbith*, which Olden (100, 180) read as a wooden rail or screen, an *ambitus altaris* separating the sanctuary from the nave, while Whitley Stokes (1901, 368–9) interpreted the same phrase as 'threshold beam', possibly at the church door. In either case the text suggests that this barrier was normally traversable. The *Rule*

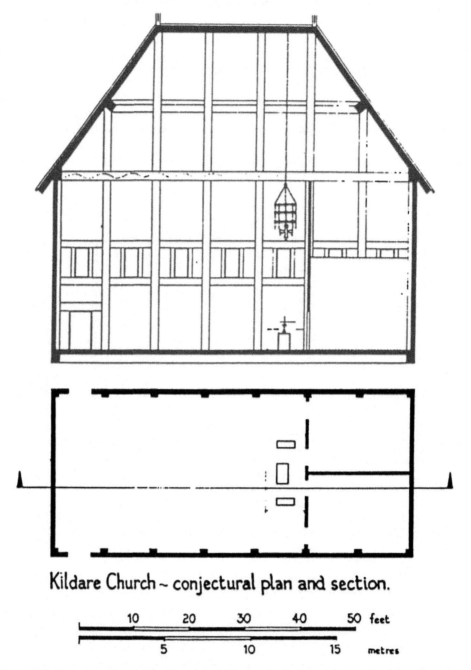

Kildare Church ~ conjectural plan and section.

Figure 10.3 Reconstruction of the church at Kildare by C.A. Ralegh Radford in his 'The earliest Irish Churches', *Ulster Archaeological Journal* 40 (1977), Fig. 9a (By permission of the Ulster Archaeological Society)

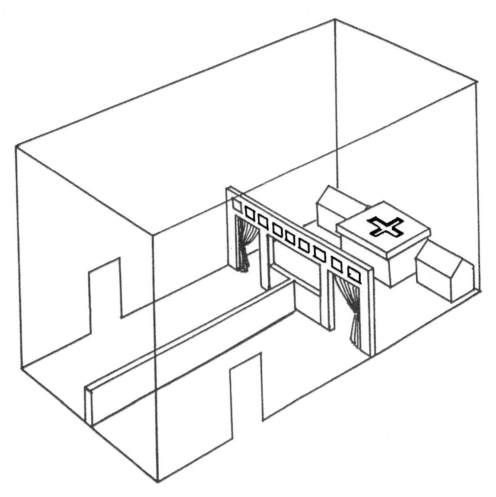

Figure 10.4 New reconstruction of the church at Kildare by the author. Drawn by Professor James Krehbiel (Ohio Wesleyan University)

of Tallaght, a ninth-century commonplace book of monastic practices in a Céli Dé community, uses different terms for barriers near the altar.

> It was not customary among them to pass between the altar and the *chlais tarsna* which is in front of the altar, and if anyone so passes, he is held to have incurred a penance. They were unwilling to kill any creature whatever between the chancel rail (*chrann-saingeal*) and the altar, for by custom only the body of Christ and his blood might be sacrificed in that space.
> (Gwynn 1927, section 16, 10–11; Kenney 1993, 471–2)

The word *clais* may mean 'ditch, trench, groove', but also 'assembly, choir'; *tarsna* translates as 'crosswise, oblique', (Ní Chatháin, O Daly, Ó Fiannachta, and O'Sullivan 1968, 222–3; Greene and Quin 1976, 86; Hamlin 1984, 119). Gwynn (11) translated *chlais tarsna* as 'transverse choir', albeit no early Irish church has a developed transept (Hare and Hamlin 1986, 133). MacAlister ([1935] 1978, 182) suggested it might be a groove for a movable screen providing access to the sanctuary as did the lateral doors in Kildare's transverse wall; if such screens existed they have left no archaeological trace. The seventeenth-century *Annals of the Four Masters* uses yet another term in reporting for the year 755 that bishop Echthigern was slain in the church at Kildare *etir an cróchaingel 7 an altóir*, 'between the chancel screen and the altar' (AFM [1854] 1966, 35). Edel Bhreathnach (2001, 118) notes that the compound *cróchaingel* 'appears to consist of *cró*, "fold, enclosure, pen" and *caingel*, "chancel screen, lattice" (borrowed from Latin *cancella*)'.[9] It is evident that where chancel screens existed in early Irish churches the terminology and perhaps also the arrangement were variable, suggesting that such spatial dividers were neither consistent in design nor mandated by common liturgical practice.

Cogitosus mentions no western entrance into the nave at Kildare, and in MacAlister's and Thomas's reconstructions, as in mine, the partition wall runs the length of the nave, precluding a centered western doorway. In this, Kildare is anomalous for its period; a central western entrance is found in every standing, or archaeologically known, early medieval church in Ireland (Hare and Hamlin 1986, 133). Textual evidence also supports this arrangement as normal for the period: the section 'On the Chapel' in the Latin A text of the *Hisperica Famina*, roughly contemporary with Cogitosus's *vita*, describes a church with a western door (Harbison 1982, 626; *Hisperica Famina*, lines 546–60). This arrangement is also anticipated in the liturgy for the consecration of churches in the *Leabhar Breac*, where the consecration of the exterior of the church is repeatedly stated to start from the western door (Olden 1900, 100; Stokes 1901, 377–81; Jensenius 1999a and 1999b). Further, psalms are to be chanted in the middle of the church and elsewhere the bishop is expected to transverse the interior of the nave diagonally; neither would be possible with a longitudinal partition wall as described by Cogitosus for Kildare, suggesting that this feature is also unusual (Olden 1900, 102; Stokes 1901, 370–1; 374–7).

Were interior partitions other than a chancel rail part of early Irish church design in general? Michael Hare and Ann Hamlin (1986, 134–5) have argued that spatial subdivisions as at Kildare must have existed at larger churches such as St. Fechin's at Fore (11.28 × 7.21 m) and the Cathedral at Glendalough (14.75 × 8.96 m), but most churches of this scale are now dated to the twelfth century. Most wooden churches of Kildare's date were considerably smaller; witness a

---

[9] Earlier annals do not specify the location of this event; the seventeenth-century annalist may be deriving his description from now-lost earlier sources or reconstructing the liturgical precinct at Kildare from forms familiar in his own time. Nonetheless, the same term also appears in the *Additamenta* in the ninth-century Book of Armagh, in a testament made by Fith Fio *iter crochaingel 7 altóir Drommo Lias*; (Bhreathnach 2001, 118; Bieler 1979, 172–3, paragraph 9[1]), and in the ninth- or tenth-century *Glossary of Cormac*, with reference to the veil of the Temple of Solomon (AFM [1854] 1966, 358–9, n. z).

document (Trinity College Dublin MS H.3.17, p. 653) which establishes a rate of payment for construction of a *dairthech* or wooden church based on its width, starting with a base design of 10 feet and working up to a larger church, defined as more than 15 feet wide (Harbison 1982, 625). Annalists' notations of the burning of 260 people in the *dairthech* at Trevet in 850, and of 150 victims in a wooden church at Drumraney in 948 are often cited as evidence for large wooden churches (Manning 2000, 46–7; Lucas 1967, 191–2). However, the dates of these massacres may indicate that the churches at Trevet and Drumraney were built significantly later than Cogitosus's church at Kildare, and the Trinity manuscript passage on construction costs suggests that such larger wooden churches were uncommon. In a smaller, narrower church, longitudinal partition walls would create a sense of hallway-like confinement and create problems of crowd circulation in the distribution of the Eucharist; it is unlikely that the smaller churches of Cogitosus's day normally had such partitions. In this, as in the absence of a western portal, Kildare was clearly unusual. These singularities may explain Cogitosus's need to describe the church at Kildare and its traffic flow patterns (Harbison 1982, 629).

Kildare was probably somewhat larger than the average Irish church of its day, but the interior width of Kildare itself should not be overestimated. Although Cogitosus uses such terms as 'spacious' and 'awesome height', to describe Kildare's interior, he writes in a context where a church measuring 15 feet in internal width was considered large. Even at Kildare a floor-to-ceiling partition wall extending the length of the nave would have blocked visibility; however intentionally hyperbolic Cogitosus's references to spaciousness may be, a complete inversion of the visual facts would have rendered his text laughable for the Kildare community. Consequently I have construed the longitudinal nave partition as a low screen wall, perhaps waist-high, ultimately modeled on the chancel screens and *solea* walls of the early Mediterranean church; Thomas (1971, 160) has noted that the construction of such partitions using panels or transennae slotted into upright posts was already known in the Insular world by the seventh century: surviving panel fragments from St. Ninian's Isle may have formed part of an altar or shrine precinct barrier. Rosemary Cramp (1984, 25) has also noted that the baluster shaft fragments found at Monkwearmouth may be 'part of a low balustrade either at the base or top of an enclosure, for example surrounding the sanctuary or choir' (Bhreathnach 2001, 118–19).

Why does Kildare diverge from the other Irish churches of its day to accommodate a longitudinal barrier down the centre of its nave to separate worshippers by gender, even to the extent of foregoing a western door? The answer may be that Kildare was copying a foreign precedent, not from North Africa or Spain as proposed by Radford and Thomas, but rather from Rome. In the Roman *ordines*, particularly in the seventh-century *Ordo I*, there are consistent parallelisms of layout and function with the approximately synchronous church at Kildare. In the *ordines*, the congregation in the nave was separated by sex with the men to the south and the women to the north, as elsewhere in the early church.[10] In Roman stational churches this segregation was made explicit by a lower choir or *solea* extending down the centre of the nave, which provided space for processions and for distribution of the Eucharist to the lower clergy. This zone was sometimes demarcated by parallel low barrier walls; at both the Lateran Basilica (Fig. 10.5) and S. Clemente these walls extended from the sanctuary almost to the central axial doorway (de Blaauw 1994, 127–9, 140–2, 504-5, figs. 1, 4; Guidobaldi 1992, 167–81).[11]

In the sequence of the offertory and the distribution of communion, *Ordo I* (*Ordines Romani* 1948, 69, 74–5, 117–22) refers to additional spaces adjacent to the altar precinct, including a *senatorium* and a comparable section on the women's side of the sanctuary which is alternatively named *pars mulierum* and *pars feminarum*; the eighth-century *Ordo IV* (1948, 41, 43, 78) calls these spaces *pars virorum* and *pars mulierum* (De Blaauw 1994, 93, 101–2). Elaine De Benedictis (1981, 71) has demonstrated that these auxiliary spaces were not intended as sites for the communion of all members of the congregation, as proposed by Thomas Mathews (1962, 73–95), but were set aside for the elite of the community to hear mass and receive the Eucharist (see also de Blaauw 1994, 100-1). De Benedictis (1981, 71–5) stresses that since *Ordo I* is very general, the spaces it does mention are standard. She cautions, however, against assuming paired enclosed precincts as suggested by Mathews; *Ordo I* only places the elite at the head of the congregation, closest to the sanctuary, and describes the distribution of their communion as separate from that of the rest of the congregation; she points out that *Ordo I*'s generalities are designed to be flexibly accommodated in the widely variable chancel arrangements of Roman churches. De Benedictis (1981, 75–85) also notes that since the term for wives of senators and even for unmarried women of the senatorial class is *matrones*, the fact that *Ordo I* does *not* refer to the space for elite secular women as a *matroneum* suggests that this term has another meaning. The term *matroneum* appears twice in the *Liber Pontificalis*; first, when Symmachus (498–514) renovates the apse at St Paul's Outside the Walls, decorates the area behind the *confessio* and builds a *matroneum* and a vault; and second, when Gregory IV (827–844) adds a *matroneum* 'enclosed all around with stones' to the north side of the presbytry at Sta. Maria in Trastevere (De Benedictis 1981, 76). Both these passages suggest a built environment. De Benedictis (1981, 79–82) suggests that the *matroneum* was for consecrated women: the *diaconissae, virgines* and *viduae*, minor orders standardized from the third century in the East and

---

[10] Separation of worshippers by gender is already a feature in the Temple of Solomon as reconstructed in Bede's *De Templo* (1995, Book 2, Chapter 17.2, 66–7); but here the purified women of Juda worshipped in an outer court rather than in a space parallel to that of the men.

[11] Late Antique extended *solea* structures are attested archaeologically for northern Italy, *inter alia* for the Basilica Maior in Milan, but regional liturgical sources of that period make no mention of their function (De Blaauw 1994, 140 n. 7). Although Irish pilgrims may have seen some of these northern Italian examples, the great Roman stational churches seem likely to have been more memorable because of their role as shrines of well-known early saints; further, there would have been no potential political advantage in copying northern Italian examples.

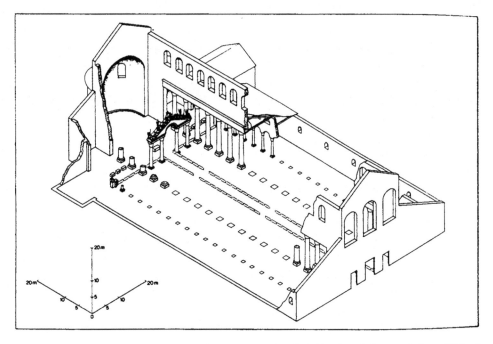

Figure 10.5 Isometric reconstruction of the Lateran Basilica (Basilica Salvatoris) from Sible de Blaauw, *Cultus et Décor: Liturgia e Architettura nella Roma tardoantica e medievale, Basilica Salvatoris, Sanctae Mariae, Sancti Petri* (Studi e Testi, Vols 355–6 Vatican City, 1994) Fig. 2 (By permission of the author and the publisher, © Biblioteca Apostolica Vaticana)

confirmed in the West from the fourth to the ninth century by references in the *Theodosian Code*, the *Liber Pontificalis* and a letter of Gregory I. Cogitosus's reference to *viduis fidelibus* among the women with the abbess in the sanctuary suggests that a minor order of widows may have existed in Ireland as well.

As described by Cogitosus, the church at Kildare echoes Roman documents and practice, but at a more modest scale. The longitudinal nave wall separates the men's and women's nave spaces. No *solea* is described, but the modest width of even a large church in early medieval Ireland and the absence of the large-scale processions of the Roman stational liturgy would have made this feature impracticable and unnecessary; the longitudinal wall is sufficient to refer to the Roman form. The separate space where the abbess and her nuns and widows (*abbatissa cum suis puellis et viduis fidelibus*) receive communion echoes the Roman *matroneum* as understood by De Benedictis.[12]

The emphasis of Cogitosus on subdivision of the congregation, 'in one vast basilica, a congregation of people of varying status, rank, sex and local origin,

---

[12] In translating Cogitosus's *puellis* as 'nuns', Connolly and Picard (1987, 26) echo both Gregory the Great and the *Penitential of Theodore* (I:14:11, 1990, 196; see also Migne 1878, 789; Niermeyer [1976] 1997, 870).

with partitions placed between them', suggests spaces for the secular elite at the east end of the nave, possibly with additional low barriers setting them off, although how such an additionally divided space would function for the distribution of communion is difficult to envision. However, a major seventh-century monastic centre such as Kildare normally included a substantial number of lay residents of both sexes, and potentially also received pilgrims who would have attended the same church as the community's religious but who were not privileged to enter the sanctuary to receive communion: how was communion distributed to them?[13] A central doorway in the chancel screen would have been blocked by the longitudinal wall bisecting the nave, and the clergy and con-secrated women standing in both halves of the sanctuary would have obstructed easy distribution of communion to the nave through the lateral sanctuary doors. In my reconstruction I suggest a low chancel rail approximately equal in height to the longitudinal median wall of the nave, flanked by the lateral doorways into the sanctuary and paralleled by a raised architrave bearing the paintings to which Cogitosus refers; the frames of the doorways serve as supports for the architrave. This results in a central space above the chancel rail that would permit both visibility from the nave of the celebrant during mass and the distribution of the Eucharist to lay congregants in the nave. The textiles mentioned by Cogitosus may have been suspended from the architrave and drawn between masses to limit visual access and create a defined sacred space for the relics of Brigit and Conleth; alternatively they may have been suspended in the lateral doorways.[14] A low chancel barrier connecting to the walls of a *solea* is not atypical in Rome in this period. The proposed combination of high open chancel screen and low parapet slabs is based on the *templon*, 'an open screen of low parapet slabs, occasionally accompanied by colonnettes supporting an architrave or epistyle' (Dodds 1990, 130 n. 84). The *templon* originated in early Christian and Byzantine churches and was widely echoed in churches in England, Gaul, Visigothic Spain, Syria and North Africa (Dodds 1990, 21–3).[15] Lavish versions in major Roman

---

[13] Jungmann (1986, II: 361–2) stresses the relative infrequency of lay communion in this period. However, as he also notes (I:73), the *ordines* of the Roman church consider the communion of the laity a norm; if Kildare is designed in *imitatio* of the great Roman stational churches and moreover anticipated pilgrims to the shrines of St. Brigit and Conleth, then a reconstruction should anticipate the possibility if not the reality of the communion of the laity.

[14] In the context of early medieval liturgical practice, Kildare's sanctuary wall and its hangings should not be reconstructed as completely blocking visibility from the nave into the sanctuary during mass. Theodor Klauser (1979, 66) emphasized the visibility of celebrant and consecrated host to the congregation in the Roman stational rite; and Thomas Mathews (1971, 162–71) made a strong case for the visibility of the celebrant in the early and middle Byzantine rite. Even the most occlusive barriers, as in Portugal at São Gião de Nazaré (note 7), are visually transparent via a central archway and flanking window-like openings. Helmut Schlunk (1971, 235 n. 38) suggested, albeit hesitantly, that these 'windows' in the chancel wall at Nazaré and between aisles and transept arms at S. Pedro de la Nave in Zamora may also served as a short-lived solution for the distribution of the Eucharist to the laity.

[15] Helmut Schlunk (1971, 214) and Jerrilyn Dodds (1990, 21–3) have argued that the number and variety of chancel screen types seen in Spain from the seventh century onward reflects the

churches, in the sanctuary of St. Peter's as well as at St. Paul's outside the Walls, would have provided memorable models for builders with an interest in *imitatio Romae* (de Blaauw 1999, 537–40, abb. 6–8).

Additional features of Kildare may demonstrate Roman influence. At St. Peter's it is unlikely that the faithful used the central western doorway; instead they used lateral doors, two on the north for women and two on the south for men (De Blaauw 1994, 504-5). Kildare, with its single gender-specific doorways in the north and south walls of the nave, may provide a scaled-down version of this aspect of St. Peter's. The draperies at Kildare were also echoed at Rome as elsewhere in the early church; De Blaauw's overview of sources indicates that draperies on display in Roman churches were very costly and would have made an impression on visitors (De Blaauw 1994, 96–7). Whatever the placement and function of the draperies of Kildare's chancel barrier, both the determination to purchase them and Cogitosus's decision to describe them may suggest knowledge of Roman practice and the prestige that costly fabrics could confer.

The evidence suggests that the community of Kildare were aware both of *Ordo Romanus I* and of specific Roman structures, possibly through pilgrims' reports, and that they were willing and able to modify received ideas to fit the more modest scale and liturgical needs of an Irish monastic church. No particular Roman church is imitated in all its particulars, but Roman precedent in general was applied effectively and with probable intent.

Why would Kildare, in reconstructing its monastic church in the mid-seventh century, depart from generalized norms of Irish church construction in order to follow Rome? The answer may lie in contemporary ecclesiastical politics. In the prologue to his life of Brigit, Cogitosus claims for Kildare a position of authority in Ireland. 'It is the head of almost all the Irish churches with supremacy over all the monasteries of the Irish and its *paruchia* extends over the whole land of Ireland, reaching from sea to sea' (Connolly and Picard 1987, 11).[16] This is more a statement of ambition than of fact, as Kildare's claims to authority were countered and eventually overpowered by those of Armagh (Ó Cróinín 1995, 152–62;

---

mandates of the First Council of Braga in 561, excluding the laity from the sanctuary, and more importantly the Fourth Council of Toledo in 633, dictating the placement of celebrants, clergy and laity in separate parts of the church at the administration of communion. Elsewhere chancel screens seem to have varied with the architectural type of the church (Dodds 1990, 130 n. 84). In seventh-century England, Reculver (Kent) had an open screen arcade, and Brixworth (Northants.) had a wall with a central archway (Taylor and Taylor 1965, I, 112–13 and II, 506-07).

[16] Kathleen Hughes (1966, 84) argued that in Cogitosus's *vita* Kildare claimed a widespread *paruchia*, not necessarily a metropolitanate (see also MacCone 1982, 136). However, Cogitosus's phrasing, *caput pene omnium Hiberniensium ecclesiarum*, suggests a more inclusive authority. Lawrence Maney (1999, 43–4) quotes David Howlett as having suggested that Cogitosus claimed primacy for Kildare in response to Wilfrid's assertion of metropolitan authority over North Britain and Ireland, which Howlett would date to 678–9. However, Eddius's *Vita Wilfridi* (1985, ch. xxi, 42–3) refers to Wilfrid's authority as extending *ad austrum super Saxones et ad aquilonem super Brittones et Scottos Pictosque*. The 'Scots to the north', possibly to be understood as physically as well as syntactically between Britons and Picts, may refer to the Irish kingdom of Dál Riata rather than to Ireland.

Aitchison 1994, 263–5). By the mid-seventh century, if current consensus is accurate in dating the *Liber Angeli*, Armagh was identifying itself with Rome in that text in a bid for metropolitan status, a concept in itself profoundly Roman (Sharpe 1984; Aitchison 1994, 198–9; Swift 1994, 61). Physical objects and the language of their description were important factors in the promulgation of Armagh's bid for central authority through *Romanitas*. Armagh held relics of major martyrs of the Roman church; Peter and Paul, Stephen, Lawrence and others, as well as a linen cloth bearing the blood of Christ; Charles Doherty (1991, 61, 69, 79) has suggested that these relics were sent to Armagh from Rome in 640 with the response to the Easter letter to Pope Severinus. Some of these relics were distributed by Armagh to bind other churches to her; the remainder were housed at Armagh in the southern church which the *Liber Angeli* calls a *basilica*, a term with ancient Roman associations also used by Cogitosus in the final sentence of his description of the church at Kildare (Migne 1878, 789; Connolly and Picard 1987, 26). Given currently accepted dates for the *Liber Angeli*, the church at Kildare, and Cogitosus's *vita*, both Cogitosus's claims for Kildare and *imitatio Romae* in Kildare's church may express Kildare's resistance to the claims of Armagh expressed through the *Liber Angeli*.[17] Kildare may not have been alone in deploying architecture as a visible statement in this struggle. By 789 Armagh had a stone church: the decision to build in stone, the medium of Roman construction, may have been a response to architectural *imitatio Romae* at Kildare. The development of masonry church construction in Ireland may have been advanced if not initiated by these ecclesiastical power struggles. That Irish churches making a bid for extended authority claimed connection to Rome is not at all surprising. Not only was Rome's church invoked frequently in the period as the ultimate authority in contemporary ecclesiastical matters, but Rome herself was also identified with the validating power of the past; as the relatively accessible site of major events of early church history and as *fons et origo* of the conversion of western Europe.

Armagh's claims in the *Liber Angeli* were raised at a moment when Kildare may have considered its political situation particularly vulnerable. Over the previous decades, the Irish churches had been deeply divided over conformity to the Roman Easter. At the Synod of Mag Léne in 629, the southern Irish churches decided to refer the matter to Rome. The letter of 633 from Cummian, abbot of Durrow, to Seghene of Iona and the recluse Beccan includes a list of the principal participants, in person or by proxy, in the synod; the successors to Bishop Ailbe

---

[17] In the *Vita Prima Sanctae Brigidae* (ch. 90), Brigit is miraculously able to hear masses said at the shrines of Peter and Paul in Rome and sends experts to learn the order of the Roman rite and 'the universal rule'; later, she sends them back when she perceives that the rite has changed (Ó Carragáin 1994, 1–2; Connolly 1989, 40–41). It is tempting to see this text as part of the Romanising efforts of Kildare, but as the *Vita Prima* has been variously dated and its authorship and place of origin debated, the contextual meaning of this passage must remain open (Sharpe 1982, 90–2; MacCone 1982, 116–7; Connolly 1989, 6; Howlett 1998, 1–23; Maney 1999, 38–92).

of Emly, and of the founder abbots Ciarán of Clonmacnoise, Brendan of Clonfert, Nessan of Mungret and Lugid of Clonfert-Mulloe (Kenney 1993, 220–1). A representative of Kildare is not listed here, although the contemporary successor to Brigit at the helm of the community of Kildare was Aéd Dub mac Colmáin, brother to King Faélán mac Colmáin of the Uí Dúnlainge dynasty of Leinster and described by the genealogists as 'rígepscop (or royal bishop) of Kildare and of all Leinster', (Ó Cróinín 1995, 55–6, 158). A parallel synod in northern Ireland is likely to have been led by the recipients of a letter from Pope Severinus written in 640: the abbots of Armagh, Clonard, Clonmacnoise, Moville and Iona, with Armagh taking pride of place.[18] By this time Aéd Dub had died, but the abbacy of Kildare had passed to his nephew, maintaining the connection between Kildare and the Uí Dúnlainge. Despite these continuing royal connections, Kildare was again out of the loop on the Easter question, the most pressing theological issue of its day.[19] If Kildare was to maintain or even further its claims of ecclesiastical authority, it would need to reinforce its visibility by making a forcible statement of its own on the question of Roman authority. The deliberate *imitatio Romae* of its splendid new monastic church, in combination with the claims to ecclesiastical power and advancement of the cult of its founder saint by Cogitosus's *vita*, may be the otherwise silenced voice of Kildare in a climate of severe competition and exclusion. Given the linkage of Kildare to the Uí Dúnlainge as a virtual *Eigenkirche* throughout the mid-seventh century, the construction of the church may have been funded by the dynasty and its plan also intended to express dynastic ambitions (Ó Cróinín 1995, 55–6; MacCone 1982, 110). Far from being a figment of scholarly imagination, the *Romanitas* of the monastic church at Kildare as described by Cogitosus may well be a stratagem in the *realpolitik* of the internal struggles of the church and the dynastic rivalries of mid-seventh century Ireland.

[18] Richard Sharpe (1984, 66) and Charles Doherty (1991, 69) note that the sequence of addressees of the papal letter probably followed the original order of signatures on the letter to Rome from the synod of 640; it does not demonstrate official recognition by Rome of Armagh's primacy, but does suggest that some Irish churches had begun to accept Armagh's preeminence. I agree with Kathleen Hughes (1966, 103–20) that arguments of regional authority advanced by Kildare and Armagh in the seventh century were not put forward for the purpose of urging conformity with Romanist practice, but it seems probable that conspicuous affiliation with Rome was useful to the political claims of both centres.

[19] Charles Thomas (1995, 61–2) has pointed out that Kildare may be part of a network of monasteries in Leinster with roots in the mission of Palladius. However, this does not explain Kildare's exclusion from the Easter synods; Ailbe of Emly was a follower of Palladius yet his successor was included at Mag Léne.

References

AFM: *Annala Rioghachta Éireann; Annals of the Kingdom of Ireland by the Four Masters from the earliest period to the year 1616*, ed. J. O'Donovan, 7 vols. (1845–51; reprint, New York, 1966).

Aitchison, N.B. 1994: *Armagh and the Royal Centres in Early Medieval Ireland: Monuments, Cosmology, and the Past* (Woodbridge).

AU: *The Annals of Ulster (to A.D. 1131)*, ed. S. Mac Airt and G. Mac Niocaill (Dublin, 1983).

Bede *On the Temple*: ed. and trans. S. Connolly with introduction by J. O'Reilly (Liverpool, 1995).

Bieler, L. 1963: *Ireland; Harbinger of the Middle Ages* (London).

—— 1979: *The Patrician Texts in the Book of Armagh*, Scriptores Latini Hiberniae 10 (Dublin).

Bhreathnach E. 2001: 'Abbesses, minor dynasties and kings *in clericatu*: perspectives of Ireland 700–850,' in Brown and Carr 2001.

Brown, M.P. and Farr, C.A (eds) 2001. *Mercia: An Anglo-Saxon Kingdom in Europe* (London) 113–25.

Bullough, D.A. 1964/1965: 'Columba, Adomnan and the Achievement of Iona', *Scottish Historical Review*, 43, 111–30, and 44, 17–33.

Butler, L.A.S. and Morris, R.K. eds 1986: *The Anglo-Saxon Church; Papers on history, architecture, and archaeology in honour of Dr H. M. Taylor*, Council for British Archaeology Research Report 60 (London).

Cogitosus *Vitae Sanctae Brigidae*, in *Acta sanctorum quotquot toto orbe coluntur, vel a Catholicis scriptoribus celebrantur, quae ex Latinis & Graecis, aliarumque gentium antiquis monumentis collegerunt ac digesserunt Seruatâ primigeniâ Scriptorum phrasi, & variis Obseruationibus illustrarunt Joannes Bollandus, Godefridus Henschenius, societas Iesu theologi; Februarius Tomus I*, new edition, ed. Joannes Carnandet (Paris, 1863) 135–41.

Cogitosus *Vitae Sanctae Brigidae*, ed. J. Basnage, in *Thesaurus monumentorum ecclesiasticorum et historicorum, sive, Henrici Canisii Lectiones antiquae: ad saeculorum ordinem digestae variisque opusculis auctae* (Antwerp, 1725) vol. 1, 413–24.

Cogitosus *Vitae Sanctae Brigidae*, ed. H. Canisius, in *Antiquae lectiones [seu] antiqua monumenta ad historiam aetatis illustrandam numquam edita. Omnia nunc primum e manuscriptis edita et notis illustrata*, 623–41 (Ingolstadt, 1604), vol. 5, part 2.

Cogitosus *Vitae Sanctae Brigidae*, ed. J. Colgan in *Trias Thaumaturga*, 518–26 (1647; reprint, Dublin, 1997).

Cogitosus *Vitae Sanctae Brigidae*, ed. S. Connolly and J.-M. Picard, 'Cogitosus: *Life of St. Brigit*,' *Journal of the Royal Society of Antiquaries of Ireland*, 117 (1987), 11–27.

Cogitosus *Vitae Sanctae Brigidae*, ed. T. Messingham in *Florilegium insulae sanctorum seu vitae et acta sanctorum Hiberniae*, 189–200 (Paris, 1624).

Cogitosus *Vitae Sanctae Brigidae* ed. J.-P. Migne, 'Sanctæ Brigidæ Virginis Vita a Cogitoso Adornata,' in *PL*. 72, 776–90 (Paris, 1878).

Cogitosus *Vitae Sanctae Brigidae*, ed. B. Mombrizio in *Sanctuarium seu Vitae Sanctorum*, 257–61 (1910; reprint, Hildesheim, 1978).

Connolly, S. 1987: 'Cogitosus's *Life of St. Brigit*; Content and Value,' *Journal of the Royal Society of Antiquaries of Ireland*, 117, 5–10.

—— 1989: 'Vita Prima Sanctae Brigidae; Background and Historical Value,' *Journal of the Royal Society of Antiquairies of Ireland*, 119, 5–49.

Cramp, R. 1984: *Corpus of Anglo-Saxon Stone Sculpture; Vol 1: County Durham and Northumberland*, Part 1 (London).

De Benedictis, E. 1981: 'The Senatorium and Matroneum in the Early Roman Church,' *Rivista di Archeologia Cristiana*, 57, 69–85.

de Blaauw, S. 1994: *Cultus et Decor; Liturgia e Architettura nella Roma tardoantica e medievale, Basilica Salvatoris, Sanctae Marie, Sancti Petri, Studi e Testi* 355–56 (Vatican City).

—— 1999: 'Die vier Hauptkirchen Roms,' in Stiegemann and Wemhoff 1999, 529–41.

Dodds, J.D. 1990: *Architecture and Ideology in Early Medieval Spain* (University Park).

Doherty, C. 1991: 'The Cult of St Patrick and the politics of Armagh in the seventh century,' in Picard 1991, 53–94.

Eddius, Stephanus *The Life of Bishop Wilfrid*, ed. B. Colgrave, (1927; reprint, Cambridge, 1985).

Esposito, M. [1912] 1988: 'On the Earliest Latin Life of St. Brigid of Kildare,' *Proceedings of the Royal Irish Academy*, 30(C), 307–26, reprint in M. Esposito, *Latin Learning in Ireland*, Variorum Reprints 9 (London).

Greene, D. and Quin, E.G., arr., 1976: *T-tnúthaigid*, in *Contributions to a Dictionary of the Irish Language* (Dublin).

Guidobaldi, F. 1992: *San Clemente: Gli edifici romani, la basilica paleocristiana e le fasi altomedievali*, San Clemente Miscellany IV, 1 (Rome).

Gwynn, E. 1927: *The Rule of Tallaght*, 2nd suppl. vol., *Hermathena* 44 (Dublin and London).

Hamlin, A. 1984: 'The study of early Irish churches,' in Ní Chatháin and Richter 1984, 117–26.

Harbison, P. 1982: 'Early Irish Churches,' in Löwe 1982, vol. 2, 618–29.

Hare, M. and Hamlin, A. 1986: 'The study of early church architecture in Ireland: an Anglo-Saxon viewpoint,' in Butler and Morris 1986, 131–45.

Hayes, R.J. 1965: *Manuscript Sources for the History of Irish Civilization* 1 (Boston).

The Hisperica Famina 1. The A-Text, ed. M.W. Herren (Toronto, 1974).

Howlett, D. 1998: '*Vita I Sanctae Brigidae*,' *Peritia*, 12, 1–23.

Hughes, K. 1966: *The Church in Early Irish Society* (London).

—— 1972: *Early Christian Ireland: Introduction to the Sources* (Ithaca).

Hughes, K. and Hamlin, A. 1981: *Celtic Monasticism: The Modern Traveler to the Early Irish Church* (New York).

Jensenius, J. 1999a: 'Wood or Stone? Tradition, Liturgy, and Law in Medieval Church Building,' unpublished paper presented at the International Congress on Medieval Studies, 11–13 May 1999, at Western Michigan University, Kalamazoo, Michigan.

—— 1999b: 'Innvielsesrituale for trekirke,' *Hikuin*, 26, 83–98.

Jungmann, J.A. 1986: *The Mass of the Roman Rite; Its Origins and Development*, trans. F.A Brunner, 2 vols, reprint (Dublin).

Kenney, J. F. [1968] 1993: *The Sources for the Early History of Ireland: Ecclesiastical*, 2nd edn, Dublin: Irish University Press, reprint (Dublin).

Klauser, T. 1979: *A Short History of the Western Liturgy; An account and some reflections*, 2nd edn (Oxford).

Löwe, H. ed. 1982: *Die Iren und Europa im früheren Mittelalter* (Stuttgart).

Lucas, A.T. 1967: 'The Plundering and Burning of Churches in Ireland, 7th to 16th Century,' in Rynne 1967, 172–229.

MacAlister, R.A.S. [1935] 1978: *Ancient Ireland: A Study in the Lessons of Archaeology and History*, reprint (New York).

MacCone, K. 1982: 'Brigit in the seventh century: a saint with three lives?' *Peritia*, 1, 107–45.

Maney, L.J. 1999: *High-Kings and Holy Men: Hiberno-Latin Hagiography and the Uí Néill Kingship, ca. 650–750*, Ph.D. diss., Harvard University (Ann Arbor).

Manning, C. 2000: 'References to church buildings in the Annals,' in Smyth 2000, 37–52.

Mathews, T.F. 1962: 'An Early Roman Chancel Arrangement and Its Liturgical Functions,' *Rivista di Archeologia Cristiana*, 38, 73–95.

—— 1971. *The Early Churches of Constantinople: Architecture and Liturgy* (University Park).

Ní Chatháin, P., O Daly, M., Ó Fiannachta, P., and O'Sullivan, A., arr., 1968: C; *Fasciculus 1*, in *Contributions to a Dictionary of the Irish Language* (Dublin).

Ní Chatháin, P. and Richter, M., eds 1984: *Irland und Europa; Die Kirche im Frühmittelalter* (Stuttgart).

Niermeyer, J.F. [1976] 1997: *Mediae Latinitatis Lexicon Minus*, reprint (Leiden).

Ó Carragáin, É. 1994: 'The City of Rome and the World of Bede,' Jarrow Lecture (Newcastle).

Ó Cróinín, D. 1995: *Early Ireland 400–1200*, Longman History of Ireland 1 (London).

Olden T. 1900: 'On an Early Irish Tract in the Leabhar Breac Describing the Mode of Consecrating a Church,' *Cambridge Camden Society Transactions* 4, 98–104 , 177–80.

Ordines Romani, ed. M. Andrieu, *Les Ordines Romani du Haut Moyen Age*, vol. 2: *Les Textes (Ordines I-XIII)* (Louvain, 1948).

Penitential of Theodore, ed. J.T. McNeill and H.M. Gamer, *Medieval Handbooks of Penance; A Translation of the Principal Libri Poenitentiales*, 179–215, (1938, reprint, New York, 1990).

Petrie, G. 1845: *The Ecclesiastical Architecture of Ireland anterior to the Anglo-Norman Invasion, comprising an Essay on the Origin and Uses of the Round Towers of Ireland* (Dublin).

Picard, J.M. ed. 1991: *Ireland and Northern France AD 600–850* (Dublin).

Radford, C.A.R. 1977: 'The Earliest Irish Churches,' *Ulster Archaeological Journal*, 40, 1–11.

Rynne, E. ed. 1967: *North Munster Studies; Essays in Commemoration of Monsignor Michael Moloney* (Limerick).

Schlunk, H. 1971: 'Die Kirche von São Gião bei Nazaré: Ein Beitrag der Liturgie für die Gestaltung des Kirchengebäudes,' *Madrider Mitteilungen*, 12, 205–40.

Sharpe, R. 1982: '*Vitae S. Brigidae*: the oldest texts,' *Peritia*, 1, 81–106.

—— 1984: 'Armagh and Rome in the seventh century', in Ní Chatháin and Richter 1984, 59–72.

Smyth, A.P. ed. 2000: *Seanchas; Studies in Early and Medieval Irish Archaeology, History and Literature in Honour of Francis J. Byrne* (Dublin).

Stalley, R. 1990: 'European Art and the Irish High Crosses,' *Proceedings of the Irish Royal Academy* 90(C), no. 6, 135–58.

Stiegemann, C. and Wemhoff, M., eds 1999: *799; Kunst und Kultur der Karolingerzeit; Beiträge zum Katalog der Ausstellung; Paderborn, 1999* (Mainz).

Stokes, W. 1901: 'The *Lebar Brecc* Tractate on the Consecration of a Church,' in *Miscellanea Linguistica in Onore de Graziadio Ascoli*, 363–87 (Turin).

Swift, C. 1994: 'Tirechán's Motives in compiling the *Collectanea*: an alternative interpretation,' *Ériu*, 45, 53–82.

Taylor, H.M. and Taylor, J. 1965: *Anglo-Saxon Architecture*, vols. I and II (Cambridge).

Thomas, C. 1971: *The Early Christian Archaeology of North Britain* (London).

—— 1995: 'Cellular Meanings, Monastic Beginnings,' *Emania*, 13, 51–67.

Webb, R. 1996: 'The Aesthetics of Sacred Space: Narrative, Metaphor, and Motion in Ekphraseis of Church Buildings,' *Dumbarton Oaks Papers*, 53, 59–74.

11

Making a Christian Landscape:
Early Medieval Cornwall

SAM TURNER

Introduction

The aim of this chapter is to consider the development of the early Christian landscape in Cornwall, the long, tapering peninsula at the far south-western tip of Britain (see Fig. 11.1). As argued below, less is known for certain of Cornwall's early Christianity than has sometimes been claimed. For example, on the Cornish mainland there is hardly any archaeological evidence for categories of early Christian site known to exist in neighbouring regions such as Ireland or Gaul (e.g. hermitages; White Marshall and Walsh 1998; Biarne 1997), and possible differences between ecclesiastical sites are commonly obscured by the lack of evidence. It is therefore hardly possible to paint a definitive picture of early Christianity in the region. What this chapter will attempt is to put the early Cornish church in context by examining some of the relationships between ecclesiastical sites and other elements of the landscape. It will also suggest that the emergence of the Christian landscape detectable by the eleventh century was neither a short nor a simple process, but was instead the result of actions over an extended period. The paper highlights the importance of the relationship between the 'sacred' and the 'secular' in early medieval society, and stresses that neither element can be properly understood without reference to the other (Markus 1997: 85–7; Fletcher 1997: 160–92; Graham 1998: 133).

The *lann Model of Early Ecclesiastical Enclosures:
a Cautious Approach

The early ecclesiastical sites of western Britain have for the last 30 years been considered in relation to the model of cemetery development proposed by Prof. Charles Thomas (1971: 49–51). With Christianity acting as the catalyst, unenclosed burial sites (commonly with long-cists or dug graves) were changed into cemeteries defined by a small curvilinear enclosure (sometimes known as a *lann; Thomas' 'undeveloped' enclosed cemeteries), and in time became 'developed'

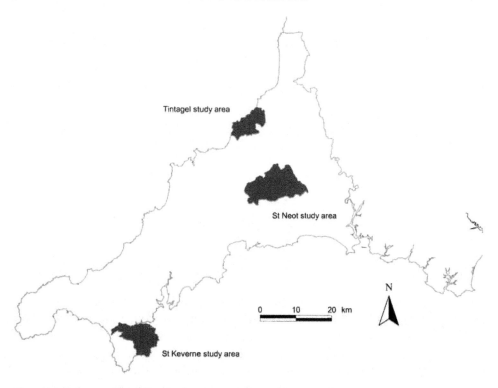

Tintagel study area

St Neot study area

N

0   10   20 km

St Keverne study area

Figure 11.1 Cornwall and the study areas mentioned in the text

enclosed cemeteries with the addition of a cross, a chapel, and then a parish church (Thomas 1971: 49–51). Some scholars have suggested that this process took place at a relatively early date in Cornwall. For example, various churchyards on the north coast have been regarded as Christian settlements founded by voyagers from across the seas to the north (see, for example, Preston-Jones 1992: 122; see also Pearce 1982; Brook 1992). Although Preston-Jones points out that not all medieval Christian cemeteries can have had very early origins, it has commonly either been stated or implied that the *lanns* are of early post-Roman date (Pearce 1978: 92; Preston-Jones 1992: 105; Thomas 1994: 305–26). Preston-Jones and Rose (1986: 155, 160) go so far as to suggest that:

> With Christianity came a whole package of ideas . . . associated site-types, place-names, monuments . . . [and that] . . . The earliest Christian foundations, or *lanns*, were settlements of people dedicated to a religious life.

Current research by Petts (2002) on early medieval burial in western Britain has questioned the relevance of Thomas' model to the period before AD *c*.800. Although several sites in Wales have been excavated and radiocarbon dated, such as Tandderwen (Clwyd), Atlantic Trading Estate (Glamorgan) and Plas Gogerddan (Dyfed), there appear to be very few examples of western British cemeteries that were enclosed in the post-Roman centuries (Petts 2002). In neither

Cornwall nor Devon does excavated evidence suggest that any simple cemeteries were enclosed before about the tenth century. Prof. Thomas' own excavations at St Dennis and Merther Uny show that these sites were only used for Christian burial from the tenth century at the very earliest (Thomas 1965; 1968b).

Documents and place-names have been used to support the model of early enclosure, but their evidence is no more supportive than the archaeology (Petts 2002). The earliest recorded use of a name in *lann* in Cornwall is possibly in a ninth-century charter granting land at Lawhitton (Sawyer 1968 [henceforth S] no.1296; Padel 1988: 108; Hooke 1994a: 16–7). Otherwise the earliest *lann* names are from tenth-century charters (e.g. Lanow: S 810; Hooke 1994a: 33–7). Prof. Wendy Davies has suggested that some of the charters from south-east Wales in the Book of Llandaf could be dated to as early as the sixth century (Davies 1978). The 159 charters contain references to many estates with *llan* names (the equivalent in Welsh of *lann* in Cornish). However, scholarly opinion on these documents is far from united: whilst some of these grants have early origins, it seems likely that the actual *names* of the estates concerned were recorded in their twelfth-century form since the charters were being used at that time to bolster the claims of a new bishop of Llandaf. The Book therefore does not provide reliable evidence for early *llan*-names (Davies 1998: 45–6).

The Cornish place-name scholar Oliver Padel has noted that *lann* may have been used to coin new names in Cornwall up to AD *c*.1200. It is therefore possible that ecclesiastical sites with *lann* names which later became parish churches were given their names in the tenth century or later. This is a particularly tempting interpretation in the light of Padel's observation that very few Christian sites that did not gain parochial status in the later middle ages (e.g. chapels or minor burial grounds) have names in *lann*, suggesting that they were specific to churches of a certain status at the time the parish system was developing (Padel 1985: 144).

These criticisms do not mean that the *lann* model should be rejected outright. Sites such as Capel Maelog in Wales show that the sequence could have occurred much as Thomas suggested, but that it took place over a period encompassing the whole of the early middle ages (Britnell 1990; Petts 2002). It is also clear that some sites did exist at an early date which comprised settlements of people dedicated to religious lives. They occupied centres which were sometimes enclosed and which accommodated activities such as Christian burial. However, these are much fewer in number than suggested by the *lann* model, and as a group they appear to have comprised early monasteries of superior status: examples include Llandough and Berllan Bach in Wales (Thomas and Holbrook 1994; James 1992: 100–1).

The *lann* model presents several problems. Most importantly, recent research has shown that there is very little evidence for the enclosure and 'development' of cemeteries in western Britain before the ninth century (Petts 2002). This conclusion makes a reconsideration of the development of the early church in Cornwall necessary. Any re-assessment also provides an opportunity to deal with other important points which have been marginalised in the *lann* model. For example, the suggestion that relatively large numbers of sites were founded in the post-Roman period has sometimes obscured potential differences between them, not only of date but also of status (Preston-Jones and Rose 1986: 157–8; Thomas 1994: 310–1). Finally, there is the question of the relationship between ecclesiastical sites and the wider community. This is crucial to understanding life in early medieval Cornwall, but as in other parts of Britain and Ireland, it is a subject in need of further research (Monk 1998; Aston 2000: 61–2).

The research reported here studies the settlement patterns of successive periods against the background of the wider landscape. Recent discussions stress that the effects of ideological change should be studied in the entire landscape rather than focusing on 'sacred sites' (e.g. van Dommelen 1999, 284; Given *et al.* 1999). In the research project on which this chapter is based, evidence from place-names, documents and archaeological sites is used to identify patterns in past landscapes (see Bender 1993, 3; Moreland 2001, 94–7). Historic landscape characterisation (see below) is used to provide a wider context against which these patterns can be analysed. The sequence of settlement patterns is used to illuminate social and cultural changes (Alcock 1993, 55–72). In this case the changes in settlement and in the structuring of the landscape between the fifth and the tenth century are interpreted as reflecting or being caused by adaptations to a new Christian ideology.

The Late Roman Landscape of Cornwall from the Third to the Sixth Century AD

The modern county of Cornwall was part of the Roman-period *Civitas Dumnoniorum*. The region was one of the least 'Romanised' in Britain, and there is a marked lack of evidence for many aspects of Roman cultural life such as the towns and villas so abundant in neighbouring *civitates* (Todd 1987). It is perhaps in the region's settlement patterns that the continuities from the Iron Age through the Roman period and beyond are most striking.

The most commonly recognised type of late Iron-Age and Roman period settlement in Cornwall are known as 'rounds'. Excavated examples show that these enclosed settlements date principally from the second century BC to the sixth century AD (Quinnell 1986). Whilst Cornwall seems to have been less 'Romanised' than other parts of Britain, it also seems to have been less severely affected than other areas by the 'ending' of Roman Britain. This is demonstrated by the settlements of Trethurgy and Grambla, both excavated rounds where finds of imported Mediterranean pottery have revealed continuing occupation in the fifth and sixth centuries (Miles and Miles 1973; Saunders 1972). It seems likely that other rounds would also have been occupied in these centuries, but may not have had access to imported wares. Quinnell has stated that the local pottery production centre of the Lizard '. . . definitely continued into the fifth century' (Quinnell 1995: 128). This interpretation is supported by recent radiocarbon dates from Tintagel (Morris *et al.* 1999: 212), and by locally produced pottery which has recently been found in association with large quantities of imported Mediterranean ceramics at the major beachmarket site of Bantham Ham in Devon (Horner 2001: 8). This new evidence could mean the final date of other rounds will be pushed from the fourth to the fifth century or later.

In addition to pottery production centres, other 'industrial' sites continued in use after AD c.400, such as Carngoon Bank and Trebarveth (McAvoy 1980: 38; Johns and Herring 1996: 84). Established patterns of trade and exchange in locally produced goods seem to have continued into the post-Roman centuries. Tin ingots have been found in several late and post-Roman contexts including Par Beach on Scilly and Praa Sands, Breage (Quinnell 1986: 130; Penhallurick 1986; Biek 1994). A large group of ingots from the Erme estuary in south Devon are also likely to date to the fifth or sixth centuries (Fox 1995; Thorpe 1997).

Several Roman-period 'high status' sites continued to be occupied in the fifth and sixth centuries. The most important example is Tintagel. Here occupation probably commenced in the third century, and continued until the seventh. During this time Tintagel may have become the main centre for the contemporary rulers of Cornwall, and it received vast quantities of imported goods including tableware, coarsewares, amphorae and glass from the eastern and western Mediterranean. In the third and fourth centuries, however, the site received a similar range of goods as important rounds like Trethurgy and Reawla (Thorpe 1997: 82). Quantities of both late and post-Roman material have also been recovered from Chun Castle in Penwith and St Michael's Mount (Thomas 1956; Herring 1993: 60–1; CAU 1998: 18). This evidence strongly suggests that the major 'post'-Roman centres of Cornwall were established as part of a late Roman-period settlement pattern (see Dark 2000: 164–70). This pattern also comprised rounds, production sites and centres for trade/exchange, many of which existed by the third century and continued into at least the sixth century.

Burial practices and burial sites also exhibit considerable continuity. Burial in cists was a standard practice from the Iron Age to the tenth or eleventh centuries AD (e.g. Harlyn Bay and Mawgan Porth; Preston-Jones 1984). No break in this tradition is apparent at the end of the Romano-British period.

With reference to the material culture of the late Roman period in Cornwall, Quinnell (1993: 40) has argued that:

> Close fostering of local traditions may have produced a community which was successful for far longer than those in regions of Roman Britain usually appraised as comparatively civilised both in classical and modern terminology.

It seems likely that the same local cultural resilience is detectable in Cornish settlements and burial practice in and around the 'Roman' centuries.

The fifth and sixth centuries was also the period when Christianity was first established in Cornwall, apparently under strong influences from Gaul and the Mediterranean (Thomas 1994). Thomas has suggested that Phillack in west Cornwall is an example of a very early Christian site (Thomas 1994: 197–201; 1998:

149). Bearing in mind the large numbers of burials reported from the vicinity of the church it seems likely that Phillack could be comparable to an early Welsh monastery such as Llandough (Somerscales 1957; Preston-Jones 1984).

Discussion over the last three decades has cast significant doubt on the theory that Tintagel Island was an early monastic centre, and it is clear that Ralegh Radford's initial interpretation of the site as an ascetic 'Celtic' monastery must be consigned to history (e.g. Thomas 1993; cf. Ralegh Radford 1935; 1962). Nevertheless, excavations at Tintagel churchyard, on a cliff-top site about half a kilometre south of the Island, revealed early Christian funerary activity. Graves in the earliest levels are surrounded by spreads of burnt clay containing sherds of imported pottery as well as foodstuffs; as the excavators argue, this could reflect the influence of Mediterranean practice in funerary rituals at the site (Nowakowski and Thomas 1992; Thomas 1994: 197–209). As at Phillack, the burial ground at Tintagel is known to extend some way beyond the confines of the modern graveyard from chance finds of cist-graves in the adjoining fields (Canner 1982). It seems likely that here at St Matheriana's church is the 'sacred' equivalent to the early royal site on the Island (Thomas 1993: 99). The recently excavated inscription from the Island also hints at a close connection between the secular elite and the literate culture of the church (see Morris et al. 1999: 213–4).

Elite literacy is further demonstrated by the monuments commonly known as inscribed stones (see Okasha 1993; Okasha, Chapter 21 in this volume; Higgitt, Chapter 20 in this volume). Although relatively few of them bear obviously Christian iconography or formulae, about half of the 35 or so monuments in Cornwall come from churchyards. It has been argued that the presence of an inscribed stone and a *lann place-name or enclosure strongly suggest an early Christian site (e.g. Thomas 1994: 312; Preston-Jones 1992: 112). However, the dating of these monuments is a contentious topic, and their context is far from certain (Okasha 1993; Thomas 1994; cf. Thomas 1998). Excavation has yet to show that any inscribed stone is contemporary with a south-western *lann-type enclosure and it is likely that some of the stones now in churchyards were transported there from other places. Though some inscribed stones were funerary monuments, many seem to have marked territorial boundaries (Handley 1998). In Cornwall the latter interpretation seems reasonable for monuments whose earliest recorded locations were close to later parish boundaries or to the edge of medieval cultivated land (e.g. the Worthyvale stone near Tintagel; the Welltown and Tawna stones near Cardinham; see Figs. 11.2 and 11.3). Some stones, such as Boslow near St Just in Penwith, may have marked both an isolated burial and a boundary. Handley has suggested the possibility that the meanings of inscribed stones changed over time, and has argued that stones associated with land ownership tend to be later in date than those whose role was solely memorial (Handley 1998: 353–4). In the context of the present discussion, this could suggest that such monuments are connected to the developments of the sixth–ninth centuries when the structure of the medieval landscape was being established (see below). Although the dates and original contexts of the inscribed stones are

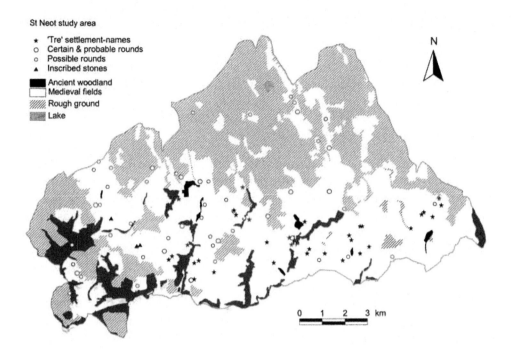

Figure 11.2 Distribution of inscribed stones, rounds, and settlements with *tre* place-names first recorded before AD 1550 plotted against the HLC in the St Neot study area

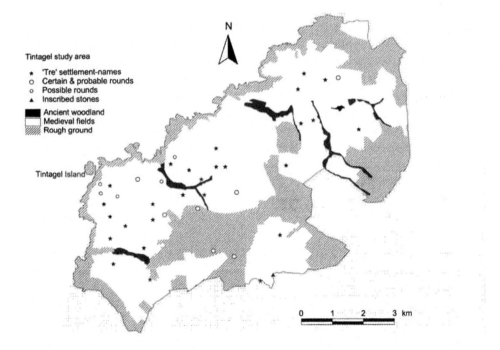

Figure 11.3 Distribution of inscribed stones, rounds, and settlements with *tre* place-names first recorded before AD 1550 plotted against the HLC in the Tintagel study area

very hard to establish, it seems plausible that they could have played a part in defining boundaries in the developing early medieval landscape.

The Early Christian Landscape of Cornwall from the Sixth to the Ninth Centuries AD

Early medieval ecclesiastical sites

Sites like Phillack and Tintagel likely to be closely linked to the post-Roman secular elite may have continued from the late- and post-Roman period into the early middle ages; there is evidence at both of Christian activity from the late Saxon period (AD *c*.900–1050; Nowakowski and Thomas 1992; Thomas 1994). Even if this means continuity can be inferred, such sites did not necessarily maintain their previous high status: at some time in the early middle ages Tintagel was eclipsed as the main ecclesiastical centre of its area by the church at Minster (Pearce 1978: 107; Thomas 1993: 113).

It is certain that religious communities did exist in Cornwall before the ninth century. Olson's analysis of the written sources demonstrates the presence of a few pre-ninth century establishments based on contemporary material (e.g. St Kew), and shows from later evidence that other communities had almost certainly existed (e.g. St Keverne, Padstow, Crantock, St Neot; Olson 1989: 105). The archaeological evidence, whilst sparse at present, seems to support Olson's identifications: it is probably significant that sites like Crantock and St Piran's stand amid extensive burial grounds with some evidence for pre-medieval activity (Olson 1982). Although Olson's book provides valuable identifications, investigation of the churches as part of the early medieval landscape is not within its scope; this topic is addressed below.

It seems likely that church and elite in Cornwall were strongly linked, as they were in other parts of Britain (see e.g. Higham 1997). The limited evidence of sixth–eighth century written sources suggests that the social elite of Cornwall were responsible for establishing the earliest churches and granting them estates. Both Gildas and Aldhelm write concerning kings of Dumnonia, and a comes, perhaps a lower-ranking member of the elite, takes part in an episode in the early *Life of St Samson*; all these men are portrayed as deeply involved in religious affairs (Winterbottom 1978: 29–30; Lapidge and Herren 1979: 155–60; Olson 1989: 16). Davies has argued that there was a British charter tradition which allowed estates to be granted from king to church (Davies 1982), and the practice is suggested at an early date in Cornwall by the record of King Gereint's early eighth-century grant of land at Maker to the church of Sherborne (Finberg 1953: 16). In addition, some tenth-century charters apparently maintain distinctive 'Celtic' elements (Olson 1989: 78–84). It is certain that some or all of Cornwall's early churches would have been provided with estates in this way.

Early medieval settlements

These new religious foundations were an important element in a wider reorgan-isation of the landscape. Although Cornish culture seems to have been relatively stable in the late and post-Roman periods, settlement studies reveal that some major changes occurred in subsequent centuries. The archaeological evidence shows that rounds ceased to be occupied in the sixth or seventh century at the latest. The most common settlement form became the 'unenclosed' farmstead. The archaeological evidence for such settlements is currently very slight. 'GM/1' near Gwithian in west Cornwall (the original place-name is lost; Thomas 1958) has been confidently ascribed to the period by its excavator. Unfortunately, the excavation has never been fully published, and the sequence of contexts described by Thomas (1968a) is unclear (Hutchinson 1979; Preston-Jones and Rose 1986: 175–6). This uncertainty means that finds from GM/1 cannot necessarily be used to date other sites.

Oliver Padel has provided a foundation for studies of early medieval settlements through his analysis of medieval Cornish place-names. He argues on linguistic grounds that *habitative* place-name elements (i.e. those denoting a settlement) such as *tre* and **bod* were used to coin names principally between the fifth and eleventh centuries (Padel 1985; 1999). Many such names must have originated by the eighth century, since the *tre* element was already in use in Devon when the English arrived (Padel 1999: 88). Preston-Jones and Rose have plotted the distributions of *tre* settlements and other place-names to analyse the early medieval settlement patterns in five different parts of Cornwall (Preston-Jones and Rose 1986; Rose and Preston-Jones 1995). They state that there is little reason to doubt that the locations of medieval (and modern) *tre* settlements represent the locations of their early medieval predecessors (ibid. 1995: 52). Several tenth–eleventh century Anglo-Saxon charter boundary clauses describe very small estates with the same names as medieval and modern settlements. In these cases the small area defined by the charter bounds implies that the early settlements cannot have moved more than a couple of hundred metres (e.g. Trethewey (S 832); Trerice (S 1019); Hooke 1994a).

It is probable that other settlements with *topographical* rather than habitative name elements were established in Cornwall during this period, although it is not yet possible to prove this. Preston-Jones and Rose (1986: 143) have shown that early medieval settlement in the upland parish of Davidstow occurred in at least two phases. They noted that places with Cornish topographical names generally occur on higher ground than sites with *tre* names, and that the former do not 'fit' into the relatively regular pattern of *tre* settlements in the valley. This suggests the topographical place-names are part of a later episode of settlement. However, Preston-Jones and Rose also found that in the Padstow area some places with topographical names do form part of a pattern otherwise made up of *tre* settlements. They concluded that whilst '. . . some topographical names must be later [than *tre* settlements], not all are' (*ibid.* 1986: 143–4). Their argument shows that in early medieval Cornwall there were 'core' areas of settlement typified by settlements with *tre* names, and implies that these areas were subject to some kind of organisation (Preston-Jones and Rose 1986: 141–4; Rose and Preston-Jones 1995: 52–6; Padel 1985: 127; 1999: 89–90). It is therefore possible to be fairly confident on both linguistic and topographical grounds that many settlements with habitative name elements (e.g. *tre*, **bod*) existed in the seventh, eighth and ninth centuries on or very close to their later medieval sites. However, it is not absolutely certain from either source that topographic name elements were given to settlements until the centuries immediately before the Norman Conquest (when they are first recorded in documents).

The exact nature of the relationship between the unenclosed *tre* settlements and the rounds is important for landscape history. One model suggests that the early medieval settlement pattern is a continuation and development of the Roman-period pattern (Rose and Preston-Jones 1995: 67). On the other hand, it has been suggested that major social and economic changes took place in or around the sixth century which led to a complete reorganisation of the country-side, resulting in an early medieval landscape of strip fields and unenclosed settlements (Herring 1999a; 1999b). Rose and Preston-Jones also argue that the end of 'defended' settlements implies an important political and social dislocation (1995: 62).

Figs. 11.2 & 11.3 represent an attempt to investigate these relationships. They show the distribution of settlements with *tre* names and rounds in two study areas. These have been plotted against a historic landscape characterisation (HLC) map of each area. HLC is a method for understanding and mapping the landscape with reference to its historical development (McNab & Lambrick 1999: 54). The HLC method recognizes that all parts of the landscape have historical significance which is the result of human activity and use over the millennia, and that archaeological features such as different types of field boundaries are characteristic of different histories. Herring has explained the basis of the HLC method developed by the Cornwall Archaeological Unit and others as follows:

> Closer examination [of the landscape] reveals that particular groupings and patterns of components which recur throughout the county can be seen to have been determined by similar histories. Cornwall's historic landscape can, therefore, be characterised, mapped and described, using a finite number of categories or types of 'historic landscape character'.
>
> (Herring 1998: 11)

The HLC maps in Figs. 11.2 & 11.3 have been produced using an adapted form of this method. The HLC plots show three different character types: medieval farmland, rough ground, and woodland. The extent of each type has been determined after an analysis of relevant features in a combination of sources for each area. Thus the extent of medieval farmland is based on the extent of enclosed field systems of medieval origin and open areas of ridge-and-furrow. The sources used include all available historic maps of each area (dating from the seventeenth century onwards), modern maps, and archaeological air and field surveys (method detailed in Turner, in progress). The maps indicate the approximate extent of all known or possible medieval farmland around the time of the climatic/demographic optimum of the thirteenth/fourteenth centuries (Johnson and Rose 1994: 114).

The distribution of *tre* place-names and rounds are plotted against the HLC maps of each study area, but it is important to note that these maps were prepared without reference to the distribution of place-names or settlements known from archaeology (unpublished data kindly supplied by Oliver Padel and Cornwall Archaeological Unit). It is clear from the maps that *tre* settlements form the core of the 'medieval farmland', and they occur exclusively within it. By contrast, both maps show rounds in areas that were uncultivated moorland or woodland even at the peak of settlement expansion in the later middle ages.

In the absence of evidence for widespread continuity from Roman to medieval settlements in Cornwall, a model emphasising the difference between Roman and early medieval settlement patterns rather than continuity is perhaps more acceptable at present. As shown by Figs. 11.2 and 11.3 there was a marked difference in the settlement patterns of the Roman period and the early middle ages. The early medieval period witnessed a retraction in the area settled, and radical changes in the form of most settlements. Rose and Preston-Jones (1995: 66) place these changes in the fifth century and link them to the decline of the Roman administration. However, as the settlement evidence discussed above shows, the late Roman pattern may have endured in Cornwall into at least the sixth century (see also Dark 2000: 168–70). The change from rounds to *tre* settlements may be associated with the changes in local power structures reflected in the decline of late and post-Roman sites such as Grambla and Trethurgy. The evidence from settlement studies suggests that the sixth or seventh centuries were more turbulent socially than the fifth.

The consolidation of royal power and the emergence of regional kingdoms have been linked to changes in settlement form in other parts of early medieval Britain (Carver 1989: 152; West 1985: 162). Similar processes may provide the context for the changes in Cornwall's settlement pattern. The exact causes of such major changes are presently uncertain. Whether one elite group, such as those who had resided at Tintagel, were replaced by a different group is not known; that site could have been abandoned in the early seventh century for some other reason (Harry and Morris 1997). What seems clear is that the new patterns of settlement and land-use formed the basis of the medieval and modern patterns. As discussed below, it is likely that the ideology of the newly established churches played an important role in structuring the new landscapes.

The early church and the landscape

The evidence discussed above strongly suggests that the early medieval settlement pattern was based around 'core' areas containing settlements and their farmland which were surrounded by outer zones of rough moorland and wood-land. How did the early medieval ecclesiastical centres relate to this pattern?

Although some have stated that Cornwall's early churches were in isolated positions (Aston 2000: 41), this opinion is not consistent with the evidence from settlement studies. As shown in Figs. 11.4 and 11.5, early ecclesiastical centres lie at the heart of the 'core' areas of early medieval settlement. The Meneage area, for example, has the densest concentration of settlements with *tre* place-names in the county; the community of St Keverne lies at its heart (Domesday Book's *Canonici Sancti Achebranni*; Thorn and Thorn 1979: 4.23). Padel's maps of Cornish habitative place-name elements (*tre* and **bod*) suggest that similar concentra-tions surround other early ecclesiastical communities such as Padstow, St Kew, Crantock and St Buryan (Padel 1999: 89–90).

With the exception of Tintagel, nothing approaching a nucleated settlement, or 'town', is known to have existed in Cornwall during the first millenium, and it is possible that Cornish ecclesiastical centres were not densely populated settlements like those Blair has suggested may have existed in Anglo-Saxon England (e.g. Blair 1996: 9). The 'monastic towns' of Ireland have recently been re-evaluated in critical terms (Valante 1998; Graham 1998) and it is clear that nowhere in early medieval Cornwall could satisfy all the normally cited criteria for an urban settlement (see, for example, Graham 1998; Halsall 1996).

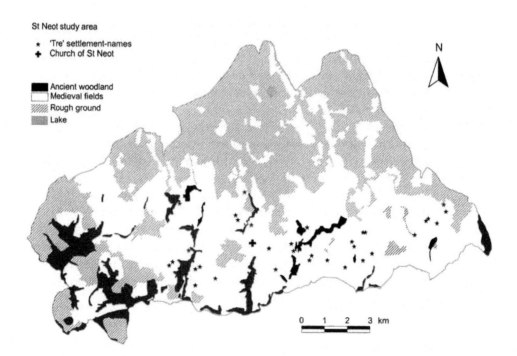

Figure 11.4 The church of St Neot and surrounding settlements with *tre* place-names first recorded before AD 1550

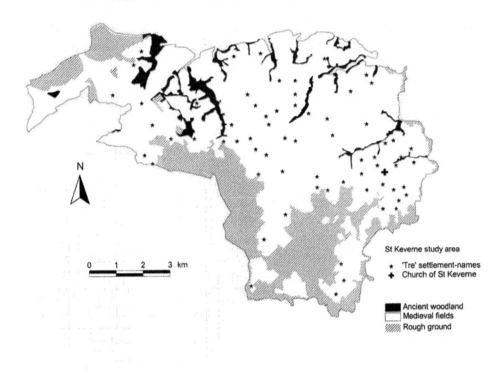

Figure 11.5 The church of St Keverne and surrounding settlements with *tre* place-names first recorded before AD 1550

However, this does not mean that the idea of the town should be dismissed as irrelevant to Cornwall's developing landscape. Carver has pointed out that the early middle ages are 'not a good period in which to employ the old-fashioned notion of "type-sites" to argue historical process from archaeological data' (Carver 2000); this was a time of considerable adaptation of existing models. Instead, Carver argues that various types of site were deployed by people with different ideological and political positions (Carver 1993; 2000). In these terms, ecclesiastical centres such as monasteries or bishops' sees represent distinctive political statements. As discussed above, Christianity was probably first introduced to Cornwall from the Roman-influenced world of Gaul and the Mediterranean. Since the fourth century at the latest Christianity had become closely interwoven with 'urban' life in the Roman world (Markus 1994). This association continued into the early middle ages, and the church took over the sites and locations of Roman towns not only in the Byzantine east (Bayliss 1999; Haldon 1999), but also in western Europe (Brogiolo 1999: 120–5; Gauthier 1999: 205). Recent studies have highlighted the importance of considering 'central places' like towns and monasteries in the context of surrounding territories or 'microregions' with which they normally had close relationships (e.g. Halsall 1996; Horden and Purcell 2000: 89–122). Just as Roman towns had functioned as central places for many economic and social activities, the monasteries and other churches which were in many cases their successors probably maintained a similar ideology of centre and associated territory. Such churches acted as centres not only through their control of spiritual power, but also by their control of temporal resources such as rural estates (e.g. Balzaretti 1996).

In Cornwall, there were no pre-existing Roman cities which could be adopted by an emergent elite eager to reinforce their claims on authority through such potent symbols. However, in the absence of ready-made towns it seems likely that the new churches themselves acted as comparable central places in the emerging medieval landscape. This may be shown by the concentration of settlements in their vicinity, and the general patterns of resources such as agricultural land, rough moorland and woodland. The former provided the settled core (with the church at its centre), with the other elements forming the (ideologically and physically) peripheral parts of the landscape.

In some cases, the surrounding settlements may represent the dwellings of members of the religious community. It is possible that the *domus* of Wrmonoc's ninth-century *Life of St Paul Aurelian* represent the dwellings of individual members of religious communities rather than separate monasteries (Olson 1989: 23). Later information such as the charter for St Buryan (S 450) and the Domesday Book entries for St Neot (Thorn and Thorn 1979; 4.28, 5.14.2) also hint that individual members of communities may have held particular farms from their churches (see also Pearce's discussion of the estates of Hartland: Pearce 1985). This raises the possibility that the ecclesiastical centre would not have had extensive living accommodation, but perhaps just churches or chapels where members of the community could congregate for meetings. There are precedents from the Mediterranean world and elsewhere for dispersed establishments (e.g. Binns 1998), and the physical form of the early ecclesiastical centres is a topic in need of urgent research.

Within the territories of the Cornish ecclesiastical centres, little is presently known of other possible holy places. The early hagiographical sources set incidents at caves, standing stones and paths; these may be commonplaces of the genre, but it seems likely that such sites were venerated (Olson 1989: 14–28). Firm evidence for continuity since pre-Christian times is lacking since little archaeological work has been undertaken on individual wells or other monuments. Although the earliest minor chapels known on the Cornish mainland date from the ninth century and later, some could incorporate sites with an earlier, 'pagan' significance (e.g. Constantine well chapel, St Merryn; Todd 1987: 293). The ability of pre-conversion ritual sites to be assimilated into the newly established territories of the Christian landscape is suggested by some of the early medieval cemeteries, particularly those showing signs of origins in the Roman-British period (e.g. Trevone (Padstow) and Penmaine (St Minver); Thomas 1971: 59). In Gaul, the acts of saints during their lives gave a kind of 'sanctity' after their deaths to the whole region associated with an ecclesiastical centre, not just the central church where their relics eventually came to rest (Pietri 1997). It seems likely that pre-existing ritual sites in Cornwall could have been incorporated into the Christian landscape by a similar power of ecclesiastical centres and their saints to reach out and 'convert' their territories.

The Christian Landscape before the Normans: the Ninth to Eleventh Centuries

Churches of the late Saxon period, AD c.900–1050

The later history of Cornwall's Christian landscape suggests that it continued to change and develop significantly in the centuries before the Norman conquest. The archaeological and historical sources suggest strongly that churches became increasingly plentiful. The evidence for early medieval church and chapel buildings comes from late Saxon sites such as Tintagel and perhaps St Gothian's (Nowakowski and Thomas 1992; Thomas 1964), and from a range of documentary evidence including Domesday Book and land charters. The documentary sources in particular suggest a large increase in the number of churches in the tenth and eleventh centuries. For example, a tenth-century list of 49 saints' names probably records the patrons of Cornish churches (Olson and Padel 1986). This rapid growth in the number of churches was also linked to changes in landholding and settlement pattern. The basic framework of the early Christian landscape was filled out and expanded both with increasing numbers of churches and holy sites, and with more settlements.

Settlement patterns before the Normans, AD c.900–1080

The settlement at Mawgan Porth is still the region's most completely excavated and best understood site of this period (Bruce-Mitford 1997). It comprised at least three houses set around small 'courtyards' and a cist-grave cemetery which was probably associated with the settlement. The site is located between two dense distributions of *tre* settlements in the areas around Padstow and Crantock which are broken by the St Breock Downs. Mawgan Porth's marginal location suggests it is a relatively late component in the pattern of settlement. Around 30 other sites have also been dated to this period on the basis of pottery similar to that from Mawgan Porth (Bruce-Mitford 1997). Perhaps the most notable example is Winnianton, site of the head manor of the hundred of Winnianton (also called Kerrier) in 1066, where large quantities of pottery have been recovered from the eroding cliff-section (Jope and Threlfall 1956; Thomas 1963).

Domesday Book provides around 350 pre-Conquest settlement names for Cornwall. Nevertheless, a distribution map of these sites is far from a representation of the full settlement pattern in 1086, since the majority of farmsteads and hamlets were not mentioned separately from their head manors. As noted above, many Cornish topographical place-names are likely to date from this period and charters demonstrate that some were in use as settlement names by the tenth century (e.g. Grugwith: *S* 832; Pennare: *S* 755). Some Domesday examples make

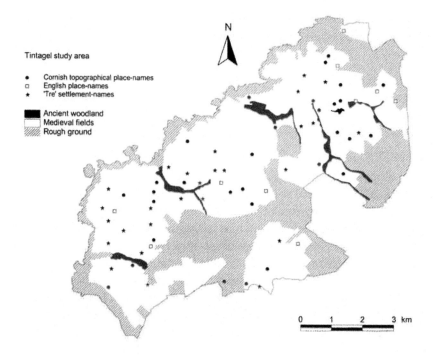

Figure 11.6 Distribution of settlements with English place-names, Cornish topographical place-names and *tre* place-names first recorded before AD 1550 in the Tintagel study area

reference to flora, locations or land-use which clearly suggest the colonization of new areas, proving that this process began in the early middle ages (e.g. Draynes (*dreyn* 'thorn bushes'), Penharget (*pen* 'top' + **hyr-yarth* 'long-ridge'), Halvana (*hyr* 'long' + *meneth* 'hill')). The name of Hammett (**havos* 'summer shieling') indicates that a once seasonal upland settlement had changed into a permanent centre by 1066 (Herring 1996). Padel has also noted that some English place-names were first given to settlements in Cornwall during the late Saxon period, in particular those with the generic *tun* (Padel 1999: 91). These are also commonly found in areas which are 'marginal' to the earlier settlement 'core' (see Fig. 11.6).

These sites were beginning the process of 'colonization' of heath, moorland and other 'marginal' areas which carried on into the later middle ages. Nevertheless, the pattern was still focused on the 'core' lowland areas where the earlier *tre* settlements had been located, and it was therefore a development based on the earlier medieval pattern (Preston-Jones and Rose 1986). The increase in the density and overall area of settlement is probably to be linked to contemporary changes in patterns of landholding. Evidence from charters and archaeology in many other parts of Britain suggest that there was a major increase in the number of small estates at this time, and that these changes were linked to alterations in settlement patterns (Richards 1999: 86–100; Faith 1997: 153–77). The overall increase in land grants in the tenth century is paralleled in the south-west, and examples such as the St Keverne group of charters probably reflect processes of estate fragmentation similar to those seen elsewhere (Hill 1981: 26; Hooke 1994b). These changes led to both greater numbers and a greater variety of landlords, and now included a substantial body of minor nobles holding their own estates.

The Christian landscape, AD c.900–1070

As in other parts of England, it was probably these developments in local lordship which provided the context for the multiplication of local churches in Cornwall (Faith 1997: 165–7). Around Tintagel in north Cornwall, for example, there is evidence of several small churches or chapels in addition to the mother church at Minster by 1066. These include Tintagel and St Juliot, and perhaps St Julitta's on Tintagel Island and St Piran's at Trethevey (Thomas 1993). The estates of the area were held by a variety of landowners, including distant churches such as St Piran's and St Petroc's at Bodmin, major secular lords and minor nobles (Thorn and Thorn 1979). The existence of these chapels in the late Saxon period seems to reflect the concern on the part of both lay and ecclesiastical landowners to provide private churches for their own estates.

This was also a period when the wider landscape was increasingly marked with Christian sites. Whenever sites such as wells, minor chapels and burial-grounds had their origins, from the late Saxon period onwards such places were increasingly elaborated with features that had a clear Christian significance.

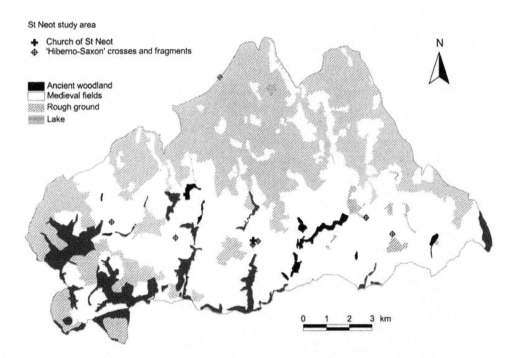

Figure 11.7 Early medieval crosses in the area around St Neot

In Cornwall the standing stone crosses with 'Hiberno-Saxon' and related ornament date mainly to this period. Some of these monuments, such as the Lanivet hogback, almost certainly marked individual burials (Langdon 1896: 412–4). As in northern England, such sculpture was probably produced for members of the local elite (Carver 1998: 24–6). However, the majority of Hiberno-Saxon monuments seem to have been related to churches and monasteries. Evidence from Cornwall and the south-west suggests that as in Wales many of these crosses probably marked the boundaries of territories associated with monastic sites (e.g. the crosses around St Neot: Turner in progress; Edwards 1999; Fig. 11.7, Pl. 11.1). It seems that the custom of marking ecclesiastical land in this way only developed from the late ninth and tenth centuries. This was the time when secular encroachment onto church lands was at its height, and the demarcation of church property may have become necessary partly as a symbolic defence against increasingly rapacious secular landlords (see Fleming 1985; Davies 1996).

Plate 11.1 The wheel-head cross at Cardinham, tenth to eleventh century

In the late pre-Conquest landscape, the provision of Christian monuments such as chapels and crosses may have provided a way to articulate competing claims to land and local authority.

Conclusion

There were significant changes in Cornish settlement patterns between the end of the Roman period and the eleventh century, and Christian institutions were at the heart of these developments. A pattern based on enclosed settlements (the rounds) was first replaced by one of open hamlets and farmsteads. Between the sixth and ninth centuries settlements with *tre* place-names were established in 'core' areas of agricultural land, within which monastic churches probably acted as the central places. In the ninth to eleventh centuries, ecclesiastical provision expanded and an increasing number of churches of lesser status was founded in association with minor estates. A large number of Cornwall's churches and *lann* sites may in fact owe their origin to this later phase. Many of the standing stone sculptures also belong to the ninth–eleventh centuries and served as boundary markers for the most important ecclesiastical centres which had continued to develop.

ACKNOWLEDGEMENTS

I am very grateful to Martin Carver for inviting me to contribute to this volume and for his valuable comments on an earlier draft. The Department of Archaeology at the University of York has generously funded the project on which this paper is based. My thanks are also due to the Cornwall Archaeological Unit and Oliver Padel for supplying and discussing data, to David Petts and Ann Preston-Jones for help with burials and sculpture in Cornwall, and to Peter Halls, Peter Herring and David Stocker for methodological advice. All the errors that remain are my own.

References

Alcock, S., 1993. Graecia Capta: *The Landscapes of Roman Greece* (Cambridge: Cambridge University Press).

Aston, M., 2000. *Monasteries in the Landscape* (Stroud: Tempus).

Balzaretti, R., 1996. 'Cities, *emporia* and monasteries: local economies in the Po valley, c.AD 700–875' in N. Christie and S. Loseby (eds), *Towns in Transition: Urban Evolution in Late Antiquity and the Early Middle Ages* (Aldershot: Ashgate), pp.213–34.

Bayliss, R., 1999. 'Usurping the urban image: the experience of ritual topography in late antique cities of the Near East' in P. Baker, C. Forcey, J. Jundi, R. Witcher (eds), *TRAC 98: Proceedings of the 8th Annual Theoretical Roman Archaeology Conference, Leicester 1998* (Oxford: Oxbow), pp. 59–71.

Bender, B., 1993. 'Introduction: landscape – meaning and action' in B. Bender (ed.), *Landscape: Politics and Perspectives* (Oxford: Berg), pp.1–17.

Biarne, J., 1997. 'L'espace du monachisme gaulois au temps de Grégoire de Tours' in N. Gauthier and H. Galinié (eds), *Grégoire de Tours et l'Espace Gaulois* (Tours: La Simarre), pp.115–138.

Biek, L., 1994. 'Tin ingots found at Praa Sands, Breage, 1974' *Cornish Archaeology* 33, pp.57–70.

Binns, J., 1998. 'The concept of sacred space in the monasteries of Byzantine Palestine' in T. Insoll (ed.), *Case Studies in World Religion: Proceedings of the Cambridge Conference* BAR Int Ser 755 (Oxford: Archaeopress), pp.26–32.

Blair, J., 1996 'Churches in the early English landscape: social and cultural contexts' in J. Blair and C. Pyrah (eds) *Church Archaeology: Research Directions for the Future* CBA Res Rep 104 (York: CBA), pp.6–18.

Britnell, W., 1990. 'Capel Maelog, Llandrindod Wells, Powys: Excavations 1984–87' *Medieval Archaeology* 34, pp.27–96.

Brogiolo, G., 1999. 'Ideas of the town in Italy during the transition from antiquity to the middle ages' in G. Brogiolo and B. Ward-Perkins (eds), *The Idea and Ideal of the Town between Late Antiquity and the Early Middle Ages* (Leiden: Brill), pp.99–126.

Brook, D., 1992 'The early church east and west of Offa's Dyke' in N. Edwards and A. Lane (eds), *The Early Church in Wales and the West* Oxbow Monograph 16 (Oxford: Oxbow), pp.77–89.

Bruce-Mitford, R., 1997. *Morgan Porth: a Settlement of the Late Saxon Period on the North Cornish Coast* (London: English Heritage).

Canner, A., 1982. *The Parish of Tintagel: Some Historical Notes* (Tintagel: Tintagel PCC).

Carver, M., 1989. 'Kingship and material culture in early Anglo-Saxon East Anglia', in S. Bassett (ed.), *The Origins of Anglo-Saxon Kingdoms* (Leicester: Leicester University Press), pp.141–58.

—— 1993. *Arguments in Stone: Archaeological Research and the European Town in the First Millennium* Oxbow Monograph 29 (Oxford: Oxbow).

—— 1998. 'Conversion and politics on the eastern seaboard of Britain: some archaeological indicators' in B. Crawford (ed.), *Conversion and Christianity in the North Sea World* (St Andrews: University of St Andrews).

—— 2000. 'Town and anti-town in first millennium Europe', in A. Buko and P. Urbanczyk (eds), *Archeologia w Teorii i w Praktyce* (Warsaw), pp.373–96.

CAU, 1998. 'Round-up for 1997–8' *Archaeology Alive 6: a Review of Work by the Cornwall Archaeological Unit 1997–98*, (Truro: Cornwall Archaeological Unit), pp.7–19.

Dark, K., 2000. *Britain and the End of the Roman Empire* (Stroud: Tempus).

Davies, J., 1998. 'The Book of Llandaff: a twelfth-century perspective' *Anglo-Norman Studies* 21, pp.31–46.

Davies, W., 1978. *An Early Welsh Microcosm: Studies of the Llandaff charters* (London: Royal Historical Society).

—— 1982. 'The Latin charter-tradition in Western Britain, Brittany and Ireland in the early medieval period' in D. Whitelock, R. McKitterick and D. Dumville (eds) *Ireland in Early Medieval Europe: Studies in Memory of Kathleen Hughes* (Cambridge: Cambridge University Press), pp.258–80.

—— 1996. 'Protected space in Britain and Ireland in the Middle Ages' in B. Crawford (ed.), *Scotland in Dark Age Europe* (St Andrews: University of St Andrews), pp.1–19.

Edwards, N., 1999. 'Viking-influenced sculpture in north Wales: its ornament and context' *Church Archaeology* 3, pp.5–16.

Faith, R., 1997. *The English Peasantry and the Growth of Lordship* (London: Leicester University Press).

Finberg, H., 1953 'Sherborne, Glastonbury and the expansion of Wessex' *Transactions of the Royal Historical Society* 5th ser 3, pp.101–24.

Fleming, R., 1985. 'Monastic lands and England's defence in the Viking Age' *English Historical Review* 395, pp.247–65.

Fletcher, R., 1997. *The Conversion of Europe: from Paganism to Christianity, 371–1386 AD* (London: Harper Collins).

Fox, A., 1995. 'Tin ingots from Bigbury bay, South Devon' *Devon Archaeological Society Proceedings* 53, pp.11–23.

Gauthier, N., 1999. 'La topographie chrétienne entre idéologie et pragmatisme' in G. Brogiolo and B. Ward-Perkins (eds), *The Idea and Ideal of the Town between Late Antiquity and the Early Middle Ages* (Leiden: Brill), pp.195–209.

Given, M., A. Knapp, N. Meyer, T. Gregory, V. Kassianidou, J. Noller, L. Wells, N. Urwin, H. Wright, 1999. 'The Sydney Cyprus Survey Project: an interdisciplinary investigation of long-term change in the north central Troodos, Cyprus' *Journal of Field Archaeology* 26, pp.19–39.

Graham, B., 1998. 'The town and the monastery: early medieval urbanization in Ireland, AD 800–1150' in T Slater and G Rosser (eds), *The Church in the Medieval Town* (Aldershot: Ashgate), pp.131–54.

Haldon, J., 1999. 'The idea of the town in the Byzantine Empire' in G. Brogiolo and B. Ward-Perkins (eds), *The Idea and Ideal of the Town between Late Antiquity and the Early Middle Ages* (Leiden: Brill), pp.1–23.

Halsall, G., 1996. 'Towns, societies and ideas: the not-so-strange case of late Roman and early Merovingian Metz' in N. Christie and S. Loseby (eds), *Towns in Transition: Urban Evolution in Late Antiquity and the Early Middle Ages* (Aldershot: Ashgate), pp.235–61.

Handley, M., 1998. 'Early medieval inscriptions of western Britain: function and sociology' in J. Hill and M. Swan (eds), *The Community, the Family and the Saint: Patterns of Power in Early Medieval Europe* (Turnhout: Brepols), pp.339–61.

Harry, R. and C. Morris, 1997. 'Excavations on the lower terrace, Site C, Tintagel Island 1990–1994' *Antiquaries Journal* 77, pp.1–144.

Herring, P., 1993. *An Archaeological Evaluation of St Michael's Mount: a Report to the National Trust* (Truro: Cornwall Archaeological Unit).

—— 1996. 'Transhumance in medieval Cornwall' in H. Fox (ed.), *Seasonal Settlement* (Leicester: University of Leicester Vaughan Paper 39), pp.35–44.

—— 1998. *Cornwall's Historic Landscape: Presenting a Method of Historic Landscape Character Assessment* (Truro: Cornwall Archaeological Unit).

—— 1999a. 'Farming and transhumance at the turn of the second millennium (Part 1)' *Cornwall Association of Local Historians. Journal* Spring 1999, pp.19–25.

—— 1999b. 'Farming and transhumance at the turn of the second millennium (Part 2)' *Cornwall Association of Local Historians. Journal* Summer 1999, pp.3–8.

Higham, N., 1997. *The Convert Kings: Power and Religious Affiliation in Early Anglo-Saxon England* (Manchester: Manchester University Press).

Hill, D., 1981. *An Atlas of Anglo-Saxon England* (Toronto: University of Toronto Press).

Hooke, D., 1994a. *Pre-Conquest Charter-Bounds of Devon and Cornwall* (Woodbridge: Boydell).

—— 1994b. 'The administrative and settlement framework of early medieval Wessex' in M. Aston and C. Lewis (eds), *The Medieval Landscape of Wessex* (Oxford: Oxbow Monograph 46), pp.83–95.

Horden, P. and N. Purcell, 2000. *The Corrupting Sea. A Study of Mediterranean History* (Oxford: Blackwell).

Horner, W., 2001. 'Secrets of the sands' *Devon Archaeological Society Newsletter* 79, pp.1, 8–9.

Hutchinson, G., 1979. 'The bar-lug pottery of Cornwall' *Cornish Archaeology* 18, pp.81–103.

James, H., 1992. 'Early medieval cemeteries in Wales' in N. Edwards and A. Lane (eds), *The Early Church in Wales and the West* Oxbow Monograph 16 (Oxford: Oxbow), pp.90–103.

Johns, C. and P. Herring, 1996. *St Keverne Historic Landscape Assessment: an Archaeological and Historical Survey* (Truro: Cornwall Archaeological Unit).

Johnson, N. and P. Rose, 1994. *Bodmin Moor: an Archaeological Survey. Vol. 1: The Human Landscape to c.1800* (London: English Heritage).

Jope, E. and R. Threlfall, 1956. 'A late dark-ages site at Gunwalloe' *Proceedings of the West Cornwall Field Club* 1.4, pp.136–40.

Langdon, A., 1896. *Old Cornish Crosses* (London and Truro).

Lapidge, M. and M. Herren, 1979. *Aldhelm – the Prose Works* (Cambridge: Brewer).

Markus, R., 1994. 'How on earth could places become holy? Origins of the Christian idea of holy places' *Journal of Early Christian Studies* 2, pp.257–71.

—— 1997. *Gregory the Great and his World* (Cambridge: Cambridge University Press).

McAvoy, F., 1980. 'The excavation of a multi-period site at Carngoon Bank, Lizard, Cornwall, 1979' *Cornish Archaeology* 19, pp.31–62.

McNab, A. and G. Lambrick, 1999. 'Conclusions and recommendations' in G. Fairclough, G. Lambrick and A. McNab (eds), *Yesterday's World, Tomorrow's Landscape: the English Heritage Landscape Project 1992–94* (London: English Heritage), pp.54–9.

Miles, H. and T. Miles, 1973. 'Excavations at Trethurgy, St Austell: interim report' *Cornish Archaeology* 12, pp.25–30.

Monk, M., 1998. 'Early medieval secular and ecclesiastical settlement in Munster' in M. Monk and J. Sheehan (eds), *Early Medieval Munster: Archaeology, History and Society* (Cork: Cork University Press), pp.33–52.

Moreland, J., 2001. *Archaeology and Text* (London: Duckworth).

Morris, C., C. Batey, K. Brady, R. Harry, P. Johnson and C. Thomas, 1999. 'Recent work at Tintagel' *Medieval Archaeology* 43, pp.206–215.

Nowakowski, J. and C. Thomas, 1992. *Grave News from Tintagel: an Account of a Second Season of Archaeological Investigation at Tintagel Churchyard* (Truro: Cornwall Archaeological Unit).

Okasha. E., 1993. *Corpus of Early Christian Inscribed Stones of South-West Britain* (London: Leicester University Press).

Olson, L., 1982. 'Crantock, Cornwall as an early monastic site' in S. Pearce (ed.), *The Early Church in Western Britain and Ireland* BAR Brit Ser 102 (Oxford: BAR), pp.177–86.

—— 1989. *Early Monasteries in Cornwall* (Woodbridge: Boydell).

Olson, L. and O. Padel, 1986. 'A tenth century list of Cornish parochial saints' *Cambridge Medieval Celtic Studies* 12, pp.33–71.

Padel, O., 1985. *Cornish Place-name Elements* English Place-name Society Vol.56–7 (Nottingham: EPNS).

—— 1988. *A Popular Dictionary of Cornish Place-Name Elements* (Penzance: Alison Hodge).

—— 1999. 'Place-names' in R. Kain and W. Ravenhill (eds), *Historical Atlas of South-West England* (Exeter: University of Exeter Press), pp.88–94.

Pearce, S., 1978. *The Kingdom of Dumnonia: Studies in the History and Tradition of South-West Britain, AD 350–1150* (Padstow: Lodenek Press).

—— 1982. 'Church and society in South Devon, AD 300–700' *Devon Archaeological Society Proceedings* 40, pp.1–18.

—— 1985. 'The early church in the landscape: the evidence from north Devon' *Antiquaries Journal* 142, pp.255–75.

Penhallurick, R., 1986. *Tin in Antiquity* (London: Institute of Metals).

Petts, D., 2002. 'Cemeteries and boundaries in western Britain' in S. Lucy and A. Reynolds (eds), *Burial in Early Medieval England and Wales*, Society for Medieval Archaeology Monograph Series 17 (London: Society for Medieval Archaeology), pp.24–46.

Pietri, L., 1997. 'Grégoire de Tours et la géographie du sacré' in N. Gauthier and H. Galinié (eds), *Grégoire de Tours et l'Espace Gaulois* (Tours: La Simarre), pp.111–14.

Preston-Jones, A., 1984. 'The excavation of a long-cist cemetery at Carnanton, St Mawgan, 1943' *Cornish Archaeology* 23, pp.157–78.

—— 1992. 'Decoding Cornish churchyards' in N. Edwards and A. Lane (eds), *The Early Church in Wales and the West* (Oxford: Oxbow Monograph 16), pp.104–24.

Preston-Jones, A. and P. Rose, 1986. 'Medieval Cornwall' *Cornish Archaeology* 25, pp.135–85.

Quinnell, H., 1986. 'Cornwall during the Iron Age and Roman period' *Cornish Archaeology* 25, pp.111–34.

—— 1993. 'A sense of identity: distinctive Cornish stone artefacts in the Roman and post-Roman periods' *Cornish Archaeology* 32, pp.29–46.

—— 1995. 'The pottery', pp.120–28, in J. Ratcliffe, 'Duckpool, Morwenstow: a Romano-British and early medieval industrial site and harbour' *Cornish Archaeology* 34, pp.81–172.

Ralegh Radford, C., 1935. 'Tintagel: the castle and Celtic monastery, interim report' *Antiquaries Journal* 15, pp.401–19.

—— 1962. 'The Celtic monastery in Britain' *Archaeologia Cambrensis* 111, pp.1–24.

Richards, J., 1999. 'Cottam: an Anglo-Scandinavian settlement on the Yorkshire Wolds' *Archaeological Journal* 156, pp.1–111.

Rose, P. and A. Preston-Jones, 1995. 'Changes in the Cornish countryside AD 400–1100' in D.Hooke and S. Burnell (eds), *Landscape and Settlement in Britain AD 400–1066* (Exeter: University of Exeter Press), pp.51–67.

Saunders, C, 1972. 'The excavations at Grambla, Wendron, 1972: interim report' *Cornish Archaeology* 11, pp.50–2.

Sawyer, P., 1968 *Anglo-Saxon Charters: an Annotated List and Bibliography* (London: Royal Historical Society).

Somerscales, M., 1957. 'A dark age site on Phillack Towans near Hayle' *Proceedings of the West Cornwall Field Club* 2(1), pp.8–14.

Thomas, A. and Holbrook, N., 1994. 'Llandough' *Archaeology in Wales* 34, pp.66–8.

Thomas, C., 1956. 'Evidence for post-Roman occupation of Chun Castle, Cornwall' *Antiquaries Journal* 41, pp.89–92.

—— 1958. *Gwithian: Ten Years' Work* (Camborne: West Cornwall Field Club).

—— 1963. 'Unpublished material from Cornish museums: 2. Gunwalloe pottery, Helston Museum' *Cornish Archaeology* 2, pp.60–4.

—— 1964. *Gwithian: Notes on the Church, Parish and St Gothian's Chapel* (Gwithian).

—— 1965. 'The hillfort at St Dennis' *Cornish Archaeology* 4, pp. 31–5.

—— 1968a. 'Grass-marked pottery in Cornwall' in Coles and Simpson (eds) *Studies in Ancient Europe* (Leicester), pp.311–32.

—— 1968b. 'Merther Uny, Wendron' *Cornish Archaeology* 6, pp.78–9.

—— 1971. *The Early Christian Archaeology of North Britain* (Oxford: Oxford University Press).

—— 1993. *Tintagel: Arthur and Archaeology* (London: Batsford/English Heritage).

—— 1994. *And Shall These Mute Stones Speak? Post-Roman Inscriptions in Western Britain* (Cardiff: University of Wales Press).

—— 1998. *Christian Celts: Messages and Images* (Stroud: Tempus).

Thorpe, C., 1997. 'Ceramics', pp.74–82 in R. Harry and C. Morris, 'Excavations on the Lower Terrace, Site C, Tintagel Island 1990–94' *Antiquaries Journal* 77, pp.1–143.

Thorn, C. and F. Thorn (eds), 1979. *Domesday Book 10: Cornwall* (Chichester: Phillimore).

Todd, M., 1987. *The South West to AD 1000* (London: Longman).

Valante, M., 1998. 'Reassessing the Irish 'monastic town'' *Irish Historical Studies* 31 (121), pp.1–18.

van Dommelen, P., 1999. 'Exploring everyday places and cosmologies' in W. Ashmore and B. Knapp (eds), *Archaeologies of Landscape: Contemporary Perspectives* (Oxford: Blackwell), pp.277–85.

West, S., 1985. 'West Stow: the Anglo-Saxon Village' *East Anglian Archaeology* 24.

White Marshall, J., and C. Walsh, 1998. 'Illaunloughan, Co, Kerry: an island hermitage' in M. Monk and J. Sheehan (eds), *Early Medieval Munster: Archaeology, History and Society* (Cork: Cork University Press), pp.102–11.

Winterbottom, M., (ed. and trans.), 1978. *Gildas: The Ruin of Britain and Other Documents* (Chichester: Phillimore).

12

Early Medieval Parish Formation in Dumfries and Galloway

CHRISTOPHER CROWE

My focus for this brief survey of the development of Church institutions in south-west Scotland is the region now known as Dumfries and Galloway, and the period under consideration is the early eighth to the tenth centuries AD. I have taken wide liberties with the lack of documentary evidence and the almost complete lack of archaeological evidence for the physical presence of an organised church in this region during this period. I turn instead to the place-names and the scant surface remains in the large number of deserted and partly abandoned churchyards throughout the area. In order to make sense of these scarce resources I also call on the work of Daphne Brooke in her discussions of the mediaeval arrangements for the parishes in both Galloway and Carrick (Brooke 1987, 1991a, 1991b), Geoffrey Barrow in tracing the significance of the place-names in 'eccles' in south-east Scotland and the existence of the small 'scir' in the administrative arrangements of the northern territories of the Anglian kingdoms (Barrow 1973, 1980) and Steve Driscoll for the archaeological survey of the power centres of both local chiefdoms and thanages in Scotland (Driscoll 1991, 1998).

I take some previous assumptions with a generous pinch of salt, especially those concerning the antiquity of church dedications, circular churchyards and land boundaries. The indications of an early foundation suggested by dedications to early saints of both the Celtic and Roman churches have proved to be of little use. An example is the list of dedications to St Kentigern in Dumfries and in present-day Cumbria. Many of the churches in Annandale have been associated with this saint in the medieval period and some of these appear in the list of lands thought to have belonged to the see of Glasgow. The list of names of the land holdings which the see of Glasgow thought ought to be rendered back to them as of ancient right in the twelfth century is, almost certainly, a bogus claim (*REG*, 4–7). This claim is reinforced in the twelfth-century biography of St Kentigern by the monk Joscelyn of Furness, a biography drawn from at least two earlier narratives, which might seem to add a legitimacy to the fabulous foundation of the see of Glasgow (*Vitae*, 32–119). The dedications are a more reliable source for the situation during the twelfth century, rather than the sixth. There has also been, for many years, an assumption that the circular or curvilinear shape of churchyards in the western parts of the British Isles reflects an early Celtic practice (Brooke 1988). But this practice seems neither particularly Celtic nor early in Dumfries and Galloway. I have many examples from this region where the foundation of a church and establishment of a churchyard may be traced as a circle on the map but firmly shown to originate in the twelfth or thirteenth centuries (Crowe 1984, 1998). I have also had to omit the study of early land boundaries. There seems little point in speculating about the exact location of territories in the possession of tribal leaders or their client nobles in the early centuries of the kingdom of Rheged or of the conquering kingdom of Bernicia. It is doubtful whether the land boundaries of the later parish and barony were static throughout the centuries between the seventh century and the twelfth century. However, it is possible to find other ways of connecting medieval parishes, and drawing from them the possibility of a pre-existing land-unit with a particular ecclesiastical organisation. This will be attempted here using sculpture, earthworks and the names of the places which are central to these proposed early territories.

The background for the study is provided by the documentary record. Our principal authority is Bede who provides the narrative, although he was an unashamed apologist for the Roman church and the Anglian supremacy in the northern kingdoms. He tells us that Pecthelm, a cleric with an impeccable Anglo-Saxon background, was appointed bishop at Whithorn in AD 731. The conversion of the people of Galloway, together with the 'southern Picts' had, however, already been achieved some years before by St Ninian of Whithorn (*HE* V.18). Pechthelm was thus an Anglian bishop in the territory of a mainly British popu-lation (Cramp 1995), possibly including an Irish immigrant group of which Peter Hill has discerned traces at Whithorn (Hill 1997, 15–16). It has been supposed that the area was part of the British kingdom of Rheged in previous centuries and that the appointment of an Anglian bishop followed the annexing of the territory by an Anglian ruling class.

It is clear that from the early eighth century onwards into the mediaeval period the institutions of the ruling class and the emerging church in Dumfries and Galloway were similar to Anglian institutions elsewhere. Local rulers formed an administrative class under the supervision of a king's court at a remote location. Each local ruler supervised a territory, often only a few miles wide, and some-times consisting of a single estate. Within these territories, taxes and obligations were owed the ruler in exchange for his protection and patronage (Foster 1998, 3). The ruling class during the eighth century could be drawn from both Anglian and native backgrounds as the place-names imply (see below). The imposition of a bishop in the territories of the nobility also carried the assumption that he controlled the central church and a surrounding ring of dependent churches to carry out baptism, bury the dead and perform such other offices as were required by the Christian community.

I now want to look at the possible arrangements in three areas within Dumfries and Galloway which seem to derive from the presence or absence of bishops and

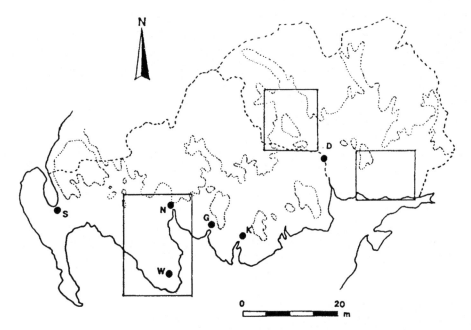

Figure 12.1 Dumfries and Galloway: present settlements are identified. Land over 150 m is defined by dotted lines. S – Stranraer, W – Whithorn, N – Newton Stewart, G – Gatehouse of Fleet, K – Kirkcudbright, D – Dumfries. Three areas discussed in this study are indicated

possibly abbots during these early years of Anglian overlordship (Fig. 12.1). The three areas are, first, the part of Galloway now called the Machars, second, the central basin of the lower Nith Valley and, third, the coastal plain to the west of Annan. In each of these areas there seems to have been a strong Christian presence from the seventh or early eighth century.

In the Machars (Fig. 12.2) the territory includes Whithorn, where we have had the benefit of much excavation at the site of the early monastic town (Hill 1997). The excavation of the southern quarter of the hill on which the present parish church stands has confirmed an early monastic presence on the site with a possible shrine and burials outside an inner precinct, but within a larger enclosed space or outer precinct (Hill 1997, 67). After about two centuries of development there was a significant change in the style of building which happened around the end of the seventh century, in the years just before the induction of Pecthelm as bishop (Hill 1997,134–182). This change signalled Anglian practices in both building and burial styles and probably followed an Anglian occupation of the western part of Galloway close to the end of the seventh century. From about 730 to 845 there followed years of continued development of an Anglian minster church with attendant clergy and a large lay population. A list of the bishops for this period from records compiled at York shows that all the incumbents had Anglian names. Records fail after 832 but the archaeological record shows that even after a widespread fire in the early ninth century the buildings were restored and improved for a further 80 years. It was during this period that there appeared a characteristic form of standing cross, with origins possibly at Whithorn and a distribution in the Machars as far to the north as Luce and Penninghame (Pl. 12.1; Fig. 12.2). This Whithorn School has been defined on art-historical grounds by Derek Craig in 1991 and, although dating is fraught with problems, his placing of these monuments in the tenth century seems to be uncontroversial (Craig 1991, 45–62). Collingwood compared some of the stylistic motifs with sculpture from Bakewell and Darley Dale in Derbyshire (Craig 1997, 52). Some Hiberno-Norse influence may be detected in the occurrence of the debased interlace which has become known as 'stopped plait' and is found on some crosses of the type identified from Whithorn (Bailey 1980, 205–6). The advent of the Whithorn School is also associated with changes in the administration and contacts of the settlement at Whithorn. Although the sculpture itself reflects a closer Anglian tradition, the cultural assemblage reflects an increased trade or exchange with the wider Hiberno-Norse trading world (Hill 1997, 54–55).

Plate 12.1 A 'Whithorn school' cross-head from Whithorn (tenth century) (National Museum of Scotland (Photo C. Crowe)

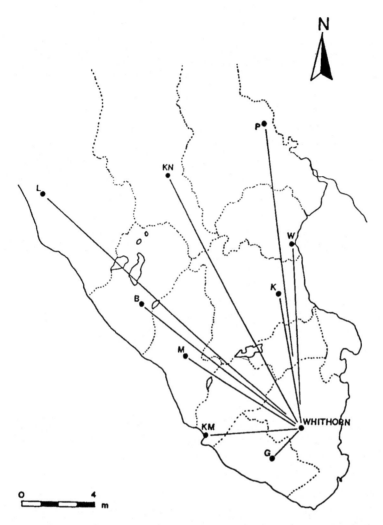

Figure 12.2 The Machars: Pre-Reformation parish boundaries and central churches with 'Whithorn school' sculptures. W – Whithorn, G – Glasserton, KM – Kirkmaiden, M – Mochrum, B – Barhobble, L – Glenluce, KN – Kirkcowan, P – Penninghame, W – Wigtown, K – Kirkinner

The distribution of the tenth-century stone crosses suggests a link with the sites of later medieval parish churches (Fig. 12.2). From this we may postulate that Whithorn was the *matrix ecclesia* for these churches even at an early date in the late ninth or early tenth century. Were there also early church buildings at these locations? Daphne Brooke (pers. comm.) has suggested that the crosses represent preaching and ministering stations where priests from Whithorn might conduct religious 'surgeries' on a regular basis, and there is little archaeological evidence for standing buildings in the ninth century at these sites. However, the earliest phases of the recently excavated church at Barhobble show Anglian activity, buildings in stone, a cashel wall to enclose the site and burials dating to the approximate period (*c.*AD 950–1125). This points to a church rather than a preaching station, even if there is no trace of a structure which might be classed as a church (Cormack 1995, 48–9). Barhobble may have been a failed parish centre, which was swallowed by Mochrum in the thirteenth century (Crowe 1998, 64–5). This would be then an example of a pre-ninth-century parish church with Anglian, Whithorn-derived, sculpture associated with it.

In addition to the medieval parish church sites shown in Fig. 12.2, other Whithorn School stones have been recorded at St Ninians Cave, Craiglemine, Knock and Monreith House. In fact, all the stones may be assigned to a church centre as the point of their original location. St Ninians Cave was a retreat used from the early Anglian period by monks or priests from Whithorn. Craiglemine is a mile from Glasserton and the location of a country house, and it is probable that a previous owner took it from the church as it lay in ruins during the late eighteenth and early ninteenth cenuries. Knock is the nearest settlement to Kirkmaiden and, almost certainly, someone saved the cross from the ruined church and re-erected it in the village. The cross at Monreith House repeats the story of rescue from the same ruined church at Kirkmaiden.

There are two other crosses, one from West Crosherie and one from Mains of Penninghame, both probably originating at the ruined church at Penninghame. It might be argued that if crosses are such moveable monuments then the crosses might all have been brought in to the parish church centres during the centuries after they were placed in the landscape as boundary markers or wayside crosses. But if we can agree that these monuments were erected as grave markers, then it is more likely that they were erected in a burial ground with a church.

It is emerging from research at different locations all over Scotland and the Borders that there was a significant change in the pattern and distribution of centres of power during this period. Such changes involved the shift of a regional power centre from isolated hilltops down into the good agricultural lands in the valleys. This shift resulted in a different type of settlement, from a fortified crag as at Mote of Mark or Trusty's Hill, to a timber hall with associated buildings. Such a hall might have been excavated (but not recognised as such) at Kirkconnell, Dumfries (Laing and Clough 1973, 128–39). Another may have been the central place of a local chieftain at Castlehill, Dalry in Ayrshire where excavation revealed a hall building beneath the motte (Laing 1975, 38).

This change in the physical location and settlement type of the centres of power happened during the period c.AD 750–950. Associated with this change was an apparent devolution of power to local rulers acting for the kings of the region. Whereas the king and his retinue used to tour the kingdom to collect and consume the rents which derived from each district within his jurisdiction, as well as appearing to his people and dispensing justice, now there is evidence that the local centres performed the functions of government and rendered the fruits of taxation in the form of service (Driscoll 1998, 39). This function would increasingly come to look like a knight's service in later centuries.

Local districts were to be known as 'scir' in northern Britain, sometimes called the 'small shire' in recent research (Faith 1997, 9), and as 'thanage' in areas further north in Pictland and the lands of Dalriada. These local districts were often no more than a few miles across and approximated in size to the later medieval parishes. At the heart of each district was a church or religious monument and each district could claim the benefits of the church's literate and standardised administration to work alongside the lord of the estate. This close link between the lord of the estate and the Church must have led to a widespread setting up of proprietary churches in the farming landscape.

The place-names in some cases indicate British origin for an estate, for example Mochrum, an an older name for Kirkinner recorded as Carnesmoel in 1319 (a name with the prefix 'caer'). Longcastle has early forms of the name which suggest a name in British 'llan', a name form more familiar in Wales, and seems to confirm a relationship with the church. The name Luce is an ancient river name which has so far not been properly ascribed to a language group (Maxwell 1930, 204). It may also be noted that there appear to be significant earthworks in many of the churchyards and the surrounding fields which suggest the presence of earlier church buildings or enclosures beneath the surface of many of the mediaeval church sites (Crowe 1998,159; Fig. 12.3).

The second of the districts where we may be able to perceive a matrix or web of churches in a relatively self-contained landscape lies in Nithsdale centred on Penpont (Fig. 12.4). A mile to the north of Penpont is a farm which bears the name Eccles. It is this name which might alert us to the possibility that the place is the central place of a 'scir' from the period of the first Anglian administration in Dumfries in the early eighth century. Sculptural fragments of Anglian-derived crosses have been found at each of the parish churches on this map. At Penpont there are three recorded, at Glencairn, two and at Closeburn, two. As with the Whithorn School we are faced with the problem of stylistic dating, but we may

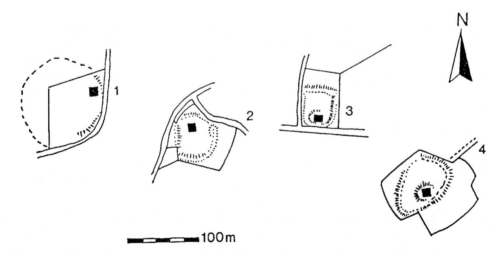

Figure 12.3 Parish church sites with remains of previous settlements. Present buildings in use are shown as solid blocks. 1. Wigtown, 2. Mochrum, 3. Sorbie, 4, Glasserton

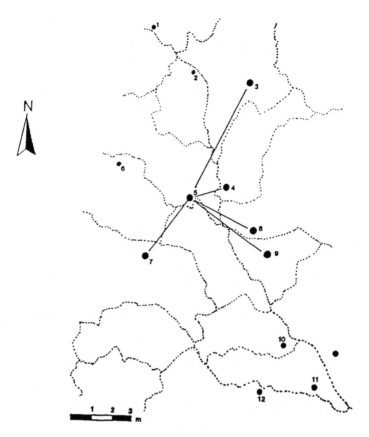

Figure 12.4 Nithsdale: Pre-Reformation parish boundaries with their churches. Heavy dots show pre-conquest Anglian sculpture. 3, Durrisdeer, 4, Moreton, 5. Penpont, 7, Glencairn, 8. Dalgarnock, 9. Closeburn

place the whole assemblage broadly within the ninth–tenth centuries. One of the pieces at Penpont is a mile away to the east of the village, perhaps in its original position beside a ford across the Nith (Pl 12.2). In such a location, it might have been intended as a milecross or boundary marker for a monastic site at Penpont – as have been traced in a ring around the monastic site at Whitby (Crowe 1996; and see O Carragáin, Chapter 9 in this volume). Alternatively, this cross has been moved by an enthusiastic landowner during the eighteenth century to ornament a part of his parkland, in which case it probably came from Penpont.

The mediaeval parish churches in the sample area are Glencairn, Closeburn, Durisdeer, Moreton (a cross base now in a tree at the ruined church site of Kirkbog) and Dalgarnock. It may be significant that the location of Penpont, on a rocky outcrop overlooking the Scar Water, might indicate an early power centre. The shape of the glebe and original kirkyard may also indicate an early monastic precinct which formed the centre for this web of churches in Nithsdale. A survey of earthwork features show that here also there are the remains of previous settlements or church buildings in several of the churchyards. Glencairn

Plate 12.2 Anglian cross at Penpont
(Photo C. Crowe)

churchyard seems to have had at least two recuts in the hillside to make the enclosure before the church was moved in the eighteenth century (Crowe 1998, 143). At Penpont an earlier church platform and earlier churchyard areas are visible.

The third of the districts under discussion here has Hoddom at the centre (Fig. 12.5). Hoddom has long been known as an early (sixth century or earlier) monastic foundation and was associated with the name of St Kentigern in the mediaeval period (Lowe 1991). It was certainly an important Anglian monastery and the centre for a bishop's see in the eighth and ninth centuries, although there is little documentation from such an early date. Hoddom has had the benefit of a recent excavation to confirm its date and importance as an Anglian centre (Lowe 1991). This set of relationships between the central church and its surrounding proto-parishes is more difficult to sustain because there is not the neat correlation between sculptures and a production centre. However, one of the results of the recent exploration has been to show that it survived as a bishops' administrative centre up to the eleventh century. The medieval parish church is now an earthwork ruin in the graveyard at the heart of the old monastic precinct. Outlying findspots of Anglian-derived sculpture have been identified at Luce, Gardyne (Applegarth), Ruthwell and Cummertrees (CBA 1993, 3). Here the range of dates seems to have been wider: from the eighth century to the tenth or eleventh and a

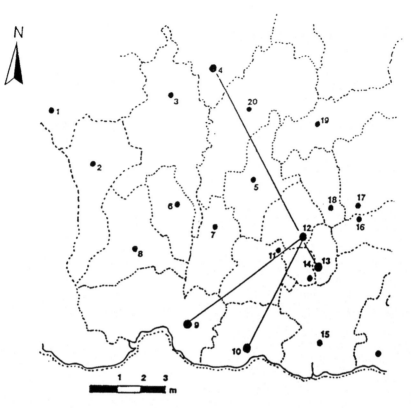

Figure 12.5 Annandale: The Anglian minster at Hoddom with its dependent churches are indicated by heavy dots where Anglian sculpture has been identified. 4. Gardyne, 9. Ruthwell, 10. Cummertrees, 12. Hoddom, 13. Luce

disproportionate number of all local examples came from Hoddom. East of Hoddom lies Ecclefechan, which contains the place-name element 'eccles', possibly indicating a scir. As at Whithorn there is also a strong undercurrent of native British name-forms in the list of surrounding mediaeval parishes. These are Cummertrees (the 'tref' of the Cymry), Trailtrow, another name with the prefix 'tref', Pennersax (the spur of the Saxons). The last name surely indicates that the Anglo-Saxon immigrants were a noteworthy addition to the population. Only Tundergarth has traces of a former churchyard and church within its current precinct.

    In all these three areas I believe we can point to a parish system in the making. The date for the formation of these central churches with surrounding estate churches is at some time between the late eighth century and the tenth. Similar patterns have been observed elsewhere in Scotland, such as on the Tarbat peninsula (Carver 1998) and in the estate centres with name forms in 'eccles' which have been explored in the region around St Andrews (Barrow 1973, 7–68; Proudfoot 1998, 68).

Not every territory in Dumfries and Galloway need have developed in Anglian mode as a network of churches linked to a central church. In the coastal plain to the west of the River Fleet, early sculptural fragments and crosses are located in the landscape but they do not seem to have been associated with church sites at all. The mediaeval parishes are Anwoth, Kirkmabreck and Kells, which seem to be later impositions, and there are also churches and burial grounds at Kirkbride 2 miles west of Anwoth, High Auchenlarie and Kirkdale. Far from there having been a central estate for each parish there seem to have been several,and therefore I am led to believe that another administrative system was in operation. There are several factors which may have led to this separate development. One is the relative poverty of the narrow coastal plain which has concentrated settlements in small pockets of viable agricultural land. The uplands which form the bulk of the available territory were, and still are, devoted to upland grazing of cattle and now sheep. A form of transhumance is reflected in the place-names: High and Low Auchenlarie, High and Low Ardwall. The small estate centres with British names may have actually controlled wide areas of the upland massif and they straddle the only viable route from east to west along the coast. They also have access to the sea which gave each estate an income which is different from the largely arable and stock rearing in the lands of the Machars and Nithsdale. Few of the medieval estate centres within the parishes have a church in association. The estates are nearly all named as a 'caer', a British word for a fort or castle: Cardoness, Kirklaugh (caer cleuch) Cairny (?), Carsluith, Cassencarie (Carskeel).

What is reflected here may be an older settlement pattern which was served by the pre-Anglian British church in a dispersed ecclesiastical system which remains elusive. The area of Dumfries and Galloway underwent at least two conversions, and it seems to have been the second of these, owed to Anglian inter-vention in the eighth century, which has most strongly marked the landscape. The discernible pattern is that of a set of pre-existing estates, each under the secular control of British or Anglian lords, which are subservient in ecclesiastical matters to a designated monastic site (minster), such as Whithorn. A major re-investment of the ninth or tenth centuries, including the Whithorn school of monuments, made the system more visible, at the same time as opening the country more widely to Irish Sea traffic.

References

Primary sources

HE: *Historia Ecclesiastica Gentis Anglorum*, in *Baedae Opera Historica*, C. Plummer (ed.) Oxford 1896.
Vitae: *Lives of St Ninian and St Kentigern*. A.P. Forbes (ed.) (1874).
REG: *Registrum Episcopatum Glaswegiensis*. (Bannatyne and Maitland Club, 1875).

Secondary sources

Bailey, R.N. 1980 *Viking Age Sculpture in Northern England*. (London).

Barrow, G.W.S. 1973 *The Kingdom of the Scots*. (Edinburgh).

Barrow, G.W.S. 1980 *The Anglo-Norman Era in Scottish History*. (Oxford).

Brooke, D. 1987 'The Deanery of Desnes Cro and the Church at Edingham', *Transactions of the Dumfries and Galloway Natural History and Antiquarian Society*. 3rd ser. LVIII: 48–65.

—— 1991a 'Gall-Gaidhil and Galloway' in R.D. Oram and G. Stell (eds) *Galloway, Land and Lordship*, (Edinburgh), 97–116.

—— 1991b 'The Northumbrian Settlements in Galloway and Carrick', *Proceedings of the Society of Antiquaries for Scotland*, 121, 295–327.

Brooke, D. 1988 'The Early Church East and West of Offa's Dyke', in N. Edwards and A. Lane (eds) *Early Mediaeval Settlements in Wales AD 400–1100*. (Cardiff), 77–89.

CBA Newsletter *British Archaeological News*, December 1993.

Carver, M. 1998 'Conversion and Politics on the Eastern Seaboard of Britain', in B.E. Crawford (ed.) *Conversion and Christianity in the North Sea World*. (St Andrews), 1–21.

Cormack W.F. 1995 'Barhobble, Mochrum', *T.D.G.N.H.A.S.*, 3rd ser. LXX.

Craig, D. 1991 'Pre-Norman Sculpture in Galloway', in R. Oram and G. Stell (eds) *Galloway Land and Lordship*. (Edinburgh), 45–62.

Cramp, R. 1995 *The Whithorn Lecture* [no pagination]. (Whithorn).

Crowe, C.J. 1984 'An Excavation at Brydekirk, Annan', *T.D.G.N.H.A.S.* 3rd ser. LIX: .33–40.

—— 1996 Scheduling documentation for MPP (English Heritage) *Hawsker Cross, The Wishing Chair and Robbed Howe*.

—— 1998 *The Development of Church Institutions in Dumfries and Galloway* (unpublished thesis, Manchester Metropolitan University).

Driscoll, S. 1991 'The Archaeology of State Formation in Scotland', in W.S. Hanson and E.A. Slater (eds) *Scottish Archaeology, New Perceptions*. (Aberdeen), 61–111.

—— 1998 'Formalising the Mechanisms of State Power', in S. Foster, A. Macinnes and R. Macinnes (eds) *Scottish Power Centres*. (Glasgow), 32–58.

Faith, R. 1997 *The English Peasantry and the Growth of Lordship*. (Leicester).

Foster, S. (ed.) 1998 *The St Andrews Sarcophagus*. (Dublin).

Hill, P. 1997 *Whithorn and St Ninian*. (Stroud).

Laing, L. 1975 *The Archaeology of Late Celtic Britain*. (London).

Laing L. and T. Clough, 1973 'Excavations at Kirkconnell, Dumfries, 1968' *T.D.G.N.H.A.S.* 3rd ser. III, 128–39.

Lowe, C.E. 1991 'New Light on the Anglian Minster at Hoddom', *T.D.G.N.H.A.S.* 3rd ser. LXVI, 11–35.

Maxwell, Sir H. 1930 *The place-names of Galloway*. (Glasgow).

Proudfoot, E. 1998 'The Hallow Hill and the Origins of Christianity in Eastern Scotland', in B.E. Crawford (ed.) *Conversion and Christianity in the North Sea World* (St Andrews), 57–74.

13

Christian and Pagan Practice during the Conversion of Viking Age Orkney and Shetland

JAMES H. BARRETT

Introduction

This paper asks when Christian practice was adopted in Viking Age Scotland. It focuses on the Northern Isles, Orkney and Shetland, which ultimately emerged as the medieval earldom of Orkney (Crawford 1987). The chronological range is from the initial phase of Norse settlement in the mid ninth century (Graham-Campbell 1998: 106; Barrett in press) to the establishment of a formal bishopric around AD 1048 (Morris 1996: 188).

It is useful to begin with three general observations. First, the available evidence is meagre from a pan-European perspective. Richard Fletcher's (1997: 375) 562 page volume, *The Conversion of Europe*, relegates it to a single pithy paragraph. Nevertheless, the region is important, both in a particularistic sense and as a possible route for early transmission of Christian ideology to Norway and elsewhere in the Norse North Atlantic (e.g. Myhre 1993; Solli 1996; Vésteinsson 1999: 18). It is worth extracting what one reasonably can, accepting that the result must presently serve as a heuristic tool.

Second, any attempt to define and recognise 'Christianisation' must confront fundamental epistemological issues. Was it the adoption of a *mentalité* (e.g. Lönnroth 1987: 27), a political ideology (Earle 1997: 143; Carver 1998: 11) or both? Did either exist as discrete facets of experience and action in early historic Britain? Can patterns in material culture provide unambiguous evidence of Christian practice as *mentalité* or ideology (Abrams 1998: 115–6; Carver 1998: 13–6)? These questions are probably unanswerable in the abstract, but must be confronted in concrete terms within the specific context of Viking Age Scotland.

Third, the study of early Christianity in northern Scotland has a complex historiography far too lengthy to review here.[1] Much of the relevant work has

---

[1] A selection of relevant works of the last hundred years might include the following: Allen and Anderson 1993[1903]; Clouston 1918a; 1918b; Scott 1926; Radford 1962a; 1962b; Wainwright 1962;

been summarised by Christopher Morris (1996; see also Smith 2001: 9–14), who identifies two broad models. The first follows medieval Icelandic tradition regarding the forced conversion of Earl Sigurd Hlodvisson of Orkney by Olaf Tryggvason c.AD 995 and Adam of Bremen's account that a bishopric was subsequently established at Birsay, by Earl Thorfinn Sigurdarson, around AD 1048. Despite its attractive simplicity, this traditional account has long been challenged by a second, alternative, view that Christianity was also practised earlier in Norse Scotland (e.g. Wainwright 1962: 158; Stevenson 1981; Lamb 1995). Ideas then differ regarding whether this should be explained as continuity of Pictish institutions (e.g. Lamb 1995; 1998) or as rapid conversion of some Norse colonists (e.g. Morris and Emery 1986; Morris 1996: 192). Surprisingly little, however, has been made of the implication that Christian and pagan practice may have been contemporary.

Given this background, the present study will begin by addressing whether or not Christian practice predated the traditional conversion of c.AD 995. Five main categories of evidence will be considered – sculpture, place-names (including church dedications), chapels with cemeteries, a ninth-century hagiography (the *Life of Saint Findan*) and pagan graves – with attention given to the interpretative complexity of each. In concluding, the paper will then address the relationship between Christian and Pagan practice.

Sculpture and Place-names

Stone sculpture, including crosses and other unambiguous Christian monuments, is one of the most important sources for the study of conversion in Northern Europe. Class II symbol stones provide the primary record of early Christian influence in 'Pictish' Scotland (Carver 1998; Driscoll 2000) and rune stones play a similar role in Scandinavia (e.g. Sawyer 1991; 2000). However, this category of evidence is weak for Viking Age Scotland.

Christian rune stones are rare and none are incompatible with the traditional – late tenth century – conversion date. Three from western Scotland, at Iona, Kilbar (Barra) and Inchmarnock (off Bute), are all likely to be products of the late tenth or eleventh centuries (Fisher 2001: 17, 107, 130). A runic cross slab from Thurso, Caithness, (within the medieval sphere of the earldom of Orkney) may belong to the twelfth century (Batey 1993: 157). In the Northern Isles themselves, the extraordinary corpus of runic inscriptions from Maes Howe includes Christian references, but is also of twelfth century origin (Barnes 1994). A handful

Thomas 1971; 1973; Lamb 1974; Crawford 1975; MacDonald 1977; Lamb 1980; Stevenson 1981; Thomson 1983 and references therein; Cant 1984; Smyth 1984; Hunter 1986; Morris and Emery 1986; Thomson 1986; Morris 1990; MacDonald 1992; Myhre 1993; Morris 1995; Lamb 1995; Morris 1996; Solli 1996; Dumville 1997; Foster 1997; Crawford 1998 and references therein; Lowe 1998; Morris and Brady 1998; Thomas 1998; Barrett *et al.* 2000a; 2000b; Harry 2000; Buteux *et al.* 2001; Smith 2001.

of other runic memorials have been found in Orkney and Shetland. Examples include fragments built into the twelfth-century church at the Brough of Birsay, Mainland Orkney, and from Cunningsburgh, Shetland, but all are late or undated (Barnes 1992; idem pers. comm.; Owen and McKinnell 1989; Graham-Campbell and Batey 1998: 42; see also Bäcklund 2001: 38–9).

The paucity of early rune stones is one symptom of a more significant anomaly. The Northern Isles did not produce a syncretic sculptural tradition, incorporating elements of early Christian and (at least nominally) pagan iconography as occurred in the Scandinavian colonies of the Isle of Man (e.g. Margeson 1983; Wilson 1983) and England (Bailey 1980: 101–42; Lang 1991; Richards 2000: 162). The search for Viking Age Christian sculpture has thus focused on a few monuments of entirely local style which might be dateable, on art historical and linguistic grounds, into the ninth or tenth centuries. The number of pieces is not large: Stevenson's (1981) key paper noted seven – although it is conceivable that a systematic treatment of the corpus might produce more candidates. As Brian Smith (2001: 9–14) has recently demonstrated, however, the entire argument essentially hinges on the traditional interpretation of an ogham inscription on one monument – the Bressay stone from an island of the same name in Shetland. It may incorporate a Norse loan word (*dattrr* for daughter), which would imply the survival of Pictish sculpture into a phase of Norse contact. Given the imprecision of art historical dating (Fisher 2001: 12; see Smith 2001: 12–3) – and uncertainty regarding when Scandinavian settlement began in the region (see Barrett in press) – the remaining fragments of sculpture fade to insignificance without this crucial argument. It is thus of considerable significance that Michael Barnes (1998 in Smith 2001: 13) has recently suggested that the word could in fact be Pictish. Unfortunately, however, ogham inscriptions in this language are so difficult to interpret (see Forsyth 1997: 33; Barnes 1999) that it is unlikely the debate will ever be resolved, leaving the related corpus of alleged Viking Age Christian sculpture in chronological limbo.

A third category of sculptural evidence may be slightly more informative. Several medieval chapel sites have produced earlier Christian monuments, such as cross slabs, fragments of corner post shrines and (in one case) a Class II symbol stone indicative of eighth–ninth-century Pictish ecclesiastical activity. Excavated examples include St Ninian's Island, Shetland (Thomas 1973; 1998), St. Boniface, Papa Westray, Orkney (Lowe 1998: 6–7), St Nicholas' chapel, Papa Stronsay, Orkney (Buteux *et al.* 2001) and the Brough of Birsay (Curle 1982: 97) (Fig. 13.1). These carvings raise the possibility of continuous Christian practice, but a definitive phase of Viking Age ecclesiastical use has not yet been identified on any of the relevant sites.

Two categories of place-names have been interpreted as evidence for early Viking Age Christianity in the Northern Isles: those incorporating *papar*, Norse for priest (MacDonald 1977; Crawford 1987: 164–6; Lamb 1995), and those where a church-site is dedicated to a saint with alleged Pictish associations (Lamb 1995; Morris 1995: 7; Lamb 1998). These names are notoriously difficult to date in the

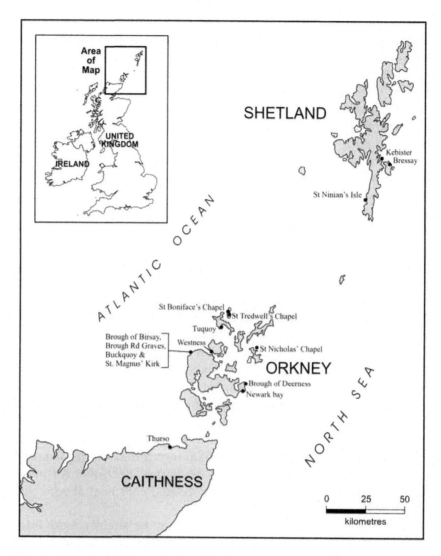

Figure 13.1 Location of main sites mentioned in the text

absence of an early inventory comparable to the Domesday Book. They are largely derived from high medieval sources, such as the late twelfth or early thirteenth century *Historia Norvegiae*, and modern Ordnance survey records (e.g. MacDonald 1977: 25–7; see Fellows-Jensen 1984: 148). Nevertheless, the *papar* names are typically viewed as early Viking Age on the assumption that they were coined in reference to native Christian communities during an initial phase of Norse colonisation (MacDonald 1977; Lamb 1995; Graham-Campbell and Batey 1998: 39). This interpretation is open to criticism on the basis of inadequate dating evidence. In the present context, however, it is more important to observe that the names need not indicate early Viking Age Christian practice even if they could be attributed to the ninth–tenth centuries. The association of papar names with early Christian communities is ultimately based on medieval Icelandic tradition, but *Landnámabók* famously interprets them as the footprints of Irish monks who had *fled* the scene on Norse settlement (Benediktsson 1968: 31–2). In light of this example, Raymond Lamb's (1995; 1998) suggestion that they indicate Viking Age survival of Pictish ecclesiastical centres cannot be sustained.

Church sites with dedications which may have Pictish (or at least pre-Viking Age) associations are even more problematic. First, Raymond Lamb (1995; 1998) has argued that a number of Orcadian chapel sites dedicated to St Peter are survivals from an eighth-century Pictish mission to Orkney. This argument has also been dissected by Brian Smith's (2001: 17–8) recent study introduced above. He simply observes that most of the sites have not been dated: the hypothesis is thus entirely conjecture. Second, the Pictish origin of St. Boniface, associated with the above-mentioned pre-Viking Age and medieval site on Papa Westray, Orkney, may be a medieval invention (MacDonald 1992: 30, 47). Third, neither this site nor the remaining examples – such as St. Tredwell's (Triduana's) chapel, also on Papa Westray (Lamb 1995: 19; Morris 1995: 7), and what may be a dedication to St Peter or St Colm on the Brough of Birsay (Lamb 1983: 41), exhibit clear Viking Age ecclesiastical phases (Morris 1993: 286–7; Lowe 1998). Although some of these sites have yielded Pictish Christian sculpture, Smith's (2001: 14) argument that they were reoccupied (and presumably rededicated) in the Middle Ages is entirely feasible.

The categories of evidence discussed thus far were those dismissed by Richard Fletcher (1997: 375), who dubbed them 'the slippery evidence of church dedications and the ambiguous evidence of certain memorial grave-stones'. One can understand his position. The sculpture cannot be closely dated and the churches with putative Pictish associations lack known Viking Age phases. If this were the only evidence for early Viking Age Christianity one might be tempted to accept the traditional conversion date of *c*.AD 995.

Chapels and Christian Burial Practice

The evidence from church architecture and burial patterns is also problematic, but it is here that one finds the first convincing indication of Viking Age Christian practice which may predate the end of the tenth century. Given the clear association of medieval chapels and Pictish sculpture at several sites it has been assumed that the critical evidence for Viking Age Christianity is likely to underlie later church architecture. This reasonable proposition has influenced excavation campaigns at a series of sites, most of which have already been mentioned (e.g. Small *et al.* 1973; Morris and Emery 1986; Morris 1993: 286–7; Barber 1996; Lowe 1998; Harry 2000; Buteux *et al.* 2001). Of these, however, it is only at St. Magnus' Kirk, Birsay, (Barber 1996) and the Brough of Deerness (Morris and Emery 1986), both in Orkney, that tenth-century phases have been proposed. Two other possible tenth-century chapels, at Kebister, Shetland (Owen and Lowe 1999: 290–3), and Newark Bay, Orkney (Brothwell 1977; Brothwell *et al.* 1986; Barrett *et al.* 2000b), do not underlie later churches and were discovered by chance (Fig. 1).

Before considering this evidence it is necessary to address the epistemological difficulties associated with identifying 'Christian' buildings and graves (Abrams 1998: 115–6; Carver 1998: 13–6). For present purposes, it is assumed that the co-occurrence of supine east-west oriented burials, a rectangular east-west oriented structure (lacking domestic or industrial features such as a hearth and sometimes including a surviving altar at the east end) and the absence of grave-goods from all or virtually all graves is sufficient to imply the existence of a church and associated cemetery. Chancels and other distinctive architectural elements are not characteristic of the earliest phase of church building in the Northern Isles (e.g. Morris and Emery 1986; Owen and Lowe 1999: 291; Buteux *et al.* 2001: 1).

The identification of individual 'pagan' and 'Christian' graves is more problematic (see Carver 1998: 13–6 and references therein). East-west orientation is of little value as it occurred in pre-Christian Scandinavia (Roesdahl 1987: 3). Grave-goods probably do indicate non-Christian belief given that they are rarely found in churchyards (see Geake 1997: 133–4 for an English parallel). The only examples from northern Scotland are an axe from St. Ola's churchyard, Whiteness, Shetland (Shetelig 1945: 4), a jet-like bracelet from grave 69/104A or 69/104B at Newark Bay in Orkney and an antler comb approximately 40 cm from the skull of burial 70/28 also at Newark (Barrett *et al.* 2000b: 538).[2] Flexed inhumations are probably also pagan given their virtual absence from churchyards in Scotland (only one occurs in the cemetery of about 250 otherwise supine burials at Newark) and their association with grave-goods (see Barrett *et al.* 2000a: Table 1). The *absence* of grave-goods, however, could relate to status in addition to worldview (Nielsen 1991: 251) and is thus an ambiguous indicator of Christian practice unless a burial is also associated with a church. In sum, single burials with grave-goods are probably indicative of pagan practice, but graves which lack them cannot automatically be recognised as Christian. Conversely, the co-occurrence of east-west oriented burials and non-domestic buildings can probably be regarded as a Christian pattern despite the fact that neither is convincing on its own.

The four putative tenth-century chapels from the Northern Isles are all east-west oriented rectangular structures which lack domestic features and are associated with burials (Morris and Emery 1986; Barber 1996; Owen and Lowe 1999: 290–3; Barrett *et al.* 2000b; see Fig. 13.2). In one instance, the Brough of Deerness, the chapel was also distinguished by an altar at its eastern end (Morris and Emery 1986: 314, 323). In all cases there seems little reason to doubt an ecclesiastical function. It is more difficult, however, to date the sites to before *c.*AD 995.

The earliest structure under the post-medieval parish church of St. Magnus' Kirk, Birsay, is the most problematic in this regard. The church is located on the mainland side of Birsay Bay, near the Brough of Birsay discussed above. Lamb

---

[2] The latter of these is not securely stratified and could have derived from an earlier souterrain passage over which the grave was placed.

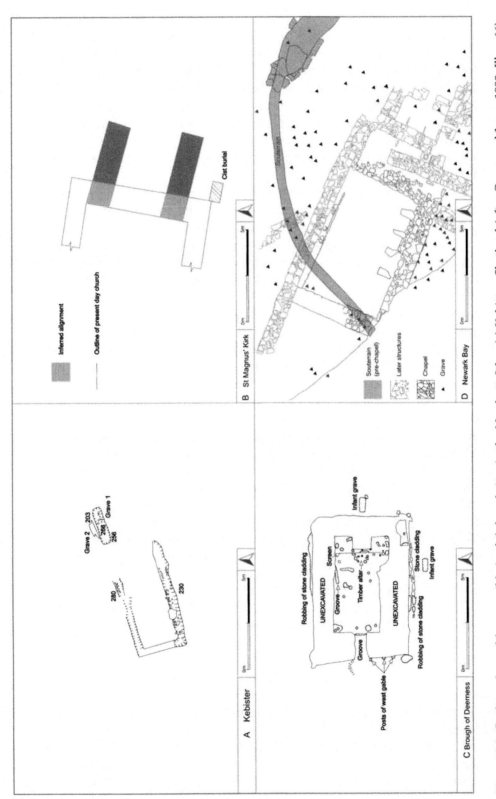

Figure 13.2 Outline plans of four possible 'early' chapel sites in the Northern Isles: (a) Kebister, Shetland (after Owen and Lowe 1999, Illus. 66); (b) St. Magnus' Kirk, Birsay (after Barber 1996, Illus. 7, Illus. 15); (c) Brough of Deerness timber phase (after Morris and Emery 1986, Illus. 8); (d) Newark Bay (Brothwell 2002)

(1983) suggests that it, rather than the Brough, may mark the location of Earl Thorfinn's eleventh-century minster, but there is insufficient evidence to choose between the alternatives (see Morris 1993: 286–7). Excavation has revealed the foundations of a twelfth-century church built in the Romanesque tradition (phase 4) and an earlier church of uncertain, but probable eleventh-century, date (Barber 1996: 28). More importantly, however, two parallel wall lines belonging to the earliest structural episode (phase 2) have been identified as an oratory of the ninth or tenth centuries based on a radiocarbon date on human bone from an adjacent burial (Barber 1996: 27–8; see Table 13.1).

Unfortunately, the latter interpretation is undermined in three ways. First, the relevant burial does not stratigraphically overlie the structure (Barber 1996: Figure 7). It cuts the same deposit as the wall lines, but could pre- or postdate the building. Second, when calibrated at two sigma using the standard atmospheric curve (Stuiver et al. 1998) the result includes the eleventh century in its error range (AD 776–1022, 1120±60 bp, GU-1631). Third, radiocarbon dates on human bone from the Northern Isles must be adjusted to account for marine reservoir effects using stable carbon isotope data. This procedure is necessary given the dietary importance of fish in the region (Barrett et al. 1999), which will bias radiocarbon results by making them appear older than terrestrial samples of the same age (Barrett et al. 2000b). In the case of the St. Magnus' Kirk date, this essential correction is not possible due to the lack of appropriate stable isotope data.

Phase 3, block 118, at Kebister has also been published as a possible tenth-century chapel (Owen and Lowe 1999: 290). The church itself is only represented by truncated, east-west oriented, foundation trenches (probably from a wooden structure), but it was associated with two graves on the same alignment (Owen and Lowe 1999: 84–6). Its identification as an ecclesiastical site is also supported by the discovery of a cross-incised stone and a fragment of green porphyry as residual objects in later phases (Owen and Lowe 1999: 290–3).

The site is dated by radiocarbon assays of coffin wood (Scots pine) from the best preserved burial, thus avoiding the pitfalls associated with marine reservoir effects (Table 13.1). The combined assay for grave one (using Stuiver et al. 1998), based on two consistent dates (1060±50 bp, GU-2332 and 1100±50 bp, GU-2623), is AD 890–1021 at the 2 sigma level. A third assay (on the same plank which yielded sample GU-2332) produced a calibrated date of AD 1163–1470 at 2 sigma (640±120 bp, GU-2334). This last sample can be rejected on the basis of low carbon yields (Owen and Lowe 1999: 140–1), but the site nevertheless falls short of demonstrating Christian practice prior to the traditional conversion date. Even when the anomalous assay is ignored the radiocarbon range for grave one extends into the eleventh century and the wood may have been old (perhaps driftwood) prior to its use.

The best evidence for earlier Viking Age churches derives from two sites in the east Mainland of Orkney: the Brough of Deerness (Morris and Emery 1986) and Newark Bay (Brothwell 1977: 182; see Barrett et al. 2000b). Both sites are dated by mid-tenth century coins (Brothwell 1977: 182; pers. comm.; Stevenson 1986: 339–40) and radiocarbon dates on associated burials (Barrett et al. 2000b).

Two superimposed chapel phases were identified at Deerness by Morris and Emery (1986). The later is of stone construction; the earlier of timber with stone cladding. Both phases were associated with a small number of graves and had altars at their eastern end (Morris and Emery 1986: 315, 322, 359). Morris (1996: 191) has suggested that they served as private chapels rather than foci of monastic activity as once thought. They stand on a small coastal stack surrounded by about 30 unexcavated rectilinear structures which are likely to be broadly contemporary (Morris and Emery 1986: 311, 365–6). It is easy to envision this high density settlement in an easily defensible location as the stronghold of a chief or earl and an associated retinue.

A worn coin of Eadgar (reign 959–975) found under the floor of the stone chapel provides a *terminus post quem* for it and a *terminus ante quem* for the earlier timber phase (Stevenson 1986: 339; Morris 1996: 192). Two radiocarbon dates exist for a burial labelled BS (the only skeleton preserved sufficiently for analysis), which stratigraphically post-dates the stone phase (Morris and Emery 1986: 350; MF3: E10; Barrett *et al.* 2000b: 541): AD 996–1260 (920±65 bp, GU-1574) and AD 1017–1211 (940±40 bp, TO-6697), both calibrated at 2 sigma. The 2 sigma estimate after marine reservoir correction is AD 1030–1249 (see Barrett *et al.* 2000b; Table 13.1).

In sum, the upstanding (stone) phase of the Brough of Deerness was built between 959 and the thirteenth century, but probably in the earlier end of this range. This date is entirely consistent with the c.AD 995 conversion tradition or with mid eleventh century developments under Earl Thorfinn. The same cannot be said, however, for the earlier wooden chapel stratigraphically below the Eadgar coin. It could belong to the eleventh century if the coin was old on deposition, but it seems likely to precede Olaf Tryggvason's alleged mission and is almost certain to pre-date Thorfinn Sigurdarson's foundation of a bishopric. Morris (1990: 13; 1996: 192) cautions that the timber chapel could conceivably represent a much earlier Pictish structure, but argued on architectural grounds that it is most consistent with a Norse milieu. He hesitated in assigning it definitively to the Viking Age based on a radiocarbon date of mammal bone (from the same phase as the Eadgar coin) which included pre-Viking Age centuries in its error range, AD 651–1015 (1220±90 bp, GU-1558, calibrated at 2 sigma; no marine reservoir correction is possible for this sample) (Morris and Emery 1986: 357; Morris 1996: 192). However, the fact that the two buildings were virtually identical in size and alignment (Morris and Emery 1986: 314) is more easily explained if the stone church immediately succeeded its timber predecessor. The construction date of the wooden phase remains uncertain, but it may well have been in use by the mid tenth century.

Newark Bay includes a sequence of Iron Age, medieval and post-medieval structural deposits (Brothwell 1977; pers. comm.; Brothwell *et al.* 1986: 56; Barrett *et al.* 2000b). The complexity of the site, and the fact that it has not been published in detail, has led to scepticism regarding the existence of a chapel phase (e.g. Lowe 2001: 66). Under the late- and post-medieval structures, however, was a

Table 13.1 Radiocarbon dates associated with putative tenth-century chapels from the Northern Isles. Marine reservoir correction (mixed atmospheric/marine calibration) has been applied where appropriate and possible. Atmospheric calibrations of the dates on bone for which this has not been possible are likely to appear too old. All calibrations are based on Stuiver *et al.* (1998).

Burial	Material	Lab Number	Date bp	Atmospheric calibration (2 σ range)
St Magnus' Kirk, Birsay, C2	Human Bone	GU-1631	1120±60	776–1022
Deerness (Between timber and stone phases)	Mammal Bone	GU-1558	1220±90	651–1015
Deerness BS (Stone phase)	Human Bone	TO-6697	940±40	1017–1211
Deerness BS (Stone phase)	Human Bone	GU-1574	920±65	996–1260
Kebister Grave 1	Scots Pine	GU-2623	1100±50	782–1022
Kebister Grave 1	Scots Pine	GU-2332	1060±50	889–1145
Kebister Grave 1	Scots Pine	GU-2332/2623		890–1021
Kebister Grave 1	Scots Pine	GU-2334	640±120	1163–1470
Newark Bay 69/33	Human Bone	TO-7176	1460±40	537–659
Newark Bay 69/11	Human Bone	TO-7180	1380±30	617–687
Newark Bay 71/3	Human Bone	TO-7193	1200±40	691–960
Newark Bay 69/x	Human Bone	TO-6942	1180±30	776–960
Newark Bay 68/16A	Human Bone	TO-7174	1190±40	693–964
Newark Bay 71/5	Human Bone	TO-6933	1170±50	694–985
Newark Bay 69/104B	Human Bone	TO-7189	1130±50	777–1017
Newark Bay 69/36	Human Bone	TO-7182	1090±40	886–1020
Newark Bay 69/99	Human Bone	TO-7187	1060±40	893–1026
Newark Bay 69/9	Human Bone	TO-7179	1030±30	978–1031
Newark Bay 69/4	Human Bone	TO-7177	1010±30	983–1149
Newark Bay 70/1	Human Bone	TO-7192	1010±60	896–1162
Newark Bay 12	Human Bone	TO-6943	960±50	988–1210
Newark Bay 69/34	Human Bone	TO-7181	930±40	1019–1214
Newark Bay 68/12	Human Bone	TO-7173	930±40	1019–1214
Newark Bay CC4	Human Bone	TO-6941	920±40	1021–1217
Newark Bay 69/69	Human Bone	TO-7184	910±40	1022–1219
Newark Bay 69/8	Human Bone	TO-7178	830±30	1161–1276
Newark Bay 70/6	Human Bone	TO-6937	700±40	1261–1388
Newark Bay 1968/2	Human Bone	TO-6940	550±40	1303–1438

[1]Mixed atmospheric and marine calibration is not possible for bone dates where appropriate $\delta^{13}C$ values are not available (see Barrett *et al.* 2000b), it is not necessary for the wood dates from Kebister.

δ¹³C (±0.2‰)	Estimated % marine carbon in collagen	Mixed atmospheric/ marine calibration (2 σ range)[1]	References
			Barber 1996
			Morris and Emery 1986
−19.4	14	130–1249	Barrett *et al.* 2000b
			Morris and Emery 1986
			Owen and Lowe 1999
			Owen and Lowe 1999
			Owen and Lowe 1999
			Owen and Lowe 1999
−19.8	10	551–671	Barrett *et al.* 2000b
−20.7	0	616–685	Barrett *et al.* 2000b
−19.3	15	778–990	Barrett *et al.* 2000b
−20.2	5	778–974	Barrett *et al.* 2000b
−20.5	2	720–972	Barrett *et al.* 2000b
−19.7	10	776–1012	Barrett *et al.* 2000b
−17.4	37	970–1163	Barrett *et al.* 2000b
−19.3	15	901–1038	Barrett *et al.* 2000b
−18.5	25	995–1166	Barrett *et al.* 2000b
−16.3	50	1129–1270	Barrett *et al.* 2000b
−19.3	16	1017–1165	Barrett *et al.* 2000b
−19.1	17	987–1221	Barrett *et al.* 2000b
−16.8	45	1160–1298	Barrett *et al.* 2000b
−21.8	0	1017–1213	Barrett *et al.* 2000b
−17.6	35	1168–1291	Barrett *et al.* 2000b
−16.7	46	1217–1306	Barrett *et al.* 2000b
−20.8	0	1023–1219	Barrett *et al.* 2000b
−19.4	14	1213–1289	Barrett *et al.* 2000b
−18.8	21	1291–1414	Barrett *et al.* 2000b
−19.7	10	1330–1449	Barrett *et al.* 2000b

rectangular stone building oriented approximately east-west with internal dimensions of 4.2 m × 9.5 m and walls about 0.85 m thick.[3] A possible chancel of later construction extended to the east, but was very disturbed. The building overlaid a souterrain of Iron Age date and, most importantly, was surrounded by approximately 250 burials (Brothwell 1977: 182; Brothwell *et al.* 1986: 56). The latter respected the structure, with the exception of two graves inserted into its floor. They also reflected its approximate east-west orientation and all but one were supine. Although full excavation details are not yet available, on gross stratigraphic grounds it would appear that most of the burials were contemporary with use of the structure (Brothwell pers. comm.).

Two coins beneath the flagstone floor of this building were minted under Eadred (reign 946–955) and Anlaf Sihtricsson (York, reign 941–944 and 948–952) (Smyth 1978; Stevenson 1986: 340). They provide a mid-tenth century *terminus post quem* for the partially excavated structure. The twenty radiocarbon dates on burials from Newark Bay – for which marine reservoir correction has been attempted – are also informative (Barrett *et al.* 2000b; Table 13.1). First, two seventh-century assays suggest that it was originally a Pictish burial place. The next earliest burials are consistent with continued or renewed use of the site by the mid tenth century at the latest. Samples TO-7193, TO-6942 and TO-7174 are particularly suggestive. The mixed marine and atmospheric calibrations for these samples are AD 778–990, AD 778–974 and AD 720–972 at the 2 sigma level: all predate the traditional conversion of Orkney. The site then continued in use into the fourteenth or fifteenth centuries.

The Life of Saint Findan

Although the Brough of Deerness and Newark Bay suggest that Christianity was practised in Orkney in the tenth century, the best evidence regarding the ninth century derives from a continental hagiography, the *Life of Saint Findan*. It was probably written in the late ninth century and purports to describe the escape of an Irishman (who was captured by Vikings) to an Irish speaking Bishop in Orkney (Christiansen 1962; Omand 1986). If historical (see Smith 2001: 18 for a sceptical view), the events must have occurred around AD 850 (Thompson 1986: 279). This account has often been interpreted as evidence for continuity of Pictish institutions (e.g. Lamb 1995: 23; Lowe 1998: 8), but the same source explicitly refers to Orkney as lying close (or next) to the land of the Picts (Christiansen 1962: 158; Thomson 1986: 280).[4] It may thus be more appropriate to view this bishop as a product of the Hiberno-Norse world, perhaps an emerging Gall-Ghaidheil community in fact if not yet in name (see Dumville 1997: 26–28; Clancy forthcoming).

---

[3] The walls of this structure remain *in situ*, but are partly obscured by overlying masonry from later phases and by backfill.

[4] The critical passage reads: 'His ita gestis, ad quasdam venere insulas iuxta Pictorum gentem, quas Orcades vocant' (Christiansen 1962:150).

Pagan Graves

Although Christian burials cannot be identified unless associated with a church, the date at which burial with grave-goods ceased in Viking Age Scotland remains relevant to the question of conversion. Approximately 130 'pagan' graves of Scandinavian style are known from northern and western Scotland (Graham-Campbell and Batey 1998: 47). On the basis of the typological evidence, Graham-Campbell and Batey (1998: 154) have argued that 'the period from about the mid-ninth to the mid-tenth century would appear to include the great majority, if not all, of the pagan Norse graves known from Scotland.' Three graves containing coins may thus mark both the beginning and the end of pagan practice. The two earliest, from King's Cross Point, Arran, and Kiloran Bay, Colonsay, both included stycas of Archbishop Wigmund of York dating between AD 837 and 854 (Graham-Campbell and Batey 1998: 152). The latest, from Buckquoy, Birsay, Orkney, included a lightly worn coin of Eadmund dating between AD 940 and 946 (Ritchie 1977: 190). Although less precise, radiocarbon assays of human and animal bone from the pagan graves of Scotland are broadly consistent with this range (Sellevold 1999; Barrett *et al.* 2000a: Table 1). The cessation of burial with grave-goods does not constitute positive evidence for Christian practice, but it is clearly compatible with this possibility.

Discussion

Despite the limitations of the available evidence, there is clearly some indication that Christian practice in the Northern Isles pre-dated the traditional conversion of *c.*AD 995. Chapels may have been erected at Newark Bay and the Brough of Deerness in the middle decades of the tenth century – broadly concurrent with the cessation of burial with grave-goods. Depending on the historicity of the *Life of Saint Findan*, it may also be necessary to envision Christian practice in the ninth century. If the latter possibility is accepted, however, one must reconcile it with evidence for explicit pagan practice: the approximately 130 known burials with grave-goods – from the mid ninth to mid tenth centuries (Graham-Campbell and Batey 1998: 47). Barrett *et al.* (2000a: 9–15) have sketched the outline of two alternative interpretations which follow from these observations: syncretism during a period of conversion or the existence of distinct Christian and Pagan factions.

The first scenario might be observable as diminishing numbers of grave-goods during the emergence of a Christian worldview or *mentalité* (see Crawford 1975: 16; Lönnroth 1987: 27). Clothed burials, with dress accessories but no true grave offerings, continued into the 'Christian' period in Scandinavia (Roesdahl 1987: 3). Scottish parallels might include four Viking Age burials on the mainland shore of Birsay Bay: Buckquoy (Ritchie 1977: 190) and Brough Road graves BJ and DT (Morris 1989) included modest assemblages of grave-goods, and Brough Road grave CU (Morris 1989) was flexed with no associated finds. Only the Buckquoy grave, with its Eadmund coin (AD 940–946) can be closely dated, but if the others are broadly contemporary all could be viewed as the last breath of paganism in a period when burial form was giving way to Christian practice. The anomalous burials at Newark Bay mentioned briefly above could be viewed in a similar light. One of the approximately 250 burials was flexed, one included a jet-like bracelet and one may have been associated with an antler comb (Barrett *et al.* 2000b: 538). The axe from St. Ola's churchyard in Shetland (Shetelig 1945: 5) may also be consistent with this interpretation.

The 'syncretic' model is most convincing if the *Life of Saint Findan* is dismissed as anecdotal evidence of little historical merit. In this case, the earliest (mid tenth century) archaeological evidence for Christian practice in Norse Orkney and Shetland is broadly contemporary with the waning of burial with grave-goods expressed at Birsay Bay. Conversely, the model is very difficult to accept if the *Life's* reference to an Orcadian bishop around AD 850 is taken at face value. There is little evidence for a century (or even several decades) of syncretism within a convert community. In particular, one can note the complete absence of sculpture combining Christian iconography with images drawn from Norse mythology of the kind known in the Isle of Man (Margeson 1983; Wilson 1983) and northern England (Bailey 1980: 101–42; Lang 1991). This lacuna is particularly striking given the existence of a pre-Viking sculptural tradition in the Northern Isles (e.g. Thomas 1973).

The alternative interpretation takes as its starting point the strong ideological – political – element involved in the adoption of religious allegiances in the early Middle Ages (Stevenson 1996; see also Myhre 1993; Earle 1997: 143). It is most convincing if the *Life of Saint Findan* is accepted as historical. The existence of an Orcadian bishop around AD 850 (Thomson 1986: 279) implies the existence of élite Christian patrons, without whom no early medieval bishop could function (Stevenson 1996). However, the concurrent existence of a pagan elite is clearly evidenced by ninth-century burials with extravagant grave-goods – at Westness in Rousay, for example (Kaland 1993; 1996).[5] One can thus envision competing factions employing different ideologies – a well known scenario elsewhere in Viking Age and medieval Scandinavia (Stevenson 1996: 182). There is no specific reason to assume that these factions would represent native and Norse groups. The earliest chapel at the Brough of Deerness was built in a Norse style (Morris 1996: 192), and based on contemporary Irish parallels (e.g. Doherty 1998: 295) one could equally envision a complex web of fluctuating alliances.

Having raised this possibility, however, is it realistic to envision competing chiefs within a polity as small as the Northern Isles? Based on analogy with the eleventh–twelfth centuries, for which *Orkneyinga Saga* provides a reasonable historical record (see Jesch 1992), the answer is clearly yes. The medieval earldom

[5] Westness did include both 'Pictish' and 'Pagan' burials, but the latter appear to postdate the former and are consistent with the replacement of Christian practice early in the Viking Age.

was frequently divided between claimants. This division was sometimes, but not always, expressed in spatial terms (e.g. Guðmundsson 1965: 28–33). Given the interdigitated network of clientship known from medieval Icelandic chiefdoms (Byock 1988: 113), complex political and ideological distinctions may well have been possible on a non-geographical basis.

Returning to the meagre archaeological record, it is conceivable that we can glimpse the configuration of competing ideological factions at one point in the tenth century. The crucial comparison is between the earliest known Christian chapels and the latest known pagan burials. The Christian sites are close together in the east Mainland, one (the Brough of Deerness) on a stack site thought to be a Norse chiefly stronghold (Morris and Emery 1986; Morris 1996: 190–2). Conversely, the latest known pagan graves are found on the west coast immediately opposite the Brough of Birsay, now thought to be another Viking Age chiefly centre (Hunter *et al.* 1993: 273; Morris 1996: 194).

It is fortuitous that the Buckquoy grave at Birsay contained a coin of Eadmund (AD 940–946), as this facilitates direct comparison with the early chapels. As discussed above, there was a worn coin of Eadgar (AD 959–975) between the two chapel phases at the Brough of Deerness and coins of Eadred (AD 946–955) and Anlaf Sihtricsson (AD 941–952) under the floor of the chapel at Newark Bay. Viking Age coins found in Scotland cannot provide absolute dates. They often remained in use – in and out of hoards – for many decades (e.g. Brennand *et al.* 1998: 21).[6] Nevertheless, it is striking that these coins are virtually contemporary. If the Birsay burials do not represent a final expression of paganism we may be seeing contemporary Christian and pagan practice at two chiefly centres positioned at the ultimate ends of an east-west axis across the Orkney Mainland.

This suggestion is offered as a hypothesis rather than a conclusion. There is little to commend it if the *Life of Saint Findan* is dismissed as an unreliable witness. The period of clear overlap between Christian and Pagan practice would then disappear. If eventually substantiated, however, the hypothesis does have novel implications for the interpretation of eleventh-century events as described by Adam of Bremen (Tschan 1959). If Birsay was indeed the centre of a tenth-century pagan faction, Adam's observation that Earl Thorfinn established a bishop's seat there around AD 1048 and brought Orkney into 'European Christendom' may deserve close scrutiny (Morris 1996: 188). His father, Earl Sigurd Hlodvisson, is traditionally thought to have died under a pagan banner at the battle of Clontarf in 1014, despite his alleged conversion by Olaf Tryggvason two decades earlier (Thomson 1987: 42). It is conceivable that Thorfinn's choice of Birsay as a centre of both political and ecclesiastical authority represented a highly symbolic act by the first Christian to achieve absolute power in the earldom.

---

[6] I thank Gareth Williams for helpful discussion regarding the numismatic evidence.

ACKNOWLEDGEMENTS

This paper develops ideas first aired in Barrett *et al.* (2000a). It has been heavily influenced by the work of Christopher Morris, my former PhD supervisor, and by helpful comments from audiences at the *Age of Conversion in Northern Europe* conference in York and the *First Millennium Studies Group* in Edinburgh. The research on which it is based was originally sponsored by the Social Sciences and Humanities Research Council of Canada. Samples of human bone were kindly provided by Anne Brundle of the Orkney Museum, Kirkwall, and Theya Molleson of the Natural History Museum, London. Don Brothwell provided details regarding Newark Bay prior to publication (including Figure 13.2d, drawn by Jen Harland) and Sarah King kindly commented on a draft version of the text.

References

Abrams, L. 1998. History and Archaeology: The conversion of Scandinavia, in B.E. Crawford (ed.), *Conversion and Christianity in the North Sea World.* 109–28. St. Andrews: St. John's House Papers No 8.

Allen, J.R. and J. Anderson. 1993[1903]. *The Early Christian Monuments of Scotland.* The Pinkfoot Press: Balgavies.

Bäcklund, J. 2001. War or peace? Relations between the Picts and the Norse in Orkney. *Northern Studies* 36: 33–48.

Bailey, R. N. 1980. *Viking Age Sculpture in Northern England.* London: Collins.

Barber, J. W. 1996. Excavations at St. Magnus' Kirk, Birsay, in C. D. Morris (ed.), *The Birsay Bay Project Volume 2: Sites in Birsay Village and on the Brough of Birsay, Orkney.* 11–32. Durham: University of Durham, Department of Archaeology Monograph series number 2.

Barnes, M. P. 1992. Towards an edition of the Scandinavian runic inscriptions of the British Isles: Some thoughts. *Northern Studies* 29: 32–42.

—— 1994. *The Runic Inscriptions of Maeshowe, Orkney.* Uppsala: Institutionen för nordiska språk, Uppsala Universitet.

—— 1998. *The Norn Language of Orkney and Shetland.* Lerwick: The Shetland Times Ltd.

—— 1999. Richard A.V. Cox *The Language of the Ogam Inscriptions of Scotland* Scottish Gaelic Studies Monograph Series I. *Northern Studies* 34: 129–39.

Barrett, J. H. in press. Culture Contact in Viking Age Scotland, in J. H. Barrett (ed.), *Contact, Continuity and Collapse: The Norse colonization of the North Atlantic.* Turnhout: Brepols, Studies in the Early Middle Ages.

Barrett, J., R. Beukens, I. Simpson, P. Ashmore, S. Poaps and J. Huntley. 2000a. What was the Viking Age and when did it happen? A view from Orkney. *Norwegian Archaeological Review* 33: 1–39.

Barrett, J. H., R. P. Beukens and D. R. Brothwell. 2000b. Radiocarbon dating and marine reservoir correction of Viking Age Christian burials from Orkney. *Antiquity* 74: 537–43.

Barrett, J. H., R. A. Nicholson and R. Cerón-Carrasco. 1999. Archaeo-ichthyological evidence for long-term socioeconomic trends in northern Scotland: 3500 BC to AD 1500. *Journal of Archaeological Science* 26: 353–88.

Batey, C. E. 1993. The Viking and Late Norse graves of Caithness and Sutherland, in C. E. Batey, J. Jesch and C. D. Morris (ed.), *Caithness, Orkney and the North Atlantic in the Viking Age.* 148–64. Edinburgh: Edinburgh University Press.

Benediktsson, J. Editor. 1968. *Íslendingabók, Landnámabók.* Reykjavík: Hið Íslenzka Fornritafélag.

Brennand, M., M. Parker Pearson and H. Smith. 1998. *The Norse settlement and Pictish Cairn at Kilpheder, South Uist: Excavations in 1998.* Dept. of Archaeology and Prehistory, University of Sheffield.

Brothwell, D. 1977. On a mycoform stone structure in Orkney, and its relevance to possible further interpretations of so-called souterrains. *Bulletin of the Institute of Archaeology* 14: 179–90.

—— 2002. Excavations at Newark Bay, Deerness, Orkney. Unpublished manuscript.

Brothwell, D., D. Tills and V. Muir. 1986. Biological characteristics, in R. J. Berry and H. N. Firth (ed.), *The People of Orkney.* 54–88. Kirkwall: The Orkney Press.

Buteux, S., L. Dingwall, J. Hunter and C. Lowe. 2001. *Excavations at St. Nicholas' Chapel, Papa Stronsay, Orkney: Data structure report 2001.* Birmingham and Edinburgh: Department of Ancient History and Archaeology, The University of Birmingham, and Headland Archaeology Ltd.

Byock, J. L. 1988. *Medieval Iceland: Society, sagas and power.* Enfield Lock, Middlesex: Hisarlik Press.

Cant, R. G. 1984. Settlement, society and church organisation in the Northern Isles, in A. Fenton and H. Pálsson (ed.), *The Northern and Western Isles in the Viking World.* 169–79. Edinburgh: John Donald.

Carver, M. 1998. Conversion and politics on the eastern seaboard of Britain: Some archaeological indicators, in B. E. Crawford (ed.), *Conversion and Christianity in the North Sea World.* 11–40. St. Andrews: St. John's House Papers No 8.

Christiansen, R. 1962. The people of the north. *Lochlann* 2: 137–64.

Clancy, T. O. forthcoming. The Gall-Ghaidheil and Galloway, in M. MacLeod (ed.), *Gall-Ghaidheil: The Western Isles in the Viking World.*

Clouston, J. S. 1918a. The old chapels of Orkney (1). *Scottish Historical Review* 58: 89–105.

—— 1918b. The old chapels of Orkney (2). *Scottish Historical Review* 59: 223–40.

Crawford, B. E. 1975. Viking Graves, in P. McNeill and R. Nicholson (ed.), *An Historical Atlas of Scotland c.400–c.1600.* 16–7. St. Andrews: Conference of Scottish Medievalists.

—— 1987. *Scandinavian Scotland.* Leicester: Leicester University Press.

—— Editor. 1998. *Conversion and Christianity in the North Sea World.* St. Andrews: St. John's House Papers No 8.

Curle, C. L. 1982. *Pictish and Norse Finds from the Brough of Birsay 1934–74.* Edinburgh: Society of Antiquaries of Scotland Monograph Series Number 1.

Doherty, C. 1998. The Vikings in Ireland: A review, in H. Clarke, M. Ní Mhaonaigh and R. Ó Floinn (ed.), *Ireland and Scandinavia in the Early Viking Age.* 288–330. Dublin: Four Courts Press.

Driscoll, S. T. 2000. Christian monumental sculpture and ethnic expression in early Scotland, in W. O. Frazer and A. Tyrrell (ed.), *Social Identity in Early Medieval Britain.* 233–52. London: Leicester University Press.

Dumville, D. N. 1997. *The Churches of North Britain in the First Viking Age.* Whithorn: Whithorn Trust.

Earle, T. 1997. *How Chiefs Come to Power: The political economy in prehistory.* Stanford: Stanford University Press.

Fellows-Jensen, G. 1984. Viking settlement in the Northern and Western Isles – the place name evidence as seen from Denmark and the Danelaw, in A. Fenton and H. Pálsson (ed.), *The Northern and Western Isles in the Viking World.* 146–68. Edinburgh: John Donald.

Fisher, I. 2001. *Early Medieval Sculpture in the West Highlands and Islands*. Edinburgh: Royal Commission on the Ancient and Historic Monuments of Scotland.

Fletcher, R. 1997. *The Conversion of Europe: From paganism to Christianity 371–1386 AD*. London: Fontana Press.

Forsyth, K. 1997. *Language in Pictland*. Utrecht: de Keltische Draak, Studia Hameliana 2.

Foster, S. M. 1997. The strength of belief: The impact of Christianity on early historic Scotland, in G. De Boe and F. Verhaeghe (ed.), *Religion and Belief in Medieval Europe: Papers of the 'Medieval Europe Brugge 1997' conference volume 4*. 229–40. Zellik: I.A.P. Rapporten 4.

Geake, H. 1997. *The Use of Grave-goods in Conversion-period England, c.600–c.850*. Oxford: British Archaeological Reports British Series 261.

Graham-Campbell, J. 1998. The Early Viking Age in the Irish Sea Area, in H. Clarke, M. Ní Mhaonaigh and R. Ó Floinn (ed.), *Ireland and Scandinavia in the Early Viking Age*. 104–30. Dublin: Four Courts Press.

Graham-Campbell, J. and C.E. Batey. 1998. *Vikings in Scotland: An archaeological survey*. Edinburgh: Edinburgh University Press.

Guðmundsson, F. 1965. *Orkneyinga Saga*. Reykjavík: Hið Islenzka Fornritafélag.

Harry, R. 2000. St. Ninian's Isle Chapel. *Discovery and Excavation in Scotland* 1999: 81.

Hunter, J. R. 1986. *Rescue Excavations on the Brough of Birsay 1974–82*. Edinburgh: Society of Antiquaries of Scotland Monograph Series Number 4.

Hunter, J. R., J. M. Bond and A. M. Smith. 1993. Some aspects of Viking settlement in Orkney, in C. E. Batey, J. Jesch and C. D. Morris (ed.), *The Viking Age in Caithness, Orkney and the North Atlantic*. 272–84. Edinburgh: Edinburgh University Press.

Jesch, J. 1992. Narrating Orkneyinga Saga. *Scandinavian Studies* 64: 336–55.

Kaland, S. H. H. 1993. The settlement of Westness, Rousay, in C. E. Batey, J. Jesch, and C. D. Morris (ed.), *The Viking Age in Caithness, Orkney and the North Atlantic*. 308–17. Edinburgh: Edinburgh University Press.

—— 1996. En vikingtidsgård og -gravplass på Orknøyene, in J. F. Krøger and H. Naley (ed.), *Nordsjøen: Handel, religion og politikk*. 63–8. Karmøy Kommune: Vikingfestivalen.

Lamb, R. G. 1974. The cathedral of Christchurch and the monastery of Birsay. *Proceedings of the Society of Antiquaries of Scotland* 105: 200–5.

—— 1980. *Iron Age Promontory Forts in the Northern Isles*. Oxford: British Archaeological Reports British Series 79.

—— 1983. The cathedral and the monastery. *Orkney Heritage* 2: 36–45.

Lamb, R. 1995. Papil, Picts and papar, in B. E. Crawford (ed.), *Northern Isles Connections: Essays from Orkney and Shetland presented to Per Sveaas Andersen*. 9–27. Kirkwall: The Orkney Press.

—— 1998. Pictland, Northumbria and the Carolingian Empire, in B. E. Crawford (ed.), *Conversion and Christianity in the North Sea World*. 41–56. St. Andrews: St. John's House Papers No 8.

Lang, J. T. 1991. *Corpus of Anglo-Saxon Sculpture Volume III: York and eastern Yorkshire*. Oxford: Oxford University Press.

Lönnroth, L. 1987. The effects of conversion on Scandinavian mentalité, in B. Sawyer, P. Sawyer and I. Wood (ed.), *The Christianization of Scandinavia*. 27–9. Alingsås: Viktoria Bokförlag.

Lowe, C. Editor. 1998. *St. Boniface Church, Orkney: Coastal erosion and archaeological assessment*. Edinburgh: Sutton Publishing and Historic Scotland.

—— 2001. Newark. *Discovery and Excavation in Scotland* 1: 66.

MacDonald, A. 1977. On 'papar' names in N. and W. Scotland. *Northern Studies* 9: 25–30.

––––– 1992. *Curadan, Boniface and the Early Church of Rosemarkie*. Rosemarkie: Groam House Lecture Series.

Margeson, S. 1983. On the iconography of the Manx crosses, in C. Fell, P. Foote, J. Graham-Campbell and R. Thomson (ed.), *The Viking Age in the Isle of Man*. 95–106. London: Viking Society for Northern Research.

Morris, C. D. Editor. 1989. *The Birsay Bay Project Volume 1: Brough Road Excavations 1976–1982*. Durham: University of Durham, Department of Archaeology Monograph Series Number 1.

––––– 1990. *Church and Monastery in the Far North: An archaeological evaluation*. Jarrow: Jarrow Lecture 1989.

––––– 1993. The Birsay Bay project, in C. E. Batey, J. Jesch and C. D. Morris (ed.), *Caithness, Orkney and the North Atlantic in the Viking Age*. 285–307. Edinburgh: Edinburgh University Press.

––––– 1995. Birsay: An Orcadian centre of political and ecclesiastical power: A retrospective view on work in the 1970s and 1980s. *Studia Celtica* 29: 1–29.

––––– 1996. Church and monastery in Orkney and Shetland : An archaeological perspective, in J. F. Krøger and H. Naley (ed.), *Nordsjøen: Handel, religion og politikk*. 185–206. Karmøy Kommune: Vikingfestivalen.

Morris, C. D. and K. Brady. 1998. *Unst Chapel Survey 1997*. Glasgow: Glasgow University Archaeological Research Division.

Morris, C. D. and N. Emery. 1986. The chapel and enclosure on the Brough of Deerness, Orkney: Survey and excavations, 1975–1977. *Proceedings of the Society of Antiquaries of Scotland* 116: 301–74.

Myhre, B. 1993. The beginning of the Viking Age – Some current archaeological problems, in A. Faulkes and R. Perkins (ed.), *Viking Revaluations*. 182–204. London: Viking Society for Northern Research.

Nielsen, L. C. 1991. Hedenskab og kristendom. Religionsskiftet afspejlet i vikingetidens grave, in P. Mortensen and B. M. Rasmussen (ed.), *Fra Stamme til Stat i Danmark 2: Hovdingsdamfund of kongemagt*. 245–68. Aarhus: Jysk Arkaeologisk Selskabs Skrifter XXII: 2.

Omand, C. J. 1986. The life of Saint Findan, in R. J. Berry and H. N. Firth (ed.), *The People of Orkney*. 284–7. Kirkwall: The Orkney Press.

Owen, O. and C. Lowe. Editors. 1999. *Kebister: The four-thousand-year-old story of one Shetland township*. Edinburgh: Society of Antiquaries of Scotland Monograph Series 14.

Owen, O. and J. McKinnell. 1989. A runic inscription from Tuquoy, Westray, Orkney. *Medieval Archaeology* 33: 53–9.

Radford, C. A. R. 1962a. Art and architecture: Celtic and Norse, in F. T. Wainwright (ed.), *The Northern Isles*. 163–87. Edinburgh: Thomas Nelson and Sons.

––––– 1962b. The Celtic monastery in Britain. *Archaeologia Cambrensis* 111: 1–24.

Richards, J. D. 2000. *Viking Age England*. Stroud: Tempus.

Ritchie, A. 1977. Excavation of Pictish and Viking-Age farmsteads at Buckquoy, Orkney. *Proceedings of the Society of Antiquaries of Scotland* 108: 174–227.

Roesdahl, E. 1987. The archaeological evidence for conversion, in B. Sawyer, P. Sawyer and I. Wood (ed.), *The Christianization of Scandinavia* 2–5. Alingsås: Viktoria Bokförlag.

Sawyer, B. 1991. Viking age rune stones as a crisis symptom. *Norwegian Archaeological Review* 24: 97–112.

—— 2000. *The Viking-Age Rune Stones*. Oxford: Oxford University Press.

Scott, A. B. 1926. The Celtic Church in Orkney. *Proceedings of the Orkney Antiquarian Society* 4: 45–56.

Sellevold, B.J. 1999. *Picts and Vikings at Westness*. Oslo: NIKV Scientific Report 010: 1–62.

Shetelig, H. 1945. The Viking graves in Great Britain and Ireland. *Acta Archaeologica* XVI: 1–55.

Small, A., C. Thomas, and D. M. Wilson. 1973. *St. Ninian's Isle and its Treasure*. Oxford: Oxford University Press.

Smith, B. 2001. The Picts and the martyrs or did Vikings kill the native population of Orkney and Shetland. *Northern Studies* 36: 7–32.

Smyth, A. P. 1978. The chronology of Northumbrian history in the ninth and tenth centuries, in R. A. Hall (ed.), *Viking Age York and the North*. 8–10. London: Council for British Archaeology Research Report No 27.

—— 1984. *Warlords and Holy Men: Scotland AD 80–1000*. London: Edward Arnold.

Solli, B. 1996. Narratives of encountering religions: On the Christianization of the Norse around AD 900–1000. *Norwegian Archaeological Review* 29: 91–114.

Stevenson, R. B. K. 1981. Christian sculpture in Norse Shetland. *Froðskaparrit* 28–9: 283–92.

—— 1986. The Anglo-Saxon silver penny and its context, in C. D. Morris and N. Emery, The chapel and enclosure on the Brough of Deerness, Orkney: Survey and excavations, 1975–1977, *Proceedings of the Society of Antiquaries of Scotland* 116: 301–74

Stevenson, J. 1996. Christianising the northern barbarians, in J. F. Krøger and H. Naley (ed.), *Nordsjøen: Handel, religion og politikk*. 162–84. Karmøy Kommune: vikingfestivalen.

Stuiver, M., P. J. Reimer and T. F. Braziunas. 1998. High-precision radiocarbon age calibration for terrestrial and marine samples. *Radiocarbon* 40: 1127–51.

Thomas, C. 1971. *The Early Christian Archaeology of North Britain*. Oxford: Oxford University Press.

—— 1973. Sculptured stones and crosses from St. Ninian's Isle and Papil, in A. Small, C. Thomas and D. M. Wilson (ed.), *St. Ninian's Isle and its Treasure*. 8–44. Oxford: Oxford University Press.

—— 1998. Form and function, in S. Foster (ed.), *The St Andrews Sarcophagus: A Pictish masterpiece and its international connections*. 84–96. Dublin: Four Courts Press.

Thomson, W. 1983. *Birsay: A centre of political and ecclesiastical power (Orkney Heritage, Volume 2)*. Vol. 2. Orkney Heritage. Kirkwall: Orkney Heritage Society.

Thomson, W. P. L. 1986. St Findan and the Pictish-Norse transition, in R. J. Berry and H. N. Firth (ed.), *The People of Orkney*. 279–83. Kirkwall: The Orkney Press.

—— 1987. *History of Orkney*. Edinburgh: Mercat Press.

Tschan, J. Editor. 1959. *Adam of Bremen, The Archbishops of Hamburg Bremen*. New York: Columbia University Press.

Vésteinsson, O. 1999. *The Christianization of Iceland: Priests, power and social change 1000–1300*. Oxford: Oxford University Press.

Wainwright, F. T. 1962. The Scandinavian Settlement, in F. T. Wainwright (ed.), *The Northern Isles*. 117–62. Edinburgh: Thomas Nelson and Sons.

Wilson, D. M. 1983. The art of the Manx crosses of the Viking Age, in C. Fell, P. Foote, J. Graham-Campbell and R. Thomson (ed.), *The Viking Age in the Isle of Man*. 175–87. London: Viking Society for Northern Research.

Part III

Christianity and the English

14

Anglo-Saxon Pagan and Early Christian Attitudes to the Dead

AUDREY L. MEANEY

Just over 1,300 years ago, according to his hagiographer Felix, St Guthlac did something until then unrecorded in England; he went to live in a burial mound. When Guthlac came to the fen 'island' of Crowland, seeking a hermit's life, he found:

> a mound built of clods of earth which greedy comers to the waste had dug open, in the hope of finding treasure there; in the side of this there seemed to be a sort of cistern, and in this Guthlac . . . began to dwell, after building a hut over it.[1]

Felix, therefore, states only that the mound was artificial; it is with archaeological hindsight that we can be virtually certain that it was a barrow. His statement appears to be the earliest extant reference to grave-robbing in England;[2] however, some Anglo-Saxon charter bounds mention 'the barrow which was dug into', and 'the broken barrow',[3] so perhaps the tradition that mounds contained treasure, and some attempts to recover it, began quite early in Anglo-Saxon England.

A metal sign to the south of Crowland abbey church announcing 'Site of St Guthlac's Cell' marks where later tradition placed it, and where the rector thought he had found it in 1908. This is no longer accepted; though it is usually believed that the cell must have been close to the present church no burial mound is known there. Another possibility is that Guthlac's cell was about 500 m to the north-east of the church, on a site known as Anchorite (or variations thereon) Hill, where a later medieval 'chapel' (so-called) apparently overlay a Bronze Age barrow, and was surrounded by an enclosure ditch, as can be seen on air photographs.[4] This

---

[1] *Felix's Life of St Guthlac* (hereafter *VG*), ch. XXVIII, ed. and trans. B. Colgrave (Cambridge 1956). See the discussion in Audrey L. Meaney, 'Felix's *Life of Guthlac*: Hagiography and/or truth', *Proceedings of the Cambridge Antiquarian Society* 90 (2001) pp.29–48.

[2] Colgrave (1956), p.183.

[3] A.C. Amos *et al.*, *Dictionary of Old English* (Toronto 1986–), *Fascicule* B. (Toronto 1991), citations under **beorg**: charter 273.7: þam beorgum þe adolfen wæs; charter 1590.3: wið eastan brocenan **beorg**. Sometimes, though not by Felix, a dragon is regarded as the guardian of the treasure; see H. Davidson, 'The Hill of the Dragon', *Folklore* 61 (1950), pp.169–85.

is near where a stone has recently (April 1999) been placed, as was shown on local television, when it was stated that this was the site of Guthlac's cell. The inscription on the stone is more circumspect, and Guthlac's establishment evidently had several cells, so that it might have been one of the others which was originally on Anchorite Hill.[5]

Along the axis of the Crowland gravel peninsula other Bronze Age barrows are known, but they have yielded only 'rude pottery . . . cinerary urns (including Roman ware) . . . flint spearheads' and the like[6] – hardly enough, it would seem, to have tempted treasure seekers. Unless a local mound, whether natural or artificial, had been used as a convenient repository for a coin hoard,[7] in England it is only burials – and, perhaps, only the richer barrows of the later sixth and seventh centuries, about a 100 years before Guthlac's arrival on Crowland – which might have yielded enough precious metal to have made the efforts of grave-robbers (as opposed to archaeologists) worthwhile. None of these Anglo-Saxon barrows is known on Crowland, but at Eye, about 5 miles (7.5 km) to the south, and on a comparable gravel peninsula, a secondary 'Saxon burial with beads datable to the mid-6th century AD' was found in an early Bronze Age barrow.[8] A similar but richer burial at Crowland as the cause of the 'robber hole' is therefore just possible.

What could Felix have meant by 'a sort of cistern' (velut cisterna)? No stone is found in the fens, and it is not used in the structure of known local prehistoric mounds.[9] Colgrave, writing before the discovery of Bronze Age barrows on Crowland, conjectured that Guthlac's might have been a Roman barrow, examples of which are found in eastern England. Some of these contained cists 'built of tiles, mortar [or] stone',[10] and one of these might have served as Guthlac's hut base. Martin Carver (pers. comm.) has suggested that the 'cistern' might have been a timber-lined chamber grave, like that at Jelling, but I remain doubtful if such a timber structure could have survived well enough in the fenland gravels

[4] P.P. Hayes and T.W. Lane (eds), *The Fenland Project Number 5: Lincolnshire Survey, the South-West Fens*, East Anglian Archaeology Report No.55, p.197 and pl.IX.

[5] D. Stocker, 'The Early Church in Lincolnshire', in *Pre-Viking Lindsey*, ed. A. Vince (Lincoln 1993), pp.101–22 at pp.104–6.

[6] See note 4.

[7] L.V. Grinsell, 'Barrow Treasure, in Fact, Tradition and Legislation', *Folklore* 78 (1967), pp.1–38.

[8] D. Hall, 'The Fenland Project 2: Fenland landscapes and settlement between Peterborough and March, *East Anglian Archaeology* 35 (1987), p.6.

[9] L. Shook's argument in 'The burial mound in *Guthlac A*', *Modern Philology* 63 (1960), pp.1–10, that a prehistoric chambered barrow is envisaged in the poem *Guthlac A* is not affected by the discussion here; the poet may not have known the landscape as Felix did.

[10] Colgrave (1956), pp.182–4. See G.C. Dunning and R.F. Jessup, 'Roman Barrows', *Antiquity* 10 (1936), pp.37–53; R.F. Jessup, 'Barrows and Walled Cemeteries in Roman Britain', *Journal of British Archaeology* 3rd ser 22 (1959), pp.1–32 and pls.I-XII, at pp.1, 4, 6, 7.

[11] See, for example, illustrations in I. Hodder and P. Shand, 'The Haddenham Long Barrow: an Interim Statement', *Antiquity* 62 (1988), pp.349–53, and in Alison Taylor, *Burial Practice in Early England* (Stroud 2001) p.36 and colour plate II. Compare the Anglo-Saxon timber chamber under excavation in Mound 2 at Sutton Hoo, M.O.H. Carver (ed.) *The Age of Sutton Hoo* (Woodbridge 1992), Plate 27.

to serve as a dwelling.[11] However, two of Felix's literary sources described anchorites in the Middle Eastern deserts as living in cisterns;[12] so perhaps he borrowed the term and used it imprecisely. Guthlac's 'cistern' could have been merely a robber pit dug into the gravel, providing a conveniently scooped-out base for a 'Sunken Featured Building' of a typically Anglo-Saxon type. Later details in one of Guthlac's visions, where devils were envisaged as entering his cell *'through floor holes and gaps; neither the hinges of the doors nor the openings in the wattle-work denied them entry'*,[13] might well indicate that his cell was very similar to the houses lovingly reconstructed with plank floors over a hollow, but with log walls instead of wattle and daub, not far away at West Stow in Suffolk.[14]

Early Anglo-Saxons belonging to the pagan or conversion periods dug graves into prehistoric burial mounds for their own dead, but seem to have avoided living near them. According to hagiographers, however, anchorites often dwelt in tombs: when Antony (the earliest and most famous of the Egyptian hermit saints, whose Latin *Life* Felix clearly used) first moved away from his village, he had himself shut into a tomb.[15] Felix's account of Guthlac's choice of an ancient devil-haunted site on which to build his hut, and the discovery of structures within it, is so hagiographically conventional, that it can scarcely be regarded as historical evidence. Nevertheless, if in real life Guthlac was indeed attempting to emulate the desert fathers, he would have regarded a burial mound as an appropriate dwelling.

Admittedly, Felix does not state anywhere that the devils which Guthlac encountered in his visions were the ghosts of the pagan dead, or even specifically associated with the barrow. Indeed, I have conjectured that when Felix described the devils which Guthlac saw in a vision as misshapen humans, he may have envisaged them as examples of the Anglo-Saxon folkloric monster, the þyrs, whose habitat was the fen. Beowulf's enemy, Grendel, was a þyrs. Usually, however, Felix's devils conform to the hagiographic norm, and are essentially identical to those which tormented Saint Antony, albeit described in a more exaggerated manner.[16]

---

[12] A.T. Thacker, *Social and Continental background to early Anglo-Saxon hagiography* (unpublished DPhil, Oxford 1977, p.296 refers to Jerome's *Vita Pauli Primi Eremitæ*, ch.5–6 (ed. J.P. Migne, *Patrologia Latina* 23 (Paris 1845), cols.17–28, at p.21): an anchorite lived in an 'old cistern' [*in cisterna veteri*]. W.F. Bolton ('The Latin revisions of Felix's "Vita Sancti Guthlaci"' *Mediaeval Studies* 21 (1959), p.37, n.7) noticed that in Aldhelm's *Prose De Virginitate*, Athanasius Bishop of Alexandria (author of the *Life of Antony*) is said to have hidden 'in the dry hollow of a cistern' for 6 years, to get away from his detractors. See Aldhelmus, *De Virginitate (Prosa)* XXXII, in *Aldhelmi Opera*, ed. R. Ehwald, *Monumenta Germaniae Historica Auct. Antiquis.* XV (Berlin 1919), pp.226–323, at p.274 l.6; translated in *Aldhelm: The Prose Works*, M. Lapidge and M. Herren (Ipswich 1979), pp.59–132, at p.94.

[13] *VG* ch.XXXI.

[14] See cover illustration to S. West, *West Stow: The Anglo-Saxon Village* I, East Anglian Archaeology Report 24 (1985).

[15] *St Athanasius: The Life of St Anthony*, trans. R.T. Meyer (London 1950) (hereafter *VA*), chs.8–13.

[16] Meaney 2001 (note 1), especially pp.33 and 37.

In one of the Old English poems on St Guthlac, however, the devils are specifically associated with the mound, and the poet's attention is focussed on the battle between them and the saint for possession of it:

> The evildoers were full of anger; they said that (beside God himself) Guthlac alone had done the greatest harm to them, when for pride he had stormed the mounds in the waste land, where they, wretched adversaries, could formerly have enjoyed refuge at times after torment, when they came from their wanderings to rest for a while.[17]

It is not explicit or even necessary for the poem that these devils represent the lost souls of the pagans buried in the barrow; and indeed some critics have argued that the poet (with a profound ignorance of the fen landscape) used **beorg** in the sense of 'hill, mountain' rather than of 'burial mound'.[18]

The idea that the anchorite is invading territory which rightly belongs to demons is also found in the Life of Antony. When he was occupying a deserted fort, '*his acquaintances . . . often spent days and nights outside. . . . They heard what sounded like riotous crowds inside . . . wailing piteously and shrieking: "Get out of our domain! What business have you in the desert?"*'[19]

Guthlac's residence in an earthen barrow rather than a stone tomb certainly had to do with the fact that he was in the English fens rather than in the Egyptian or the Judaean desert; all these hagiographic encounters with the devil are meant to recall those of Christ in the wilderness, however different the landscape.

The early royal minsters in England seem to have often occupied the same kinds of sites as the Middle Eastern monasteries: that is, for example, within a Roman fort (for example, at Chesterfield in Derbyshire, and Bradwell-on-Sea in Essex, like Castellion in the Judaean desert); or within the ruins of a Roman town, as at Bath; or on or beside a Roman building, as at Cheddar Somerset. Sometimes, perhaps, a minster may have been on the site of an earlier Christian shrine, and sometimes, where one lies just outside a Roman town, Blair suggested that it might 'perpetuate a tomb-cult in a Roman suburban cemetery'. Blair wrote:

17

Wæron teonsmiðas tornes fulle,
cwædon þæt him Guðlac eac Gode sylfum
earfeþa mæst ana gefremede,
siþþan he for wlence on westenne
beorgas bræce, þær hy bidinge,
earme ondsacan, æror mostun
æfter tintergum tidum brucan
ðonne hy of waþum werge cwoman
restan ryneþragum, rowe gefegon (lines 205–213)

The Exeter Book, eds. G.P. Krapp and E. van K. Dobbie (New York and London 1936), pp.49–72, at p.55.

[18] See P.F. Reichardt, 'Guthlac A and the Landscape of Spiritual Perfection', *Neophilogus* 58 (1974), pp.331–8.

[19] *VA*, ch.13.

The reasons for so frequent a choice of Roman sites . . . must go beyond the purely practical. . . . It still seems best to invoke a general sense of historical and even architectural fittingness. The Continental missionaries could recognize a Roman town, and knew that it was the right and proper place for a great church.[20]

Within the English context, there may have been other reasons for choosing a site where earlier peoples had made their mark. As already remarked, a would-be hermit saint needed not only a deserted place where he could worship God uninterrupted, but also a site haunted by demons, so that he could demonstrate God's power and his own reliance on Him. Something of the same attitude may have been exhibited by the founders of the early minsters. The remains of masonry buildings and walls may have been recognizable as Roman to the educated (even to the Reeve of Carlisle, who showed St Cuthbert a Roman fountain in the city walls),[21] but the Old English literary tradition indicates that in poetic imagination they were the work of ancient giants (**enta geweorc**):

> Cities (those which are on this earth) are visible from afar,
> skilful work of giants, wondrous construction of wall-stones.[22]

Though there are two sets of charter bounds where a 'giant's' or 'a giants' barrow' (**enta hlewe/ entan hlew**) is mentioned, some of the details in other poems (such as *Beowulf* and *The Ruin*) reinforce our impression that when Anglo-Saxon poets used the term **enta geweorc** it was usually in reference to Roman ruins. The word **ent** is native, but it is not to be forgotten that, for Anglo-Saxons from King Alfred's time onward (at least), the builder of the Tower of Babel (which would certainly have been visible from afar) was an **ent**.[23] The futility of such constructions is thereby hinted at, for those who were able to pick up the reference.[24]

---

[20] J. Blair, 'Minster Churches in the Landscape', in *Anglo-Saxon Settlements*, ed. D. Hooke (Oxford 1988), pp.35–58, at pp.40–7; see also R. Morris, *The Church in British Archaeology*, CBA Research Report 47 (1983), pp.26, 40–5. P.H. Hase ('The Church in the Wessex Heartlands', in *The Medieval Landscape of Wessex*, ed. M. Aston and C. Lewis (Oxford 1994), pp.47–81, at p.54), however, has pointed out that there may be local variations in siting; that churches in Wessex (such as those at Dorchester, Dorset, and Ilchester, Somerset) are more likely to have been founded immediately outside Roman towns than inside them, and that the proximity to water is of the greatest importance in the siting of a church.

[21] *Two Lives of St Cuthbert*, ed. B. Colgrave (Cambridge 1940); *Anonymous Life* IV.8; *Bede's Prose Life*, Ch 27.

[22]
> Ceastra beoð feorran gesyne
> orðanc enta geweorc, þa þe on þysse eorðan syndon,
> wrætlic weallstana geweorc

Cotton Gnomic Verse, lines 1b–3a; in *Sweet's Anglo-Saxon Reader*, ed. D. Whitelock (Oxford 1967), pp.174–6.

[23] See R. Venezky and A. Di Paolo Healey, *A Microfiche Concordance to Old English* (Newark NJ and Toronto 1980) under **ent, enta, entan, entas, entum.**

[24] See P.J. Frankis, 'The thematic significance of *enta geweorc* and related imagery in *The Wanderer*', *Anglo-Saxon England* 2 (1973), pp.253–69. I am grateful to Professor K O'Brien O'Keeffe who pointed out this article to me after most of the above was written.

Blair has pointed out that the practice of siting monasteries in Roman forts and small towns took place in Europe before the conversion of the English, and the 'channel of influence' from Gaul to England was probably the most important in encouraging the practice here.[25] Roman sites may have been avoided by the pagan Anglo-Saxons as places to live because they were (at the least) uncanny, and so were available for minsters as 'brown-field sites', themselves unsuitable for agriculture, even if surrounded by good soil. They may have been within the gift of the local rulers – Bede tells how the kings of Wessex, East Anglia, Essex, Kent and Northumbria all gave away Romano-British enclosures 'so that saints could build cathedrals or minsters in them'[26] – but, as Blair remarked concerning Dorchester on Thames, a king would not have given away his own residence.[27]

Martin Biddle considers that churches would not have been founded where there were only ghosts, unless it was to exorcize them. He drew attention to the circle of pagan Anglo-Saxon cemeteries outside Winchester, as evidence of a considerable population in the vicinity, perhaps indicating some kind of continuing authority within the Roman town.[28] Yet the argument could go in the other direction: if *Venta Belgarum* itself was as empty as archaeology appears to show it was throughout the pagan period,[29] it would have made a very good centre for missionary activity in the surrounding villages. The remains of Roman masonry may have provided a good basis and good raw material for the stone buildings which the missionaries may have preferred to build, and have seemed more like home to them. The respect shown to the ancient remains may also have been part of a design to bring the pagan barbarians into civilized European society.

Yet pre-Roman sites were also re-used by minsters; Blair has commented:

> A handful at least of mid-Saxon English minsters, such as Hanbury (Worcestershire), Tetbury (Gloucestershire), Breedon-on-the-Hill (Leicestershire), and Aylesbury (Buckinghamshire) are within Iron Age forts, and the practice was echoed by the eighth-century missionaries to Germany in their foundations at Fulda, Würzburg, Büraburg and Erfurt.[30]

[25] J. Blair, 'Anglo-Saxon minsters: a topographical review', in *Pastoral Care Before the Parish*, ed. J. Blair and R. Sharpe (Leicester 1992), pp.226–66, at pp.235–7, 265–6.

[26] Ibid. pp.235–7. The same points were made more briefly, but 20 years earlier, by C. Thomas, *The Early Christian Archaeology of North Britain* (Oxford 1971), pp.32–3.

[27] Blair (1988), p.44; Blair (1992), pp.239–40.

[28] M. Biddle, 'Winchester: the development of an early capital', in *Vor- und Frühformen der europäischen Stadt im Mittelalter*, ed. H. Jankuhn, W. Schlesinger and H. Steuer (Göttingen 1973), pp.229–61, at pp.232–42.

[29] For example, B. Kjølby-Biddle 'A cathedral cemetery: problems in excavation and interpretation', *World Archaeology* 7.i (1975), pp.87–108, at p.92, states, concerning the Old Minster at Winchester, that 'apart from sporadic "dark-age" levels, nothing intervened between the Roman levels and the first church'.

[30] Blair (1992), p.234. However, Hase (1994) p.54, has commented that in Wessex 'only Malmesbury of known Middle Saxon churches is believed to be built within an ancient hillfort. Wessex has more hillforts than anywhere else in England: in these circumstances, the few early churches to be found in hillfort enclosures suggests that the Anglo-Saxons in this part of England deliberately *avoided* such places when they founded their churches: it is interesting to note that Malmesbury was founded by an Irish pilgrim and not by a West Saxon.'

Though a prehistoric fort would have provided an earth bank and ditch to serve as the *uallum monasterii*,[31] in other respects it would have been inferior to a Roman town: no re-usable stone or brick, no hard-standing, no veneer of civilization. Yet the monks and nuns living within it would still have been able to advertise to the surrounding populace that they could rely on God's power to repel any evil spirits infesting the ancient sites, like Guthlac's pagan burial-mound.

A second event throwing light on the Anglo-Saxon attitude to the dead comes at the end of Felix's *Life*, where he describes Guthlac's *post mortem* history. Guthlac's body, first buried with honour 3 days after his death was found a year later on its translation to a shrine to be incorrupt.[32] In this it resembles the bodies of four of the virgin saints mentioned by Bede: Cuthbert and three with East Anglian connections (the Irishman Fursey, and two daughters of King Anna, Æthelburh abbess of Farmoutier-en-Brie, and her better-known sister Æthelthryth of Ely). The accounts of all five translations are very similar, though the intervals between their deaths and their translations vary.[33]

Felix knew and used the *Life* of Fursey[34] and Bede's *Life* of Cuthbert, and (since he was himself East Anglian) he must surely have heard of Æthelthryth and probably her sister too. It is therefore not surprising that he ascribed this symbol of sanctity to Guthlac. Indeed, it is possible that candidates for sainthood in Anglo-Saxon England were among those embalmed at the time of their death. There is some archaeological evidence for the practice in later Saxon England[35] and if, at the time of translation, the embalming was shown to be successful, it would have confirmed the saintliness.

Stephen Wilson has commented that, though an ascetic, living saint may have resembled a corpse, a dead saint did not. Ideally, his body was not merely incorrupt, but gave off sweet odours. It was not buried in the ground, but raised above it in a shrine where, in the popular imagination, the saint himself remained.[36] In early Christian western Europe it was not acceptable that a saint's body should be moved or dismembered to provide relics for other churches,[37] and this seems to have been still the case in England in Felix's time. Only later did it

---

[31] Blair (1992), p.232.

[32] *VG*, ch.L-LI.

[33] For Æthelthryth (*HE* iv.19) it was 16 years, for Cuthbert 11 years (*HE* iv.30), for Æthelburh 7 years (*HE* iii.8), for Fursey 27 days until his first translation, 4 years until the second (*HE* iii.28). B. Colgrave and R.A.B. Mynors, *Bede's Ecclesiastical History of the English People* (Oxford 1969), p.240 n. 2; see also p.234 n.1. The index confuses Æthelburh (*HE* iii.8), with her namesake the abbess of Barking, sister of Eorcenwold bishop of London (*HE* iv.6). Bede also used the *Life of Fursey*, edited as *Vita et Miracula S Fursei* in W.W. Heist *Vitae Sanctorum Hiberniae*, Subsidia Hagiographica 28 (Brussels 1965), pp.37–55.

[34] Colgrave (1956), passim; Thacker (1977), p.305

[35] W. Rodwell, *The Archaeology of the English Church* (London 1981), pp.149, 155–6 and fig.74.

[36] S. Wilson, Introduction to *Saints and their Cults: Studies in Religious Sociology, Folklore and History* (Cambridge 1983), pp.1–53, at pp.10–11.

[37] See J. McCulloch, 'The Cult of Relics in the Letters and 'Dialogues' of Pope Gregory the Great: A Lexicographical Study', *Traditio* 32 (1976), pp.145–84.

become common here to steal relics in order to gain a saint's protection for a site distant from those he had known in his life-time.[38] However, Bede's account of the history of King Oswald's remains prefigures the way that things were to go. Oswald was killed in 642 in battle against Penda of Mercia, who ordered his head and hands to be severed and put on stakes. A year later when Oswald's brother Oswiu found them, he buried the head in the church at Lindisfarne and put the hands and arms in a silver shrine in St Peter's church in Bamburgh (*in regia uero civitate*), where they were still incorrupt when Bede was writing.[39] Bede does not relate where the rest of Oswald's body was first buried, but it did not remain incorrupt (presumably because he was not a virgin), and his bones were subsequently translated by his niece Osthryth (wife of Æthelred of Mercia) to Bardney in Lincolnshire, where they were received with some reluctance.[40] Oswald also generated many incorporeal relics.[41]

Peter Brown has demonstrated how distasteful all this handling of dead bodies and human bones would have been to a 'Mediterranean man of traditional background'. In pagan times Romans buried their dead outside towns, away from the living, but as Christian cults of the saints took hold, relics came to be housed within the walls, and graves of ordinary people clustered around them, so that 'normative public worship and the tombs of the dead were made to coincide in a manner and with a frequency for which the pagan and Jewish imagination had made little provision'.[42]

Brown is fortunate in the area which he has chosen for comparison of early Christian and heathen customs, in that information on the ideas and ceremonials of literate Mediterranean pagans is abundant, whereas in England Christianity replaced a heathenism for which we have virtually no evidence in writing, and precious little of any kind. Even our knowledge of early Christian custom has largely to be deduced rather than taken from clear historical accounts. When attempting to compare pagan and early Christian attitudes to the 'ordinary' dead, we are forced to rely on archaeological evidence, which may be capable of more than one explanation. Therefore much of what I am about to say is on the one hand conjectural: many may disagree with it, and I may even come to agree with them (in time). On the other hand I may be thought to be stating the obvious, or

---

[38] P.J. Geary, *Furta Sacra: The Thefts of Relics in the Central Middle Ages* (Princeton NJ, rev. edn 1990), esp. pp.37–43.

[39] *HE* iii.6,12.

[40] The later complex history of Oswald's remains is set out by C. Plummer, *Venerabilis Baedae Opera Historica* (2 vols, Oxford 1896), II, pp.157–8, but does not concern us here.

[41] Earth from the place where Oswald was killed, and from where the water which had washed his bones at Bardney was poured away, the stake on which his head was first placed, and the cross which he had set up at Heavenfield were also regarded as holy, and performed healing miracles, mostly by means of water in which chips from them had been soaked (*HE* iii.9–11, 13). Charles Thomas has pointed out that sometimes these cures involved five steps from the original (*The Early Christian Archaeology of North Britain* (1971), pp.132–7).

[42] P. Brown, *The Cult of the Saints* (Chicago and London 1981), pp.4–5.

repeating what others have already said better, especially since generalization is necessary here for the sake of brevity.

Donald Bullough was of the opinion that 'the early Church showed itself surprisingly indifferent to where Christians were laid to rest'.[43] Was this the case in early England? Large early graveyards have been found with interments packed close around churches and the shrines of saints, but nevertheless identifying the earliest Anglo-Saxon Christian churchyard burials is not easy since the earliest burials found in a churchyard may not have been Christian, or may have been British. For example, those at Deerhurst Gloucestershire 'were recognised . . . precisely because they had been disturbed by the foundations of the first stone church'.[44] At Hereford Castle Green, the earliest burials discovered were associated with apparently religious buildings, but radio-carbon dating (centred on AD 700) 'leaves open the possibility of an eighth-century date, well after the conversion period – and a pre-Anglo-Saxon date in the sixth or seventh centuries cannot be excluded either.[45]

At Burgh Castle, Suffolk, a post-Roman cemetery of about 200 supine burials of adults and children was virtually without grave-goods. The graves were in parallel rows, aligned EW, more or less, but more with a large rectangular timber building (which the burials respected) up against the southern wall of the fort. The excavator, Charles Green, associated the post-Roman activity with the Irish saint Fursey, who is documented as having established a monastery at a Roman camp called *Cnobheresburg* near the sea, given to him by Sigeberht of East Anglia (ruled *c*.630-*c*.634?).[46] Unfortunately, there are difficulties in identifying Burgh Castle as *Cnobheresburg*, let alone the timber building found there as Fursey's church. The grave-yard, with its children's burials and, in places, 'at least three layers of overlying graves', apparently continued in use for over 200 years (from *c*.AD 800 to the early tenth century, according to radio-carbon dating).[47]

From the foregoing, in spite of the difficulties of identifying the earliest churchyard burials, their character, once established, appears clear enough. The bodies were normally buried in shrouds (sometimes also in coffins), but with nothing to distinguish their age, rank or even gender (unless they were priests buried with chalice and patten). That is strange, since the Anglo-Saxon laws, with their varying penalties for offences against men of differing hierarchical ranks,

[43] D. Bullough, 'Burial, Community and Belief in the Early Medieval West', in *Ideal and Reality in Frankish and Anglo-Saxon Society: Studies presented to J.M. Wallace-Hadrill*, ed. P. Wormald (Oxford 1983), pp.177–201, at p.186.

[44] P. Sims-Williams, *Religion and Literature in Western England 600–800* (Cambridge 1990), pp.59–60.

[45] *Ibid*. See also R. Shoesmith, *Hereford City Excavations I* (1980), pp.11 (Fig.7), 12–13, 24–5. Two adult males excavated in 1960 were associated with an earth platform, on which a timber building (? a church) may have stood. Three burials excavated in 1973 were of two adult males and a small child. All these burials were supine and on a different orientation (slightly north of east) from overlying graves and from the wall of a stone building near the 1973 discoveries. There were no signs of coffins or grave-goods, or that any grave-markers had been used.

[46] *HE* iii.19, based on the earlier *Life of Fursey* (op cit).

[47] S. Johnson, *Burgh Castle, Excavations by Charles Green 1958–61*, East Anglian Archaeology Report 20 (1983), pp.3–4, 47–55, 63–5, 119–21.

make it clear that status was of vital importance in earthly life. However, John Blair surmises that in the seventh and eighth centuries burial in a churchyard may itself have been 'more a matter of privilege than compulsion'.[48] Only the positioning near the body of a saint in hope of sharing his resurrection was important,[49] and likely to have been much more available to the rich and powerful than to the ordinary run of mankind.

How did this differ from the disposal of the dead in pagan times? It is a fair assumption that all those buried in graves dated by fifth or sixth-century grave-goods were pagans, since the foreign missionaries had not yet arrived.[50] Heathen cemeteries have not often been found close to settlements, though modern excavations, such as those at Spong Hill Norfolk,[51] and Mucking Essex,[52] have shown that some of the earliest invaders placed their dwellings and cemeteries close together. The pagan burial-grounds are not defined by visible boundaries, though at times the burials abruptly end at what appears to us an arbitrary line.[53]

Pagan burials come in more than one style. Cremations are by definition pagan, for the Church did not approve of them.[54] Though it is sometimes believed that the purpose of burning the body is to release the spirit, the specific significance of cremation varies in traditional societies, and for the Anglo-Saxons is virtually irrecoverable.[55] There are resemblances between the cremation and inhumation rituals: women appear to have been laid on the pyre wearing the same kind of clothes as are evident in the inhumation burials, but the cremation rite had some special features; for example, the burning of animal bodies with the corpse, and the lack of weapons with male burials (though they sometimes had their playing-pieces with them), but the provision of miniature (symbolic?) toilet implements, unburnt, placed with the ashes in the urns. However, the incoming missionaries would have encountered few cremating Anglo-Saxons, since the practice was in

---

[48] Blair (1988) p.52.

[49] Geary (1990) p.30.

[50] I leave open the possibility that some unfurnished burials in the 'heathen' cemeteries may have been those of crypto-Christians, whether Britons or not.

[51] R. Rickett, *The AngloSaxon Cemetery at Spong Hill, North Elmham, Part VII: The Iron Age, Roman and Early Saxon Settlement*, East Anglian Archaeology Report 73 (1995), p.xii, pp.41–4, 147, 154–8.

[52] M.U. and W.T. Jones, 'An Early Saxon Landscape at Mucking, Essex', in T. Rowley (ed.), *Anglo-Saxon Settlement and Landscape*, British Archaeological Reports 6 (1974), pp.20–35; Fig.2, p.26.

[53] Consider, for example, the western edge of the Spong Hill cemetery (*op.cit.*).

[54] The arguments against cremation by the early Christian fathers are complicated by their need to counter the idea that a part of the soul remained with the body until it had been entirely destroyed by time, and by the doctrine of the resurrection of the body. Though little more is expressed than a preference for inhumation, cremation seems to have been avoided by Christians until about 200 years ago. See, for example, Minucius Felix *Octavius* Ch 11.2, 4–5; 34.9, ed. in *Tertullian, Apology, De Spectaculis: Minucius Felix* (Loeb repr. 1966), pp.340–3; 420–1; *Quinti Septimi Florentis Tertulliani, De Anima* ch. 51.4, ed. in J.H. Waszink (Amsterdam 1947), pp.68–70, notes pp.526–34, trans. R Arbesmann *et al.* in *Tertullian, Apologetical Works, and Minucius Felix, Octavius*, Fathers of the Church X (Washington DC 1950, 2nd ed. 1962); J. Hastings, *Encyclopaedia of Religion and Ethics* IV (Edinburgh and New York 1911), p.457; Dorothy Watts, *Christians and Pagans in Roman Britain* (London 1991), p.52 and note 1, p.238.

[55] Howard Williams (pers. comm.) has conjectured a connection between the cremation ritual and shamanism.

decline when they arrived. Some of the missionaries probably did encounter another rite implying a different kind of otherworld journey, boat burial, found only in high-status burials in Suffolk.[56]

Superficially and generally there is not a great deal of difference visible between the inhumation burial of a pagan and a Christian. Pagan burials are less regularly aligned than those in the Christian churchyards, though sometimes there was, even in the sixth century, a prevailing orientation. Many of the pagan inhumation burials are supine and neatly laid out, but often the postures vary and sometimes family groups using the same cemetery appear to have positioned their dead differently.[57]

The most noticeable characteristic of the pagan inhumations is the provision of grave-goods with the dead: both males and females regularly had at least a knife with them. Many men were provided with weapons, probably indicating their status;[58] evidence for what they wore is slighter, though a belt buckle is found not infrequently. In contrast, women were apparently displayed for burial in their best clothes, fastened by brooches and pins, adorned with beads and pendants. Less often, they were buried with domestic items, the commonest being spindle-whorls and keys, whether actual or symbolic, which had sometimes been kept in a waist bag. John Hines has speculated that this pagan society was virilocal, and that brides brought their distinctive local jewellery with them to their new homes, where (presumably) they were buried.[59] The splendour of the female funereal display may therefore have defined a womans' identity as daughter, as wife and as desirable mother for the next generation. To put it another way, it may be that man's weapon-burial illustrated his active role in the wider society, whereas a woman's dressed burial illustrated her intrinsic value within the family.[60] Some of the richer burials, both male and female, were

---

[56] The significance of boat burial is uncertain: Audrey L. Meaney, 'Scyld Scefing and the dating of Beowulf – Again' *Bulletin of the John Rylands University Library of Manchester* 71 (1989), 77–40, at 22–37. M.O.H. Carver supposes that the rite was drawn from a long-lived ideological mind-set reified at certain moments in history for political purposes: 'Boat burial in Britain: Ancient custom or political signal?' in O. Crumlin-Pedersen and Birgitte Munch Thye (eds), *The Ship as Symbol in Prehistoric and Medieval Scandinavia* (National Museum of Denmark, 1995), pp.111–24.

[57] E-J. Pader, *Symbolism, Social relations and the Interpretation of Mortuary Remains*, British Archaeological Reports, International Series 130 (1982). See also A. Taylor, C. Duhig and J. Hines, 'An Anglo-Saxon cemetery at Oakington, Cambridgeshire', *Proceedings of the Cambridge Antiquarian Society*, 86 (1997), pp.57–90, burials 12a and b (two apparently unrelated children, one probably a girl aged about 15 with a little jewellery, the other, a child about 8, lying sprawled both face down), and burial 23 (a child aged about 6, with a cattle bone between its legs). The orientation and position of the Oakington burials as a group was more than usually varied.

[58] Heinrich Härke, 'Warrior graves? The background of the Anglo-Saxon weapon burial rite' *Past and Present* 126 (1990) pp.22–43; but see M. Parker Pearson *The Archaeology of Death and Burial* (Stroud 1999), pp.119–21.

[59] Tim Malim and John Hines, *The Anglo-Saxon Cemetery at Edix Hill (Barrington A) Cambridgeshire* (CBA RR 112, 1998), pp.301–8; 313–17. For waist-bags or pockets see pp.268–9.

[60] I am deliberately avoiding the question of race. The possibility that men and women buried with a full early Anglo-Saxon kit of artefacts related to those found in North Germany may have nevertheless been Britons seems to me unlikely; that those buried without grave goods in the same cemeteries may have been Britons, is as yet unproven.

supplied with vessels, either pottery or glass, which may have contained beverages. Occasionally, there are remains of food: bones from cuts of meat, or hazel nuts in bronze bowls. Whether these were envisaged as food for the dead, or as offerings to show respect (as with our provision of flowers), is unknown. The quantity and quality of grave-goods seems to have been regulated by both wealth and age: the youthful and the elderly usually have a more restricted kit than those who died in the prime of life, and small children seldom have anything recognisable with them. Before the conversion period therefore, status may have been achieved rather than inherited.

It seems, then, that to the fifth- and sixth-century pagans the provision of a good funeral which reflected the status of the dead (even to the very occasional provision of a sacrificed slave, horse or dog) was all-important. But what happened if later heathens disturbed a grave? We can only tell that this has happened where a later pagan burial with grave-goods has disturbed an earlier one, and (for example) skull or long bones are tossed back into the grave fill. However, this is found rarely enough for us to be able to assume that pagans usually took care to respect earlier graves. In contrast, although the Christian emphasis upon the resurrection of the body would seem to imply that corpses should be treated reverently,[61] the practice was otherwise. One of the major problems in identifying the earliest of the English churchyard burials is that they are at the bottom of the sequence in a confined space that was used over and over again.[62]

The earliest identifiable unfurnished churchyard burials cannot have been the burials of the earliest Anglo-Saxon Christians; the chronological gap between them and the sixth-century pagan inhumations is too great. The gap is filled (and indeed overlapped) not only by the occasional furnished churchyard burial,[63] but also by a series of cemeteries and individual burials (not associated with churches) which can be dated to the seventh century or later.[64] At the earlier end of the seventh century are some burials which are as richly furnished as the richer sixth-century interments, or are even wealthier, but in a different style; they seem to have been affected by political, social and even fashion changes brought in along with the introduction of Christianity.[65] However, there cannot have been an

[61] See St Augustine, *The City of God against the Pagans* I, xii-xiii, ed. and trans. G.E. McCracken (London and Cambridge, Mass. 1957), pp.58–67.
[62] See A. Morton, 'Burial in Middle Saxon Southampton', in *Death in Towns: Urban Responses to the Dying and the Dead, 100–1600*, ed. S. Bassett (Leicester 1992), pp.69–77; Kjølbye-Biddle (1975 see n.29).
[63] See Table V in R. Morris, *The Church in British Archaeology*, Council for British Archaeology Research Report 47 (1983), pp.59–60, Figs.11,17.
[64] *Ibid.* pp.24–5, 55–6; A. Boddington, 'Models of Burial, Settlement and Worship: The Final Phase Reviewed', in *Anglo-Saxon Cemeteries: A Reappraisal*, ed. E. Southworth (Stroud 1990), pp.177–99; Sims-Williams (1990, see n.44), pp.64–72.
[65] Audrey L. Meaney, *Anglo-Saxon Amulets and Curing Stones* (BAR 96 Oxford 1981) *passim*, esp. 262–9.

exact correlation between religious belief and burial rite.[66] Some of the (usually male) richer seventh-century burials in large and often solitary barrows exhibit more concern with status – sometimes perhaps even with land division – than with religion. It is also possible that some of them show an 'aggressively pagan' reaction to Christianity, though we cannot be sure of this unless the cremation rite is used, as at Asthall Barrow Oxfordshire.[67]

Early Anglo-Saxon cemeteries show gradual changes in ritual, beginning perhaps even before the conversion. More graves are aligned east-west, and grave-goods become steadily rarer. Spears, shields and swords disappear from male graves (though certainly not from everyday life); only a large seax is found as a possible weapon. Dressed burial, in the height of fashion, particularly for women, lasted longer. Though there are a very few burials with grave-goods which can be dated to the mid and later eighth century, for the most part grave-goods were suddenly abandoned about AD 730,[68] about 15 years after Guthlac's death. Surely some of these late furnished graves could have been of Christians, like those in unfurnished graves lying beside them. But we cannot tell who was pagan and who Christian (even if they wore pendant crosses), and so the evidence of these cemeteries is ambiguous.[69] In time, however, all these traditional distinguishing features of the old pagan burial rites were eliminated, leaving only the anonymity of the pared-down Christian churchyard inhumation rite which has only been affected by minor changes in the centuries since.[70]

---

[66] M.O.H. Carver, 'Sutton Hoo in context' in *Angli e Sassoni al di qua e al di là del Mare* (Settimane di Studio del Centro Italiano di Studi sull'alto medioevo 32, 1986), pp.77–117, at pp.94–99.

[67] E. Thurlow Leeds 'An Anglo-Saxon Cremation Burial of the seventh century in Asthall barrow, Oxfordshire' *Antiquaries J.* 4 (1924), pp.13–126; Tania M. Dickinson and George Speake 'The seventh century cremation burial in Asthall Barrow Oxfordshire' in M. Carver (ed.) *The Age of Sutton Hoo* (Woodbridge 1992), pp.95–130.

[68] H. Geake, *The Use of Grave-Goods in Conversion-Period England, c.600–850*, British Archaeological Reports, British Series 261 (1997).

[69] D. Hadley, 'Equality, Humility and Non-Materialism? Christianity and Anglo-Saxon burial practices', *Archaeological Review from Cambridge* 17.2 (2000), pp.149–78.

[70] Indeed, the rite used in late Roman Christian cemeteries appears to have been virtually identical. See Watts (1991), pp.38–89.

15

The Adaptation of the Anglo-Saxon Royal Courts to Christianity

BARBARA YORKE

As is the case with many Germanic provinces far more is recorded about the conversion of the ruling houses of Anglo-Saxon England than about that of the bulk of the population. Looking at the conversion of élites may provide a way to understand broader issues of a province's conversion, though the ruling classes are also likely to be atypical; their conversion involved concerns which were not applicable to the greater part of the population. Political issues of the Anglo-Saxon conversion, in terms of the operation of overlordship and dynastic alliances, have received close attention in many previous studies.[1] Though such factors undoubtedly could have been very important in encouraging acceptance or rejection of Christianity, or of a particular missionary faction, we should not forget also that the attitudes of Germanic élites to the new religion would have been conditioned by their pre-existing religious beliefs and practices especially where these reinforced power and authority. In considering some facets of the conversion of the Anglo-Saxon kings from this perspective, I shall in effect be providing an Anglo-Saxon case study of the approaches championed by Przemyslaw Urbanczyk, both at the conference and elsewhere, for understanding the acceptance of Christianity by early medieval elites.[2]

Conversion and the Elites

As Dr Urbanczyck has reminded us, the Latin 'official' versions of royal conversion are not concerned to see matters from the royal point of view, and he has

---

[1] In particular, H. Mayr-Harting, *The Coming of Christianity to Anglo-Saxon England* (3rd edn, London, 1991), 64–8; J. Campbell, 'Observations on the conversion of England', *Essays in Anglo-Saxon History* (London, 1986), 69–84, esp. 74–7; D.P. Kirby, *The Earliest English Kings* (London, 1991); N. Higham, *The Convert Kings* (Manchester, 1997).

[2] P. Urbanczyk, 'The meaning of Christianization for medieval pagan societies', in *Early Christianity in Central and East Europe*, ed. P. Urbanczyk (Warsaw, 1997), 31–8; *idem*, 'Christianization of early medieval societies: an anthropological perspective', in *Conversion and Christianity in the North Sea World*, ed. B. Crawford (St Andrews, 1998), 129–33; *idem*, Chapter 2 in this volume.

shown how theoretical and anthropological models may help in reconstructing non-Christian perspectives. To tackle the history of the conversion of the Anglo-Saxons therefore involves a certain amount of deconstruction of our main source, Bede's *Historia Ecclesiastica*, and among the important developments in the historiography of the Anglo-Saxon conversion in recent years has been the appreciation that Bede's narrative of conversion is one conditioned by his own ecclesiastical perspectives, and that other narratives are possible.[3] An example of the problems of Bede's approach can be provided by the way he dealt with the initial phase of conversion. What was especially significant to Bede was the primary conversion that led to the establishment of a bishopric, and the appearance of any unbaptised king after that point was presented by him as apostasy. In Bede's analysis kings and their kingdoms were either Christian or pagan; no other combinations were possible.

But the material Bede presents on the first phase of conversion could be open to other interpretations in which it would appear royal houses saw matters rather differently. For the initial period after conversion could be seen as one in which the different religions co-existed, a state of affairs symbolised by the well-known description of how Raedwald, on returning home to East Anglia after baptism at the Kentish court, 'seemed to be serving both Christ and the gods whom he had previously served; in the same temple he had one altar for the Christian sacrifice and another small altar on which to offer victims to devils (*daemoniorum*)'.[4] Such a period in which practitioners of both religions could be found at the same time within the royal houses would help to explain the frequency with which princes who had not been baptised came to the throne.[5] For instance, in the case of the East Saxons it was not only the three sons of Saebert, the first East Saxon ruler to be converted, who remained unbaptised, but also several of their successors from more distant branches of the royal house for a period of some 50–60 years after Saebert's initiation into the new religion.[6] Adherence to more than one god at the same time would, of course, have seemed natural behaviour to people who practised a polytheistic religion, and comparable reactions can be found at a later date in the Scandinavian world.[7] What Bede saw as an unforgivable apostasy,

---

[3] For instance, it can be suggested that the British may have played a much more positive role in the conversion of the Anglo-Saxons than Bede allows: P. Sims-Williams, *Religion and Literature in Western England, 600–800* (Cambridge, 1990), esp. 54–85.

[4] *Bede's Ecclesiastical History of the English People*, eds B. Colgrave and R.A.B. Mynors (Oxford, 1969) [henceforth *HE*], II, 15. Here we see one of the ways in which Christian apologists sought to accommodate non-Christian deities by demonising them; for the alternative route of euhemerisation whereby gods were converted into heroes, see below n. 42.

[5] A. Angenendt, 'The conversion of the Anglo-Saxons considered against the background of the early medieval mission', *Angli e Sassoni al di qua e al di là del Mare, Spoleto Settimane di Studio*, 32 (1986), II, 747–81 suggests that the eldest son was deliberately left unbaptised as a kind of 'insurance policy', but the incidence of unbaptised males in the Anglo-Saxon royal houses seems to go deeper than that.

[6] B.A.E. Yorke, 'The kingdom of the East Saxons', *Anglo-Saxon England* 14 (1985), 1–36.

[7] For instance, the Icelandic althing eventually recognised Christianity as the country's official

may have been a pragmatic decision by royal houses that may have felt they needed the support and associations of both religions. Although one individual might honour both Christian and non-Christian gods, it may also have been the case that the worship of different deities was shared between members of a royal kin-group, so producing the situation apparently recorded by Bede in which there appeared to be 'Christian' and 'pagan' adherents within the same royal family at the same time. Only gradually was it accepted that recognition of one God was a non-negotiable tenet of Christianity. This point was reached at different dates within the different kingdoms. A sign of transition from the first phase to the next could be a royal initiative like the edict ordering the abandonment of pagan worship that Bede records was passed in Kent during the reign of King Earconbert (640–664);[8] but generally it is something that has to be inferred from the cessation of unbaptised princes succeeding to the throne. It is a transition that occurred between 40–60 years after the introduction of Christianity in most of the Anglo-Saxon kingdoms for which sufficient written evidence survives.[9]

The Monk-Kings and Sainted Kings

This paper will concentrate on some of the features of the second phase of conversion when Christianity became the only religion practised by the Anglo-Saxon royal houses, and the only religion officially allowed within their kingdoms. Kings had, of course, supported the church before this point through the foundation of bishoprics and grants of land to churches, but it was only in the second phase that they founded religious houses which members of their immediate families entered. What is most surprising of all is that the active personal involvement of royalty in monasticism seems to have been initiated by kings themselves. For it is at this transitional stage that the phenomenon of, in Clare Stancliffe's felicitous phrase, 'kings who opted out' is found, that is kings who voluntarily resigned their thrones to enter monasteries.[10]

The first Anglo-Saxon king known to have renounced his throne in order to enter a religious community was Sigebert of the East Angles who retired to an unnamed monastery at some unspecified point after his succession in 630 or 631.[11]

religion, but allowed that pagan sacrifices and various other practices (infanticide, the eating of horse flesh) could be carried out in the privacy of an individual's home. For fuller discussion of the first phase of conversion and references, see B.A.E. Yorke, 'The reception of Christianity at the Anglo-Saxon royal courts', in *St Augustine and the Conversion of England*, ed. R. Gameson (Stroud, 1999), 152–73.

[8] *HE* III, 8.

[9] See further, Yorke, 'Reception of Christianity'.

[10] C. Stancliffe, 'Kings who opted out', in *Ideal and Reality in Frankish and Anglo-Saxon Society*, eds P. Wormald, D. Bullough and R. Collins (Oxford, 1983), 154–76.

[11] *HE* III, 18. According to twelfth-century tradition recorded at Ely Sigebert's monastery was at *Betricesworde*, by which Bury St Edmunds is probably meant; *Liber Eliensis*, ed. E.O. Blake, Camden Society 3rd ser 92 (London, 1962), I, 1.

The next such recorded abdication is that of Centwine of Wessex in 685. His departure allowed the aggressive ætheling Caedwalla to come to the throne, and there is some temptation to see Centwine's entry into a religious community as less than voluntary, like some examples recorded from Northumbria in the following century.[12] However, Aldhelm, whose poem written for Centwine's daughter abbess Bugga is the only source for the king's retirement, does not make any such insinuations.[13] Voluntary retirement is also stressed in Bede's account of King Saebbi of the East Saxons and his long desire to give up his throne 'preferring a private life in a monastery to all the riches and honours of a kingdom'.[14] In the event he did not have to do without his royal trappings for very long, because he only became a monk at St Paul's in London shortly before his death in 694 while already suffering from the illness that would kill him. The final example, Æthelred of Mercia who retired in 704 to become a monk in the monastery he had founded at Bardney, seems to have done so while in better health for he may have survived until 716.[15]

In considering these four rulers as a group, one can observe first that examples of such voluntary abdications to enter monasteries are very rare in early medieval Europe,[16] and that their example was not (voluntarily) followed by any of their successors in their respective kingdoms. However, the circumstances in which these monk-kings made their decisions to withdraw from the world were not identical. Sigebert of the East Angles, who initiated the abdication of kings in order to live a religious life, may have had different experiences from the others. He had spent an earlier phase in exile in Gaul where he had been converted, and so may have experienced at first hand the enthusiasm for monasticism generated among the nobility of northern Francia and Burgundy by the activities of Columbanus.[17] Felix, whom he appointed to the East Anglian see, came from

---

[12] The *Continuatio* in the Moore Manuscript of *HE* records that in 731 King Ceolwulf was captured and tonsured, apparently as a means (unsuccessful in this instance) of forcing him from the throne. He later voluntarily entered the monastery of Lindisfarne.

[13] *Aldhelmi Opera*, ed. R. Ehwald, *Monumenta Germaniae Historica, Auctores Antiquissimi*, XV, 14–15; *Aldhelm: The Poetic Works*, eds M. Lapidge and J. Rosier (Woodbridge, 1985), 40–1 and 47–9; Stancliffe, 'Kings who opted', 154–5.

[14] *HE* IV, 11 – the refusal of his wife to agree to a separation is said by Bede to have been the reason that he did not opt out earlier.

[15] *The Chronicle of John of Worcester*, vol. II, eds R.R. Darlington and P. McGurk (Oxford, 1995), 172–3; A. Thacker, 'Kings, saints and monasteries in pre-Viking Mercia', *Midland History* 10 (1985), 1–25, at 1–4.

[16] Stancliffe, 'Kings who opted'.

[17] I. Wood, 'A prelude to Columbanus; the monastic achievement in the Burgundian territories', *Columbanus and Merovingian Monasticism*, ed. H.B. Clarke and M. Brennan, British Archaeological Reports, International Series 113 (Oxford, 1981), 3–32; P.J. Geary, *Before France and Germany: The Creation and Transformation of the Merovingian World* (Oxford, 1988), 171–89; A. Dierkens, 'Prolégomènes à une historie des relationes culturelles entre les Îles Britanniques et le continent pendant le haut moyen âge', in *La Neustrie. Les Pays au Nord de la Loire de 650 à 850*, ed. H. Atsma (2 vols, Sigmaringen, 1989), II, 371–94.

Burgundy and, it has been suggested, may have been a follower of Columbanus.[18] We should perhaps even consider the possibility that Sigebert had spent time in a Frankish monastery before returning to England to claim the East Anglian throne. The tradition concerning him which Bede has passed on was that he was in exile in Gaul to escape the enmity of Raedwald. In Francia by the early seventh century there was a tradition of nobles and princes out of favour with royal courts seeking sanctuary in religious houses (though for the most part these were native Franks rather than foreign visitors). A possible parallel for such a pattern in Sigebert's life can be found in the early years of Dagobert II, who as a young prince was spirited away to the safety of an Irish monastery until the time was favourable for him to return to Francia to claim the throne.[19]

Some 50 years or more separated Sigebert's entry into the religious life from that of the others, by which time there was a developing aristocratic enthusiasm for the monastic life which they could be seen as sharing. Æthelred of Mercia, for instance, could be seen in a similar light to Benedict Biscop, a leading noblem an at the Northumbrian court who founded the celebrated monasteries of Wearmouth and Jarrow to which he eventually retired.[20] The case of Saebbi is rather different, for he entered the monastic life on the point of death, a pattern to be followed by many other noblemen in the middle ages; approaching death brought sharply into focus the need for penance for the lives that had been lived. The monk-kings could have been a by-product of the impact of Christianity, as preached by Irish missionaries in particular, with an emphasis on the transience of earthly power and the need for penance, as Clare Stancliffe has so cogently argued.[21] But it may be that other factors should be considered. Motivations for entering monasteries could have been mixed, and although there may have been a significant personal sacrifice for a king in entering a monastery, the way of life was not necessarily particularly ascetic nor lacking in many of the luxuries and pastimes of the royal court.[22]

The stage within the conversion process at which these royal retreats into monasticism occurred may be significant. All the monk-kings can be said to have made their decisions to enter the monastic life at a comparable point in the history of conversion in their respective kingdoms, that is at the transition point from the first to second phases of conversion. Sigebert succeeded the last recorded pagan

[18] N. Brooks, *The Early History of the Church of Canterbury* (Leicester, 1984), 65; J.M. Wallace-Hadrill et al., *Bede's Ecclesiastical History of the English People. A Historical Commentary* (Oxford, 1988), 77–8, 223.

[19] J-M. Picard, 'Church and politics in the seventh century: the Irish exile of King Dagobert II', *Ireland and Northern France*, ed. J-M. Picard (Dublin, 1991), 27–52.

[20] P. Wormald, 'Bede and Benedict Biscop' in *Famulus Christi: Essays in Commemoration of the Thirteenth Centenary of the Birth of the Venerable Bede*, ed. G. Bonner (London, 1976), 141–69.

[21] Stancliffe, 'Kings who opted'.

[22] P. Wormald, 'Bede, Beowulf and the conversion of the Anglo-Saxon aristocracy', in *Bede and Anglo-Saxon England*, ed. R.T. Farrell, British Archaeological Reports 46 (Oxford, 1978), 32–95. For complaints about the type of lay aristocratic life lived in Anglo-Saxon monasteries see C. Cubitt, *Anglo-Saxon Church Councils c.650-c.850* (London, 1995) *passim*.

king of the East Angles,[23] while Saebbi had begun by sharing the reign with Sigehere who had resorted to traditional cults during the plague of 663–664 and is the last known East Saxon king to have sponsored pagan rites.[24] Centwine as well seems to have abdicated at a crucial stage in the full commitment of the West Saxon rulers to Christianity, for Caedwalla who succeeded him was the last unbaptised king to come to the throne, though he seems to have already made a major decision to support the Church in the form of bishop Wilfrid.[25] Caedwalla abdicated after 3 years in order to travel to Rome to be baptised by the Pope.[26] King Æthelred may appear a little more distant from the transition point, for his brother Wulfhere who ruled before him appears to have been a fully Christianised king, but, like the others, he was still of the first generation of his family to commit themselves to the new religion.

Before exploring the monk-kings any further, it may be appropriate to view them alongside what happened in Northumbria at the same transition point. For in Northumbria, rather than monastic retreat in the seventh century, we find kings who died a violent death being culted as saints. A relatively large body of evidence survives concerning the early promotion of the cult of King Oswald of Bernicia who died in battle in 642 against Penda of Mercia, though it has to be studied largely through the medium of Bede's *Historia Ecclesiastica*.[27] The cult began almost immediately after Oswald's death at the place where he was slain, apparently as a spontaneous response by local inhabitants,[28] and then through promotion by his brother King Oswiu. When Oswiu had gained control of Northumbria in 643, he retrieved the king's head and arms from the stakes on which the victorious Penda of Mercia had displayed them, then gave the head to his episcopal centre on Lindisfarne and enshrined the arms in a royal chapel at Bamburgh which according to Alcuin had been expressly founded for that purpose.[29] As Alan Thacker has stressed in his illuminating study of the cult, its official promotion was done on the king's initiative, apparently without episcopal support, and there was a marked difference in the treatment of the relics at Lindisfarne and Bamburgh.[30] The latter became an active shrine at which miracles

---

[23] *HE* III, 15; it is not clear if Ricbert who had slain Sigebert's brother Eorpwald was ruler for the 3 years between the latter's death and the accession of Sigebert when Bede says 'the province reverted to error'.

[24] *HE* III, 30.

[25] *HE* IV, 15–6; *The Life of Bishop Wilfrid by Eddius Stepahanus*, ed. B. Colgrave (Cambridge, 1927), ch. 42.

[26] *HE* V, 7; he died soon after and was buried in Rome in his baptismal robes.

[27] *Oswald. Northumbrian King to European Saint*, eds C. Stancliffe and E. Cambridge (Stamford, 1995).

[28] *HE* III, 9–10; C. Cubbitt, 'Sites and sanctity: revisiting the cult of murdered and martyred Anglo-Saxon royal saints', *Early Medieval Europe* 9 (2000), 53–84, esp. 60–3.

[29] *HE* III, 6 and 12; *Alcuin: the Bishops, Kings and Saints of York*, ed. P. Godman (Oxford, 1982), 28–30 (lines 304–11).

[30] A. Thacker, '*Membra Disjecta*: the division of the body and the diffusion of the cult', in *Oswald. Northumbrian King*, 97–127, esp 98–102.

were performed;[31] Bede records that Oswald's right hand, which had been blessed by Bishop Aidan because of the king's generosity in sending a silver dish piled with food to the poor, remained incorrupt in its silver shrine.[32] In contrast, at Lindisfarne the head was buried and only seems to have become a valued relic at a later date.[33] The next stage in the promotion of the cult was also made on royal rather than ecclesiastical initiative, when Oswiu's daughter's Osthryth, at a date between 679 and 697, exhumed the body from its burial place on the battlefield and translated it to the monastery at Bardney in the province of Lindsey which she had founded with her husband King Æthelred of Mercia.[34] It was probably only after this translation that Bishop Wilfrid and his followers at Hexham became enthusiastic proponents of Oswald's cult, and it was largely because of this promotion, perhaps especially through the advocacy of Bede's friend and diocesan Acca of Hexham, that Oswald became the main exemplar of a sanctified king in the *Historia Ecclesiastica*.[35]

The cult of King Edwin of Deira, although less well recorded and successful seems to have followed a similar sequence. Edwin had also been slain by Penda (in 633) and his remains may have been treated in a similar way to Oswald's, for his head was housed separately from his body at an early stage and placed in his episcopal centre of York.[36] Unfortunately it is not clear from Bede's account when this took place, who was responsible and whether it occurred before or after Oswiu's promotion of Oswald's cult. There are also signs of a cult at the place where Edwin fell in battle and was buried, and his body was also translated and enshrined by a daughter of Oswiu, Abbess Ælfflaed who removed it to her nunnery at Whitby.[37] The similarities between these two enshrinements by the two sisters suggest that they were either part of a co-ordinated campaign or else that one was done in imitation of the other. Although Edwin was not promoted as a saint in the *Historia Ecclesiastica*, it is quite clear from the Whitby *Life* that he was regarded as a saint there and reputed to have performed miracles.[38] No details are given of miracles at his tomb, but the dreams of a priest that led to the *inventio* of the body are described at some length and conform to hagiographic conventions.[39]

The early phases of the cults of Oswald and Edwin are characterised by having been promoted by members of the royal house apparently with very little episcopal encouragement or support. They are the earliest cults of native

---

[31] *Alcuin. Bishops, Kings and Saints*, 30 (lines 308–11).

[32] *HE* III, 6.

[33] *HE* III, 12; Thacker, '*Membra disjecta*', 101–2.

[34] *HE* III, 11.

[35] Thacker, '*Membra disjecta*', 107–12.

[36] *HE* II, 20.

[37] *The Earliest Life of Gregory the Great*, ed. B. Colgrave (Cambridge, 1968), ch. 18–19.

[38] *Life of Gregory the Great* ch. 18 states that 'the light of Christ shines from this King Edwin in the glory of his miracles'.

[39] *Life of Gregory the Great* ch. 18.

Anglo-Saxons and date before a tradition of culting native-born churchmen had been established. Although the translations of the bodies of Edwin and Oswald in particular seem to show a knowledge of contemporary western European conventions for the creation of saints, the production of multiple relics from dismembered bodies was not accepted practice in the early medieval church at this date.[40] Oswiu and his daughters were acting in knowledge of the contemporary cults of saints, but seem to have been prepared to innovate to achieve their goals. The cult of the murdered and martyred king was to develop a long and successful tradition in Anglo-Saxon England and beyond. It seems likely, as Catherine Cubitt has argued, that both the royal promoters and the lesser laymen, who apparently quickly and independently appreciated the powers of the bodies, decapitated heads and blood of fallen kings, drew upon pre-Christian popular traditions of royal sacrality.[41] Nevertheless, in choosing to promote kinsmen as saints the initiators of the cults of Edwin and Oswald may be presumed to have been also following their own specific agendas. Through their promotions they demonstrated a willingness to take the initiative as leaders of the Christian cult and made a public statement about the sacrality of kingship and how it manifested itself in the Christian religion. Such things must have been all the more important to do if, as there is good reason to believe, one of the planks supporting kingship was a belief in divine descent symbolised in genealogies by descent from Woden and other gods.[42] It is just the kind of behaviour we might expect to find in the secondary phase of conversion where royal concern would have been to ensure that issues of royal status, specifically the sacrality of kings, which had been met in certain ways under the pagan regime were transferred effectively to Christian sponsorship now that pagan rites had ceased to be observed.

The kings who entered monasteries also had the potential to become saints as Susan Ridyard has discussed.[43] Although Bede stops short of describing Saebbi as a saint, he does reproduce two miracles concerning his death and burial that he says came from the *libellus* of Barking that also provided him with miracle stories concerning Abbess Æthelburh and other nuns of Barking.[44] Barking was a double monastery with close associations with the royal house as well as with St Paul's, where Saebbi was buried, as Bishop Eorcenwald of London (c.675–693)

[40] Thacker, '*Membra disjecta*'.

[41] Cubitt, 'Sites and sanctity', which puts the approach on an altogether more authoritative standing than that achieved by W.A. Chaney, *The Cult of Kingship in Anglo-Saxon England* (Manchester, 1970).

[42] K. Sisam, 'Anglo-Saxon royal genealogies', *Proceedings of the British Academy* 39 (1953), 287–348; H. Moisl, 'Anglo-Saxon royal genealogies and Germanic oral tradition', *Journal of Medieval History* 7 (1981), 215–48; R. North, *Heathen Gods in Old English Literature* (Cambridge, 1997); Yorke, 'Reception of Christianity', 153–5.

[43] S.J. Ridyard, 'Monk-kings and the Anglo-Saxon hagiographic tradition', *The Haskins Society Journal* 6 (1994), 13–28.

[44] *HE* IV, 11 and 19; Ridyard, 'Monk-kings', 16–17.

was brother of Æthelburh and involved in the foundation of Barking.[45] It seems likely that Saebbi was being promoted as a saint in the East Saxon kingdom within a few years of his death. Æthelred and his wife Osthryth were evidently culted at the monastery they had founded for they appear in the late Saxon list of saints' resting-places under Bardney.[46] It cannot be known when the cult was established, but the entry comes in the first part of the list that is generally believed to be of pre-viking origin.

Founders of early Anglo-Saxon religious communities were particularly likely to be revered as saints, and it may even have been the case that every minster at one stage had had its own saint, though the vagaries of history and the varying survival of traditions has meant that evidence for all has not survived.[47] Sigebert and Centwine who founded communities therefore also had the potential to have been seen as saints even though no specific evidence for their cults survives. There are various factors that could explain why any such cults had failed to flourish. Neither king, as far as is known, was succeeded by his own descendants. The destruction caused to the earliest religious foundations in East Anglia by the activities of Penda may have left little of Sigebert and his church for future generations.[48] In Wessex, on the other hand, there are very few local saints for the pre-viking period recorded, and no tradition of a male saint in its royal house before the late Saxon Edward the Martyr. Either Wessex differed significantly from other early Anglo-Saxon kingdoms or later ecclesiastical and dynastic policies effaced the traditions of earlier saints. The cult of Oswald was exceptional partly because Bede took it up in the *Historia Ecclesiastica*, but also because Oswald's direct descendants continued to rule into the eighth century so that they and their ecclesiastical supporters had additional reasons for continuing to cultivate his reputation as a saint.[49] In Kent there appears to have been neither kingly saints nor abbots, but there is an attested early cult of two murdered male princes promoted at the royal nunnery of Thanet that may have filled similar needs.[50] However, the princes came from a side-lined cadet branch of the royal house so there are different ways in which their cult might be interpreted, both in the seventh century when the cult was apparently initiated and in subsequent centuries.[51]

---

[45] C.R. Hart, *Early Charters of Eastern England* (Leicester, 1966), 117–45.
[46] D. Rollason, 'Lists of saints' resting-places in Anglo-Saxon England', *Anglo-Saxon England* 7 (1978), 61–94, at 89.
[47] J. Blair, 'A saint for every minster? Local cults in Anglo-Saxon England', and 'A handlist of Anglo-Saxon saints', *Local Saints and Local Churches*, ed. R. Sharpe and A. Thacker (Oxford, forthcoming). I am very grateful to Dr Blair for making this material available to me in advance of publication.
[48] Ridyard, 'Monk-kings', 20–1.
[49] D.P. Kirby, 'Northumbria in the time of Wilfrid', in *Saint Wilfrid at Hexham*, ed. D.P. Kirby (Newcastle upon Tyne, 1975), 1–34.
[50] D. Rollason, *The Mildrith Legend. A Study in Early Medieval Hagiography in England* (Leicester, 1982).
[51] D. Rollason, 'Cults of murdered royal saints', *Anglo-Saxon England* 11 (1983), 1–22, at 17–19 and 21; S. Hollis, 'The Minster-in-Thanet foundation story', *Anglo-Saxon England* 27 (1998), 41–74.

Viewing the early monk-kings and sainted kings together seems to produce a significant pattern. In all the major Anglo-Saxon kingdoms soon after pagan worship was finally abandoned (with the possible exception of Kent), we find promotion of kings, by themselves or by members of their immediate families, as men who can demonstrate a close link with the new source of supernatural power through a manifestation of saintlinesss, achieved either through 'martyrdom' – though Bede carefully avoids promoting Oswald as a martyr[52] – or through life as a monastic that might also lead to canonisation. The rulers whose initiatives seem to have been most significant in establishing the trend – Sigebert of the East Angles and Oswiu of Northumbria – had both lived in exile in Christian communities, in Francia and Ireland respectively, and so had had the opportunity to see how Christian cult might be adapted to underpin Anglo-Saxon kingship. They were not trying to outmanoeuvre or replace the growing band of cult specialists, the bishops and priests, but do appear to want to have had some active role in the new religion and to demonstrate that kings could be an embodiment of political and spiritual power in the way that evidence suggests they had been seen under the pagan religion.[53] Under paganism kings and other members of the royal house may have played an active role in some cult practices. Not many such references have survived the careful presentation of aspects of paganism by Christian commentators like Bede who wished to emphasize that kings should leave intervention in ecclesiastical matters to their bishops and priests, and probably for this reason preferred to stress the role of a parallel pagan priesthood.[54] But some references have slipped through. Quotations provided by Bede from the letters of Pope Boniface V to King Edwin of Northumbria and to his wife Æthelburh (which alludes to Kentish practice)[55] refer to divination at pagan shrines with the implication that kings were involved in these ceremonies.[56] The expectation of kings and royal houses as they made the transition to full acceptance of Christianity was that they would have some active involvement in Christian cult, and a particular area of concern would have been that they should continue to be seen as having an inherent tendency towards sacrality. These two aspects were presumably to their minds closely interlinked; the one was the guarantor and demonstration of the latter. Monasticism and the cult of saints seemed to offer a solution to both these concerns.

---

[52] V.A. Gunn, 'Bede and the martyrdom of St Oswald', *Studies in Church History* 30, ed. D. Wood (Oxford 1993), 57–66. Bede's efforts were in vain for Oswald was presented as a martyr in later manifestations of his cult; see *Oswald, King and Martyr passim*.

[53] Urbanczyk, 'Christianisation of early medieval societies', and Chapter 2 in this volume.

[54] R. Page, 'Anglo-Saxon paganism: the evidence of Bede', *Pagans and Christians. The Interplay between Christian Latin and Traditional Cultures in Early Medieval Europe*, eds. T. Hosfra, L. Houwen and A. MacDonald. Germania Latina II (Groningen, 1995), 99–130.

[55] *HE* II, 10 and 11.

[56] For discussion of other examples of Germanic leaders involved in divination, and other evidence for early Germanic paganism, see I. Wood, 'Pagan religions and superstitions east of the Rhine from the fifth to the ninth century', *After Empire. Towards an Ethnology of Europe's Barbarians*, ed. G. Ausenda (Woodbridge, 1995), 253–79.

From Holy Kings to Royal Abbesses and Princess-Saints

However, the phenomenon of the holy king, and especially the monk-king, was to be shortlived (though any king or prince who died a violent death in the Anglo-Saxon period, no matter how unvirtuous their life, had the potential to become a martyr).[57] The king-saint was not a phenomenon that early Anglo-Saxon churchmen seem to have been keen to promote. Alan Thacker has remarked that clergy of Lindisfarne seem to have been reluctant to do anything with Oswald's head besides burying it.[58] Bede commended Saebbi's religious enthusiasm, but observed that 'many people thought and often said that a man of his disposition ought to have been a bishop rather than king'.[59] The same individual should not try to do both; different qualities were needed for two very different roles. A king, like Oswald as presented by Bede, should be advised by his bishop and help him as instructed, but he should not be a religious leader himself.[60] Apart from the desire to eradicate any trace of pre-Christian royal cultic roles, the early medieval church believed that those in holy orders should have no involvement with secular warfare and in particular they had to avoid the taint of the shedding of blood. Their apprehensions about the undesirability of kings becoming monks would have included a consciousness of some unfortunate precedents from neighbouring societies when royal and monastic roles had been conflated. Gildas, for example, provided the chilling example of King Constantine of Dumnonia who had apparently murdered two kinsmen in the church to which he had retired as abbot.[61]

Other factors may have encouraged rulers to reach similar conclusions about the desirability of not combining royal and monastic roles. In Francia, princes who retired to monasteries were regarded as having lost their royal power, not as having added a spiritual dimension to it. Enforced retirement to a monastery was a way of removing rivals as an alternative to killing them, as Clotild was reminded when two of her sons, having captured some unwanted nephews, suggested she chose between letting them live with their hair cut short (i.e. tonsured) or having them killed. 'If they are not to ascend the throne, I would rather see them dead than with their hair cut short', she is reputed to have said.[62] Forcible tonsuring not only humiliated, but removed a sign of princely

---

[57] Rollason, 'Cults of murdered royal saints'; Cubitt, 'Sites and sanctity'.

[58] Thacker, '*Membra disjecta*', 101–4.

[59] *HE* IV, 11.

[60] J. Wallace-Hadrill, *Early Germanic Kingship on England and the Continent* (Oxford, 1971), 83–5.

[61] *Gildas. The Ruin of Britain and Other Documents*, ch. 28. ed. M. Winterbottom (Chichester, 1978), 99–100.

[62] Gregory of Tours, *Libri historiarum decem*, ed. B. Krusch and W. Levison, *Monumenta Germaniae Historica. Scriptores Rerum Merovingicarum* 1 (Hannover, 1951), III, 18; translated *Gregory of Tours, History of the Franks*, ed. L. Thorpe (Harmondsworth, 1974), 180–2. See also II, 41 for the enforced tonsuring of Chararic and his son Clovis and V, 14 for Merovich, son of King Chilperic tonsured and packed off by his father to be turned into a priest after a rebellion.

status – their long hair.[63] These messages were not lost on the Anglo-Saxons, and when rivals sought to topple King Ceolwulf from power in 731 he was captured and tonsured (though subsequently restored to power).[64] It was a precedent followed with enthusiasm in eighth-century Northumbria. Therefore for a king or prince to enter a monastery came to have connotations of failure, and the real risk that a prince who had taken holy orders would be barred from inheriting the throne as the supporters of Coenwulf seem to have argued successfully in the case of the Kentish claimant Eadbert Praen.[65]

However, there was a possible compromise that all parties appeared to find acceptable. Instead of kings and princes going into the church, widowed queens and princesses became the religious specialists of the royal houses. The relative chronology is significant here. For in most of the kingdoms for which we have adequate records the first royal nunneries were founded soon *after* the attempts discussed above whereby kings sought to establish a specifically Christian sacral identity for themselves and their families.[66] For instance, the daughters of Sigebert of East Anglia's successor Anna were the first Anglo-Saxon princesses to go into the church,[67] and Centwine's daughter Bugga founded the first known royal nunnery in Wessex.[68] The entry of royal women into the church was a movement apparently taken up with enthusiasm in all the major kingdoms in the last quarter of the seventh century, after precedents set by princesses from East Anglia and by their Deiran in-laws. At a conservative estimate, some 25–30 royal nunneries were established in the late seventh or early eighth centuries.[69] It was a movement that also had Frankish antecedents, as Bede indicates by naming significant nunneries of the lower Seine such as Faremoutiers-en-Brie, where two East Anglian princesses and their Kentish niece were installed,[70] though these Frankish nunneries had been founded by leading noble families rather than by members of the royal house.[71] In families like that of Burgundofara, first abbess of Brie, the sons established the family position through public service and the daughters nurtured the family's spirituality on paternal lands. In the words of Patrick Geary, they added 'a family tradition of supernatural power to that of traditional lordship'.[72]

---

[63] E. James 'Bede and the tonsure question' *Peritia* 3 (1984), 85–98; R. Bartlett, 'Symbolic meanings of hair in the middle ages', *Transactions of the Royal Historical Society* 6th ser., 4 (1994), 43–60.

[64] *HE*, continuation in the Moore Manuscript, 532–3.

[65] B. Yorke, *Kings and Kingdoms of Early Anglo-Saxon England* (London, 1990), 31–2.

[66] The claims that some Kentish nunneries were founded in the first half of the seventh century are not considered here as they are of doubtful reliability; see material included in Rollason, *Legend of St Mildrith*.

[67] *HE* III, 8.

[68] B. Yorke, 'The Bonifacian mission and female religious in Wessex', *Early Medieval Europe* 7 (1998), 145–72, at 157–8 and 161–4.

[69] For full details see B. Yorke, *Nunneries and the Anglo-Saxon Royal Houses* (London, 2003).

[70] *HE* III, 18.

[71] Dierkens, 'Prolégomènes à une historie des relationes culturelles', 371–94.

[72] Geary, *Before France and Germany*, 173.

The royal women presumably would have been more acceptable to the Church than kings or princes as they were not eligible to hold royal office or military commands, even though many had lived as married women and exercised secular power as queens. Though virginity may have remained the ideal, especially for female sainthood, loss of it was not an insurmountable obstacle for a monastic career and the position of abbess.[73] The royal nunneries proved to be convenient bases for nurturing the cults of royal saints including that of Edwin at Whitby and Saebbi at Barking, as well as functioning like any other monastic centre in praying on behalf of the welfare of living and dead benefactors. But the princess-saints could also take on the role of embodying the spiritual power of the royal lines. In the absence of a specific statement to this effect in Anglo-Saxon sources, we can turn to the tenth-century continental Saxon author Hrostwitha of Gandersheim for an interesting insight into how such matters may have been viewed in the Anglo-Saxon royal houses as well as in Ottonian Germany. The occasion for her comments was the marriage of Edith, daughter of Edward the Elder, in 929 or 930 to the future Emperor Otto I. For Hrostwitha, Edith of Wessex was distinguished not only by descent from 'a race famous for its grand kings', but also from a *beata stirps*, a blessed line descended from saintly ancestors.[74] Hrostwitha implies that the Ottonians had the first category of descent from powerful rulers, but not the second which Edith was expected to pass on to her descendants and so make her children by Otto I more fitting than their rivals to rule. She is not saying that saintliness, *sanctitas*, was transmitted as such, but rather that a tendency towards it and to greater virtue than the norm was. Her views were apparently justified by the miracles at Edith's tomb after her death – even though Edith had never lived the life of a religious.[75] Only her own premature death, followed by that of her son, prevented a major cult from developing.

Hrostwitha may provide us with a gateway into the thought world of seventh-century Anglo-Saxon royal houses. When Christianity was introduced kings probably already had an established convention in which, to return to Patrick Geary's phrase, 'a family tradition of supernatural power [was added to] that of traditional lordship'. Kings were at first anxious to continue with certain traditional cultic practices in which they played a prominent part and which could be interpreted as underpinning their positions. When obliged to accept that any attempt to continue to find support from non-Christian spiritual powers was

---

[73] M. Lapidge and M. Herrren, *Aldhelm: The Prose Works* (Woodbridge, 1979), 55–67; see further Yorke, *Nunneries*.

[74] *Gesta Ottonis*, in H. Homeyer (ed.), *Hrotsvithae Opera* (Munich, 1970), v. 83–97; P. Corbet, *Les Saints ottoniens; sainteté dynastique, sainteté royale et sainteté féminine autour de l'an Mil*, Beihefte von Francia, bd 15 (Sigmaringen, 1986), 46–50, 111–19. The supposed saintly ancestor who seems to have most impressed Hrostwitha was Oswald of Northumbria who could only have been seen as a direct ancestor of the West Saxon royal house through a female line or by adoption.

[75] The miracles are also recorded by Thietmar of Merseburg; Corbet, *Les Saintes Ottoniens*, 48–9.

unacceptable to the new religion, kings sought to demonstrate that they were both spiritual and military leaders by retiring to monasteries and by becoming saints. The final stage was to accept that the task of manifesting the spiritual strength of the royal house could be delegated to royal women. For as Hrostwitha, herself a nun, believed, Anglo-Saxon royal women could be interpreted as being particularly prone to saintly behaviour because they had been born into a *beata stirps* – they were a manifestation of blessings enjoyed by all members of their families, including, perhaps especially, the kings.

Possibly by becoming the monastic specialists of the royal house, Anglo-Saxon queens and princesses were adapting cult roles that they had played under traditional Germanic paganism. The role of women in pagan cult is a controversial area and one particularly difficult to discuss for the Anglo-Saxons in the absence of relevant written sources, especially if one feels it wise to avoid both Tactitean claims of an inherent Germanic respect for female spirituality and the lures of the late Old Norse written tradition. But possible evidence for the involvement of some Anglo-Saxon women in pagan cult may come through the study of jewellery with pagan symbolism. Most work to date has been on the symbolism and significance of bracteates which were worn by elite women in Scandinavia, but also in Kent and, more rarely, in other parts of eastern England.[76] However, various brooch forms may also have had a significant pagan symbolism,[77] and there is a possible line of enquiry here on the importance of display of such symbolism by elite women to win protection or support from the gods for the household and, perhaps in the case of royal women, for the kingdom as well. After conversion elite women began wearing objects of Christian symbolism instead,[78] suggesting the custom was considered to be sufficiently important to be adapted to the new religion and that women were among the first members of the royal house to have a prominent role in the promotion of Christianity.

Conclusion

The surviving written accounts of Anglo-Saxon conversion are not concerned with foregrounding the perspectives of the lay community including those of the royal houses, though Bede in particular does display an awareness of some of the problems and tensions that occurred when different traditions of morality and religious belief clashed.[79] By using such evidence and allowing the actions of

[76] M. Gaimster, 'Scandinavian gold bracteates in Britain. Money and media in the Dark Ages', *Medieval Archaeology* 36 (1992), 1–28; *idem, Vendel Period Bracteates on Gotland. On the Significance of Germanic Art*, Acta Archaeologica Lundenensia 27 (Lund, 1998).

[77] D. Leigh, 'Ambiguity in Anglo-Saxon Style: I Art', *Antiquaries Journal* 64 (1984), 34–42.

[78] H. Geake, *The Use of Grave-Goods in Conversion-Period England c.600-c.850*, British Archaeological Reports, British series 261 (Oxford, 1997).

[79] Wormald, 'Bede and the Conversion'; J. Campbell, 'Elements in the background of the life of St Cuthbert and his early cult', *St Cuthbert, His Cult and His Community to AD 1200*, ed. G. Bonner, D. Rollason and C. Stancliffe (Boydell, 1989), 3–19.

rulers to suggest something of lost thought processes, together with a broader contextualisation of royal conversion, we may be able to reconstruct something of how matters were viewed from the perspective of the royal courts. It has been suggested here that one of the priorities of royal houses, once Christianity had been accepted as sole religion, was to ensure that the sacrality of the royal line, and above all that of kings, continued to be recognised. To be fully accepted into the Anglo-Saxon royal houses Christianity had to meet their expectations of the conjunction of spiritual and temporal power, but this also had, of course, as far as their ecclesiastical hierarchies were concerned, to be done in a way that was compatible with Christian practices and belief. A certain experimentation was necessary before a balance was achieved that was acceptable to all sides. The final abandonment of pagan worship, some years after the initial introduction of Christianity, was marked by the appearance of the short-lived phenomenon of saintly and monkish kings in most of the major Anglo-Saxon kingdoms. It was a phenomenon that it appears occurred only once in the history of each royal house that pursued this option in the conversion period. That may be an indication of the opposition in ecclesiastical circles to the outbreak of holy kings, but might also mean it was considered sufficient for one king to establish the sacrality of the royal houses before it could be left to royal women (and the occasional accidental kingly martyr) to continue the demonstration of the line's susceptibility to holiness. Although such considerations are unlikely to have applied to all classes of society, nevertheless this royal Anglo-Saxon case study may have a wider relevance for understanding something of the processes and compromises involved in the conversion of early medieval peoples to Christianity.

16

The Control of Burial Practice in Anglo-Saxon England

HELEN GEAKE

> We still do not know for certain *why* grave-goods were placed in the grave.
> ... Who *is* responsible for the ceremony of burial? Did that person allow a
> choice of different customs? ... Or was burial left to the heirs, or to the
> family? (James 1989, 34)

The question of who was responsible for the funeral in early Anglo-Saxon
England, or for the management of burial sites, has often been raised in passing
by archaeologists, but has generally not been examined in detail. This is, perhaps,
due to the difficulty of finding archaeological evidence for ceremony and its
underlying motives which is independent of the analogies available to the
observer (Carver 1993, v-vi). This paper represents an attempt to search for such
evidence. The identification of who or what might have been responsible for
patterns and variations in burial could have far-reaching consequences. If there
was some form of social control, this could change the theoretical basis from
which we extract meaning from these patterns, as of course the meanings of these
patterns will vary depending on who deliberately created them and whose ideologies they reflected. At the very least, it might help us understand phenomena
such as the speed and uniformity of change in Anglo-Saxon burial practice across
England, or the underlying principles by which the landscape position and layout
of pre-Christian cemeteries was planned. Understanding the social control of
burial may also shed light on one of the thorny problems of burial practice in the
Age of Conversion: the seemingly immense effect of the coming of the Church on
burial practices, which took place apparently without any detectable institutional
intention. These are wide inferences; let us see how far we can push the evidence
to justify them.

   After well over a century of analysis, we now know that the process of the
disposal of the dead in early Anglo-Saxon England required a great many decisions to be made (Filmer-Sankey and Pestell 2001, 262). The appropriate cemetery
had to be selected, and the choice between inhumation and cremation made.
If cremation was chosen, the pyre had to be constructed, with another set of

decisions to be made. If the rite was to be inhumation, the grave had to be dug in the correct place, with the right orientation. If there was to be a mound, the height and diameter had to be selected. Coffins and other structures had to be chosen; or, for cremations, a container, such as a pot, of the correct size and with the right decoration. The dead body had to be laid out in the grave or on the pyre, and any objects had to be selected and added in their correct places.

The focus of funerals today is the lowering of the body into the grave, but in the early Anglo-Saxon period it seems to have been the viewing of the tableau; the body laid out in the grave or on the pyre, with its jewellery or weapons and other accoutrements. To achieve the correct tableau, with the uniform patterning observed by the archaeologist, the task of laying the body out had to be deliberately and carefully performed. In the case of inhumation burials, the dead body would have had to be carefully laid out in the bottom of the grave. If it had simply been lowered in, necklaces would have slipped round the back, pots would have fallen on their sides, swords and spears would have ended up across the body. The person responsible for the laying-out must also have had knowledge of the significance of the selection and placing of grave-goods. Those responsible for this have usually been loosely categorised as the 'mourners' or 'family', but these layouts, as well as the assemblages of objects, were complex and meaningful (Pader 1982; Malim and Hines 1998, 34–42) and it has hitherto been unclear how the knowledge for their proper arrangement was disseminated.

Anglo-Saxon cremation burials are similar to inhumations in that they show an equal level of uniformity across the areas of England in which they occur. Experience and special knowledge would have been necessary in order to build the pyre, lay the body out on the pyre with any grave-goods or accompanying animals, light the fire and keep it burning evenly for the right length of time at the correct temperature, select bones and grave-goods from the ashes, clean the bones, select any additional grave-goods, and finally place everything within the correct pot (or other container) for that particular person (McKinley 1994; Richards 1987).

The decisions made about the disposal of the dead vary across England, but a remarkable synchronic uniformity can also be seen. Although different people are doing different things in different places, there are a number of changes that happen swiftly and simultaneously across the country. Most obvious is the steady rate of change over time in the styles of women's jewellery and other grave-goods such as glass vessels, presumably related to changing fashions in worldly life. Other more peculiar changes might include the relationship between horse burial and harness burial; in the sixth century, horses in human cemeteries are buried in their harness, but in the seventh they are buried naked and bridles appear in the graves of humans (Oexle 1984, 123). More significant shifts in funerary practice include a movement away from cremation in the late sixth or early seventh century; the widespread adoption of mound-burial for high-status graves in the later sixth and seventh centuries (Shephard 1979); the use of new types of grave-goods in the seventh century (Geake 1997; 1999); and the abandonment of grave-goods altogether in the early eighth century (Geake 1997, 125). These changes over time are surprisingly fast and homogeneous across England, and this homogeneity implies that the disposal of the dead is being actively controlled and managed.

When we turn to look at cemeteries which are spatially related to churches, however, decision-making and control is very much harder to see. It is well known now that the major change in burial practice in the eighth century, away from cemeteries containing furnished burials, has surprisingly little to do with any deliberate decision on the part of the institutionalised Church (Morris 1983, 50; Bullough 1983). The Church is not entirely silent on the matter of burial – in the Penitential attributed to Theodore, Archbishop of Canterbury from 669 to 690, there is a brief description of the funeral customs of members of the Roman Church (II.v.1; MacNeill and Gamer 1938, 202–5; and see below) – but there is no mention of furnished burial at all within Church law, no suggestion that it was thought of as a pagan or heretical rite, and no stricture against it.

A generalised effect of the Church on burial, however, is never really called into question by modern scholars. This is probably for two reasons. The first is the remarkable lack of conventionally furnished burials, even of the early seventh century, in or around English churches (Geake 2002); the second is the rather sudden ending of the use of grave-goods in other cemeteries in the early eighth century (Geake 1997, 125). These combine to imply a sharp break between burial grounds containing furnished burials on the one hand, and churchyard cemeteries on the other. It seems obvious that the Church must be having an effect on burial, but there is little documentary evidence of any intent or decision in this process.

The third phenomenon to look at in an investigation of the control of burial is the landscape position and layout of burials. Some work has been done on the reasons underlying the particular locations of cemeteries, but this has mainly concentrated on identifying nearby parish boundaries or pre-existing visible monuments (Williams 1997; Lucy 2000, 124–30); an exception is the analysis of landscape visibility and prior land-use at the Sutton Hoo mound cemetery (Carver in press). At the moment we cannot explain why certain such visible places, boundaries or monuments should have been used for early Anglo-Saxon burial, yet others ignored. Not only do we know little about how land was held in early Anglo-Saxon society, and therefore which areas would have been available for burial, but our tendency to excavate only small areas of cemeteries means that we are unsure about how they were fitted into the overall Anglo-Saxon landscape and how their boundaries had to relate to other contemporary landscape features.

In addition, the lack of theories about intra-cemetery planning has hampered efforts to interpret early Anglo-Saxon society from its burials. Organisation and discipline is evident in the layout of many sites. At some, such as Spong Hill, the inhumations are consistently orientated and are zoned away from the cremations (Hills et al. 1984, Fig. 3). Even in ostensibly disorganised cemeteries such as Great

Chesterford in Essex, where the cremations and inhumations are jumbled up and there is no clear pattern to the orientations of the inhumations, potentially meaningful groups of burials can be identified (Evison 1994, 36–43; see also, for example, Malim and Hines 1998, 34–42). In most cemeteries burials appear to avoid each other, implying that they were visibly marked (Hirst 1985, 24).

But because we do not know how cemeteries were planned and managed, we cannot be sure that the inferences about society which we draw from these plans – family groupings, special treatment for one age or sex, those outcast from or marginal to mainstream society, high-status individuals whose burials became foci, or were separated from mainstream society, and so on – were real, intended patterns, or can only ever have been coincidences.

If we are to be optimistic, and assume that cemetery layouts were intentional, and that the patterning of graves and their contents within these layouts was meaningful, we must then ask who within Anglo-Saxon society could exercise this intention. One possible answer is that there was a specific person or persons within a community whose role was to make decisions and keep control over all aspects of the disposal of the dead. A burial specialist could have provided knowledge not just of where graves were and in what direction they were orientated, but also of who was buried in each one and what grave-goods had been included in the grave. Without the expert knowledge of burial specialists, the transmission of a meaningful use of space is unlikely over many generations, especially in an oral culture and when much of the relevant information is buried below ground.

Attention has been drawn to the possibility of the control of burial in Merovingian areas, but conclusions have so far been essentially negative. Young has argued that there is no evidence that pre-Christian burial was regulated, citing the apparent indifference of the early Church and the apparent lack of unity within pre-Christian cemeteries (Young 1975, 61–2 and 106; quoted in Hirst 1985, 24). If he is right, the situation in Francia must have been very different to that in England, where pre-Christian burial sites certainly show a high degree of organisation. Churchyard burials in Francia are certainly very different, with well-known rich burials within churches such as at Paris St-Denis and Cologne Cathedral (Werner 1964; James 1992, 247–8; Geake 2002).

In the quest for burial specialists our first port of call should perhaps be the cemeteries themselves. The person or persons who organised burial in a community must also have died and been buried, and it may be expected that those who controlled burial within their communities would have received a special type of burial on their own death, whether or not this event coincided with the transfer of control to another person. The grave of the person responsible for allocating the rite, position, orientation, layout and furnishing of a grave may be unusually cremated, positioned, orientated, laid out or furnished.

A small group of individual graves have been defined by Audrey Meaney as those of 'cunning women' (1981, 249–62). These graves are almost indefinably strange. They contain female inhumations, and have collections of peculiar small objects of no obvious practical or decorative use, laid out in unusual positions and combinations. In addition, the location and orientation of 'cunning woman' graves within cemeteries seems to imply that they would have been in some way special within the community, or at least that their honouring in death was special.

Identifying 'cunning women' graves as those of ritual specialists on the grounds of their grave-goods alone is risky, as almost every type of Anglo-Saxon female grave-good has, at one time or another, been identified as possessing amuletic or magical significance, if not from its material or form then from its ornamentation. Because of this, all those buried (for whatever reason) with many objects begin to look like jingling, glittering magicians. Case studies must, therefore, concentrate on examples of women who look, in death, so unlike the majority that we are forced to interpret them as something out of the ordinary.

Grave HB2 at Bidford-on-Avon in Warwickshire is so unusual in its grave-goods that it inspired Tania Dickinson, normally a most sober and cautious writer, to talk of 'a glimpse of ritual and superstition' and to suggest that 'this was the grave of someone with special powers' (1993, 45; 53). The grave was that of a young adult woman buried in the first three-quarters of the sixth century. The layout of the grave-goods was unusual. A group of bronze objects consisting of four lace-tags, a disc pendant and twelve bucket pendants stitched to a leather backing, were found *underneath* the shoulder, implying that the objects were either deliberately concealed or that the body did not receive the full laying-out for viewing typical of the furnished early Anglo-Saxon burial. There were also some peculiar objects, such as an antler cone and a very odd long-handled knife, which were found in a bag by the hip together with an iron and a bronze ring. HB2 was found at the extreme northern edge of the excavation, but as the cemetery was not fully excavated it is impossible to know whether this was a truly liminal location (Dickinson 1993).

Grave 27 at Wheatley in Oxfordshire is another candidate for 'cunning woman' status (Meaney 1981, 32–4). The cemetery at Wheatley was excavated in the nineteenth century and at least 70 graves are known. Grave 27 contained a considerable number of objects in two groups. First, in a squarish mass between the left arm and the ribs, were 61 amber beads, 16 glass beads, a bone bead, a bronze wire bead, two dog or wolf teeth, a boar's tusk, two Roman bronze coins, a pair of disc brooches, an ear scoop, an Iron Age pin, and some scraps of textile and iron (Dickinson 1976, 229–30). The location of these objects was unusual: in a bag or box rather than on the body, again as if the objects were either concealed, or as if the person had not been dressed properly for burial.

The second group of objects was between the feet, and consisted of two iron rings, a bronze weight, a triangular bronze plate and a fragment of glass. Further grave-goods were unlocated; half a rectangular bronze plate, half a tinned bronze disc, a bit of a bronze wrist-clasp, an iron rod with a bronze wire ring through a perforation at one end, and one iron and one bronze ring.

This odd collection of scrap is typical of the bag collections cited by Meaney as one of the attributes of the cunning woman. Meaney and Dickinson both interpret these women as ritual specialists whose roles included those of healers and fortune-tellers. There is no direct evidence to connect them with the control of burial, but as their graves are full of odd objects and do not seem to have received the usual preparation for burial, it seems reasonable to suggest that they could also be the controllers and managers of burial. Modern ethnographic parallels, for example in rural Greece, show that women, particularly old women, often look after mortuary practices. Such women could be termed 'death-midwives', taking a person out of this world safely and properly.

It is harder to find possible examples of burial specialists within cremation burials. This is to some extent counter-intuitive; as the rite of cremation involves more difficult techniques and is more complicated, it might be expected to need more specialist expertise. It is of course possible that there was something about cremation burial that made the entire rite inappropriate for a burial specialist. But also we should remember that although cremation burials have received much less detailed analysis, one aspect that does seem certain is that the selection of grave-goods during the cremation rite was very different to that in the inhuma- tion rite. Age and gender are not nearly so clearly differentiated within cremation grave-goods, and it may be that other social roles are also not best approached by studying this dataset. Differences in the laying-out of the body and the grave- goods are also harder to see within a cremation burial, as the bones and objects go through a further process of selection and organisation as they are placed in the burial container. A remaining possibility is that the social role of the burial controller was expressed through a particular type of container; this suggestion may, however, be hard to test using current analytical techniques.

It is often assumed by modern writers that a burial controller, or undertaker, should be connected with other aspects of ritual or spiritual life, even though there is no *prima facie* reason for this assumption. In fact, the limited view of pagan ritual given us by contemporary writers might be argued to contradict it. Theodore's Penitential specifies penances both for 'a woman [who] performs diabolical incantations or divinations' and 'he who celebrates auguries, omens from birds, or dreams, or any divinations according to the custom of the heathen' (I.xv.4; MacNeill and Gamer 1938, 194–5) but these people, in common with the pre-Christian priests mentioned by writers such as Bede or Eddius Stephanus, are not recorded as having anything to do with the disposal of the dead. Theodore also gives no penances for organising inappropriate burials; the furthest he goes is to specify a 5-year penance for those who burn grain when a man has died, for the purification of the house and of the living (I.xv.3; Wilson 1992, 97). Of course, these writers are operating in a Christian milieu, and we already know that the ritual specialists of the early Church did not care much about funerals. It could be argued that we should hardly believe them when they imply that their claimed pagan counterparts did not either.

The role of burial controllers may, however, be described in a single non-Christian documentary source, albeit from the other end of Europe, and many centuries later; the famous description by the Arab traveller Ibn Fadlan of the extravagant and theatrical burial of a Rus' chief soon after 920 AD (Warmind 1995). Ibn Fadlan was part of a Moslem embassy sent from Baghdad to Bulgar, on the Volga near modern Kazan, and his description is full of interest for the student of burial.

He tells how the dead man was temporarily buried for 10 days, with temporary grave-goods, while preparations were made for the funeral proper; the making of special clothes is particularly mentioned. On the day of the funeral, the chief's ship was dragged up onto the river bank and perched on a great stack of wood. The dead man was exhumed, dressed in his elaborate burial clothes and laid in a tent on the ship. Food and drink were laid out around him, together with all his weapons. A number of animals – exhausted horses, cows, a dog and chickens – were killed and cut up and thrown into the ship. The rest of the day was filled with various elaborate sexual and mystical ceremonial involving a 'volunteer' slave girl, who is given a great deal to drink and in the end is strangled and stabbed. Finally the closest kinsman of the dead man walks backwards, naked, with a hand over his *bab ishtihi* ('gate of the buttocks'), and with a lighted torch ignites the ship. When it has burnt completely they raise up a mound over it with a post with the man's name on top.

The significant part of Ibn Fadlan's account for our purposes is that the entire funeral service is presided over by a woman called by him the *Malak al Maut*, which can be translated as 'Messenger of Death', assisted by her daughters. There has been debate over whether the 'Messenger of Death' was herself Scandinavian, or perhaps a local Slav (Warmind 1995, 133; Ellis Davidson 1992, 331). So many features known to be characteristic of north-west European burial practices are contained within the story, however, that it seems inescapable that the 'Messenger of Death' knew what was right for Vikings to do; she also appears to have known their language. It seems possible that the 'cunning woman', so curiously honoured in death, and the 'Messenger of Death' observed by Ibn Fadlan, could have carried out the same function within their societies – women who, perhaps among other spiritual duties (Bierbrauer, Staecker, Lager, Gräslund, Chapter 27, 29, 31 and 30 in this volume), ensured that the correct burial customs and rituals were observed.

Communication between the burial specialists of different communities would provide a mechanism for the speedy transfer of new burial trends across the country. The comprehensive nature of these new trends – in method of disposal of the body, grave-good types, grave structures, cemetery location, and so on – implies that the burial specialists had a hand in all aspects of the treatment of the dead. Ibn Fadlan's description of the 'Messenger of Death' as being assisted by her daughters might imply that the role was at least occasionally hereditary, which would help in the transmission of knowledge through time as well as over distance.

The identification of a class of female ritual specialists, responsible for the control and maintenance of burial tradition, has wide-ranging implications for many aspects of the interpretation of cemeteries and graves. Not least among these may be our views on the ideological and political interpretations of burial evidence, which may be heavily dependent on whose ideas and desires could have influenced the burial controllers. These are wide and weighty questions which deserve more considered treatment; this paper will concentrate instead only on the possible implications of this idea on the transition to burial around churches.

The relationship of Christianity to archaeologically observed changes in burial practice is complex. One of the most obvious changes, in the use of grave-goods, coincides with the period of the Christian missions, and another change, in the location of the burial place, follows soon after, around 720 AD (Geake 1997). Carver has suggested that exceptionally demonstrative burial rites being practised in the early seventh century reflect a high-status reaction to the Christian mission (1998, 136). Those of the later seventh and eighth centuries may be connected with the growing influence not only of the formal Church, but also of other forms of Christianity. The influence of informal Christianity may, perhaps, be detectable in burials outside churchyards, although other linked factors such as the development of dynastic kingship are equally important (Geake 1997, 132–3; 1999). There is a natural expectation that the Church should have been interested in burial practice, but the available (admittedly negative) evidence suggests it was not.

An early Anglo-Saxon society used to the control of burial practices by ritual specialists, however, might quite plausibly expect the men of the Church, when they took over the role of ritual specialists, therefore also to act as burial controllers. A similar unfulfilled expectation is seen in Bede's story of the reaction of a group of 'everyday people' to the misfortune of some monks who were being blown out to sea: 'Let no man pray for them, and may God have mercy on none of them, for they have taken the immemorial rituals from men and nobody knows how the new ones are to be observed' (Fletcher 1997, 285–6). The fact that the Church apparently did not tell the Anglo-Saxons what to do with their dead (beyond the neutral description of the custom of the 'Roman Church') may not have prevented its members from actually wielding great influence, particularly when some of their strictures (such as those against those who perform diabolical incantations or divinations) could be interpreted as warnings against heeding the words of non-Christian ritual advisers.

The factors underlying the siting of churches have been examined by many scholars (Blair 1988; Morris 1989, 274; Pestell forthcoming), and are generally considered to relate primarily to aspects of landholding and aristocratic convenience. However, when an early date for a church has been established by archaeological excavation, it is often found that the earliest features are unfurnished burials, possibly indicating that the church was built on a pre-existing burial ground (Morris 1989, 152; Geake 1997, 135). A faint echo can perhaps be heard here of the foundation of many urban churches across Europe, within extramural cemeteries in which Roman saints and martyrs were buried; it may be that burials attract churches as much as churches attract burials.

The burial rite appropriate to a churchyard, the rows of unfurnished orientated graves, is very specific and recognisable, but is nowhere laid down in Church law. Theodore tells us that:

> According to the Roman Church, the custom is to carry dead monks or religious men to the church, to anoint their breasts with the chrism, there to celebrate masses for them and then with chanting to carry them to their graves. When they have been placed in the tomb a prayer is offered for them; then they are covered with earth and stone.
>
> (II.v.1; MacNeill and Gamer 1938, 194–5)

Even if this was the model followed, there is scope within these parameters to add many additional features, and indeed the English variety of this rite is subtly different from the 'Christian' burial practices found in other parts of Europe.

Both the new rite and the initial placing of a new burial site may therefore represent an interpretation of the new ideology by a special group, whose ancestral task had always been the easing of the inevitable passage out of life rather than the censoring of behaviour within it. The new rites may, perhaps, represent the last contribution of the Anglo-Saxon female burial controllers. The supervision of burial is now less demanding. The location is dictated by the church, which also owns the space; grave-goods are absent and do not need positioning; and within the tight confines of the churchyard, graves are routinely cut through and mortal remains disturbed. The burial controllers might instead have turned their attention to pre-burial ceremonies, taking their activities out of the sphere of archaeological visibility.

It may be felt that there is comparatively little positive evidence for the existence of burial specialists – a couple of odd female inhumations, a tenth-century story of Viking activity on the Volga – and that their existence can therefore be dismissed as a flight of fancy. But it has been argued here that circumstantial evidence of decision-making, planning and organisation requires some control of burial practice and managment of burial sites. The theoretical consequences of this idea are enormous, as we now have to ask not only 'what did these burials mean?' but also 'whose message were they communicating?' An answer to the latter question will inevitably change our views about the former.

ACKNOWLEDGEMENTS

I would like to thank Barbara Wills for giving me the initial idea, and Chris Knüsel for the discussions that gave me the courage to share it. I would also like to thank Martin Carver for reading a version in draft and adding many inspired thoughts, and Angus Wainwright for rescuing me from some errors. None of them, however, should be blamed for the final form in which these conjectures have been presented.

References

Blair, J. 1988. 'Minster churches in the landscape' in D. Hooke (ed.) *Anglo-Saxon Settlements* (Basil Blackwell, Oxford) 35–58.

Bullough, D. 1983. 'Burial, community and belief in the early medieval West' in P. Wormald, D. Bullough and R. Collins (eds) *Ideal and Reality in Frankish and Anglo-Saxon Society: studies presented to J. M. Wallace-Hadrill* (Blackwell, Oxford) 177–201.

Carver, M.O.H. 1993. 'In search of cult' in M. O. H. Carver (ed.) *In Search of Cult* (Boydell and Brewer, Woodbridge) v–ix.

Carver, M.O.H. 1998. *Sutton Hoo: Burial Ground of Kings?* (British Museum Press, London).

Carver, M.O.H., in press. *Sutton Hoo: A Seventh-century Princely Burial Ground and its Context* (British Museum Press, London).

Dickinson, T.M. 1976. *The Anglo-Saxon Burial Sites of the Upper Thames Region and Their Bearing on the History of Wessex, c.AD 400–700* (unpublished DPhil dissertation, University of Oxford)

Dickinson, T.M. 1993. 'An Anglo-Saxon "cunning woman" from Bidford-on-Avon' in M. O. H. Carver (ed.) *In Search of Cult* (Boydell and Brewer, Woodbridge) 45–54.

Ellis Davidson, H. 1992. 'Human sacrifice in the late pagan period in north-western Europe' in M.O.H. Carver (ed.) *The Age of Sutton Hoo* (Boydell and Brewer, Woodbridge) 331–40.

Evison, V. I. 1994. *An Anglo-Saxon Cemetery at Great Chesterford*, Essex (CBA Research Report 91, York).

Filmer-Sankey, W. and Pestell, T. 2001. *Snape Anglo-Saxon Cemetery: excavations and surveys 1824–1992* (East Anglian Archaeology 95, Ipswich).

Fletcher, R. 1997. *The Conversion of Europe* (HarperCollins, London).

Geake, H.M. 1997. *The Use of Grave-Goods in Conversion-Period England, c.600-c.850* (British Archaeological Reports British Series 261, Oxford).

Geake, H. M. 1999. 'Invisible kingdoms: the use of grave-goods in seventh-century England' in T.M. Dickinson and D. Griffiths (eds) *The Making of Kingdoms* (Anglo-Saxon Studies in Archaeology and History 10, Oxford).

Geake, H.M. 2002. 'Persistent problems in the study of Conversion-Period burials in England' in A. Reynolds and S. Lucy (eds).

Hills, C., Penn, K. and Rickett, R. 1984. *The Anglo-Saxon Cemetery at Spong Hill, North Elmham, Part III: catalogue of inhumations* (East Anglian Archaeology 21, Norfolk Archaeological Unit, Dereham).

Hirst, S. M. 1985. *An Anglo-Saxon Inhumation Cemetery at Sewerby, East Yorkshire* (York University Archaeological Publications 4, York).

James, E. 1989. 'Burial and status in the early medieval west', *Transactions of the Royal Historical Society* 5th ser, 39, 23–40.

James, E. 1992. 'Royal burials among the Franks' in M. O. H. Carver (ed.) *The Age of Sutton Hoo* (Boydell and Brewer, Woodbridge) 243–254.

Lucy, S. 2000. *The Anglo-Saxon Way of Death* (Sutton, Stroud).

Malim, T. and Hines, J. 1998. *The Anglo-Saxon Cemetery at Edix Hill (Barrington A), Cambridgeshire* (CBA Research Report 112, York).

McKinley, J. 1994. *Spong Hill, Part VIII: the cremations* (East Anglian Archaeology 69, Gressenhall).

MacNeill, T. and Gamer, H.M. 1938. *Medieval Handbooks of Penance* (Columbia University Press, New York).

Meaney, A. L. 1981. *Anglo-Saxon Amulets and Curing Stones* (British Archaeological Reports British Series 96, Oxford).

Morris, R. K. 1983 *The Church in British Archaeology* (Council for British Archaeology Research Report 47, London).

Oexle, J. 1984 'Merowingerzeitliche Pferdebestattungen – Opfer oder Beigaben?' *Frühmittelalterliche Studien* 18, 122–72.

Pader, E.-J. 1982 *Symbolism, Social Relations and the Interpretation of Mortuary Remains* (British Archaeological Reports International Series 130, Oxford).

Pestell, T. forthcoming. *Monasteries and Landscapes: foundation in East Anglia c. 650–1200* (Studies in Anglo-Saxon History, Boydell and Brewer, Woodbridge).

Richards, J. D. 1987 *The Significance of Form and Decoration of Anglo-Saxon Cremation Urns* (British Archaeological Reports British Series 166, Oxford).

Shephard, J. 1979. *Anglo-Saxon Barrows of the Later Sixth and Seventh Centuries AD* (unpublished PhD thesis, University of Cambridge).

Warmind, M.L. 1995. 'Ibn Fadlan in the context of his age' in O. Crumlin-Pedersen and B. M. Thye (eds) *The Ship as Symbol in Prehistoric and Medieval Scandinavia* (Publications from the National Museum, Studies in Archaeology and History vol. 1, Copenhagen) 131–7.

Werner, J. 1964. 'Frankish royal tombs in the cathedrals of Cologne and St Denis', *Antiquity* 38, 201–16.

Williams, H. 1997. 'Ancient landscapes and the dead; the reuse of prehistoric and Roman monuments as early Anglo-Saxon burial sites', *Medieval Archaeology* 41, 1–32.

Wilson, D.R. 1992. *Anglo-Saxon Paganism* (Routledge, London).

Young, B. 1975. *Merovingian Funeral Rites and the Evolution of Christianity: a study in the historical interpretation of archaeological material* (unpublished PhD thesis, University of Pennsylvania).

17

The Straight and Narrow Way: Fenland Causeways and the Conversion of the Landscape in the Witham Valley, Lincolnshire

DAVID STOCKER AND PAUL EVERSON

Introduction

John Ruskin's Romantic view of the world compelled him to look beyond the scientific reality of landscape and see in it, additionally, symbols of his Christian beliefs. 'The simplest forms of Nature are strangely animated by the sense of the Divine', he wrote in the third volume of *Modern Painters* (1899, 72). This is a paper about symbolic meanings which have been 'read' into the landscape in the past; but, unlike Ruskin, it concentrates not on a single ideology, but on a single area of landscape, the superficially uninteresting valley of the River Witham in Lincolnshire. The topic is a difficult one. Documentary history tells us very little of such matters, whilst archaeological evidence has to be used with great care. The concept that there might be a symbolic meaning in landscape, that it has been exploited ritualistically, has been more fully developed in prehistoric studies and attempts to discuss such ideas in medieval archaeology are rare. Even so, certain small-scale studies have attempted the task (Everson 1993; Everson and Williamson 1998), and it is inconceivable that such meanings were not perceived in the medieval period, as they still are today. In recent years there has been an upsurge in interest in ritual uses and meanings in the prehistoric landscape (e.g. Tilley 1994; 1996), and in the symbolic value accorded to monuments placed within it (Bradley 1993; Bradley 1998a). Even more relevant to our purposes here, Richard Bradley's earlier book *The Passage of Arms* (1998b) explored the multifarious meanings of votive deposits within the diverse landscapes of Western Europe. Studies such as these have shown that functional explanations need be neither the first, nor the only ones, applied to the material remains of past cultures. In the case of monumental structures in particular, the prehistorian agrees with more modern architectural critics that built structures deliberately set out to embody a symbolic meaning within their contemporary environment, often in addition to having a functional role. Indeed, such embodiments of larger meanings, in addition to the purely functional, might be an integral part of the definition of a monument.

This study focuses on the central part of the Witham valley in Lincolnshire, an area which is rightly famous for its spectacular finds of votive metalwork from the river (Fig. 17.1) (Davey 1971; Davey 1973; White 1979a; 1979b; 1979c; Fitzpatrick 1984). Here also, Naomi Field's 1981 excavations revealed a timber causeway-like structure of later prehistoric date, near the village of Fiskerton. In publishing those excavations, Mike Parker Pearson concludes that the mass of votive artifacts recovered, which were originally deposited in watery contexts, have to be seen as a small part of a much larger 'ritual landscape' (Field 1986; Field nd.; Parker Pearson and Field 2003). In this Parker Pearson is following the lead set by Francis Pryor in his interpretations of the prehistoric ritual land-scape excavated at Flag Fen over many years (Pryor 1990; 1991; 1992). Similar explanations are now being offered for many prehistoric artifacts recovered from other sites in the Fenland (e.g. Coles and Hall 1998, 29, 37–9, 45). This paper sets out both to define more closely the 'ritual landscape' of the prehistoric Witham valley and then to trace its development forward into the medieval period. Our suspicions that this was an area of considerable 'ritual interest' between the seventh and the sixteenth centuries are confirmed immediately by the extra-ordinary density of monastic sites in this short length of river valley. But it is not enough merely to point out the density of monastic sites. We need to look, also, at the siting of these monasteries relative to the causeways across the river valley. Specifically, we need to understand whether the monasteries were the creators of causeways which lead towards them across the fenland, or rather whether they were merely the medieval custodians of a much longer, prehistoric, tradition of marking passages across the fen ritualistically. How did the monasteries approach these necessary items of highways infrastructure, which had previously been, also, potent symbols in the landscape? Do we have any evidence that the monastic causeways were viewed as anything other than a means by which travellers could cross the wetlands? And, if so, what if anything can we say about their symbolic meaning?

Geomorphological Background

The two central reaches of the river Witham extend between the Brayford Pool at Lincoln and its confluence with the rivers Slea and Bain just below Tattershall. Most of the Lincolnshire causeways lie between these two points, and the great majority of the famous metalwork finds have been made along these two reaches. The broad valley extends east from the Brayford Pool for about 10 km to the confluence with the Barlings Eau and Snakeholme Drain before turning south-eastwards towards Tattershall. From the late Bronze Age onwards, the rising water levels have generated a wetland in the valley floor, characterised by a slow-flowing river in an area of alder-carr fen with many stagnant pools and meres

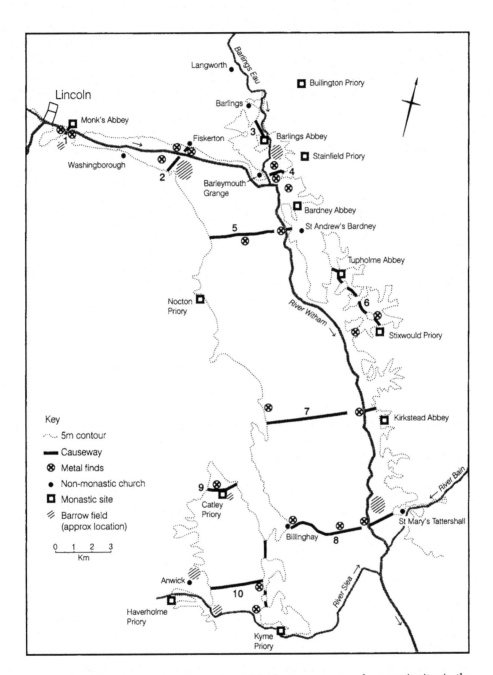

Figure 17.1 Map showing locations of metal finds, causeways and monastic sites in the central Witham valley (© English Heritage)

(Wilkinson 1986–7). The 'upland' boundary of the former wetland area is marked today by a peat blanket that fills the valley floor below the 5 m contour. Below Lincoln, the modern river channel, which flows along the north and east sides of the valley, is close to the line of the medieval river (a line it had already found by Domesday). It is thought, however, to have occupied a completely different line, closer to the centre of the valley, in the early medieval period (Lane and Hayes 1993, 20). The river channel cuts through a valley floor filled with a layer of peat, which can reach as much as 6–8 m in depth, but is more typically 2–3 m deep. There is no evidence that the causeways discussed below ever hindered navigation along the Witham and, until relatively recently, all were broken in the middle where they met the main channel of the river. Typically the journey across the main channel was undertaken by ferry. In the period under discussion, therefore, the causeways were in effect pairs of opposed jetties of considerable length to the west or south of the river channel, but much shorter to the east or north. Extensive archaeological research in Lincoln itself has shown that the Stamp End causeway, at least, influenced water levels in the river upstream (Jones, Stocker and Vince 2003). It is possible that some of the other causeways had a similar effect, restricting the river flow with the result that the pools and meres that characterised the valley may have been more abundant upstream of the barriers.

Summary of Evidence from Causeways Studied, Based on the Billinghay-Tattershall Example

For some years the authors have been undertaking a detailed study of one of the most interesting of the Witham valley monasteries (Barlings Abbey) in its landscape setting and, as part of that work, we have collected information about all the Witham valley monasteries, and about the medieval causeways which led towards them across the fens (Everson and Stocker forthcoming). The final publication of this project will include a full account of the data collected on ten such sites, which is summarized below in the Table 17.1.

All ten causeways share a striking range of diagnostic characteristics, which together strongly suggest that they are pre-monastic in origin. The causeway linking Billinghay and Tattershall effectively illustrates many of these pre-monastic characteristics. It is the longest of the causeways and furthest down-stream in the valley, providing a link between southern Lindsey and the densely occupied Slea valley in Kesteven. This key location, in itself, might arouse expectations of its early significance, but the distribution of monuments and finds along its line demonstrates the distinctive clustering of archaeological evidence which we find along and around all ten causeways. The Billinghay-Tattershall causeway forms the second leg of the journey across the fenlands at this point. The first leg, across the embayment east of Anwick, carries the route to Kyme island; it then turns north to join the long peninsula of higher ground extending into the larger Witham fen at Billinghay. From Billinghay to Tattershall there is

Table 17.1 Summary of data from Witham causeways

Causeway name	Approximate length metres	Ferry?	Minimum number of finds	Date range of finds	Monastic site(s) associated with causeway
Lincoln Stamp End	350	?	26	BA-11th Cent	Monks Abbey
Washingborough-Fiskerton	1100	perhaps	70	BA-14th Cent	Fiskerton Manor
Barlings Abbey	950	no	none reported[3]	–	Barlings Abbey
Short Ferry	1050	yes	12	IA-14th Cent	Barleymouth Grange
Branston Booths-Bardney	4200	yes	22	BA-14th Cent	Bardney Abbey
Stixwould-Tupholme	3100[1]	no	6	BA-13th Cent	Tupholme Priory and Suxwould Priory
Martin-Kirkstead	5600	yes	13	BA-15th Cent	Kirkstead Abbey
Billinghay-Tattershall	5500	yes	10	BA-Roman	Tattershall Church
Catley Priory	1500[2]	no	1	BA only	Catley Priory
Anwick-Kyme	2800	yes	15	BA-Roman	Haverholme Priory and South Kyme Priory

Notes
[1] Total length – figure includes three causeways and higher ground between.
[2] Total length – figure includes two causeways and higher ground between.
[3] Does not include finds from Langworth causeway.

another causeway, now carrying the A153 along the line of the 1793 turnpike, but which is potentially of great antiquity. Archdeacon Trollope commented on dugout canoes, flint axeheads, Romano-British pottery 'and various other relics of the British, Roman and Saxon Period' from Billinghay parish (1872, 489), and some of these finds may have had their origins in the known group of barrows around the Billinghay end of the causeway. Certainly this is the likely origin of the fine decorated beaker which he illustrates, and a looped palstave has also come from this same area (Davey 1973, 68, No.108). This is an unusual density of prehistoric finds from the core of a single Lincolnshire parish and may indicate a zone of special ritual interest in the Bronze Age. Furthermore, we now have evidence of another barrow cemetery emerging from the peat blanket just to the north of the causeway's eastern bridgehead, north-west of Tattershall church (APs in NMR, TF 1957). Although the Billinghay-Tattershall causeway may have had barrows at either end, six of the other Witham causeways have similar monument groups near one or other terminal. At the Anwick end of the Anwick-Kyme causeway there is a remarkable concentration of barrows, in at least two groups, which date from the early Bronze Age (Oliver 1846, 29–35; Chowne 1980, 300–3; Chowne and Healey 1983, 38), although barrows at the Kyme end are probably later in date (Everson and Stocker forthcoming). Similarly, there is a group of 24 barrows at the eastern end of the Catley Priory causeway (Oliver 1846, 19; Chowne 1980, 300–3; Healey and Hurcomb 1988–9), whilst to the north-west of the eastern terminal of the Short Ferry causeway, lie another group of at least 33 such barrows which have been surveyed as part of the Barlings Project (Everson and Hayes 1984, 36; Everson and Stocker forthcoming). A cemetery with at least a dozen barrows has been identified near the southern end of the Washingborough-Fiskerton causeway (Wilkinson 1986–7, 55), whilst a number of early Bronze Age barrows have been identified near both ends of the Stamp End causeway in Lincoln (Jones and Stocker 2003). All of these barrow cemeteries were buried by encroaching peat deposits, formed during the rise in water levels in the late Bronze Age. These peats have been sampled and dated around the Catley Priory barrows to 590 BC (+/− 100)(Chowne 1980, 300–3) or to 820–515 CalBC (Lane and Hayes 1993, 13).

It seems clear, however, that these locations retained their sacred character, regardless of their changed environment. At Billinghay-Tattershall, for example, some indication of the date of the causeway across the new wetlands is probably provided by the two late Bronze Age/early Iron Age swords found c.1852 not far from its centre (Trollope 1872, 29; Davey 1973, 93; May 1976, 107). Davey suggests that a sword found in 1852 and now in Lincoln Museum is a third sword from the same site (1973, 93). A looped palstave (Davey 1973, No.81) could represent a votive offering made around the barrow field north-west of Tattershall church prior to the inundation, but two leaf-shaped swords, found nearby (Davey 1973, Nos. 418 and 419), are less likely to be offerings of this sort; votive swords tend to be later in date than typical barrow burials and are characteristic of depositions in wetland (Bradley 1998b, 97). Again Billinghay-Tattershall is comparable with all of the other causeways studied: two late Bronze Age swords and possibly as many as eleven palstaves and axes have come from the vicinity of Anwick-Kyme (Davey 1973; Healey 1986; Owen 1992); Martin-Kirkstead has produced a single late Bronze Age sword and a spearhead of similar date (Davey 1973); Stixwould-Tupholme has produced a single palstave (Davey 1973). There are three spear-heads and a palstave from the vicinity of Branston Booths-Bardney (Davey 1973; Anon 1850, xxviii). Washingborough-Fiskerton has produced the astonishing total of at least 27 late Bronze Age metal work finds of weaponry, including five swords (Davey 1973); whilst Stamp End has produced at least three swords and two daggers, in an assemblage of at least fourteen late Bronze Age finds (Davey 1973). This makes a total of at least 64 metalwork finds of late Bronze Age date from sites adjacent to the causeways. Not all the finds sites are recorded precisely, but using patterns of precisely located finds, and the known dates at which work was undertaken on specific river improvement projects, we can be reasonably confident that these finds are not scattered randomly along the length of the river, but are quite closely focused around the terminals of the causeways (Everson and Stocker forthcoming) (Fig 17.1).

At Billinghay-Tattershall, and at most of the other causeways, votive depositions continued into the Iron Age and Roman-British periods. In 1768 the famous Iron Age *carnyx* – a form of war-trumpet – and a Romano-British *skillet* were found at a place called 'Tattershall Ferry' (Pearson 1796). For many years commentators presumed that these finds were made at the site of the modern Tattershall Bridge, within the Billinghay-Tattershall causeway. In 1958, however, Sir Cyril Fox stated that the 'Tattershall Ferry' in question was in the parish of Fiskerton, 13 km to the north-west. His radical new identification was based in his being 'told locally that most of the nineteenth-century finds came from the longitude of Fiskerton – a village on the northern bank, 5 miles east of Lincoln – which has an ancient ferry 'Tattershall', still nominally existent' (1958, p.31 n.14). We should note that the name of this ferry, which occurs on no contemporary map, is provided by a verbal source and that, anyway, the finds in question were those made in the nineteenth century and not those made in 1768. Regardless of the weakness of this re-identification, it has been repeated by subsequent scholars and is now embedded in the literature (e.g. May 1976, 165–6). If we disregard Fox's informant, we have no other evidence that the ferry at Fiskerton was called 'Tattershall Ferry'. Furthermore, the sixteenth-century antiquary John Leland, made it clear that 'Tatershaul Ferry' was 8 miles south of Short Ferry and one mile north of Dogdyke (Toulmin Smith 1964, 29; Barley 1937, 8; Hunt 1996) – in other words it was near Tattershall, not Fiskerton. *Pace* Fox, then, it seems much more likely that these two superb artefacts came, not from Fiskerton, but from the ferry within the Billinghay-Tattershall causeway. The time-span of ritual deposition from the Billinghay-Tattershall causeway is, consequently, extended forward into the Iron Age and Romano-British periods and in this, also, it is typical of the other Witham causeways. A group of spearheads from the Anwick-Kyme causeway may be of this date (Davey 1973; Trollope 1872, 77–8) whilst the gold torc from the western end of Martin-Kirkstead certainly was (Oliver 1846, 55). Similarly, two exceptionally fine swords with decorated scabbards from the Short Ferry causeway date from the later Iron Age (Anon. 1850 xxxi-ii; White 1979a, 4–5), as do at least fifteen finds from Washingborough-Fiskerton (Coles *et al.* 1979; Field nd.; White 1979a, 6; Anon. 1893; Anon. 1894; Page and Field 1985) and a further six finds from Stamp End (White 1979a 3–5; Meyrick 1831; Whitwell 1970, 15 and n20). The finds from Washingborough-Fiskerton and Stamp End are mostly weaponry and include items such as armour, a helmet and a shield, as well as swords.

The pattern of votive finds along the Billinghay-Tattershall causeway, then, suggests that the causeway here may existed long before its occurrence in late medieval documentation. But how the hypothetical causeway at Billinghay-Tattershall related to early church sites is, unfortunately, less clear than in some other cases. We have no real evidence that the parish church at Billinghay, close to the western end of the causeway, is of great antiquity, but it is possible that the church at Tattershall may have an early background. The settlement at Tattershall was evidently comprehensively re-planned around its market square in the late Middle Ages. It is often said that this re-planning is associated with the foundation of the College, School and other charitable institutions by Ralph Lord Cromwell in the first half of the fifteenth century, even though the market was granted as early as 1201 (Simpson 1960, xii) and the *caput* of the Tattershall barony was established on the castle site following a licence of 1231 (*Calendar of Patent Rolls*, 1225–32, 435). Prior to these developments, the main settlement and manorial centre seems to have been at Tattershall Thorpe, 1.5 km north of modern Tattershall, where Domesday Book records two manors, with two attached churches (Foster and Longley 1924, 136). Unfortunately it proves difficult to establish where those churches were. One of them might have been that dedicated to St Mary at modern Tattershall, which had twelfth-century features, and was pulled down to make way for Ralph Cromwell's Holy Trinity College (Simpson 1960, xi). Despite having a burial ground, St Mary's seems to have been of chapel status (Owen 1975, 21), and was presumably dependent on a parochial church located elsewhere in the parish – alongside the earlier manorial centre, at Tattershall Thorpe for example.

Furthermore, the great Cistercian Abbey of Kirkstead, which was eventually located in the north-western corner of Tattershall, was originally founded at an unknown site somewhere else within the parish. This first site was called *Kirkstead* – a place-name that indicates that there was a church here before the abbey came, although the *stead* element may suggest that there was no settlement. Given to the monks in 1139, this site was described as a 'place of horror like a vast solitude. A level plain surrounded by brushwood and marsh' in Tattershall parish (Page 1906, 135). In these circumstances, it seems possible (perhaps even likely) that St Mary's Tattershall was the *kirk* after which *Kirkstead* was originally named. The site at *Kirkstead* proving unsatisfactory, the monks moved a short distance to their final site between the late 1150s and 1187 (Fergusson 1984, 131; Wilson 1986, 108n; Jecock 1994, 1–2). A case can be made, then, that the *kirk* recorded in the place-name *Kirkstead* was represented in the twelfth century by St Mary's chapel at Tattershall. This was a notable isolated church, with burial rights, located at the eastern bridgehead of the causeway, whose importance was subsequently appropriated and eclipsed by Kirkstead Abbey. We have no further information about the likely date of foundation of St Mary's, but presumably the kirk was in existence by the time of the formation of the place-name, i.e. perhaps between the ninth and eleventh centuries. The possibility that there was an institution of pre-Viking date hereabouts may be suggested by the discovery of a single sherd of Middle-Saxon 'Ipswich ware' in excavations east of the later collegiate church (Addyman and Whitwell 1970, 98).

At Billinghay-Tattershall, then, the causeway, with its evidence for votive deposits over an extended time-span, can be associated with a potentially early Christian site. Fortunately, in most other cases the presence of an early ecclesiastical site has been more clearly identified. The monastery at Bardney enjoyed the seventh-century patronage of the Mercian royal house (Thacker 1985; Stocker 1993), whilst there is good circumstantial evidence for an early monastery on the island site at Kyme (*ibid.*). Monks Abbey in Lincoln belonged to the Benedictines of St Mary at York when first heard of in the early twelfth century; but there was a tradition – collected by Leland (Toulmin Smith 1964, I, 30) – that it had been the site of the seventh-century monastery of *Icanho* mentioned by Bede, and its estate might even have been the medieval successor of a large block of land laid out in the fourth century around the so-called 'villa' at Greetwell Road (Stocker 2003). The manor of Fiskerton was farmed in demesne throughout the Middle Ages by the Benedictines of Peterborough, after they acquired it in the eleventh century (Mellows 1948–9). Their policy of acquiring defunct early church sites in Lincolnshire, including Hibaldstow and perhaps Castle Bytham, is best documented with St Chad's ancient monastic estate at Barrow / Barton-on-Humber (Everson 1984; Everson and Knowles 1992–3). At Barlings, too, the ecclesiastical guardian of the causeway was an alien Benedictine priory founded on a pre-existing church (Everson and Stocker forthcoming). This pattern lends confidence to the interpretation developed above about an early ecclesiastical site at Tattershall. It is also clear that, for those causeways that cross the Witham valley proper, the causeways' ecclesiastical guardian stands, without exception, at its northern or eastern, Lindsey end.

The location of these early monastic sites at the causeway's end was not due solely to topographical convenience. In a number of cases, obligations of maintenance for the causeways were given to the associated monastic house, probably at their foundations. We know this to have been the case at Bardney Abbey (which had responsibilities for the Branston Booths-Bardney causeway – Thompson 1913–14, 77), Tupholme Abbey (for the Stixwould-Tupholme causeway – Dugdale 1817, 871) and Stainfield Priory (for the Short Ferry causeway – Everson nd.; White 1976; White 1984). Monk's Abbey probably had responsibilities for the Stamp End causeway (HMC 1895, 15–6) whilst Peterborough Abbey's manor at Fiskerton may have been responsible for the ferry (and presumably any surviving causeway terminals) at Washingborough-Fiskerton.

There are occasional hints, too, of ceremonies or special practices that took place on the causeways, which may have had their origins in pre-Christian river-based rituals. Medieval fishing rights around the confluence of the Witham and the Barlings Eau belonging to Bardney Abbey were habitually leased to the nuns of Stainfield Priory. The terms of Stainfield's lease specifically permitted the monks of Bardney to visit the grange at Barleymouth – that is, presumably, the causeway – to fish the river for one day on the vigil of St Oswald (Dugdale 1817,

I, 633–4). Yet the numbers of fish caught on this single day cannot have been important in the monastic diet or economy. The specific connection between this ceremonial fishing expedition and the vigil of the saint for whom Bardney was the pre-Viking cult centre makes it highly likely that this was an ancient monastic observance. Although we know nothing about the specific rituals undertaken on these occasions, we may guess that they included casting nets into the river and may wonder whether such ceremonies belong to that large group of pagan festivals that were christianised in the conversion period. In this case at least, it seems, the connection with the river is explicit.

More important than the rather incomplete documentary evidence for monastic involvement in the maintenance of the causeways that lead towards them, however, is the unambiguous archaeological evidence for the continuation of votive deposition as late as the fourteenth or fifteenth century. Furthermore these medieval finds are not rare; in some cases (such as Martin-Kirkstead, Branston Booths-Bardney and Stixwould-Tupholme) medieval finds outnumber prehistoric ones. Although Anwick-Kyme, Catley Priory and Billinghay-Tattershall have no medieval finds, the remainder have produced at least 32 finds of medieval date, including ten swords, five daggers/long knives, six axe heads and six spearheads (Everson and Stocker forthcoming). Some of the swords carry incantations inscribed into their blades, which emphasise the superstitious (and presumably ritualistic) character of their depositions.

Discussion

Our ten causeways follow a remarkably consistent pattern (see Table 17.1). At most of them the archaeological record begins with evidence for an early or middle Bronze Age barrow cemetery on the lower valley sides, presumably located close to the course of the original river. Once the valley had succumbed to inundation and become a landscape of meres and pools in the late Bronze Age and early Iron Age, the sacred significance of these locations started to be marked by a series of votive depositions, predominantly of weapons and other military objects. At most of the sites this sequence of votive depositions seems to have continued through the Iron Age and Romano-British periods, and in 70% of cases, deposition continued into the medieval period. The latest securely dated depositions in these sequences were made in the fourteenth century or later. Typically, neither the prehistoric offerings, nor those of the medieval period, were disabled or 'killed' before deposition. These votive depositions are associated with causeways, but were the causeways constructed at the same time and in association with the votive depositions? Only that at Fiskerton has been excavated and those excavations showed a date of first construction around 600 BC, contemporary with the votive depositions associated with it. We can show that all the causeways (except Fiskerton) already existed by the medieval period, but without excavation it can only be an assumption made on the strength of the finds associated with them that the causeways go back to the late Bronze or early Iron Age. Even so, the similarity between the assemblages from the other causeways and that from Fiskerton is close enough to make entirely credible the suggestion that the medieval causeways may have had such early origins.

It is very noticeable that the finds from the River Witham are clustered around the locations of the causeways, and there are long stretches from which no finds are reported (Fig 17.1). This patterning makes it likely, perhaps, that the small group of twelve finds whose find-location is not recorded more precisely probably came from one of the known causeway sites rather than from elsewhere along the river. Equally, however, it is clear that only a small proportion of the depositions can have been made from causeways on the medieval alignments themselves. A substantial number of the finds, like those from Church Field Fiskerton, lie up-river of the known causeway alignments, and so cannot have been deposited from the causeway and carried downstream with current or tide. One possible explanation for this would be a multitude of causeways; there may have been many jetties projecting into the watercourses throughout the prehistoric period, with only one becoming fossilised at each location during the agricultural drainage schemes of the eleventh to thirteenth centuries. A more likely explanation for the scattering of finds 100 m and more to the west of the excavated Fiskerton causeway, however, is that such depositions were made by boat. At other causeways, the finds also occur within easy reach, but probably only a minority were actually thrown from the causeways themselves. This in turn suggests that the important consideration in making such depositions was not the causeway itself, but the presence of pools and meres, which could presumably have been accessed by boat from a single causeway. This is not to say that the causeway was not relevant to the ritual of deposition. All the causeways were broken by a gap for the main stream of the river and, in the medieval period, these terminals were moorings for ferries. If this was also true in the prehistoric period, depositions made from boats in pools up- or down-stream of the causeway would have begun at the causeway terminals. Thus the pattern of finds in the Witham, with artefacts distributed away from the causeways themselves, does not invalidate Pryor's assumption that the ritual significance of the causeways was directly related to their role as a symbolic path representing rites of passage (Prior 1992, 529).

The Witham provides abundant evidence that votive depositions, continuing these prehistoric traditions, were still taking place in the medieval period. The early Christian period is represented by objects like the eighth-century Fiskerton hanging bowl, but reported objects of Middle Saxon date are fewer in number than those of later medieval date. The great majority of offerings of the Christian era are of swords, and this also demonstrates a continuity of ritual with earlier periods, where weaponry had also been predominant. By the date these medieval swords were deposited in the river, however, the causeways were under the control of a chain of monastic houses. Clearly, the practice had been Christianised in some way. The prehistoric ritual had been given a meaning that sat acceptably within the ideology of the new religion: a 'conversion' had taken place.

Bede's report of the miracle of the washing of the bones of St Oswald on their arrival at Bardney may provide us with a glimpse of the process of conversion (Colgrave and Mynors 1969, 247–9). The bones of the saint were washed in water, presumably from the Witham, and that water immediately acquired the power of healing, simply through contact with the saint's bones, as indeed did the dust from the ground on which it had been poured. Is it too fanciful to see in this simple miracle the 'conversion' of the sacred power of the water? By the action of washing St Oswald's bones in the Witham waters, the traditional power of those waters was henceforward attributed to the saint, rather than to whatever water-spirits might have been resident previously.

Given the documentary and locational evidence for the custody of the cause-ways by the monasteries, it seems likely that the casting of swords into the river waters must have been approved of, and was probably supervised, by the Church, although we have no documentary evidence recording such practices. By the fourteenth century, however, such gestures must have been considered merely 'traditional' rather than a threat to good order within the church. It may be, for example, that casting the lord's sword, his symbol of lordship, into the river represented a symbolic termination of that lordship, in the same way that the staffs of officers of the royal household were traditionally broken at their funerals (Cherry 1992, 25). Furthermore, it may be no coincidence that the first recorded instances of aristocrats hanging military equipment around their tombs come from the fourteenth century also (Alexander and Binski 1987, 479–80), just when the practice of depositing such equipment in the river apparently ceased. This new tradition was officially sanctioned by the Crown itself, when the armour of Edward the Black Prince was permanently displayed on his tomb in Canterbury Cathedral in 1376 (Stanley 1883, 129–85; Arnold 1993). Did this new behaviour replace earlier customs of reverent disposal of the trappings of lordship, such as depositing them in a local river? Despite the Church's reluctance to accommodate weaponry in ecclesiastical buildings, one can see that it might sponsor such a move; by finally bringing the deposition within the church itself, it eventually assimilated completely this evidently pre-Christian practice.

But why was there such a *concentration* of these distinctive finds at certain points on the river Witham? Economic motivations provide the commonplace explanation: the founders of monastic houses in the late eleventh and twelfth centuries were expecting that each new house would improve an unused or marginal corner of their estate. Furthermore, the connections between early church sites and early markets have been the subject of much comment and investigation (Sawyer 1981, 1986; Ulmschneider 2000, 81–92). But the extra-ordinary concentration of monastic sites along the Witham prompts speculation that their location within the landscape was due to something more than a simple desire to capitalise on fisheries and ferries. The Witham valley is, of course, pre-eminently liminal. The river formed not just the boundary for estates, parishes and manors, but in earlier times it was the boundary of the independent political state of Lindsey. It was, and still is, a boundary marked by important deep-rooted cultural differences, such as dialect (Ellis 1984). Nor was it merely a boundary of water; even today the Lindsey bank of the river on which the monasteries are set is relatively densely wooded, and it was even more so at Domesday (Sawyer 1998, 22–5). The remarkable line of Witham monasteries along this boundary, therefore, are visible entries and exits into a different place; secular as well as spiritual. They were all founded by Lindsey lords, and one could see them as symbolic guardians of the entry into the territory. In such circumstances, the causeways leading to these symbolic entries would necessarily become the foci of ritualised processions. This must be one level of meaning that can be read into the story of the admission of St Oswald's relics into Bardney Abbey. Having been reverently recovered by Queen Osthryth and processed from Northumbria to Lincolnshire, the relics were shut outside the monastery in their wagon, whilst the monks deliberated whether they should be granted admission (Colgrave and Mynors 1969, 247). Presumably whilst they waited, the relics were stationed at the causeway's end awaiting their grant of safe passage through the symbolic gateway to Lindsey. For the pilgrim of the later Middle Ages also, such a journey to the monastic house, across the causeway, could be invested with just as much Christian meaning, replicating both Christ's journey from Galilee to Jerusalem towards his death and the crossing of the Jordan, the symbol of rebirth.

Although Bardney Abbey was initially the burial place of the saintly king of Northumbria, and of members of the Mercian royal house aspiring to sanctity, it was re-founded in the eleventh century as the mausoleum of the de Gant family, probably the most important aristocratic family of their period in Lincolnshire. Barlings Abbey was founded as the burial place of the de la Hayes, the twelfth-century lords of Lincoln Castle, and it became the mausoleum of the de Lacy Earls of Lincoln in the fourteenth century (Everson and Stocker forthcoming). Kirkstead Abbey was the burial place of the twelfth-century lords of Tattershall, whilst Tattershall College was founded on the site of the ancient chapel of St Mary specifically as the mausoleum for the mighty Lord Cromwell and his family. Just as the funeral cortege of St Oswald travelled across the causeway to Bardney, so the processions of all of these later great figures would have approached their monasteries from the south-west, across the causeways. Such a journey would have carried just as much symbolic freight as the Bronze-Age rites of passage, including ceremonial funerals, such as might have taken place on the Flag Fen causeway (Pryor 1992, 529; Coles and Hall 1998, 29). What is more, the deposition of swords – the symbols perhaps of those Lindsey lordships – in the boundary river might be seen as a symbolic 'defence' of the approaches to Lindsey, much as *Excalibur* was the symbol of Arthur's defence of his kingdom and had to be returned to the spiritual guardian of the state, the Lady of the Lake, once it had served its purpose in this world. Were the Witham swords similarly seen as the obligatory military offering by the community's nominal war-leaders to mark their frontier?

So what conclusions should we draw from the Witham valley about the process of conversion, in what was clearly a meaningful symbolic landscape when

Christianity arrived? We have become familiar with the notion that, rather than destroying individual artefacts and structures belonging to the indigenous ideologies, the success of the Christian church in the seventh century lay in its concern to appropriate and 'convert' them to serve the causes of the new religion. Such a procedure was recommended to the missionaries in Pope Gregory's often-quoted injunctions to Abbot Mellitus, to convert the temples of the heathen rather than destroy them (Colgrave and Mynors 1969, 107–9). The Witham valley offers an example of a very similar process of assimilation of the trappings of the old religions, but on a landscape scale. It seems clear that the central part of the river valley was 'sacred' in pre-Christian times. Along its length there had been a more-or-less continuous ritual tradition, focused at regularly spaced locations, where community rituals had occurred from the Bronze Age onwards. At each, the initial focus was a conventional barrow cemetery, but when these were flooded by rising water levels, the rituals became transferred to watery features in the new landscape. Perhaps their new focus was the river itself, but evidence from Tacitus and other classical writers (e.g. Chadwick 1971, 147–9) and from Scandinavian archaeology (Glob 1977, 144 ff.) suggests that activity was more likely to have centred on the pools and meres along its course. Such rituals would have been the justification either for the initial construction, or for the occasional appro-priation of causeways, to provide access directly to the pools and river, or to the boats by means of which the appropriate parts of the landscape were reached. The arrival of Christianity did not result in a sudden discontinuation of these ancient practices. Indeed, there are more votive finds of the period between the eleventh and fourteenth centuries than there are of the Roman and early Medieval periods. Instead the river valley became the location of a succession of monastic founda-tions, which became remarkably thick on the ground. The earliest was probably at Bardney, although around the embayment to the north of the island there may have been a group of early church sites over which Bardney had some superior control, reflected in the ancient rights Bardney held over fishing at Barleymouth Grange. Many of the Witham monasteries – perhaps, originally, all of them – were given specific responsibilities for the maintenance of the causeways. Certainly Bardney would have been subject to an injunction of a synod at *Clofesho* in 749 by which, according to William of Malmesbury, monasteries were freed from all public services *except bridge-building* (Deansley 1963, 223). In many cases perhaps, the causeways themselves would have been rebuilt at this stage. Nothing would make so effective a symbol of the triumph of the new church over the old religion as the construction of a causeway across the formerly sacred pools. Indeed, it may have been with precisely this symbolic purpose in mind that so many of the causeways in eleventh-century Scandinavia were dedicated or re-dedicated by members of the incoming Christian hierarchy (Roesdahl 1982, 50; 1998, 79–81). In England, as in Scandinavia, economic motives may have coincided with symbolic ones. The war on paganism and the contemporary draining of the fenlands were both processes undertaken, almost exclusively, by the monasteries and both campaigns were largely completed by the end of the twelfth century. The draining of the fens and the re-construction of the causeways ensured that rituals formerly centred on the river and its pools became focused instead on the monastic church and on the causeway that now led straight to it. Like the Roman Emperors before them, individual medieval bishops, including Remigius of Lincoln (1067–1092), sometimes styled themselves *pontifex*, 'bridge-builder' (Lewis and Short 1879, 1397; Smith 1980, liii), and no doubt they had many different types of bridge in mind. One implication of the bishops' appropriated title expressed another appropriation, however; the church's ideological re-orientation of ancient causeways, like those in the Witham valley, which could symbolise the conversion of a whole landscape.

ACKNOWLEDGEMENTS

The authors wish to thank Philip Sinton for drafting Fig. 17.1, and Naomi Field and Dr Mike Parker Pearson for discussing the paper with the authors and for sight of their important forthcoming publication of the 1984 excavations at Fiskerton.

References

Addyman, P.V. and Whitwell, J.B., 1970, 'Some Middle Saxon Pottery types in Lincolnshire', *The Antiquaries Journal* 50, 96–102.

Alexander, J. and Binski, P., 1987, *The Age of Chivalry. Art in Plantagenet England 1200–1400*, London.

Anon 1850, 'Catalogue of Antiquities, exhibited in the Museum', *Memoirs illustrative of the History and Antiquities of the County and City of Lincoln communicated to the annual meeting of the Archaeological Institute of Great Britain and Ireland held at Lincoln, July 1848*, London, xxvii–lx.

Anon 1893, 'An account of some ancient arms and utensils found in Lincolnshire, chiefly in the bed of the River Witham, between Kirkstead and Lincoln, when it was scoured out in 1787 and 1788', *Lincolnshire Notes and Queries* 3, 196–201, 232–6.

Anon 1894, 'An account of some ancient arms and utensils found in Lincolnshire, chiefly in the bed of the River Witham, between Kirkstead and Lincoln, when it was scoured out in 1787 and 1788 – continued', *Lincolnshire Notes and Queries* 4, 20–1, 61–2, 124–7, 184–5, 238–41.

Arnold, J., 1993, 'The *jupon* or coat-armour of the Black Prince in Canterbury Cathedral', *Journal of the Church Monuments Society* 8, 12–24.

Barley, M.W., 1937, 'Lincolnshire Rivers in the Middle Ages', *Lincolnshire Architectural and Archaeological Society Reports and Papers* 1, 1–22.

Bradley, R., 1993, *Altering the Earth. The origins of Monuments in Britain and continental Europe. The Rhind Lectures 1991–92. Society of Antiquaries of Scotland Monograph Series* 8, Edinburgh.

—— 1998a, *The Significance of Monuments. On the shaping of human experience in Neolithic and Bronze Age Europe*, London.

—— 1998b, *The Passage of Arms. An Archaeological analysis of prehistoric hoards and votive deposits* (2nd edn), Oxford. (1st edn 1990, Cambridge.)

Chadwick, N., 1971, *The Celts*, Harmondsworth.

Cherry, J., 1992, 'The Breaking of Seals', *Art and Symbolism. Pre-printed papers of a conference on medieval archaeology in Europe 21–24 September 1992, at York* 7, 23–7.

Chowne, P., 1980, 'Bronze Age Settlement in South Lincolnshire', *Settlement and Society in the British Later Bronze Age* (eds. Barrett, J., and Bradley, R.). *British Archaeological Reports British Series* 83, Oxford, 295–305.

Chowne, P. and Healey, F., 1983, 'Artefacts from a Prehistoric Cemetery and Settlement in Anwick Fen, Lincolnshire', *Lincolnshire History and Archaeology* 18, 37–46.

Coles, J.M. and Hall, D., 1998, *Changing Landscapes: The Ancient Fenlands*, Cambridge.

Coles, J.M., Orme, B.J., May, J. and Moore C.N., 1979, 'Excavations of Late Bronze Age or Iron Age Date at Washingborough Fen', *Lincolnshire History and Archaeology* 14, 5–10.

Colgrave, B. and Mynors., R.A.B., 1969, *Bede's Ecclesiastical History of the English People*, Oxford.

Davey, P.J., 1971, 'The Distribution of later Bronze Age Metalwork from Lincolnshire', *Proceedings of the Prehistoric Society* 37/1, 96–111.

―― 1973, 'Bronze Age Metalwork from Lincolnshire', *Archaeologia* 104, 51–127.

Deansley, M., 1963, *An Ecclesiastical History of England. The Pre-Conquest Church in England*, London (2nd edn).

Dugdale, Sir W., 1817, *Monasticon Anglicanum . . .* 6 vols. (eds. Caley, J., Ellis, H. and Bandinel, B.), London.

Ellis, S., 1984, 'Lincolnshire Dialect', *A Prospect of Lincolnshire, being collected articles on the history and traditions of Lincolnshire in honour of Ethel H. Rudkin* (eds. Field, N. and White, A.), Lincoln, 109–14.

Everson, P., 1984, 'The pre-Conquest estate of *Æt Bearuwe* in Lindsey', *Studies in Late Anglo-Saxon Settlement* (ed. Faull, M.), Oxford.

―― 1993, 'Pre-Viking Settlement in Lindsey', *Pre-Viking Lindsey. Lincoln Archaeological Studies* 1 (ed. Vince, A.G.), Lincoln, 91–100.

―― nd. 'Archive of unpublished notes deriving from the RCHME survey of West Lindsey' (NMRC Swindon).

Everson, P. and Hayes, T., 1984, 'Lincolnshire from the Air', *A Prospect of Lincolnshire, being collected articles on the history and traditions of Lincolnshire in honour of Ethel H. Rudkin* (eds. Field, N. and White, A.), Lincoln, 33–41.

Everson, P. and Knowles, G.C., 1992–3, 'The Anglo-Saxon Bounds of *Æt Bearuwe*', *Journal of the English Place-Name Society* 25, 19–37.

Everson, P. and Stocker, D.A., forthcoming, *Barlings Abbey, Lincolnshire: an abbey in its landscape*.

Everson, P. and Williamson, T., 1998, 'Gardens and designed landscapes', *The archaeology of landscape. Studies presented to Christopher Taylor* (eds. Everson, P. and Williamson, T.), Manchester, 139–165.

Fergusson, P., 1984, *The Architecture of Solitude: Cistercian Abbeys in twelfth-century England*, Princeton.

Field, F.N., n.d. (1984), *Fiskerton in the Iron Age*, Lincoln.

―― 1986, 'An Iron Age timber causeway at Fiskerton, Lincolnshire', *Fenland Research* 3, 49–53.

Fitzpatrick, A.P., 1984, 'The Deposition of La Tène Iron Age Metalwork in Watery Contexts in Southern England', *Aspects of the Iron Age in Central Southern Britain* (eds. Cunliffe, B. and Miles, D.). *Oxford University Committee for Archaeology Monograph Series* 2, Oxford, 178–90.

Foster, C.W. and Longley, T. (trans. and ed.), 1924, *The Lincolnshire Domesday and the Lindsey Survey. Lincoln Record Society* 19, Horncastle.

Fox, Sir C., 1958, *Pattern and Purpose. A survey of early Celtic art in Britain*, Cardiff.

Glob, P.V., 1977, *The Bog People*, London.

Healey, R.H., 1986, 'A Bronze Age Socketed Axe from South Kyme', *Lincolnshire History and Archaeology* 21, 75.

Healey, R.H. and Hurcombe, L., 1988–9, 'A Bronze-Age barrow group in Walcott, Lincolnshire', *Fenland Research* 6, 17–20.

HMC 1895, *Historical Manuscripts Commission, 14th Report for 1895, Appendix Part 8. The Manuscripts of Lincoln . . .* , London.

Hunt, W.M., 1996, 'The Promotion of Tattershall Bridge and the Sleaford to Tattershall Turnpike', *Lincolnshire History and Archaeology* 31, 42–5.

Jecock, H.M., 1994, 'Field survey report. Kirkstead Abbey, Lincolnshire', unpublished RCHME report (NMRC, Swindon).

Jones, M.J. and Stocker, D.A., 2003, 'Prehistoric Settlement in the Lincoln Area – Archaeological Discussion', in Jones, Stocker and Vince op. cit.

Jones, M.J., Stocker, D.A. and Vince, A.G., 2003, *The City by the Pool. An Archaeological Assessment of Lincoln* (ed. Stocker, D.A.) Oxford.

Lane, T.W. and Hayes, P. *et al.*, 1993, *The Fenland Project Number 8: Lincolnshire Survey, the Northern Fen-Edge. East Anglian Archaeology* 66, Norwich.

Lewis, C.T. and Short, C., 1879, *A Latin Dictionary*, Oxford.

May, J., 1976, *Prehistoric Lincolnshire. The History of Lincolnshire* 1, Lincoln.

Mellows, W.T., 1948–9, 'The Estates of the Monastery of Peterborough in the County of Lincoln', *The Lincolnshire Historian* 3 and 4, 92–114, 128–66.

Meyrick, S.R., 1831, 'Description of two antient British Shields, preserved in the Armoury at Goodrich Court, Herefordshire', *Archaeologia* 23, 92–7.

Oliver, G., 1846, *The Existing Remains of the Ancient Britons, within a small district lying between Lincoln and Sleaford*, London and Uppingham.

Owen, D., 1975, 'Medieval Chapels in Lincolnshire', *Lincolnshire History and Archaeology* 10, 15–22.

Owen, J., 1992, 'Three Bronze Socketed Axes from South Kyme', *Lincolnshire History and Archaeology* 27, 40–1.

Page, A.B. and Field, F.N., 1985, 'A Roman Bowl from Fiskerton', *Lincolnshire History and Archaeology* 20, 77–8.

Page, W. (ed.), 1906, *The Victoria History of the County of Lincoln* 2, London.

Parker Pearson, M. and Field, N., 2003, *Excavations at Fiskerton*, London.

Pearson, G., 1796, 'Observations on some ancient metallic Arms and Utensils; with Experiments to determine their composition', *Philosophical Transactions* 86, 395–451.

Pryor, F.M.M., 1990, 'The many faces of Flag Fen', *Scottish Archaeology Review* 7, 114–24.

—— 1991, *Flag Fen: Prehistoric Fenland Centre*, London.

—— 1992, 'Discussion: the Fengate/Northey landscape', *Antiquity* 66, 518–31.

Roesdahl, E., 1982, *Viking Age Denmark* (trans. Margeson, S. and Williams, K.), London.

—— 1998, *The Vikings*, Harmondsworth (2nd edn).

Ruskin, J., 1899, *Selections from the writings of John Ruskin, D.C.L., LL.D*, Orpington (4th edn).

Sawyer, P., 1981, 'Fairs and Markets in Early Medieval England', *Danish Medieval History: New Currents* (eds. Skyum-Nielsen, N. and Lund, N.), Copenhagen, 153–68.

—— 1986, 'Early Fairs and Markets in England and Scandinavia', *The Market in History* (eds. Anderson, B.L. and Latham, A.J.H.), London, 59–77.

—— 1998, *Anglo-Saxon Lincolnshire. The History of Lincolnshire* 3, Lincoln.

Simpson, W.D. (ed.), 1960, *The Building Accounts of Tattershall Castle 1434–1472. Lincoln Record Society* 55, Lincoln.

Smith, D.M. (ed.), 1980, *English Episcopal Acta I . Lincoln 1067–1185*, London.

Stanley, A.P., 1883, *Historical Memorials of Canterbury*, London.

Stocker, D.A., 1993, 'The Early Church in Lincolnshire: A Study of the Sites and their Significance', *Pre-Viking Lindsey* (ed. Vince, A.G.). *Lincoln Archaeological Studies* 1, Lincoln, 101–22.

—— 2003, 'Settlement in the Lincoln Area in the Prehistoric and Roman Eras – The Archaeological Agenda', in Jones, Stocker and Vince op. cit. and Vince op. cit.

Thacker, A., 1985, 'Kings, Saints and Monasteries in Pre-Viking Mercia', *Midland History* 10, 1–25.

Thompson, A.H., 1913–14, 'Notes on the History of the Abbey of St Peter, St Paul and St Oswald, Bardney', *Associated Architectural Societies Reports and Papers* 32, 35–96, 351–402.

Tilley, C., 1994, *A Phenomenology of Landscape: Places, Paths and Monuments*, Oxford.

—— 1996, 'The power of rocks: topography and monument construction on Bodmin Moor', *World Archaeology* 28/2. *Sacred Geography* (ed. Bradley, R.), 161–76.

Toulmin Smith, L. (ed.), 1964, *The Itinerary of John Leland*, 5 vols., Carbondale (Illinois).

Trollope, E., 1872, *Sleaford and the Wapentakes of Flaxwell and Aswardhurn*, London and Sleaford.

Ulmschneider, K., 2000, *Markets, Minsters, and Metal-Detectors. The archaeology of Middle Saxon Lincolnshire and Hampshire compared. British Archaeological Reports British Series* 307, Oxford.

White, A.J., 1976, 'Fiskerton', *Lincolnshire History and Archaeology* 11, 58.

—— 1979a, *Antiquities from the River Witham. Part 1 Prehistoric and Roman. Lincolnshire Museums Information Sheet, Archaeology Series* 12, Lincoln.

—— 1979b, *Antiquities from the River Witham. Part 2 Anglo-Saxon and Viking. Lincolnshire Museums Information Sheet, Archaeology Series* 13, Lincoln.

—— 1979c, *Antiquities from the River Witham. Part 3 Medieval. Lincolnshire Museums Information Sheet, Archaeology Series* 14, Lincoln.

—— 1984, 'Medieval Fisheries in the Witham and its Tributaries', *Lincolnshire History and Archaeology* 19, 29–35.

Whitwell, J.B., 1970, *Roman Lincolnshire. The History of Lincolnshire* 2, Lincoln.

Wilkinson, T.J., 1986–7, 'Palaeoenvironments of the upper Witham Fen: a preliminary view', *Fenland Research* 4, 52–6.

Wilson, C., 'The Cistercians as missionaries of Gothic in northern England', *Cistercian art and architecture in the British Isles* (eds. Norton C. and Park, D.), Cambridge, 86–116.

18

Three Ages of Conversion at Kirkdale, North Yorkshire

PHILIP RAHTZ AND LORNA WATTS

Introduction

The subject of conversion is here examined with reference to Kirkdale, North Yorkshire, where we have been working since 1994. Kirkdale is the site of a historic church situated about 50 kms north-east of York in a long narrow valley on the north side of the Vale of Pickering, just to the south of the North York Moors (Fig. 18.1; Pl. 18.1). Here we have defined sculptural, epigraphic and historical evidence which relates to processes of conversion in Britain between the fourth and eleventh centuries AD. There is no modern village in the lower part of the valley, just the isolated church known as St Gregory's Minster (Watts *et al.* 1996–97, 6). This is famous for its sundial, set in the exterior wall of the church above the south door (Pl. 18.2). This carries a complete inscription in Old English, which has most recently been translated by Elisabeth Okasha as:

> Orm, son of Gamal, bought St Gregory's church when it was completely ruined and collapsed, and he had it constructed recently from the ground to Christ and St Gregory, in the days of King Edward and in the days of Earl Tosti. And Haward made me and Brand the priest. (Watts *et al.* 1997, 81)

This is dated (by the reference to Earl Tosti and King Edward) to AD 1055–1065. St Gregory's is thus one of the few Anglo-Saxon churches in England with a close date for one phase of its building or rebuilding.

It is suggested that this mid-eleventh century rebuilding of St Gregory's Minster is the final event in a long history of the use of the church area as a nucleus for religious activities, including human burial, possibly as early as the fourth century AD.

The three ages of conversion at Kirkdale which are to be discussed are, first, the fourth century (pagan Roman to Christian); second, the seventh–ninth centuries ('pagan Germanic' to Christian); by the latter date, we suggest Kirkdale was the site of an important Anglo-Saxon monastery; and, third, the late ninth–earlier eleventh centuries (pagan Scandinavian to Christian); the last ultimately culminating in the rebuilding by Orm Gamalson.

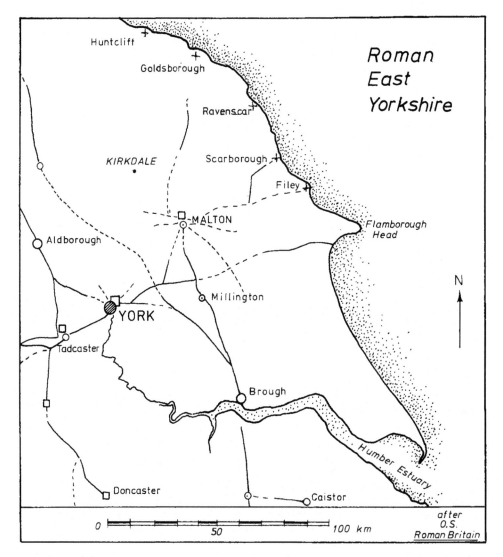

Figure 18.1 Map of Roman east Yorkshire

The evidence for evangelical activities at Kirkdale in these periods is tenuous, but this paper attempts to put what we do know in the wider context of the Vale of Pickering in these centuries, and especially to consider the theoretical function of Kirkdale as a catalyst for Christian activity.

The Background of Study

Kirkdale has been studied using both written and archaeological sources, including field work, recording of earthworks and the fabric of St Gregory's; and small-scale excavation (Watts *et al.* 1996–7; Watts *et al.* 1997; Rahtz and Watts

Plate 18.1 St Gregory's minster at the foot of the North York Moors

1998–99). In setting this evidence in a wider context, we discuss a background of historical and archaeological work extending from the seventeenth century to the present day. This includes especially the study of Roman and later settlements and cemeteries, and Anglian and Anglo-Scandinavian sculpture, of which there are many examples in the Vale of Pickering (Lang 1991).

We have been fortunate at Kirkdale to have increased the understanding of the structural history of St Gregory's Minster. We have also demonstrated the use of the area for a complex series of burials, possibly dating back to late Roman times, and have found two artefacts (another inscription, on lead, and a filigree glass rod fragment) which emphasise the high status of the putative Anglo-Saxon monastery in the seventh–ninth centuries (Rahtz and Watts 1998–1999).

Late Roman – the First Age of Conversion

The Vale of Pickering, especially the margins of its north and south sides, were densely settled in prehistoric times, from the eighth or ninth millennium BC onwards. In Roman times, it became part of the hinterland for two important Roman sites, the fortress city of York (EBORACUM) to the south and the fortress and town of Malton[1] to the north-east. The question of linking routes in the area, including to and from the coast, also needs to be considered (Fig. 18.1).

---

[1] Malton's Roman name, previously thought to be DERVENTIO, is now uncertain (Lawton 1999).

Plate 18.2 The sundial and inscription recording the revival of the Anglian minster by the Scandinavian lord Orm Gamalson in the eleventh century

York

There is very little evidence for Roman Christianity in North Yorkshire. EBORACUM, the capital of *Britannia Secundum*, did, however, have a bishop, Eborius, who attended the Council of Arles in 314 (Rollason *et al.* 1998, 44 and 108–9). We must assume, therefore, that there was a Christian community in York and indeed that it was an important centre in the Romano-British church (Rollason *et al.* 1998, 441). There is, nevertheless, very little positive archaeological evidence for Christianity in the city, though there are features and finds which have been considered as such, at least potentially.

The massive excavations under York Minster (Phillips and Heywood 1995) did not find any evidence for a Roman Christian presence, not even for the historically attested seventh-century church, or for the later Anglo-Saxon cathedral. The only find from these excavations which may hint at some Roman Christian presence was found beneath the east end of the Minster, north of the Roman *principia*. This was a chi-rho *graffito* on a tile fragment. Thomas suggests it had been on the roof of the *principia*, where 'it had no doubt served, as an intended, if unofficial, Christian antefix' (Thomas 1981, 89, 107 and Fig. 5, no. 6).

The only structure in York which has been suggested to be a church is that of St Mary Bishophill Senior (in the *colonia*); but this identification is ambiguous (Ramm 1976; Tweddle *et al.* 1999, 145; also see Rollason *et al.* 1998, 157).

Although there are no row cemeteries, such as that at Poundbury outside Roman Dorchester (Dorset), there are a number of excavated Roman cemeteries in the city. Ottaway (1993, 108) suggests that the abrupt changes noted in the cemetery area at 37–41 Blossom Street, in mortuary practices and orientation, could indicate the spread of Christianity; the later (fourth-century) burials were in wooden coffins, but unfurnished, without gravegoods, except (interestingly) those of infants (with shale bracelets). About 50 burials have been found in York where the skeletons were packed with gypsum, of which seventeen are attributed to the fourth century (Ottaway 1993, 108). Sparey-Green (1977 and Chapter 6 in this volume) has discussed these as a sign of Christian burial. Thomas has also mapped the find-spots of other possible Christian material in York (Thomas 1981, Fig. 29.1). The best-known of these is a stone coffin with gravegoods, in Sycamore Terrace; the finds include a three-line open-work bone mounting, reading S. ROR AVE/VIVAS/IN DEO O [Sister, hail! May you have life in God] (Thomas 1981, 126–8).

In spite of the sparsity and ambiguous evidence for Roman Christianity in York, the historical references to the bishopric and, significantly, the association with Constantine the Great (see Tweddle *et al.* 1999, 120), we may expect there to have been a substantial Christian presence in York, and this would have had some repercussions in the surrounding hinterland.

The villas

Ottaway (1993,107), in discussing villas in the area, points out that 'York was, like some of the towns in Britain, not a focus for them', perhaps because of the existence of a legionary *territorium*. 'Civilian landowners may . . . have been veterans and government officials who, unlike the native aristocrats preferred to have their principal dwelling in a town' – a point relevant to our discussion below. He considers, however, that the mosaics in both town and country reflected 'a consuming interest in religious matters', including doubtless Christianity.

Nevertheless, there are a large number of villas in the hinterland north of York and near Malton, notably by comparison with areas further north. They have been found west of York (as at Dalton Parlours), on the Wolds (notably Rudston (Stead 1980)) and those in the Wharram area (Rahtz *et al.* 1986) (Fig. 18.2). Of these, only Rudston has been extensively excavated; its mosaics are very 'pagan' in their

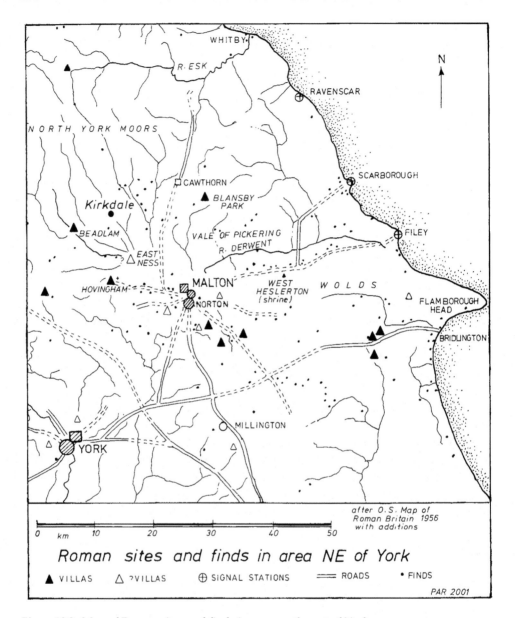

Figure 18.2 Map of Roman sites and finds in area north-east of York

subject matter; there was intensive use of the villa up to the later part of the fourth century, but nothing to indicate a Christian presence.

The villa at *Hovingham* (Fig. 18.2) is known only by illustrations of fine mosaics discovered in the eighteenth century (Kitson Clark 1935, 88–92, with full details and references). Hovingham is the only one of our three or four villas to have what may be an associated barrow, just to the east on the road to Malton. It is conical in form, and believed to be Roman.[2] The coin list extends to the end of the fourth century and the latest coins were worn (*inf.* T. Pacitto); there is also a *styca*, indicating a post-Roman use of the area (Kitson Clark 1935, 92), but there is no evidence of Roman Christian structures or finds. However, about 100 m from the presumed location of the villa is a church with an Anglo-Saxon tower and fine pieces of Anglo-Saxon sculpture, including a panel dated to the eighth century (Hawkes 1993). If the wealthy owner of the villa had Christian faith or sympathy, we might consider the possibility of a Christian nucleus which blossomed into an early missionary centre and church.

Beadlam, near Helmsley, is the only villa in the Vale to have been extensively excavated (Neal 1996). Like Hovingham, it must have had a wealthy owner, having three wings (one still visible), mosaics, baths and hypocausts. Finds include a remarkable group of late Roman glass and the only potentially Christian find in the villas. This is a bronze nail-cleaner in the form of a fish (Neal 1996, 45 and Fig. 31.2). This was included by Thomas in his review of Christian finds (Thomas 1981, 93 and Fig. 8 no. 11).

The third villa is that recently found at *Blansby Park*, just north of Pickering, by the Pickering Beck (Rahtz *et al.* 2001). Much building debris and other finds have recently been found in ploughing. A geophysical survey commissioned by the North York Moors National Park (the site is in the Park) delineated linear features and a circular building. An evaluation excavation was done in May-June 2000, after moles had uncovered over a hundred tesserae. Part of a hypocaust of what is likely to be a bath-house by the beck was excavated. Most of the finds so far are of late Roman date, with coins extending to the Valentinian dynasty. Fragments of a small statue of Italian stone (from the Apennines) suggest that this, like Beadlam, is a high-status complex.

There is likely to be a fourth villa in the vicinity of the small hamlet of *East Ness*, a few kilometres east of Hovingham, near the River Rye.[3] A stone coffin was found here in ploughing in the early seventeenth century (Young 1817, 712); the sarcophagus was subsequently lost, but an inscription on the side was transcribed soon after its discovery, translated as follows (Kitson Clark 1935, 79–80):

> Valerius Vindicianus had this made for his wife Titia Pinta, aged 38 and his sons Valerius Auditor, aged 20, and Variolus, aged 15.

These are the only named Romans in the Vale. The name Vindicianus occurs also in the inscription at Ravenscar, referring to the building of the signal station on the coast (Fig. 18.1) (Kitson Clark 1935, 121–2) in the later decades of the fourth century. It has been suggested (e.g. by Young 1817, 712) that this was the same person as that in the East Ness inscription. If it were, we might see the putative associated villa as the country retreat of a military officer associated with the coast defences.

---

[2] E.g. on the Ordnance Survey Roman Britain map. There is no record that it has been excavated.
[3] All these villas, like Kirkdale, are close to water.

Young also suggested that this person is the same Vindicianus as that on an inscription on a monument at Old Penrith erected by him to the memory of his brother Crotilus Germanus, aged 26, and of his daughter, Greca, aged 4 years (Young 1817, 712–3). Young also pointed out that the Penrith stone inscription is prefixed by the usual *D.M.* (*Dis Manibus*), but that this is not the case in the East Ness inscription. Perhaps, Young comments, Vindicianus had become a Christian between the date of the Old Penrith inscription and that at East Ness, and thus omitted the *D.M.* prefix. Professor Peter Salway has commented (pers. comm. 26.9.2000) that it is difficult to be sure about the precise lettering, since both the East Ness and the Old Penrith inscriptions are lost. Salway made further comments on the Vindiciani; he suggested that the family origins of the Vindicianus in the Old Penrith inscription were Germanic, since it seems to refer to a brother called Crotilo Germanus, if *frater* does mean brother rather than the colloquial 'friend'/comrade common in the Vindolanda letters. Salway further suggests that Vindicianus (of the Old Penrith inscription) was an ethnic German officer in the Roman army like the Emperor Magnentius, but – like Stilicho – he could easily be at least second generation Roman. If the Old Penrith Vindicianus is the same man as that in the East Ness inscription, his 'Valerius' here

> ... may suggest Roman citizenship acquired by the family as early as the reign of Diocletian. This does not really tell us anything about religion: the determinedly pagan Flavius Arbogastes, after all, managed to rise to be commander-in-chief of the western Roman army – and to be a personal friend of St Ambrose! Still, any reasonably ambitious officer stationed in the fourth century at or near a provincial capital and military HQ (let alone one so prestigious as the scene of the elevation of Constantine) is perhaps more likely to want to appear Christian – or sympathetic to Christianity – than not.
>   (Salway pers. comm.)

Salway's observations may apply indeed to any of the villa-owners in the area, but may not be reflected in the material culture of the villas.

At **Kirkdale** excavations at the west end of the church in 1997 (Rahtz and Watts 1998–99) defined a series of burials on two different orientations. The earliest graves were west-east (heads to west), in line with an associated building, presumably a church (but not the present structure). These were followed by a series orientated approximately 30° away from the earlier graves (SW–NE, heads to SW). This orientation is that of the north churchyard wall and of a cemetery beyond it, in the present field north of the church; finally, a series of later graves reverted to the orientation of the church.

In the lowest part of the burial area by the church were a coin of Constantine the Great and half a melon bead. While neither could be directly associated with a grave (the area had been disturbed), either or both could be from a grave in the earliest series.

In 2000, further excavations in advance of drainage operations exposed the foundations of the south side of the nave of the church. Beneath an offset course of limestone, attributed to the rebuilding of the Minster in 1055–65 (see above), was a lower step foundation, comprising a number of long blocks of sandstone. These have been compared, especially their tooling, with Roman structures in York. While not being *in situ* as part of a Roman structure (being reused in an Anglo-Saxon church), they raise the strong probability that there was a substantial Roman structure in the vicinity of St Gregory's Minster. Within the church, close to this point, reused columns inset into the piers below the arch between nave and chancel have also been suggested to be of Roman origin.[4]

There is enough food for thought here to propose an age of conversion in the fourth century in the area around the bishopric of York, at whatever levels of society it may have been successful.

Anglo-Saxon – the Second Age of Conversion

Anglo-Saxon monasteries in the Vale (Fig. 18.3)

The seventh–ninth centuries are the classic age of conversion in east Britain, well documented in written sources, notably those of Bede. His pages are especially relevant to Northumbria and there are references to two named places in the vicinity of the Vale of Pickering: Hackness and Lastingham (Fig 18.3). Both are described as monasteries, the former founded in AD 680 by Abbess Hilda of Whitby (Bede 1990, 243, 246). Lastingham was founded in AD 655 by Cedd (bishop of the East Saxons), who fell ill and died there in 659 (Bede 1990, 181–2). The land was granted to him by Ethelwald, King of Deira (Charles-Edwards 1974). Chad (bishop of the Mercians) also resided at Lastingham, although he would be buried at Lichfield (Bede 1990, 182, 207). Bede tells us that he himself had direct contact with the brethren of Lastingham, who had given him information used in his *History* (Bede 1990, 42). A third documented monastery was at Stonegrave, just beyond the Vale, close to Hovingham, described as such in a papal document at Rome in 781 (Whitelock 1955, 184).

The nature of the earlier Anglo-Saxon monasteries (documented as *monasterium* or *minster*) has been a major question for historians and archaeologists. It is generally accepted that many such institutions were founded in the later seventh century and that their foundation is relevant to the process of the conversion of the English as a whole. Discussion has revolved around the physical characteristics of such monasteries, their function, whether they were relatively closed communities with little contact with neighbouring people, and whether they made positive attempts to convert local communities to Christianity.

Lastingham, Hackness (and Kirkdale) are isolated places now, but in John Blair's words, 'Minsters were fixed points as the world changed round . . . centres of exotic and high culture and religion, and also of secular importance' (Blair forthcoming). Lastingham is not described by Bede specifically as a centre from which evangelism proceeded, but principally as a place where monastic discipline

---

[4] First noted by Jane Grenville.

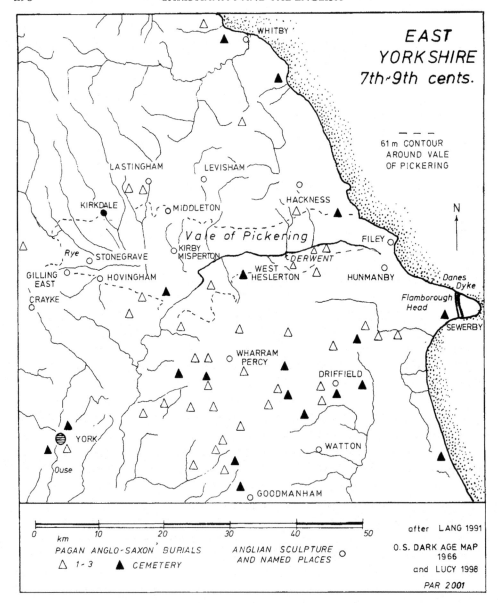

Figure 18.3 Map of seventh to ninth-century east Yorkshire, showing pagan Anglo-Saxon burials, Anglian sculpture and named places

reigned, in 'the observance of the usages of Lindisfarne' (that is, in the Irish manner – see Charles-Edwards 1974). It was also intended to be the burial place of King Ethelwald of Deira.

The existence of ecclesiastical establishments in pre-Viking times (650–850) is also attested by an impressive range of sculpture (especially decorated crosses) found in the Vale, mostly at sites which are certainly or possibly monastic (Lang 1991, Carver 1998; Fig. 18.3). At Lastingham, there is additional evidence of architectural worked stone (including part of a probable door jamb) presumed to have been part of structures of the eighth-century monastery, which was at least partly built in stone (Lang 1991, 171).

The monastery at Kirkdale

The evidence for a monastery at Kirkdale is both direct and indirect. The sundial inscription, featuring Orm's dedication of 1055–65, refers to a *minster* which had been rebuilt or restored from 'ruins' (above; Okasha in Watts *et al*. 1997). This seems to indicate the existence of a minster church earlier than Orm. It was by the eleventh century dedicated to St Gregory, but we do not know how long this had been true. The rare dedication, assumed to be to the first, sixth-century, pope of that name, suggests that a church could have been in existence since the later seventh or earlier eighth century, when the name of Gregory was prominent, notably in the pages of Bede (1990, ch. 23), as the instigator of the English conversion. This dedication may also suggest other points of contact for Kirkdale. York and Whitby also had two of the few dedications to Gregory (cf. Watts *et al*. 1997, 88 and 98, note 152).[5]

St Gregory's Minster is now isolated from the villages and towns which are strung along the northern margins of the Vale, from Helmsley to Pickering and beyond towards Scarborough. It is a few hundred metres north of the present main road. This is, however, of nineteenth-century date; the older route along the northern margin of the Vale passed very close to the Minster; it crosses the Hodge Beck by way of a ford, sometimes impassable to vehicles after heavy rain (Watts *et al*. 1996–97, 2). The ford is in a very unsuitable location, and may have been crossed by a bridge in earlier centuries. It was the inconvenience of this ford which necessitated the construction of the present road – a by-pass which crosses the beck over a masonry bridge (Watts *et al*. 1996–7, 6).

The church lies in the base of the dale, but just above the level of maximum floods. To its north, west and south are large graveyards with hundreds of gravestones, surprising in a church with no associated settlements (the smaller area on the east side is bordered by the Hodge Beck).[6] Further north, beyond the present north churchyard wall, is a pasture field, the North Field; and, further south, another area of pasture, the South Field, close to the ford.

There are a number of fragments of Anglian sculpture at Kirkdale, a few described in detail in the Lang *Corpus* (Lang 1991), others (found since that was compiled) briefly reported in our monographs (Watts *et al*. 1996–7 and Rahtz and Watts 1998–99). Two of those included in Lang's *Corpus* are of considerable importance: they are stone slabs, now set within the church. These, Lang suggests, are tomb-shrines, set on a container or grave (above ground, as now set), within

---

[5] The pre-Viking name of Kirkdale is unknown; its Anglo-Saxon form may be one of the unlocated places in Bede.

[6] The deceased come from surrounding hamlets and farms and a few, by request, from further afield.

which were all or some of the bones of what Blair (pers. comm.) believes were very important people, possibly local 'saints'. The western slab is of late eighth–early ninth-century date; it is elaborately decorated with an embellished cross; there is a small recess which may originally, as with Lastingham 4, have held a metal or jewel inset; the stone is one of the largest of its type known (Lang 1991, no. 7, 161–2, illus. 558–62). The eastern slab is similar in size, of the early ninth century (Lang 1991, no. 8, 162–3, illus. 563–7). Three of the four edges have a running pattern of tassels; the fourth is plain, implying that this end was against a wall. Collingwood suggested that the decoration was in imitation of actual embroidery (Lang 1991, 163). Embroidery is known to have been used in eighth–ninth-century Gaul for palls on tomb-shrines for saints of especial interest. 'At Kirkdale the depiction of the embroidery was an assertion of sanctity – a statement that this slab did indeed cover the bones or relics in the tomb's interior' (Blair forthcoming). Both slabs would probably have been painted.

Indeed, the richness of design of both these slabs, with implied access to exemplars and all the associated cultural resonances akin to the creation of the great jewellery pieces of the pagan period, suggests a rich aristocratic background (secular and/or ecclesiastical). These highly decorated slabs must have been inside a contemporary building, probably St Gregory's church, perhaps on either side of the principal altar at the east end of the chancel or a neighbouring *porticus* (cf. Bede 1990, 182) – a church likely to be earlier than that ruinous in the mid-eleventh century.

Excavations since 1994 have also added further evidence both of the antiquity of the church and also the importance of Kirkdale in pre-Viking times. An excavation in the North Field (Rahtz and Watts 1998–99) defined, first, a cemetery of males, females and children orientated on a NW–SE orientation. This is not yet dated.

Secondary to this was a structure, of which several large postholes were located. Associated with it, but possibly of its destruction phase, was a layer of dark soil, with charcoal, slag and other 'craft' debris. In this layer were two very significant finds. The first was the partly melted remnant of an inscribed lead plaque (Watts *et al.* 1997). The inscription is incised, in Old English, of eighth–ninth century date. The key word in the surviving script is interpreted as *BANCYST*, 'bone-container'. It seems that the plaque was attached to a box or bag in which were bones, relics of an important person. The inscription would have included the name of the person thus commemorated – another indication of important people at Kirkdale.

The second remarkable find in this layer was a very small segment of glass rod, with spiral trails of opaque white and yellow (Rahtz and Watts 1998–99, Figs 6–7). Such glass rods are known from a few monastic sites in Britain (but not in the NE), and also from the major trading towns in the Baltic, such Ribe and Birka. The best parallels are from San Vincenzo, a Carolingian (ninth-century) monastery south-east of Rome (Hodges 1993; Rahtz and Watts 1998–99, Fig. 7). Hundreds of such filigree rods were made at San Vincenzo for use as decoration on altar lamps. This find reflects the Mediterranean and European trade, gift and exchange network, in which Kirkdale was distantly involved; and the contacts both intellectual and physical to which it was exposed – as doubtless were other monasteries in the area, which have not been excavated.

The excavated sequence in the North Field made it clear that a substantial part of the complex lay in this field. The two finds, with the evidence of tomb-shrines, demonstrate the high status of the community at a pre-Viking date.

Archaeological examination of the foundations of St Gregory's Minster have demonstrated two, and possibly three, phases before that of the mid-eleventh century rebuilding (of which parts remain visible), including the reused ?Roman blocks (above). At the west exterior, there were three phases of burial.[7] The middle one, orientated NW–SE like those in the North Field (above), included a sarcophagus of ninth–eleventh-century date (Rahtz and Watts 1998–99, 10–11). This is not certainly pre-Viking (see below), but again indicates prestigious burial. To this may be added the discovery that the mid-eleventh century sundial inscription is cut on the side member of another sarcophagus (Watts *et al.* 1997, 89).

Kirkdale has thus been demonstrated to have been an important nucleus of Anglian religious activity as early as the eighth century (and possibly earlier); we may safely call it a monastery, in the light of its being known as a 'minster' with a putative early foundation. The relative proximity of Kirkdale to Lastingham (Fig. 18.3) may suggest a close relationship, and a broadly contemporary origin, Kirkdale perhaps being an offshoot, or even a sister monastery. It may be that evangelism was promoted in the Vale not from places like Lastingham, which may have been essentially remote from the contemporary world, up in the hilly terrain of the North York Moors, but from minsters, such as Kirkdale, closer to the Vale on the main routes through the area. Lastingham may have functioned as a place of private retreat, while Kirkdale was a more public place.[8]

Who were the pagan people of the area, and to what extent was the Kirkdale community involved in converting them?

Pagans and conversion in the Vale during the Anglo-Saxon period

In East Yorkshire, there are many 'Anglo-Saxon' cemeteries which have long been regarded as pagan; with graves of the fifth–earlier seventh centuries, often with numerous gravegoods, many of 'Germanic' style; putative graves of immigrants from areas east of the North Sea.

---

[7] The changing orientation needs to be investigated in detail, to see whether Irish- and/or Northumbrian-derived Christianity and Roman-derived Christianity all observed the same customs in burial orientation; also whether Anglo-Scandinavian burial followed similar customs to those of an earlier time.

[8] It is possible that Ethelwald owned Lastingham in 655 when he established a monastery there. At the time of Domesday Book, it is possible that Lastingham and Kirkdale were at least partly held in common (see Watts *et al.* 1997, note 158); could this situation go back to the seventh century?

We are now, however, in the beginning of the third millennium, not so sure. While the general post-Roman date for these cemeteries is still accepted, there is no longer certainty that those people buried in the graves were all immigrants, or their descendants; instead they may include Britons still living in the area (Lucy 1998, 2000). We are also less certain that they were all pagans; and we now also ask whether some elements of fourth-century Roman Christianity survived. It is in addition not so certain that all the gravegoods owe their characteristics to overseas styles, rather than local British affinities, in some cases derived from a late Roman background.

Nevertheless, neither cemeteries nor their rarer associated settlements of the fifth–seventh centuries can be shown to have any Christian features, such as specific finds or structures like churches. It is a truism that here and elsewhere, churches, whether Anglo-Saxon or later, are associated with later cemeteries and settlements, belonging to times when Christianity had been widely accepted as the religion of the English and the Britons.

It is probably still the case that the cemeteries near the coastal points of entry to East Yorkshire, such as Sewerby (Hirst 1985), are likely to have had a larger proportion of immigrants or their descendants than those further inland such as West Heslerton (see below).

Indeed, as one moves further west, away from the chalk uplands of the Wolds, what are usually called Anglo-Saxon cemeteries become more scarce. Moreover – and this is of considerable significance – not one substantial cemetery has been discovered on the north side of the Vale of Pickering (Fig. 18.3); and it is on this side where most of our early monasteries are located. Not only are 'Anglo-Saxon pagan' cemeteries absent from the west side of the Vale, but there is no positive evidence of settlement here (nucleated or otherwise) in the period between the Roman settlements and villas and the date of the early monasteries.

We may thus see a possibility of a dichotomy in the Vale, between an 'Anglo-Saxon' or mixed pagan area to the east, and a Christian population (?British or mixed) to the west. This is, of course, a gross over-simplification, but hints at least at some cultural and ideological differences between the sides of the Vale; this may be a reflection of a political divide, the Kingdom of Deira to the east of the River Derwent (cf. Higham 2000, 41) and a British area or 'kingdom' to the west (Fig. 18.3).

On the east side of the Vale, only one settlement has been investigated on a sufficiently large scale to provide a useful body of data relevant to this paper. This is West Heslerton (for location, see Fig. 18.3). As Kirkdale has been suggested to speak for many monasteries, West Heslerton may be set up as representative of what seem to be a number of early Anglo-Saxon settlements on the east side of the Vale. The site is doubly useful, in having not only a cemetery (of fifth–seventh centuries: Haughton and Powlesland 1999), but also a large and complex settlement (of about 17 ha), extending from late Roman times to the middle Saxon period, with hundreds of structures and other features.

The cemetery is conventionally pagan, but those phases of the settlement which can be shown to be contemporary with the graves may be seen as in use by a community which could have been the target of early missionaries. If conversion was successfully achieved, it was at least notionally complete by the later eighth–ninth centuries, with the probable establishment of the local village church. The archaeological evidence from West Heslerton extends into the 'post-pagan' phases – there are coins of the ninth century.

The situation we may envisage, as between our type-monastery of Kirkdale and our type-pagan settlement at West Heslerton, must have taken place in many areas in complex ways. We do not know how conversion was carried out. It is most likely that missionaries moved among the people to be converted, preaching and seeking political and other support in the upper echelons of society; a scene familiar in numerous historical accounts. An alternative is that perhaps (or additionally) large assemblies were set up at places accessible and well-known, where preaching and baptism took place on a large scale. Such a scene is familiar to us in Bede's description of Paulinus' preaching at Yeavering and also mass baptism in the River Glen (Bede 1990, 131–2). This was dramatically brought to light in the archaeology of that place – the discovery of a 'grandstand' near to the royal centre close to the river (Hope-Taylor 1977). This kind of occasion may be seen in modern times, with the rhetoric of latter-day missionaries such as Billy Graham.

Anglo-Scandinavian – the Third Age of Conversion

The Viking capture of York in 866–7 (Rollason *et al.* 1998, 63) was followed by Scandinavian settlement of the area of the north of York, including the Vale of Pickering. We may expect some violence in the initial stages of the land-taking, in the later ninth–tenth centuries, and some damage to the pre-existing Anglian monasteries. The Scandinavian leaders and settlers are now seen as having been assimilated and integrated rather than converted as such, either fairly swiftly or protracted over several decades. Assimilation in this context is generally taken to be, at least initially, the fusion of a new god with the northern pantheon with which the Vikings were familiar (cf. Hadley 2000, especially ch. 5).

It was clearly important for the new Scandinavian lords to control any institutions, places or buildings that had been of earlier significance to legitimise their power. These would have included churches and the sites of monasteries such as Kirkdale, even if they did not survive physically in the new regime, and especially if they had been also places of prestigious burial, of 'saints' or kings. It has long been realised that some Scandinavian lords continued to use existing burial places for their own graves, notably those recently discovered in the key context of Repton (Richards, Chapter 24 in this volume). In doing so, they were allying themselves with any advantage that Christian burial offered, but also consolidating their presence and power as new magnates.

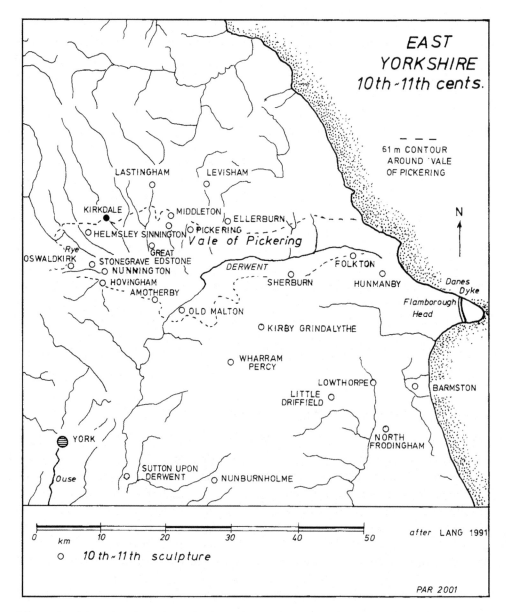

Figure 18.4 Map of tenth to eleventh-century east Yorkshire, showing distribution of sculpture

In the Vale of Pickering, no Viking burials or gravegoods have been found; this is not surprising, since only at Kirkdale have there been any excavations of potentially ninth–tenth century burial areas. There are however in the Anglo-Saxon churches or graveyards in the Vale numerous pieces of Anglo-Scandinavian sculpture (Lang 1991), indeed many more than of Anglian date (Figs 18.3 and 18.4). They comprise parts of crosses, with a fusion of Anglian and Scandinavian iconography, such as a slab at Middleton which includes a depiction usually taken to be of a Viking armed warrior, with Christian motifs (Lang 1991, no. 2, 182–3, illus. 676–81).

There has been extensive debate on the significance of these crosses, the extent to which they were originally associated with graves, set up in commemoration of important people, or set up as symbols of their control of places already well-known. Many were placed alongside existing sculpture of pre-Viking times.

Another facet of the debate concerning Viking-age sculpture is the extent to which the status or function of the churches, and any monasteries associated with them, changed radically. Were they now more directly associated with the new lords or their estates as personal and private possessions? Even this allows the continuation of the presence of priests, or even an attenuated community. The quality of the Viking-age sculpture has generally been considered to be inferior technically and aesthetically to the Anglian examples; they were probably made by local workmen, usually from local stone (cf. Lang 1991, 27). Martin Carver has proposed (1998, 24–6) that the Scandinavians 'dissolved' the Anglian monasteries and replaced a primarily monastic system with a broader network of private churches, marked by the numerous find-spots of Anglo-Scandinavian sculpture (see Lang 1991, 26–7).

At Kirkdale, where the very form of the place-name belongs to this period, there is some evidence relevant to the Scandinavian settlement and their assimilation to Christianity. First, the sculpture, including a 'bound Christ', on a cross-shaft set in the south wall of St Gregory's Minster, incorporated in the 1827 rebuild[9] (Watts et al. 1997, 78 and Fig. 7). Other pieces (e.g. the cross-shaft in the west wall, north of the (1827) tower) are set in masonry which can be argued to be part of the masonry of Orm Gamalson's rebuild or restoration in 1055–65 (Weatherill 1959; Watts et al. 1996–7, 12).

The surfaces and edges of the sandstone foundations at the junction of nave and chancel, attributed to an Anglian church (above), were burnt bright red. The ground level associated with this burning was 10–20 cms *lower* than that associated with the putative mid-eleventh century limestone foundation of Orm's church. The Anglian-period inscribed lead plaque (above) was partly melted. We are, not surprisingly, tempted to associate these burning episodes with the destruction of the church and its shrines in the later ninth or earlier tenth century, and attribute it to the initial violence of the Scandinavian conquest. If this is the case, then it could be argued that the church remained ruinous for nearly two centuries before the 1055–65 rebuild. But there are of course other causes of fire besides marauding Viking hordes!

The Anglo-Scandinavian investment at Kirkdale included both the rebuilding of the church and the burial of élite persons in its graveyard. Among the anomalously orientated graves was a reused stone sarcophagus (but with its contents very disturbed in post-medieval times). Anglo-Saxon or Anglo-Scandinavian

---

[9] This may reflect an Irish element in the Scandinavian conquest (cf. Lang 1991, 42).

sarcophagi are not common[10] and there is at present no parallel to the form of this one. It is slightly bowed in both plan and elevation (Rahtz and Watts 1998–99, Fig. 10), similar to some late Anglo-Saxon secular buildings.[11] This may point to the sarcophagus itself being (in this area) of Anglo-Scandinavian date. It could just have been (in its original location) the resting place of one of the Anglo-Scandinavian lords of the Kirkdale area in the tenth or eleventh centuries.

At Kirkdale, we cannot yet be certain which phase of the church building belongs to the Anglo-Scandinavian lord or community, but the sculptures certainly indicate their continuing interest into the later tenth–eleventh centuries, as may the graves.[12] Places like Kirkdale, where there are Anglian and Scandinavian sculptures, offer the best contexts in which our third age of conversion may be understood. Excavations to these ends need, however, to be on a large scale, including the churchyard, as carried out by Martin Biddle at Repton. We have, however, shown the kinds of evidence which can survive.

The consequences of conversion

By the later tenth century, it would generally be argued that the Anglo-Scandinavians were Christian, even with some fusion with the ancestral Nordic pantheon; and that those who were practising Christians, or wished to be seen as such, worshipped in churches, and were buried inside them or in the associated graveyards.

Among the monastic sites in the Vale, Kirkdale is unique in having a complete inscription set up by the last pre-Conquest lord of the area, a local magnate, to commemorate with 'some pomp and self-satisfaction' (Blair forthcoming) his restoration or rebuild of the Minster.

This tells us several points relevant to this discussion:

1. Orm Gamalson rebuilt (or restored) the church; he is probably the same person who is named in written sources as a local magnate (cf. Watts *et al.* 1997, 87 and note 162); his name associates him with the Anglo-Scandinavian community; he was probably (but not certainly) of Scandinavian descent, at least in part of his lineage.
2. He bought the church, implying that it was 'for sale' (from whom?), and was not already in his possession. It was thus a legitimate transfer of ownership that is referred to, not theft etc.
3. It was at that time known as a minster church, dedicated to St Gregory.
4. He was not building *de novo*, but was replacing a church which was by that time ruinous and collapsed, which was clearly in existence before his day; though

---

[10] There is surprisingly no major published research on this topic.
[11] Cf. also the reconstructed buildings in the tenth-century forts in Denmark, such as Trelleborg.
[12] The identification of DNA and of isotope affiliations for defining genetic affiliation will be important in defining the character of the population at Kirkdale.

it is possible that he may have exaggerated the totality of the rebuild; 'from the ground' may mean literally using only the earlier foundations to rebuild on, or making at least a new ground foundation to support his rebuilt church. Or he may have been exaggerating in that he only restored a church which was in a bad way. Any discussion about exactly what he did do awaits a final discussion on the whole structure and its archaeological phasing.

5. The dedication to St Gregory is reiterated, but Orm may personally have added the dedication to Christ.
6. The work was done 'recently', presumably in the decade 1055–65, in the light of the people mentioned (Watts *et al.* 1997, 87 and note 165).

What we do not know is the reason *why* Orm carried out his reconstruction (also see Okasha 1994, 73–4). One possibility is that he was establishing a new church for his own purpose, and chose to build on a site already well-known as a church, perhaps as a place both ancient and sacred. Orm knew what the church was called, and to whom it had been dedicated; and he may have known that the dedication suggested an origin up to five centuries before his time.

He may have authorised his work in a spirit of piety to a place revered as one of considerable importance in pre-Viking times, as the archaeology tells us today. It is possible that his restoration was rekindling the light of an earlier age of faith. If the recent history of this part of England was known to him or to his advisers, Orm may have been cognisant of the armed conflict that initiated the Scandinavian take-over, and even that it had begun with the sacking of a monastery further north at Lindisfarne, in 793; and that there had been similar violence offered to similar monasteries in later years, even perhaps Kirkdale, as we have hinted above.

Was there any element of restitution in his reconstruction of St Gregory's, especially if he knew that he was in the same lineage as those who had been responsible? Orm was a powerful person by the eve of the Conquest. He is likely to have been born at some time in the earlier eleventh century, of parents who had been born in the later tenth century. Their grandparents may have known of or even participated in any sacking of St Gregory's. So perhaps Orm was expiating the sins of his great-great-grandparents?

The recognition of the importance of the Minster in earlier times may be attested by the incorporation of some of the earlier sculpture. The current view is that the lower parts of the western wall of the church are extant parts of the mid-eleventh century reconstruction (Watts *et al.* 1996–7, 12). In this were incorporated the two great tomb-shrine slabs, of pre-Viking date (discussed above), in the lowest courses of this wall. They were set on either side of the western doorway with their decorated faces visible;[13] the implication is that they were still visible

---

[13] They were taken out and moved to their present position in the earlier twentieth century, when it was demonstrated that they were part of the wall when it was constructed, not inserted at a later date (Weatherill 1959; Watts *et al.* 1997, note 94).

somewhere in the ruinous church or in its vicinity. An Anglo-Scandinavian cross is still *in situ* higher up in this wall (on the north side of the 1827 tower); and two more were probably set in the south wall of the nave, re-set in similar location in the 1827 rebuild of this part of the church.

The sundial inscription provides a neat capping for the process of conversion at Kirkdale as, a century earlier, an inscription by King Harold Bluetooth did at Jelling for the Christianisation of Denmark (cf. Randsborg 1980, Fig. 3A, B, C,).

Conclusion

We have discussed here a number of observations and speculations on the character of St Gregory's Minster, its possible role in the processes of conversion, asking in particular if it was at any time a nucleus for attempts to convert the local population to Christianity. The evidence from Kirkdale must be seen in the context of the local settlement and history. It is currently too thin to support or refute any detailed hypothesis about the ages of conversion at Kirkdale itself, but can be used to throw light on the general processes involved, and shows how archaeological investigation can help to bring that picture into ever sharper focus.

References

Bede 1990 *Ecclesiastical History of the English People* trans. L. Sherley-Price and R.E. Latham (London).

Blair, J. forthcoming *The Anglo-Saxon Church in the Vale of Pickering* (The Kirkdale 2000 Lecture, to be published by the Friends of St Gregory's Minster).

Carver, M.O.H. 1998 'Conversion and politics on the eastern seaboard of Britain; some archaeological indicators' in B. Crawford (ed.) *Conversion and Christianity in the North Sea World* (St Andrews): 11–40.

Charles-Edwards, T.M. 1974 'The Foundation of Lastingham', *The Ryedale Historian* 7: 13–21.

Hadley, D.M. 2000 *The Northern Danelaw, Its Social Structure c 800–1100* (Leicester University Press).

Haughton, C. and Powlesland, D. 1999 *West Heslerton: The Anglian Cemetery*, 2 vols (Landscape Research Centre).

Hawkes, J. 1993 'Mary and the Cycle of Resurrection; the Iconography of the Hovingham Panel', in R.M. Spearman and J. Higgitt (eds) *The Age of Migrating Ideas* (National Museums of Scotland), ch. 31.

Higham, N. 2000 'King Edwin of the Deiri: Rhetoric and the Reality of Power in Early England', in H. Geake and J. Kenny (eds) *Early Deira* (Oxbow Books), 41–9.

Hirst, S.M. 1985 *An Anglo-Saxon Inhumation Cemetery at Sewerby, East Yorkshire*, York University Archaeological Publications 4.

Hodges, R. 1993 *San Vincenzo al Volturno 1* (British School at Rome).

Hope-Taylor, B. 1977 *Yeavering, An Anglo-British Centre of Early Northumbria* (Department of the Environment Archaeological Report no. 7).

Kitson Clark, M. 1935 *A Gazetteer of Roman Remains in East Yorkshire* (Roman and District Report no. 5, Yorkshire Archaeological Society).

Lang, J.T. 1991 *York and Eastern Yorkshire, Corpus of Anglo-Saxon Stone Sculpture in England*, vol. 3 (British Academy and Oxford University Press).

Lawton, I.G. 1999 'Derventio – a Roman Stamford Bridge Update', *Forum* (CBA Yorks): 7–11.

Lucy, S. 1998 *The Early Anglo-Saxon Cemeteries of East Yorkshire* (BAR British Series 272).

Lucy, S. 2000 *The Anglo-Saxon Way of Death* (Stroud).

Neal, D.S. 1996 *Excavations on the Roman Villa at Beadlam, Yorkshire*, Yorkshire Archaeological Report no. 2 (Yorkshire Archaeological Society).

Okasha, E. 1994 'The Commissioners, Makers and Owners of Anglo-Saxon Inscriptions', *Anglo-Saxon Studies in Archaeology and History 7*, 71–7.

Ottaway, P. 1993 *Roman York* (London).

Phillips, A.D. and Heywood, B. 1995 *From Roman fortress to Norman Minster. Excavations at York Minster Vol. 1* (London).

Rahtz, P.A., Hayfield, C. and Bateman, J. 1986 *Two Roman Villas at Wharram Le Street*, (York University Archaeological Publications 2).

Rahtz, P.A., Watts, L. and Jones, A. 2001 'Blansby Park 2000 – Interim Report', *Yorkshire Archaeological Society Roman Antiquities Section Bulletin 18*, 3–12.

Rahtz, P.A. and Watts, L. 1998–99 *Kirkdale Archaeology*, Supplement to *The Ryedale Historian* 19, 16pp.

Ramm, H. 1976 'The Church of St Mary Bishophill Senior, York: Excavation 1964', *Yorkshire Archaeological Journal 48*, 35–63.

Randsborg, K. 1980 *The Viking Age in Denmark* (London).

Rollason, D., with D. Gore and G. Fellows-Jensen 1998 *Sources for York History to AD 1100, The Archaeology of York*, vol. 1 (York Archaeological Trust).

Sparey-Green, C. 1977 'The Significance of Plaster Burials for the Recognition of Christian Cemeteries', in R Reece (ed.) *Burial in the Roman World* (CBA Research Report 22).

Stead, I.M. 1980 *Rudston Roman Villa*, (Yorkshire Archaeological Society).

Thomas, C. 1981 *Christianity in Roman Britain to AD500* (London).

Tweddle, D., Moulden, J. and Logan, E. 1999, *Anglian York: A Survey of the Evidence* (The Archaeology of York 7/2).

Watts, L., Grenville, J. and Rahtz, P.A. 1996–97 *Archaeology of Kirkdale*, Supplement to *The Ryedale Historian* 18, 19pp.

Watts, L., Rahtz, P.A., Okasha, E., Bradley, S.A.J., and Higgitt, J. 1997 'Kirkdale – the Inscriptions', *Medieval Archaeology 41*, 31–99.

Weatherill, J. 1959 *On Stones Built into Kirkdale Tower* (MS; copies now with authors and with The Borthwick Institute).

Whitelock, D. (ed.) 1955 *English Historical Documents I c500–1042* (Oxford).

Young, G. 1817 *History of Whitby* (2 vols) (Whitby).

19

The Confusion of Conversion: Streanæshalch, Strensall and Whitby and the Northumbrian Church

P.S. BARNWELL, L.A.S. BUTLER AND C.J. DUNN

Introduction

A little under 40 years after the formal conversion by baptism of Edwin, first Christian king of the Northumbrians, a synod was held to resolve tensions created by the fact that the kingdom was subject to sometimes opposing influences from the continental ('Roman') and western ('Celtic') churches.[1] The interest of both traditions in Northumbria is apparent from the time of Edwin's conversion itself for, while Bede records that his baptism in 627 was conducted by Paulinus, emissary of the Roman church, there is an alternative, British, tradition that it was performed by Rhun, son of Urien of Rheged.[2] Under Oswald (634–642), who had been baptised while exiled among the Scots during Edwin's reign, missionary activity in Northumbria was conducted by adherents to the Celtic tradition, most notably Aidan, whom the king had brought in from Iona.[3] It was Oswald's brother and successor, Oswiu, who had also been exiled and brought up in the British tradition,[4] who presided at the 664 Council, traditionally said to have been held at Whitby on the Yorkshire coast, at which the Northumbrians decided in favour of the 'Roman' rather than the western or Celtic tradition.

Bede's account of the Council narrates the events in narrowly ecclesiastical terms, concentrating on the form of monastic tonsure and, more especially, the date

---

[1] Bede, *Historia ecclesiastica gentis anglorum* (H.E.), iii.25 (ed. C. Plummer, 2 vols, Oxford, 1899). See Yorke, Chapter 15 in this volume for an overview of conversion processes in Anglo-Saxon England.

[2] H.E., ii.15, contrasted with Nennius, *Historia Brittonum*, 63 (ed. and trans J. Morris, *Nennius: British History and the Welsh Annals* (Chichester, 1980, Arthurian Period Sources, 8), and *Annales Cambriae*, *s.a.* 626 (ed. as Nennius). For a recent discussion of these two traditions, see C. Corning, 'The Baptism of Edwin, King of Northumbria: a new analysis of the British tradition', *Northern History*, 36 (2000), pp. 5–15, which suggests that Paulinus performed the baptism, Rhun acting as sponsor.

[3] H.E., iii.3.

[4] H.E., iii.29.

at which Easter should be celebrated.[5] The implications of the outcome were, however, of much greater significance than that suggested by this. In religious terms, the decision to reject Celtic teaching brought the Northumbrian kingdom into line with the main Southumbrian kingdoms, and with the mainstream of continental Christianity as represented by the papacy. But there were also important political dimensions to the decision, particularly in relation to Oswiu's ability to control the southern, Deiran, part of his kingdom, despite his having married Eanflæd, daughter of the Deiran King Edwin.[6] It was not until 655, some 13 years after his accession in Bernicia, that Oswiu had managed to gain full power in Deira,[7] and he then sought to strengthen his position by associating Alhfrith, his son by a previous liaison, with his rule as sub-king in the region.[8] The marriage to Eanflæd, however, only increased the religious tension in Oswiu's immediate circle, for she, like her father, was an adherent of the Roman tradition, and the situation was later exacerbated by Alhfrith's espousal of the Roman party,[9] partly, perhaps, in order to consolidate relations with his Deiran subjects, but also to challenge the authority of his father.[10] The decision taken at the 664 Council therefore had implications for the unity of Northumbria and for the future of Oswiu's own power; there were also implications in terms of whether the main future political allegiance of the kingdom would lie in the Celtic or Anglo-Saxon spheres.

Locating the Synod

The site of the Council which was convened to resolve these matters was an important monastic foundation closely associated with the Northumbrian royal house. It had been established in 657 as one of a number of churches founded by the King Oswiu in thanksgiving for his victory over the Mercian king, Penda, 2 years earlier,[11] in the same campaign which gave him mastery in Deira; it followed in the tradition of his earlier foundation, in 651, of a monastery at Gilling in expiation for his murder of Oswine, his cousin, who had ruled Deira during the first part of his reign.[12] The first three abbesses of the new monastery were Hild, Eanflæd and Ælfflæd – respectively, great-niece, daughter and grand-daughter of

---

[5] *H.E.*, iii.25; cf. Stephen, *Vita Wilfridi*, 10 (ed. B. Colgrave, *The Life of Bishop Wilfrid by Eddius Stephanus* (Cambridge, 1927)).

[6] *H.E.*, iii.15.

[7] After defeating the Mercians and Œthelwold of the Deirans at the Battle of the *Winwæd*: *H.E.*, iii.24.

[8] There is no explicit primary evidence that Alhfrith was sub-king in Deira as such, but there is good circumstantial evidence; for discussion, see E. John, 'The Social and Political Problems of the early English church', in J. Thirsk (ed.), *Land, Church and People: essays to H.P.R Finberg*, Supplement to *Agricultural History Review*, 18 (London, 1970), p. 41 n. 2.

[9] *H.E.*, iii.25.

[10] For the political dimension to the Council, see John, 'Social and Political Problems', pp. 42–50, H. Mayr-Harting, *The Coming of Christianity to Anglo-Saxon England*, 3rd edn (London, 1991), pp. 108–9, cf. pp. 7–8; R. Abels, 'The Council of Whitby: a study in early Anglo-Saxon politics', *Journal of British Studies*, 23 (1983), pp. 1–25.

[11] *H.E.*, iii.24, for the subsequent history of the monastery, see ibid., iii.25, iv.23, 26, v.25.

[12] *H.E.*, iii.14, 24.

Edwin – and under them the monastery became the dynastic burial place.[13] In the time of Hild in particular, it had a reputation as a centre for learning, and several later bishops were educated there, including Bosa and Wilfrid II of York, John of Hexham and York, Ætla of Dorchester and Oftfor of the Hwicce.[14]

Despite its importance, there are significant gaps in our knowledge of the history of the monastery, particularly after the death in 713 of Ælfflæd, part of whose epitaph has been claimed to have been found during excavations at Whitby in the 1920s.[15] In 867 the place was destroyed by Scandinavian raiders[16] and, shortly before 946, monks from Glastonbury removed relics, claimed to be those of Hild and Oswiu, from the site,[17] the ruined buildings of which were apparently visible. They could still be seen later, in the 1070s, when a new monastery was founded by Reinfrid of Evesham who selected the location largely on account of its association with the famous events of the early Anglo-Saxon past.[18]

The traditional location of the Council and monastery at Whitby is problematic, for the place is only ever referred to as *Streanæshalch* in the near-contemporary sources, Bede's *Ecclesiastical History*, Stephen's *Life of Wilfrid*, and the anonymous *Life of Gregory the Great*.[19] The first documented occurrence of the name 'Whitby' is in Domesday Book[20] and, as it is of Scandinavian form, it cannot have been applied to the place earlier than the ninth century: while this means that there must have been an earlier name, there is no firm evidence to suggest what that name was. A further complication arises from the fact that a second name of Scandinavian form, Prestby, indicating a foundation or possession of secular priests, was also associated with what is now Whitby in the late eleventh century.[21] The relationship between the two Scandinavian-period names is unclear, though Philip Rahtz has suggested that Prestby could have referred to the area on the headland occupied by the church and monasteries, which may

---

[13] The relevant evidence is conveniently assembled in K. H. Krüger, *Königsgrabkirchen der Franken, Angelsächsen und Langobarden bis zur Mitte des 8. Jahrhunderts. Ein historischer Katalog*, (Munich, 1971), pp. 309–11.

[14] *H.E.*, iv.23.

[15] C. Peers and C.A.R. Radford, 'The Saxon monastery of Whitby', *Archaeologia*, 89 (1943), pp. 41–4. See below for further discussion.

[16] J.C. Atkinson (ed.), *Cartularium abbathiae de Whitby*, 2 vols (Surtees Society 69 and 72, Durham, 1878–9), vol. i pp. xvi, xx.

[17] William of Malmesbury, *Gesta regum Anglorum*, i.50 (ed. R.A.B. Mynors, R.M. Thomson and M. Winterbottom, 2 vols (Oxford, 1998–9)); *idem*, *De gestis pontificum Anglorum*, ii.9 (ed. N.E.S.A. Hamilton (London, 1870)); *idem*, *De antiquitate Glastoniae ecclesiae*, 21 (ed. and trans. J. Scott (Woodbridge, 1981)).

[18] See Symeon of Durham, *Libellus de exordio atque procursu istius, hoc est Dunhemlensis ecclesie*, ed. D.M. Rollason (Oxford, 2000), iii.22. The re-foundation of the monastery is discussed in J. Burton, 'The monastic revival in Yorkshire: Whitby and St Mary's York', in D. Rollason, M. Harvey and M. Prestwich (eds), *Anglo-Norman Durham 1093–1193* (Woodbridge, 1994), pp. 41–53.

[19] *H.E.*, iii.24, 25, iv.23, 26, v.24; Stephen, *Vita Wilfridi*, 10; *Vita Gregorii Magni*, 18 (ed. B. Colgrave, *The Earliest Life of Gregory the Great, by an anonymous monk of Whitby* (Cambridge, 1968)).

[20] Domesday Book, i, 309a, 380c cf. 373a.

[21] William of Malmesbury, *Gesta regum Anglorum*, i.50; Atkinson, *Cartularium*, vol. i, document I (Memorial of the foundation and of the early benefactions); cf. Domesday Book, as n. 20.

later have been subsumed into a harbour settlement in the Esk valley, perhaps called Whitby.[22]

Whatever the explanation for the later names, neither helps in elucidating what the place was called in Anglian times. The first author explicitly to link *Streanæshalch* with Whitby was Symeon of Durham, writing in the twelfth century[23] – that is, after Reinfrid had established the new Benedictine monastery and claimed the association with Hild's foundation. There are, however, considerable problems both in relating *Streanæshalch* to the site at Whitby, and in the 'translation' of the name, given by Bede, as 'Sinus Fari', or 'Bay of the Lighthouse'.[24] The second element – *halch* – may refer to a secret or secluded place: this is difficult to relate to a cliff-top monastery, notwithstanding the dangers of access posed by a treacherous and fog-prone coast. The more likely reference is to a corner, angle or nook of land, usually associated with a river by which it may have been partly enclosed.[25] This relates equally poorly to the headland at Whitby, though it could perhaps have been applied to a low-lying site by the River Esk. Bede's translation of *halch* as *sinus* in the sense of a 'bay' is therefore stretching the term, and could be evidence of an attempt to fit the name to a place to which it does not belong. The first part of the name, *strēon*, is rare: it could be the personal name, *Strēon(a)*, but is thought more likely to be related to *(ge)strēon* and to refer to 'property', 'gain' or 'the reward of labour', or to a 'lineage' or 'clan'.[26] The latter possibility would relate it to the Latin *fara*, but that is not the same as Bede's *fari* (genitive of *pharos*), again giving rise to the suspicion that he may have been attempting to fit the name *Streanæshalch* to an alien place. The real meaning of the name would suggest a piece of property of angular shape, probably low-lying, and perhaps in the angle of a river:[27] that is precisely the situation of the two places called Strensall in Worcestershire (one on the outskirts of Evesham and the other in Wick Episcopi, near Worcester itself)[28] and of the Strensall five miles (8 km) north of York. It is difficult to see any similarities between those places and either the harbour or headland sites at Whitby.

The actual identification of *Streanæshalch* with the Strensall north of York has on occasion been considered in the past, though it has generally been thought to be precluded by the results of the excavations at Whitby in the 1920s,[29] which

---

[22] P.A. Rahtz, 'Whitby 1958', *Yorkshire Archaeological Journal*, 160 (1962), pp. 605–6.

[23] Symeon of Durham, *Libellus*, iii.22, cf. *idem*, *Historia regum*, 161 (ed. T. Arnold, *Symeonis monachi opera omnia*, 2 vols (London, 1882–5)).

[24] M. Gelling, *Signposts to the Past: place-names and the history of England* 3rd edn (London, 1997), p. 189.

[25] A. Mawer, *The chief elements used in English place-names, being the second part of the Introduction to the Survey of English Place-Names* (Cambridge, 1930), pp. 34–5.

[26] See J.R. Clark Hall, *A concise Anglo-Saxon Dictionary*, 4th edn (Cambridge, 1960), p. 324, and R. Coates, 'The slighting of Strensall', *Journal of the English Place-Name Society*, 13 (1980), pp. 50–3.

[27] For an alternative interpretation, see Coates, 'Slighting of Strensall', pp. 50–3.

[28] Gelling, *Signposts*, p. 189.

[29] Hunter Blair, 'Whitby as a centre of learning in the seventh century', in M. Lapidge and H. Gneuss (eds), *Learning and literature in Anglo-Saxon England: studies presented to Peter Clemoes on the occasion of his sixty-fifth birthday* (Cambridge, 1985), p. 10 n. 3.

found evidence consistent with a high-status monastic community.[30] Those excavations uncovered the foundations of buildings which can be interpreted as those of a monastic settlement, while the finds include high-status domestic items and articles for toiletry, hanging bowls, styli and an early baluster shaft. There is also a quantity of sculpture, including crosses and stones with carvings and inscriptions, two of which are of particular note. The first is part of a cross, which bears an inscription which the excavators read as *ABBAE +*, perhaps confirming the monastic nature of the site. More recently, however, John Higgitt has tentatively suggested that the true reading is *AHHAE +*, which could refer to Edwin's sister,[31] Acha, who could have been one of the unnamed *nobiles* Bede states were buried at *Streanæshalch* alongside Oswiu, Edwin, his daughter, Eanflæd, and grand-daughter, Ælfflæd,[32] the last two having been joint abbesses there. A second inscription was claimed by the excavators to be the epitaph of Ælfflæd herself, but Higgitt has in this case argued that the identification is unsafe, since the initial reconstruction of the relevant part of the text as *[+ AEL]FLEAEDA* does not take account of the fact that, in an Anglian context, 'Ælfflæd' should be 'Ælfflēd', a reading precluded by the only four letters (*EAED*) which can be read with certainty.[33] Even if this view is rejected, the epitaph cannot be demonstrably linked to the second abbess: the name of none of her successors between 713 and 867 is known, and an abbess of any monastic foundation in the area could have adopted the name out of respect for the earlier nun, wherever she was based, in the same way as John of Beverley's successor in the see of York was named Wilfrid after the earlier saint. A final piece of archaeological evidence, found in 1874, long before systematic excavation, takes the form a lead papal *bulla*, bearing the name 'Boniface' and the word 'archdeacon'.[34] Assuming that the object is of seventh-century date, it could belong to one of two Roman archdeacons of that name, one active in 685 and the other, with whom Wilfrid had dealings, some 30 years earlier:[35] there is, however, no way of knowing when the object reached Whitby, which need not have been immediate.

The sum of the excavated evidence from Whitby therefore suggests that the existence of a high status early site there is indisputable, and the plan of the buildings, together with the number, type and quality of the finds, indicate that

---

[30] For the excavations, see Peers and Radford, 'The Saxon monastery of Whitby', and Rahtz, 'Whitby 1958', with R.J. Cramp, 'Monastic sites', in D.M. Wilson (ed.), *The Archaeology of Anglo-Saxon England* (Cambridge, 1976), pp. 223–9, and her, 'Analysis of the finds register and location plan of Whitby Abbey', in the same volume, pp. 453–7 ,with P.A. Rahtz, 'The building plan of the Anglo-Saxon monastery of Whitby', also in the same volume, at pp. 459–62.

[31] J. Higgitt, 'Monasteries and inscriptions in early Northumbria. The evidence of Whitby', in C. Bourke (ed.), *From the isles of the north: early medieval art in Ireland and Britain* (Belfast, 1995), pp. 231, 233.

[32] *H.E.*, iii.24.

[33] Higgitt, 'Monasteries and inscriptions in early Northumbria', p. 232.

[34] D. Haigh, 'The Monasteries of St Heiu and St Hilda', *Yorkshire Archaeological and Topographical Journal*, 3 (1875), p. 371; cf. A. White, 'Finds from the Anglian monastery at Whitby', *Yorkshire Archaeological Journal*, 56 (1984), 35, 37–8.

[35] *H.E.*, v.19.

it was monastic in character.[36] While nothing conclusively demonstrates the identity of that site with *Streanæshalch*, there are enough pieces of circumstantial evidence for the identification not to be easily discounted, despite the problem of the inappropriate nature of the place name for the site.

During the course of nearly 200 years more than one hypothesis has been devised to overcome the problems of the name and, particularly, by Bede's 'translation' of it. As early as 1817, the Reverend George Young not only recognised the difficulty in his account of Whitby Abbey, but also suggested that the 'translation' represented an interpolation into Bede's original text,[37] though later manuscript scholarship suggests that such is unlikely to be the case. In the 1970s, Peter Hunter Blair ingeniously suggested that Bede's precise phraseology indicates that, rather than providing a translation of the Old English name, *Sinus Fari* represents an exegetical interpretation of Whitby as the place from which the light of the traditions of the Roman Church shone over the whole of Britain.[38] More recently, notwithstanding the etymological difficulties, an attempt has been made to find evidence of a Roman lighthouse or watchtower at Whitby, though the conclusion drawn is that Bede's 'translation' of *Streanæshalch* 'remains one of the most suggestive pieces of evidence for a signal station at Whitby'.[39] None of these is entirely satisfactory, and what follows is an approach to the problem through an examination of the topography of Strensall near York, which has never before been discussed in this or any other context, and a consideration of its possible implications for the understanding of the relationship between *Streanæshalch* and Whitby. It is acknowledged in advance that the conclusions are only tentative, but they may point towards a possible source of further clarification.

The Site at Strensall

Strensall village is situated in a bend of the River Foss some 5 miles (8 km) north of the historic centre of York (Fig. 19.1). The church (now a nineteenth-century building)[40] stands immediately above the flood plain, adjacent to a medieval

[36] *Pace* D. Tweddle, 'The Anglian City', in D. Tweddle, J. Moulden and E. Logan (eds), *The Archaeology of York*, 7 fasc. 2, *Anglian York: a survey of the evidence* (York, 1999), p. 136; see P.A. Rahtz, 'Anglo-Saxon and later Whitby', in L.R. Hoey (ed.), *Yorkshire Monasticism: archaeology, art and architecture from the seventh to sixteenth centuries* (London, 1995), p. 8, despite his earlier hint at questioning this by drawing an analogy between the plan and that of a town, as well as pointing out its relationship to that of a fully developed monastery, in his 'Building plan', p. 462. On the significance of the finds for a monastic context, see R. Cramp, 'A Reconsideration of the monastic site at Whitby', in R.M. Spearson and J. Higgitt (eds), *An Age of Migrating Ideas: early medieval art in northern Britain and Ireland* (Edinburgh and Stroud, 1993), p. 64.

[37] G. Young, *A History of Whitby and Streoneshalh abbey: with a statistical survey of the vicinity to the distance of twenty-five miles*, 2 vols (Whitby, 1817), vol. ii, pp. 142–3.

[38] P. Hunter Blair, 'Whitby as a centre of learning' pp. 11–2.

[39] T.W. Bell, ' A Roman signal station at Whitby', *Archaeological Journal*, 155 (1998), pp. 303–13.

[40] The present building is of 1865–6: N. Pevsner, *The Buildings of England. Yorkshire: the North Riding* (Harmondsworth, 1966), p. 460. It replaces the medieval church, which was substantially re-built

moat,[41] and is prominently visible from the west and north (Pl. 19.1). The historic village, which lies to the east, consists of a main street at the north and a back lane (now Southfields Road) to the south, beyond which are the remnants of the open fields. The church is set with its east end slightly to the south of Grid east, while the north and south sides of the partially surviving, but apparently trapezoidal, moat are similarly (but not identically) aligned. By contrast, the area of the village to the west of the present road north over Strensall Bridge to Sheriff Hutton lies east-north-east, while the east end of the settlement, beyond the Sheriff Hutton road, stands almost exactly east–west. The deflection in the village plan may indicate that its two sections were laid out at different periods. If that is correct, the east end of the village, although more closely aligned with the moat, may represent the later element: it is too small to have formed a complete village, whereas the area between it and the manor is more regularly laid out, and generally akin to other small villages in the vicinity.

The church and moat are not fully integrated into the village plan, but appear to occupy a separate area within the angle of the Foss: both the 1849 Tithe Map and the first edition 25-inch Ordnance Survey map of 1893 show a large, undivided and empty area around them.[42] To the south-west of the church is a small area, of which both the morphology and main road name suggest it represents an addition to the village. The road, West End, forms its southern side, being a continuation of the line of the back lane of the village (rather than of the main street), and the properties along it therefore face south rather than north as in the main part of the settlement. Between West End and the main village is an irregularly shaped block of land with haphazard internal subdivision. It interrupts the line formed by the West End and the back lane of the main village and, at its south, terminates on the sinuous north end of what is now York Road, beyond which lies the mid nineteenth-century Old Vicarage.

The road pattern as shown on the first edition 25-inch map reflects the morphology of the settlement as a whole. York Road approaches from the south, turns sharply east at the Old Vicarage for about 30 yards (27 m), north for a further 30 yards (27 m), east again on to the line of the back lane for slightly longer, then north again for a short distance before finally swinging east to form the line of the main street or The Village. At the east end of what was apparently the earlier

in 1801: G. Lawton, *Collectio rerum ecclesiasticarum de Diœcesi Eboracensi; or Collections relative to the churches and chapels within the Diocese of York. To which are added collections relative to churches and chapels within the Diocese of Ripon*, 2nd edn, 2 vols (London, 1842), vol. i, p. 461.

[41] For the moat, see H.E.J. Le Patourel, *The moated sites of Yorkshire* (Society for Medieval Archaeology, Monograph series, 5, London, 1973), p. 121; the present Hall was largely built in 1695 see H.M. Colvin, *A biographical dictionary of British architects, 1600–1840*, 3rd edn (New Haven, 1995), p. 354.

[42] The tithe map is conveniently reproduced in T. Mitchell, *Strensall in the mid-19th century* (York, 1989), pp. 28–9; the OS sheet numbers are Yorkshire (North Riding) clvii.3–4.

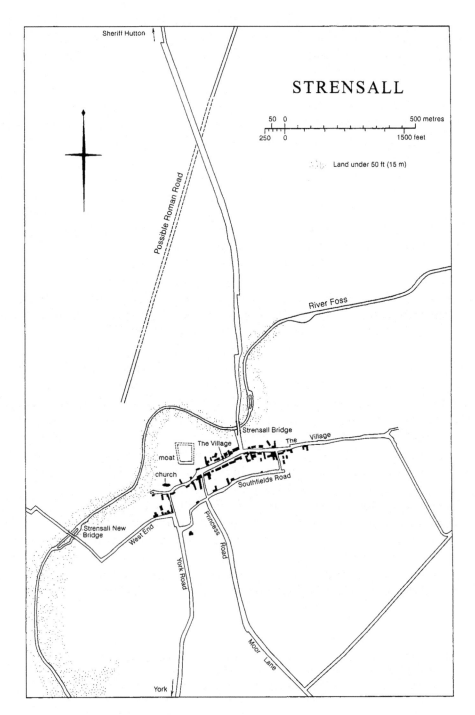

Figure 19.1 Map of the modern village of Strensall north of York

Plate 19.1 Strensall church and the river Foss, viewed from the north

block of the village is the road to Sheriff Hutton. At the west end of the village, making a slightly staggered junction with the back lane, a further road, Moor Lane, leads south, apparently being an Enclosure road to the Common. The presence of Moor Lane suggests that, despite its meandering approach, York Road formed the route to Strensall from York. Where it first turns east, its line is continued to the north for some 30 yards (27 m) by West End before a sharp turn west on to the line of the back lane. At that corner a narrow lane continues northwards until the church is reached. This may suggest that York Road originally continued north to the church.

It is not clear whether the road stopped at the church or whether, before the church was built in its present position, it continued north to a now lost crossing of the Foss. Such an interpretation is uncertain, partly since there are other villages in the vicinity, such as Stillington (5 miles (8 km) north-west of Strensall), where the main road is dog-legged. In favour of such a hypothesis, however, is the fact that a projection of the line of York Road across the River not only links with the Sheriff Hutton Road at the parish boundary some three-quarters of a mile to the north, but would also intersect with a possible Roman road which runs across the northern part of the parish in a north-easterly direction,[43] passing near to a first- or

---

[43] The evidence, derived from aerial photographs, is discussed in V.G. Swan, B.E.A. Jones and D. Grady, 'Bolesford, North Riding of Yorkshire: a lost wapentake centre and its landscape', *Landscape History*, 15 (1993), p. 20. Since that work, the English Heritage National Mapping Programme has identified a further section of the possible road, approximately 400 m north-west of Strensall; see National Monuments Record SE 66 SW 4.

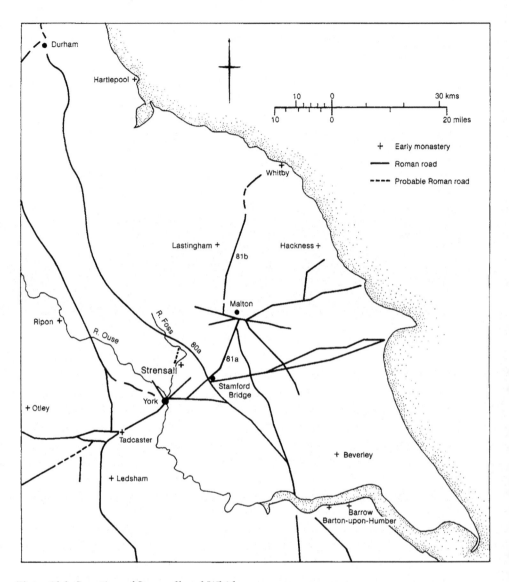

Figure 19.2 Location of Strensall and Whitby

second-century settlement, apparently of some status, not very far from the church.[44] The Roman road presumably started in York, may have lain entirely on the west side of the Foss, and probably connected with the Roman route from

[44] The settlement was revealed by field-walking undertaken by John Bateman (formerly of the Department of Archaeology at the University of York), and published in J. and D. Bateman, 'Roman finds from the Vale of York', in the *Bulletin* of the Roman Antiquities Section of the Yorkshire Archaeological Society, 4 (Winter 1986–7), pp. 26–9. The landowner requested that the precise location of the site should not be revealed. We are grateful to Mr Bateman for sharing his information with us, and for supplying a fuller version of his report than that which was published.

Stamford Bridge to Durham (Fig. 19.2). From there the road which went from York to Malton and thence towards Whitby would have been easily attained.[45]

If this reading of the topography is correct in general terms, it is possible to suggest the following development. First, a Roman settlement and probable road on the west side of the River Foss, the latter extending from York to link with the Roman road system further north. Second, the creation of an enclosure in the bend of the Foss. If York Road, on the east side of the River, was in existence before the enclosure, it is possible that the creation of the latter led to the deflection of the road and created its present sinuous course towards the village and the present Sheriff Hutton Road. Third, the laying out of the main (western) part of the village, followed, fourthly, by the extension of the village to the east and, finally, by the development of West End.

Given the early date of the place name – much earlier than the planned part of the village, which is unlikely significantly to pre-date the Norman Conquest – it is probable that the earliest surviving element of the settlement was the enclosure in the bend of the river in which the church and moat stand, rather than the enclosure and village being the result of a single act of planning. During the later middle ages, Strensall was a prebend within York Minster, the prebendary being the lord of the manor of Strensall,[46] the hall of which presumably lay within the moat. The church lies in the centre of the enclosed area, and it is possible with the eye of faith to trace the remnants of the south-eastern quadrant of a curvaceous boundary around it and the adjacent prebendal manor. This could suggest that the enclosure was formed around an area of ecclesiastical land.

If it is accepted that the name *Streanæshalch* does not fit the site of Whitby, and that the topographical evidence of Strensall contains possible hints of an ecclesiastical enclosure, then it is necessary to consider whether any other early monastic sites occupy similar positions in the landscape. The location of Strensall, a few miles outside the royal centre of York, has some general similarities with Lindisfarne, near the royal residence at Bambrough, Lichfield, near that at Wall (*Letocetum*) and, perhaps, with St Augustine's at Canterbury, as well as with continental examples.[47] Similarly, although many of the best known sites in and beyond the north-east of England occupy coastal positions (from Abercorn in the north to Lindisfarne, Jarrow and Wearmouth, Hartlepool and Whitby, and to Barrow and Barton-upon-Humber in the south), other situations are equally possible: Hexham, Ripon, Otley (unless that was an episcopal estate[48]) and Beverley are all inland, as are Lastingham and Hackness, which stand in secluded

---

[45] The roads from Stamford Bridge to Durham and from York to Malton and thence to Whitby are, respectively, nos 80a and 81a and 81b in I.D. Margary, *Roman roads in Britain*, 3rd edn (London, 1973).

[46] Lawton, *Collectio rerum ecclesiasticarum*, vol. i, p. 461. Strensall was one of the first prebends, established before the middle of the twelfth century.

[47] Tweddle, 'The Anglian City', p. 136.

[48] I.N. Wood, 'Anglo-Saxon Otley: an archiepiscopal estate and its crosses in a Northumbrian context', *Northern History*, 23 (1987), pp. 20–38.

valleys, and Ledsham which, like Strensall, is near a Roman road; Tadcaster, to which Heiu, Hild's predecessor at her earlier monastery of Hartlepool, moved, is also low-lying and near a Roman road.[49] Although the situation of none of these is identical to that of Strensall, there are enough general similarities for Strensall to represent a possible monastic site.

In terms of the events which are reported to have occurred at *Streanæshalch*, there is no conclusive evidence in favour of either Whitby or Strensall. Perhaps the strongest argument in favour of Whitby is that Bede stated that the associated monastery of *Hacones* was 13 miles from *Streanæshalch*,[50] suggesting that it should be identified with the modern Hackness, 13 miles from Whitby, where Anglian sculpture and an inscription referring to an abbess have been found.[51] Conversely, unless one believes that Celtic saints and abbots would only use water transport, remote Whitby would seem an inconvenient site for the holding of the 664 Council, whereas Strensall was in easy reach of York, the capital of Deira. Other factors suggest that both locations are equally possible. Hence, for example, the body of King Edwin, whose head had been buried at York,[52] was later moved from Edwinstowe in Nottinghamshire, near Hatfield Chase where he was killed, to *Streanæshalch*:[53] Whitby would have been convenient if water transport were used, while Strensall was near York (which was itself accessible by water) whence it was easily reached by the Roman road system. In addition, if *Streanæshalch* was near York, Hild's move thence from Hartlepool would have been directly parallel to Heiu's earlier move from Hartlepool to Tadcaster.[54] Further straws in the wind may be the fact that three of York's bishops (Bosa, John and Wilfrid II) were associated with Hild's monastery, suggesting that it at least had close connections with York;[55] that the sculpture at Whitby has closer parallels with a Deiran (and specifically York-based) tradition than with the great monasteries of Bernicia;[56] and that an association between York and Hild may be reflected in the dedication to Evorilda (*Euforhilda*, or York-Hild), of the church at Nether Poppleton, near York.[57] Finally, the early eighth-century author of the Life of Gregory the Great, who was associated with the place where Edwin was buried (and, as a result,

[49] The nearby name of Healaugh could be derived from 'Heiu'; see Plummer's note to Bede, *Historia ecclesiastica*, iv.24.

[50] *H.E.*, iv.23.

[51] J.T. Lang, *Corpus of Anglo-Saxon Sculpture, 3, York and East Yorkshire* (Oxford, 1991), pp. 135–42.

[52] *H.E.*, ii.20.

[53] *H.E.*, iii.12.

[54] *H.E.*, iv.24.

[55] R.K. Morris, 'York, Alcuin and the *alma sophia*', in L.A.S. Butler and R.K. Morris (eds), *The Anglo-Saxon Church: papers on history, architecture and archaeology in honour of Dr H.M. Taylor* (London, 1986), pp. 81 and 87 n. 6. An association of both Hild and John of Beverley with Strensall, rather than Whitby, was accepted in T. Fuller, *The Worthies of England*, 3 vols (London, 1662, repr. 1840), iii, pp. 402–3. We are grateful to David Palliser for this reference.

[56] Cramp, 'Reconsideration', pp. 68–70; cf. Higgitt, 'Monasteries and inscriptions', p. 230.

[57] L.A.S. Butler, 'Church dedications and the cult of Anglo-Saxon saints in England', in Butler and Morris, *The Anglo-Saxon Church*, p. 49 n. 11.

generally considered to be at Whitby),[58] was very familiar with York, suggesting that he may have had readier access to the city than if he had lived at Whitby.

If, on all these grounds, Strensall can be considered at least a possible location for the monastery Bede described as *Streanæshalch*, the remaining question is how the name could have come to be associated with Whitby. There are several possibilities, none of which is susceptible of proof on the basis of existing evidence, particularly as written material for eighth-century Northumbria is notoriously sparse. One option is that Strensall and Whitby formed a twin monastery, like Monkwearmouth-Jarrow, and that both were subsumed under a single name. If that were the case, the question of which events occurred at which place would remain open. A second possibility is that in 657 Hild founded a monastery at Strensall near York, in the same way as Heiu did 2 years earlier at Tadcaster, and that it later spawned a daughter house at Whitby which carried the name 'Strensall' with it and later rose to outshine it in importance. Finally, it is conceivable that a monastery was founded at Strensall prior to 657, either in the reign of Oswald (633–642) or, more likely, early in the reign of Oswiu (642–670). If this were correct, it might be that when Oswiu subsequently gave Hild land near Whitby, he also gave her the fledgling monastery at Strensall, either as an additional donation and nucleus of monks, or as a retreat in case the new foundation failed. In either case, the new foundation could have taken the name of *Streanæshalch* from the older monastery, and the relationship could have been similar to that which existed much later between Llanthony in the wilds of the Black Mountains and Llanthony *secunda* in the safety and comfort of Gloucester. An explanation of this kind could, perhaps, explain two features of Bede's account of the foundation of *Streanæshalch*. Although it seems that the house was one of the six founded by Oswiu in Deira in thanksgiving for his victory at the Battle of the *Winwæd*, the fact is nowhere explicitly stated:[59] a new foundation combined with an older one on a different site could offer an explanation for the uncertainty. Further, the precise phrase Bede used to describe the foundation of *Streanæshalch* is unusual, for he states that Hild was given land 'to construct or else ordain [construendum siue ordinandum] a monastery in the place which is called *Streanæshalch*'.[60] This is the only occasion in the *Ecclesiastical History* on which Bede uses 'ordain' in relation to an institution rather than to a person, and all his other references to the foundation of monasteries only contain the idea of 'construction'. It could therefore be that two sites were involved: Whitby, which was 'constructed' or founded, and Strensall, which had already been founded a short time before, but was still to be fully organised or 'ordained'.

---

[58] *Vita Gregorii Magni*, 18, 19, with pp. 45–6 of Colgrave's Introduction to the text.

[59] N. Higham, *The Convert Kings: power and religious affiliation in early Anglo-Saxon England* (Manchester, 1997), p. 251.

[60] *H.E.*, iv.23: '... construendum siue ordinandum monasterium in loco, qui uocatur Streaneshalch ...'.

Under any of the three options outlined above, Whitby could have risen to outshine Strensall itself, either in Hild's time or later, though none resolves the location of the 664 Council. Two contexts may tentatively be suggested for the flourishing of Whitby rather than Strensall. The first possibility could be provided by the dynastic turmoil of the Northumbrian kingdom in the eighth century, which saw the replacement of the descendants of Oswiu by those of one Leodwald.[61] The occupants of a monastic enclave as closely associated with Oswiu's family as was *Streanæshalch* might have found proximity to York uncomfortable, and have removed themselves, perhaps even with their dynastic relics, to the relative safety of the more remote Whitby, carrying the name with them. The second, and perhaps more likely, context for the rise of Whitby lies in the circumstances of the seventh century itself, and stems from the existence of a degree of tension between Hild and Ælfflæd.[62] In contrast with Ælfflæd, grand-daughter of Edwin, Hild's dynastic and ecclesiastical connections were centred in Bernicia rather than in Deira. Partly as a consequence, Hild opposed Wilfrid, who was a representative of the Roman church and a protégé of Alhfrith, who put him in charge of the monastery at Ripon in place of the Celtic Eata, who returned to the Bernician territory where he had been educated by Aidan;[63] Ælfflæd, on the other hand, was one of Wilfrid's chief supporters. Of more direct significance in the present context is the fact that the two women backed different sides at the 664 Council, Hild supporting the losing Celtic faction. These circumstances could perhaps render it possible to envisage an initial foundation at Strensall having become so riven by rivalry that Eanflæd and her daughter, Ælfflæd, moved away to Whitby, but carrying the name with them, perhaps to maintain a link with the past, particularly if the 664 Council had taken place at Strensall. Thereafter, Ælfflæd seems to have appropriated the site as a monument to the Deiran dynasty and her own forbears.[64] This, combined with Ælfflæd's immense power in the Northumbrian church,[65] perhaps building on the success of the Roman party with which her mother, Eanflæd, was associated, contrasts with Hild's position on the losing side at the Council, and may have led Bede to say relatively little about her: it is not known where she was buried, and, exceptionally for so significant a figure, he reports none of her actual words.[66] If Hild had indeed been associated with Strensall, and Eanflæd and Ælfflæd had left for Whitby, there might be a convincing context for the decline of Strensall after, if not before, Hild's death, leaving little trace other than the name as applied to the monastery at Whitby.

---

[61] D.P. Kirby, *The earliest English kings*, 2nd edn (London and New York, 2000), pp. 118–33.

[62] C.E. Karkov, 'Whitby, Jarrow and the commemoration of death in Northumbria', in J. Hawkes and S. Mills (eds), *Northumbria's Golden Age* (Stroud, 1999), pp. 129–35.

[63] Bede, *Vita sancti Cuthberti*, 7, 8 (ed. B. Colgrave, *Two Lives of Saint Cuthbert: a Life by an anonymous monk of Lindisfarne and Bede's prose Life*, (Cambridge, 1940)); *H.E.*, iii.26.

[64] Karkov, 'Whitby, Jarrow and the commemoration of death', pp. 129–30 and 133–5.

[65] A. Thacker, '*Membra Disjecta*: the division of the body and the diffusion of the cult', in C. Stancliffe and E. Cambridge (eds), *Oswald: Northumbrian king to European saint* (Stamford, 1995), p. 110.

[66] Karkov, 'Whitby, Jarrow and the commemoration of death', pp. 129–30.

The factors which conditioned the later history of Strensall would have been the same whichever interpretation of the reasons for its initial decline is favoured. Either at the moment of decline, or after the destruction of Whitby in the mid ninth century, it passed to the archbishops of York (who owned land there in Domesday Book[67]). In the twelfth century it re-emerged as a prebendal manor within York Minster; if not the wealthiest of the prebends, it was, in the sixteenth century, known as the 'Golden Prebend'.[68] Following its own destruction, Whitby itself, by contrast, was in lay hands by the time of the Domesday survey.

Conclusion

The suggestions made here are almost entirely informed speculation, but they could account for the use of the name *Streanæshalch*, for the hints of a close association between that monastery and York, for the later demise of Strensall, and for the later identification of Whitby with *Streanæshalch*. They could also help to explain why so little is left to mark the early importance of Strensall: there have never been any chance archaeological finds to suggest its significance; the parish, although large, is not abnormally so; there are no daughter churches as there are for some other, longer-lived, early sites such as Dewsbury and Gilling; and there is no documentary evidence. All we have are the topography, the location of a prebendal manor, the use of the name *Streanæshalch* by early authors, some suggestive hints concerning the relationship of *Streanæshalch* with York, and a scatter of archiepiscopal holdings around that at Strensall, which could be a relic of a once larger estate.[69] None of this amounts to more than an empty shell. That major early ecclesiastical sites could disappear almost without trace is observable elsewhere, as at Wing in Buckinghamshire and, perhaps most famously, at Brixworth in Northamptonshire, where the great seventh-century church is notoriously devoid of context or place in history; apart from the church building, the evidence for a significant, even if short-lived, ecclesiastical site at Strensall could be considered relatively good by comparison. It could be tested further by geophysical survey and excavation both in the churchyard (which may have been disturbed by the early nineteenth-century restoration and subsequent re-building of the church) and in the area to its north which has not been built upon, at least in recent times (Pl. 19.1). Perhaps if physical evidence were forthcoming there would be some possibility of adding a little flesh to the skeleton presented here, and finally solving the riddle posed by the name of the site of one of the seminal events in early English Christianity.

[67] Domesday Book, i.303c.

[68] In 1291 it ranked joint eighth in terms of annual value, out of 36 prebends. By 1535 its value had risen, and 12 years later it was the third wealthiest of the 29 prebends which survived the Reformation. See B. Dobson, 'The Later Middle Ages, 1215–1500', in G.E. Aylmer and R. Cant (eds), *A History of York Minster* (Oxford, 1977), pp. 55–6, and C. Cross, 'From the Reformation to the Restoration', in the same volume, p. 227.

[69] Especially Towthorpe, Earswick and Haxby, but perhaps also including Stillington and 'Corburn': Domesday Book, i.303b–c. We are grateful to Peter Addyman for this suggestion.

ACKNOWLEDGEMENTS

We gratefully acknowledge the encouragement, assistance and comments of several individuals, both at the Conference and elsewhere: Dr Peter Addyman, John Bateman, Tessa Mitchell, and Professors David Palliser, Philip Rahtz and Barbara Yorke. We are also grateful to Allan Adams for drawing the figures and to Bob Skingle for the photograph.

20

Design and Meaning in Early Medieval Inscriptions in Britain and Ireland

JOHN HIGGITT

The Roman-letter inscriptions on stone from early medieval Britain and Ireland are surprisingly diverse in content and form, a reflection no doubt of the diverse cultural contexts in which they were made. Latin is the preferred language in the British West and the vernacular in Ireland, whereas both are widely used in England, sometimes on the same monument. The inscriptions have tended to be studied for their textual information, as a source of linguistic evidence and, sometimes, for their letter-forms. Less attention has been paid to their design. My aim in this paper is to investigate some of the ways in which the physical form, or at least the layout, of inscribed texts could enhance the message and perhaps complement the ostensible meaning of the words.

In a series of recent publications, and in particular in his *Christian Celts: Messages and Images*, Charles Thomas (1998) has argued eloquently that a number of early medieval Christian inscriptions in Wales, south-west Scotland and Cornwall should be seen as highly complex literary productions with layers of encoded messages behind their surface texts. He sees their texts as examples of the 'biblical style' expounded in many publications by David Howlett.[1] Charles Thomas' principal method with early medieval British inscriptions has been to subject them to numerical analysis based on totals of words, syllables and letters, on the use of letters as numerals, and on the identification of embedded Roman numerals. Other devices that he employs are the subdivision of texts in accordance with numerical approximations to the golden section, and the rearrangement of whole texts or of sections of text on geometrical grids. Through such means he identifies patterns that he sees as revealing intentional number symbolism and concealed messages such as the name of the author of the text. He maintains that these messages were there to be decoded by other members of the same small literate élite as the authors with the use of the same sets of rules by which they were composed – and, presumably, with the aid of a wax-tablet.

---

[1] For an excellent introduction to Howlett's arguments see the open-minded but sceptical review article by Allan Hood (1999).

The aspect of Charles Thomas' theory that touches on the use of visual design to convey meaning is his claim that some of these inscriptions were also devised to reveal, through various types of pattern, what he calls 'mental images', that is simple plans or profiles either in the inscription as it appears on the stone or in the text as rearranged in geometric grids (Thomas 1998, 132–7). Two examples will illustrate his approach. On the fifth-century Latinus stone at Whithorn in south-west Scotland, which he interprets as a form of building inscription rather than a memorial stone, he has identified features in the inscription that lead him to see in it a plan of the Temple of Solomon as described in 2 Chronicles, 3 and 4 (Thomas 1998, 110–4). (The last three lines appear to be secondary and are therefore excluded from this analysis.) His main clues are groups of letters within the text which he interprets as incomplete 'labels'. Examples, in which the letters in brackets must be supplied by the reader are (P)O(RT)I(C)V(S) (the porch), DOMIN(I) D(O)MVS (the house of the Lord), (DOM)VS (MAI)OR (the greater house), (S)AN(CT)V(M) S(A)N(CTOR)VM (the holy of holies), A(QUILO) (north), (MERIDIES) (south) and VVVV (four 5s, that is 20 cubits). That in some cases even the initial letters have to be supplied confirms the arbitrariness of the identifications. A more serious objection to the hypothesis is that the meandering layout of the lettering as it appears on the stone cannot be made to fit the superimposed Temple plan. His solution is to require the reader to draw up and work with a neatly laid out 'model form' of the inscription, in which the abbreviations have been expanded (Thomas 1998, Fig. 37).

Thomas's interpretation of the sixth-century memorial of a certain Carausius now in Penmachno in North Wales identifies images in profile (rather than in plan) suggested again by groups of letters both on the stone and in a triangular grid based on the second part of the text (Thomas 1998, 142–9 and figures). Letters in the body of the inscription forming (when rearranged) the name CARAVSIVS are taken as a profile seated image of the deceased. In the triangular grid a similar profile includes six of the nine letters of his name. He reads another loose grouping of letters as VIOLA, who, he suggests, was both Carausius's fiancée and the author of this encoded text.

This is not the place to comment in detail on Charles Thomas's methods or to do justice to his dense and imaginative arguments. These need to be followed step by step in order to understand the hypotheses and in order to judge the plausibility of the various assumptions and stages in the arguments.[2] I remain sceptical about most of this and in particular about the 'mental images', but I will limit myself at the moment to observing the surprising contrast between the sophistication claimed for the texts and the informal execution on the stones, on which the relaxed lettering follows no underlying system of ruling or regular layout. Thomas' suggested messages and images are strangely disconnected from the visual aspect of arranging lettering on stone.

I would like now to turn to the visual evidence. At a much more basic level than

---

[2] For a critical discussion of Thomas' methodology see the review by Thomas Clancy (2000).

that with which Charles Thomas concerns himself, the layout of some of these Western British inscriptions can be seen to echo the emphases of their texts. The division into lines of what appears to be the original part of the text (lines 1–9) on the seemingly irregular Whithorn Latinus stone (Thomas 1998, 106) corresponds with word-endings and also with subdivisions of the text according to meaning (see Appendix (1) below). It may have been headed with the name of Christ in the form of a Constantinian *chi- rho* monogram (Craig 1997, 614–16). The opening of the text can be reconstructed as a two-line invocation: TE DOMINVM LAVDAMVS (We praise thee, the Lord). The subjects of the principal statement, Latinus aged 35 and his daughter aged 5, occupy five lines, Latinus having a line to himself. The predicate follows in two lines, probably: [I]C [S]INVM FICERV[N]T. That is to say they made a *signum* (a sign, perhaps a monument or cross) or, less probably, a *sinus* (perhaps in the unattested sense of church) (Thomas 1992, 6). What we seem to have here is a continuation of the orderly presentation of epigraphic texts found in many official and memorial inscriptions from the period of the Roman Empire, although without the ruled layout and the frequent centring of the lines, or devices such as the use of lines of larger lettering at the start of the inscription (e.g. Gordon 1983, Pls 23, 28–30, 32–5, 39–41, 43–5, 47, 49–50, 55–7, 59).

A simple but still effective device is to place the name of the commemoratee prominently at the beginning or end. The name is allowed to occupy the whole of the first line of Carausius's monument at Penmachno or of that to King Cadfan at Llangadwaladr (Nash-Williams 1950, 55–7, 92, Pls VII and VIII). The perhaps eighth-century memorial to Catuoconus on Caldey Island, combines emphasis with humility by giving him the last line, following a request for the reader's prayers (Nash-Williams 1950, 180–2, Pl. XXIII).

I would like now to look more broadly at early medieval Insular inscriptions to see how far and in what ways the designer or letter-cutter might contribute to the message. Whilst many inscriptions show little concern for effective lay-out, many are clearly the product of careful and satisfying planning. We can start with two eighth-century stone slabs with texts in skilfully cut, neatly set-out and balanced lettering on either side of a cross. At Monkwearmouth (Okasha 1971, no. 101; Higgitt 1979, 360–5, Pls LXIIb, LXIII) an epitaph opens with an enlarged initial, like a manuscript text, and runs in six lines downwards from the top of the cross, ending at the bottom with the name of the deceased: HIC IN SEPVLCHRO REQVIESCIT CORPORE HEREBERICHT PR(ES)B(YTER) ('Here in the tomb rests in the body Herebericht the priest.') (The name has been recut but the original name must have stood in the same place.) The request for prayers on the slab at Tullylease in County Cork resembles patronage inscriptions on free-standing stone crosses in Ireland in being placed at the foot of the cross, perhaps as a sign of humility (Okasha and Forsyth 2001, 119–23; Higgitt 1986, 142–3): (QVI CVM QVÆ HVNC TITVLV(M) LEGERIT ORAT PRO BERECHTVINE.) ('Jesus Christ. Whoever reads this inscription prays for Berechtuine.' Or, if ORAT is taken as an error for ORET: 'Jesus Christ. May whoever reads this inscription pray for Berechtuine.') Here the upper fields are reserved for the names of Christ. The name of the deceased, or perhaps the patron, since there is no mention of death, comes again at the bottom as the sole occupant of the last line.

The long and magnificent mid-ninth-century inscription on the so-called Pillar of Elise at Llandysilio-yn-Iâl near Llangollen, now eroded into nearly total illegibility but copied by Edward Lhuyd in 1696, opened with the name of the king, Concenn or Cyngen, who raised the monument (Nash-Williams 1950, 123–5; Bartrum 1966, 1–3 and plates). Lhuyd's copy shows that the reader of the 31-line text was given some assistance by the crosses that introduced the principal subdivisions of the text. Furthermore it suggests that the designer may have honoured the names of Concenn, his father and his grandfather in the first two lines with larger lettering.

The slightly earlier Anglo-Saxon cross-shaft from Wycliffe in North Yorkshire (Cowen and Barty 1966; Lang 2001, 266–8) preserves an extant but damaged inscription in which taller letters seem to have been used deliberately to stress key words. It was in Old English and read (with line numbers):

> [1] BA[DA] | [2] [—T—] | [3] [A]EFTE | [4] [R] [:] BERE | [5] HTVINI : | [6] BE[C]VN | [7] [A]EFTER [. .] | [8]—

A literal translation might be: 'Ba[da] [erected?] in memory of Berehtuini, a monument in memory of —'. The taller lines (1, 4, 5 and 6) contain personal names and the word 'becun' (for monument or cross). The first word seems also to have been distinguished by more decorative letter forms.

Greater complexities can be seen on the eighth-century Ruthwell Cross with its wealth of inscriptions in both Latin and Old English. Here the designer has had to devise ways in which to arrange texts relating to carved imagery on framing strips around the carvings. I will limit my comments to the Latin inscriptions on the broad faces of the better preserved lower stone of the cross. As Paul Meyvaert (1982) has shown, the normal pattern, with various exceptions, was for the text to start in the upper margin of a panel, to continue into the right margin and to conclude in the left margin. One exception to the basic pattern can be seen around what is the principal and largest panel, that showing Christ adored by the beasts in the desert (see Appendix (2) below). The inscription opens in the upper margin and continues down the right but then breaks off a third of the way down and resumes in the left margin and concludes in the remaining space in the right margin. Meyvaert (1982, 12–13) is right to explain this apparent eccentricity as a way of separating two distinct sections of the text: a title identifying the standing figure as 'Iesus Christus, iudex aequitatis' (Jesus Christ, judge of equity), and the statement that the beasts and dragons recognized the saviour of the world in the desert. The designer has arranged the first section of this inscription so that, following the introductory cross, abbreviated forms of 'Iesus Christus' are centred immediately above the cruciform halo of Christ. The inscriptions around the lower two panels on this face of the stone also begin in the margin above the scenes and, as they open with the names of the protagonists, they also act as labels identifying the principal figures, St Paul the Hermit and the Virgin Mary (good plates in

Cassidy 1992, Pls 23–5). In another case the positioning of three words echoes, perhaps deliberately, the action of the protagonist, Mary Magdalen, as she wipes Christ's feet. The arrangement of the words CAPILLIS CAPITIS SVI (the hair of her head) around the bottom left-hand corner of the panel seems to mimic the flow of her hair (Okasha 1971, 111; Cassidy 1992, Pl. 16).

The French epigrapher Robert Favreau (1992, 682) maintains that there was a gradual shift in early medieval inscriptions recording acts of patronage from an emphasis on the work commissioned to an emphasis on the individual who ordered it. The inscription commemorating the dedication of St Paul's church at Jarrow in 685 (see Appendix (3) below; and Pl. 21.1, p. 341) is a good example of the earlier type (Okasha 1971, no. 61; Higgitt 1979). It opens with the name of Christ in the form of the *chi-rho* monogram and the rest of the first line is occupied by the two words DEDICATIO BASILICAE (the dedication of the basilica), a clear heading and statement of the significance of the event recorded. Line 2 contains the name of the dedicatee, St Paul, and the date of the dedication. The secular and ecclesiastical founders of the monastery, King Ecgfrith and Abbot Ceolfrith, then follow in the dating formulae that conclude the text.

The small group of late Anglo-Saxon building inscriptions illustrate Favreau's later type, although of course the estate and town churches from which they came were very different sorts of foundations from the great Northumbrian monastery of Jarrow. In these the secular patron normally comes first. Shortly before the Conquest, in the building inscription flanking the sundial at Kirkdale (see Appendix (4) below; and Pl. 18.2, p. 292), the emphasis is very clearly on the patron and owner of the church, Orm son of Gamal, whose generously spaced name opens the inscription at the beginning of the panel on the left (Okasha 1971, no. 64; Lang 1991, 163–6; Watts *et al.* 1997; Rahtz and Watts, Chapter 18 this volume). Hawarth and Brand the priest, who are named as makers, are given an even greater epigraphic prominence in the centre of the panel beneath the sundial. These emphases and the choice of the vernacular seem appropriate for the secular patron and for the no doubt predominantly secular audience who would see and read, or be told about, this act of patronage by the most powerful man in the locality. At first sight this inscription seems to have been informally, even care-lessly laid out. The crowded lettering in the panel on the right suggests poor planning. This may be true but the most important part of the text, from the patron's point of view, was on the more generously spaced left. Further, there is a perhaps deliberate symmetry in the repetition in the middle lines of both side panels of the name of the patron saint of the church, Gregory. The designer seems also to have been influenced by scribal practice in the use of *signes de renvoi* in the form of two outline crosses to lead the eye of the reader from the end of the second panel of the patronage inscription to the maker formulae. The third section of the inscription, that which comments on the sundial itself, is distinguished from the other two sections by the smaller size of the lettering, by its position and by its own introductory, medial and final crosses. On closer examination the layout turns out to be a little more sophisticated than often thought.

The stone selected to record the building of the church of St Mary-le-Wigford in Lincoln (see Appendix (5) below) was a Roman tombstone, in its way as conspicuous as a sundial and symbolic of the Roman origins of Lincoln (Okasha 1971, no. 73; Everson and Stocker 1999, 214–16). The vernacular inscription was cut into the gable of this stone and again opens, after an introductory cross, with the name of the patron, one Eirtig, who, we are told, 'had me made and endowed with possessions to the glory of Christ and St Mary'. The way in which the inscription is laid out, however, inverts the order of the text by setting the first line along the base of the triangular gable and continuing upwards in four more lines of decreasing length, so that Eirtig's name is at the base of the triangle and Mary's occupies the apex. This graceful visual inversion is surely more than accidental and is a subtler device than the quality of the lettering might lead one to expect. Furthermore the Christian text is set triumphantly (and presumably deliberately) over the pagan inscription, a counterpart to a long tradition of images of victory seen for example in the personifications of Virtues trampling on defeated Vices in the illustrations to Prudentius' *Psychomachia* (Katzenellenbogen 1939, Figs 13–22).

The dedication inscription from the chapel built at Deerhurst by Earl Odda (see Appendix (6) below; and Pl. 21.5, p. 344), a kinsman of Edward the Confessor, is on the other hand a very handsome and well executed piece of lettering (Okasha 1971, no. 28; Higgitt forthcoming). The language is Latin and we are told that the chapel was raised for the soul of Odda's brother Ælfric, who died at Deerhurst in 1053, and that the dedication was performed by Ealdred, bishop of Worcester, in 1056. This inscription resembles its less sophisticated contemporaries in opening with the name of the secular patron (immediately after the introductory cross). The name ODDA DVX is given plenty of room. The inscription closes with the name of his royal kinsman at the end of the dating formula, so that secular authority is commemorated at either end of the inscription. The name of Ælfric, Odda's dead brother, seems to be lost in the body of the nine-line inscription, until you notice that it is the middle word of the middle line and that its middle letter (R) falls at the centre of this face of the stone. There are further symmetries in the placing of forms of the verb *dedicare* two lines above and two lines below the middle line and perhaps also in the balancing of the names of the dedicatee, the Holy Trinity, and of the officiating bishop, Ealdred, in the lines immediately above and below the centre. The emphasis on the aristocratic patron and his brother and the other symmetries seem to have been the result of careful planning.

The classical treatment of the capitals at Deerhurst and the subtleties of layout suggest a level of clerical literacy of a different order from that of the designer of the Kirkdale sundial. Perhaps the well-travelled Bishop Ealdred, who had recently spent a year in Cologne (cf. Hare 1997, 50–2, 59–60), provided the contacts that brought this epigraphic sophistication to Deerhurst.

The nearest parallel, however, that I have so far found for Deerhurst's apparent use of symmetry to lay stress on key elements of the text is no less an inscription than the marble memorial slab that Charlemagne ordered, perhaps at Aachen, for Pope Hadrian I after his death in 795 and had sent to St Peter's in Rome

(Favreau 1997, 64–8, Fig. 5; Scholz 1997). It seems once again more than coincidence that the epitaph has been drawn up so that the names of the pope and of the king are arranged in symmetrical pairs (see Appendix (7) below). The deceased, HADRIANVS, is named at the beginning of the second and towards the end of the penultimate line, whilst the patron and the first-person voice of these verses, KAROLVS, appears twice, towards the middle of the line four lines above the middle of the inscription and of the line four lines below (lines 17 and 24 of the 40 lines).[3] It is true that the name HADRIANVS also appears unsymmetrically just before the KAROLVS in line 24 where the epitaph speaks of joining the two names together, but it could be argued that this image explains the balanced repetitions of the two names that we have just seen.

Deerhurst's use of the middle word of the middle line and the exact middle of the inscription to commemorate Ælfric has an equally illustrious precedent in the seven-line mosaic foundation inscription in the fifth-century church of Santa Sabina in Rome (Oakeshott 1967, 89–90; Krautheimer et al. 1970, 91, 98, C. Dates (422–440); Gray 1986, Fig. 34) (see Appendix (8) below).[4] The PETRVS on whom this inscription centred was Peter the Illyrian, the founder of the church, who, to judge from the wording, was perhaps already dead by the time the inscription was devised.

So far I have found five other inscriptions from Rome or nearby in which a key name or word is placed in the middle of a line at or near the centre. The name is that of the pope in at least three papal epitaphs: Boniface III (d. 607: line 7 of 14); Boniface V (d. 625: line 11 of 20); and Benedict III (d. 858: line 3 of 6) (Montini 1957, 115, 119–20, 139). The name of the principal patron (BENEDICTVS PR(ES)B(YTER)) stands in the centre of the three-line inscription on a ciborium of the time of Pope Leo III (795–816) (Stiegemann and Wemhoff 1999, II, 624–5). Finally, is it a coincidence that it is the word SOPHIAE (wisdom) that falls at the centre of the thirteen-line epitaph of Pope Sylvester II (d. 1003)? The wisdom in question is that with which both pope and emperor ornamented the age (Morison 1972, Pl. 111; Montini 1957, 165–70).

The honorific use of the middle of a line can also be seen in at least one prestigious inscription in Ottonian Germany. The inscription around the top of the shrine that Archbishop Egbert of Trier (977–993) had made for St Andrew's sandal was devised so that the names EGBERTVS and S(AN)C(T)I ANDREAE APOSTOLI would appear in the middle of the two longer sides (Westermann-Angerhausen 1987, Pl. 7).[5]

---

[3] The first 38 lines are in verse and last two in prose. The symmetries relate therefore to the 40 lines as they appear on the stone and not to the verses alone, although they are made possible by the structure of the verses.

[4] This device requires a middle line and the inscription needs therefore to be set out in an odd number of lines.

[5] I am very grateful to Dr Rüdiger Fuchs for telling me of this example. I would also like to thank Professor Robert Favreau for drawing my attention to some short twelfth- and thirteenth-century funerary inscriptions in which the name of the deceased is given a line to itself, sometimes the middle line (e.g. Favreau et al. 1982, Figs 55, 73, 96).

Was one meant to notice these effects? It is possible that colour was used to pick out key names on the stone inscriptions, but in the Santa Sabina mosaic all the letters are in gold against blue, so that the name PETRVS is not specially distinguished. In the case of Hadrian's epitaph we are told by two nearly contemporary sources that the letters were gilded (Ramackers 1964, nn. 10 and 14). We do not know whether a contrasting metal or pigment was used to bring out the names of the pope and the king. This handful of examples suggests that, by the eleventh century, there was a long-established tradition of using the centre of an inscription or symmetrical pairings to mark out the names of distinguished individuals, especially those of patrons or of the dead. It looks as if these devices may have originated in Rome and they appear to have remained very unusual. It may never be possible to work out by what stages they were communicated to eleventh-century Deerhurst but it is possible that they were adopted because of their Roman connotations.

What conclusions can we draw from this rapid and selective survey of Roman-letter inscriptions on stone in Britain and Ireland? We have seen a variety of design techniques ranging from the common and simple device of highlighting a significant name by isolating it at the beginning or end of a text, perhaps a fairly universal rule in the grammar of layout, to the carefully tailored layouts of the Latin inscriptions designed to accompany individual scenes on the Ruthwell Cross. We have seen the top of an inscription being reserved for the patron saint of a church and the bottom being used perhaps to indicate humility. The cosmopolitan designer of the Deerhurst inscription adopted, perhaps from Rome, a distinguished and venerable tradition of honorific layout that involved the centre of an inscribed panel and symmetry about the centre. The devices that he used seem to be unique amongst surviving Insular inscriptions but, for all we know, they may once have been familiar in the now lost inscriptions of the major Anglo-Saxon churches. We have seen the layouts of inscriptions being used to enhance the meaning of their texts in a variety of contexts and for various purposes; but most of the examples that we have noticed have been intended either to draw attention to, or to distinguish in a less obvious way, personal names, generally those of patrons or of the dead. The simple highlighting of names, which were a matter of general interest, might be noticed even by those with minimal literacy, whereas other less obvious effects were probably thought of as effective or appropriate design, forms of visual rhetoric, rather than encoded messages. These devices are very modest compared with those that Charles Thomas has argued for in some of the Western British inscriptions. They also differ from those in being visual effects, and therefore visually testable, rather than codes requiring mental decoding. They were intended to enhance surface messages rather than to communicate hidden meanings.

APPENDIX

The texts of the principal inscriptions discussed in this paper are set out below to illustrate how they are divided into lines on the stone. They are given here in edited form with abbreviations expanded in brackets rather than as exact transcriptions. The originally runic graph *wynn* is here transcribed as W. The arabic numeral '7' represents the Tironian sign for *et*, which was adopted for Old English *and* (or *ond*). In (1) and (3) below 'chi/rho' represents the 'Constantinian' form of the monogram of the first two letters of the name of Christ in Greek, that is *chi* and *rho*.

(1) The 'Latinus' stone at Whithorn

```
                [chi/rho]
                TE[DOMI]NV[M]
                LAVDAM[VS]
                LATINV[S]
                ANN[OR]V[M]
                XXXV E[T]
                FILIA SV[A]
                ANNI V
                [I]C [S]INVM
                [FI]CERV(N)T
(Later?)        N[I]PVS
                BA[R]ROV[A]
                    DI
```

Lines 1-9: '[chi/rho] We praise thee, the Lord. Latinus, aged thirty-five, and his daughter, aged five, made a *si[g]num* [*or* a *sinus*] here.' (A *signum*, literally a sign, might perhaps refer to a monument or a cross. A *sinus* was a curved surface and, by extension, a fold or a bosom, and with possible figurative meanings of protection, refuge, etc., which led Thomas (1992, 6) to suggest that the word might also have been used for a church (in the sense of the building).)
Lines 10–12: 'The grandson [*or* nephew, *or* descendant] of Barrovadus.'

(2) The Ruthwell cross (Christ adored by the beasts panel)

Top margin; upper section of right margin:
```
        + IE(SV)S CHR(ISTV)S
        IVDEX : AEQVITATIS :
```

Left margin; lower section of right margin:
```
        BESTIAE : ET : DRACONES : COGNOVERVNT : IN DE :
        SERTO : SALVATOREM : MVNDI :
```

Top margin; upper section of right margin:
'+ Jesus Christ. Judge of equity.'

Left margin; lower section of right margin:
'The beasts and dragons recognized the saviour of the world in the desert.'

(3) Jarrow dedication inscription

Upper stone: chi/rho DEDICATIO BASILICAE
                S(AN)C(T)I PAVLI VIIII K(A)L(ENDAS) MAI(AS
                ANNO XV ECFRIDI REG(IS)

Lower stone: CEOLFRIDI ABB(ATIS) EIVSDEMQ(VE)
                Q ECCLES(IAE) D(E)O AVCTORE
                CONDITORIS ANNO IIII

Upper stone: 'chi/rho The dedication of the basilica of Saint Paul on the ninth day before the kalends of May [23rd April] in the fifteenth year of King Ecgfrith'

Lower stone: 'in the fourth year of Ceolfrith, abbot and, by the direction of God, founder of the same church'

(4) Kirkdale

The main text is set out in two columns, one on each side of the sundial, and the maker formula runs underneath the dial.

+ ORM GAMAL	CAN 7 TOFALAN 7 HE
SVNA BOHTE S(AN)C(TV)S	HIT LET MACAN NEWAN FROM
GREGORIVS MIN	GRVNDE CHR(IST)E 7 S(AN)C(TV)S **GREGORI**
STER ÐONNE HI	**VS** IN EADWARD DAGVM C(I)NG
T WES ÆL TOBRO	7 (I)N TOSTI DAGVM EORL +

+ 7 HAWARÐ ME WROHTE 7 BRAND PR(EO)S(T) [*or* PR(E)S(BYTER)]

'+ Orm the son of Gamal bought St Gregory's Minster when it was utterly ruined and collapsed and he had it built recently [*or* had it rebuilt] from the foundations (in honour of) Christ and St Gregory in the days of King Edward and in the days of Earl Tosti. +
+ And Harwarð made me and Brand the priest. [*or* Harwarð made me and Brand, priests.]'

(5) Lincoln

Reading from bottom line to top:

[MA]RIE
O[F]E [7] S(AN)C(T)E
N [C]RISTE TO [L]
—V [.F]I[O...T.]—
[+] EI[R]TIG [M]E LET [W]I[R.E]—

'+ Eirtig had me built [and endowed with property?] to the glory of Christ and St Mary.'

(6) Deerhurst

+ **ODDA DVX** IVSSIT HANC
REGIAM AVLAM CONSTRVI
ATQVE **DEDICARI** IN HONO
RE S(ANCTE) TRINITATIS PRO ANIMA GER
MANI SVI **ÆLFRICI** QVE DE HOC
LOCO ASV(M)PTA E(ST) ALDREDVS VERO
EP(ISCOPV)S QVI EANDE(M) **DEDICAVIT** II IDI
BVS AP(RI)L(IBVS) XIIII AVTE(M) ANNO $ REG
NI **EADWARD REGIS ANGLORV(M)**

'+ Earl Odda ordered this royal hall (*i.e.* church) to be built and dedicated in honour of the Holy Trinity for the soul of his brother Ælfric which was taken up from this place. And Bishop Aldred [*or* And Aldred [is/was] the bishop] who dedicated it on the second day before the Ides of April (12th April) in the 14th year of the reign of Eadward King of the English.' (I present the arguments elsewhere (Higgitt forthcoming) for reading E(ST) ALDREDVS instead of the usual reading, EALDREDVS. The $ in this transcription represents an apparently redundant S. A lightly incised line runs through it and was perhaps intended to cancel it.)

(7) Rome, St Peter's, Epitaph of Pope Hadrian I (lines 1-2, 17, 23-4, 39-40 only)

1.   HIC PATER ECCLESIAE ROMAE DECVS INCLYTVS AVCTOR
2.   **HADRIANVS** REQVIEM PAPA BEATVS HABET
      [..]
17. POST PATREM LACRIMANS **KAROLVS** HÆC CARMINA SCRIBSI
      [..]
23. NOMINA IVNGO SIMVL TITVLIS CLARISSIME NOSTRA
24.   HADRIANVS **KAROLVS** REX EGO TVQ(VE) PATER
      [..]
39. SEDIT BEATAE MEMORIAE **HADRIANVS** PAPA
40.   ANNOS XXIII MENSES X DIES XVII OBIIT VII KL IAN

1.   'Here the Father of the church, the glory of Rome, the illustrious master,
2.   blessed Pope Hadrian has his rest.'
17.   'Afterwards, weeping for the Father, I, Charles, wrote these verses.'
23.   'Oh most illustrious of men, I join our names together in this inscription,
24.   Hadrian and Charles, I the king and you the Father.'
39.   'Pope Hadrian of blessed memory reigned
40.   for twenty-three years, ten months and seventeen days. He died on the seventh day
      before the kalends of January [26th December].'

(8) Rome, Santa Sabina all'Aventino

CVLMEN APOSTOLICVM CVM CAELESTINVS HABERET
PRIMVS ET IN TOTO FVLGERET EPISCOPVS ORBE
HAEC QVAE MIRARIS FVNDAVIT PRESBYTER VRBIS
ILLYRICA DE GENTE **PETRVS** VIR NOMINE TANTO
DIGNVS AB EXORTV CHRISTI NVTRITVS IN AVLA
PAVPERIBVS LOCVPLES SIBI PAVPER QVI BONA VITAE
PRAESENTIS FVGIENS MERVIT SPERARE FVTVRVM

Walter Oakeshott (1967, 90) translates this as follows: 'When Celestinus [Pope Celestinus I, 422–32] held the highest apostolic throne and shone forth gloriously as the foremost bishop of the whole world, a presbyter of this city, Illyrian by birth, named Peter and worthy of that great name, established this building at which you look in wonder. From his earliest years he was brought up in the hall of Christ – rich to the poor, poor to himself, one who shunned the good things of life on earth and deserved to hope for the life to come.'

References

Bartrum, P.C. 1966: *Early Welsh Genealogical Tracts* (Cardiff).

Cassidy, B. (ed.) 1992: *The Ruthwell Cross: papers from the colloquium sponsored by the Index of Christian Art, Princeton University 8 December 1989* (Princeton).

Clancy, T. 2000: review of Thomas, C., *Christian Celts: Messages and Images* (Stroud, 1998), *The Innes Review*, 51.1: 85–88.

Cowen, J.D. and Barty, E. 1966: 'A lost Anglo-Saxon inscription recovered', *Archaeologia Aeliana*, 4th series, 44: 61–70.

Craig, D. 1997: 'The provenance of the Early Christian inscriptions of Galloway' in Hill, P., *Whithorn and St Ninian: the excavation of a monastic town, 1984–91* (Stroud), 614–9.

Everson, P. and Stocker, D. 1999: *Lincolnshire*, Corpus of Anglo-Saxon Stone Sculpture, V (British Academy, Oxford).

Favreau, R., Michaud, J. and Leplant, B. 1982: *Ville de Toulouse*, Corpus des inscriptions de la France médiévale, 7 (Paris).

Favreau, R. 1992: 'Les commanditaires dans les inscriptions du haut moyen âge occidental' in *Settimane di studio del Centro Italiano di Studi sull'Alto Medioevo*, 39 (Spoleto), 681–722 [reprinted in Favreau, R., *Études d'épigraphie médiévale*, 2 vols, I (Limoges, 1995), 469–504].

Favreau, R. 1997: *Épigraphie médiévale*, L'atelier du médiéviste, 5 (Turnhout).

Gordon, A.E. 1983: *Illustrated Introduction to Latin Epigraphy* (Berkeley, Los Angeles, London).

Gray, N. 1986: *A History of Lettering: creative experiment and letter identity* (Oxford).

Hare, M. 1997: 'Kings, crowns and festivals: the origins of Gloucester as a royal ceremonial centre', *Transactions of the Bristol and Gloucestershire Archaeological Society*, 115: 41–78.

Higgitt, J. 1979: 'The dedication inscription at Jarrow and its context', *Antiquaries Journal*, 59: 343–74.

Higgitt, J. 1986: 'Words and crosses: the inscribed stone cross in early medieval Britain and Ireland' in Higgitt, J. (ed.), *Early Medieval Sculpture in Britain and Ireland*, British Archaeological Reports British Series 152 (Oxford), 125–52.

Higgitt, J. forthcoming: *Odda, Orm and Others: patrons and inscriptions in later Anglo-Saxon England* (Deerhurst Lecture for 1999).

Hood, A.B.E. 1999: 'Review article: Lighten our darkness – Biblical style in early medieval Britain and Ireland', *Early Medieval Europe*, 8.2: 283–96.

Katzenellenbogen, A. 1939: *Allegories of the Virtues and Vices in Mediaeval Art from Early Christian Times to the Thirteenth Century* (Warburg Institute, London).

Krautheimer, R., Corbett, S. and Frankl, W. 1970: *Corpus Basilicarum Christianarum Romae: The Early Christian Basilicas of Rome (IV-IX cent.)*, 5 vols (1937–77), IV (Città del Vaticano).

Lang, J. 1991: *York and Eastern Yorkshire*, Corpus of Anglo-Saxon Stone Sculpture, III (British Academy, Oxford).

Lang, J. 2001: *North Yorkshire*, Corpus of Anglo-Saxon Stone Sculpture, VI (British Academy, Oxford).

Meyvaert, P. 1982: 'An Apocalypse panel on the Ruthwell Cross' in Tirro, F. (ed.), *Medieval and Renaissance Studies (Proceedings of the Southeastern Institute of Medieval and Renaissance Studies, Summer 1978)*, Medieval and Renaissance Series 9 (Durham, N.C.), 3–32.

Montini, R.U. 1957: *Le Tombe dei papi*, Istituto di Studi Romani (Rome).

Morison, S. 1972: *Politics and Script: Aspects of authority and freedom in the development of Graeco-Latin script from the sixth century B.C. to the twentieth century A.D.* (Oxford).

Nash-Williams, V.E. 1950: *The Early Christian Monuments of Wales* (Cardiff).

Oakeshott, W. 1967: *The Mosaics of Rome from the third to the fourteenth centuries* (London).

Okasha, E. 1971: *Hand-list of Anglo-Saxon non-runic Inscriptions* (Cambridge).

Okasha, E. and Forsyth, K. 2001: *Early Christian Inscriptions of Munster: a corpus of the inscribed stones* (Cork).

Ramackers, J. 1964: 'Die Werkstattheimat der Grabplatte Papst Hadrians I', *Römische Quartalschrift*, 59: 36–78.

Scholz, S. 1997: 'Karl der Grosse und das 'Epitaphium Hadriani': ein Beitrag zum Gebetsgedenken der Karolinger', in Berndt, R. (ed.), *Das Frankfurter Konzil von 794: Kristallisationspunkt karolingischer Kultur*, Quellen und Abhandlungen zur mittelrheinischen Kirchengeschichte, 80/1 (Mainz), 373–94.

Stiegemann, C. and Wemhoff, M. (eds) 1999: *799 – Kunst und Kultur der Karolingerzeit: Karl der Große und Papst Leo III. in Paderborn*, Katalog der Ausstellung Paderborn 1999, 3 vols (Mainz).

Thomas, C. 1992: *Whithorn's Christian Beginnings*, Whithorn Lecture.

Thomas, C. 1998: *Christian Celts: Messages and Images* (Stroud).

Watts, L., Rahtz, P., Okasha, E., Bradley, S.A.J. and Higgitt, J. 1997: 'Kirkdale – the inscriptions', *Medieval Archaeology*, 41: 51–99.

Westermann-Angerhausen, H. 1987: 'Spolie und Umfeld in Egberts Trier', *Zeitscrhift für Kunstgeschichte*, 50: 305–36.

21

Spaces Between Words: Word Separation in Anglo-Saxon Inscriptions

ELISABETH OKASHA

The title of this paper refers to the title of a book by Paul Saenger entitled *Space between Words: The Origins of Silent Reading* (Stanford University Press, 1997). In this book Saenger examines one of the conventions of printed and written texts that we tend to take for granted: the fact that spaces are used in writing to indicate where one word ends and the next begins. He argues convincingly that the ability to read silently and rapidly is a direct result of the introduction of this convention. Literacy was introduced to these islands by the Romans in the pre-Christian era. However, with the coming of Christianity, literacy was zealously promoted by the Church, with much emphasis being placed on the role of the written word. A convention that made comprehension of the written word easier to master was obviously of considerable benefit.

In the Roman world, manuscripts were generally written in unseparated text, otherwise known as *scriptura continua*. Saenger illustrates this from a page of the fifth-century text, Livy's *History of Rome* (Paris BN, lat. 5730, f. 59r: Saenger 1997, p. 5, Fig. 1). There are no spaces between words, no punctuation, and frequent run-on of words from one line to the next. It was in this sort of form that writing entered Britain under Roman occupation. Some of the inscribed stones from Roman Britain are indeed rather similar in layout, for example a dedication slab from South Shields, Co Durham, now kept in the Arbeia Roman Fort and Museum, South Shields (Collingwood and Wright 1965, no. 1060, p. 354 and Fig. 1060). The text on this stone commemorates the installation of a supply of water for the Fifth Cohort of Gaul. The words in the text are unseparated except that, by utilising the idiosyncratic abbreviation typical of Romano-British inscribed stones, almost all the lines begin with a new word.

However, not all Romano-British stone inscriptions have texts like this. There is, for example, an altar from Lanchester, Co Durham, now kept in Lanchester Parish Church, on which there is some attempt made to indicate word division by means of dots (Collingwood and Wright 1965, no. 1074, p. 358 and Fig. 1074). The use of dots, or interpuncts, to separate words had been used to some extent in manuscripts in antiquity, and this is presumably the origin of it on Romano-British stone inscriptions. In the text on the Lanchester altar, most of the words are separated by a medial dot although some words are divided between two lines of text.

The earliest manuscripts from Anglo-Saxon England are Christian: they are in Latin and use unseparated text. A clear illustration of this occurs in the Moore manuscript of Bede's *Historia Ecclesiastica*, dating from *c*.737 (Cambridge UL, Kk.v.16: folio 16 is illustrated in Webster and Backhouse 1992, no. 2, p. 19 and Fig. 2). Here there is minimal use of word separation, although it is occasionally indicated by a dot or space. From the eighth century onwards, Latin manuscripts written in Anglo-Saxon England are increasingly unlikely to use unseparated text. However, fully separated text, with spaces after every word, does not appear immediately. Saenger has coined the term 'aerated' to describe manuscripts with some, but not consistent, use of spaces. An early example occurs in the mid-eighth century Cotton manuscript of Bede's *Historia Ecclesiastica* (London BL, Cotton Tiberius A xiv: folio 84 is illustrated in Webster and Backhouse 1992, no. 92, pp. 128–9 and Fig. 92). Here there are spaces after many words, but not all, and there is the occasional use of incorrect word-division. Dots are used in this manuscript, but usually to indicate abbreviation rather than as word-division signs.

Texts written in the vernacular, even explicitly Christian texts, were slower to adopt consistent word spacing. Aerated text is still being used in the early tenth century, for example in the Old English translation of Orosius' *Seven Books Against the Pagans* (London BL, Add. 47967: folio 5b is illustrated in Webster and Backhouse 1992, no. 238, pp. 262–3 and Fig. 238). Prepositions frequently occur without a following space, the word *is* is often joined to the word that follows and many words are divided between one line and the next.

Saenger's book is almost entirely concerned with manuscript texts, not inscriptions, and it is interesting to examine Anglo-Saxon inscriptions in roman script to see whether Saenger's conclusions also hold good for them. Two of Saenger's conclusions are considered in this paper. The first is that from the ninth century onwards, in Latin manuscripts written in Anglo-Saxon England, separated text 'had already become habitual' (Saenger 1997, p. 90). The second is that from this same period, while Latin manuscripts are being written in separated text, manuscripts in Old English are still using aerated text, which they continued to do 'at least until the mid-eleventh century' (Saenger 1997, p. 97).

Although there is a sizable body of epigraphic material from Anglo-Saxon England, over 200 inscriptions in roman script, unfortunately not all are suitable for this study. To be useful, the texts have to be legible, to consist of more than one word and to be complete or largely complete. They also have to be datable, within broad limits, and it has to be certain whether they are written in Old English or in Latin (something that is not always obvious). When all these provisos are taken into account, the number of texts that can furnish any evidence is considerably reduced. In the period of the seventh, eighth and ninth centuries, only some 25 inscriptions can be considered. In the later period, the tenth and eleventh centuries, there are more, some 40 inscriptions. In both chronological brackets, but especially in the earlier, there are more texts in Latin than in Old English.

In order to investigate the texts of the inscriptions for this study, they have been divided into three broad categories. First, there are those which use unseparated text, that is, with no word-division indicated by any means. Second, there are those which are aerated by means of dots and/or crosses; that is, not all words are separated but, when they are, the separation is indicated not by spaces but by dots or crosses in the text. Third, there are those which use aerated text proper, that is with some word-division indicated by spaces or other means, and some words unseparated. The seven texts used to illustrate these categories are printed in the appendix.

An illustration of the first category is the dedication stone from Jarrow, Co Durham, dating from c.AD 685 (Pl. 21.1; appendix, Piece 1). The text is in Latin and has no word separation indicated at all, though there may have been a conscious attempt to end words at the ends of lines. A similarly unseparated text in Old English is the well-known Alfred jewel of the ninth century (Pl. 21.2; appendix, Piece 2).

The second category contains those texts which are aerated by means of dots and/or crosses. The eighth- or ninth-century cross-shaft from Yarm in North Yorkshire (Pl. 21.3; appendix, Piece 3) contains an Old English text which is incomplete. There is enough of it, however, to show that crosses were used to

Plate 21.1   Dedication stone in Jarrow parish church, Co Durham

Plate 21.2 The Alfred Jewel, now in the Ashmolean Museum, Oxford

separate the first four words of the remaining text, while the final four words were not separated. It is possible that some attempt was made to exploit the ends of lines to indicate the ends of words, for example at the ends of lines two and four, but if so the attempt does not seem to have been made very strenuously.

Other texts in this category are aerated by dots, as for example an Old English text on an eleventh-century stone from Ipswich (Pl. 21.4). The main part of the text (appendix, Piece 4) is set beneath the carving and is aerated by means of a triple dot which is also used at the beginning and end of the text. In addition, the text is fitted in around the carving so that each line starts with a new word; however, two of the words, *feht* and *wið*, are not separated by either dots or the beginning of a line.

An example of a Latin text aerated by dots is the dedication stone from Deerhurst dated to AD 1056 (Pl. 21.5; appendix, Piece 5). In the first two lines of this text, the first two words are separated by dots, the next two are not separated while the line-end separates the fourth and fifth; the next three are unseparated. Overall in this text, about one quarter of the words are separated by dots, and there was clearly some attempt to utilise line-ends to indicate the ends of words, but the majority of the words are not separated at all.

The third category contains those texts that use aerated text proper, that is with some word-division indicated, by spaces and other means, and some words unseparated. An Old English text in this category is the piece of verse on the late tenth- or eleventh-century brooch from Sutton in Cambridgeshire (appendix, Piece 6; Okasha 1971, no. 114, pp. 116–17 and Fig. 114). About one quarter of the

Plate 21.3 Cross-shaft from Yarm, North Yorkshire, now in the Monks'
Dormitory, Durham Cathedral

Plate 21.4 Stone in St Nicholas' church, Ipswich, Suffolk

Plate 21.5 Dedication stone from Deerhurst, Gloucestershire, now in the Ashmolean Museum, Oxford

words of this text are separated by spaces but the divisions between the rest are not marked. An example with Latin texts is the late tenth- or eleventh-century altar now in the Musée de Cluny, Paris, (appendix, Piece 7; Okasha 1983, no. 172, pp. 95–6 and Fig. VIII). The texts on this portable altar describe the figural decoration. Eight of the twelve words have dots following them, although this includes the two words at the ends of the lines, while the remaining words are either separated by spaces or are run together.

There is only one inscription which has a completely separated text. This text is on a stone cross-slab of the eighth or ninth century (appendix, Piece 8; Henderson and Okasha 1992, pp. 1–36 and figs.) but in many ways it stands apart from the other inscriptions. This stone is not from Anglo-Saxon England at all, but from Tullylease, Co Cork, in Ireland. However, it does contain an Old English name, a form of *Beorhtwine*, in its otherwise Latin text and the design on the cross–slab bears a striking resemblance to one of the carpet pages of the Lindisfarne Gospels (London BL, Cotton Nero D iv, f. 26v). If this inscribed stone is rather different from many Anglo-Saxon ones, it is markedly different from contemporary Irish inscribed stones, in terms both of its carving and of its text. Its text is closely related to the texts of manuscript colophons, in particular to that on the Macregol Gospels (Oxford Bodleian Library, Auct. D. 2. 19 (S.C. 3946) f. 169v). In view of this, and of its location in Ireland, this inscription seems to stand in a class of its own. It may well be that it should be considered as more closely related to manuscripts than to other epigraphic texts. For these reasons it has been omitted from the discussion that follows.

Saenger suggested that from the ninth century onwards all manuscript texts in Latin from Anglo-Saxon England use largely separated text, but that manuscripts written in Old English continue to use aerated text until the eleventh century. The position with inscriptions is, however, rather different. In the seventh, eighth and ninth centuries, there is not a single inscribed text from Anglo-Saxon England that uses separated text. The majority of the texts, whether in Latin or in Old English, have the words unseparated. The few texts that are aerated indicate word-division not by spaces but by means of crosses and/or dots and/or by judicious use of line-ends. Moreover, texts in Latin are no more likely than texts in Old English to be aerated; the proportions are in fact exactly the same. This is clearly different from the position in manuscripts.

In the tenth and eleventh centuries more than half the inscribed texts are still totally unseparated. There is still not a single example of a text that is fully separated. However, some of the aerated texts have started to indicate word-division by means of spaces as well as by using crosses and dots. There is also beginning to be a difference between Latin texts and those in the vernacular. Old English texts are considerably more likely to be unseparated than to be aerated; however, in the case of texts in Latin, aerated text is just as common as unseparated text. Moreover, none of the aerated Old English texts makes use of spaces after words, preferring instead dots and/or crosses, whereas spaces occur quite often in Latin texts, often combined with dots.

The same sort of pattern that Saenger observed in manuscripts does then seem to be observable in inscribed texts, but only after a considerable time delay. In addition, in inscribed texts there is the use, and the retention, of conventions typical of inscriptions. The use of crosses to separate words seems to be confined to epigraphic texts. This is scarcely surprising in view of the difference in length between a typical manuscript text and a typical inscription: we would hardly expect word-division to be marked by the use of crosses throughout several folios of a manuscript. Dots are certainly used in some manuscripts to mark word-division, as well as other things like abbreviation, but the use of dots for word separation seems to be more prevalent in inscribed texts, and to continue in use for considerably longer.

Why then did unseparated and aerated text remain in use in Anglo-Saxon inscriptions when their use had been abandoned in contemporary manuscripts? There were probably several contributory factors. One was no doubt the fact that inscribed texts are generally much shorter than manuscript texts and readers were therefore less in need of help in understanding them. Another factor may have been that such texts were usually quite predictable and the meaning was therefore easier to grasp. Many inscribed stones, for example, request prayers for some-one's soul, while many metal objects, weapons, jewellery and so on, record the name of their maker and/or owner. Another factor may have been that those who carved stones or inscribed metal objects were less under the eye of an overseer than were those who copied manuscripts. The chief scribe of the scriptorium may not have always travelled to the place where a mason was carving a stone in order to make sure that the work was being done satisfactorily.

Another factor may have been that inscribed texts may not always have been produced with the express intention of their being read. The Ipswich stone (Pl. 21.4; appendix, Piece 4), for example, not only describes in words the carved scene of St Michael fighting the dragon but also labels which figure is St Michael and which the dragon. This was clearly not done to aid an audience, who would scarcely need the labels to differentiate between the dragon and St Michael. It looks more as if the carver was exhibiting his or her skill and, perhaps, making a statement about the high status of the carving by associating it with an act of literacy. In the case of most manuscript texts, however, the primary purpose was certainly that they should be read. Greater importance was therefore no doubt attached to helping readers to comprehend what was written in manuscripts.

Another possible factor concerns the nature of the intended audience of manuscript and epigraphic texts. Most manuscripts were written, and copied, in order to be read by literate people. Some inscriptions were no doubt incised with the same intention. But in some cases, as with the Ipswich stone, the intended literate audience may have been small. In other cases, as with grave-stones buried beneath the ground, the intended audience may not have been human at all but these requests for prayers may have been directed towards God and the saints. Clearly a divine readership would not be in need of reading aids like word-division, designed to help a fallible human audience.

A final factor might be the different levels of importance attached to manuscripts and inscriptions. Word separation certainly makes reading easier. We might expect that the more important, and more difficult, texts would therefore introduce word separation first. The majority of texts from Anglo-Saxon England are concerned with the church, its beliefs, its teaching and its organisation. It might well have been considered essential to make the reading of such texts as easy as possible.

Many inscriptions are also overtly Christian, for example those describing a religious carving or those which request prayers for someone's soul. A sizeable minority was clearly secular, with texts recording the maker of a sword or the owner of a finger-ring. It might well have been that at least some inscriptions were considered minor, of lesser importance than manuscript texts like the Gospels, the liturgy or homilies. Perhaps texts of lesser importance, especially if they were also short and predictable, were less in need of useful reading aids like word separation.

In the inscriptions of Anglo-Saxon England the same sort of pattern that Saenger pointed out in manuscripts can be observed. That is, word separation, especially as time goes on, tends to be marked more often and more consistently in Latin texts than in vernacular ones. Nevertheless the whole process is considerably retarded in epigraphic texts, indeed by several centuries. Separated inscriptional texts are all but unknown before the Conquest, both in Latin and in Old English. This cannot be because those who designed the texts of inscriptions were unfamiliar with manuscript texts. Instead the reasons may be sought in the different conventions within which inscriptions were made and the reasons why such texts were produced. Moreover, inscribed texts may well have emanated from a slightly separate milieu from manuscripts, perhaps derived from, and directed towards, a different class of Anglo-Saxon society.

Appendix

The texts are given in the order in which they are mentioned in the paper. In each case the transliteration is given with the abbreviations unexpanded but spaces between the words added. Part of the research for this paper was supported by a grant from the Arts Faculty Research Fund, University College Cork, for which I am most grateful.

Piece 1: text on the dedication stone from Jarrow, Co Durham, c. AD 685

+ *dedicatio basilicae sci pauli viiii k̄l mai anno xv ecfridi rēg ceolfridi abb̄ eiusděm q q: eccles dō auctore conditoris anno iiii* '+ the dedication of the church of St Paul was on the 23 April in the 15th year of King Ecgfrith and the 4th year of Ceolfrith, abbot and under God's guidance founder, of this same church'.

Piece 2: text on the Alfred jewel, now in the Ashmolean Museum, Oxford, ninth century

aelfred mec heht gewyrcan 'Alfred ordered me to be made'

Piece 3: text on the stone cross-shaft from Yarm, North Yorkshire, now in Durham Cathedral Library, eighth or ninth century

-[m]berehct + sāc + alla + signum aefter his breoder a[s]etae +, '-[m]berehct the priest; Alla set up this cross in memory of his brother'. The lost part of the text probably contained the first part of the personal name and perhaps the word *aefter*.

Piece 4: text on a stone from Ipswich, Suffolk, eleventh century

: her : sc̄e mihael : feht wið ðane : draca :, 'here St Michael fights (*or* fought) against the dragon'.

Piece 5: text on the dedication stone from Deerhurst, Gloucestershire, now in the Ashmolean Museum, Oxford, 1056 A.D.

+ odda : dux iussit : hanc regiam aulam : construi : atque : dedicari in honore s̄ : trinitatis : pro anima germani sui œlfrici que : de hoc loco : asūpta ealdredus vero ep̄s qui : eandē : dedicavit ii idibus : apl̄ xiiii aute anno s regni eadward regis anglorū '+ Earl Odda ordered this royal hall (*or* church) to be built and dedicated in honour of the Holy Trinity for the soul of his brother Ælfric which (was) taken up from this place. And Ealdred was the bishop who dedicated the same on 12 April and in the fourteenth year of the reign of Edward King of the English'.

Piece 6: text on the silver brooch from Sutton, Cambridgeshire, now in the British Museum, late tenth or eleventh century

The text is in Old English verse

+ Ædvwen me ag	*age hyo drihten*
drihten hine awerie	*ðe me hire œtferie*
buton hyo me selle	*hire agenes willes*

'+ Ædwen owns me; may the Lord own her. May the Lord curse him who takes me from her, unless she gives me voluntarily'.

Piece 7: text on the Paris altar, now in the Musée de Cluny, Paris, late tenth or eleventh century

+ discipulus plorat : raphael quem : semp̄ : adorat : +
[ge]nitrix : meret : ḡabriel : cui sc̄s adheret : +
'the disciple mourns him whom Raphael always worships; the Mother mourns, to whom the holy Gabriel cleaves'

Piece 8: text on the cross-slab from Tullylease, Co Cork, Ireland, eighth or ninth century

quicumquœ hunc titulū legerit orat pro berechtuine 'whoever will (*or* might) have read this inscription, let him/her pray (*or* pray) for Beorhtwine'.

References

Collingwood R.G. and R.P. Wright 1965 *The Roman Inscriptions of Britain*, I *Inscriptions on Stone* (Oxford University Press).

Henderson I. and E. Okasha 1992 'The Early Christian Inscribed and Carved Stones of Tullylease, Co. Cork', *CMCS* 24, 1–36.

Okasha E. 1971 *Hand-list of Anglo-Saxon Non-runic Inscriptions* (Cambridge).

—— 1983 'A Supplement to Hand-List of Anglo-Saxon Non-Runic Inscriptions', *Anglo-Saxon England* 11, 83–118.

Saenger, P. 1997 *Space between Words: The Origins of Silent Reading* (Stanford University Press)

Webster L. and J. Backhouse eds. 1992 *The Making of England. Anglo-Saxon Art and Culture AD 600–900* (London: British Museum Press).

22

Sacraments in Stone: The Mysteries of Christ in Anglo-Saxon Sculpture

JANE HAWKES

Probably the earliest use of the monumental cross in Anglo-Saxon England
was that as a standard of the faith and a center for preaching the Gospel.
(Stevens 1904, 63)

Generally speaking, in the pre-Norman period we have no indication of the
use of carefully carved stones as 'preaching crosses' . . . a missionary would
not wait, even if he had the means, for such a work before delivering his
message. He would set up his walking-stick with its crossed head, or cut a
sapling and make a staff-rood in ten minutes. (Collingwood 1927, 4–5)

Introduction

For those studying the material culture of early Christian Anglo-Saxon England,
it is well established that the large-scale stone monuments set up in the landscape
between the eighth and ninth centuries were an ecclesiastical construct (e.g. Bailey
1980, 81–2; 1996a, 23–41). As such, they can be considered as much a part of the
public display of the presence of the Church in the land as the utilization of stone
for church buildings, and have clearly been recognized as such by generations of
scholars, although the exact nature of their function is still a topic for debate.
Nevertheless, while they may be considered less prominent features in the landscape than large-scale buildings, in their original form and setting the stone
monuments, whether crosses, shafts, obelisks or columns, were undoubtedly
intended, at a very primary level, to impress all who encountered them.

Being constructed of the permanent medium of stone, many being brightly
colored with paint and inset with paste glass and metal, it is hard to under-
estimate the impact they would have had in the Anglo-Saxon landscape
– whether their setting was that of the stone-built ecclesiastical complex or more
isolated surroundings, as perhaps at Bewcastle, Cumbria. In such instances,
however, current physical isolation can be misleading; here (as at Ilkley,
Yorkshire), the backdrop for the monument was that of the ruined, but still
upstanding, Roman fort, a structure that would undoubtedly have provided an

added dimension to the setting of the monument, functioning as a physical manifestation of the old *imperium* that, with the erection of the Anglo-Saxon monument, was being appropriated and redefined by the highly visible and permanent expression of the establishment of the Church in Anglo-Saxon England (Bailey 1996a, 5–11; 1996b, 32–6; Hawkes 1999a, 213–15; 1999b, 405; forthcoming 2003a; forthcoming 2003b).

Given the prominent appearance and settings of these monuments and the considerable investment in materials and labour represented by their production (Morris 1989, 302; Parsons 1991, 15–17; Eaton 2000, 14), it is not unlikely that the choice of images carved on them was also the result of deliberate planning. This is particularly the case with the crosses decorated with figural images, a type of monument that was always comparatively rare in the early Christian period. For example, of the 113 pieces of Anglian (pre-Scandinavian) sculpture surviving in present-day Northumberland, only nine have figures carved on them, and three of these were part of the same monument: the Rothbury cross (Bailey 1980, 22–5; 1996a, 11; Hawkes 1999a, 204–5). This is not just the case for Northumberland; it is the pattern of survival repeated across the country. It suggests that not only were stone monuments an impressive feature of the ecclesiastical culture of Anglo-Saxon England, but that those carved with figures were even more so. It also implies that the process by which those figural images were selected and arranged on the monuments was unlikely to have operated on a haphazard or entirely serendipitous basis.

The Nature of the Surviving Images

Turning to consider these figural images, it is worth noting at the outset that, despite the recent development of iconographic studies and the concomitant growth of interest in the narrative scenes carved on the monuments (scenes such as the Road to Calvary featured at Sandbach in Cheshire; Hawkes 1998), this type of image is not common in the extant corpus of Anglo-Saxon figural carvings of pre-Scandinavian date. Most of the surviving figural images are, in fact, iconic portraits: of Christ, the Virgin Mary, the apostles or saints, and angels. A brief (but by no means exhaustive) survey of the material indicates that approximately eleven images of Christ in Majesty have survived, varied in detail, but all functioning iconographically to signify the majesty and authority of the Divine. Of the angels, some fifteen different iconic portraits survive, while there are at least twelve instances of the Virgin and innumerable iconic images of apostles or saints preserved on monuments at over a dozen different sites across the country (see Appendix 1).

This may not seem an excessive number of carvings, but it certainly exceeds the extant narrative images depicting episodes from the Incarnation and Life (Ministry) of Christ, of which only twelve different episodes survive on stones from ten different sites (see Appendix 2). To put this into perspective, 33 different narrative episodes survive in the corpus of early Christian Irish sculpture (see

Harbison 1992). Furthermore, most (although not all) of the Anglo-Saxon narrative carvings survive as single examples. There is only one image of Christ's Nativity, figured by the Adoration of the Manger on the North cross at Sandbach, a monument which also depicts the only extant portrayal of the Adoration of the Magi, and there is only one depiction of the Presentation of the Christ Child, at Wirksworth in Derbyshire (Hawkes 1995a, 213; 1995b, 260–1, 270–1; forthcoming 2003a). Thus, even when the vagaries of production and survival are taken into account, it would seem that figural sculpture in pre-Viking Anglo-Saxon England was an unusual phenomenon, and that narrative images were even more unusual.

In addition, when we turn to examine the nature of these narrative images we find that they tend to cluster (perhaps not surprisingly) around the events of the Incarnation of Christ, with episodes from the Passion and Resurrection forming another group (see Appendix 2), the Crucifixion, of course, being the most popularly illustrated scene (Coatsworth 1979). Thus, apart from the Nativity, the Adoration of the Magi and the Presentation in Temple, the Incarnation of Christ is illustrated by the Annunciation, Visitation and the Journey from (and possibly to) Bethlehem with, perhaps, the Massacre of the Innocents at Bakewell (Bailey 1988, 2). From the events surrounding the Passion and Resurrection, there is the Washing of the Disciples' Feet (*Pedilavum*) and the Road to Calvary, the Descent into Hell (*Anastasis*), the Women at the Sepulchre and the Ascension.

Set against such (comparatively) concentrated interest in the narrative events of the Incarnation and Passion-Resurrection of Christ, the range of events selected to illustrate the Life and Ministry of Christ is very limited indeed. Apart from the iconic representations of the Transfiguration at Sandbach (where the 'narrative' has been excised with the exclusion of the disciples, rendering the image a portrayal of Divine Majesty recognized and attended by the Law and the Prophets; Hawkes 1995a), and the similarly iconic and hieratic portrayal of Christ standing in Majesty attended by 'Mary Magdalene' at Ruthwell (Cassidy 1992, Pl. 16), the Life of Christ is illustrated exclusively by the depiction of four miracles: the Wedding at Cana, the Healing of the Blind Man, the Multiplication of the Loaves and Fishes, and the Raising of Lazarus. There are no examples of narrative events such as the Baptism or Temptation of Christ, or of Christ with the Woman taken in Adultery; nor are there any illustrations of the parables – all of which survive in other media in Anglo-Saxon and Carolingian contexts (see surveys in e.g. Wilson 1984; Hubert *et al.* 1970). Equally significantly, there are no examples in the early Anglo-Saxon sculptural record of miracles such as Christ stilling the tempest or casting out demons, no examples of him healing lepers or the man sick with palsy or the woman with the issue of blood – all of which feature among the miracles surviving in the early Christian art of western Europe (including that of the Insular world).

Such absences, taken in conjunction with what has survived, suggest that the processes informing the design and production of stone monuments carved with figural images in pre-Scandinavian Anglo-Saxon England were extremely selective; as such they clearly provide insights to the way in which the early

Anglo-Saxon Church sought to express itself in the decoration of its public monuments. And, although there is ample scope for hypothesis in the apparent focus on the Incarnation and Passion of Christ, it is the significance of the smaller group of images depicting the Miracles of the Ministry of Christ that will be examined here.

Miraculous Carvings

The Healing of the Blind Man (John 9:1–12; cf. Matthew 9:27–31, 20:30–4; Mark 8:22–6, 10:46–52)

The Healing of the Blind Man, found only on the monument at Ruthwell, Dumfriesshire (Pl. 22.1), was, as has long been recognized, regarded by patristic writers as an image of the enlightenment available to the individual Christian through faith (Saxl 1943; Schapiro 1944; Ó Carragáin 1988, 39; 1995, 631–2 and note 4). As Augustine put it in his treatise on the subject:

> If we reflect then on what is signified by the deed here done, that blind man is the human race; for this blindness had place in the first man through sin, from whom we all draw our origin, not only in respect of death, but also of unrighteousness. . . . [For] unbelief is blindness, and faith enlightenment.
> (Schaff 1888, 245)[1]

Such general concerns, however, were not the only significance that could be invoked by an image of Christ Healing the Blind Man. Liturgically, as Ó Carragáin has shown, the gospel account of the healing of the Blind Man, particularly that recorded in the Gospel of John (9:1–12), which is referred to in the inscription accompanying the carving at Ruthwell and which was the version used most commonly as the Gospel lesson in the Roman liturgy, the episode was very much associated with the observances of Lent. In fact, in the eighth century (and there is evidence for this being the case in Anglo-Saxon England), it formed the Gospel for the Wednesday of the fourth week in Lent, the week during which ceremonies important to the catechumenate were observed (Klauser 1979, 47–8; Ó Carragáin 1988, 39; 1995, 631–2 and note 4; Lenker 1997, 314). Again, as Augustine went on to say in his treatise:

> [When] the Lord came: what did he do? He set forth a great mystery . . . He baptised him [the blind man], in a manner in Himself; he then enlightened him, . . . he made him a catechumen. (Schaff 1888, 245)[2]

---

[1] 'Si ergo quid significet hoc quod factum est cogitemus, genus humanum est iste caecus; haec enim caecitas contigit in primo homine per peccatum, de quo omnes originem duximus, non solum mortis, sed etiam iniquitatis. Si enim caecitas est infidelitas, et illuminatio fides' (Augustine, *Tractatus XLIV in Iohannis Evangelium*1, C.C.S.L. 36, 381).

[2] 'Venit Dominus; quid fecit? Magnum mysterium commendauit . . . Si ergo quando eum in seipso quodammodo baptizauit, tunc illuminauit; . . . fortasse catechumenum fecit' (Augustine, *Tractatus XLIV in Iohannis Evangelium* 2, C.C.S.L. 36, 382). Homilies on the healing of the blind narrated in the other gospels also tended to be Lenten homilies (see e.g. Gregory the Great, Homily 13 on Luke 18:31–43, in Hurst 1990, 94–100, note 1).

Plate 22.1 The Healing of the
Blind Man: Ruthwell,
Dumfries (Photo: Author)

In other words, the enlightenment available to each believer through the gift
of faith was inextricably linked with the rituals of baptism, the process by which
the individual was formally initiated into the Community of the Church – the
Body of Christ. Thus the narrative image of the Healing of the Blind Man at
Ruthwell can be understood, at the very least, to have provided the (informed)
onlooker with an iconographic discourse on the rituals of baptism and the
ideologies attendant on them.

Raising of Lazarus (John 11:1–46)

The Raising of Lazarus is figured three times in the extant corpus of Anglo-Saxon
sculpture: on the remains of the shaft in the churchyard at Heysham in Lancashire
(Pl. 22.2; Collingwood 1927, 72); on a small fragment from Great Glen, Leicestershire (Pl. 22.3; see Bailey 1988, 2, 5 and Fig. 2 for reconstruction); and at the top of
the cross-shaft from Rothbury, Northumberland (Pl. 22.4; Hawkes 1989; 1996,
85–7; although see Cassidy 1996).

Plate 22.2 The Raising of Lazarus: Heysham, Lancs. (Photo: Author)

Plate 22.3 The Raising of Lazarus: Great Glen, Leics. (Photo: David Parsons)

Plate 22.4 The Raising of Lazarus: Rothbury, Nld (Photo: Society of Antiquaries of Newcastle upon Tyne)

By the eighth century, the gospel account of this event formed the reading for the Friday of the fourth week in Lent – that week which, as noted, was dominated by ceremonies for the catachumenate. In the patristic literature, therefore, the episode was regarded very much as a general prefiguration of the Resurrection, but, more specifically, it was also interpreted as an example for the individual Christian of the spiritual awakening from sin that is necessary for salvation (Schiller 1971, 181–4; Farr 1999, 392–3). As Augustine put it, the death of Lazarus:

> . . . is distinguished as a habit of wickedness. For it is one thing to fall into sin, another to form the habit of sinning. . . . He who has become habituated to sin, is buried, and has it properly said of him, 'he stinketh'; for his character, like some horrible smell, begins to be of the worst repute. Such are all who are habituated to crime, abandoned in morals. . . . And yet the power of Christ was not unequal to the task of restoring such a one to life.
>
> (Schaff 1888, 271)[3]

---

[3] 'Est genus mortis immane, mala consuetude appellatur. Aliud est enim peccare, aliud peccandi consuetudinem facere. Qui autem peccare consueuit, sepultus est, et bene de illo dicitur: "fetet;" incipit enim habere pessimam famam, tamquam odorem teterrimum. Tales sunt omnes assueti sceleribus, perditi moribus . . . Nec ad ipsum tamen resuscitandum minor fuit virtus Christi' (Augustine, *Tractatus XLIX in Iohannis Evangelium* 3, C.C.S.L. 36, 421).

So, while Christ's action of resuscitating Lazarus proved the possibility of resurrection, Lazarus' death demonstrated the state of man prior to the loosing of the bonds of sin at confession. For, again quoting Augustine:

> While you despise Him [Christ] you lie in the arms of death; . . . but when you make confession, you come forth. For what is this coming forth, but the open acknowledgement you make of your state, in quitting as it were, the old refuges of darkness? But the confession you make is effected by God when he . . . calls you in abounding grace. Accordingly, when the dead man had come forth, still bound; confessing, yet guilty still, that his sins might be taken away, the Lord said to his servant: 'Loose him, and let him go'.
> (Schaff 1888, 277–8)[4]

Thus, the shrouds binding Lazarus, figured in all the Anglo-Saxon carvings, were the means of expressing, iconographically, the sins binding humankind which fall away after confession is made in the faith of Christ's redemption. In the Rothbury scene, with the shrouds falling from him, Lazarus is shown literally waking into the light of the living world from the darkness of death; as he rises, and the grave-clothes fall away, so he is released, through Christ's intervention, from the habitual bonds of sin and wickedness which kept him in the grave.

In this way the example of Lazarus was not simply a proof or type of the Resurrection. Rather, it was an example of the faith that was required by each Christian and demonstrated by confession. More importantly, it was a prerequisite for participation in the salvation on offer through Christ. In fact, the figure of Martha in the Rothbury scene, deliberately included and responsible for the confusing setting of that scene on its side, was the iconographic means of emphasising this aspect of the episode. Because Christ addressed himself to Martha (with the words from John 11:25: 'I am the resurrection and the life; he that believes in me, though he were dead, yet shall he live'), she became, in exegetical literature, the focus of discussions on such exemplary faith (see above, note 4; Hawkes 1989; 1996, 86–7; Farr 1999, 392–3).

Thus, the portrayal of Lazarus' resurrection can be understood to provide the onlooker with a fairly complex iconographic narrative expressing the notion that through faith, humanity is redeemed by Christ and purged of sin through confession.

---

[4] 'Quando contemnis, mortuus iaces; . . . quando confiteris, procedis. Quid est enim procedere, nisi ab occultis uelut exeundo manifestari? Sed ut confitearis, Deus fecit magna uoce clamando, id est, magna gratia uocando. Ideo cum processisset mortuus adhuc ligatus, confitens et adhuc reus; ut soluerentur peccata eius, ministris hoc dixit Dominus: "Soluite illum, et sinite abire"' (Augustine, *Tractatus XLIX in Iohannis Evangelium* 24, C.C.S.L. 36, 431). See also, Ambrose, *De Excessu Fratris sui Satyrii* II:77–79 (*P.L.* 16, 1395–6); Hilary of Poitiers, *De Trinitate* VI:47 (*P.L.* 10, 195); Psuedo-Bedan/Alcuinian text, *In S. Johannis* XI (*P.L.* 92, 777–8).

Plate 22.5 The Miracle of the Loaves
and Fishes: Hornby, Lancs.
(Photo: Author)

The Miracle of the Loaves and Fishes (John 6:1–15; cf. Mattew 14:13–21,
15:32–9; Mark 6:30–44; Luke 9: 10–11; John 6:25–59)

Apart from the fragmentary remains of the narrative scene at Dewsbury in
Yorkshire (Pl. 22.6; Cramp 1999, 9), the Miracle of the Multiplication of the Loaves
and Fishes is also preserved on the shaft at Hornby in Lancashire (Pl. 22.5), where
Christ and another figure (presumably an apostle) stand over the loaves and
fishes, flanking a vine-tree growing from the loaves.

    Richard Bailey's work (1996b, 26–8) on this piece has demonstrated that this
particular version of the scene makes explicit the Eucharistic frame of reference
inherent in any image of this miracle (Schiller 1971, 164–5). Indeed, the equation
of the miracle with the Eucharist is present even in the biblical narratives of the
discussions that took place after the miracle between Christ and his disciples.
During these Christ, in a fairly lengthy discourse, interpreted the event by
equating himself with the bread of the loaves:

Then Jesus said unto them: verily, verily I say unto you . . . my Father gives you that true bread from heaven. For the bread of God is He who comes down from heaven and gives life unto the world. . . . And [then] Jesus said unto them, I am the bread of life; he that comes to me shall never hunger, and he that believes in me shall never thirst. . . . And this is the will of him that sent me, that every one who sees the Son and believes on him may have everlasting life, and I will raise him up at the last day. . . . I am the living bread which came down from heaven; if any man eat of this bread he shall live for ever: and the bread that I will give is my flesh which I will give for the life of the world. . . . Except ye eat the flesh of the Son of man and drink his blood, ye have no life in you.   (Jn 6:32–53)

While John's account of the miracle itself formed the gospel reading for the fourth Sunday in Lent in Anglo-Saxon England (Lenker 1997, 314), the language used to contextualize the event in the biblical narrative accentuates the association of the miracle with the Eurcharist; it is very much that which, echoed

Plate 22.6 The Miracles of the Loaves and Fishes and the Wedding at Cana: Dewsbury, Yorks. (Photo: Author)

at the Last Supper, became enshrined in each enactment of the Eucharist (John 13:16–20; cf. Matthew 26:26; Mark 14:22; Luke 22:14–20; I Cor. 10). It is thus not surprising that the association was a commonplace in the patristic literature. As Augustine's sermon on John 6:9 makes clear:

> Who is the bread of heaven but Christ? But in order that man might eat angels' bread, the Lord of Angels was made man. For if he had not been made man, we should not have his flesh; if we had not his flesh we should not eat the bread of the altar.   (Schaff 1887, 499)[5]

A primary reference point in any iconographic reading of an image depicting the Miracle of the Loaves and Fishes, therefore, will be to the celebration of the Eucharist. What the scene at Hornby does, with the inclusion of the vine-tree, is to make that reference both explicit and multivalent: Christ is depicted as himself, performing the miracle, but he is equally figured in the symbols of the fish and the vine (with its evocation of Christ's words at John 15:1 that 'I am the True Vine'). Furthermore, Christ as Eucharist is figured in the loaves of bread and the wine-producing grapes of the vine. Then there is the manner in which the vine-tree frames the image that could also be read as a reference to the way in which those receiving spiritual sustenance from the fruit of the vine are often figured as enclosed within its branches.

Thus, the Anglo-Saxon carvings of the Miracle of the Loaves and Fishes can be understood, like any such images, to have had a primary Eucharistic significance which, at Hornby, was exploited to convey more explicitly its multiple and complex references. In addition, as John 6:40 makes clear,[6] the images would probably have had an eschatological frame of reference with a concomitant emphasis on the necessity of believing in such consequences.

The Miracle at Cana (John 2:1–11)

The miracle by which Christ converted water into wine during the Wedding at Cana is preserved most completely on the fragment at Dewsbury (Pl. 22.6; Cramp 1999, 9), but it may also have figured at Breedon-on-the-Hill, in Leicestershire (Pl. 22.7; Jewell 2001, 259–61). Here the leg and feet of the servant and two of the water jugs are preserved on a fragment inserted into the south wall of the south aisle of the church. These are elements that compare with details featured in elaborate narrative depictions of the miracle as, for instance, in certain Carolingian ivories of ninth-century date (e.g. Goldschmidt 1918, Pl. XXII.46, 47; Gaborit-Chopin 1978, Pl. 87).

---

[5] 'Quis est panis coeli, nisi Christus? Sed ut panem Angelorum manducaret homo, Dominus Angelorum factus est homo. Si enim hoc non factus esset, carnem ipsius non haberemus: si carnem ipsius non haberemus, panem altaris non manducaremus' (Augustine, Sermo CXXX(a): De verbis Evangelii Joannis, ubi narratur miraculum de quinque panibus et duobus piscibus 2, P.L. 38, 726).

[6] 'This is the will of him that sent me, that every one which sees the son and believes on him may have everlasting life, and I will raise him up at the last day.'

Plate 22.7 The Wedding at Cana:
Breedon-on-the-Hill, Leics.
(Photo: Author)

By the fourth century the account of the wedding and its attendant miracle, preserved only in the gospel of John, formed one of the readings for the liturgical celebrations of Epiphany, and patristic homilies on the event make it clear that its significance lay in the association of the Incarnation (celebrated at the Feast of Epiphany) with the Second Coming (the presence of the Virgin at the Wedding functioning as a link between the Incarnation and the Crucifixion), the marriage itself providing an opportunity to expound on the nature of the 'Bridegroom' and the Last Judgment (Schiller 1971, 162–3). Furthermore, within this all-embracing subject matter, the homiletic discourses also tended to feature an exposition on the theme of the ages of the world, as typified by the water jugs.

Taking as an example Bede's homily on the subject, which closely follows those of Augustine, the episode overall is interpreted (succinctly) as indicating 'that the Lord came to link the Church to himself' (Martin and Hurst 1991, 136).[7] For:

---

[7] '... sed tertio tempore saeculi dominum ad aptandam sibi ecclesiam uenisse designat' (Bede, *Homelia 14: Post Epiphanium (Ioh. ii.1–11), C.C.S.L.* 122, 96, based on Augustine's commentaries on John 2, *Tractatus VIII-IX, C.C.S.L.* 36, 91–100).

... looking at the literal sense of this [story] we clearly learn what great diligence we should have in placing ourselves under the mysteries (*mysteria*) of the gospel faith, seeing that he, himself the lawgiver ... took care to receive, and at the same time to hand on the new mysteries (*sacramenta*) of grace. (Martin and Hurst 1991, 142)[8]

These 'mysteries' are understood by Bede to have been initiated by Christ's incarnation, his circumcision (on the eighth day after his nativity), and his presentation in the temple (on the thirty-third day after this). They thus allowed (metaphorically) for:

... cleansing the contagion of sin, for giving drink from the joys of life, and for bringing cleaner flowing waters to others. [Thus] in the circumcision of the eighth day you may understand baptism, which has redeemed us from the death of our sins into the mystery of the Lord's resurrection. In [Jesus'] being led into the temple and the offering of the sacrificial victims of purification, you may recognize a prefiguration of any of the faithful entering from the baptistry to the holy altar and needing to be consecrated by an exceptional sacrificial victim, the Lord's body and blood. [If you have this understanding of the story], you have been granted wine made from the water, and it is a most undiluted wine. Furthermore, you can interpret the day of circumcision as the general resurrection of the human race ... and you can understand the leading of the circumcised into the temple with the sacrificial offerings as the time after the resurrection when the universal judgment is finished, and the saints, then made incorruptible will enter with their offerings of good works ... [If you understand the story in this way] you will unquestionably see wondrous wine made from the water, concerning which you should testify to its Maker and say 'And your inebriating cup, how splendid it is' [Ps 23:5].

(Martin and Hurst 1991, 142–3)[9]

This patristic tradition, articulated by Bede and Augustine before him, clearly regarded the miracle at Cana as signifying, in an extraordinarily complex manner, the rituals of baptism and the Eucharist, the faith necessary to participate in such rituals, their place in the life of the Church, and the manner in which this Church

---

[8] 'Haec intuentes ad litteram aperte discimus quanta nobis diligentia sunt euangelicae fidei subeunda mysteria quando ipse benedictionem gratiae adferens qui legem litterae dedit ueterum primo caerimoniarum tiru consecrari qui cuncta diuinitus consecrat et sic noua gratiae sacramenta suscipere simul et tradere curauit' (Bede, *Homilia 14*, C.C.S.L. 122, 101).

[9] 'Ecce hydria sexta ad abluenda peccati contagia ad potanda uitae gaudia mundiorem ceteris adferens undam. Verum si in octaui diei circumcisione baptisma quod in mysterium dominicae resurrectionis a peccatorum nos morte redemit intellegis in inductione in templum et oblatione hostiae purificantis figuratum cognoscis fideles quosque de baptisterio ad altare sanctum ingredi ac dominici corporis et sanguinis uictima singulari debere consecrari, uino quidem de aqua facto et quidem meracissimo donatus es. Porro si circumcisionis diem ad generalem humani generis resurrectionem quando mortalis propago cessabit mortalitas tota in immortalitatem mutabitur interpretaris et circumcisos induci in templum cum hostiis intellexeris quando post resurrectionem uniuersali expleto iudicio sancti iam incorruptibiles facti ad contemplandum perpetuo speciem diuinae maiestatis cum bonorum operum muneribus intrabunt, mirandum profecto uinum de aqua fieri uidebis cuius conditori necte protesteris et dicas: "Et poculum tuum inebrians quam praeclarum est"' (Bede, *Homilia 14*, C.C.S.L. 122, 101–2).

was founded on Christ. At a macrocosmic level, this was situated within the scheme laid out by the Divine Will that encompassed all humanity from Creation to the re-establishment of heaven on earth at the Second Coming.

As such, the Miracle at Cana can perhaps be understood to situate and encapsulate the ideas highlighted in the iconography of the other three miracles favored by those responsible for the design and decoration of the Anglo-Saxon stone monuments. The Healing of the Blind Man takes as its primary significance the theological issues surrounding the rituals of Baptism; the Raising of Lazarus refers to the ideas attendant on the faith necessary for partaking of salvation which could be demonstrated in confession of one's 'habitual sins'; and the Miracle of the Loaves and Fishes focuses on the theological questions relating to the rituals of the Eucharist. In other words, these four miracles, selected from all the miracles potentially available to those responsible for the design of the Anglo-Saxon carved monuments of the pre-Viking period, are those which focus quite specifically on the matrix of ideas surrounding the two major rituals of participation in the mystery of Christ as they were understood in the pre-scholastic Church and which are best elucidated by the term *sacramentum*.

In exegetical contexts this concept involved both the senses of the Greek word *mysterion* (mystery) for which it functioned as a synonym (see above note 8) and, in its Latin tradition, a sense of contractual obligation and oath taking. Thus, in biblical literature (particularly the Pauline epistles) *sacramentum* refers to God's design to save humanity through the life, death and resurrection of Christ (e.g. Rom. 6:1–11; I Cor. 2, 4; Eph. 3; cf. Ferguson 1990 1011–4). Because Christ embodied God's plan to save humanity, he was the mystery (*sacramentum*) and so, by extension, the Church, as the body of Christ, was where the believer gained access to that mystery. The manner in which this access was to be accomplished was the central concern of the patristic debates on such matters, and here the Anglo-Saxon interest in the four miracles featured on the stone monuments can probably be regarded as the visual means of articulating these concerns. The answer, as intimated in the iconographic excursus of the carvings, was through symbolic participation in Christ's life, death and salvation – through participation in the liturgical rites of baptism and the Eucharist, the signs that were regarded as embodying Christ, for as Leo the Great put it: 'What was visible in our Redeemer has passed over into the sacraments'.[10]

Symbolic participation thus involved, not just observing the ritual of the mysteries (as mediated through the Church), but being part of a transaction through which the believer and their deity bound themselves to each other in a sacred commitment: the iconographic remit of the Lazarus image with its emphasis on confession and faith. On one side, God was considered to have made union with humanity in the person of Christ who, as Bede put it 'came to link the

---

[10] 'Quod itaque Redemptionis nostri conspicuum fuit, in sacramenta transiuit' (Leo, *Tractatus LXXIV: Item Alius De Ascensione Domini* 2, C.C.S.L. 138A, 457); cf. Augustine, *Tractatus VI: in Iohannis Evangelium* 1: 32–3 8, C.C.S.L. 36, 57.

Church to himself'; on the other, each believer was obliged to demonstrate their obedience (through faith) in the divine will lying behind the Incarnation, Life, Passion and Resurrection of Christ. This was the crucial element in the ability of the individual to receive God's gifts dispensed by the Church through the rituals of baptism and the Eucharist. Put another way: through symbolic participation, undertaken with faith, in the 'mysteries of grace' (*gratiae sacramenta*), each Christian became a 'figure' in Christ's salvation in a manner not unlike that by which the miracles themselves figured that salvation.

Summary

Thus the decision to use figural images in the decoration of the carved stone sculptures of the early Christian Church in Anglo-Saxon England seems to have been a relatively rare, and quite deliberate phenomenon. More specifically, the images selected to illustrate the Ministry of Christ on these monuments were, in all likelihood, chosen because of their iconographic potential to illustrate the two rituals of initiation and participation in the mystery of Christ as mediated by his Church. It would seem that in this particular instance (in the almost exclusive interest in these four episodes), the Church in the pre-Viking period was using figural stone carving as a means, not of 'converting' a population to Christianity through images selected to tell a story as has often been assumed (e.g. Stevens 1904, 63; Bonner 1999, 366); rather, such carvings, displayed on highly visible large-scale monuments in very specific settings, were intended, at a number of levels, to exhibit and celebrate, in permanent and public form, the function and identity of the Church in Anglo-Saxon England as the means by which each believer was able to participate in the mysteries of Christ. To paraphrase Bede, the Church, through its figural stone monuments, was presenting itself as the means by which each believer could be linked to Christ, as Christ came to link the Church to himself.

Appendix 1 Iconic Portraits in (Pre-Viking) Anglo-Saxon Sculpture

Majestas Christi	Peterborough, Cambs.
	Bewcastle, Cu.
	Hoddam, Dumfries
	Ruthwell, Dumfries
	Newent, Gloucs.
	Halton, Lancs.
	Rothbury, Nld
	Dewsbury, Yorks.
	Easby, Yorks.
	Ilkley, Yorks.
	Masham, Yorks.

Appendix 1 *continued*

Virgin	Peterborough, Cambs. Fletton, Cambs. Sandbach, Ches. (with Child × 2 examples) Bakewell, Derbys. Derby St Alkmund (with Child) Eyam, Derbys. (with Child) Deerhurst, Gloucs. (with Child) Breedon-on-the-Hill, Leics. Dewsbury, Yorks. (with Child)
'Saints'	Peterborough, Cambs. Fletton, Cambs. Castor, Cambs. Bakewell, Derbys. Auckland St Andrew, Co. Dur. Halton, Lancs. Heysham, Lancs. Hornby, Lancs. Breedon-on-the-Hill, Leics. Norham, Nld Eccleshall, Staffs. Collingham, Yorks. Otley, Yorks.
Angels	Fletton, Cambs. Sandbach, Ches. Bradbourne, Derbys. Bakewell, Derbys. Eyam, Derbys. Auckland St Andrew, Co. Dur. Deerhurst, Gloucs. Halton, Lancs. Hornby, Lancs. Breedon-on-the-Hill, Leics. Hexham, Nld Cundall, Yorks. Dewsbury, Yorks. Ilkley, Yorks. Otley, Yorks.
(Agnus Victor)	Wirksworth, Derbys. Hart, Co. Dur. Hoddam, Dumfries

Appendix 2 Narrative Images of the Life and Passion of Christ (Excluding Crucifixion) in Pre-Viking Anglo-Saxon Sculpture

INFANCY **Annunciation**	Sandbach, Ches.: North cross Wirksworth, Derbys. Ruthwell, Dumfries Hovingham, Yorks.
Visitation	Hovingham, Yorks.
Journey to/from Bethlehem	Bakewell, Derbys. Ruthwell, Dumfries
Nativity	Sandbach, Ches.: North cross (Adoration of the Manger)
Adoration of the Magi	Sandbach, Ches.: North cross
Massacre of the Innocents	Bakewell, Derbys.
Presentation in the Temple	Wirksworth, Derbys.
LIFE AND MINISTRY **Miracle at Cana**	Dewsbury, Yorks. Breedon-on-the-Hill, Leics.
Healing of the Blind Man	Ruthwell, Dumfries
Multiplication of the Loaves **and Fishes**	Hornby, Lancs. Dewsbury, Yorks.
Raising of Lazarus	Heysham, Lancs. Great Glen, Leics. Rothbury, Nld
(Christ and Mary Magdalene)	Ruthwell, Dumfries
(Transfiguration)	Sandbach, Ches.: 1 × North cross; 1 × South cross
PASSION AND RESURRECTION **Pedilavum**	Wirksworth, Derbys.

Appendix 2 *continued*

Road to Calvary	Sandbach, Ches.: North cross
Resurrection	Wirksworth, Derbys. (*Anastasis*) Hovingham, Yorks. (3 women at the Sepulchre)
Ascension	Wirksworth, Derbys. Reculver, Kent Rothbury, Nld
(Last Judgement)	Eyam, Derbys.

References

Bailey, R.N. 1980: *Viking Age Sculpture in Northern England*, London.

—— 1988: 'The Meaning of Mercian Sculpture' (Vaughan Paper 34), *Brixworth Lecture*, Leicester.

—— 1996a: *England's Earliest Sculptors*, Toronto.

—— 1996b: '"What Mean These Stones?" Some Aspects of Pre-Norman Sculpture in Cheshire and Lancashire' (Toller Memorial Lecture), *Bulletin of the John Rylands University Library of Manchester* 78.1 (1996), 21–46.

Bonner, G. 1999 'Bede: scholar and spiritual teacher' in Hawkes and Mills, 1999, 365–70.

Cassidy, B. 1992: ed. *The Ruthwell Cross: Papers from the Colloquium Sponsored by the Index of Christian Art, Princeton University, 1989*, Princeton, New Jersey.

—— 1996: 'The Dream of Joseph on the Anglo-Saxon Cross from Rothbury', *Gesta* 35.2 (1996), 149–55.

C.C.S.L. 36: *Corpus Christianorum. Series Latina 36: Aurelii Augustini Opera Pars VIII: In Iohannis Evangelium Tractatus CXXIV*, ed. R. Willems (Turnholt, 1954).

C.C.S.L. 122: *Corpus Christianorum. Series Latina 122: Bedae Opera Pars III. Opera Homiletica / Pars IV. Opera Rhythmica*, ed. D. Hurst (Turnholt, 1955).

C.C.S.L. 138A: *Corpus Christianorum. Series Latina 138A: Sancti Leonis Magni, Romani Pontificis Tractatus Septem et Nonaginta*, ed. A. Chavasse (Turnholt, 1973).

Coatsworth, E. 1979: *The Iconography of the Crucifixion in pre-Conquest Sculpture in England* (unpublished Ph.D. thesis, University of Durham, 2 vols).

Collingwood, W.G. 1927: *Northumbrian Crosses of the Pre-Norman Age*, London (repr. Lampeter 1989).

Cramp, R.J. 1999: 'The Northumbrian Identity', in Hawkes and Mills 1999, 1–11.

Eaton, T. 2000: *Plundering the Past: Roman Stonework in Medieval Britain*, Stroud.

Farr, C. 1999: 'Questioning the Monuments: Approaches to Anglo-Saxon Sculpture through Gender Studies', in Karkov 1999, 375–402.

Ferguson, G. 1990: ed. *Encyclopedia of Early Christianity*, New York.

Gaborit-Chopin, D. 1978: *Ivoires du Moyen Age*, Paris.

Goldschmidt, A. 1918: *Die Elfenbeinskulpturen aus der zeit der Karolingischen und Sächsischen Kaiser: VIII-XI Jarhundert*, Berlin (repr. Oxford, 1969).

Harbison, P.1992: *The High Crosses of Ireland: an Iconographical and Photographic Survey*, 3 vols, Bonn.

Hawkes, J. 1989: 'The Miracle Scene on the Rothbury Cross-shaft', *Archaeologia Aeliana*, ser. 5, 17 (1989), 207–11.

—— 1995a: 'A Question of Judgment: the Iconic Programme of Sandbach, Cheshire', *From the Isles of the North*, ed. C. Bourke (Belfast, 1995), 213–20.

—— 1995b: 'The Wirksworth Slab: an Iconography of Humilitas', *Peritia* 8 (1995), 1–32.

—— 1996: 'The Rothbury Cross: an Iconographic Bricolage', *Gesta* 35.1 (1996), 77–94.

—— 1998: 'Breaking the Silence: the Road to Calvary at Sandbach', *Le Isole Britanniche e Roma in Età Romanobarbarica*, ed. A. M. Luiselli Fadda and É. Ó Carragáin (Rome, 1998), 37–48.

—— 1999a: 'Anglo-Saxon Sculpture: Questions of Context', in Hawkes and Mills 1999, 204–15.

—— 1999b: 'Statements in Stone: Anglo-Saxon Sculpture, Whitby and the Christianization of the North', in Karkov 1999, 403–22.

—— Forthcoming 2003a: 'Reading Stone', *Theorizing Anglo-Saxon Stone Sculpture*, ed. C.E. Karkov and F. Orton (West Virginia University Press).

—— Forthcoming 2003b: '*Iuxta Morem Romanorum*: Stone and Sculpture in Anglo-Saxon England', *Anglo-Saxon Styles*, ed. G. Hardin Brown and C. Karkov (Kalamazoo, W. Michigan).

Hawkes, J. and S. Mills 1999: (eds) *Northumbria's Golden Age*, Stroud.

Hubert, J., J. Porcher and W.F. Volbach 1970: *The Carolingian Renaissance*, New York.

Hurst, D. 1990: *Gregory the Great: Forty Gospel Homilies Translated from the Latin* (Cistercian Studies Series, 123), Kalamazoo, W. Michigan.

Jewell, R. 2001 'Classicism of Southumbrian sculpture' in *Mercia: an Anglo-Saxon kingdom in Europe*, ed. M.P. Brown and C.A. Farr (Leicester), 246–62.

Karkov, C.E. 1999: ed. *The Archaeology of Anglo-Saxon England: Basic Readings*, New York and London.

Klauser, T. 1979: *A Short History of the Western Liturgy*, Oxford.

Lenker, U. 1997: *Die Westsächsische Evangelienversion und die Perikopenordnungen im Angelsächsischen England*, Munich.

Martin, L.T. and D. Hurst 1991: (eds) *Bede the Venerable: Homilies on the Gospels 1*, Kalamazoo, W. Michigan.

Morris, R.K. 1989: *Churches in the Landscape*, London.

Ó Carragáin, É. 1988: 'The Ruthwell Crucifixion Poem and its Iconographic and Liturgical Contexts', *Peritia* 6–7 (1987–8), 1–71.

—— 1995: 'Rome Pilgrimage, Roman Liturgy, and the Ruthwell Cross', *Akten des XII. internationalen Kongresses für christliche Archäologie, Bonn, 22 bis 28 September 1991* (*Jahrbuch für Antike und Christentum*, Ergänzungsband 20, 2 parts, Münster), 2, 630–9.

Parsons, D. 1991: 'Stone,' *English Medieval Industries*, ed. J. Blair and N. Ramsey (London, 1991), 1–28.

P.L. : *Patrologiae Cursus Completus, Series Latina*, ed. J-P. Migne, 221 vols (Paris, 1844–64).

Saxl, F. 1943: 'The Ruthwell Cross', *Journal of the Warburg and Courtauld Institutes* 6 (1943), 1–19.

Schaff, P. 1887: *A Select Library of the Nicene and Post-Nicene Fathers of the Christian Church* 6 (repr. Michigan, 1978).

—— 1888: *A Select Library of the Nicene and Post-Nicene Fathers of the Christian Church* 7 (repr. Michigan, 1979).

Schapiro, M. 1944: 'The Religious Meaning of the Ruthwell Cross', *Art Bulletin* 26 (1944), 232–45.

Schiller, G. 1971: *Iconography of Christian Art* 1, London.

Stevens, W.O. 1904: *The Cross in the Life and Literature of the Anglo-Saxons*, (repr. 1977 with a new preface by T.D. Hill, in *The Anglo-Saxon Cross*, Hamden, Connecticut, 7–109).

Wilson, D. 1984: *Anglo-Saxon Art from the Seventh Century to the Norman Conquest*, London.

23

Alcuin's Narratives of Evangelism: The Life of St Willibrord and the Northumbrian Hagiographical Tradition

KATE RAMBRIDGE

As for those churches that do not have priests, it is a dangerous thing that the flock of Christ should remain a long time without a pastor . . . truly is it said that 'There is a great harvest, but there are few labourers; pray therefore the lord of the harvest, that he send forth his labourers into his harvest.' And I tell you, my cherished friend, that there is a great harvest to be had in a Christian people, but there are no preachers in these places. It is you who should ask my beloved David, the lord of the harvest, that he send labourers into his harvest: and that he should say to them, just as his own protector, God, and matchless lover Christ said to his disciples: 'Go: behold, I send you forth.'[1]

This passage is taken from a letter written in 796 by Alcuin to Megenfrid, one of Charlemagne's officers in the campaigns he led, from 791, against populations settled east of the Frankish territory.[2] In this letter, Alcuin urges Megenfrid that he should represent to Charlemagne (*dominum messis, id est David meum dilectum*) the importance of supporting a missionary pastorate in his expanding empire. In a number of the letters written by Alcuin during the 790s and early 800s, there recur similar expressions of concern related to the moral and practical dimensions of evangelism in the Carolingian empire.[3] These concerns are articulated with a consistency and a force eloquent of Alcuin's commitment to the continuing mission of the Church – a commitment essentially characteristic of the Northumbrian monastic and ecclesiastical tradition in which he had been

---

[1] *Monumenta Germaniae Historica*, Epistolae IV, ed. E. Duemmler (Berlin, 1895), no.111, pp. 161–2 (hereafter, Alcuin, *Epistolae*).
[2] See R. Collins, *Charlemagne* (London, 1988), pp.89–97.
[3] See for example *Epistolae* 107, pp.153–4; 110, pp.156–9; 113, pp.163–6; 134, pp.202–3; 136, pp.205–10.

educated.[4] Alcuin, like Gregory and Bede before him, knew that he and his contemporaries lived in an age of conversion.[5] He also shared with his forerunners the conviction that participation in this age conferred great responsibilities upon those who guided and governed the Church. In his letter to Megenfrid, Alcuin calls upon Charlemagne to recognise his sacral secular role in this age: the emperor, as a new David, must understand and fulfil his responsibility towards the Church and its community.[6] In voicing his concerns, and in presenting Charlemagne with an agenda for the fulfilment of his role in an age of conversion, Alcuin aspires through his eloquence to contribute as a writer to the mission of the Church. The subject of this paper is Alcuin's understanding of his own responsibility, as author and educator, and the ways in which he aspires to fulfil this responsibility.

As his letters make clear, the moral and practical considerations that arise from the importance attributed to the continuing mission of the Church represent, for Alcuin, an issue of immediate concern in the context of late eighth-century Francia.[7] Donald Bullough, in an appraisal of Alcuin's Carolingian career, describes the issue of adult baptism as being for Alcuin a particular 'preoccupation in his final years at [Charlemagne's] court . . . the recent rapid success of Carolingian arms in the south-east, a decade after the painfully achieved victory over the Saxons, had brought to the fore major problems of pastoral theology

---

[4] Conversion and evangelism and are important themes of a number of eighth-century Northumbrian texts that form a part of Alcuin's literary background: see for example Bede's prose *Vita S. Cuthberti*, ed. and trans. B. Colgrave, *Two Lives of St Cuthbert, A Life by an Anonymous Monk of Lindisfarne and Bede's Prose Life* (Cambridge, 1940), pp.142–307, c.9, pp.184–7, c.13, pp.198–9, c.13, pp.200–3; *The Earliest Life of Gregory the Great, by an Anonymous Monk of Whitby*, ed. and trans. B. Colgrave (Kansas, 1968; reprinted Cambridge, 1985), cc.5–6, pp.80–5; *Bede's Ecclesiastical History*, ed. B. Colgrave and R.A.B. Mynors (Oxford, 1969), I.23–33, pp.68–117; II.9–17, pp.162–97; III.3–6, pp.218–31; IV.27, pp.430–5; V.9–11, pp.474–87. On the ways in which Alcuin's historical writing reflects his familiarity with Northumbrian literature, and his special respect for Bede as an historian, see P. Godman, 'Alcuin's Poem on York and the Literature of his Times', Ph.D. thesis (Cambridge, 1980), pp.14–45, 121–212.

[5] On the force of the idea of mission in Anglo-Saxon England see W. Levison, *England and the Continent in the Eighth Century* (Oxford, 1946), pp.45–93; C.H. Talbot, *The Anglo-Saxon Missionaries in Germany* (London, 1954); R. McKitterick, *Anglo-Saxon Missionaries in Germany: Personal Connections and Local Influences*, University of Leicester Vaughan Paper, 36 (Leicester, 1981). G. Kiesel and J. Schroeder (eds), *Willibrord: Apostel der Niederlande – Gründer der Abtei Echternach* (Luxemburg, 1989); H. Mayr-Harting, *The Coming of Christianity to Anglo-Saxon England*, 3rd edn (London, 1991); D. Dales, *Light to the Isles: A Study of Missionary Theology in Celtic and Early Anglo-Saxon Britain* (Cambridge, 1997); R. Gameson (ed.), *St Augustine and the Conversion of England* (Stroud, 1999).

[6] On the context of reform within which Alcuin felt it appropriate to address Charlemagne in these terms see: G. Brown, 'The Carolingian Renaissance' in *Carolingian Culture: Emulation and Innovation*, ed. R. McKitterick (Cambridge, 1994), pp.1–51; Collins, *Charlemagne*, pp.102–24; M. Garrison, 'The Franks as the New Israel? Education for an Identity from Pippin to Charlemagne', in *The Uses of the Past in the Early Middle Ages*, ed. Y. Hen and M. Innes (Cambridge, 2000), pp.114–61; M. de Jong, 'The Empire as *Ecclesia*: Hrabanus Maurus and Biblical *Historia* for Rulers', in Hen and Innes, *Uses of the Past*, pp.191–226.

[7] See note 3 above.

... Frankish conquest had recreated the adult catechumenate.'[8] The conversion of new subject peoples was a contentious issue: Alcuin was a highly principled advocate for the Christian education of these groups, maintaining that 'a man may be drawn into the faith, but he cannot be compelled to it'.[9] Alcuin refers (both writing to Megenfrid and in a contemporaneous letter to Charlemagne) to Augustine's *De Catecezandis Rudibus* as a work that sets a pastoral standard for the Carolingian church: he reiterates Augustine's emphasis on catechesis as an essential precursor to baptism.[10] His tone in the passage from the letter to Megenfrid quoted above, as in others associated with the continuing work of evangelism in this context, is urgent, hortatory: he presents dedication to this work as a moral imperative to which he demands that his audience respond.

In this letter, Alcuin asserts his conviction that the labour of evangelism is an apostolic responsibility conferred on the Church by Christ. He drives home his argument with emphatic reference to two passages from the Gospels which are crucial to the role of the Church in the age of conversion: these are Luke 10.2–3, which records Christ's instruction to his disciples to preach amongst the people,[11] and Matthew 20.1–16, which gives the parable of the labourers in the vineyard. These two passages deploy a figurative theme that recurs throughout the Bible: imagery of irrigation, nourishment and cultivation is common in both Old and New Testaments.[12] In the Gospels, it occurs most often in Matthew[13] and Luke,[14] as well as in the letters of St Paul.[15] The language of nurture and nourishment, variously expressed in the images and narratives of sowing, irrigation, harvest and the provision of food – loaves and fishes, milk and meat, the bread of life – is, in the Bible, the language of spiritual health and growth. The conjunction of this figurative theme with Christ's command to his apostles resonates throughout the early medieval Church, and it is fundamental to Alcuin's understanding of the imperative of evangelism.

While the primary application of his reference to Matthew and Luke in the letter to Megenfrid is clearly to persuade secular authority of its moral responsibility to promote the development of the Church, further analysis of his figurative language reveals that in Alcuin's conception the relevance of the evangelists' words is much broader than this. The injunction delivered by these passages touches not only kings, but also missionary teachers and all proselytisers of the faith, including those who perform their labour through the text, the authors and educators of the monastic Church. Alcuin's quotation of Christ's command, as

---

[8] D. Bullough, 'Alcuin and the Kingdom of Heaven', in *idem*, *Carolingian Renewal: Sources and Heritage* (Manchester, 1991), pp.161–239 (188).

[9] *Epistolae* 111, p.160.

[10] *Epistolae* 110, p.158; *Epistolae* 111, p.160. See also *Epistolae* 134, pp.202–3.

[11] See also Matthew 9.37–8.

[12] See for example Deuteronomy 7.12–15; Job 5.1–27; Psalms 1.1–3, 92.12–14, 104.1–35.

[13] Matthew 3.7–10; 4.1–4.

[14] Luke 3.8–9, 6.43–4, 8.4–15; 13.6–9; 20.9–16.

[15] I Corinthians 3.1–9.

recorded by Luke, is intended to persuade his audience of their duty but, as I shall show, it also represents his own response to that same imperative, as an author and an educator.

Alcuin's models for a literary 'labour in the harvest' were Gregory and Bede. In the Northumbrian ecclesiastical tradition in which Alcuin was educated, both of these writers were venerated as fathers of the Church, and both were strong advocates for Her continuing mission in their own times.[16] Gregory had interpreted Luke 10.1–7, in his Gospel homilies, as a moral injunction for the members of the sixth-century Italian Church.[17] His exposition of Luke's text is characterised by that hortatory, even polemical tone which is associated with Alcuin's deployment of the same passage in his letter to Megenfrid:

> Let us listen to what the Lord says after he sent out his preachers: 'The harvest indeed is great, but the labourers are few; so ask the Lord of the harvest to send labourers to his harvest.' The harvest is now great, but the labourers are few, because – I cannot speak of this without sorrow – although there are many to hear good things, there is no one to tell them. The world is full of priests, but seldom do we find a labourer in God's harvest. We do indeed receive the priestly office, but we do not carry out its work.[18]

Gregory expresses a number of concerns which arise from his fear that the Church is failing in its responsibility to fulfil this injunction. In particular, he voices grave doubts about the integrity of those who should respond to this imperative but who fail to understand or to live up to their responsibility.[19]

This Gregorian homily informed several of Bede's commentaries, including those on Mark and Luke.[20] Moreover, Bede's great investment in the pastoral work of the monastic church was profoundly indebted to Gregory's thought and

---

[16] See R.A. Markus, 'Gregory the Great and a Papal Missionary Strategy', *The Mission of the Church and the Propagation of the Faith*, ed. G.J. Cuming, Studies in Church History, 6 (1970), pp.29–38; W.D. Macready, *Signs of Sanctity: Miracles in the Thought of Gregory the Great*, Pontifical Institute of Medieval Studies: Studies and Texts, 91 (Toronto, 1989), pp.33–64; A. Thacker, 'Bede's Ideal of Reform', in *Ideal and Reality in Frankish and Anglo-Saxon Society*, ed. P. Wormald (Oxford, 1983), pp.130–53; *idem*, 'Bede and the Irish', in *Beda Venerabilis: Historian, Monk, and Northumbrian*, ed. L.A.R.J. Houwen and A.A. Macdonald (Gröningen, 1994), pp.31–59 (34–50).

[17] See C. Straw, *Gregory the Great: Perfection in Imperfection* (Berkeley and Los Angeles, California, 1988), pp.200–12; R.A. Markus, *Gregory the Great and his World* (Cambridge, 1997), pp.17–34;

[18] Gregory the Great, homily on Luke 10.1–9, *Homilia in Evangelia Libri Duo*, ed. J.P. Migne, *Patrologia Latina*, 76 cols 1075–1312 (1138–49); trans. D. Hurst, *Gregory the Great: Forty Gospel Homilies* (Kalamazoo, MI, 1990), no.19, pp.134–50. Compare Alcuin's expression of concern about the abuse and neglect of clerical and episcopal responsibility in *Epistolae* 136, p.209.

[19] On Gregory's conception of the preacher's role as one of nurture see in particular Straw, *Gregory*, pp.206–7.

[20] See Hurst's notes to this Gregorian homily, and also his editions of Bede's commentaries on Luke and Mark, *In Lucae Evangelium Expositio*, ed. D. Hurst, CCSL, 120 (Turnhout, 1960), pp.5–425; *In Marcae Evangelium Expositio*, ed. D. Hurst, CCSL, 120 (Turnhout, 1960), pp.431–648. See also M. Stansbury, 'Source-marks in Bede's Biblical Commentaries', in *Northumbria's Golden Age*, ed. J. Hawkes and S. Mills (Stroud, 1999), pp.383–9.

writing on the same subject, exemplified in this homily.[21] Bede, like Gregory, assumed the authority to speak out on matters concerning the state of the Church in his day, most famously in his letter to Egbert[22] but also in his historical and exegetical writings.[23] The *Historia Ecclesiastica* evidently influenced Alcuin's *Versus de Patribus, Regibus et Sanctis Euboricensis Ecclesiae* which is heavily indebted for its subject-matter to Bede's historiography.[24] Godman has argued that Bede influenced Alcuin's thought on the working relationship between secular and ecclesiastical authority, and that the long historical poem on York also confirms and extends Bede's representation in the *Historia Ecclesiastica* of the shared responsibilities of ecclesiastical and secular authority.[25]

Alcuin held Bede in a regard comparable to that which Bede had for Gregory. For Alcuin, both Gregory and Bede were servants of God who had responded positively to the Gospel injunction to labour, fulfilling through their lives of writing the responsibility that this conferred upon them. Alcuin's use, in his *Versus*, of the figurative language of irrigation and cultivation, shows how their dedication had been fundamental to the nurture and gathering of the Lord's harvest in Northumbria. Alcuin describes the outstanding contribution made by Bede to the intellectual and spiritual culture of Northumbrian monasticism, and refers emphatically to the authority of his works:[26] this repeated assertion of his reliance upon Bede's literary authority culminates in the description he gives of the Aelberht's library at York Minster, where Alcuin, *'doctrinae sitiens'*,[27] thirsting for knowledge, had been educated. Among the works with which Aelberht satisfied his pupil's thirst – books which are described as showers of refreshing rain from Heaven – are the works of *Beda magister*.[28] Bede's dedication to his scholarly and literary vocation produces books that are a source of spiritual sustenance for Alcuin in his youth and throughout his life.[29] Similarly, to celebrate the contribution made by Gregory to the establishment and growth of the Northumbrian church Alcuin draws again upon the figurative language of spiritual nurture, describing the pope as 'a thoroughly ardent tiller of the fields

---

[21] For analyses of Gregory's important influence on Bede, see P. Meyvaert, *Bede and Gregory the Great,* Jarrow Lecture (Newcastle-upon-Tyne, 1964); G.H. Brown, *Bede the Venerable* (Boston, Mass., 1989), pp.44–6, 48; S. DeGregorio, 'The Venerable Bede on Prayer and Contemplation', *Traditio,* 54 (1999), pp.1–39 (3–15).

[22] *Epistola ad Ecgberctum,* ed. C. Plummer, *Baedae Opera Historia,* 2 vols. (Oxford, 1896), I., pp.405–23.

[23] Thacker, 'Bede's Ideal of Reform', pp.130–46.

[24] *Alcuin: The Bishops, Kings and Saints of York,* ed. and trans. P. Godman (Oxford, 1982), pp.lxxv-lxxviii; lines 681–750, pp.56–63; lines 1301–19, pp.102–5.

[25] Godman, *Bishops, Kings and Saints,* pp.lviii-lx.

[26] See note 17 above.

[27] Godman, *Bishops, Kings and Saints,* line 1527, pp.120–1.

[28] *Ibid.,* lines 1394–1562, pp.108–27.

[29] See G.H. Brown, 'The Preservation and Transmission of Northumbrian Culture on the Continent: Alcuin's Debt to Bede', in *The Preservation and Transmission of Anglo-Saxon Culture: Selected Papers from the 1991 Meeting of the International Society of Anglo-Saxonists,* ed. P.E. Szarmach and J.T. Rosenthal, Studies in Medieval Culture, 40 (Kalamazoo, MI, 1997), pp.159–75.

of Christ'.[30] Alcuin would also describe himself, as abbot of Tours, as a kind of spiritual gardener, eager to graft onto the stock of his Frankish monks the learning of his native York:

> But I, your humble servant, lack sorely such scholarly books of the best erudition as I had in my native land through the virtuous and most devoted efforts of my teacher and through my own labour, such as it was. Therefore I suggest to your excellency . . . that I should send abroad some of our pupils, who might gather from there certain texts necessary to us, and bring back into Francia the flowers of Britain, so that York will no longer remain a garden enclosed, but the sproutings of Paradise and fruits of its orchard may be found in Tours, and so that as the east wind, when it comes, blows on the gardens of the river Loire, and their perfumes flow through the air, that which follows in the Song of Songs, from which I have added the following lesson, may be renewed: 'My love comes into the garden, and eats the fruit of his trees', and says to his youths, 'Eat, my friends, drink and be joyful, my beloved. I sleep, and my heart wakes'; or again the prophet Isaiah's exhortation to wisdom, 'Come to the waters, all you who thirst. And whoever has no money, take and eat without delay; come, take without money and without any trading wine and milk'.[31]

The use of this figurative language to describe the work of the Christian educator is a recurrent and an important motif of Northumbrian narratives of evangelism. It is particularly associated with veneration of Gregory: the earliest life of this pope, written at Whitby between 704–714 uses this theme to support the argument that he was the special patron and teacher of the Northumbrians, who continues to nurture their faith through the influence of his writings:

> To speak truly, there are some now, and indeed there have been some before us, who through the Holy Spirit were so conspicuous by their teaching that innumerable people throughout the world have been watered by the rain-showers of their words, and 'bring forth fruit in patience', imitators of Him who 'gave himself for us, an offering and a sacrifice to God in a sweet odour'. Among these we number Gregory, the man mentioned previously, our apostolic saint, and would that we too might be numbered with him.[32]

The saintly pastor Cuthbert is represented in comparable terms in Bede's metrical *vita*,[33] and so are the exemplary founder abbots of Lindisfarne and Jarrow, Aidan and Ceolfrid in the accounts of their lives given in the *Historia Ecclesiastica*[34] and the *Vita S. Ceolfridi*.[35] This figurative language is, in fact, used consistently throughout the surviving works of Northumbrian history, to describe the work

[30] Godman, *Bishops, Kings and Saints*, lines 79–89, pp.10–11.
[31] Alcuin, *Epistolae*, 121, pp.176–8.
[32] *The Earliest Life of Gregory*, c.5, p.80.
[33] *Bedas Metrische Vita S. Cuthberti*, ed. W. Jaeger, *Palaestra*, 198 (Leipzig, 1935), lines 13–18, p.59, lines 690–2, p.110.
[34] *Bede's Ecclesiastical History*, ed. B. Colgrave and R.A.B. Mynors (Oxford, 1969), III.5, pp.228–9.
[35] *Vita Abbatum auctore anonymo*, ed. C. Plummer, *Baedae Opera Historica*, I, pp. 388–404, c.11, p.392.

of abbots, bishops and saints, and is deployed with considerable resource and elegance. It unifies, in the Northumbrian historiographical tradition, the narratives of evangelism which so strongly inform the sense of continuing mission in the Anglo-Saxon Church.

Alcuin's adoption of this same figurative language of spiritual nurture to describe the contributions of Gregory and Bede as authors to this continuing mission is significant because it clearly has implications for his own self-conception as an author. If monastic writers such as Gregory and Bede can respond to Christ's injunction through their literary labour, in a way which complements the more active pastoral and missionary role of saints like Aidan and Cuthbert in the Northumbrian church, this defines Alcuin's own responsibility in the expansion of the Carolingian Church. The language of Luke's gospel is important not only because its imagery gives resonance to the historical narrative of conversion,[36] but also because it expresses with authority a continuing imperative. Gregory, Bede and Alcuin all respond to Christ's injunction in Luke 10.1–7 by recognising this as a call to evangelism during the present and in the future of the Church.[37] The labour that Christ commands defines the role of the Christian author, both as it is described in retrospect and as it should be fulfilled in the present – for example, by Alcuin in Charlemagne's Francia. This leads us to the question of how this understanding informs Alcuin's writing: how does literary strategy perform apostolic labour in the fields of the Carolingian Christian empire?

It has been shown already that in hortatory letters Alcuin urges upon Charlemagne the relevance of the Gospel injunction to the work of the Church in Francia. During the 780s and 790s and the early years of the ninth century, the period during which he sent these letters, Alcuin also wrote four works honouring missionary saints who were celebrated for their apostolic role in the expansion of the church: these were St Richarius, who led a mission among the Britons (781x804);[38] St Vedastus, who had been instrumental in the conversion of Clovis (c.796);[39] a relative, compatriot and near contemporary, Willibrord, the apostle of Frisia (785x97);[40] and Martin of Tours (802–4).[41] It is to the *Vita S. Willibrordi* that I shall turn briefly now, in order to illustrate how Alcuin, in writing hagiography, participates as an author in the labour of the harvest.

---

[36] On the relationship between rhetoric and historical narrative see C.B. Kendall, 'Bede's *Historia Ecclesiastica*; the Rhetoric of Faith', in *Medieval Eloquence*, ed. J.J. Murphy (Berkeley and L.A., 1978), pp.145–72.

[37] Compare *Epistolae* 113, p.164, in which Alcuin points out to Arno, bishop of Salzburg, the continuing force, for the contemporary Frankish church, of Christ's commands to 'teach all nations'.

[38] *Vita Richarii Confessoris Centulensis*, ed. B. Krusch, *MGH* Scriptores Rerum Merovingicarum, IV, pp.381–401.

[39] *Vita Vedastis Episcopi Atrebatensis*, ed. B. Krusch, *MGH* Scriptores Rerum Merovingicarum, III, pp.414–27.

[40] *Vita Willibrordi Archiespiscopi Traiectensis* (prose), ed. W. Levison, *MGH* Scriptores Rerum Germanicarum, VII, pp.81–141. *Vita Willibrordi Archiespiscopi Traiectensis* (verse) ed. D. Dummler, *MGH* Poetarum Latinorum Medii Aevi, I, pp.207–20.

[41] *De Vita S. Martini Turonensis*, PL, 101, cols. 657–64.

The *Vita S. Willibrordi* is the longest of Alcuin's *vitae*, a bi-partite work comprising prose and metrical versions of the narrative of Willibrord's career. In his preface to the *Vita*, in which he dedicates the work to the Echternach community who claim Willibrord as their special patron, Alcuin explains his decision to adopt this distinctive form:

> I have compiled two little books, one pacing in prose speech which (if it seems to you worthy) might be publicly read to the brothers in the church, and the other running in Pyrrhic metre, which should be meditated upon among your scholars, in private.[42]

Clearly, Alcuin sees the relationship between the style and the function of the text as important: in the fulfilment of his literary responsibility towards the Echternach community, Alcuin tells us that he has assessed the different capacities and needs of members of this community, and that he exploits the potential of prose and verse style in order to meet these.[43] Decisions about literary strategy are explicitly related to Alcuin's responsibility, as an author commissioned by Abbot Beornraed to write the *vita* of Echternach's patron, to produce a text which will contribute to the spiritual life of the community.

Alcuin's preface to his *Vita S. Richarii*, which represents a revision of existing writings associated with the saint's cult, indicates his sensitivity to the relation between the text's language and its function: here he claims that he has respected the preference of the audience for which he writes for simple, 'unpolished' prose.[44] In the deliberately sophisticated *Vita S. Willibrordi*, however, the deployment of figurative language makes an important contribution to a text of spiritual education. A prominent stylistic element of Alcuin's literary strategy in the bi-partite *Vita* is his use of the figurative language of spiritual nurture, which as we have seen is closely associated with the continuing narrative of evangelism.

Alcuin's use of figurative language in this text is complex, but brief reference to three examples will be sufficient to demonstrate the cornerstones of his strategy. The first use of the figurative language of spiritual nurture, which establishes its significance in the *Vita S. Willibrordi*, occurs in the fifth chapter of the prose life. Here, Alcuin describes the inception of Willibrord's mission to the Frisians:

---

[42] *Vita S. Willibrordi* (prose), p.113.
[43] On the relationship between the style and function of the hagiographical text see M. Lapidge, 'Bede's Metrical *Vita S. Cuthberti*', in *St Cuthbert: His Cult and his Community to AD 1200*, G. Bonner, D. Rollason and C. Stancliffe (Woodbridge, 1990), pp.77–94; see also Godman, 'Alcuin's York Poem', pp.149–77; M. Garrison, 'Alcuin's World through his Letters and Verse', Ph.D. thesis (Cambridge, 1996), pp.64–130. On the relationship between literary language, the educative potential of the text, and the competence of the reader, as this was perceived in the Anglo-Saxon educational tradition, see M.H. King, 'Grammatica Mystica; a Study of Bede's Grammatical Curriculum', in *Saints, Scholars and Heroes: Studies in Medieval Culture in Honour of CW Jones*, ed. M.H. King and W. Stevens, 2 vols. (Collegeville, MN, 1979), I, pp.145–59.
[44] *Vita S. Richarii*, p.389.

> In the thirty-third year of his age, the fervour of [Willibrord's] faith had reached such an intensity that he considered it of little value to labour at his own sanctification unless he could preach the gospel to others and bring some benefit to them. He had heard that in the northern regions of the world the harvest was great but the labourers were few. . . . [Pippin] received him with every mark of respect; and as he was unwilling that he and his people should lose so great a teacher, he made over to [Willibrord] certain localities within the boundaries of his own realm, where he could uproot idolatrous practices, teach the newly converted people and so fulfil the command of the prophet [Jeremiah]: 'Drive a new furrow, and sow no longer among the briars'.[45]

Here, Alcuin draws again on the Gospel account of Christ's words that drives the polemic of his letter to Megenfrid. Willibrord's sense of vocation is represented here as a direct response to Christ's injunction, while Pippin's part is clearly presented as an enlightened compliance that contributes to the fulfilment both of this injunction and of Jeremiah's prophecy.

Alcuin's introduction of the figurative language of spiritual nurture in this chapter is as deliberate as it is crucial to the narrative of the *Vita*. He proceeds to build upon this image of Willibrord as a labourer in Christ's fields, driving his furrow amongst the Frisians, through the reiteration of this figurative language throughout the two versions of the *Vita*. Willibrord's commitment to preaching and conversion, and the achievements of his mission, are consistently represented in terms of sowing, irrigation, cultivation, and nourishment.[46] This figurative language of spiritual nurture informs the metrical version of the *Vita*, in which Alcuin describes Willibrord 'watering the hearts of all with the dew of Christ' as strongly as it does the prose.[47] Through the consistent use of this language Alcuin prompts his audience to interpret Willibrord's mission as an apostolic continuation of the labour enjoined upon the disciples by Christ.

Moreover, Alcuin uses the same figurative language in the homily which he appends to the *Vita S. Willibrordi*, in order to encourage his Echternach audience to regard themselves as the fruit of that labour: their faith is the flowering of Willibrord's initiative. In a prayerfully apostrophic passage, appealing for Willibrord's benevolent intercession on their behalf, the Echternach brethren are described as his sons who, in the words of psalm, multiply 'like the cedars of Lebanon'.[48] Alcuin's sustained use of the figurative language of spiritual nurture is directed towards this celebratory confirmation of the identity and unity of the present Ecthernach community, a fruition that arises from and witnesses to Willibrord's apostolic labour in the Lord's harvest.

---

[45] *Vita S. Willibrordi* (prose), pp.119–20.
[46] See for example *Vita S. Willibrordi* (prose), c.8, p.123, c.9, p123, c.12, p.126; (verse), c.8, p.123; c.16, p.212.
[47] *Vita S. Willibrordi* (verse), c.6, p.210.
[48] *Homily*, appended to *Vita S Willibrordi* (prose), p.140; see Psalm 91.12–14.

This flowering of the narrative of evangelism in the representation of the Echternach community can be read in relation to Alcuin's vision of a mission that continues to grow in the present, and which has a future as well as a past. Alcuin's sustained use of the figurative language of spiritual nurture, springing from Christ's injunction to labour in the Lord's fields, creates a strong resonance between the *Vita S. Willibrordi* and Alcuin's polemical letter to Megenfrid. If the letter urges Carolingian secular authority to fulfil Christ's imperative in the new fields of the empire, the *Vita S. Willibrordi* complements that argument by providing a paradigm for this labour. This *Vita* articulates many of the same moral and practical concerns about the labour of conversion that recur in Alcuin's letters, through narratives which provide clear examples for the conduct of the missionary preacher and, equally importantly, the secular and ecclesiastical authorities which support his work.[49] I have mentioned that Pippin's support for Willibrord is approvingly described as a contribution to the fulfilment, in the saint's mission, of the prophecy of Jeremiah. The *Vita* also records Pope Sergius' support for Willibrord: by consecrating him as archbishop and by establishing his see at Utrecht Sergius complies with divine instruction revealed through an angelic messenger.[50] In particular, Alcuin illustrates in his vitae the principle, expounded in his letters with reference to Augustine's *De Catechizandis Rudibus*, that an adult catechumenate must be converted through education, if their faith is to be well-founded.[51] Willibrord's attempt to convert the pagan King Radbod, although it is unsuccessful, is carefully described because it is an opportunity for Alcuin to present a paradigm for the kind of education advocated by Augustine: Willibrord attempts to convert the King through instruction – faith must arise from understanding.[52] Alcuin also describes Willibrord's evangelical forward planning: although the Danes reject the faith when the saint goes to preach to them, he decides instead to adopt and educate their boys as a future missionary labour-force.[53] In his *Vita S. Vedasti* also, Alcuin places particular emphasis on the importance of the education of the catechumen, in preparation for baptism.[54] These *Vitae* can be read, like Alcuin's letters, as purposeful interventions in their contemporary political and ideological contexts. Alcuin's *Vitae* reflect, both through their sustained use of figurative language associated with the theme of evangelism, and through the prominent place they give to exemplary narratives of missionary labour, their author's conception of his literary responsibility as a rhetorical, even perhaps polemical, contribution to the continuing mission of the church.

[49] Although constraints of space preclude discussion of the *Vitae* of Vedastus and Richarius, similar interests are evident in Alcuin's narratives of their saintly careers: see for example *Vita S. Vedasti*, c.2, pp.417–8; *Vita S. Richarii*, cc.8–9, pp.393–4.

[50] *Vita S. Willibrordi* (prose), cc.6–7, pp.121–2.

[51] See Bullough, 'Alcuin and the Kingdom of Heaven', pp.188–92

[52] Compare Bede's account of the conversion of Edwin by Paulinus: *Historia Ecclesiastica* II.9–14, pp.162–89.

[53] *Vita S. Willibrordi* (prose), c.9, pp.123–4.

[54] *Vita S. Vedastis*, c.4, p.419.

Although it is dedicated to an Echternach audience, the *Vita S. Willibrordi* articulates through its sustained and resonant figurative language, and through its exemplary narrative, principles that have broad relevance within an expanding Carolingian church. Alcuin invests in his *Vita S. Willibrordi* a degree of literary skill that matches the energy with which he exhorts Megenfrid to promote the cause of evangelism with Charlemagne. The consistency between these writings, united in spite of their generic difference by the crucial references to the gospel account of Christ's command to his disciples, is eloquent of Alcuin's commitment to his own responsibility as an author in an age of conversion. By devoting his literary skills – demonstrated here in his expertly sustained use of the figurative language of spiritual nurture – to the service both of the Echternach community and of the Carolingian church as a whole, Alcuin aspires to emulate the authorial role that he attributes to Gregory and Bede. Alcuin's *Vita* is a work written in conformity with his sense of the moral responsibility of literary authority: it is a form of labour in the harvest, which uses language and narrative as the means of reinforcing the imperative of, and providing a paradigm for, continuing evangelical effort. The *Vita S. Willibrordi*, like Bede's *Historia Ecclesiastica* or Gregory's *Dialogi*, represents the fulfilment of this responsibility through an historical narrative that articulates principles which should inform the present and the future of the age of conversion.

24

Pagans and Christians at a Frontier: Viking Burial in the Danelaw

JULIAN D. RICHARDS

The Vikings are the victims of cultural stereotyping (see e.g. Wawn 2000). In the popular imagination they provide the comic-book archetypal pagans: marauding shaggy war bands living and dying by the sword, with no respect for person or property, and least of all for the hallowed monasteries and clerics of Anglo-Saxon England. They worshipped violent and unforgiving Gods who inhabited the dark places of Northern Europe and they sacrificed animals and humans with complete disregard for Christian ethics. The Viking warrior aspired to the glorious death which would convey him on the journey to Valhalla where he would feast until Ragnorök.

On the other hand, the scholarly world, faced with an acute lack of archaeological evidence for Pagan hordes, has created an alternative stereotype of the peaceful immigrant and trader eager to take on all the trappings of the host society, including its religion. In Anglo-Saxon England, within the space of a single generation, pagan warriors had become Christian farmers. Christian burial was rapidly adopted (Wilson 1967), many choosing to be buried in churchyards (Graham-Campbell 1980). By the tenth century their ferocious leaders were commissioning stone crosses and establishing private chapels on their new estates.

> [the] Evidence . . . all points to wide acceptance of the new faith already by the end of the ninth century. In the first decade of the tenth century the Danes can still be classed 'pagans' by their enemies, but this is the last indication of any continuation of heathen religion. (Whitelock 1941, 175)

Those Vikings who, after the late ninth-century partitions of land in East Anglia, Northumbria and Mercia, settled in the area later known as the Danelaw, were amongst the first Scandinavians to adopt Christianity. They were Christian at least two or three generations before Harold Bluetooth's claim to the conversion of Denmark (Roesdahl 1997). The rapid conversion of Scandinavian settlers, so we are led to believe, demonstrates the weakness of their own pagan religions in the face of an all-embracing Christianity, and provides another example of their eagerness to become assimilated.

Both stereotypes, however, mask a variety of strategies and circumstances, and a number of recent contributions have highlighted this diversity. Abrams (2000, 2001) has suggested that the act of conversion should be distinguished from a longer process of Christianisation. Several authors (e.g. Sidebottom 2000, Stocker 2000, Stocker and Everson 2001) have shown how the adoption of Anglo-Scandinavian sculptural traditions may be linked to wider secular agendas. Hadley (2000; 2001) and Halsall (2000) have described the variety of burial practices in Late Saxon England which defies simple classification into pagan and Christian. Even within a relatively small Scandinavian colony different approaches might be adopted in different situations. At Balladoole, for example, on the south-east coast of the Isle of Man, a Christian cemetery was deliberately disturbed and desecrated when a Viking ship burial was inserted and the partially articulated remains of recent Christian burials were re-interred within the mound (Richards 1991, 106; Tarlow 1997). At Peel Castle, by contrast, on the west coast of the island, the so-called 'Pagan Lady' and other accompanied 'Scandinavian-style' burials were actually interred in a Christian style stone-lined cist grave which respected existing graves (Richards 1991, 103). Elsewhere, such as in the case of the ship burial at Scar on Orkney, it has been suggested that the pagan burials might not be those of the first generation settlers, but might date instead to a later phase during which a small group sought to reassert paganism (Owen and Dalland 1999).

It is the purpose of this chapter to demonstrate further that conversion might not be so much a matter of individual conscience as a question of social and political expediency. Religion may be used actively in the process of the creation and re-invention of group identities. Furthermore, it is performed within a social and political landscape of allegiances and obligations, but it also takes place within a physical landscape, and geographical space may be used to define distinct spheres of activity. For archaeologists, burial is one of the most observable physical manifestations of this.

I will discuss burials in the vicinity of Repton, Derbyshire, associated with a specific historically attested event, that is, the over-wintering of the Viking Great Army in 873–4 (Fig. 24.1). This provides a case study of the adoption of paganism and Christianity according to political expediency and of the promotion of alternative burial rites as part of the creation and reinforcement of group identity within a landscape setting.

Repton is extremely unusual for the concentration of pagan burials within a small area. Around the church and shrine of St Wystan there are a number of individual accompanied burials, including an exceptional warrior grave, as well as a large burial mound apparently incorporating a central inhumation set within a substantial charnel deposit. This is in itself a unique phenomenon but only 4 km away, at Heath Wood, Ingleby, there are the remains of the only known Scandinavian cremation cemetery in the British Isles. Both sites have become better understood in recent years. Excavations at Repton in 1974–93 by Martin Biddle and Birthe Kjølbye-Biddle have revealed the remains of the Viking winter

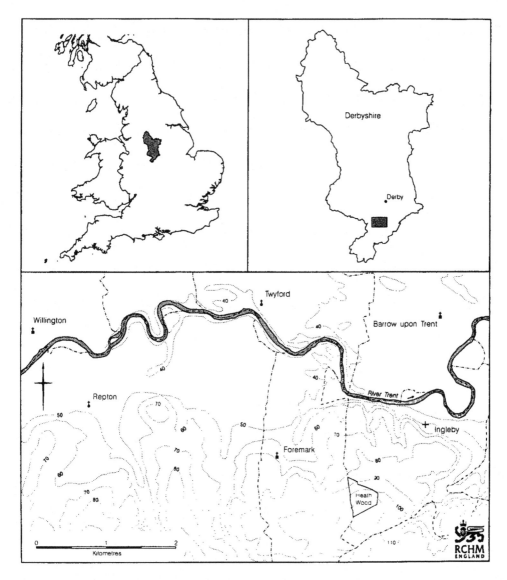

Figure 24.1 Map of the central Trent area showing the location of Repton and the burial mound cemetery at Heath Wood (Crown copyright)

camp. Although full publication is awaited, the interim accounts (Biddle and Kjølbye-Biddle 1992, 2001) provide sufficient detail to allow provisional interpretation. Antiquarian investigations and more recent topographic survey at Heath Wood have been summarised (Richards *et al.* 1995) and (whilst the full report is also in preparation) the results of excavation in 1998–2000 have been outlined (Richards 2000, 148) (Fig. 24.2). Understanding the survival of pagan burial in this small part of South Derbyshire may help illuminate the nature of conversion elsewhere.

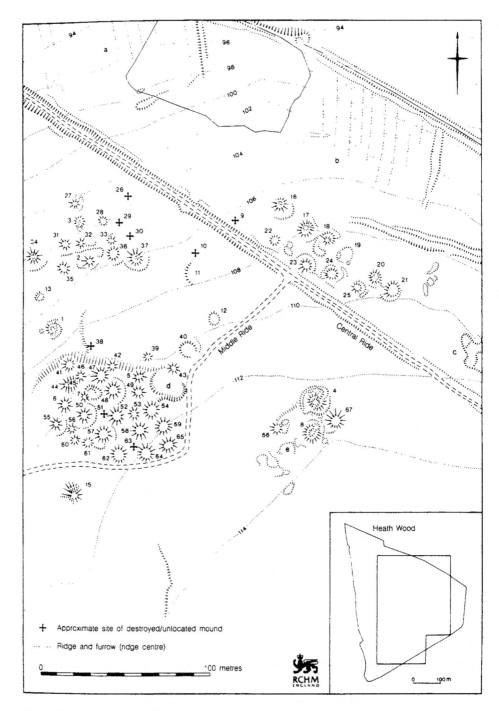

Figure 24.2 Topographical map of the Heath Wood cemetery (Crown copyright)

The first question must focus on why such a range of burial strategies is found concentrated in this location, when it is not found elsewhere in the Danelaw. To answer this we must consider the political and ideological significance of Repton. By the late ninth century Repton was one of the principal ecclesiastical centres of England, and was closely associated with the power of the Mercian royal family. A monastery had been established here in the seventh century. It appears to have been a double house for men and women ruled by an abbess of noble, possibly royal, rank (Biddle and Kjølbye-Biddle 2001, 50). Several of the kings of the Mercian house were buried at Repton, including Aethelbald after his murder at Seckington in 757. In 849 Wigstan (Wystan) was brought to Repton after his murder in a struggle over the succession to the Mercian throne. Wigstan was buried in the mausoleum of his grandfather Wiglaf (827–840). This is almost certainly the crypt which survives beneath the chancel. Miracles took place at the tomb and the entrances to the crypt were lengthened to deal with the flow of pilgrims (Biddle and Kjølbye-Biddle 2001, 52). Before the end of the ninth century, Wigstan had come to be regarded as a saint. By this stage the church had a north and south porticus, and a chancel over the mausoleum, with burials to the south and east. Excavation has revealed evidence for multi-coloured window glass and exceptional stone sculpture. To the west, now within the area of the vicarage garden, there was also a two-roomed stone structure, probably a mortuary chapel.

From 865 England was subject to escalating Viking raids by a highly mobile force led by Ivar the Boneless and his brother Halfdan. It is difficult to get a clear understanding of the size of this army, beyond the fact that the Anglo-Saxon Chroniclers considered it to be 'Great', and the fact that it regularly over-wintered in England. After the conquest of Northumbria in 866, and East Anglia in 869, Alfred Smyth has suggested that the Great Army was reinforced by what the Anglo-Saxon Chronicle describes as the Summer Army, before it forced Wessex to make peace in 871 (1977, 240–3). The combined force was subsequently active in various parts of the extended kingdom of Mercia.

In the autumn of 873 the Great Army arrived at Repton and took over the monastic complex, driving the Mercian king Burgred into exile in Rome, and placing one of his thegns, Ceolwulf, on the throne as their puppet king. The Anglo-Saxon Chronicle records that the army took *wintersetl*, or winter quarters, there. Their choice had a symbolic as well as a tactical significance. The seizure of one of the holy places of Christendom could not have gone unnoticed; its continued occupation suggests a desire to gain whatever authority might rub off by association. But Repton also occupied a strategic location. The church of St Wystan was built on a prominent bluff on the south side of the flood plain of the River Trent. The river now flows on the far side of the valley, 1 km to the north, but originally flowed on the Repton side, at the foot of a low cliff. Repton therefore lay at an important junction of the main routes across the Trent and along the valley. In late ninth-century England this was an important frontier and a key point for the control of the Midlands.

The Great Army invested considerable effort in remodelling the site, and the monastic church, into a defensive enclosure. A large V-shaped ditch, 4 m deep × 8 m across at the top, was dug to create a D-shaped enclosure, enclosing an area of 1.46 ha (3.65 acres) with the church in the middle of its south side, so that the doors in the north and south sides of the nave provided a defended entrance way, and the cliff of the Trent valley providing the long straight side of the D.

Several groups of burials have been associated by the Biddles with the over-wintering of 873–874, including inhumations adjacent to the chancel, and the charnel deposit with its central burial in the former mortuary chapel. In their published interpretations of these graves the Biddles have cogently argued for the pagan Viking character of several aspects of their discoveries (Biddle and Kjølbye-Biddle 1992, 2001). Although the evidence is persuasive, some qualification is necessary.

The most obvious 'Viking' is the warrior aged at least 35–45 (Grave 511) buried immediately to the north of the chancel, within the defended enclosure. A second male, aged 17 to 20 (Grave 295), buried soon after and adjacent to the warrior, is interpreted by Martin Biddle and Birthe Kjølbye-Biddle as perhaps representing his weapon bearer. The man buried in Grave 511 had met a very violent death, presumably in battle. It now appears that he had been killed by the thrust of a sharp implement through the eye which had penetrated the orbital socket and gone into the brain, presumably caused by a sword point finding a vulnerable spot on the head which was unprotected by the helmet (*Blood of the Vikings* 2001). However, before or after death he had also received several cuts to the arm, and a great slashing blow to the top of his left femur which would also have removed his genitals. Cuts to the lower vertebrae, inflicted from the stomach cavity also imply he was disembowelled. This detailed description is necessary in order to emphasise the grisly treatment that at least one of the Viking Great Army had received from the Christian defenders of a Mercian royal monastery. In most aspects his burial was that appropriate for a great pagan warrior, slain in battle. He was buried wearing a Thor's hammer amulet, and his sword was placed by his side. A boar's tusk was placed between his thighs, presumably to make up for what he had lost, in case it proved necessary in Valhalla. Further down a jackdaw, or ?raven, humerus was also placed between his legs, perhaps invoking Odin. On the other hand we should note that, although not in the monastic cemetery, he was buried on an east-west alignment immediately adjacent to a Christian shrine, and that the mausoleum to St Wystan was apparently retained intact during the Viking occupation. Given the powerful associations of burial next to saintly relics, at the very least this was someone for whom the options were being kept open.

Martin Biddle and Birthe Kjølbye-Biddle state that 'there are several other burials of Scandinavian type' adjacent to the chancel (Biddle and Kjølbye-Biddle 2001, 65). These are listed as Grave 529, a man aged 25–35 also buried north of the chancel, with a gold finger ring and five silver pennies datable to the mid-870s. They also note that burial continued south of the chancel, in the established monastic cemetery. Individually itemised graves from this area include Grave 83, a man aged about 50 with a copper alloy ring, and Grave 84, a younger man, aged about 20, adjacent. There is also Grave 203, a woman aged about 45 with an iron knife and a strike-a-light, although it is suggested that the latter could have been buried up to a generation later. Although these graves include a few personal objects there does not appear to be anything particularly Scandinavian or pagan about them, and the evidence for them being Scandinavian appears to rest upon their association with Grave 511. Grave 52 is also singled out as being the possible source of a bearded axe, but as this was found as a chance find in 1923 the association has to remain uncertain.

Martin Biddle and Birthe Kjølbye-Biddle also suggest that the charnel deposit from the western mortuary chapel and its central burial should be seen in the context of the 873–874 over-wintering. They present persuasive arguments that the central burial, disturbed c.1686, was probably that of Ivar the Boneless (2001, 81–4). I see no reason to argue with that, but would question their identification of the charnel deposit as comprising mainly the remains of the Viking Great Army. The dating, derived from a second packet of five coins, is consistent with 873–874, and certainly associates the general assemblage with the over-wintering, even if the precise provenance of the coins is uncertain. The critical factor about the deposit, however, is that it is very clearly derived from disinterred and reburied skeletons. The total minimum number of individuals is 264, based on 253 left adult femurs and 11 juvenile right tibias. However, the percentage of the smaller bones recovered from these individuals is much lower, with only 32% of the vertebrae, for example, and less than 2% of the finger and toe bones. When decayed bodies are disturbed and re-buried it would be expected that the smaller bones would be lost. The other pertinent facts are that approximately 20% of the bodies were female, and that the sixteen radiocarbon dates show at least two populations, the first dated to the late seventh or early eighth centuries, and the second group to the later ninth century. The Biddles (2001, 79) propose three possibilities for the origins of the earlier bones: that they represent the primary burials in the mortuary chapel, that they are ancestral Viking remains brought with the Army from Scandinavia, and that all the bodies were brought from elsewhere. Although they conclude that the latter explanation is the most likely they still argue that the later bodies are those of the Great Army disinterred from their primary resting places and brought to Repton, having become contaminated with earlier burials. The principle evidence for a substantial Scandinavian component to the charnel deposit is the physical anthropological evidence, from which the Biddles conclude that 'the male bones from the mass burial are massive and suggest a selected group, such as would be the case if the cemetery of a Guards regiment was studied and compared with the contemporary local population' (Biddle and Kjølbye-Biddle 2001, 78).

However, a robust and predominantly male group need not necessarily equate with an incoming military elite, and the well-fed and aristocratic inhabitants of a Mercian monastery are also likely to have had a larger stature than the average

Anglo-Saxon peasant or slave. Is there any reason to look further than the burials of the original monastic cemetery for the origins of the Repton charnel? In digging the great V-shaped ditch the Great Army cut through the established area of burial south of the chancel. It might have seemed a natural, if not particularly pagan, activity to collect the more obvious bones for reburial, and the existing mortuary chapel, outside the enclosure, would have provided a logical home. This explanation would fit the long date range of the charnel deposit and also, given Repton was a double house, the small proportion of female bones. It would also be in keeping with the general lack of weapon trauma on the charnel bones. The smaller proportions of older and younger individuals in the charnel deposit compared to the monastic cemetery might initially suggest it was drawn from a different population, but this can again be explained by differential survival and recovery of smaller and more fragile bones.

This is not to say that the Great Army was not responsible for the Repton charnel; or that they did not choose to bury one of their leaders as the central grave. The charnel bones might still include a few remains of re-interred warriors, but this was not its primary purpose. Nonetheless, it would be a mistake to regard it simply as a rather convenient and prosaic collection point for bones disturbed in the course of earthwork construction. The symbolism of re-arranging the bones of Mercian monks and aristocrats around the psychopath Ivar would not have been lost on the conquering Army. They also truncated the Mercian royal mortuary chapel, levelled it with sand, gave it a stone kerb, and turned it into a mound. The Biddles further suggest that four teenagers, buried together next to the mound, were sacrificed as part of the burial ritual. This may be the case, although their skeletons bear no signs of violent injury.

I am certainly not suggesting that the Repton charnel deposit is not the work of pagans, but would argue that it was designed to reflect a degree of accommodation with the existing establishment. This includes a continuity of purpose, and a deliberate and clear association between Mercian and Viking remains, and between the Anglo-Saxon shrine and the Viking winter camp. This continuity is also reflected by the fact that the area of the charnel mound continued in use for aristocratic burial, with a later cemetery, including burials of those with fine jewellery and costume, drawn up around it. Similarly, in 1801–2 a hogback monument was found to the west of St Wystan's church. This is too late to be associated with the Great Army, and should date to the period 920–970. We know little of the immediate history of St Wystan's church after the Great Army departed, although by the first quarter of the tenth century it was an important minster church, serving a large region of South Derbyshire (Biddle and Kjølbye-Biddle 2001, 53). Apparently those continuing to require burial associated with the shrine also continued to include members of the local Danish aristocracy. Given that the Great Army gained control of Mercia not by its destruction but by putting their own candidate on the throne, none of this should be surprising. Those Vikings buried at Repton were seeking to legitimate their own succession by their association with the Mercian royal house, and whilst a few maintained

Plate 24.1 Burial mound at Heath Wood under excavation (Richards)

some pagan trappings, the majority found it expedient to allow themselves to be converted to Christianity.

This strategy was not, however, shared by everyone who was in the Viking Army that arrived at Repton in 873. Repton is overlooked by a number of low hills that run parallel with the Trent Valley. Some 4 km to the south-east is a block of woodland known as Heath Wood. The plantation is relatively recent and in the ninth century this was open heath land commanding impressive views northwards across the Trent Plain. Further east lies the village of Ingleby, perhaps distinctive because it was a surviving enclave of the English in an area that was now under Danish control. It was on the brow of the hill now known as Heath Wood, however, that another group of Vikings chose to commemorate their dead with a more conventional pagan burial rite than that adopted by their compatriots in Repton. Excavations at Heath Wood, Ingleby, have revealed a Scandinavian cremation cemetery of some 60 mounds, of which about a third have now been excavated (Pl. 24.1).

Excavations have revealed that many of the mounds contain *in situ* cremation hearths comprising charcoal, ash and burnt bone, of people as well as animal offerings, including remains of cow, horse, sheep, pig and dog. Despite the poor preservation conditions there are also traces of objects which had been deliberately placed on the pyres, as well as items of personal dress. The former include two mutilated swords (from Mounds 1 and 7), a large number of nails (also from Mound 7), possibly from the binding of a leather shield, and a number of nails from other objects. The latter include a number of iron buckles and copper alloy loops, a fragment of wire wool embroidery (from Mound 11), and a ring-headed pin (from Mound 56). Previous accounts have suggested that many of the mounds were empty, and may have represented a cenotaph style memorial for those given Christian burial elsewhere (Posnansky 1956, Richards *et al.* 1995). However these conclusions were based on partial trenching of the burial mounds. Open area excavation of two mounds, Mounds 50 and 56, in 1998–2000, has revealed two forms of the cremation rite. Mound 50 contained an *in situ* cremation hearth with a mass of charcoal and cremated bone covering an area of approximately 2 m × 3 m within the centre of the mound. Mound 56, on the other hand, contained only a small patch of redeposited charcoal and bone, as well as the ring-headed pin, on the edge of the mound. This body must have been cremated elsewhere, and only a token deposit placed within the mound, which was otherwise completely empty. Incomplete excavation would have quite easily missed these ephemeral traces, so it seems likely that each of the Heath Wood mounds represented at least one cremation. Indeed, analysis of the remains from Mound 50 suggests the presence of at least two individuals (J. McKinley pers. comm.), and this could also have been the case for those bone assemblages examined in the 1940s and 1950s.

Although further analysis may provide more precise dating, at the moment there is nothing to definitely link the Ingleby burials to the over-wintering of 873–874. However, it is very difficult to see any other possible context. Given that St Wystan's church and the winter camp and Heath Wood would have been inter-visible and also that the presence of the Great Army in 873–874 is beyond doubt, it would be perverse to try to associate the Heath Wood burials with some unidentified and unassociated event. Furthermore the excavated evidence appears to show that the Heath Wood mounds were erected within a relatively short space of time. Indeed, given the almost complete lack of cremation burial from elsewhere in the Danelaw, it is intrinsically unlikely that settled farmers in South Derbyshire, and they alone, would retain an alien burial rite. There is also one specific similarity with Repton. The mortuary chapel was prepared for the charnel deposit by levelling it with a layer of clean sand. The erection of Mounds 50 and 56 was undertaken by first removing the topsoil from across the area, and then digging into the bed rock to create a ring ditch, giving an approximate outline for the mound. The interior of each mound was then levelled with a 10 cm thick layer of clean sand. In the case of Mound 50 the cremation pyre was then built directly on this surface, and the mound thrown up over it. In each case the layer of clean sand can be interpreted as having some ritual cleansing function.

The Heath Wood burials are otherwise very different from those at Repton. Cremation goes back to the pagan burial forms as practised in ninth-century Sweden, Denmark and Norway. In *Heimskringla*, Snorri Sturluson notes that Odin's Law:

> decreed that all the dead should be burned, and put on the funeral pyre with all their possessions. He also said that everyone should come to Valhalla with all the property that he had on the pyre, and he should also enjoy the

use of what he had himself buried in the earth, and mounds should be raised in memory of men of rank. (Sturluson 1964)

A very definite commitment to paganism is demonstrated at Heath Wood by the performance of cremation rites and animal sacrifice in conjunction with mound burial. Rather than peaceful, permanent, stable settlement the barrow cemetery at Heath Wood seems to reflect instability and insecurity of some sort. In this way, the Heath Wood burials might represent a deliberate and physically imposing allusion to the pagan homeland of those who produced them: a statement of religious, political and military affiliation in unfamiliar and inhospitable surroundings.

The outstanding question is then why did those over-wintering at Repton react to the local circumstances in such different ways? To answer this I have suggested (Richards 2001) that we need to go back to the disparate composition of the Great Army:

> The invaders cannot be treated as a large amorphous mass under the convenient label of the Great Army on the assumption that the *micel here* which arrived in 865 was the only significant body of invaders
> (Smyth 1977, 241)

On its departure from winter quarters in Repton the army split into two bands, perhaps reflecting the two forces which had been combined:

> For nine years the miscellaneous Danish force had acted as a single military unit. In the autumn of 874 it fell apart into two armies which were never reunited   (Stenton 1943, 250–1).

This was not simply spontaneous fragmentation because of numbers but the result of a specific agreement between Halfdan and Guthrum. Halfdan's army was tired of war and returned to Northumbria where in 876 he and his men 'shared out the land of the Northumbrians, and they proceeded to plough and support themselves' Guthrum, Oscytel and Anund, on the other hand, left Repton to march on East Anglia and then to wage renewed war on Wessex.

One explanation for the different burial and conversion strategies represented at Repton and Heath Wood, therefore, might be that the two cemeteries represent a division in the Viking camp, the first group preferring legitimation through association with the Mercian site, the other preferring traditional pagan values. If the Biddles are correct that the central burial in the Repton charnel deposit is that of Ivar the Boneless then it is tempting also to speculate that it was Halfdan and his men, the original joint leader of the force that first arrived in 865, who were responsible for the appropriation of the mortuary chapel, whilst it was those reinforcements who had arrived in the summer of 871 under Guthrum who preferred cremation at Heath Wood.

In the environs of Repton we are therefore able to observe the playing out of a major ideological drama in the 870s. This war-torn frontier zone acted as a stage, first, for the demonstration of the power of the Great Army, but then for an unfolding drama of dissent within its ranks. With its tradition of royal Mercian patronage and its prestige as a focus of pilgrimage, Repton would have provided the perfect location for a demonstration of new spiritual convictions combined with political/military subjugation. The Mercian landscape and even the royal church and mausoleum were appropriated by one section of the Great Army in order to legitimate their political control. However, on a hill top to the south-east a traditional ritual of cremation, animal sacrifice and mound burial was being performed.

In this small area of South Derbyshire we can therefore see the creation of a ritual landscape, and the re-invention of a small piece of pagan Scandinavia in Heath Wood. Viking armies were not homogenous groups; they contained those of diverse beliefs and ideologies. Standard pagan and Christian stereotypes may be of little use if we wish to understand the nature of conversion in the Danelaw. In this single case study we are able to observe a number of alternate strategies and accommodations between pagans and Christians in a frontier society.

References

Abrams, L. 2000 'Conversion and assimilation', in D.M. Hadley and J.D. Richards (eds) *Cultures in Contact: Scandinavian settlement in England in the ninth and tenth centuries*, Study in the Early Middle Ages 2, Turnhout: Brepols, 135–53.

Abrams, L. 2001 'The conversion of the Danelaw', in J.Graham-Campbell, R.Hall, J.Jesch and D.N. Parsons (eds) *Vikings and the Danelaw. Selected Papers from the Proceedings of the Thirteenth Viking Congress*. Oxford: Oxbow Books, 31–44.

Biddle, M. and Kjølbye-Biddle, B. 1992 'Repton and the Vikings', *Antiquity* 66, 36–51.

Biddle, M. and Kjølbye-Biddle, B. 2001 'Repton and the "great heathen army", 873–4', in J. Graham-Campbell, R. Hall, J. Jesch and D.N. Parsons (eds) *Vikings and the Danelaw. Selected Papers from the Proceedings of the Thirteenth Viking Congress*. Oxford: Oxbow Books, 45–96.

Blood of the Vikings 2001 Television series BBC2.

Graham-Campbell, J. 1980 'The Scandinavian Viking-Age burials of England: some problems of interpretation', in P. Rahtz, T. Dickinson, and L. Watts (eds) *Anglo-Saxon Cemeteries 1979*, British Archaeological Reports British Series 82, Oxford, 379–82.

Hadley, D.M. 2000 'Burial practices in the Northern Danelaw, c.650–1100', *Northern History* 36, 199–216.

Hadley, D.M. 2001 *Death in Medieval England*. Stroud: Tempus.

Halsall, G. 2000 'The Viking presence in England? The burial evidence reconsidered' in D.M. Hadley and J.D. Richards (eds) *Cultures in Contact: Scandinavian settlement in England in the ninth and tenth centuries*, Study in the Early Middle Ages 2, Turnhout: Brepols, 259–76.

Owen, O., and Dalland, M. 1999 *Scar: A Viking Boat Burial on Sanday, Orkney*. Phantassie: Tuckwell Press.

Posnansky, M. 1956 'The pagan-Danish barrow cemetery at Heath Wood, Ingleby', *Derbyshire Archaeological Journal* 76, 40–56.

Richards, J.D., with Jecock, M., Richmond, L. and Tuck, C. 1995 'The Viking barrow cemetery at Heath Wood, Ingleby, Derbyshire', *Medieval Archaeology* 39, 51–70.

Richards, J.D. 1991 *Viking Age England*. London: English Heritage/ B.T.Batsford.

Richards, J.D. 2000 *Viking Age England*. Second edition. Stroud: Tempus.

Richards, J.D. 2001 'Boundaries and cult centres: Viking burial in Derbyshire', in J.Graham-Campbell, R. Hall, J. Jesch and D.N. Parsons (eds) *Vikings and the Danelaw. Selected Papers from the Proceedings of the Thirteenth Viking Congress*. Oxford: Oxbow Books, 97–104.

Roesdahl, E. 1997 'Landscape sculpture in Viking Age Denmark', *Aarhus Geoscience* 7, 147–55.

Sidebottom, P. 2000 'Viking Age stone monuments and social identity', in D.M. Hadley and J.D. Richards (eds) *Cultures in Contact: Scandinavian settlement in England in the ninth and tenth centuries*, Study in the Early Middle Ages 2, Turnhout: Brepols, 213–35.

Smyth, A. 1977 *Scandinavian Kings in the British Isles 850–880*. Oxford: Oxford University Press.

Stenton, F. 1943 *Anglo-Saxon England*. Oxford: Oxford University Press.

Stocker, D. 2000 'Monuments and merchants: irregularities in the distribution of stone sculpture in Lincolnshire and Yorkshire in the tenth century', in D.M. Hadley and J.D. Richards (eds) *Cultures in Contact: Scandinavian settlement in England in the ninth and tenth centuries*, Study in the Early Middle Ages 2, Turnhout: Brepols, 179–212.

Stocker, D. and Everson, P. 2001 'Five towns funerals: decoding diversity in Danelaw stone sculpture', in J. Graham-Campbell, R. Hall, J. Jesch and D.N. Parsons (eds) *Vikings and the Danelaw. Selected Papers from the Proceedings of the Thirteenth Viking Congress*. Oxford: Oxbow Books, 223–43.

Sturluson, S. 1964 *Heimskringla*, Everyman edition, trans. S. Laing. London: Dent.

Tarlow, S. 1997 'The dread of something after death: Violation and desecration on the Isle of Man in the tenth century', in J. Carman (ed.) *Material Harm: Archaeological studies of war and violence*. Skelmorlie: Cruithne Press, 133–42.

Wawn, A. 2000 *The Vikings and the Victorians: Inventing the Old North in nineteenth-century Britain*. Cambridge: D.S. Brewer.

Whitelock, D. 1941 'The Conversion of the Eastern Danelaw', *Saga-Book* 12/3, 159–76.

Wilson, D.M. 1967 'The Vikings' relationship with Christianity in northern England', *Journal of the British Archaeological Association*, 3rd series, 30, 37–46.

25

The Body of St Æthelthryth:
Desire, Conversion and Reform in
Anglo-Saxon England

CATHERINE E. KARKOV

Conversion and the Golden Age

The conversion of England is, on one level, all about sex and desire for the female body. Some time before 580, 20 years or so before Pope Gregory sent Augustine north to preach to the English, Bertha, the Christian daughter of the Merovingian king, Charibert, married the pagan prince (later king) Æthelberht of Kent.[1] Freedom to practice her own religion was one of the conditions of her marriage, and she was accompanied to England by her own bishop, Liuthard. Bede tells us that, through his wife, Æthelberht was already familiar with Christianity before the Gregorian mission, and the implication is that it was the knowledge imparted by the queen that led him to welcome Augustine and his retinue so warmly.[2] The pattern was repeated when, sometime before 625, Bertha and Æthelberht's daughter, Æthelburh, married the Northumbrian king, Edwin, their marriage becoming the 'occasion' for the conversion of Northumbria.[3] One could, of course, argue that it was the desire for sons, or advantageous political alliances, rather than the desire for the women themselves, that motivated these kings; nevertheless, one cannot erase either desire or the female body from the process.[4]

---

[1] See Ian Wood, 'Augustine and Gaul', in *St Augustine and the Conversion of England*, ed. Richard Gameson (Stroud: Sutton, 1999), 68–82, at 71; and Richard Gameson, 'Augustine of Canterbury: Context and Achievement', in *ibid.*, 1–40, at 16, for a discussion of the chronology of the marriage and conversion.

[2] *Bede's Ecclesiastical History* (hereafter *HE* i.25 (ed. Colgrave and Mynors), p. 72. See also Richard Gameson, 'Augustine of Canterbury', 16–7.

[3] *HE* ii.9, p. 162: 'Huic autem genti occasio fuit percipiendae fidei, quod praefatus rex eius cognatione iunctus est regibus Cantuariorum, accepta in coniugem Aedilbergae filia Aedilbercti regis'.

[4] On queens and conversion in general see Jo Ann McNamara, '*Imitatio Helenae*: Sainthood as an Attribute of Queenship', in *Saints: Studies in Hagiography*, ed. Sandro Sticca (Binghamton: State University of New York Press, 1996), 51–80.

Conversions are not just about those who do the converting or are converted; they are equally about those who record the histories, stories and myths that arise from that process. Conversion, like history, comes down to us through narrative: chronicles, hagiography, and the narratives we compose around the material record. The only direct textual account of the conversion of England to survive is Bede's *Ecclesiastical History*, and Bede provides us largely with the doings and voices of men. In Bede, queens become the objects through which Christianisation is achieved, rather than active agents in conversion. The desired body disappears behind a mask of text. For example, we know that in 601 Pope Gregory wrote to both Æthelberht and Bertha, and that he praised Bertha for the help she had given Augustine with his mission, but Bede transcribes only the letter to Æthelberht.[5] Similarly, while Boniface, in a letter to Æthelburh, acknowledged the ability of the queen to influence her husband with both her body and her voice, writing his acknowledgment in words that borrow from the language of carnal passion, Bede gives us only the voice of Boniface,[6] and we learn nothing of Æthelburh's actions or response.

Nowhere is desire for and denial of the female body and voice more evident than in Bede's account of the virgin queen and abbess Æthelthryth (d. 679). Æthelthryth lived in the years immediately following the conversion, but she became for both Bede and the later writers of the reform era an emblem of the newly Christianised country and the golden age of the Anglo-Saxon church. Æthelthryth's story as told in Book iv.19 of the *Ecclesiastical History* is well known. She was the daughter of King Anna of East Anglia, and managed to maintain her virginity through two marriages – the first to Ealdorman Tondberht of the South Gwyre, and the second to King Ecgfrith of Northumbria. During her reign as queen she was the supporter of, and supported by, Bishop Wilfrid, finally receiving the veil from him and entering the monastery at Coldingham after 12 years of marriage. A year later she founded the monastery of Ely and became its first abbess. Bede tells us that after entering the church she lived the life of an extreme ascetic, was renowned for her teaching, and became 'the virgin mother of many virgins'.[7] Æthelthryth was, then, in turns princess, wife, queen, nun and abbess, enjoying every possible position of power a woman could claim in early Anglo-Saxon England. If her story is to be believed, she was clearly a learned, powerful and persuasive woman, able to maintain her position at court – and perhaps that of Wilfrid too[8] – on her own terms for 12 years. It is also clear that Bede genuinely admired her; but even so, Æthelthryth, as a politically and spiritually influential woman, disappears beneath the layers of text and trans-

---

[5] Gregorius Magnus, *Registrum epistularum*, ed. D. Norburg, 2 vols. (Turnhout: Brepols, 1982), XI, 35. See also, Fiona Gameson, 'Goscelin's Life of Augustine of Canterbury', in *St Augustine*, ed. Richard Gameson, 391–409, at 394; Richard Gameson, 'Augustine of Canterbury', 17; *HE* i.32.

[6] *HE* ii.11.

[7] *HE*, p. 392.

[8] See Stephanie Hollis, *Anglo-Saxon Women and the Church* (Woodbridge: Boydell, 1992), 70.

lation with which Bede and later writers cover her. Indeed, by the tenth century the real woman had given way to the fetishistic object defined and manipulated by the men who controlled her cult. Beginning with Bede, her body is never revealed to us by those who wrote about her, yet it remains the focus of our, and their, attention, an unfulfilled desire established in the first instance through Bede's words. Narrative is itself a structure of desire and a means of, or at least an attempt at, possession. As Susan Stewart notes, narrative 'both invents and distances its object and thereby inscribes again and again the gap between signifier and signified that is the place of the generation of the symbolic'.[9] It is also the place of the lack that generates the fetish. In the case of Æthelthryth we are left not with the woman, her voice, or her actions, but with what she stood for to a series of male voices and their various agenda. Possession of the body of Æthelthryth is from the very start of the story a desired but unobtainable goal.

Bede begins his account of Æthelthryth with a series of sentences that clearly define her as the object of exchange within a secular, male economy of marriage: 'Accepit autem rex Ecgfrid coniugem nomine Aedilthrydam, filiam Anna regis Orientalium Anglorum, cuius saepius mentionem fecimus, uiri bene religiosi ac per omnia mente et opere egregii; quam et alter ante illum uir habuerat uxorem, princeps uidelicet Australium Gyruiorum uocabulo Tondberct. Sed illo post modicum temporis, ex quo eam accepit, defuncto, data est regi praefato'.[10] She entered the monastery at Coldingham only with her husband's permission, and under the guidance of Wilfrid, and was *appointed* abbess of Ely a year later – though Bede does credit her with building the monastery.[11] The rest of her life Bede acknowledges as being based on tradition or the words of a third party, prefacing his remarks with the phrase 'De qua ferunt quia' ('It is stated that'). Within this chronology, Bede weaves a story of desire and denial. Ecgfrith offered Wilfrid estates and money if he could convince Æthelthryth to consummate their marriage, but to no avail; however, the absence of a sexualised Æthelthryth is a potent reminder of the role her royal body was meant to fulfil. (This was certainly the case for one modern author, who commented that 'we may envisage Etheldreda not as the stubborn, cold, remote, and frankly unlovable religious fanatic to whom Victorian historians are so committed, but as someone soft in nature. Let us think of her additionally as rather immature, unsure of herself, and with the kind of vulnerability irresistible to the most hard-hearted of men.'[12]) Moroever, Æthelthryth's own ascetic practices – wearing woollen garments,

---

[9] Susan Stewart, *On Longing: Narratives of the Miniature, the Gigantic, the Souvenir, the Collection* (Baltimore and London: Johns Hopkins University Press, 1984), ix.

[10] *HE*, p. 390–1: 'King Ecgfrith married a wife named Æthelthryth, the daughter of Anna, king of the East Angles, who has often been referred to, a very religious man in both mind and deed. She had previously been married to an ealdorman of the South Gwyre, named Tondberht. But he died shortly after the marriage and on his death she was given to King Ecgfrith.'

[11] *HE*, p. 392: 'Post annum uero ipsa facta est abbatissa in regione quae uocatur Elge, ubi constructo monasterio'.

[12] Norman Sneesby, *Etheldreda: Princess, Queen, Abbess and Saint* (Ely: Fern House, 1999), 73.

refusing to bathe or eat, rejoicing in the pain of her tumour – also serve to focus our attention on the body they were designed to deny.[13] At the heart of Bede's story, however, is Æthelthryth's burial and translation; it is here that the body is simultaneously covered and exposed, concealed and never quite revealed. Æthelthryth is originally buried in a simple wooden coffin in the monastic cemetery, but 16 years later her sister, now abbess, orders her to be translated into the church. Her grave is covered by a tent surrounded by singing nuns and monks who, like us, do not see the body, but only hear of its miraculous preservation; in fact, they might be described as forming yet another layer of covering between us and the saint's body. The body itself is intact, fresh and healed of the one physical intrusion made into it: the neck wound made by the surgeon's knife in his attempt to relieve her of the ailment that killed her. Even the surgeon's account of the translation and miraculous healing of the wound adds to the tension between the body and its coverings. He describes her body as wrapped, yet partially exposed; the wound he tells us Æthelthryth had compared to the necklaces of gold and pearls with which she had once covered her neck, has now become a necklace marked on the body by 'cicatricis uestigia parerent' ('the slightest traces of a scar'). The body is unwrapped, washed and reclothed, safely surrounded by a screening curtain of nuns, and placed in a miraculous white marble sarcophagus that fits it exactly. The sarcophagus, like Æthelthryth's body is shining, white and intact. There is an element of spectacle in all this that generates our desire to witness the events described, our voyeuristic impulses; yet that desire is frustrated and made all the stronger by the fact that we cannot see, but only read about, what was or was not seen.

Interestingly, Æthelthryth's translation also becomes a symbolic re-enactment of the conversion. The marble sarcophagus, as Colgrave and Mynors point out, is almost certainly a Roman sarcophagus.[14] Æthelthryth's body thus converts what was once a pagan monument into a site of Christian worship. But the covering of the sarcophagus, like that of the original coffin, or the burial shroud, invites exposure. The cover, as Stewart emphasises, 'always bears the potential of striptease'; it invites us to imagine the body beneath,[15] an invitation realized throughout the Middle Ages in the viewer's desire to see, touch and interact with the bones of the saints. There was, moreover, something miraculous about the saint's (or relic's) very survival, and its existence as both a person and a thing. One might compare the collection, translation and display of saints and relics to the collection, stripping and display of Egyptian mummies – 'objects' that, like relics, existed in the nebulous area between the living and the dead. There is very

---

[13] The same is, of course, true for the ascetic practices of most saints. See, for example, Caroline Walker Bynum, *Holy Feast and Holy Fast: The Religious Significance of Food to Medieval Women* (Berkeley: University of California Press, 1987).

[14] *HE*, p. 394 n1. We might also note here that it is the brothers of the monastery who locate the sarcophagus near *Grantacæstir* (Cambridge) and bring it back to Ely.

[15] Stewart, *On Longing*, 114.

little, other than avowed religious intent, that separates the collecting and translating of the bodies of the saints from the collecting and unwrapping of Egyptian
mummies, and both can be understood as objects of desire, if not fetish. In
his study of the body of the mummy, Dominic Montserrat notes that 'there is
an element of display involved in the keeping of the mummy – the preserved
body is to some extent a contained spectacle in itself'. He goes on to note that
'Mummies themselves are expensive commodified objects. Covered with costly
linen wrappings, impregnated with exotic perfumes and decorated with gold,
mummies represent a conspicuous consumption and an aesthetic of surface.'[16]
Saints and relics too became luxury commodities, an aspect of saints' cults and
their devotees explored most notably by Patrick Geary. Covered with eastern
textiles, gold and jewels, the relic, like the mummy, was both person and thing, a
beautiful and precious ecclesiastical object within the medieval system of
exchange. According to Geary:

> Human remains could go through a life-cycle closely related to the
> production-circulation context: a human bone, given by the Pope as a sacred
> relic, thereby became a sacred relic if the receiver was willing to consider it
> as such. Likewise, a corpse once stolen (or said to have been stolen) was
> valuable because it had been worth stealing. Solemn recognition, by means
> of ritual authentication normally involving the miraculous intervention of
> the saint himself, provided assurance that the value assigned by the transfer
> was genuine. The value endured so long as the community responded by
> recognizing miraculous cures and wonders and ascribing them to the
> intervention of the saint. In general, however, enthusiasm tended to wane
> over time, and the value of the relic had to be renewed periodically through
> a repetition of transferral or discovery, which would then begin the cycle
> anew. So long as the relic continued to perform as a miracle worker, it
> maintained its value as a potential commodity and could be used to acquire
> status, force acknowledgement of dependency, and secure wealth through
> its whole or partial distribution.[17]

Æthelthryth's body and cult went through just such a life-cycle.

Reform and the Golden Virgins

Little is known of Ely between the late-eighth and the tenth century, and it has
been suggested that monastic life there was interrupted by the arrival of the
Vikings. By the 940s Æthelthryth's shrine at Ely is known to have been in the care
of a community of married priests, and there were rumours of neglect. With the

---

[16] Dominic Montserrat, 'Unidentified Human Remains: Mummies and the Erotics of Biography', in
Changing Bodies, Changing Meanings: Studies on the Human Body in Antiquity, ed. D. Montserrat
(London and New York: Routledge, 1998), 162–9, at 166.

[17] Patrick Geary, 'Sacred Commodities: The Circulation of Medieval Relics', in *The Social Life of
Things: Commodities in Cultural Perspective*, ed. Arjun Appadurai (Cambridge: Cambridge
University Press, 1986), 169–91, at 187–8.

accession of Edgar in 959 the monastery passed into royal control. Ely was reformed (or refounded) by Bishop Æthelwold of Winchester c.970 with the approval of King Edgar, and amidst some local tension.[18] The double community of nuns and monks over which Æthelthryth had ruled was replaced by a community of Benedictine monks and an abbot. The relics of Æthelthryth were a key component in Æthelwold's legal claims to the monastery,[19] as well as in his attempts to create a new golden age for the Anglo-Saxon church, and it was thus necessary that he re-establish their value. This he did by continuing the tradition of translation (both textual and physical) established in the pages of the *Ecclesiastical History*. His efforts not only succeeded in bringing new wealth and importance to the community, but also in creating a direct relationship between the age of the reform and the age of conversion via a fetishistic collection of objects and images that took the place of the concealed saint. To be sure, Æthelwold endowed a number of churches with important relics, but only at Ely did collection involve a program of replication, and only at Ely do we find such a consistent emphasis on the body of the saint as a contained object rather than an active participant in the reform process.

During his reconstruction of the abbey's church, Æthelwold is said to have 'invenit' ('discovered') the body of the 'holy virgin and queen Æthelthryth' beside the high altar.[20] The choice of verb is significant, as *invenio* can carry the active meaning of 'to invent or effect' as well as the more passive meaning of 'to discover' in the liturgical sense. The word suggests not only that Æthelthryth had been lost and recovered from the past, but also perhaps that Æthelwold had 'invented', literally recreated or reanimated her. The description is contained in the later *Liber Eliensis*, the history of the abbey compiled in the twelfth century, but incorporating earlier written sources; however, the implication that Æthelwold was discovering and animating the saint may be a straightforward development of an idea implicit in the blessing for the Feast of St Æthelthryth contained in Æthelwold's private benedictional, and thought to have been written by Æthelwold himself (see below). Building on his discovery, Æthelwold then oversaw the translation to Ely of the relics of Æthelthryth's sister and successor Seaxburh, and Seaxburh's daughter Eormenilda, while Byrhtnoth, a former prior of Winchester and Æthelwold's appointee as abbot of Ely, procured the remains of Withburga of Dereham, Æthelthryth and Seaxburh's sister, for the abbey through a 'theft of faith'.[21] While all four bodies were said to have been incorrupt we should bear in mind that the importance of the last three women lay only in their relationship to Æthelthryth, and that in a certain sense they

---

[18] Susan Ridyard, *The Royal Saints of Anglo-Saxon England: A Study of West Saxon and East Anglian Cults* (Cambridge: Cambridge University Press, 1988), 187–90.

[19] Ridyard, *Royal Saints*, 191.

[20] E.O. Blake, ed., *Liber Eliensis* (London: Royal Historical Society, 1962), ii.52, p. 120 (hereafter *LE*).

[21] Ridyard, *Royal Saints*, 185; David W. Rollason, *Saints and Relics in Anglo-Saxon England* (Oxford: Basil Blackwell, 1989), 180.

merely replicated her royal, saintly and even virginal status. It need hardly be pointed out that the multiple translations continued, indeed expanded on, the process of concealing and revealing the female body begun by Bede; but where Bede had only Æthelthryth, Æthelwold and Byrhtnoth had a whole family of royal 'virgins' whose shrines were now displayed in the east end of their rebuilt church. At some point before his death c.999, Byrhtnoth donated four gem-studded gold and silver statues of these virgin saints to the abbey, literally translating the flesh and blood bodies of the women into precious objects for display.[22] If made before Æthelwold's death in 984, the donation would certainly have been made with his knowledge and support. The statues became highly visible signs of the power and sanctity of the enclosed, invisible bodies of the saints themselves, and by extension signs of the wealth and institutional memory of the abbey.[23] Like Æthelthryth's white marble sarcophagus, the golden images were also signs of the intact nature of the virgins, but these were statues, not shrines or reliquaries. They represented rather than contained the bodies of the women, and thus took one step further the process of objectification begun by Bede. Byrhtnoth's actions either paralleled or were paralleled by those of Æthelwold.

The date at which Byrhtnoth's golden images were produced is uncertain, but they certainly influenced, or were influenced by, the more famous golden image of St Æthelthryth on folio 90v of the Benedictional of Æthelwold (London, British Library, Additional 49598), produced at Winchester between 971 and 984, according to Robert Deshman, probably c.973 (Pl. 25.1).[24] Resplendent in gold and surrounded by a golden inscription, Æthelthryth stands on the golden bar of an elaborate acanthus frame. She faces an initial page with the opening words of the benediction for her feast ('Omnipotens unus et aeternus deus') and the image of Christ blessing contained in the initial 'O' (Pl. 25.2). As Deshman has noted, this is the only feast in the manuscript illustrated with both a full-page miniature and an historiated initial.[25] Certainly the combination is indicative of Æthelthryth's

---

[22] While life-sized gold and silver Crucifixion groups are known to have existed in Anglo-Saxon England, this is the only surviving record of precious statues of local or national saints.

[23] The statues eventually became part of a larger narrative programme. The *Liber Eliensis* records the presence at Ely of an effigy made for abbot Ælfsige (981–c.1019) of the Virgin made of gold, silver and precious gems, noting that the throne was 'as large as a man', and a less unusual Crucifixion with life-sized figures of Christ, Mary and John worked in silver donated by Archbishop Stigand (1052–70). (See *LE* ii.61, p. 132 and ii. 98, p. 168; C.R. Dodwell, *Anglo-Saxon Art: A New Perspective* (Manchester: Manchester University Press, 1982), 211 and 215. See also John Crook, *The Architectural Setting of the Cult of Saints in the Early Christian West c.300–c.1200* (Oxford: Oxford University Press, 2000), 193–4.) The Ely virgins became part of a tableau in which their iconographic similarity to, and positioning alongside of, Mary made clear their role as emulators of Mary and brides of Christ. Byrhtnoth was here developing an association first suggested for Æthelthryth in the hymn that Bede composed for her (see *HE* iv.20, pp. 396–400).

[24] Robert Deshman, *The Benedictional of Æthelwold* (Princeton: Princeton University Press, 1995), 261.

[25] Deshman, *Benedictional*, 122.

importance, but it can also be read as a reference to (or model for) the three-dimensional icons within the church, and the bodies they represented.[26] The scintillating surface of the manuscript with its multiple washes of colour and lavish use of gold is clearly related to the gilded and gem-studded statues standing in Æthelwold's church, and is itself an object of desire.[27] Of equal interest are the style and iconography of the page, which help to set it apart from the other miniatures in the manuscript. While over half the illustrations in the Benedictional are devoted to representations of saints, only four figures appear as non-narrative portraits: John the Evangelist (fol 19v), Swithun (fol 97v), Benedict (fol 99v) and Æthelthryth. John is shown as a conventional evangelist type seated with book and symbol against a background of clouds, a device used in the manuscript to indicate divine or heavenly space. The images of Swithun, Benedict (Pl. 25.3) and Æthelthryth are similar in that each of the three saints is depicted on a verso page, standing or sitting in a motionless pose, and facing the opening of the accompanying benediction. Æthelthryth is the only one of the three to appear isolated against a plain vellum background devoid of any architectural or landscape elements and, as noted, the only one to face an historiated initial. The lack of depth or space in the Æthelthryth miniature emphasises simultaneously the text, Æthelthryth's position within the text, and the surface of the page. The effect is enhanced by the way in which the saint perches on the border rather than stands within the space of the miniature, and by the golden inscription that surrounds her. Benedict is also surrounded by an inscription, but its text receives much less attention, not only because it is written in small black rather than large golden letters, but also because both it and Benedict appear within an elaborate architectural setting. The setting is a likely reference to the monastic life within which the Benedictine Rule was central, a reference picked up in the wording of the inscription which identifies the figure as Saint Benedict, abbot. The difference in the wording of the inscriptions that surround Benedict and Æthelthryth is significant. The figure on folio 99v is Saint Benedict, the figure on folio 90v *is* the *image* of Saint Æthelthryth, abbess and perpetual virgin, the word 'image' distancing the figure on the page from the historical woman it is meant to represent.

Conversely, the way in which the golden inscription surrounds Æthelthryth unites her to the blessing Christ contained in the historiated initial on the facing page. The juxtaposition serves to identify Æthelthryth as a bride of Christ, and

---

[26] According to the *LE*, Æthelthryth's shrine was to the south of the altar (to Christ's left), and Seaxburh's shrine to the north, but clearly the arrangement in the manuscript was necessary if the text of the prayer was to be read and displayed without interruption. See *LE* ii.,146, p. 231: 'In turre vero regina Æðeldreða et celebris virgo ad altare proprium ab australi parte tumulata resplenduit'. ('Indeed, Æthelthryth, queen and celebrated virgin, shone from her tower at the high altar, having been buried on the south side.')

[27] The relationship between manuscript representation and the collection of precious objects is also noted by Michael Camille in his discussion of Jean de Berry as collector ('"For Our Devotion and Pleasure': The Sexual Objects of Jean, Duc de Berry', *Art History* 24 (2001), 169–94, at 169.

Plate 25.1 St Æethelthryth (London, British Library, Additional 49598, fol 90v) (Reproduced by permission of the British Library)

an emulator of the Virgin Mary, and suggests her resurrection into the kingdom of heaven.[28] The similarity in the compositions of the two pages is also important: Æthelthryth, like Christ, is framed by golden letters. On one level, the inscription focuses our attention on her saintly, virginal status, underscoring her identification with Mary and her position as bride of Christ; on another, it serves to incorporate her quite literally into the benediction for her feast. She is contained within the inscription, which flows almost seamlessly into the blessing:

[28] Deshman, *Benedictional*, 121–4.

Plate 25.2 Christ (London, British Library, Additional 49598, fol 91) (Reproduced by permission of the British Library)

Imago sanctae Æþeldryþe abbatissa ac perpetue virgin. Omnipotens unus et aeternus deus pater et filius et spiritus sanctus, qui beatae aeðeldryðe animum septiformis gratiae ubertate ita succensum solidauit, ut duorum coniugum thalamis asscita immunis euaderet, castamque sibi piissimus sponsam perpetim adoptaret, uos ab incentiua libidinum concupiscentia muniendo submoueat, et sui amoris igne succendat. Amen.

Et qui eius integritatem per imputribile corpus post obitum manifeste designauit, signisque miraculorum ineffabiliter ostendit, uos in sanctis operibus castos fideliter usque ad uitae terminum perseuerare concedat. Amen.

'Image of saint Æthelthryth abbess and perpetual virgin. May the omnipotent and eternal God, the Father and the Son and the Holy Spirit, who made the will of blessed Æthelthryth steadfast and so ablaze with the

Plate 25.3 St Benedict (London, British Library, Additional 49598, fol 99v) (Reproduced by permission of the British Library)

bounty of seven-fold grace that, summoned to the marriage beds of two husbands, she avoided them, remaining intact, and was taken as a chaste bride in perpetuity by the most just one, remove you from the burning desire of lust by protecting you, and kindle the fire of his own love. Amen. And may he, who displayed her purity manifestly through her incorruptible body after death, and revealed her ineffably by signs of miracles, allow you to persevere faithfully in holy works, chaste to the end of your life. Amen.'[29]

In the prayer Æthelthryth is portrayed as the passive yet pliable object of an active Christ who 'animated her will', 'displayed her purity', and 'revealed her'

---

[29] Deshman, *Benedictional*, 122.

through miracles, a portrayal that further reveals her status as an image within a text rather than a figure introducing a text. It is the second verse that is the most interesting: 'And may he, who displayed her purity manifestly through her incorruptible body after death, and revealed her ineffably by signs and miracles . . .' 'He' is of course God (or Christ as Æthelthryth is cast as a bride of Christ); but in reading the blessing the bishop and his words became the point of contact between the divine blessing and those who were being blessed,[30] and the parallels between God/Christ's revelation and display of the saint and Æthelwold's revelation and display of her relics would probably not have been lost on a contemporary audience, and certainly not on Æthelwold himself. Like Christ, and like Bede, Æthelwold (and Byrhtnoth) 'displayed' and 'revealed' the saint through his discovery of her shrine (a type of symbolic elevation) and through the golden images of her and her 'sisters' that stood in the church. Like Christ, Æthelwold also 'animated' the saint, through his revival of her cult, and the record of the new miracles attributed to the saint and her shrine after her tenth-century rediscovery.[31] But unlike Bede, Æthelwold and Byrhtnoth seem to have focussed on Æthelthryth as a body to be collected. Once Æthelwold had discovered her bodily remains, the two men set about collecting those of her sisters and her niece; one or both created the golden statues, the surrogate bodies through which the virgins could be represented and displayed publicly, and Æthelwold commissioned the two-dimensional 'image' of Æthelthryth in his private benedictional. Æthelthryth here becomes a fetish in both Freudian and Marxist terms. The multiplication of the image, the presence that masks the absence, becomes Freud's excess of image. It is also a mode of collection that Marx labelled the fetishism of the object (*das Dinge*), a type of fetishism that is a feature of various forms and periods of conspicuous consumption.[32] As thing, object or shrine, any relic might be classed as fetishistic because fetishism grants autonomous power to the object,[33] but the multiplication of bodies and images adds an extra dimension in the case of Æthelthryth. Fetishism, as contemporary scholars have come to recognize, is a discourse in which human desire, the physical object and social power all meet, and one that is above all characterized by the love of looking (Freud's *scopophilia*).[34] In Freudian terms it is the image and not the relics of Æthelthryth that becomes the fetish, as it is the image that both stands for the

---

[30] A point noted by Andrew Prescott in *The Benedictional of Saint Æthelwold: Commentary* (London, 2001), p. 40.

[31] See *LE* xxxii. Blake notes that some, if not all, of the miracles recorded in the twelfth-century manuscript 'must have been taken from older miracle collections'.

[32] See Karl Marx, *Das Kapital: Kritik der politische Ökonomie*, vol. 1: *Der Produktinsprozess des Kapitals* (Frankfurt am Main: Ullstein, 1969), 50.

[33] Laura Mulvey, 'Some Thoughts on Theories of Fetishism in the Context of Contemporary Culture', *October* 65 (1993), 3–20, at 7.

[34] Sigmund Freud, 'Fetishism', in *The Standard Edition of the Complete Psychological Works of Sigmund Freud*, ed. James Strachey, vol. 21: *The Future of an Illusion, Civilization and its Discontents and Other Works* (London: Hogarth Press, 1961), 149–57. See also, Emily Apter and William Pietz, *Fetishism as Cultural Discourse* (Ithaca and London: Cornell University Press, 1993), x.

object, and is collected in its place. For Freud, the fetish was a substitute, sign or object set up to conceal a lack – the image of Æthelthryth, and not the woman herself. Here fetishism and collection go hand-in-hand. In his exploration of the phenomenon of collecting, Baudrillard points out that objects only acquire 'exceptional value' through their absence, and that multiplication of an object is a frequent means of masking absence: 'the impulse of physical possession . . . can only be satisfied by a string of objects, or by the repetition of the same object, or by the superimposition of all objects of desire.'[35]

Image and Identity

It is also possible that the image(s) of the saint came to represent the living as well as the dead – a multiplicity of Æthelthryths, as it were. By inscribing the name Æthelthryth on the page, and stating clearly that this was not Æthelthryth but the image of her, a connection might be established between the historical saint and her contemporary namesake, Æthelthryth, abbess of Nunnaminster, like Byrhtnoth an Æthelwold appointee. Æthelwold's reform era had its abbess Æthelthryth just as Bede's golden age had the saint of the same name, and in the image they could become one. The age of Bede could not only be resurrected, it could be recreated, or repossessed, via the image. The names of both women, along with the foundation and refoundation of their respective houses are explicitly linked in Wulfstan's *Life of St Æthelwold*, written *c*.996:

> Mandras sanctimonialium ordinauit quibus matrem de qua superius paululum tetigimus Æthelthrytham. . . . Est enim quaedam regio famosa in prouincia Orientalium Anglorum sita, paludibus et aquis in modum insulae circumdata, unde et a copia anguillarum quae in eisdem paludibus capiuntur Ælig nomen accepit. In qua regione locus omni ueneratione dignus habetur, magnificatus nimium reliquiis et miraculis sanctae Æthelthrythae reginae et perpetuae uirginis ac sororum eius; sed in ipso tempore erat destitutus et regali fisco deditus. Hunc ergo locum famulus Christi pro dilectione tantarum uirginum magnopere uenerari coepit, datoque precio non modicae pecuniae emit eum a rege Eadgaro, constituens in eo monachorum gregem non minimum. Quibus ordinauit abbatem Byrhtnodum praepositum suum.[36]

---

[35] Jean Baudrillard, 'The System of Collecting', in *The Cultures of Collecting*, ed. John Elsner and Roger Cardinal (London: Reaktion Books, 1974), 7–24, at 13 and 8.

[36] 'Here [Nunnaminster] he established flocks of nuns, placing over them Æthelthryth. . . . There is a well-known spot in East Anglia, surrounded like an island by swamps and water. From the quantity of eels taken in these marshes it has been given the name Ely. Here there is a place held to deserve all reverence, for it is made glorious by the relics and miracles of St Æthelthryth, queen and perpetual virgin, and her sisters. But at this time it was abandoned and pertained to the royal fisc. The servant of Christ began to reverence this place greatly, out of his love for the distinguished virgins, and he paid a large sum of money to buy it from King Edgar. In it he established a group of monks, ordaining his prior Byrhtnoth as abbot.' Michael Lapidge and Michael Winterbottom, eds, *Wulfstan of Winchester Life of St Æthelwold* (Oxford: Clarendon Press, 1991), 36–39. See also Ælfric's account, based on Wulfstan's *Life*, in *ibid.*, 70–80.

There is also a possible third Æthelthryth, the abbess/nurse of the Nunnaminster who interpreted Æthelwold's mother's prophetic dream of the future greatness of her unborn son.[37] It is unclear whether this woman and the abbess Æethelthryth named above are the same woman or not, but it is doubtful that a woman already an abbess before Æthelwold's birth would still have been an abbess by the time he became bishop.[38] It might be possible to read an example of female agency into the episode in which Æthelthryth the nurse interprets the dream telling of Æthelwold's future glory, just as Æthelwold would tell of St Æthelthryth's past glory, but Wulfstan denies us that possibility by not giving us her interpretation, and by stating quite clearly that 'We too may act as interpreters of these dreams'.[39] In other words, her abilities were no greater than ours. There is also the possibility that this Æthelthryth is nothing more than a literary topos, and that the name was used simply for what the name and image had come to signify – the self-generating value of the Marxist fetish.

The abstract space of Æthelthryth's portrait in the Benedictional, and the prominence of the inscription, can be seen as part of a tradition in which her body and name were continually revealed and displayed through the words and actions of others – Bede, Æthelwold, Wulfstan, Ælfric (who wrote a life of Æthelwold based on Wulfstan's) and Christ (in the text of the benediction). Her golden image, both in the Benedictional and in its three-dimensional form beside the high altar at Ely, embodied the spiritual, economic and historical values, which she had come to represent. But they are images that come down to us only as text. The inscription of the Benedictional portrait ensures that the image of the body is written into the text and does not stand on its own.[40] It is the ultimate step in Æthelwold's translation of Æthelthryth from living body into a lack of body that began with the discovery of the relics (the real body), and progressed through three-dimensional representation (the statues), two-dimensional representation (the painted portrait), and ended in the words written by Æthelwold himself, words in which Christ's animation of the woman is made to echo Æthelwold's animation of the object. For Freud, the fetish was a sign, a covering for, and a commemoration of a site of lack. For Æthelwold, the image of Æthelthryth became all these things. It was a sign of the missing woman, as well as the missing history of Ely that separated the age of conversion from the age of reform; it was a covering, a painted image that masked or substituted for the body concealed within the shrine, perhaps also masking the fear that the body might not actually be as incorrupt as claimed. It was also a commemoration of the absent

[37] Lapidge and Winterbottom, *Life of St Æthelwold*, 4–7.
[38] For the problems see Lapidge and Winterbottom, *Life of St Æthelwold*, 4 n3.
[39] 'Nos quoque eorundem somniorum coniectores esse possumus.' Lapidge and Winterbottom, *Life of St Æthelwold*, 6–7.
[40] See also Gwen Griffiths, 'Reading Ælfric's Saint Æthelthryth as a Woman', *Parergon* ns 10.2 (1992), 35–49, at 35.

woman, the unrecoverable past and the tradition of history writing for which Æthelthryth had become both symbol and souvenir. Susan Stewart sees the boundary between collection and fetishism as 'mediated by classification and display in tension with accumulation and secrecy.' The collection is for display (often for public consumption), is systematic, and is both a part of and authenticated by the past.[41] The fetish, on the other hand, is private, visually appealing, timeless, yet dependent upon the reification of a particular cultural or originary reference (Stewart's example is the transformation of the corporeal body into representation in contemporary consumer culture).[42] It is possible to understand Æthelthryth and the Ely virgins as crossing the boundaries between the two. Like the collection of souvenirs, the Ely virgins united past and present, the age of Bede and that of Æethelwold; the shrines and golden statues were objects of public display, and the collection was, if anything, systematic. Like the fetish, however, the object was made to stand for the absent body: the corporeal bodies of the saints concealed within their tombs. It also had a private component in the image of Æthelthryth in Æthelwold's private benedictional. All these objects – the white marble sarcophagus that held the body of Æthelthryth, the golden and jewel encrusted statues, and the richly coloured and gilded painted image – were both visually and tactilely appealing surfaces that enclosed and then replaced the desired object, and all were dependent on the one present yet absent body of Æthelthryth and the reification of her story and her role in the creation of the English church. The story of Æthelthryth, like Bede's story of the conversion, is all about sex, desire and the absent woman.

---

[41] Stewart, *On Longing*, 150, 163. For a different interpretation of these terms see Susan M. Pearce, *Museums, Objects and Collections: A Cultural Study* (Leicester and London: Leicester University Press, 1992). While Pearce's definition of the terminology is different, her view of the way in which the collection functions generally within cultural and historical discourse is similar to Stewart's.

[42] Stewart, *On Longing*, 163–4.

Part IV

From the Alps to the Baltic

26

From a Late Roman Cemetery to the *Basilica Sanctorum Cassii et Florentii* in Bonn, Germany

CHRISTOPH KELLER

Introduction: Late Roman and Early Medieval Bonn

The modern city of Bonn is situated west of the Rhine on the high river bank, which is intersected by several old river beds (Fig. 26.1), most of which remained small streams or stagnant channels until the Middle Ages. This provided an easily defendable site with natural obstacles to the west, north and south. The situation also allowed control over trade on the river as well as on the ancient route to south-western Germany. This favourable location attracted settlers from the late Iron Age onwards. Several small settlements or farmsteads, already known as *bonna*, have been discovered in the area of the later city (Joachim 1988, 20–2).

When Drusus was running his military campaigns in Germany in 12–9 BC he used the site for building a small camp and a bridge across the river (Rösger and Will 1985). During the first century AD *Legio I* was moved to the site and a legionary fortress was constructed (Horn 1987, 364–76). With the arrival of the Roman army at least some of the local inhabitants changed their main business from farming to supply production. Pottery kilns, iron smelting furnaces and the remains of antler, bone and leather working indicate the new craft activities. With the rising numbers of civilian inhabitants, two adjacent settlements – a *canabae legionis* and a *vicus* – developed and flourished until the end of the third century (Fig. 26.2A). While most of the buildings clustered alongside the main north-south road, industrial activities concentrated along the fringes of the settlements. Graveyards can be found to the west of the fortress and the *canabae*. Contrary to Roman legislation, burials were not excluded from the residential areas but can also be found inside both the *vicus* and *canabae* (Kaiser 1996, 487–488).

The conflicts with invading Germanic groups in AD 275/276 and 353/355 left the military and civilian settlements in ruins. As far as we know today, life continued only within the re-fortified legionary fortress and at a few rare spots in close vicinity. Two cemeteries remained in use. One was situated to the west of the fortress, while the other lies to the south right in the heart of the ruined *canabae*

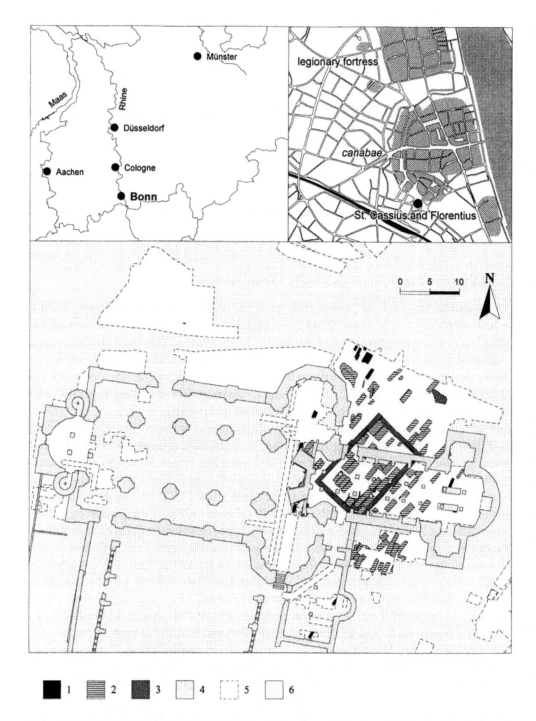

Figure 26.1 Roman and early medieval burials underneath the church St. Cassius and Florentius in Bonn: 1 Roman burial; 2 early medieval burial; 3 church D; 4 medieval church; 5 excavated area; 6 unexcavated area

Figure 26.2 Roman and early medieval Bonn: A – Roman Bonn; B – early medieval Bonn: 1 civilian settlement; 2 legionary fortress; 3 industrial area; 4 burial

(Kaiser 1996, Fig. 7). During the late fourth and fifth century, there were Frankish graves among the burials, but so far no settlement remains can be assigned to the period. By the sixth century an area in the south-western corner of the old fortress and alongside its southern wall shows settlement activity again, or there might even have been continuous use of that site from late Roman times on (Fig. 26.2B, north). A second settlement developed by the church of SS Cassius and Florentius, which is the main subject of this paper (Fig. 26.2b, south). The church, which is first mentioned in AD 691/692, was attracting others to live in the vicinity of its college of priests from the sixth century onwards. There are only a few archae-ological features – mainly pits – indicating activity. All structural remains have been removed by later disturbances. By the eighth century a third settlement had come into being close to the river (Fig. 26.2b, centre). It was the home of a growing trading community which took advantage of the easy access to the river in this area. Merovingian burials were found not only alongside the church of SS Cassius and Florentius, but also by the medieval chapel of St Paul and to the northwest of the fortress on the old Roman cemetery (Böhner 1978, Fig. 7; Dietz 1962, 133). The topography of early medieval Bonn was strongly influenced by its Roman roots and the Romano-Celtic part of its population.

Historic sources tell us little about Christian communities in the late Roman province of *Germania secunda* (Kremer 1993, 323–6). In AD 313 Maternus, who also founded the diocese of Tongern, is the first bishop to be mentioned in Cologne (Dassmann 1993, 108–9). In other major cities like Mainz and Trier, Christian communities were established before the end of the Roman administration in Germany (Dassmann 1993, 43–104). Likewise a Christian community might have existed in Bonn from the early fourth century onwards. But we do not know whether pagan cults were still practised or even dominated the religious scene (Kremer 1993, 325). It is also unclear whether a Christian community survived the troubled times of Frankish raids during the later fourth and fifth century as there are, even in Cologne and Tongern, no records of church building or clergy until the first half of the sixth century.

We do not know, therefore, whether a Christian community existed and survived within the late Roman population or whether it was introduced during the late sixth and seventh century, when the Frankish population was converted. Even archaeological finds indicating individual Christians are scarce in Bonn. Only four objects decorated with religious motifs are known. In 1972 a sandstone coffin was discovered on a construction site. It contained a late Roman military belt, a spatha, a knife, a brooch and a glass bottle and cup (Cat. Bonn 1991, 29–34). Both brooch and cup were decorated with a chi-rho monogram. But this does not necessarily reflect the buried soldier's religion. Two other finds with Christian symbols were discovered in the nineteenth century. A glass cup shows biblical scenes like Moses opening the water-source and Lazarus being raised from the dead (Cat. Bonn 1991, 285–9). A grave-stone fragment shows part of the inscription and a chi-rho monogram. It was found near the chapel of St Paul, in an area where late Roman and Merovingian graves have been found (Cat. Bonn 1991, 115). All these finds are either difficult to date or the Christian decoration does not necessarily reflect its owner's faith. Altogether they do not prove a late Roman Christian community in Bonn. To get a more precise idea of the introduction and expansion of Christianity, we have to look for other evidence. Churches provide the best indication, but there are problems in identifying them. Early churches may not have diagnostic features, and early Christians may have gathered in pre-existing private buildings.

Investigations at the Site of SS Cassius and Florentius

The minster church in Bonn, formerly dedicated to SS Cassius and Florentius (Fig. 26.1), is an excellent location at which to address some of the questions related to the process of Christianisation of a frontier town in late Roman and Merovingian Germany. The church is first mentioned in a record for 28 July 691 (or 692) when Helmgarius presents a vineyard to the *basilica sanctorum Cassii et Florentii* (Levison 1932, 236 No. 5). According to a medieval legend recorded in 1236 the church was founded by Helena, mother of the emperor Constantine, when she buried the bodies of Cassius, Florentius and Malosius on the location of the later church. The three men were soldiers of the so-called Thebean legion and suffered martyrdom during the reign of emperor Diocletian (Höroldt 1957, 36). Major excavations in the interior and just outside the church provide the archaeological background to verify the date of the Merovingian or even late Roman origin suggested by the written sources.

The first archaeological observations date back to the mid ninteenth century, when graves were discovered inside and in close vicinity to the church (Lehner and Bader 1932, 4–5). In 1920 a first archaeological excavation was conducted by Hans Lehner, after road-works unearthed the remains of a small chapel on the northern side of the nave (Lehner 1925). Seven years later, several small-scale trenches were opened inside the crypt and to the north and south of it. The discovery of 'Roman' graves, including a number of stone coffins, as well as a stone wall running south-west/north-east led to a 3-year excavation campaign between 1928 and 1930 (Lehner and Bader 1932).

Hans Lehner and Walter Bader investigated the Romano-Frankish cemetery and the remains of different buildings predating the existing Romanesque church. By 1930 they had recorded more than 100 graves and structural remains dating from late Roman times to the eighteenth century. The most striking discovery was a small building identified as a *cella memoriae* used for ceremonial meals in remembrance of the deceased (Fig. 26.3). It contained two low stone benches on either side of two stone tables (Fig. 26.4). The north-eastern end was constructed as a dry stone wall. The entire building had a sunken floor and must have had some kind of timber walls and roofs. It was used only for a rather short period as the soft plaster of the stone benches showed no sign of wear. A layer of burned wood was seen as signs of a violent destruction a short time after its construction. According to Bader this resulted from a violent clash between pagan and Christian inhabitants of Bonn (Bader 1985, 183).

Lehner and Bader saw the *cella memoriae* as the starting point of a cemetery and a successive number of small church buildings. Its alignment followed a nearby road running in a south-west/north-east direction. They dated the cella to the late third century and associated it with the medieval legend of the martyrs SS Cassius and Florentius. The *cella* was thus claimed as one of the oldest Christian build-ings in Germany. Lehner and Bader also assigned a number of graves to this first phase. Immediately after the *cella* was destroyed, a first church (termed 'Church D', see Fig. 26.1) was constructed on the site. It was a rectangular building 13.7 m long by 8.9 m wide, with a choir area originally separated by a screen. The foundations consisted of three layers of Roman altar-stones resting on a layer of undressed stones. The 1.3 m high massive foundation was used to support a stone superstructure. The inside of the church was finished by laying out a floor made of mortar mixed with crushed bricks to give it a terrazzo-like surface. The inside walls were covered with plaster and whitewashed, while the outside walls were left un-plastered. Crosses marked in the mortar floor indicated the position of two graves (see below). It is therefore possible to call the building a church even without any trace of an altar. Coin finds were used to date this church to just before AD 400 (Lehner and Bader 1932, 184). It was said to have been altered and enlarged during the early fifth and again from the eighth century onwards

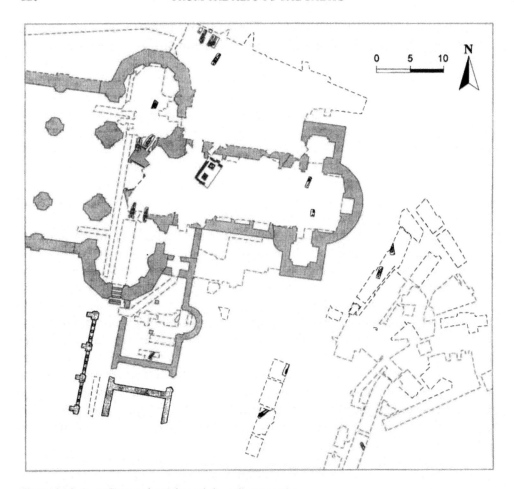

Figure 26.3 Late-Roman burials and the *cella memoriae*

(Lehner and Bader 1932, 186). The early dating of the cella and the late fourth-century date of church D have been matters of much debate over the past 70 years, and have now been substantially revised (see below).

Fresh information was added in excavations by Wieland between 1946 and 1948 (Oelmann 1949). He found the remains of Roman and early medieval structures in the northern transept and south of the crypt. In 1965 Hugo Borger re-excavated the entrance hall north of the nave. His work there as well as on the adjacent Minster Square in 1963/1964 gave no evidence of the Roman and Merovingian cemetery extending to the north and west. More than 1250 m² has now been excavated, amounting to almost half of the church. Only the 1928–1930 excavations have been published by Lehner and Bader in an extensive preliminary report in 1932. Most of the burials, the architectural remains and coins were discussed but hardly any of the pottery was published.

New work has concentrated on re-examining the old evidence and analysing the pottery, which has resulted in changes to most of the previously accepted

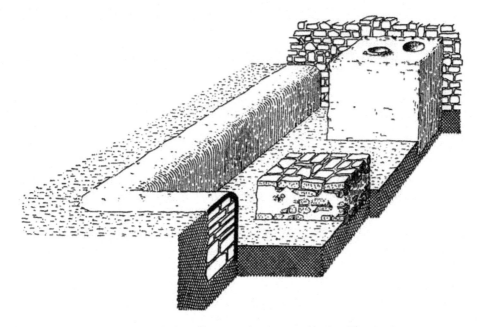

Figure 26.4 Reconstruction of the *cella memoriae* (Lehner/Bader 1932, Pl. 3)

dates. This work is summarised below. An analysis of the Merovingian burials is also in progress and will be published by Ulrike Müssemeier as part of her PhD thesis.

The Early Christian Sequence at Bonn: a New Model

The site of the minster church is situated on the slope of high river bank down to the old river bed called 'Gumme'. In Roman times an industrial area separated it from the *canabae*. The pottery finds indicate massive rubbish-tipping on the slope during the second and early third century. Material of this date inevitably found its way into later features. The first burials on the site probably belong to the second half of the third century: Grave 45 is dated to this period by its grave goods. Two of the three ceramic vessels have almost no comparison and seem to be a local cup type (Haupt in: Petrikovits 1967/1968, 117). The Roman pottery in Grave 31 was redeposited in a sixth-century burial (Keller/Müssemeier 2001, 295–6).

Several other burials can be assigned to the late Roman graveyard by virtue of their stratigraphy and alignment. All of them are inhumation burials, some of them in wooden coffins. They have the same alignment as the cella which differs from that of Church D and the later graves by more than 5 degrees. One of these burials, Grave 106, can be dated to the fifth century by a Mayen-ware sherd. Several other graves discovered during excavations between 1946 and 1951 can be assigned to this group. This leaves us with a cemetery consisting of graves scattered loosely over an area 50 metres square (Fig. 26.3).

Figure 26.5 Finds from the *cella memoriae*

The *cella memoriae* itself was erected on the already existing cemetery and not as Lehner and Bader assumed as its starting point. The late third-century date given by Lehner and Bader was based on the *terminus post quem* provided by the inscription on a reused stone altar (after AD 235) and a samian ware bowl set into the mortar of one of the two stone tables (Lehner and Bader 1932, 176–8). However, among the pottery recovered from below the stone benches and the earth fill of the *cella* were two vessels which can be assigned to the mid and second half of the fourth century (Fig. 26.5).

The lack of artefacts in the graves and religious objects or inscriptions in the *cella* leaves us with the question of whether the *cella* and its contemporary graves were of Christian or non-Christian affiliation. Lehner and Bader believed in a direct relation between the excavated *cella* and the burial of the two martyrs known from the medieval legend (Lehner and Bader 1932, 208). Bader always suspected that their graves lay beneath the cella-building and that the two stone *mensae* were used to commemorate them (Bader 1948; Bader 1985, 183). Therefore a Christian cult could have been practised on the site right from its beginning to the present day. But it was never possible to test this idea as safety reasons restricted excavation beneath the *cella* floor. The hypothesis was criticised by Theodor Klauser, who held that there was no proof of the Christian origin of the *cella* or of the existence of martyrs' burials (Klauser 1947, 37); but in spite of this, the Christian character of the *cella* became unquestioned fact (Kremer 1993, 280–94).

The argument remains finely balanced. On the one hand, memorial buildings are a common feature on urban Roman cemeteries and not restricted to Christian use (Naumann-Steckner 1997, 41–6). The religious beliefs of the *cella*'s builders, or of those buried in the contemporary graves, cannot be deduced from archaeological finds nor from development of the site. The medieval legend of the Roman martyrs cannot be used to validate or date archaeological features, and the recent finds analysis has shown that the first certain Christian building was 150 years later (see below). There is however one aspect in favour of a special character for these early burials. *Cella* and cemetery are some distance away from all the other fourth-century burial grounds. The first contemporary graves are more than 150 m away, the first cemetery 350 m, and the fourth-century settlement is more than 1000 m to the north (Fig. 26.6). Even more striking is the topographical setting. All other burials are located on the top of the river bank and often in close proximity to roads. But the minster burial ground is on the

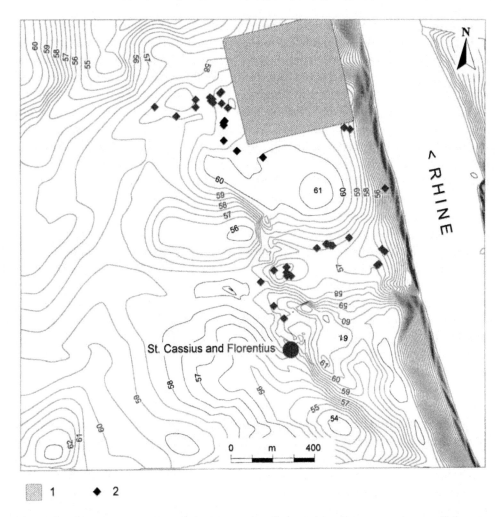

Figure 26.6 Fourth-century burials in Bonn (after Kaiser 1996): 1 legionary fortress; 2 burials

western slope of the bank. It is situated in a small depression almost on the bottom of the old river bed. The derelict area of the former industrial production sites separates it from the rest of late Roman Bonn. The remote setting has already been noted by Bader (Bader 1985, 183). This location – out of sight and far from the settled areas – might give an answer to our question. From medieval times onwards we know examples of burial sites with similar settings. These burial grounds were used by groups of people not fully integrated in the local social system (Maier and Winghart 1982, 197). In our case the burial customs do not show an ethnic distinction, but conform to Bonn's Roman population (Bierbrauer 1996, 111–3), so they might have merited separation by virtue of their religious belief. It might thus be possible to argue that there was a Christian burial ground on the minster site beginning in the late third century, the *cella memoriae* being a construction added a century later.

After the destruction of the cella the area remained in use for simple inhumation burials. Due to the occasional flooding of the old river bed the ground level rose steadily by more than a metre, after which the stone building known as 'Church D' was erected on the site (Fig. 26.7.1). With hardly any pottery recovered from the foundation trenches the construction can only be dated vaguely to the mid sixth century (Keller and Müssemeier 2001, 291–5), it being on a different alignment to the cella. Oral tradition could have handed down the location and might have already linked it to the legendary martyrs. Just after the building was finished, and prior to the laying out of a mortar floor, the first tombs were installed. Grave 32, dated to the second half of the sixth century was built from several large sandstone slabs. It contained the remains of a woman with gold-wire-decorated cloth, a necklace of 21 glass beads, a needle, a late Roman coin and a silver fitting. The position of the tomb (as also Grave 31) was marked with a cross in the newly laid mortar floor. Lehner and Bader believed that at least some of the stone coffins pre-dated Church D, but there is no stratigraphic evidence for this, and the identical alignment of all graves inside the building points to a date after the construction of the church (Keller and Müssemeier 2001, 290–2). The floor of mortar mixed with crushed brick was laid before the end of the sixth century.

With the construction of the church for the first time furnished graves appear in the cemetery. According to the grave goods these people are not Romans but Franks. They belong to the wealthier part of the population and have long-distance contacts (Keller and Müssemeier 2001, 295). It looks as though the leading members of the Frankish population in Bonn were the first to be converted to Christianity. A similar process can be observed in different places in Francia and Alamania (Böhme 1993, 519).

All through the seventh century the church was popular for burials. More than a dozen stone coffins and stone slab-lined graves were erected. Some of them were re-used up to four times for secondary burials. The cemetery on the outside extended to the south and east. During this period rooms were added at the south-west corner and the north west end (Fig. 26.7.2), which probably served as memorial chapels for Graves 8 and 74 respectively. At the north-east corner two more rooms with a dividing corridor and an exterior annexe were built. No graves were found inside the two small rooms separated by a corridor, which may have served as living quarters for the local clergy. This could be the building complex termed *basilicam sanctorum Casii et Florentii sociorum* first mentioned in AD 691 (Levison 1932, 236 No. 5).

With the beginning of the eighth century a period of intensive rebuilding began (Fig. 26.7.3). First, a new mortar floor was laid, as the old one was severely damaged by the numerous burials. Soon afterwards, rooms on the north-eastern side as well as the northern wall of the church itself were pulled down so that the church could be enlarged. The ground was leveled and additional foundations were laid out. A choir measuring 8.7 m by 7.5 m was added, and separated from the nave by a screen or barrier indicated by a wall footing. The mortar floor of the

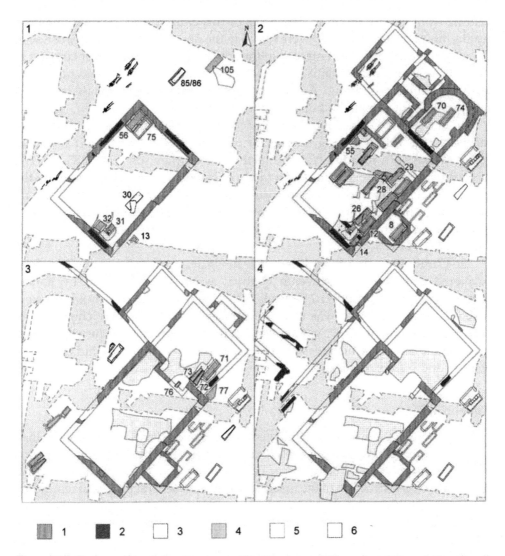

Figure 26.7 Early medieval development of St. Cassius and Florentius: 1 foundation; 2 wall; 3 mortar floor; 4 burial; 5 reconstructed wall; 6 unexcavated area

new choir was raised 20 cm above the one inside the old church. Raised by a similar height was a small rectangular alcove or chancel. The choir of the church might have served as a presbytry for the growing number of clergy attached to SS Cassius and Florentius.

A short time after the extended church was finished it probably burned down. We can see this from the pieces of molten lead, which dropped down from the burning roof. In a reconstruction (Fig. 26.7.4) the chancel at the east end was demolished, to make room for an even larger one, of which only fragments of the mortar floor have survived. In the other parts of the church a new mortar floor was laid. The barrier dividing the nave and presbytery was replaced by a ramp leading from one to the other. The walls of this church were probably painted inside: bits of decorated fresco were found in the demolition rubble (deposited in the eleventh century). The entrance in the south-western wall was enlarged. On the outside walls and remains of a mortar floor might have formed part of an atrium or similar building. A coin and pottery finds date this last period of rebuilding to the second half of the eighth century.

The new entrance probably became necessary when the remains of the two martyrs attracted a growing number of people. For the first time it is said in 798/799 that both martyrs rest within the church (Levison 1932, 255 No. 27). According to the historical sources a *tumba* of some kind was visible to mark the graves from the early ninth century onwards, although there have been no archaeological traces found of a commemorative construction. This phase may also equate with the monastery which is first mentioned in AD 804 (Levison 1932, 242 No. 13).

The Carolingian church and the monastic buildings seem to have remained unaltered until the mid eleventh century, when were replaced by a new Romanesque church (Kubach/Verbeek 1976, 110–2). After the old buildings were taken down, the ground was leveled in order to build the new church in an east/west-alignment. The crypt and part of the western apse of this church survived in the minster which was built between the mid twelfth to mid thirteenth century and stands to this day.

Conclusion

Investigations at the site of Bonn minster have uncovered remains of a late Roman burial ground which may have included Christians. The site was redeveloped in the mid sixth century by members of Bonn's newly converted Frankish population, with the construction of the first known church. Several phases of rebuilding and enlarging this church during the seventh and eighth century shows its growing importance as a monastery and for burial at a place associated with the legendary martyrs Cassius and Florentius. The site was again redeveloped on the same spot in the eleventh century with a church on a new alignment.

References

Andrikopoulou-Strack, J.-N. 1966 Der römische Vicus von Bonn. *Bonner Jahrb.* 196, 421–68.

Angenendt, A. 1995 *Das Frühmittelalter. Die abendländische Christenheit von 400 bis 900*, 2nd rev. ed. (Stuttgart/Berlin/Cologne).

Bader, W. 1948 Zur Kritik des Bonner Märtyrergrabes. *Bonner Jahrb.* 148, 1948, 452–3.

Bader, W. 1985 *Sanctos. Grabfeld, Märtyrergrab und Bauten vom 4. Jh. bis um und nach 752–768 n. Chr. Die Stiftskirche des hl. Victor zu Xanten I.1* (Xanten).

Bierbrauer, V. Romanen im fränkischen Siedelgebiet. In: A. Wieczorek *et al.* (eds), *Die Franken. Wegbereiter Europas*. Exhibition catalogue Mannheim 1996 (Mainz) 110–20.

Böhme, H.W. 1993 Adelsgräber im Frankenreich. *Jahrb. Röm.-German. Zentralmus. Mainz* 40, 1993, 397–534.

Böhner, K. 1978 Bonn im frühen Mittelalter. *Bonner Jahrb.* 178, 1978, 395–426.

Cat. Bonn: J. Engemann and Ch. B. Rüger (eds) 1991 *Spätantike und frühes Mittelalter. Ausgewählte Denkmäler im Rheinischen Landesmuseum Bonn.* Exhibition catalogue Bonn 1991. Kunst u. Altertum am Rhein 134 (Cologne).

Dassmann, E. 1993 *Die Anfänge der Kirche in Deutschland.* Urban-Taschenb. 444 (Stuttgart/Berlin/Cologne).

Dietz, J. 1962 Topographie der Stadt Bonn 1. Hälfte. *Bonner Geschichtsbl.* 16.

Gechter, M. 1979 Die Anfänge des Niedergermanischen Limes. *Bonner Jahrb.* 179, 1–129.

Höroldt, D. 1957 Das Stift St. Cassius zu Bonn von den Anfängen der Kirche bis zum Jahre 1580. *Bonner Geschichtsbl.* 11.

Horn, H.G. 1987 *Die Römer in Nordrhein-Westfalen* (Stuttgart).

Joachim, H.-E. 1988 Die vorgeschichtlichen Fundstellen und Funde im Stadtgebiet von Bonn. *Bonner Jahrb.* 188, 1–96.

Kaiser, M. 1996 Die römischen Gräber von Bonn und ihr Bezug zur topographischen Entwicklung des Legionsstandortes. *Bonner Jahrb.* 196, 469–88.

Keller, C. and U. Müssemeier 2001 Die merowinger- und karolingerzeitlichen Bauten unter der Münsterkirche in Bonn. In: E. Pohl, U. Recker and C. Theune (eds), Archäologische Zellwerk Festschrift für Helmuth Roth (Stud. Honoraria 16: Rahden), 287–318.

Klauser, Th. 1947 Bemerkungen zur Geschichte der Bonner Märtyrergräbern. In: F. Nußbaum (ed.), *Bonn und sein Münster. Festschrift für Msgr. Johannes Hinsenkamp.* Bonner Geschichtsbl. 3, 35–9.

Kremer, J. 1993 *Studium zum frühen Christentum in Niedergermanien* (PhD thesis Bonn).

Lehner, H. 1925 Die Ausgrabung auf dem Münsterplatz in Bonn. *Bonner Jahrb.* 130, 201–15.

Lehner, H. and W. Bader 1932 Baugeschichtliche Untersuchungen am Bonner Münster. *Bonner Jahrb.* 136/137, 1–211.

Levison, W. 1932 Die Bonner Urkunden des frühen Mittelalters. *Bonner Jahrb.* 136/137, 217–70.

Maier, R.A. and S. Winghart 1982 Nichtchristliches Totenbrauchtum auf einem neuzeitlichen Bestattungsplatz bei der Stadt Erdingen, Oberbayern. *Das arch. Jahr Bayern* 1981, 196–7.

Naumann-Steckner, F. 1997 *Tod am Rhein. Begräbnisse im frühen Köln* (Cologne).

Oelmann, F. 1949 Fundbericht Bonn. *Bonner Jahrb.* 149, 356–61.

Petrikovits, H.v. 1967/68 Die Zeitstellung der ältesten frühchristlichen Kultanlage unter der Bonner Münster. *Kölner Jahrb. Vor- u. Frühgesch.* 9, 112–8.

Rösger, A. and W. Will 1985 Die Drususbrücke zu Bonn. Nochmals Flor. epit. 2, 30, 26. *Bonner Jahrb.* 185, 27–39.

27

The Cross Goes North: From Late Antiquity to Merovingian Times South and North of the Alps[1]

VOLKER BIERBRAUER

In this chapter I examine the process of Christianisation among the Franks, Alamans and Bavarians as revealed by the wearing of the cross, and in particular the wearing of the symbol of the cross on brooches and pendants as part of female dress. I begin by describing the practice among the Roman peoples south of the Alps, and then how it was adopted – or not- among the Germanic peoples north of the Alps, and I offer an explanation for the differences. In the space available I can give only a brief sketch of the background of Christianity among the peoples either side of the Alps, in order to interpret this particular use of the *signum* of the cross, and to put it into context.

Roman and Post-Roman Christianity in Italy

In the well-known decree *cum cunctos populos*, the Emperor Theodosius made the Nicean creed obligatory for the Roman Empire in 380, an act which turned the Romanised population into a congregation of the Church and vice versa. Although paganism was not completely abolished, either by this decree or by imperial laws which were to follow immediately afterwards, Christianity had firmly established itself by the fifth century in both town and country in northern Italy. The map in Fig. 27.1.1 shows the network of bishoprics in the Metropolitan districts of Milan, Aquileia and Ravenna and in the rural surroundings where Christian communities had now emerged.[2] A more detailed map of north-east Italy, in Friuli (Fig. 27.1.2), that is in the surroundings of Aquileia, shows the

---

[1] Cf. the thematically related study by M. Müller-Wille, The Cross as a Symbol of Personal Christian Belief in a Changing Religious World. Examples from Selected Areas in Merovingian and Carolingian Europe. *Konferenser* 40 (Stockholm 1998) 179–200.

[2] P. Golinelli, Il Cristianesimo nella VENETIA altomedievale. Diffussione, istituzionalizzione e forme di religiosità dalle origini al sec. X. In: A. Castagnetti and G.M. Varanini (ed.), *Il Veneto nel medioevo. Dalla 'Venetia' alla Marca Veronese I* (1989) 239–59.

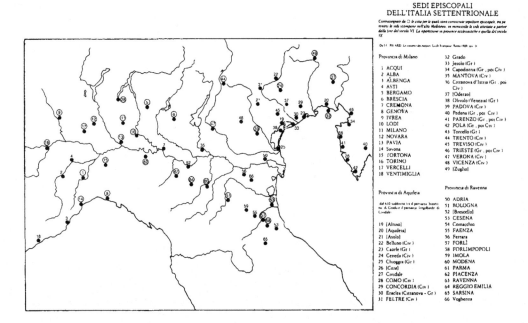

Figure 27.1.1 Network of bishoprics in the Metropolitan districts of Milan, Aquileia and Ravenna (after Golinelli, note 1, 252–253)

distribution of church foundations, almost all of them from the first half of the fifth century.[3]

In the fifth to the seventh centuries, Christianity is manifested in northern Italy by the wearing of specific types of personal dress and jewelry.[4] The evidence comes from the study of cemeteries of this period (Fig. 27.2.1)[5] which have shown that the local population had already started to wear cross-shaped brooches in the fifth century, both in Friuli and over the Central Alps as a whole.[6] The distribution map (Fig. 27.2.2) shows the location of the fifth and sixth-century examples which have been found in cemeteries. But since the native Roman population generally used to bury their dead without grave-goods, the map only illustrates the exceptions to the rule, and the wearing of cross-shaped brooches was probably far more widespread than the map implies. This is endorsed by the fact that some of these brooches have also been discovered in settlement sites.[7]

---

[3] V. Bierbrauer, Friaul im 5.–8. Jahrhundert: Siedlungsgeschichtliche Grundlinien aus archäologischer Sicht. In: R. Bratož (ed.), *Slowenien und die Nachbarländer zwischen Antike und karolingischer Epoche. Kongreß Ljubljana 1998* (2000) 314–7, with Fig. 7.

[4] Bierbrauer, 'Friaul im 5.–8. Jahrhundert'.

[5] Bierbrauer, 'Friaul im 5.–8. Jahrhundert' 320–4, with Fig. 8.

[6] Bierbrauer, 'Friaul im 5.–8. Jahrhundert' with Fig. 12; V. Bierbrauer, Kreuzfibeln in der mittelalpinen romanischen Frauentracht des 5.–7. Jahrhunderts: Trentino und Südtirol. Archivio per l'Alto Adige. *Rivista di Studi alpini* 86, 1992, 1–26; E. Riemer, *Romanische Grabfunde des 5.–8. Jahrhunderts in Italien* (2000) 116–20.

[7] Bierbrauer, 'Friaul im 5.–8. Jahrhundert'.

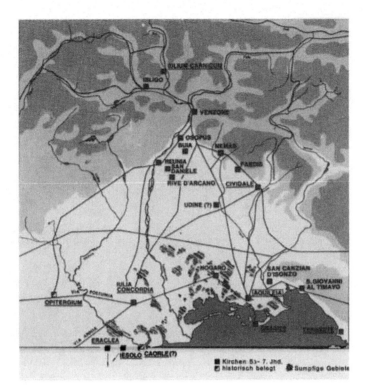

Figure 27.1.2 Distribution map of churches dating from fifth to seventh century in east upper Italy (Friuli), historical references and marshy places

The cross-shaped brooches and other types of brooches mentioned below were worn by women and served to fasten their upper garments.[8]

The typology of the cross-shaped brooches has been discussed elsewhere.[9] We can add to them other types of brooch which are not just crosses, but may be interpreted as Christian by association. Some feature doves (Fig. 27.3.1–2), the Christian symbol of the Holy Spirit,[10] worn by native Roman women in the fifth–sixth centuries.[11] Closely related to Christian symbolism are also the peacock, dove or cock-shaped brooches (Fig. 27.3.5). The peacock symbolises the idea of paradise, that is of eternal life, and the cock mainly symbolised resurrection.

---

[8] M. Martin s.v. 'Fibel und Fibeltracht'. *Reallexikon der Germanischen Altertumskunde* Vol. 8 (1994) 544f., 567–74; Riemer, 'Romanische Grabfunde' 237.
[9] Bierbrauer, 'Kreuzfibeln'; Riemer, 'Romanische Grabfunde'.
[10] Bierbrauer, 'Kreuzfibeln' 13 with Fig. 2,4–5 and plate 1,2–4; Riemer, 'Romanische Grabfunde' 119.
[11] Riemer, 'Romanische Grabfunde' 111–3; V. Bierbrauer, Tier- und Kreuzfibeln als Zeugnisse persönlichen Christentums in der oberitalienischen Romania des 5.–7. Jahrhunderts. In: S. Gelichi (ed.), *Studi di archeologia e storia dell'alto medioevo. Gedenkschrift f. Otto von Hessen* (2002); here is listed locations of the distribution maps, Figs 27.2.2 and 27.3.5.

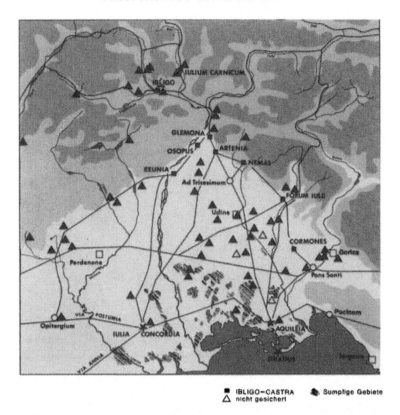

Figure 27.2.1 Distribution map of cemeteries of the local Roman population in east upper Italy, fifth to seventh century (Friuli)

Animal brooches had already been worn in the pagan context of the second to fourth centuries. However, we cannot have any doubt about an *interpretatio cristiana* here, as endorsed by the combination of dove and cross on some of the brooches (Fig. 27.3.1–2).[12] The precious cross-shaped pectoral ornament (Fig. 27.3.3) is also an example of personal, plainly confessed Christian belief,[13] just as the thin silver and bronze pendants which were probably integrated onto a chain (pectoral crosses), but which could also have been brought into rural churches as votive crosses (Fig. 27.3.4).[14]

In the sixth and seventh century personal Christian belief shows itself in the region in additional types of brooches. Particularly in south Italy ring-shaped brooches featuring the cross, a Christian stereotyped dedication and the name of a person, were also exceptionally worn by men (for example, a brooch from

---

[12] Bierbrauer, 'Tier- und Kreuzfibeln'.
[13] Riemer, 'Romanische Grabfunde' 83f.; Bierbrauer, 'Friaul im 5.–8. Jahrhundert' 16f.
[14] Bierbrauer, 'Kreuzfibeln' 16f. with Fig. 3, 5–7; H. Vierck, Folienkreuze als Votivbeigaben. In: W. Hübener (ed.), *Die Goldblattkreuze des frühen Mittelalters*. Symposium Freiburg 1974 (1975) 125ff., 131ff.

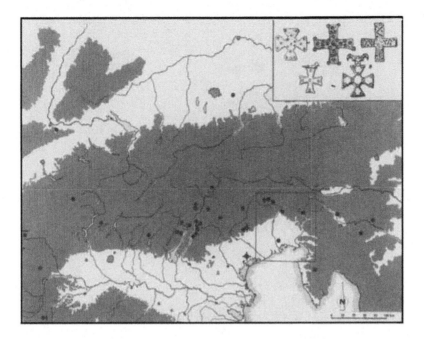

Figure 27.2.2 Distribution of cross-shaped brooches in the Alpine region, fifth to seventh century

Lupus with the dedication *biba* (= vivas) in Deo (Fig. 27.4.1).[15] Other examples include disc-shaped brooches with the cross[16] and with the motif of the peacocks either side of a chalice (Fig. 27.4.2).[17] This motif can also be observed in the context of jewelry, for instance on precious Mediterranean earrings made of gold: peacocks again at the side of a chalice, or at the side of a cross (Fig. 27.4.3), or a peacock alone or a cross alone.[18]

This brief survey of the fifth to seventh centuries in north Italy can be summarized up as follows. Apart from churches with their interior decoration, their church treasures, liturgical requisites as well as sarcophagi and so on, personal Christian belief is demonstrated completely independently from any social structures in all ranks of the population by displaying the sign of the cross and other Christian symbols in dress and jewelry. This is just as natural as the display of the cross by the upper class on tableware, for example on spoons with a Christian dedicatory formula and the nielloed cross beneath,[19] or on helmets of

[15] Riemer, 'Romanische Grabfunde' 121–4.
[16] Riemer, 'Romanische Grabfunde' 125–8.
[17] Riemer, 'Romanische Grabfunde' 127 with Fig. 15, 128.
[18] Riemer, 'Romanische Grabfunde' 67–9; the earring (Fig. 27.4.3) of unknown mediterranean provenance is part of the Collection of prince Otto von Hessen, now in the 'Archäologische Staatssammlung', Munich (in preparation).
[19] For instance Desana (Italy): V. Bierbrauer, *Die ostgotischen Grab- und Schatzfunde in Italien* (1975) 180–8 Pl. 13–16.

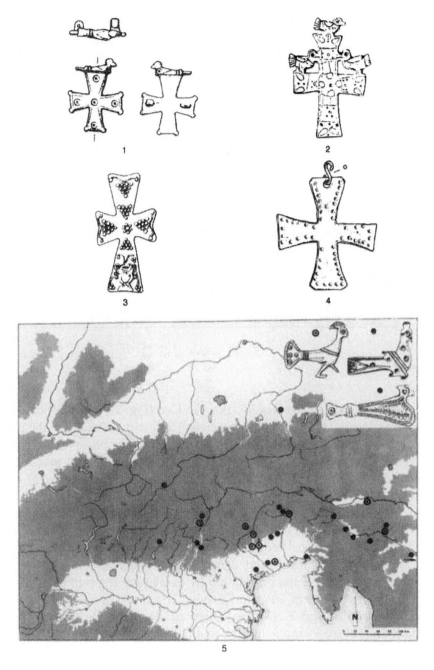

Figure 27.3 1 Cross-shaped brooch from Caraglio, San Lorenzo, Pr. Cunevo (E. Micheletto and L. Paroli (eds) *L'Italia Centro-settentrionale* (1997), 309, Fig. 4); 2 cross-shaped brooch from Korita (Bosnia-Herzegovina) (Bierbrauer, note 6, Fig. 2.4); 3 cross-shaped pectoral pendant from Desana, Pr. Vercelli (V.Bierbrauer *Die ostgotischen Grab- und Schatzfunde in Italien* (1975), Pl. 8.4); 4 cross-shaped pendant from Kučar (Slovenia) (T. Knific and M. Sagadin Pismo Brez Pisave (1991), 50, Fig. 5 [Nos 1–4 not to scale]; 5 distribution of peacock, dove and cock-shaped brooches in the Alpine region, fifth to seventh century

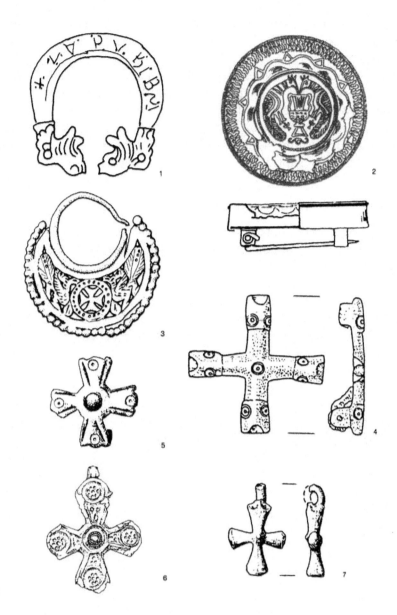

Figure 27.4 Ring-shaped brooch from region of Benevento (M.Salvatore *Vetera Christianorum* 14 (1977) 343; 2 disc-shaped brooch of Cirò Marina, Pr. Crotone (F.A. Cuteri in R. Francovich and G. Noyé (eds) *La Storia dell'alto Medioevo Italiano (VI-X secolo) alla luce dell'archeologia* (1994), 347, Fig. 6; 3 ear-ring of unknown Mediterranean provenance (collection of Otto von Hessen, unpublished); 4 cross-shaped brooch from Iversheim, Kr. Euskirchen (Ch. Neuffer-Müller, *Das fränkische Gräberfeld von Iversheim, Kr. Euskirchen* (1972), Pl. 11; 5 cross-shaped brooch from Gondorf, Kr. Mayen-Koblenz (M. Schulze-Dörlamm *Die spätrömischen und frühmittelalterlichen Gräberfelder von Gondorf, Kr Mayen-Koblenz* (1990) Pl. 37.7); 6 cross-shaped pectoral pendant from Friedberg, Kr. Augsburg; 7 cross-shaped pectoral pendant from Oberstotzingen, Kr. Heidenheim (R. Christlein in W. Hübener (ed.) *Die Goldblattkreuze des frühen Mittelalters* (1975, 82, Fig. 9.1). [Not to scale]

Mediterranean manufacture with the *crux gemmata* at the front[20] or on the golden cross-bow brooches, which were worn by high-ranking civil or military dignitaries.[21]

These manifestations of personal Christian belief on female dress, the cross-, dove-, cock- and peacock-shaped brooches, identify their bearers as Christians by symbols which are essentially based on their use in the New Testament. They reveal a process of conversion among the people of north Italy developing from the fifth century. All this will be very different when we look at the Germanic people north of the Alps.

The Early Cross-signum North of the Alps

The manifestations of Christianity differ either side of the Alps, but there are also differences between the northerners themselves, particularly the Franks on one hand and the Alamans and Bavarians on the other. In the Frankish area of settlement in North Gaul up to the Rhine, there is likely to have been a continuity of Christian institution and clerical organisation from the late Roman period into the fifth century.[22] Then, beginning with Chlodwig's baptism in 498, a dynamic process of Christianization is without doubt taking place in the sixth century. It expresses itself, however, exclusively in church buildings: the Royal Family built dynastic burial churches[23] and the Frankish nobility followed their example with their *Eigenkirchen*.[24] We know nothing about the conversion to Christianity of the majority of the Frankish population, who were buried in large cemeteries, the so-called Reihengräberfriedhöfe, some hundreds of metres away from their settlements. At best the Frankish cemeteries which surround royal burial churches, as for instance round the Apostle's Church of Chlodwig in Paris[25] or round some few *Eigenkirchen*, for instance the graves round the church at Hordain,[26] can be interpreted as Christian burial grounds of the populace. It is striking, however,

---

[20] J. Werner, Neues zur Herkunft der frühmittelalterlichen Spangenhelme vom Baldenheimer Typus. Germania 66, 1988, 521–8; D. Quast, *Merowingerzeitliche Grabfunde aus Gültlingen* (1993) 30–42; K. Böhner, Die frühmittelalterlichen Spangenhelme und die nordischen Helme der Vendelzeit. *Jahrb. Römisch-Germanisches Zentralmuseum Mainz* 41, 1994, 471–532 with Fig. 6–8.

[21] For instance: Bierbrauer 'Die ostgotischen Grab- und Schatzfunde' 122–5 Pl. 5 and 32,6.

[22] M. Weidemann, Die kirchliche Organisation der Provinzen Belgica und Germania vom 4. bis zum 7. Jahrhundert. In: P. Bange and A.G. Weiler (eds), *Willibrord, Zijn wereld en zijn werk. Kongreß Nijmwegen 1989* (1990) 285–316; F. Staab, Heidentum und Christentum in der Germania Prima zwischen Antike und Mittelalter. In: F. Staab (ed.), *Zur Kontinuität zwischen Antike und Mittelalter am Oberrhein* (1994) 117–52. Also see Pearce, Chapter 4 in this volume.

[23] M. Müller-Wille, Königsgrab und Königsgrabkirche. Funde und Befunde im frühgeschichtlichen und mittelalterlichen Europa. *Ber. Römisch-Germanische Kommission* 63, 1982, 350–8.

[24] H.W. Böhme, Adelsgräber im Frankenreich. Archäologische Zeugnisse einer Herrenschicht unter den merowingischen Königen. *Jahrb. Römisch-Germanisches Zentralmuseum Mainz* 40, 1993 (1995) 397–534.

[25] M. Müller-Wille, Zwei religiöse Welten: Bestattungen der fränkischen Könige Childerich und Chlodwig. *Abhandl. Akad. d. Wiss. u. Lit., Geistes- u. Sozialwissenschaftl. Kl. Jahrg. 1998, Nr. 1*, 27–30.

[26] Böhme, 'Adelsgräber im Frankenreich' 406–9.

that manifestations of personal Christian belief are found neither in the graves of the upper class nor in the supposed graves of the populace; if those Franks had not been buried in churches they would not be recognized as Christians at all. This remarkable result is valid until the first half of the seventh century; the few exceptions confirm the rule, as for instance the pair of disc-shaped brooches of Queen Arnegundis buried in St Denis near Paris at the end of the sixth century,[27] or the disc-shaped brooch of Rosmeer in Belgium with a cross-shaped hollow on the back, which served also as a recipient for secondary relics.[28]

Among the Franks, manifestations of personal Christian belief are found on a significant scale only from the middle of the seventh century onward. Now we find cross-shaped brooches (Fig. 27.4.4–5) in graves as well as occasionally in settlements, but distributed only in a narrowly defined region of the East Franks between the Rhine and Mosel (Fig. 27.5.1).[29] The use of these cross-shaped brooches on female dress, reflecting their use in north Italy, is no doubt connected with a late Roman Christianity which still survived in this area in the fifth and sixth centuries. It is in this same region and same period that inscribed Roman-type tombstones also dominate.[30] We may reasonably suppose that at least some of the bearers of these cross-shaped brooches are women who are culturally Roman.[31] However, the adoption does not include peacock, cock or dove-shaped brooches such as we have seen (above) formed part of the repertoire for Christian women in north Italy. In the western Frankish settlement area cross-shaped brooches do not seem to be worn at all. We may therefore ascertain that the Italian-Mediterranean manifestations of personal Christian belief, connected with very specific types of brooches and with a very specific Christian meaning, were not generally adopted by the Franks.

A similar variety of response in the signals of Christianity is observable among the Alamans and Bavarians, to whom we shall briefly turn our attention now. With the exception of the Alamans in northern Switzerland, where late Roman Christianity had remained continually active, the conversion to Christianity of the Alamans and the Bavarians was brought about from the outside: the Alamans were converted through the bishoprics on the River Rhine – like Mainz, Worms,

---

[27] P. Périn, Pour une révision de la datation de la tombe d'Arégonde, épouse de Clotaire Ier, découverte en 1959 dans la basilique de Saint-Denis. *Arch. Medievale* 21, 1991, 21–50 with Fig. 2,3.

[28] H. Roosens and D. Thomas-Goorieckx, Une fibule mérovingienne en orfèvrerie cloisonnée trouvée a Rosmeer. *Arch. Belgica* 123, 1970, 67–81 with Fig. 1–3.

[29] Müller-Wille, 'The Cross as Symbol' 190–3 with Fig. 9–11 and list 4, 199f.; in addition: J. Krier, Echternach und das Kloster des hl. Willibrord. *Die Franken. Wegbereiter Europas.* Ausstellungskatalog Mannheim Vol. 1 (1996) 470 Fig. 361.

[30] W. Schmitz, Grabinschriften und Grabsteine. In: J. Engemann and Ch.B. Rüger (eds), *Spätantike und frühes Mittelalter* (1991) 7–19 with Fig. 4; Müller-Wille, 'Zwei religiöse Welten' 27 with Fig. 14.

[31] Frankish ethnicity of the women buried with the cross-shaped brooches can only be evidenced in exceptional cases because of the lack of ethnically significant other finds: cf. Müller-Wille, 'The Cross as Symbol' with list 4; nevertheless Frankish ethnicity is mostly supposed, for instance E. Wamers, *Die frühmittelalterlichen Lesefunde aus der Löhrstraße (Baustelle Hilton) in Mainz* (1994) 135; W. Schmitz, Kreuzfibel (note 30) 203–5.

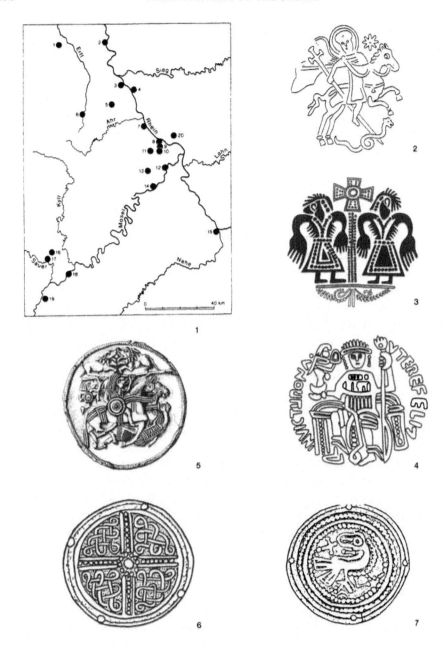

Figure 27.5 1 Distribution map of late Merovingian cross-shaped brooches in the central Rhine and Mosel area (after Müller-Wille, note 1, 192, Fig. 11); *Pressblechscheibenfibeln* from: 2 Oron-le-Châtel (Switzerland) (after M. Klein-Pfeuffer *Merowingerzeitliche Fibeln und Anhänger aus Pressblech* (1993), 177, Fig. 55.2); 3 Kirchheim, Ries (after G Haseloff *Kunststile des frühen Mittelalters* (1979), 97, Fig. 54b); 4 Wiesbaden-Dotzheim (after M. Klein-Pfeuffer *Merowinger-zeitliche Fibeln und Anhänger aus Pressblech* (1993), 200, Fig. 63.3); 5 Pliezhausen, Kr. Reutlingen (after K. Böhner *Fundberichte aus Baden-Würtemberg* 19 (1994), 389, Fig. 4c); 6 Rheinsheim, Kr Karlsruhe (after H.W. Böhme in *Germania* 74 (1996), 498–500); 7 Berghausen, Kr. Karlsruhe (*ibid.*). [Not to scale]

Speyer, Straßburg, Basel and Konstanz – as well as by the Hiberno-Frankish mission, the so-called Luxueil mission, encouraged by the Frankish state through self-interest from 590 onwards and mainly connected with Columbanus. The Bavarians were converted exclusively by the Luxueil mission, connected above all with Columbanus's successor Eustasius from 612/615 onwards.[32] As with the Franks, the initial success of the mission was seen only in the feudal *Eigenkirchen* with the graves of the nobility within the churches or nearby, dating back to 600 with regard to the Alamans and to the Bavarians since the first third of the seventh century.[33] At no time during the seventh and early eighth centuries did these two *gentes* display on female dress the personal manifestations of Christianity such as the cross- and bird-shaped brooches with the Christian associations argued for north Italy.

The Alamans instead took from north Italy another very specific custom, that of gold-foil crosses sewn on fine cloth or leather and placed on the mouth of a dead person. The dense distribution of this practice among the Alamans is remarkable[34] and possibly represents the results of a mission to the Alamans from Upper Italy.[35] The precious golden cross-shaped brooch covered with gems from Lauchheim[36] stands for an exception to the rule described before. The few pectoral crosses (Fig. 24.4.6–7) represent a Mediterranean tradition, too. Because of the comparatively rare finds, however, we cannot speak of a large adoption of the type.[37]

As among the Franks, the Alamans and Bavarians adopted the *signum* of the cross in a significant density only in the seventh century, beginning hesitatingly in the first half of the seventh century and becoming more and more frequent in the second half of the seventh century. Its use in female dress is then widespread and diverse. It appears on disc-shaped brooches,[38] on chain-pendants,[39] on decoration discs[40] and on amulet cases, the so-called *bullae*, 'eo ipso Christian

---

[32] H.W. Böhme, Adel und Kirche bei den Alamannen der Merowingerzeit. *Germania* 74, 1996, 477–507; idem, Neue Aspekte zur Christianisierung Süddeutschlands während der jüngeren Merowingerzeit. In: W. Berschin, D. Geuenich and H. Steuer (eds), *Mission und Christianisierung am Hoch- und Oberrhein (6.–8. Jahrhundert)* (2000) 75–109; G. Fingerlin, Kirchen und Kirchengräber in der frühmittelalterlichen Alemannia Südwestdeutschlands. *Denkmalpflege in Baden-Württemberg* 1997, 2, 44–51; S. Lorenz, Die Christianisierung von der Spätantike bis in karolingische Zeit. In: *Die Alamannen. Begleitband zur Ausstellung* (1997) 441–6.

[33] Böhme, 'Adel und Kirche' 482ff. with Fig. 2–4; idem, 'Neue Aspekte' 89–97 with Figs 1 and 3.

[34] Böhme, 'Adel und Kirche' 493–6 with Fig. 5; E. Riemer, Zu Vorkommen und Herkunft italischer Folienkreuze. *Germania* 77, 1999, 609–36.

[35] Böhme, 'Adel und Kirche' 494f.; idem, 'Neue Aspekte' 101.

[36] I. Stork, Fürst und Bauer, Heide und Christ. 10 Jahre archäologische Forschungen in Lauchheim/Ostalbkreis. *Arch. Informationen aus Baden-Württemberg* 29 (1995) 28 with Fig. 24 and Frontispiz.

[37] M. Knaut, Goldblattkreuze und andere Kreuzzeichen. Gedanken zu einer süddeutsch-italischen Beigabensitte. In: C. Dobiat (ed.), *Festschrift für Otto-Hermann Frey zum 65. Geburtstag* (1994) 327f. with Fig. 6; Müller-Wille, 'The Cross as Symbol' 184 with Fig. 4–5.

[38] For instance W. Müller and M. Knaut, *Heiden und Christen* (1987) 18f. with Fig. 3–5, 9, 11–13.

[39] For instance Müller and Knaut 21 with Fig. page 23.

[40] For instance Müller and Knaut 21.

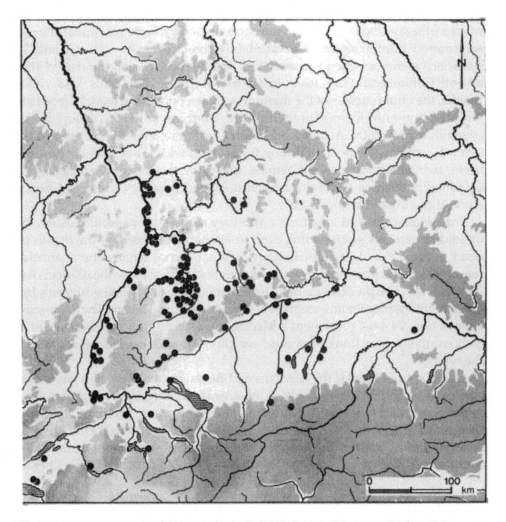

Figure 27.6 Distribution of bracteate-brooches of the later seventh-century (after Böhme, note 32, Fig. 8)

Phylakterien'.[41] The so-called *Preßblechfibeln* or bracteate-brooches are the most important carriers of Christian ornamentation from the second third of the seventh century onwards, but especially in the second half of the seventh century with a dense distribution east of the Rhine and south of the Main (Fig. 27.6)[42] Among them are those with the sign of the cross and with a bird (Fig. 27.5.6–7).[43]

[41] T. Vida, Frühmittelalterliche scheiben- und kugelförmige Amulettkapseln zwischen Kaukasus, Kastilien und Picardie. 76. *Ber. Römisch-Germanische Kommission* 1995, 234, 250–6, 263–78 with Fig. 35.
[42] M. Klein-Pfeuffer, *Merowingerzeitliche Fibeln und Anhänger aus Preßblech* (1993); Böhme, 'Adel und Kirche' 497 with fig. 8; U. Koch, Frühmittelalterliche Brakteatenfibeln – christliche oder heidnische Amulette? *Jahrb. Histor. Verein Heilbronn* 28, 1976, 19–28.
[43] Böhme, 'Adel und Kirche' 498 Fig. 6–7.

These bracteate brooches are mainly characterised by a great variety of Christian pictorial representation which all, without exception, derive from Mediterranean prototypes, for instance the Holy Knight with the cross-shaped lance (Fig. 27.5.2),[44] representations of angels at each side of a crosier (Fig. 27.5.3)[45] or the enthroned Mary (Fig. 27.5.4).[46] Frequently we come across the Christian symbol of the eagle, often with a cross.[47] Its distribution (and that of the bracteate brooches on which the front surface is bent over the rim) clearly point to an origin in the East-Frankish areas.[48] Together with the *bullae* and with the church buildings, of which 40% have Martin or Remigius as Patron Saints, all this testifies to a new mission originating from the Frankish *regnum*.[49]

Conclusion

In the course of the process of Christianization of the Franks, Alamans and Bavarians in the sixth and seventh centuries the *signum* of the cross was eventually adopted. However, concerning some essential aspects it was adopted in a very different way from that of its origins in the Christian-Mediterranean region of northern Italy, where cross, dove, peacock and cock were worn from the fifth century as brooches as part of female apparel in a matter-of-fact way. North of the Alps the display of the cross on dress occurs rarely until the mid seventh century. Then the Roman custom of north Italy was adopted, but only partially and in a narrowly defined area between Rhine and Mosel, where it can be ascribed to a continuing late Roman tradition among Christian women. The specific custom of marking the dead with gold-foil crosses was adopted from the Mediterranean region by the Alamans and partly by the Bavarians. Later in the seventh century, Franks, Alamans and Bavarians used Christian symbolism more widely in the form of pictorial representations on the bracteate-brooches also derived from the Mediterranean region.

What lies behind this striking result? One possibility is that the corresponding symbolic content of the simpler Mediterranean brooches was not understood by the Germanic Christians, that is the cross and cock as symbols of resurrection, the dove as a sign for the Holy Spirit and the peacock as a promise of eternal life, all of which require exegesis from the New Testament. The message of Christianity – and we can understand this very clearly from both literary and archaeological sources – could be made comprehensible to the Germanic peoples in this syncretic period of the sixth and seventh centuries in another, better way: that is through Christ who brings victory and grants protection. This religious imaginary world, still connected with and in relation to the old heathen world of Gods, could be

---

[44] Klein-Pfeuffer, 'Merowingerzeitliche Fibeln' 173–9 with Fig. 56.
[45] Klein-Pfeuffer, 'Merowingerzeitliche Fibeln' 180–3.
[46] Klein-Pfeuffer, 'Merowingerzeitliche Fibeln' 199–201 with Fig. 63.
[47] Böhme, 'Adel und Kirche' 499 Fig. 7.
[48] Klein-Pfeuffer, 'Merowingerzeitliche Fibeln' 50f. with map 6.
[49] Böhme, 'Adel und Kirche' 495.

more easily communicated visually. One example may stand for many: the triumphant horseman, seen first in pagan form on a *Phalera* adapted into a brooch from Pliezhausen (Fig. 27.5.5), his spear directed by a miniature divine bringer of victory,[50] and second, as the knightly Saint with the cross-shaped lance (Fig. 27.5.2). As all the Christian visual motifs, whether as crosses or on bracteates, originate from the Mediterranean area, we are observing without doubt a very conscious choice on the part of the peoples living north of the Alps.

The time for the widespread wearing of cross-shaped brooches was to come much later, mainly in the ninth century, at a time when, apart from the building up and enlarging of bishoprics, the organisation of lower churches (*Nieder-kirchenorganisation*) came about with a very dense network of parishes. This is the period of ecclesiastical development in which the cross in its iconic sense could be understood. In the sixth and seventh century, however, the Germanic world north of the Alps was still deep in syncretism.[51] The most expressive example of this syncretism is the continuity of the old pagan custom of grave goods, including the very heathen idea of living in eternity as one had lived on earth. This was expressed, for example, in furnished burial in mounds, in horse-graves and pagan amulets, and even in burial churches. This shows how very far we still are from the Christian belief of the New Testament, as manifested in earlier north Italy: that the body decays, and after death a *corpus spirituale*, a spiritual body was hoped for, exemplified in the cross- and bird brooches, worn by women in otherwise empty graves.

(translated by Heidrun von Wolffersdorf and Martin Carver)
(Figures prepared by Dieter Dahlmanns, Institute of Prehistory,
University of Munich)

---

[50] K. Böhner and D. Quast, Die merowingerzeitlichen Grabfunde aus Pliezhausen, Kr. Reutlingen. *Fundber. Baden-Württemberg* 10, 1994, 388–98; K. Böhner, Die frühmittelalterlichen Silberphaleren aus Eschwege (Hessen) und die nordischen Preßblechbilder. 38. *Jahrb. Römisch-Germanisches Zentralmuseum Mainz* 1991 (1995) 707–17.

[51] D. Quast, Opferplätze und heidnische Götter. In: *Die Alamannen. Begleitband zur Ausstellung* (1997) 433–40.

28

The Cross Goes North: Carolingian Times between Rhine and Elbe

MICHAEL MÜLLER-WILLE

Introduction

The region between the Central/Lower Rhine, Main, Saale/Elbe and the coastal zones of the North Sea and the Baltic was mainly Christianised during the phase of the northern expansion of the Carolingian Empire in the eighth and ninth centuries. At the end of the eighth and the first part of the ninth centuries many bishoprics were founded in the region between the Rhine and the Elbe, such as Münster, Paderborn, Osnabrück, Minden, Hildesheim, Halberstadt, Bremen, Verden and Hamburg. During the ninth and tenth centuries, the Mediterranean custom of wearing cross-shaped brooches can be widely observed on this northern periphery of the Carolingian empire. The type and distribution of these brooches, reviewed in this paper, gives an indication of the direction and timing of the process of conversion.

Thanks to a number of major exhibitions during the past few years it is now possible to get a clear idea of the archaeological, historical, art-historical and architectural sources related to the period of conversion in the northern lands. For the Alamans, Bavarians and Franks the catalogues and supplementary volumes accompanying the exhibitions in Mannheim 1996 (Paris-Berlin 1997), Stuttgart 1997, and Rosenheim 1998 provide comprehensive information, and the volumes accompanying the exhibition in Paderborn 1999 do the same for the understanding of situation of the Saxons and Franks. On the occasion of the exhibitions which were held in Budapest 2000 (Berlin, Mannheim, Prague, Bratislava, Cracow 2001–2003) and Magdeburg 2001, catalogues and accompanying volumes were also published, and these give an overview of the regions between the Elbe, Weichsel and Danube (that is the western Slavonic and Hungarian areas). Finally, the exhibition which was held in Berlin 1992 (Paris and Copenhagen 1992–93) dealt with contacts between Scandinavia and Europe and included the material evidence for conversion. The accessibility and dating of this material means that we can use it to reflect, at a personal level, that great change in northern Europe which we know only as a broad historical outline.

Historical Outline

In the wake of Charlemagne's conquest of Saxony from AD 772 to 805, the Christianisation of the Saxons proceeded from the regions adjacent to the south and to the west of the newly subjected areas. These regions, which include parts of the modern Netherlands, Hesse, Thuringia and Bavaria, had already adopted Christianity during the late seventh and eighth centuries, through the missionary activities of the Anglo-Saxons Willibrord and Boniface and the subsequent foundation of the bishoprics of Utrecht, Büraburg, Würzburg and Erfurt (Angenendt 1999, 424 Fig. 2). After the final conquest of Saxony around 800, bishoprics were founded at Paderborn, Münster, Osnabrück, Bremen, Verden and later at Hildesheim, Halberstadt and Hamburg (Fig. 28.1). These were closely connected with the two previously converted regions mentioned above (Angenendt 1999; Johanek 1999). The first bishops came from Fulda, Würzburg, the Rhine-Main area, or from Frisia – Liudger, first bishop of Münster had been educated in Utrecht and York (Gerchow 1999) – or from England, for example Willehad, bishop of Bremen. The itinerary of Liudger shows the main focus of activity in his native land of Frisia and in his mission area of western Westphalia (Fig. 28.2). At a later phase Ansgar exemplifies the close ties to imperial Francia

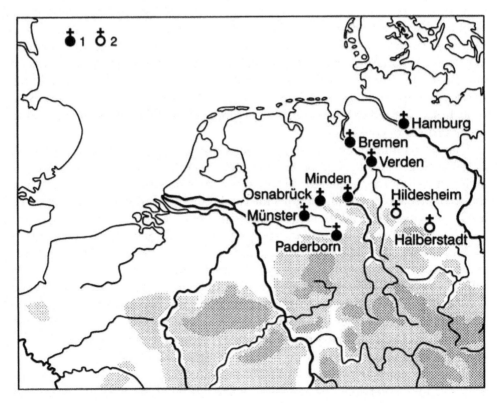

Figure 28.1 Foundations of bishoprics in Saxony: 1 under the reign of Charlemagne; 2 under the reign of Louis the Pious

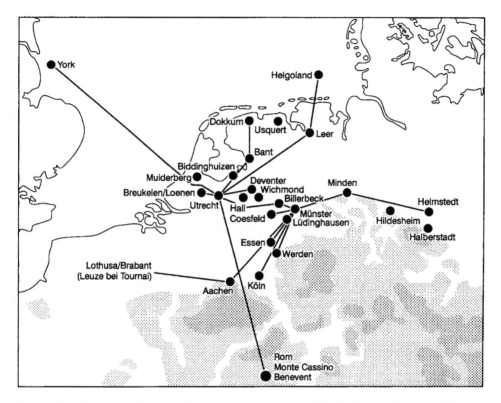

Figure 28.2 Itinerary of Liudger, first bishop of Münster, 805–809 (After Gerwing 1997)

as he went from the mother-community at Corbie near Amiens to the newly established monastery of *Nova Corbeia* – Corvey.

Among the earliest churches in the areas conquered by the Franks after 772 is the church of Christ the Saviour (*Salvatorkirche*) at Paderborn, which was built in 777 at Charlemagne's behest along with an *aula regia*. These buildings have been revealed by excavation. The church consisted of a single nave 25 m long with an eastern chancel and a western atrium, with an associated cemetery inside and outside the atrium; the hall was rectangular building of a similar size on a slightly different alignment (Gai 1999, 184 Fig. 1). Churches dating to the late eighth and the first half of the ninth centuries were mostly of stone rather than wood and their distribution (Fig. 28.3) shows the area of missionary activity in Saxony reaching from the Lower Rhine to the Lower Elbe region and from the German low mountain range to the North Sea coast (Lobbedey 1999, 500 Fig. 4).

Following the conversion of Saxony, the acquisition of relics established several focal points of saints' cults in the region between Lower Rhine and Elbe. There is evidence that the earliest translations of saints' bodies, meant to consolidate the new church on the northern periphery of the Caroligian Empire, occurred as early as the late eighth century, just as the historically defined Viking Age began with the first Scandinavian attacks on the British Isles and the Atlantic coasts (Schieffer

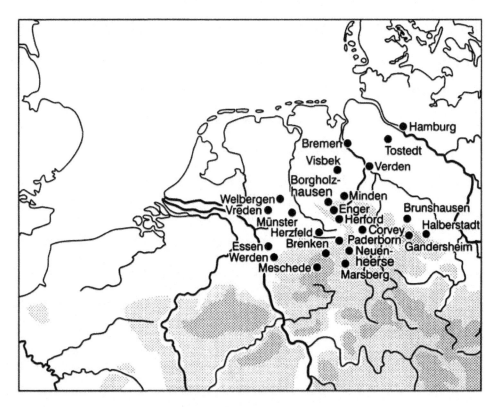

Figure 28.3 Distribution of the earliest churches (late eighth/first half of ninth century) in Saxony (After Lobbedey 1999)

1999, 485 Fig. 1). Donors of relics from outside the Frankish kingdom included Rome, Gorze, Würzburg and Northumbria, while the newly established bishoprics of Paderborn, Osnabrück and Minden and the minsters of Werden and Herford are reported to have received them. At that time the ecclesiastical infrastructure stretched as far north as Bremen (Müller-Wille 2001, 135 Fig. 1). The 'need for relics' climaxed for the first time in the first half of the ninth century during the reign of Louis the Pious. Apart from Rome and Ravenna, donations are known from Reims, St-Denis, Le Mans and Aachen (*ibid.* 136 Fig. 2). One of the best known examples from that time is the translation of St Liborius from Le Mans to Paderborn in 836. After a 4-week journey to Paderborn via Chartres and Paris the relics of St Liborius – a whole body – were buried in a ring-shaped crypt of the cathedral's western transept – following the example of Boniface's grave at Fulda (Jacobsen 1999, 630 Fig. 15). The remains of this church, including its crypt, were unearthed during the archaeological excavations within the cathedral of Paderborn (Gai 1999, 191 Fig. 9).

Cross-shaped Brooches

One of the grave-pits of the cemetery south of the church of Christ the Saviour at Paderborn contained a cross-shaped brooch (*Kreuzfibel*) cast in copper-alloy with expanding arms and a boss at each corner of the straight ends (Catalogue Paderborn 1999, I, 324 Fig. VI. 1). A similar brooch comes from grave 47 – a female inhumation oriented west-east – of the inhumation cemetery of Wünnenberg-Fürstenberg near Paderborn dating to the time around 800 (*ibid.* I, 223 Fig. IV. 47). Another similar example has been recorded from grave 192 of the Drantum cemetery near Oldenburg in Lower Saxony (Müller-Wille 1998, 193 Fig. 12, 1).

These cross-shaped brooches represent variant **a** of Egon Wamers' group of 'cross-shaped brooches with terminal bosses' (*Kreuzfibeln mit Eckrundeln*) (Fig. 28.4). There is evidence that variants **a** and **d** (see Fig. 28.4) are derived from Mediterranean and southern prototypes which were current from the fourth century onwards; in Saxony brooches of this type appear for the first time at the end of the eighth century. The distribution of the cross-shaped brooches with bosses extends from the Alps to the coastal zone, most finds being known from north of the Main (*ibid.* 194 Fig. 13). According to Wamers, the brooches of the

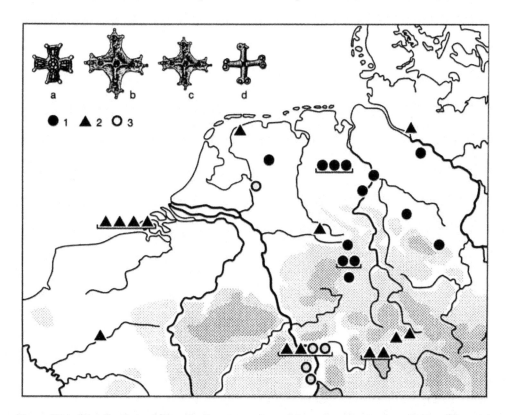

Figure 28.4 Distribution of Carolingian cross-shaped brooches (variants **a–d** after Wamers) from the area between the Rhine, the Main and the Elbe: 1 Grave/cemetery; 2 Settlement; 3 Without context (After Müller-Wille 1998, with finds list)

Rhine-Main area have mainly been found in settlements, while the Saxon finds come exclusively from graves.

A number of new examples have now been recorded from settlements in Westphalia (Bergmann 1999, 440 Fig. 1): cross-shaped brooches related to variant **a** (Fig. 28.5, nos 5–6) and cross-shaped brooches with central lozenge ornament and gemmiform trefoil-shaped terminals, related to variant **c** (Fig. 28.5, nos 8–11). A cross-shaped brooch of variant **a**, found in York, Coppergate, is described as of 'a type common in eastern Francia' which 'must have been imported into York' (Catalogue York 2001, 28 no. 20).

A survey of cross-shaped brooches with a boss in each inner angle of the cross and three bosses at the convex or triangular terminals of each arm, termed 'Worms' type, has recently been carried out by Mechthild Schulze-Dörrlamm (1997). Brooches of this general category are known from the Central Rhine and the Main regions, from Worms (Fig. 28.6, nos 1, 2, 5) and Karlburg (Fig. 28.6, no. 4), with scattered finds from the areas adjacent to the north, such as Woltwiesche, Lower Saxony (Fig. 28.6, no. 3). Among this group M. Schulze-Dörrlamm (1998, Fig. 2) counts delicately decorated examples, such as a gilded brooch with glass inlay which was found outside the fortification ditch of the first half of the ninth century at Ribe (Fig. 28.6, no. 6). The brooch probably gives evidence of Ansgar's

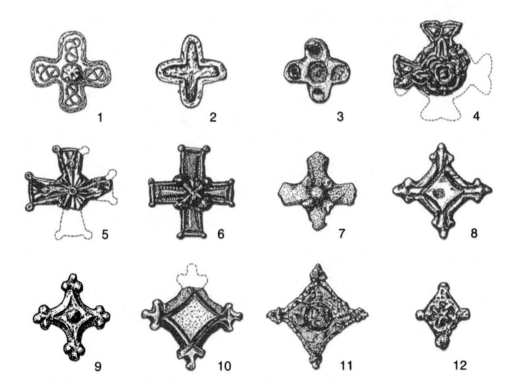

Figure 28.5 Cross-shaped brooches from Westphalia (After Bergmann 1999). Scale 1:1

Figure 28.6 Crossed-shaped brooches of 'Worms' type, including variant 'Ribe': 1 Worms-Abenheim; 2 Worms; 3 Woltwiesche; 4 Karlburg; 5 Worms; 6 Ribe; 7 Probably northern France (After Schulze-Dörrlamm 1997; 1999). Scale 1:1

missionary activities around the middle of the ninth century. By comparison with the example from Karlburg it is fair to assume that the brooches of this simple type are copies of more elaborate types (Fig. 28.6, no. 4).[1] The brooch in the Metropolitan Museum of Art, New York probably originates from northern France (Fig. 28.6, no. 7). It was made of gilded silver decorated with enamel, beads and glass inlays – a magnificent object, perhaps a royal possession. The miniature from the Milan Psalter Clm 343 depicting King David indicates that Carolingian rulers of the ninth century might actually have fastened their cloaks with large, cross-shaped brooches of extraordinary quality (Schulze-Dörrlamm 1997, 343 Pl. III). The distribution of cross-shaped brooches of the 'Worms' type shows a thin scatter, reaching from the Upper Rhine, and River Inn via the Rhine-Main area to

Lower Saxony and Denmark (Fig. 28.7). The potential loss of elaborately worked examples is exemplified by the brooch of supposed French origin (*ibid*. 344 Fig. 3; Müller-Wille 2000, 238 Fig. 7). Brooches of the 'Goddelsheim' type, which were in use in northern Switzerland, South Tyrol and the Trentino into the eighth century, are regarded as predecessors of the brooches of the 'Worms' type. The map illustrates the differing distribution patterns of both types (Fig. 28.7).

Among cross-shaped brooches from Westphalia – 25 are known according to Bergmann (1999) – two additional types can be distinguished. The first are in the style of a Maltese cross with a St Andrew's cross with a raised square-shaped

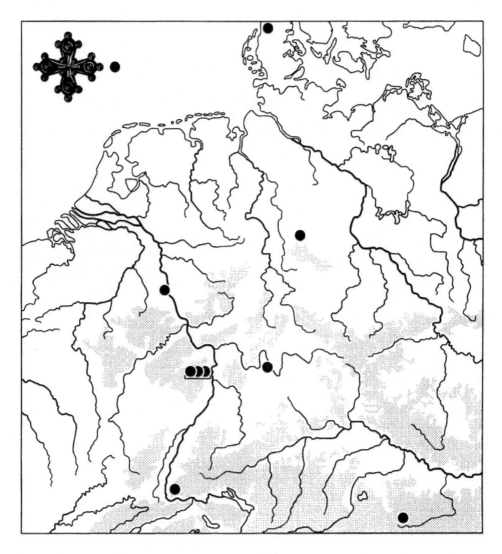

Figure 28.7 Distribution of Carolingian cross-shaped brooches ('Worms' type, including variant 'Ribe') (After Schulze-Dörrlamm 1997, with finds list)

centre. To the few examples from Westphalia, brooches of the same type from the Moselle-Rhine-Main area can be added (Wamser 1999, 228 Fig. 11; Catalogue Paderborn 1999, I, 409 Fig. VI. 146–7). These may be compared with the copper-alloy examples from Mainz, from the fortified cathedral mound (Domburg) of Münster, from the precincts of the monastery of Zellingen on the Main and from the settlement Paderborn-Balhorn (Fig. 28.8, nos 1–4; compare Fig. 28.5, no. 4). Presumably the brooches of this type originate from workshops in the Central Rhine-Moselle area in the time around 800. As regards the shape it closely resembles a small cross brooch from York, Paragon Street, with cells originally filled with coloured enamel, which is dated earlier: 'This type of highly coloured geometrical decoration would have been very familiar in York in the seventh and eighth centuries' (Catalogue York 2001, 27 no. 10).

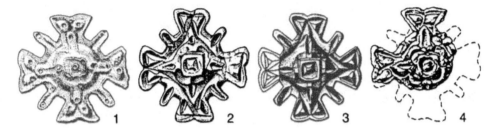

Figure 28.8 Cross-shaped brooches in the style of Maltese cross and St. Andrew's cross: 1 Mainz; 2 Münster; 3 Zellingen am Main; 4 Paderborn-Balhorn (After Wamser 1999). Scale 1:1

Among the cross-shaped brooches with simple convex ends, the gold brooch from the Carolingian-Ottonian stronghold/hillfort on the 'Gaulskopf' (district of Höxter) stands out, with an ornament of interlaced filigree wire (Fig. 28.5, no. 1). There are four other examples from settlements near Soest and Paderborn, dating to the ninth century – probably the second half (Fig. 28.5, nos 2–3).

Crosses on Brooches

The cross motif appears elsewhere, too, such as on square brooches, rectangular brooches and disc brooches (Wamser 1999, 224 ff. Fig. 8 and 13: square brooches). Square and rectangular examples (*Quadratfibel, Rechteckfibel*) bearing the cross-motif in the style of the St Andrew's cross on their enamelled panels and especially the variants with three-tipped lugs at each corner are widely known from Karlburg and its surroundings in the Main area (Fig. 28.9, nos 1–3, 5–6). The square brooches (type 'Karlburg' and variants) are concentrated in the Main area with a thin scatter of finds stretching to the mouth of the Rhine and the Lippe area. They date to the (early) ninth century (Fig. 28.10). In Westphalia, sixteen square brooches are recorded according to the recent article of Bergmann (1999). Among them there are only few brooches with a framed cross-ornament (*ibid.* 443 Fig. 5 nos 7 and 13). Some brooches of that plain style are known from the Netherlands,

Figure 28.9 Square brooches of different types, mostly from Bavaria, Hesse and Westphalia (After Wamser 1999). Scale approximately 1:1

Lower Saxony, Schleswig-Holstein, and Denmark – all of them being finds from settlements or stray finds of the late ninth century, although there is one example known from a grave from Georgenberg, Upper Austria (Müller-Wille 2000, 238 Fig. 6).

The deposits of the early medieval *terp* at Hassenbüttel situated on the west coast of Schleswig-Holstein, Dithmarschen have produced a 14 mm by 14 mm

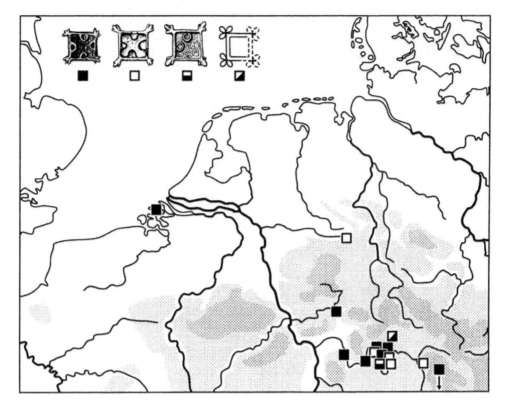

Figure 28.10 Distribution of square brooches, type 'Karlburg' and variants (After Wamser 1999, with finds list)

square-shaped brooch (Fig. 28.11, no. 2), and also two disc brooches (*Scheibenfibeln*). The large disc brooch of lead, with a central animal as a decoration in the inner circle (Fig. 28.11, no. 3) can be paralleled with an example of the tenth century from Bird-in-Hand Court, Cheapside, London. The copper-alloy disc brooch (22 mm in diameter) has a decoration in the shape of an equal-armed cross with expanding arms and four roundels (*Peltenzier*) in the inner angles executed in champlevé enamel (*Grubenemail*) (Fig. 28.11, no. 1).

The distribution of enamelled cross-shaped brooches with roundels in the inner angles (*Kreuzemailfibeln mit Peltenzier in den Kreuzzwickeln*) covers the Rhine-Main area, Westphalia, Lower-Saxony and the northern parts of the Netherlands with a single outlier in Norfolk (Fig. 28.12). The example from Hassenbüttel has two counterparts in Schleswig-Holstein: one comes from Hedeby and one from the Slavonic fortified island of Olsborg near Plön. The brooch from Hassenbüttel is paralleled by examples from the *terp* of early urban Emden, and from three *terps* in the Dutch part of Frisia (*ibid*. 237 Fig. 5). Grave-finds are known from three cemeteries in northern Lower Saxony, including the graveyard at Brunswick, Kohlmarkt.

According to Frick (1992/93) and Wamers (1994), enamelled cross-shaped brooches of the Hassenbüttel type have been recorded from 30 sites; most are

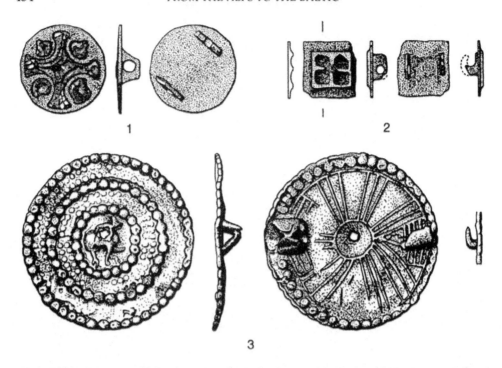

Figure 28.11 Square and disc brooches from the terp at Hassenbüttel, Schleswig-Holstein (After Müller-Wille 2000). Scale 1:1

stray finds or come from settlement sites, and only a few are finds from graves (Müller-Wille 2000, 231 ff.). The large number of brooches from Mainz suggested to Wamers that there was a workshop there. Enamelled cross-shaped brooches of the type described are commonly thought to be of ninth century date, mainly the second half of the ninth century.

There are now many new finds from Westphalia, which will fill in the distribution pattern and partially change it (Bergmann 1999, 442 Fig. 4; Dickmann 1997, 30 Fig.). They give evidence of numerous variants of cross-shaped ornaments which run from the ninth to the first half of the eleventh century (Fig. 28.13). One example can be compared to the Hassenbüttel find (Fig. 28.13, no. 3; compare Fig. 28.11, no.1).

Among the large number of disc brooches from the settlement complex of Karlburg along the Main near Würzburg there are brooches with cross ornament and roundels in the angles (Wamser 1999, 224 ff.). The distribution map of comparable disc brooches outside Karlburg clearly shows a main area of concentration between the Rivers Main, Rhine and Elbe (Fig. 28.14), which incorporates Saxony as well as the probable centre of production in Middle Rhine area and/ or East Frankish area. Moreover the picture is broadened by finds from East Anglia, and the Saxon-Danish region, especially from Hedeby (Ulriksen 1999). Missionary activity, trade and exchange are all implied here.

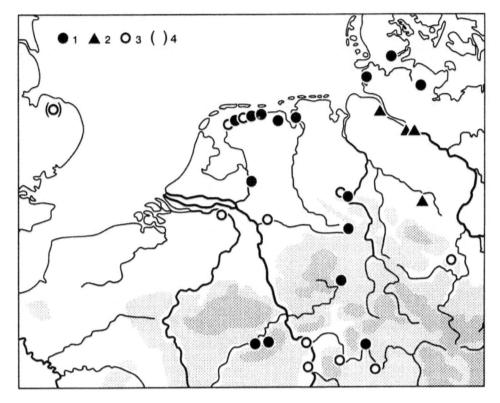

Figure 28.12 Distribution of disc brooches with a decoration in the shape of an equal-armed cross with expanding arms and four roundels, in the inner angles executed in champlevé enamel: 1 Settlement; 2 Grave; 3 Without context; 4 Find spot unknown (After Müller-Wille 2000, with finds list)

Wamser interpreted the distribution pattern of the different types and variants of enamelled brooches from Karlburg, as giving the 'probable political context of missionary activities. . . . The apparently sustained production and purposeful distribution of brooches depicting Christian motifs emanated primarily from the East Frankish area' (1999, 228). At the same time he has referred to the 'production of regional imitations or local developments in the politically annexed and ecclesiastically incorporated areas east of the Rhine, with their early missions and subsequent bishoprics' (1999, 230). This is supported by the evidence of a mould of a disc brooch decorated with an equal-armed cross with expanding terminals from Dortmund (Catalogue Paderborn 1999, I, 403 Fig. VI. 133) – so far the only example of Wamers' *Kreuzemailfibeln*, type-3 brooches (cf. Fig. 28.13, no. 1). Although larger in diameter, one brooch from the settlement area of the Balhorner Feld near Paderborn still has preserved much of the red enamel-filling (*ibid.* 361 Fig. VI. 52).

Among the Carolingian disc brooches belonging to the 'northern-zone-types' (*nördlicher Formenkreis*) – that is the area of the Saxon-Frisian mission zone – are those examples which feature the bust of a saint (*Heiligenfibel*), such as one

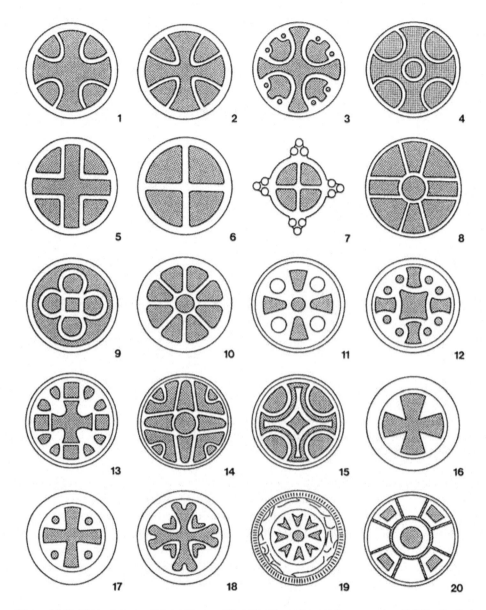

Figure 28.13 Decoration variants of enamelled disc brooches with a cross motif. New finds from Westphalia. Schematic design (After Bergmann 1999)

example from Karlburg (Fig. 28.15). The widespread schematic design of the figure occasionally occurs with cross-decorations, as is the case with an example from Karlburg (Wamser 1999, 236 Fig. 14). As with the enamelled cross-shaped brooches, it is assumed that they were manufactured in the areas of the Central Rhine, Moselle and Main areas, where the mission directed by the Franks started from. Most of them have been found in the region between Main, Rhine and Elbe,

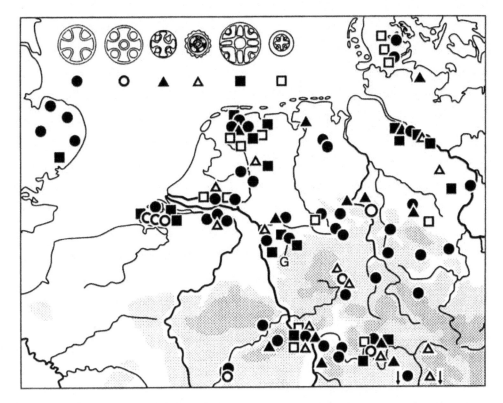

Figure 28.14 Distribution of different variants of enamelled disc brooches, which have been found in Karlburg. G = mould (Gußform) of the first variant (After Wamser 1999)

some of them in Eastern England and in Hedeby (Fig. 28.16). The technology, chronology and distribution of these brooches has recently been discussed by Krüger (1999). A small number of dove brooches (*Taubenfibeln*) with a cross on the back are known from the Saxon area, such as the example of fire-gilded silver from a burial ground near the Osnabrück Cathedral, probably of the first half of the ninth century (Catalogue Paderborn I 1999, 359 Fig. VI. 47).

Crosses on Other Objects

In the archaeological record the cross-motif has also been found on objects other than brooches, and it should be sufficient to point to some examples from the Saxon area. From the Carolingian convent at Vreden north-west of Münster a (decorative) disc made of non-ferrous metal is known, which has a cross-fleury design (*Lilienkreuz*) of red, blue and white colour executed in cloisonné enamel (Catalogue Paderborn 1999, I, 343 Fig. VI. 24). The fitting probably came from a cross, a portable altar, a reliquary, a liturgical vessel (chalice, paten) or an ecclesiastical garment.

Figure 28.15 Disc brooch with design of bust of saint from Karlburg (After Wamser 1999). Diameter 2.4 cm

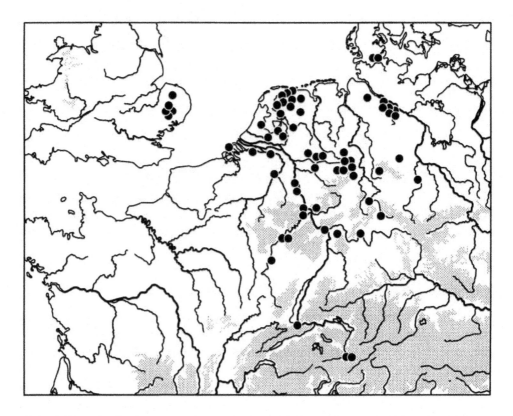

Figure 28.16 Distribution of saint's brooches (After Krüger 1999,161 Fig. 11 with finds list and Hamerow 1999, 198 Fig. 3, 3 and 4, 2)

A number of Tating ware jugs are decorated with crosses, such as the reconstructed vessel from Birka grave 597; equal-armed crosses with expanding terminals decorate the base of the jug (*ibid.* I, 147 Fig. III. 39; and see Staecker, Chapter 29 in this volume). Tating ware jugs have so far been found in an area which stretches from the Main-Rhine-Moselle and Seine region to both southern and northern Norway and central Sweden, with Staraja Ladoga featuring as the north-easternmost find spot (Wamser 1999, 215 Fig. 6). Evidence from quite a number of Anglo-Saxon sites can be added. Jugs with cross decoration were recorded from the Saxon-Frisian mission zone (Paderborn, Dorestad) and from Scandinavia, but not from the Seine region or the Rhine, Moselle and Main regions.

The coins of the emperor Charlemagne, minted in the time between 800 and 814, show two crosses connected with a church, an imitation of the pagan temple on Roman imperial coins, and the inscription 'Christiana religio' – the ideological expression of his political and religious programme (Kluge 1999, 84 Fig. 5–6; Schulze-Dörrlamm 1999).

A recent find from the settlement site of the Balhorner Feld near Paderborn is perhaps expressive of the way that these cross-bearing objects can be used to infer the process of conversion. Within the fill of a ninth–tenth century pit-house (*Grubenhaus*), a 39 mm long pendant of walrus ivory decorated with a crucifixion group was found. An initial and preliminary art-historical study, published in the Paderborn catalogue (1999, I, 363 Fig. VI. 57), ascribes the pendant to early eighth-century northern England relating it among other comparisons to St Cuthbert's shrine: 'It is therefore quite possible to associate the find with Anglo-Saxon missionaries, whose efforts to convert the Saxons of Westphalia to Christianity are well known from written accounts' (Georg Eggenstein, in Catalogue Paderborn 1999, I, 364).[2]

Conclusion

In the region between the Central/Lower Rhine, Main, Saale/Elbe and the coastal zones of the North Sea the use of the cross motif followed the Carolingian conquest and mission. Many of the cross-shaped brooches and brooches with Christian symbols from the Saxon and Frisian areas are of a later date than the phase of missionary activities in about 800. Several variants of cross-shaped brooches (*Kreuzfibeln*) can be distinguished, as E. Wamers and M. Schulze-Dörrlamm have shown, and their distribution extends from the Alps to the coastal zone. Most finds are known north of the Main, partly from graves, partly from settlements. Other brooches with Christian symbols, in the form of enamelled disc brooches with a cross (*Kreuzemailfibeln*) or with a bust of a saint (*Heiligenfibeln*) or square brooches with a cross (*Quadratfibeln mit Kreuzzier*) and others, are mainly distributed between Rhine and Elbe.

These finds originate for the most part from settlements, with only a small number from graves (Catalogue Magdeburg 2001, vol. I, 104 Fig. 12). Finds from settlements cannot be associated with individuals and during Carolingian times the growing number of burials without any grave goods was accompanied correspondingly by a considerable reduction of objects from burials. The nature of the context of the finds makes it difficult to prove that items of cross-shaped jewellery were specially associated with women, as was the case during the Merovingian period (Bierbrauer, Chapter 27 in this volume) and would be again in the next century in Scandinavia (Staecker, Chapter 29 in this volume; Gräslund 2001 and Chapter 30 in this volume).

Notes

1 The cross-shaped fittings from Mikulčice, Moravia, and Budeč, Bohemia, resemble the cross-shaped brooches of the 'Worms' type. Each of the arms is decorated with the face of Christ: Schulze-Dörrlamm 1997, 343 Fig. 2, 6; Catalogue Budapest 2000, III, Fig.: 235 and 251.
2 Two other fragments of similar pendants have been found in Mergerzen near Brakel and Fürstenberg near Neheim, North-Rhine Westphalia. In a recent analysis the art historian Victor H. Elbern prefers a dating of the pendants to the tenth century and a local Saxon production: Eggenstein and Elbern 2001.

(Drawings: Holger Dieterich, Institut für Ur- und Frühgeschichte, Universität Kiel)

References

Angenendt, A. 1999 'Die Christianisierung Nordwesteuropas' in Catalogue Paderborn 1999, II: 420–33.
Bergmann, R. 1999 'Karolingisch-ottonische Fibeln aus Westfalen. Verbreitung, Typologie und Chronologie im Überblick' in Catalogue Paderborn 1999, III: 438–44.
Catalogue Berlin 1992: *Wikinger, Waräger, Normannen. Die Skandinavier und Europa 800–1200.* 22. Kunstausstellung des Europarats (Berlin).
Catalogue Budapest 2000: Wieczorek, A. and Hinz, H.-M. (eds), *Europas Mitte um 1000.* Vol. I-III. 27. Europaratsausstellung (Stuttgart).
Catalogue Essen 1997: Seibt, F., Borsdorf, U. and Grütter, H. Th. (eds) *Transit Brügge – Novgorod. Eine Straße durch die europäische Geschichte.* Katalog Ruhrlandmuseum Essen (Bottrop, Essen).
Catalogue Essen 1999: Gerchow, J. (ed.) *Das Jahrtausend der Mönche. Kloster Werden 799–1803* (Köln).
Catalogue Magdeburg 2001: Puhle, M. (ed.), Otto der Große, Magdeburg. 27. Europarats- und Landesausstellung Vol. I-II (Mainz).
Catalogue Mannheim 1996: Wieczorek, A., Périn, P., von Welck, K. and Menghin, W. (eds), *Die Franken. Wegbereiter Europas. Vor 1500 Jahren: König Chlodwig und seine Erben.* Vol. 1–2 (Mainz).
Catalogue Paderborn 1999: Stiegmann, Chr. and Wemhoff, M. (eds) *799 – Kunst und Kultur der Karolingerzeit. Karl der Große und Papst Leo III. in Paderborn.* I-II Katalog der Ausstellung, III Beiträge zum Katalog der Ausstellung (Mainz).
Catalogue Rosenheim 1988: Dannheimer, H. and Dopsch, H. (eds), *Die Bajuwaren.* Von

Severin bis Tassilo 488–788. Gemeinsame Landesausstellung des Freistaates Bayern und des Landes Salzburg. Rosenheim/Bayern, Mattsee/Salzburg (Korneuburg).

Catalogue Stuttgart 1997: Archäologisches Landesmuseum Baden-Württemberg (ed.), *Die Alamannen* (Stuttgart).

Catalogue York 2001: Garrison, M., Nelson, J.L. and Tweddle, D. in Hartley, E. (ed.) *Alcuin and Charlemagne. The Golden Age of York* (York).

Dickmann, E. 1997 *Archäologie in Castrop-Rauxel*. Ausstellungskatalog (Dülmen).

Eggenstein, G. and Elbern, V.H. 2001 'Ein mittelalterlicher Anhänger mit Kreuzigungsgruppe aus Balhorn bei Paderborn' *Archäologisches Korrespondenzblatt* 31: 637–54.

Frick, H.-J. 1992/93 'Karolingisch-ottonische Scheibenfibeln des nördlichen Formenkreises' *Offa* 49/50, 1992/93: 243–463.

Gai, S. 1999 'Die Pfalz Karls des Großen in Paderborn. Ihre Entwicklung von 777 bis zum Ende des 10. Jahrhunderts' in Catalogue Paderborn 1999, III: 183–96.

Gerchow, J. 1999 'Liudger, Werden und die Angelsachsen' in Catalogue Essen 1999: 49–58.

Gerwing, M. 1997 'Dreimal Ostmission: Liudger, Adalbert, Norbert' in Catalogue Essen 1997: 145–54.

Gräslund, A.-S. 2001: *Ideologi och Mentalitet. Om religionsskiftet i Skandinavien från en arkeologisk horisont.* Occasional Papers in Archaeology 29 (Uppsala).

Hamerow, H. 1999 'Angles, Saxons and Anglo-Saxons: Rural centres, trade and production' in Hässler, H.-J. (ed.) *Studien zur Sachsenforschung 13* (Oldenburg): 189–205.

Jacobsen, W. 1999 'Die Renaissance der frühchristlichen Architektur in der Karolingerzeit' in Catalogue Paderborn 1999, III: 623–42.

Johanek, P. 1999 'Der Ausbau der sächsischen Kirchenorganisation' in Catalogue Paderborn 1999, II: 494–506.

Kluge, B. 1999 'Nomen imperatoris und Christiana Religio. Das Kaisertum Karls des Großen und Ludwig des Frommen im Licht der numismatischen Quellen' in Catalogue Paderborn 1999, III: 82–90.

Krüger, K. 1999 'Eine Heiligenfibel mit Zellenemail aus Ochtmissen, Stadt Lüneburg, Ldkr. Lüneburg' *Die Kunde* N.F. 50, 1999: 129–204.

Lobbedey, U. 1999 'Der Kirchenbau im sächsischen Missionsgebiet' in Catalogue Paderborn 1999, III: 498–511.

Müller-Wille, M. 1998 'The Cross as a Symbol of Personal Christian Belief in a Changing Religious World. Examples from Selected Areas in Merovingian and Carolingian Europe' in Larsson, L. and Stjernquist, B. (eds) *The World-View of Prehistoric Man* (Kungl. Vitterhets Historie och Antikvitets Akademien Konferenser 40, Stockholm): 179–200.

—— 2000 'Drei Fibelfunde aus der mittelalterlichen Dorfwurt von Hassenbüttel, Dithmarschen' in *Studia Antiquaria. Festschrift für Niels Bantelmann zum 60. Geburtstag* (Universitätsforschungen zur Prähistorischen Archäologie 63, Bonn): 231–41.

—— 2001 'Wanderungen von Heiligenreliquien. Zu Ereignissen im nördlichen und westlichen Karolingerreich: Christlicher und heidnischer Kontext' in Magnus, B., Orrling, C., Rasch, M. and Tegnér, G. (eds) *Vi får tacka Lamm* (Studies 10. Museum of National Antiquities, Stockholm): 133–41.

Schieffer, R. 1999 'Reliquientranslationen nach Sachsen' in Catalogue Paderborn 1999, III: 484–97.

Schulze-Dörrlamm, M. 1997 'Unbekannte Kreuzfibeln der Karolingerzeit aus Edelmetall' *Archäologisches Korrespondenzblatt* 27, 1997: 341–54.

—— 1998 'En frankisk korsfibel fra 9. århundrede fra Ribe'. *By, marsk og geest. Årbog for Ribe-egnen* 10, 1998: 2–28.

—— 1999 'Münzfibeln der Karolingerzeit' *Archäologisches Korrespondenzblatt* 29, 1999: 271–88.

Staecker, J. 2000 'The Mission of the Triangle: The Christianisation of Saxons, West Slavs and Danes in a comparative analysis' *Archaeological Review from Cambridge* 17: 2, 2000: 99–116.

Ulriksen, J. 1999 'Vikingetide korsemailjefibler fra Roskildeegnen' *ROMU Årsskrift fra Roskilde Museum* 1999: 11–30.

Wamers, E. 1994 *Die frühmittelalterlichen Lesefunde aus der Löhrstraße (Baustelle Hilton II) in Mainz* (Mainzer Archäologische Schriften 1, Mainz).

Wamser, L. 1999 'Zu einer Tatinger Kanne und ausgewählten Kleinfunden aus Karlburg am Main. Anmerkungen zu Handel und Verkehr, Weinbau und Missionierung im Nordosten des Karolingerreiches' in L. Wamser (ed.) *Dedicatio Hermann Dannheimer zum 70. Geburtstag* (Kataloge der Prähistorischen Staatssammlung, Beiheft 5, Kallmünz): 206–42.

29

The Cross Goes North: Christian Symbols and Scandinavian Women

JÖRN STAECKER

In recent decades research has focused intensively on the Christanisation of Scandinavia. The point of departure has mainly been the change of religion, i.e. the issue of which forces in society triggered the changes, which missionary elements generated the process of Christanisation and, finally, what happened to pagan elements of cult after the conversion. We realize today that it was not only the nobility which backed up the process of Christanisation, that German and English missionaries were probably much more confrontational than earlier believed, and that the question of continuity of cult still needs to be assessed. But there are two questions in particular which remain to be solved. The first one deals with the issue of when Christanisation actually started according to archaeology. Early medieval archaeology is often very closely connected with history and the dates offered by that discipline, so it is often difficult for archaeologists to develop independent models of interpretation. Dates like AD 965 for the conversion of the Danish King Harald Bluetooth, around AD 1000 for the Swedish King Olaf Skötkonung and around AD 995 for the Norwegian King Olav Tryggvason are like monoliths. But we have to consider whether Christanisation had its starting point with the conversion of the king and his retinue, or whether the introduction of Christanisation was a long process stretching over centuries preceding the official breakthrough.

The second question is concerned with the issue of who had the principal role in a conversion. As E.-M. Göransson (1999, 247ff.) has recently pointed out, research on Scandinavia's Christanisation quite often describes the actors as males or as genderless individuals. This is linked to the discussion about social status, where for example the Swedish term *storman* (noble man) implies a male person. But the supernumerary role of women is far from certain. As research by A.-S. Gräslund (1996) for the Viking Age and by J. Wienberg (1997) for the twelfth century has demonstrated, certain women within the nobility had a leading role in the conversion of Scandinavia.

Early Insular Influence

According to the written sources there is hardly any evidence for an early insular mission to Scandinavia. In the seventh and eighth centuries, the mission to the Frisian and Germanic areas was substantially initiated by Anglo-Saxon monks, educated in Northumbrian monasteries. After a successful mission in *Fresia citerior* Willibrord,the archbishop in Utrecht, travelled to Jutland and was well received at the court of King Ongendus. According to Alcuin's *De Vita Sancti Willibrordi* the mission was only an episode, finishing with the return of Willibrord together with 30 Danish youths, who were baptised during the sea crossing.

Amongst the finds from Scandinavia with an origin in Britain (AD 700–850), the croziers and reliquaries are particularly striking. Only a few items, namely two croziers and six reliquaries, were included in burials. The croziers date to the eighth century, but in one case there is a gap of 200 years between the date of production and that of deposition (Staecker 1997, 423ff.). The reliquaries indicate a similar pattern. They originate between AD 700 and 850 and were deposited 100 or even 200 years later. Half of the reliquaries were used in secondary contexts, as their new function as fibulae give proof (Wamers 1985). The majority of the graves are female burials and there are also two double-graves (Fig. 29.1).

How can the presence of these croziers and reliquaries be explained? Earlier researchers had no doubts: the finds were clearly identified as plunder which reached Scandinavia during the Viking Age. There is clear evidence for plundering, which began at the latest in 793, the legendary date of the destruction of Lindisfarne, and ended only during the course of the eleventh century. In the documentary sources there are accounts of the break-up and removal of several shrines between 797 and 895. According to Wamers the re-use of these objects and the context in which they were found contradict their peaceful acquisition by means of trade, gift exchange or indirect missionary activity, i.e. baptism abroad (Wamers 1985, 42). But it is remarkable that the sacred objects primarily ended up in female graves.

Could we look at the items in different way? Could the objects of Christian liturgy be seen as evidence for a mission instigated from the Irish/Northumbrian area, of which only slight echoes (Alcuin) are found in the documentary sources? Or even if a mission never took place, is there another explanation why especially women got these items? Do women necessarily long for 'a compensation for the absence of husband and son', as expressed by Wamers (1985, 42)? The gap between the production and deposition and the re-use of the items in many cases contradicts an alternative interpretation, and there is no evidence for an early Anglo-Saxon mission in Scandinavia. But it is remarkable that objects related to a Christian context are linked to gender.

Figure 29.1 Sex-determination of eighth–tenth-century burials with croziers and reliquaries: ♀ female graves; ♀♂ double-graves; ? no sex-determination

Early German Influence

In the ninth century another type of material with Christian symbolism appeared in the graves. In eleven Swedish, three Norwegian and one medieval Danish examples, jugs of the so-called Frisian or Tating-ware type form a central part of the burials. Most of such burials are cremations (there are only three inhumations), and – with one exception – all the graves are those of women (Fig. 29.2). The jugs are decorated with a symetrically armed cross in the lower section. The production centre was probably somewhere in the region of the Rhine, possibly Mayen, in addition to there being local imitations. Even if there is still a discussion going on as to whether the objects can be regarded as parts of the Christian liturgy or not, and as to whether the cross must be seen as a symbol, or as pure decoration, it cannot be denied that the time-frame of the burials – late eighth and early ninth century – fits nicely with the written records (Gabriel 1988, 134f.; Staecker

Figure 29.2 Sex-determination of late eighth and ninth-century burials with Frisian or Tating-ware jugs: ♀ female graves; ♂ male graves

1997, 430ff.). It is said in the *Vita Anskarii*, that in the year 829 a Swedish legation asked Emperor Ludwig for a missionary to visit their country, as many of their inhabitants wanted to adopt the Christian faith. Two monks, Ansgar and Witmar, both from the monastery of Corvey, were appointed to make the journey to Birka. By common consent of King Björn and his retinue they were given permission to preach the Gospel. Amongst the baptised was an important individual, namely the governor of the town of Birka. Some years later a church was built, but a revolt against the preachers led to a suspension of pastoral activities until AD 854. On his second trip to Birka Ansgar succeeded in re-establishing the mission after the decisions of two *things* on Birka and one in another place on the mainland. In addition he received permission to build churches and appoint priests.

How do we interpret cremations with Christian symbols? Is it the burial rites, the furnishing and the pagan symbols, which reflect the belief of the dead person or is it the imported pottery with Christian symbolism? We need not assume that the ideals of a newly converted Scandinavian woman were expressed as an unfurnished grave. Other factors would have played an important role here. In the absence of a priest or outside a demarcated zone where he had responsibility, there would be no model for Christian burial to follow. The jug could have simply been a token of the high regard in which a converted woman was held. But the association with female graves is striking. It suggests the possibility of a direct association with the story of Friedburg and Katla, as recounted by Rimbert. Shortly before her death the rich Friedburg requested her daughter Katla to divide all her possessions amongst the needy of Dorestad, as was then carried out. For her dying hour the widow had given explicit instructions for wine (*viaticum*) to be purchased. Even if it is impossible to prove that the wine was purchased in jugs of the Frisian type, it is still remarkable that once again an object with Christian symbolism seems to be related to the female gender.

Thor's Hammer: Symbol of Christianization

Between the late ninth and early tenth centuries we have no record of a mission and the silence could give us the impression that the first attempts of the ninth century have failed. According to written sources, mainly the ecclesiastical history of Hamburg-Bremen by Adam of Bremen, a new mission was launched in 936. In this year, Unni, the archbishop of Hamburg-Bremen, visited both the Danish King Gorm and his son Harald Bluetooth, and he even made a journey to Birka. According to Adam of Bremen Gorm had the intention of wiping out Christianity by killing the priests and by expelling them from the country. But at the same time his son Harald allowed the archbishop to hold Christian services in public, to ordain priests and to make a visit to the Danish islands. Afterwards Unni continued his journey to Birka. The *Sueones et Gothi* had in the meantime forgotten the Christian faith and were not easily brought back into the fold. Shortly before his return home Unni took ill and died.

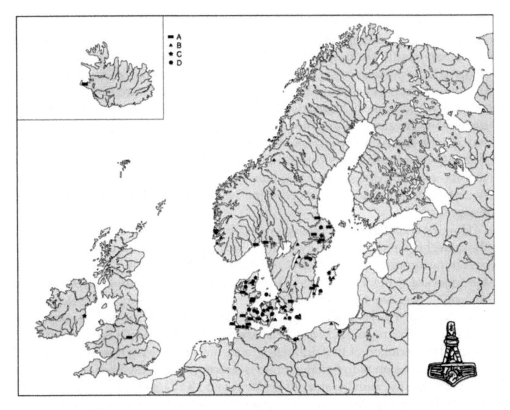

Figure 29.3 Distribution of single Thor's hammers: A grave find; B hoard find; C settlement find; D single find

Is it possible to trace Christianity in this early phase of the tenth century? There are only a few items with Christian symbolism known from the period. Objects like crosses and crucifixes are not common before the late tenth century. But there is one object, which might give us a hint that a change of religion is taking place already during the early tenth century, namely Thor's hammer. In contrast to Thor's iron hammer rings, which appear as early as the late eighth century, the single pendant is typical of the tenth century. The pendants are made of iron, amber, lead, bronze, silver and even gold. The distribution is limited to Scandinavia and the Viking colonies. Although there is an ongoing debate about how to interpret the Thor's hammer, it seems obvious that the item must be regarded as a symbol of pagan reaction against Christianity. An analysis of the Thor's hammer in Viking Age hoards and coin-dated graves demonstrates that the pagan symbol is replaced by the cross around the year 1000 in medieval Denmark, between 950 and 1000 in Sweden and around 1100 on Gotland (Fig. 29.3). The distribution of the single Thor's hammer in space and time does demonstrate that the pagan symbols occur during the initial phase of the mission in medieval Denmark and Sweden. Among the 28 Scandinavian tenth-century graves with a Thor's hammer, the dominance of female graves is apparent.

Figure 29.4 Sex-determination of ninth–eleventh-century burials with single Thor's hammer:
♀ female graves; ♂ male graves; ? no sex-determination

Nineteen graves belong to females, four to males and five are not determined (Fig. 29.4). The dominating role of the Thor's hammers in female graves might be explained by their function as symbols and jewellery, but it is again obvious that it is in the female graves that the religious symbol is mainly represented.

The Wagon Grave: Purely Pagan?

A special role in tenth-century graves is that of the carriage-bodies, that is the upper part of a wagon which could be removed from the lower chassis. The wagon with detachable body was already known from the early ninth-century

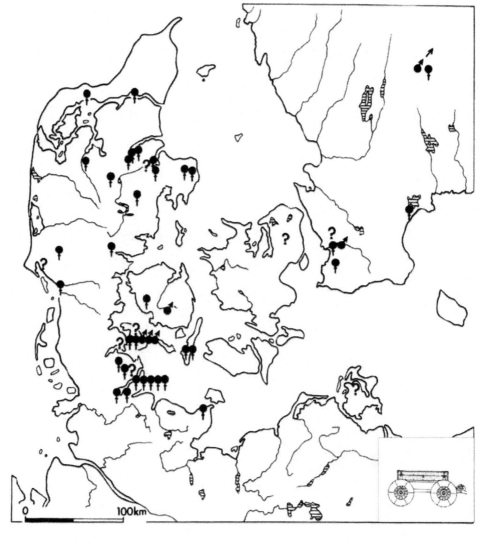

Figure 29.5 Sex-determination of tenth-century graves with carriage: ♀ female graves; ♂ male graves; ? no sex-determination

Oseberg ship-burial in Norway, where it was part of the furnishing of a chamber containing two women. A similar type of wagon-body was first observed in tenth-century burials in the 1970s by E. Roesdahl and J. Nordquist (1971, 15 ff.) and later by M. Müller-Wille (1976, 13 ff.). Iron-fittings which could be connected with a wooden wagon have since made it possible to identify a lot of wagon-graves among old excavations (Eisenschmidt 2000, 62ff.). Even graves with pairs of snaffle-bits were counted in this group. The importance of gender and the social position of the dead was quite soon pointed out by different researchers. It could be observed that the majority of the graves belonged to women of the upper classes (Fig. 29.5). Of 50 burials, 34 were female, six male and ten not determinable.

During the 1970's the role of the wagon-graves in society was under discussion. Roesdahl and Nordquist (1971, 30) wrote concerning the Fyrkat grave IV:

> You do not get the impression that this is a noble, Nordic woman. She seems to have travelled, perhaps she is a foreigner who has bought some nice goods at different places on her way to Fyrkat and uses these items like a tourist in her own way. Another possibility is that some of the objects are gifts, and one is struck by the idea that she could have been a lady belonging to a group of 'camp followers'.

But with the magnificent Oseberg burial in mind, where not only a complete wagon but also textiles illustrating the use of wagons were discovered, it became quite clear that these women were not exotic elements in society or even prostitutes, but instead members of the highest stratum of the local community. The interpretation of the wagon as a medium of transport and as an expression of vassalage (Randsborg 1980, 131) changed slightly to an interpretation of a carriage to the other world, comparable with the ship (Gabriel 1988, 223; Roesdahl 1992, 161; Andrén 1993, 46 ff.). To the group of real objects A. Andrén has added the image of wagons on four Gotlandic picture stones. In his view these wagons are representations of pagan mythology, like the story that the heroine Brynhild went to Hel in a carriage. Ships and carts were the main attributes of the Vanir, the divinities of fertility and death. The goddess Freyja had a wagon drawn by cats and the goddess Nerthus, mentioned by Tacitus, was placed in a wagon drawn by cows (Andrén 1993, 46 f.; Göransson 1999, 236).

There is still another question to be addressed: why do the wagon-graves begin during the most intensive phase of Christanisation? One possibility is that they had no religious significance. According to I. Gabriel (1988, 223) pagan attributes could equally be interpreted in a Christian way and burial-parties of Christian dead were not forced 'to sacrifice their status-symbols'. Another thesis is offered by M. Carver (1995, 122). He interprets innovative local elements in burials (here ships) as the result of the provocation of Christianity. D. Meier (1997, 213) has argued that the burials must be regarded as 'a reaction of the upper class society on meeting with the faith, which transferred new and strange values'. The leading stratum was afraid of being reduced to a lower social level when getting buried without gravegoods. But this view seems to be rather too simplistic.

The proximity of the burials to the church and the position inside the church were of highest importance (Staecker 2001). The 'pagan revival' is the wrong expression for a phenomenon, which was defined by G. Kossack (1974, 28) as a *Prunkgräbersitte*. The meeting between a socially stratified culture and an exotic culture of high standing urged society's leaders to emphasise their own rank. Graves with wagons are in this case an expression of a transition period but not necessarily of religious affiliation. Several graves, like Thumby-Bienebek, Jelling, Hørning and Oldenburg in the Slavonic territory, indicate a direct connection with Christianity by the furnishing (cross-pendant), or the topography (inside the church or on the churchyard) (see Staecker 1999; 2001; 2002).

In this context, it is necessary to mention the Gotlandic picture stones which feature wagons. As opposed to Andrén's interpretation, it is argued here that the stones in general may not be regarded as part of pagan custom. It is imporant to stress that the inscriptions on these picture-stones give us no hint of that. On the contrary, of four preserved stones with a wagon-motif, the Levide church (Go 77) stone tells us '. . . son, like his father . . . on one. That was . . . God (help) the souls of this couple'. The Gotlandic picture-stones from Levide, Ekeby, Alskog and Grötlingbo must further be differentiated into two groups: in some the wagon dominates the scene while in others it is only part of the scene. These different iconographical concepts of using the wagon centre stage or as part of the narrative may even be of importance in relation to religion. The first could be connected with Christian belief while the second refers to pagan tradition.

At the same time it is obvious that the burials with wagon-bodies are widely spread in early medieval Denmark, with usually only a single burial in each cemetery. Exceptions can only be found at Thumby-Bienebek and Ketting with five burials each. J. Callmer (1990, 683) has suggested that we should not distinguish between richer and poorer furnished wagon graves but rather interpret the female individuals as 'leaders of the cult in a pagan religious context'. If this is the case, the female graves should be looked upon as part of a transition-period phenomenon, where the women had a special function in the pagan cult and where their task could have been to prepare society for the change of religion. This thesis might get support from the fact that some of the burials are furnished with Thor's hammer (Thumby-Bienebek 7, 21; Bjerrehøj; Ketting 18) or cross-pendants (Thumby-Bienebek 21; Jelling). The wagon can in this context not only be regarded as a part of pagan mythology, but even as a part of Christian Viking-age iconography, where Christ's journey into Jerusalem must not necessarily have been made on a donkey but perhaps on a wagon drawn by horses.

The use of the wagon by women also seems to be of high importance during the eleventh century. A large number of women are mentioned on the rune stones as erectors of bridges (Sawyer 1991, 221). The practical need of building better communications-systems for the wagon is here connected with the meritorious act and in the eyes of the builder probably even regarded with the Christian idea of Christ as pontifex, i.e. the conception that the bridge builder will have a place in heaven (Andrén 1993, 51).

German and English Missionaries

According to Adam of Bremen, the mission to Denmark and Sweden was mainly influenced by Germanic tradition, whereas the Anglo-Saxon contribution played a secondary role. One cannot blame Adam of Bremen as his view could partly be explained by the fact that he was ultimately writing a history of the church of Hamburg-Bremen and naturally defended the opinions and interests of his patrons. Adam makes reference to there being numerous English bishops in the entourage of King Cnut on his return to Denmark following the conquest of England. Belonging to this personal circle was Bernhard, who would be appointed in Scania, Gerbrand with responsibility for Zeeland and Reginbert covering Fünen. Adam, however, failed to mention that Sven Gabelbart had

●ₐ ◑ᵦ ○c

Figure 29.6 Distribution of cross and crucifix-pendants from the Ottonian/Salian area with imported or style-influenced objects: A import; B style influence; C uncertain production or influence by the German Reich or England

already installed Bishop Gotebald in Scania and that Bernhard would be his official successor. Gerbrand was recognised as bishop only after the following interlude: in 1025 the archbishop of Hamburg-Bremen, Unwan, forced Gerbrand, who was travelling through Bremen at the time, to swear allegiance to Germany. It became clear that the competition between the two countries, which was deliberately incited by the Danish royal house, developed from the fear that the Germans were going to dominate church politics.

English influence in Sweden in the eleventh century is harder to substantiate. Adam names only one *Sigafrid* who operated out of Norway. Of more interest is his nephew Osmund. He went to Rome in order to be ordained a bishop, a position which he was denied. Finally he was ordained as bishop through the *archiespiscopus Polaniae* in Gnesen, Poland. Osmund was appointed as bishop by King Emund Slemae and clearly demonstrated his subordination to church

$\bullet_A$ $\mathbf{\Theta}_B$

Figure 29.7 Distribution of cross and crucifix-pendants from the Insular area with imported or style-influenced objects: A import; B style-influence

politics by meeting a delegation from Hamburg-Bremen with Swedish resistance. Osmund's career in Sweden appears to have ended with the death of Emund Slemae in 1060.

During the tenth and especially the eleventh century a large number of cross- and crucifix-pendants are found in the Scandinavian countries. When the mission was successfully completed in the late eleventh century, the objects disappear. The items reflect the impact of missionary activities and they give us a hint about the people who were willing to get baptised. The analysis of the cross-pendants indicates that several pendants in early medieval Denmark had their origin or were indirectly influenced by Germany. The most important group are here the local products; these reflect the reception of ideas and the local image (Fig. 29.6). But there is also a large number of pendants which were produced according to English models, either in England or under English influence (Fig. 29.7). A lot of

●ₐ   ○ᵦ

Figure 29.8 Distribution of cross and crucifix-pendants from the Russian area with imported or style-influenced objects: A import; B uncertain production or influence by Russia or England

●ₐ ◑ʙ

Figure 29.9 Distribution of cross and crucifix-pendants from the Byzantine area with imported or style-influenced objects: A import; B style-influence

British missionaries were active in Germany during the eighth and ninth century. Bremen was for example founded by an English bishop. The material culture may therefore in some parts look identical, so that it is difficult to say where it originates. But it is important to point out that there are no known pendants from Germany which are finished in an 'Anglo-Saxon' style. The English influence in the metalwork endorses the picture which has already appeared in the analysis of the written sources.

A similar conclusion can be reached by analyzing the Swedish cross-pendants. Since the pendants are not – as believed by Gräslund (1984, 115) – of German origin but seem to have closer links with English art, this makes a mission from there even more likely (Fig. 29.7). The German influence in Sweden is almost nonexistent, and the success of Bishop Unni's missionary activities in Birka may be doubted (Fig. 29.6). This could explain the harsh reaction against Osmund by the German missionaries. Besides the German and English influence there might

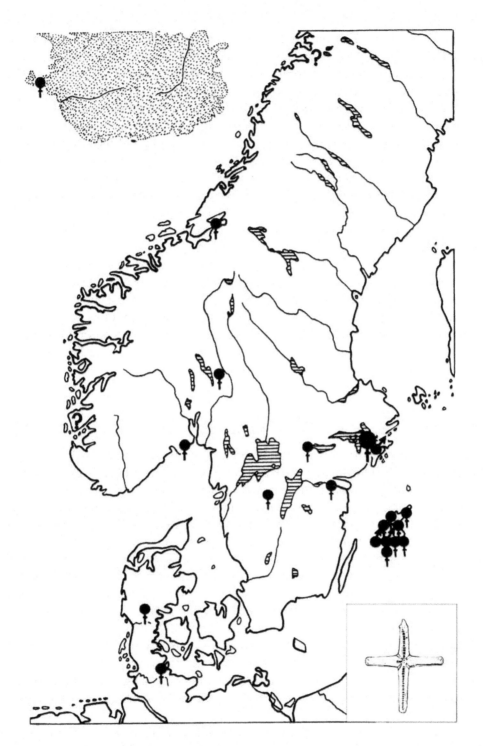

Figure 29.10 Sex-determination of tenth–eleventh-century burials with cross or crucifix-pendants: ♀ female graves; ♂ male graves

even have been a Polish initiative, as recently pointed out by W. Duczko (1999, 131f.). Concerning Christian items a high percentage of Russian imported finds can be observed, especially on Gotland (Fig. 29.8). It is not unlikely that the silence of the German writers, who completely ignored the island of Gotland in spite of its importance, has to be explained by an individual mission, which was initiated by Gotlandic farmers and Russian priests. But on the other hand the fact that a major part of the Russian items were imported and not imitated makes it more difficult to support this theory. Probably Gotland and the eastern coast of Sweden used their good contacts with Russia (through marriage and trade) to keep the German mission at a distance by using their own images and by keeping the process of Christianisation in their own hands. Another impression is given by the items of Byzantine origin (Fig. 29.9). The objects were probably regarded as high quality productions, which could be transferred by trade, gifts or even by pilgrimage.

In this initial phase of the mission it is of course interesting to take a closer look at the people who provided backing for the process. While most eleventh-century rune-stones with a cross-symbol were raised in memory of male individuals (about 70%, compared with 30% for females), the situation looks quite different for the tenth and eleventh-century burials. Of 28 inhumation and two cremation burials in Scandinavia with cross- or crucifix-pendants, 25 are females, three males and two cannot be determined (Fig. 29.10).

The Role of Women in a Conversion Period

As we can see, the majority of burials containing Christian signs are female: these are the burials with insular imports, Frisian jugs, cross-pendants, Thor's hammers and wagon-bodies. What is the reason for the fact that most of the material culture with Christian symbolism is spread among women? According to A.-S. Gräslund, men had a higher mobility and while travelling they would more easily make contact with Christianity. Women on the other hand were tied to their home. If there was a mission stationed at the trading place (like Birka), 'one could expect that the new belief would bear fruit among women' (Gräslund 1984, 117). B. Sawyer has pointed especially to the social and religious factors which might have attracted women to Christianity. 'The belief in paradise may have filled a gap, especially for women who were excluded from Valhalla and who could just look forward to the black pit of Hel'. There are even other factors like the equality of the sexes in front of god, the value of the individual, irrespective of fertility, belonging to a house, the position in society. Even a change in attitude towards children, where infanticide was forbidden, might have been one of the reasons (Sawyer 1992, 81).

These arguments sound quite convincing, but there is one problem: usually there is not more than one grave with a cross or crucifix pendant existing in each cemetery and, if we bear in mind 'classical pagan' gravegoods like Thor's hammer and the wagon, favoured at the same time, it seems that the reason might be another, or at least a more complicated one. What do we know about the position of woman in the Viking-age? Is she a free, proud and independent individual or an oppressed and powerless one (Sawyer 1991, 214)? Christianity is mainly transferred by males like bishops, missionaries and priests. But what was the situation in pagan religion? Could women have a position in cult which gave them the possibility to be part of those who had control over the pagan cult and its transition to Christianity? (See also Geake, Chapter 16 in this volume) As pointed out by E.-M. Göransson (1999, 163ff.) we can make a distinction between different types of women in Norse mythology. There is the virgin (mö), the wife, the widow, the concubine (frilla), the slave and the seeress or cunning-woman (völva). The wife could be married in a kind of 'contract-marriage' without having necessarily intensive contact with the husband. In this case strong economic or political interests of the families may have provided the reason for marriage. The concubine could have children with her lover, but the children belonged to the father. Both the contract-marriage and the relation with concubines were heavily attacked by the church, where the ideal of a monogamous marriage with children was either fulfilled by marrying the concubine or by begetting children with the wife (Sawyer 1992, 38ff.). A special status among single women was given to the widows and the seeress. The living circumstances of the widows did not necessarily mean a turn for the worse. Inheritance of land was widespread and the basis for pious generosity of women in a Christian society. This is clearly illustrated by Rimbert's account of Frideborg and Katla (above). Finally, there is the witch. She was asked for help on special occasions, to give a prognosis for the season, to foretell the future and to tell men other things they wanted to know. Unlike the mythical völva, the human seeress did not have direct access to the desired information, but had to engage in a magic ritual involving seidr (shamanism) (Jochens 1996, 113ff.).

Turning back to the archaeological record it would be useful to know to which group these commemorated 'high-status' women belonged. The position of the warrior-wife has been pointed out concerning the wagon-graves without solving the riddle that there is a gap in time between the male (early tenth-century) and female (middle tenth-century) graves (Eisenschmidt 1994, 86ff.). Other positions in society like the old woman, the concubine (apart from Roesdahl and Nordqvist's article) and the witch have never been discussed. There is only the material of 2000 Scandinavian rune stone inscriptions which has been thoroughly investigated by B. Sawyer. As already mentioned Sawyer focused especially on the widows and their social status. This group of individuals makes it possible for us to understand the vital interest in pious actions like bridge-building in eleventh-century Scandinavia which would explain the necessity of wagon-graves, and it even explains to a certain degree the presence of Frisian jugs in ninth-century graves. But the regular distribution of both pagan and Christian attributes in Viking Age cemeteries, which is quite striking with the exception of three places, could have another reason. We cannot exclude that women had a close contact with religion (not only in the sense of witches) which made it possible for them to integrate Christian elements and thoughts at an early stage in Scandinavian society. The role of a priestess cannot be determined, we know too little about pagan religion. But the archaeological record suggests that special functions in cult were carried out not by just anybody but assigned to certain persons. Since there are still hundreds of graves hidden in the ground and the symbolic role of artefacts is open to many interpretations, this thesis may turn out to be wide of the mark. But still, it is time to turn from defining social trends which are too general and investigate the role of the smaller communities and the individual.

The distribution of the different items with its concentrations and blank areas makes it even clearer that regional differences must have played an important role in Viking Age society. Concerning the erection of rune stones B. Sawyer has stated that in areas like Denmark, Norway, Småland and Gotland only a small number was commissioned by women to commemorate men. In Uppland, Södermanland and on Öland a high proportion of female erectors could be observed due to the fact that many of the stones were commissioned by men and women together. In these areas women were not hiding behind their male relatives. They could possess and dispose of property and did not have to submit to distant male relatives. It was these widowed and single women who took on the roles of men (Sawyer 1991, 214ff.). This concept could perhaps explain the fact that the distribution of ninth-century Frisian-jugs (and especially of the tenth and eleventh-century cross and crucifix pendants) was not accidental but could have its origin in the inheritance-system. In other words, widows and single women had perhaps a stronger interest in symbolising their Christian faith, especially in areas where their status was regarded as lower (with the exception of Gotland). At the same time the large number of graves with a wagon or with a Thor's hammer inside early medieval Denmark presents us with a problem. If we regard the wagon as a materialisation of a phenomenon which is later documented in the raising of bridge-builder rune-stones, the problem could be solved in a chronological way. Tenth-century rune-stones in early medieval Denmark are quite different from eleventh-century rune-stones in Uppland in their inscriptions and images. The status of a widow or a single woman could have been the same in Denmark, but it was expressed in burials rather than on rune stones. Or could it be that these women with wagons and pagan symbols belonged to a different group in society, like the witches? This was a group which may have expressed its role in different ways in different parts of Scnadinavia. It was a group which disappeared after the Christianisation of Scandinavia, even if they had been major players in its success.

References

Andrén, A. 1993. Doors to other worlds: Scandinavian death rituals in Gotlandic perspectives. *Journal of European Archaeology* 1, 33–55.

Callmer, J. 1990. Review of M. Müller-Wille, Das wikingerzeitliche Gräberfeld von Thumby-Bienebek (Kr. Rendsburg-Eckernförde). Teil 2. *Germania 68*, 682–6.

Carver, M.O.H. 1995. Boat-burial in Britain: ancient custom or political signal?' In: O. Crumlin-Pedersen and B. Munch Thye (eds), *The Ship as Symbol in Prehistoric and Medieval Scandinavia* (National Museum Copenhagen), 111–24.

Duczko, W. 1999. Real and imaginary contributions of Poland and Rus to the conversion of Sweden. In: P. Urbanczyk (ed.), *Early Christianity in Central and East Europe*. Congress Lublin 1996. Institute of Archaeology and Ethnology. Polish Academy of Sciences. Warszawa, 129–35.

Eisenschmidt, S. 1994. *Kammergräber der Wikingerzeit in Altdänemark*. Universitätsforschungen zur prähistorischen Archäologie 25. Bonn.

—— 2000. *Grabfunde des 8. bis 11. Jahrhunderts zwischen Kongeå und Eider. Zur Bestattungssitte der Wikingerzeit im südlichen Altdänemark*. Dissertation University of Kiel. Kiel.

Gabriel, I. 1988. Hof- und Sakralkultur sowie Gebrauchs- und Handelsgut im Spiegel der Kleinfunde von Starigard/Oldenburg. Oldenburg – Wolin – Staraja Ladoga – Novgorod – Kiev. Handel und Handelsverbindungen im südlichen und östlichen Ostseeraum während des frühen Mittelalters. Konferenz Kiel 1987. *Bericht der Römisch-Germanischen Kommission 69*, 103–291.

Gräslund, A.-S. 1984. Kreuzanhänger, Kruzifix und Reliquiar-Anhänger. In: G. Arwidsson (ed.), *Birka II:1. Systematische Analysen der Gräberfunde*. Kungl. Vitterhets Historie och Antikvitets Akademien. Stockholm, 111–18.

—— 1996. Kristnandet ur ett kvinnoperspektiv. In: B. Nilsson (ed.), *Kristnandet i Sverige. Gamla källor och nya perspektiv*. Projekt Sveriges kristnande. Publikationer 5. Uppsala, 313–34.

Göransson, E.-M.Y. 1999. *Bilder av kvinnor och kvinnlighet. Genus och kroppsspråk under övergången till kristendomen*. Stockholm Studies in Archaeology 18. Stockholm.

Jochens, J. 1996. Old Norse Images of Women. University of Pennsylvania Press Middle Ages Series. Philadelphia.

Kossack, G. 1974. Prunkgräber. Bemerkungen zu Eigenschaften und Aussagewert. In: G. Kossack and G. Ulbert (eds), *Studien zur vor- und frühgeschichtlichen Archäologie. Festschrift J. Werner. Teil 1. Allgemeines, Vorgeschichte, Römerzeit*. Münchner Beiträge zur Vor- und Frühgeschichte. Ergänzungsband 1/I. München, 3–33.

Meier, D. 1997. Siedlungen – Gräberfeld – Kirche. Das Beispiel Kosel bei Hedeby/Haithabu. In: M. Müller-Wille (ed.), *Rom und Byzanz im Norden. Mission und Glaubenswechsel im Ostseeraum während des 8.-14. Jahrhunderts*. Konferenz Kiel 1994. Akademie der Wissenschaften und der Literatur, Mainz. Abhandlungen der Geistes- und Sozialwissenschaftlichen Klasse Nr. 3, I. Mainz, 201–19.

Müller-Wille, M. 1976. *Das wikingerzeitliche Gräberfeld von Thumby-Bienebek (Kr. Rendsburg-Eckernförde)*. Teil I. Offa-Bücher 36. Neumünster.

Roesdahl, E. 1992. Princely Burial in Scandinavia at the Time of the Conversion. In: C.B. Kendall and P.S. Wells (eds), *Voyage to the Other World. The Legacy of Sutton Hoo*. Medieval Studies at Minnesota 5. Minneapolis, 155–70.

Roesdahl, E. and Nordquist, J. 1971. De døde fra Fyrkat. *Nationalmuseets Arbejdsmark*, 15–32.

Randsborg, K. 1980. *The Viking Age in Denmark. The Formation of a State*. London.

Sawyer, B. 1991. Women as Bridge-builders: the role of women in Viking-age Scandinavia. In: I. Wood and N. Lund (eds), *People and Places in Northern Europe 500–1600. Essays in Honour of Peter Hayes Sawyer*. Woodbridge, 211–24.

—— 1992. *Kvinnor och familj i det forn- och medeltida Skandinavien*. Occasional Papers on Medieval Topics 6. Skara.

Staecker, J. 1997. Legends and Mysteries. Reflections on the Evidence for the Early Mission in Scandinavia. In: H. Andersson, P. Carelli and L. Ersgård (eds), *Visions of the Past. Trends and Traditions in Swedish Medieval Archaeology.* Lund Studies in Medieval Archaeology 19. Riksantikvarieämbetet Arkeologiska undersökningar Skrifter nr 24. Stockholm, 419–54.

—— 1999. *Rex regum et dominus dominorum. Die wikingerzeitlichen Kreuz- und Kruzifixanhänger als Ausdruck der Mission in Altdänemark und Schweden.* Lund Studies in Medieval Archaeology 23. Stockholm.

—— 2001. In atrio ecclesiae. Die Bestattungssitte der dörflichen und städtischen Friedhöfe im Norden. In: M. Auns (ed.), *Lübeck Style? Novgorod Style? Baltic Rim Central Places as Arenas for Cultural Encounters and Urbanisation 1100–1400 AD.* Conference Taalsi 1998. CCC-papers 5. Riga, 187–258.

—— 2002. Jelling – Mythen und Realität. In: D. Kattinger (ed.), *The Baltic Rim and Continental Europe (1100–1600). Influence – Reception – Changes.* Symposium Greifswald/ Weitenhagen 2000. Greifswald.

Wamers, E. 1985. *Insularer Metallschmuck in wikingerzeitlichen Gräbern Nordeuropas. Untersuchungen zur skandinavischen Westexpansion.* Offa Bücher 56. Neumünster.

Wienberg, J. 1997. Stormœnd, stormandkirker og stormansgårde. *Meta* 4, 53–61.

30

The Role of Scandinavian
Women in Christianisation:
The Neglected Evidence

ANNE-SOFIE GRÄSLUND

Introduction

Literary evidence tells us that, in the Old Norse religion, women played an important role. In the mythology we meet goddesses and other female beings such as the giantesses, the *valkyries*, who took care of the fallen warriors at the battle-field and afterwards in Valhalla, the *disir*, important in the fertility cult and the *norns* who span the threads of fate of every person. Archaeologically, the valkyries feature as ornaments in the form of small silver ladies found in graves and on the pictorial stones of Gotland (Pl. 30.1), often with a mead cup or horn in their hands. On the tapestry from the famous Oseberg ship burial in Norway (ninth century), many women are depicted as participating in a procession that has been interpreted as an activity within the cult of Freya, the fertility goddess. It has also been suggested that the buried woman at Oseberg was a Freya priestess (Ingstad 1992, 240 ff.).

But what happened at the conversion? It has been argued that Christianity was a disaster for women, partly as there was no Christian goddess and partly as the Christian cult was headed by men, which meant that the women lost all the religious influence that they had earlier held (Næss 1981, 6 ff.; Steinsland 1985, 130). In my opinion, this is not a valid suggestion for the conversion period. It was not until the end of the twelfth century, when the Church was finally established and organised, that the difficulties with the contemptuous view of women on the part of the Church began.

There is very little space given to women in traditional Church history. However, during the past two decades, a general pattern of women who play an important role at conversions has become apparent. For the ancient Church, this has been shown through a study of Philippian women in Macedonia in the first century AD, where women were usually the first to accept the new faith, and where joy is stressed as a most important reason for women to convert: the joyful message and the sisterhood (Portefaix 1988, 181, 199). The fact becomes clear

Plate 30.1 Picture stone from Tjängvide, Gotland (After Steinsland 1992)

when studying ancient historians such as Gregory of Tours in his history of the Franks or Paul the Deacon in his history of the Langobards or the Venerable Bede in his ecclesiastical history of the English people. The same thing can be found in modern missionary history; examples can be taken from India, Africa or Greenland – everywhere women were very often the first in the family to convert (Lennemyr 1989, 27 ff.; Berge 2000, 228, 271 f., 379; Lidegaard 1991, 66).

Turning to Viking Age Scandinavia, we should recall the saga about Erik the Red and his wife Tjodhilde. Erik held on to the old faith, but Tjodhilde converted and built the first church on their farm Brattahlid (Krogh 1967, 19 ff.). It is said in the saga that the church was located to the side, so that Erik would not see it, standing on the tun. Using the archaeological evidence as well as the runic inscriptions, my conclusion is that the pattern of women as prime actors in the conversion is true (Gräslund 1989).

The Archaeological Evidence

From the *Vita Ansgarii* we know about the early Viking town or trading place Birka on a small island in the Lake Mälaren, twice visited by Ansgar as a missionary in 829 and 850, and where he formed a small congregation. From recent excavations of the settlement we now know that the town existed from *c*.750 to *c*.975 (Ambrosiani 1995, 39). On this site, more than 1100 graves had already been excavated in the nineteenth century, leaving a vast archaeological material (Gräslund 1980, 4 ff.). When looking for evidence of conversion, two categories are of importance: burial customs and artefacts. Concerning the Scandinavian Viking Age burial customs in general, a gradual transition can be followed from pagan cremation graves to oriented inhumation graves both with full equipment, to oriented inhumation graves without grave-goods located at the old pagan cemeteries (and this sequence ending up with the graves at churchyards). This is also true for Birka, even though the structure of the population, occasionally composed by many different groups, meant that some of the different steps in this sequence occured simultaneously. An important fact concerning burials is that they can reflect the religion of the deceased as well as that of the surviving family, and can also mirror the normative religion.

As to the location of the graves, men's, women's and children's graves are distributed all over the cemeteries; the impression we get is that of cemeteries where family members have their graves close to each other (Gräslund 1980, 73). The graves certainly lie next to each other, but they never overlap. In a delimited area in the cemetery north of Borg, however, the graves lie so close that they more or less overlap, and in several cases new burials destroyed earlier graves; but this is very unusual, not to say unique. Great care seems here to have been taken to keep the burials within a limited area – in all probability a consecrated site (1980, 83 f.). Of the sex-determinable graves in this small area, seven are female and four are male. Chronologically, most of these graves belong to the ninth century and it is tempting to connect them with Ansgar's mission.

Another aspect of the burials with relevance for the question of Christianisation are the coffins. Most coffins seem to have been rectangular, but there are 73 coffins of a more or less trapezoidal shape, which constitute 29% of all recorded coffins. Generally, trapezoidal coffins are seen as a clearly Christian feature for Continental cemeteries by Weidemann (referred to in Schmid 1965, 173). Among the Birka graves with trapezoidal coffins in which the sex of the deceased can be determined, women's and children's burials are strongly over-represented: there are 22 women, twelve children and nine men. This supports the idea of women's interest in Christianity at this time.

Looking at the Birka artefacts, the most striking example is that all the nine pendant crosses and the single pendant reliquary were found in women's graves (Gräslund 1984, 111) (Pl. 30.2). One of the pendant crosses was found in a double grave, but the cross probably belonged to the woman. (In the same grave there is also a Thor's hammer, but judging from the location it belonged to the man).

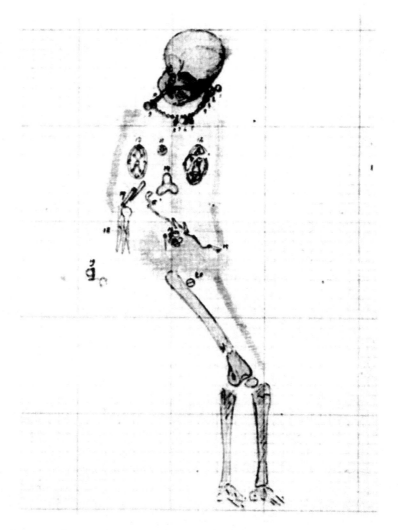

Plate 30.2 Detail of Hjalmar Stolpe's field drawing of chamber-grave Bj 968, Birka, where the dead woman wore a pendant cross (nr 8) on her necklace

It can of course be argued that pendants are ornaments, naturally connected with women, but that is not necessarily so. From the point of view of the quality of craftsmanship, several of the crosses are very simple, plain and carelessly made (Pl. 30.3). This is never the case with normal Viking Age silver ornaments. The symbolic value may have been much greater than the ornamental value (Gräslund 1984, 117).

   Another type of artefact probably connected with the Christian mission comprises bronze keys, almost always found in women's graves, both in Birka and elsewhere. The bronze keys are not specifically Scandinavian: they have a wide distribution in north-west Germany and in southern England, coinciding with the spread of Christianity (Almgren 1942, 7 ff.). In Birka they are found in ninth

Plate 30.3 Pendant crosses from women's graves in Birka. The cross from grave Bj 968 is left in the upper row (After Arbman 1940)

century graves, and if their interpretation as Christian symbols is correct – the keys to heaven or the keys of St Peter – the buried persons in the key-graves may be some of the women who had listened to Ansgar's preaching. The key is an ancient symbol, used for example as an amulet for women in labour (Ament 1992, 19 ff). This does not, however, in my view prevent a later Christian interpretation; we can compare the keys with the pendant crosses, which developed from Roman pagan amulets (Staecker 1999, 51 ff.).

Furthermore, in Birka there are some vessels (five so-called Tating-ware jugs with cruciform decorations), which could have belonged to a Christian milieu. The jugs have even been interpreted as liturgical vessels (Selling 1951, 275 ff.; Ring and Wieczorek 1979, 360). It can be argued that when they were deposited in the graves, the jugs had lost their religious meaning, but they were all found in women's graves datable to the ninth century. Two of the graves are cremations, the others are one chamber-grave, one coffin-grave and one coffin-less inhumation grave. Chamber-grave 854 is very rich with several items imported from Western Europe (Arbman 1943, 325 ff.), including a Tating-ware jug and an Irish hanging-bowl of bronze with fish-shaped mounts. The bowl is possibly a liturgical object, originally used for ritual hand-washing in connection with the Mass. This grave is unusually difficult to resolve as to the faith of the dead woman. She was not cremated but inhumed in an east-west orientation; she wore a Thor's hammer ring round the head and her other grave-goods included two possible Christian vessels: the Tatinger jug with a cruciform decoration and the hanging-bowl. Her rich jewellery included two rectangular brooches of continental type with a cross shape (see Müller-Wille, Chapter 28 in this volume). This could be an example of a mixed religiosity, partly Christian, partly Old Norse at a time when people were hesitant as to which was the better religion.

Leaving Birka and turning to the Middle Ages, Scandinavian women are known as founders of churches. A good example is the Norwegian gravestone from about 1300, saying *Here lies Ragna Asolf's daughter who had this church built. She died on Christmas Eve.* The picture shows Ragna, presenting the church to St

Plate 30.4 Grave slab from *c.*1300, Eidfjord Church, Hardanger, Norway, showing Ragna Asolf's daughter presenting the church to the patron, St Jacob (After Skre 1988)

Jacob, the patron of the church (Pl. 30.4). In this connection, female graves in west towers of churches are of great interest. Danish scholars have pointed out that these graves could be those of the founders of the churches (Stiesdal 1983, 7 ff.). There are many examples from the Continent of women being buried in so-called *Stiftergräber* or *Gründergräber* (Stein 1967, 162 ff.; Theune-Grosskopf 1989, 284 ff.; cf. Borgolte 1985, 27 ff.). One example from Northern Sweden is the female grave beneath the west tower of the church of Västerhus in Frösön, Jämtland (Gejvall 1960, 96, Pl. 6). From the province of Södermanland there are two early medieval examples of church names with female prefix, *Ulfhildakirkia* and *Sigridakirkia*, that support the idea of female church founders in the Early Middle Ages (Wahlberg 1975, 45 ff.).

Several examples of royal women playing an important role in the foundation of communities as well as acting as powerful abbesses can be found in the history

of early monasticism. Originally they could have been heads of double communities, i.e. both a monastery and a nunnery. One example of this was Theodechilde,
abbesse of Jouarre, east of Paris, in the middle of the seventh century (Müller-Wille
1996, 218). Queen Ulvhild in Sweden was the one who asked Bernard of Clairvaux
to start the first Swedish monastery, Alvastra, in 1143. The Varnhem monastery
was founded in 1150 by an aristocratic woman, Sigrid, and the monastery of Viby
in 1160 through a donation of a woman called Doter. An example of an early
Swedish royal abbess is Ingegerd (d. 1204), sister of king Karl Sverkersson, who
was the prioress of Vreta nunnery for 40 years (Karlsson 1996, 16 ff.).

The Evidence of the Rune Stones

Let us return to the Viking Age in Central Sweden and look at the rune stones
as witnesses of the conversion. In Sweden, there are about 2500 known runic
inscriptions dating to the Viking Age (Pl. 30.5). The provinces around the Lake
Mälaren are the richest, with Uppland as number one, with approximately 1300

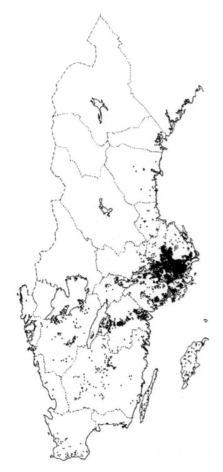

Plate 30.5 Distribution map of Swedish Viking
Age rune stones (After Jansson 1987)

rune stones. The primary purpose of the rune stones was as memorial stones; they were raised in memory of dead family members by the surviving family. As the vast majority of the stones either contain a prayer in the text or are decorated with a cross, there is an obvious link between the fashion for raising them and the introduction of Christianity to Sweden (see also Lager, Chapter 31 in this volume).

The rune stones are often seen as a purely male concern (and the most common type of inscription is in fact a son raising the stone in memory of his father), but a study of all Upplandic inscriptions shows that women were mentioned in 39% of them, either alone or together with men (Gräslund 1989, 223 ff.). In inscriptions that mention the building of bridges for the soul(s) of the dead, the female component is clearly more frequent, 55%, or more than half the total number of

Plate 30.6 Rune stone U 489, Morby, Lagga parish, Uppland, raised by the mother Gullög who had a bridge made for her daughter Gillög's soul (After *Upplands runinskrifter*)

inscriptions. In order to promote the building of roads and bridges the Catholic Church had already at an early stage incorporated this in the system of indulgence, comparable to the giving of alms or going on a pilgrimage. In return the Church offered intercession for the soul and/or absolution. Bridge stones can be found from the beginning of the eleventh century up to the end of the century (for the dating of rune stones see Gräslund 1994). Interesting early examples are the Sigurd carving from Ramsund in Södermanland (Sö 101) and the stone from Bro parish in Uppland (U 617), both raised by women in memory of their husbands. Dated to the last quarter of the century, a beautifully ornamented stone from Lagga parish in Uppland (U 489) has the inscription *Gullög had this bridge made for her daughter Gillög's soul* . . . , (Pl. 30.6). The famous Dynna stone from southern Norway should also be mentioned, raised by a mother who made a bridge in memory of her daughter, *the most handy girl of Hadeland*. This is decorated in a classical Ringerike style and can therefore be dated to the first half of the eleventh century. The pictures on the stone show scenes from the Christmas Gospel: Christ, the star, the three wise men and the stable with the crib (Pl. 30.7). In

Plate 30.7 Two details from the rune stone from Dynna, Opland, raised by a mother who had a bridge made in memory of her daughter. Scenes from the Christmas Gospel, to the right Christ, the star and the three wise men, to the left the stable with the crib (After Fuglesang 1980)

all probability, the mother and her daughter were familiar with the Christmas story.

Worship of the Virgin Mary can be viewed as a compensation for the pre-Christian goddesses that were abandoned in Christianisation, e.g. Freya, who was not only the goddess of fertility, but also, according to the Edda, the one who cared for half of the dead. The importance of the Virgin already during the eleventh century in the Lake Mälaren region is evident from the runic inscriptions. These inscriptions also provide the basis for an assumption that worship of the Virgin attracted women in particular, as the female component of the texts with the prayer *may God and God's mother help his/her soul* is much larger than for the prayer *may God help his/her soul* (Gräslund 1987, 92).

There are only two inscriptions mentioning pilgrimage, both on stones raised by women. A wife raised one in memory of *her husband who went to Jerusalem and died in Greece* (U 136). The other was erected by *Ingerun, Hård's daughter, who had these runes carved for herself. She wanted to go eastwards, out to Jerusalem* (U 605). Really, it is a fascinating thought that a woman in the middle of the eleventh century would plan such a journey!

A stone, contemporary with the Ingerun inscription, reads *Gisl and Ingemund, good young men, had this stone raised in memory of Halvdan, their father, and Ödis, their mother. May God help her soul* (U 808; see Chapter 31, Plate 1 for a picture of this stone). This is notable. Normally, if a stone is raised in memory of more than one person the prayer should be *May God help their souls*. In this case I get the impression that the sons and their mother were Christians, but that the father was not. This can be compared to the story told about Erik the Red and Tjodhilde.

Conclusions

In my opinion, both the archaeological and the runological evidence support the idea of women playing an active role in conversion. But we should reflect over whether the change was positive or negative for them. Obviously, the women had played an important role in the Old Norse religion, as well. So why change? Were they receptive simply because they were curious about something new and unknown? Maybe, but several other possible causes should also be pointed out:

- Conditions in the afterlife were much better. Of course it sounded preferable to go to 'light and paradise', compared to the dark, dreary and depressing Hel.
- The Christian message was less violent.
- The Christian attitude to small children, who were usually the responsibility of women. Infanticide was forbidden.

And perhaps the most important:

- Christianity stressed the individual instead of the collective, the family.

That meant equality and a possibility of salvation for everybody. If you were a good person, you could affect your own fate and afterlife. The formulation *May God help his soul better than he deserved* in runic texts probably alludes to the grace of God, perhaps against family members who had not converted. One archaeological argument for the emphasis of the individual could be the sex segregation of the early medieval churchyards. Women were buried to the north of the church and men to the south. This custom only exists in the Early Middle Ages. In *c.*1250 there is a return to the system of family graves, a fact that can be explained through a new ecclesiastical law, which gave the father a stronger power over the members of his family and his household (Nilsson 1994, 99).

As mentioned above, it has been argued that Christianity was bad for women, since the cult was headed only by men. I am convinced that the situation was completely different at the time of conversion compared with later centuries, when the Church had been established. In the history of mission, there are many examples of how women could act as priestesses at this pioneer stage but, later on, they lost this possibility. For Sweden, the history of the revivalist movement of the pietism in the eighteenth century can provide an analogy. At first, women acted as preachers, but later this possibility was closed to them (Haettner Aurelius 1996, 260 f.). In a wider context, this is the problem of institutionalisation. During radical changes in society, women have turned out to have a very strong position with good possibilities for important influence, as for example at the Reformation in southern Germany in the 1520s. Afterwards, when things had settled down, the normal patriarchal pattern returned (Roper 1989, 2 f.). There are also many examples of activities, initially run by women, which are gradually taken over by men. The activity is given higher status and finally becomes institutionalised, whereby women become totally excluded.

The Christian practice of stressing individuality made people aware of their own identity. Historians and historians of literature are often of the opinion that it was not until the eighteenth century that people began to be self-aware. The reason for this seems to be that the earliest autobiographies are from that period. However, I find it very strange that people of earlier periods should not have had an idea of their own personal identity. The Viking Age group of rune stones raised in memory of the raiser himself/herself (e.g. Ingerun) well supports this.

Returning to the comparison between the conversion and the revivalism in the eighteenth century, there could be another clue to why women were attracted by Christianity. The difference between the very severe and censorious Swedish Lutheran eighteenth century church and the much softer and more emotional religiosity of the pietism could possibly be a parallel to the distinction between Old Norse religion and the Christian message. One explanation of the fact that women seem to be attracted by an emotional type of religion can be taken from developmental psychology. Studies of small children have shown that boys and girls develop their identities in different ways (Macoby and Jacklin 1974). The socialising process for boys is characterised by separation, to encourage them to manage on their own, to have a group of friends, to take part in competitions and to go out into the wide world. Key words for the girls' identity formation are: relation, dependence, the little world, one's best friend, community and the fear for separation. The regressive and symbiotic element in the softer form of religion fits well with such a female identity (Eriksson 1990, 51). There is a strong emotional, not to say sexual, element in the songs of the pietism. It must have been easier for a woman to feel like the Bride of Christ than for a man.

In a study of the Brethren of Moravia in Sweden, the historian Arne Jarrick has pointed out that the strong emotional component in this movement could be an explanation as to why the proportion of women was so high in this congregation and their position so strong in contrast with their modest position in other fields of public life (Jarrick 1987, 69). That coincides well with the picture of women raising rune stones and building bridges, both with a strong Christian element. This was also an exception, deviating from the traditional gender role.

Note

Scandinavian chronology:
Viking Age c. 750/800 – 1050/1100
Early Middle Ages c. 1050/1100 – 1200

The numbers of the rune stones refer to the corpus Sveriges runinskrifter.
Sö = Södermanlands runinskrifter. Granskade och tolkade av E. Brate & E. Wessén. Sveriges runinskrifter 3. Stockholm 1924–1936.
U = Upplands runinskrifter. Granskade och tolkade av E. Wessén & S.B.F. Jansson. Sveriges runinskrifter 6–9. Stockholm 1940–1958.

References

Almgren, B. 1942. Thors märke och himmelrikets nycklar. *Uppland*.

Ambrosiani, B. 1995. Excavations at Birka 1990: Interim report. In: *Excavations in the Black Earth 1990*. Eds B. Ambrosiani and H. Clarke. Birka Studies 2. Stockholm.

Ament, H. 1992. *Das alamannische Gräberfeld von Eschborn*. Materialien zur Vor- und Frühgeschichte von Hessen 14. Wiesbaden.

Arbman, H. 1940–1943. *Birka I. Die Gräber*. Text (1943) und Tafeln (1940). Stockholm.

Berge, L. 2000. *The Bombatha Watershed. Swedish Missionaries, African Christians and an Evolving Zulu Church in Rural Natal and Zululand 1902–1910*. Studia Missionalia Uppsaliensia 78. Uppsala.

Borgolte, M. 1985. Stiftergrab und Eigenkirche. Ein Begriffspaar der Mittelalterarchäologie in historischer Kritik. *Zeitschrift für Archäologie des Mittelalters* 13.

Eriksson, A-L. 1990. *Livsåskådningar hos kvinnor och män i Sverige. Delrapport från projekter Livsåskådningar i Sverige*. Teologiska institutionen, Uppsala universitet. Uppsala.

Fuglesang, S.H. 1980. *Some aspects of the Ringerike style*. Odense.

Gejvall, N-G. 1960. *Westerhus. Medieval population and church in the light of skeletal remains*. Stockholm.

Gräslund, A-S. 1980. *Birka IV. The burial customs. A study of the graves on Björkö*. Stockholm.

——— 1984. Kreuzanhänger, Kruzifix und Reliquiar-Anhänger. In: *Birka II:1. Systematische Analysen der Gräberfunde*. Ed. G. Arwidsson. Stockholm.

—— 1987. Pagan and Christian in the age of conversion. In: *Proceedings of the Tenth Viking Congress. Larkollen, Norway 1985.* Ed. J. Knirk. Universitetets Oldsaksamlings Skrifter, ny rekke 9. Oslo.

—— 1989. 'Gud hjälpe nu väl hennes själ'. Om runstenskvinnorna, deras roll vid kristnandet och deras plats i familj och samhälle. *Tor* 22.

—— 1994. Rune stones – on ornamentation and chronology. In: Developments around the *Baltic and the North Sea in the Viking Age.* Eds B. Ambrosiani and H. Clarke. Birka studies 3. Stockholm.

Haettner Aurelius, E. 1996. *Inför lagen. Kvinnliga svenska självbiografier från Agneta Horn till Fredrika Bremer.* Lund.

Hermansson, K. 1991. 'Cherubim and Seraphim' och kvinnorna. In: *Det mångreligiösa Jos. Om kyrkoliv och kristen-muslimska relationer i Nigeria. En fältstudierapport.* Teologiska institutionen, Uppsala universitet. Uppsala.

Ingstad, A-S. 1992. Oseberg-dronningen – hvem var hun? In: *Oseberg-donningens grav: vår arkeologiske nasjonalskatt i nytt lys.* Eds. A.E. Christensen, A-S. Ingstad and B. Myhre. Oslo.

Jansson, S.B.F. 1987. Runes in Sweden. Stockholm.

Jarrick, A. 1987. *Den himmelske älskaren. Herrnhutisk väckelse, vantro och sekularisering i 1700-talets Sverige.* Stockholm.

Karlsson, J.O.M. 1996. *Tidig cistercienserarkitektur i det medeltida Sverige.* Unpublished manuscript (doctoral thesis forthcoming). Uppsala.

Krogh, K. 1967. *Viking Greenland.* Copenhagen.

Lennemyr, M. 1989. Kristna kvinnors identitet i Indien. En 'case study' från Dornakalstiftelsen i Sydindien. In: *Vilket Indien!? Rapport från ett missionsvetenskapligt fältstudium våren 1989.* Teologiska institutionen, Uppsala universitet. Uppsala.

Lidegaard, M. 1991. Kristendommen og den eskimoiske kultur. *Tidsskriftet Grönland* 1991:3.

Macoby, E.E. and Jacklin, C.N. 1974. *The psychology of sex differences.* Stanford.

Müller-Wille, M. 1996. Königtum und Adel im Spiegel der Grabfunde. In: *Die Franken, Wegbereiter Europas. Vor 1500 Jahren: König Chlodwig und seine Erben.* Mainz.

Naess, J.R. 1981. På kant med gyldne gubber i arkeologien. *Nicolay* 36.

Nilsson, B. 1994. *Kvinnor, män och barn på medeltida begravningsplatser.* Projektet Sveriges Kristnande. Publikationer 3. Uppsala.

Portefaix, L. 1988. *Sisters rejoice. Paul's letter to the Phillipians and Luce-Acts as seen by first-century Philippian women.* Coniectanea Biblica. New Testament Series 20. Stockholm.

Ring, E. and Wieczorek, A. 1979. Tatinger Kannen aus Mainz. *Archäologisches Korrespondenzblatt* 9.

Roper, L. 1989. *The holy household. Women and morals in Reformation Augsburg.* Oxford.

Schmid, P. 1965. XVI. Symposion für Arbeitsgemeinschaft für Sachsenforschung in Oldenburg. *Die Kunde* N.F. 16.

Selling, D. 1951. Problem kring vikingatida keramikkannor. *Fornvännen* 46.

Skre, D. 1988. *Gård og kirke, bygd og sogn.* Rigsantikvarens rapporter 16. Oslo.

Staecker, J. 1999. *Rex regum et dominus dominorum. Die wikingerzeitlichen Kreuz- und Krucifixanhänger als Ausdruck der Mission in Altdänemark und Schweden.* Lund Studies in Medieval Archaeology 23. Lund.

Stein, F. 1967. *Adelsgräber des achten Jahrhunderts in Deutschland.* Text und Tafeln. Germanische Denkmäler der Völkerwanderungszeit A 9. Berlin.

Steinsland, G. 1985. Husfruer, gydjer og vølver. In: *Kvinnenes kulturhistorie. Fra antikken til år 1800.* Eds K. Vogt et al. Oslo.

—— 1992. Scandinavian paganism. In: From Viking to Crusader. The Scandinavians and Europe 800–1200. Eds. E. Roesdahl and D. Wilson. Nordic Council of Ministers, Copenhagen.

Stiesdal, H. 1983. Grave i tidlige vesttårne. Nogle nyere iakttagelser. *Hikuin* 9.

Theune-Grosskopf, B. 1989. Ein frühmittelalterlichen Kirchenbau mit Gründergrab in Cognin (Savoyen). *Archäologisches Korrespondenzblatt* 19.

Wahlberg, M. 1975. Sockennamnet Sighridhakirkia. *Ortnamnssällskapets i Uppsala årsskrift*.

31

Runestones and the
Conversion of Sweden

LINN LAGER

Introduction

A shift in religion in a fundamentally religious society involves all aspects of society as well as all the individuals that live in it. The traces of these events are consequently very diverse and often problematic both to identify and to interpret. Even the term 'conversion' in itself is problematic, since it can have both particular and general connotations. Either it can be treated as a sudden and clearly detectable event or as a long drawn-out series of many different and interconnected processes. One way to get around these problems is to divide the one complex transformation into several shorter transformations or phases, as has been done by Fridtjov Birkeli in a study of the conversion of Norway. He separates the conversion into a phase of infiltration, a phase of mission and a phase of institution (Birkeli 1973:14). The phase of *infiltration* is the period during which the population gets passive information about Christianity through their own travels and contacts with Christian countries (*ibid.*: 14 ff.). The phase of *mission* is characterised by active missionary activities from the continent and from the growing number of Scandinavian Christians (*ibid.* 20 ff.). The phase of *institution* is characterised by the establishment of an ecclesiastical organisation and the building of churches (*ibid.*: 26 ff.). While the phase of infiltration is predominantly 'heathen', the phase of mission is both 'heathen' and Christian, and the phase of institution is predominantly Christian. The different religious 'phases' are also accompanied by, or perhaps rather spring from, different political considerations.

If we want to use these phases as analytical tools for studying the conversion of Sweden, several adjustments have to be made. The phases from infiltration to institution represent the conversion as a whole in chronological order, as Birkeli used them. But since the conversion of Sweden was a very slow and diverse process it seems reasonable to assume that several of Birkeli's phases occurred at the same time in different parts of the country. Setbacks in the conversion might also have put a region back into the characteristics of an earlier phase (see

Welinder, Chapter 32 in this vol.). Even though this separation of the conversion
into different phases might seem very artificial, it puts focus on the fact that the
terms Christian and Christianity are very relative concepts during the conversion,
both from our point of view and from the perspective of the converts. From the
phase of infiltration and onwards there were most likely people in Sweden who
considered themselves to be Christian, but the way in which they were Christian
and the context in which this Christianity was practised varied considerably. Even
for those who lived their lives in the midst of the conversion, being Christian
would have been a relative term in comparison with other areas or earlier times.
Christianity as it was practised in the middle of the eleventh century probably
differed both from the Christianity that was practised a hundred years earlier and
hundred years later. Even though the conversion rolled back and forth in the
country, many Christians would have had the experience of considering themselves to be 'the most Christian' that people in that area had ever been. In this
article I will use Birkeli's phases when discussing Christianity in Sweden during
the conversion with a basis in my own research on runestones (Lager 2002).

The Runestones as a Source of Information about the Conversion

The conversion of Sweden occurs at a time when Sweden theoretically is making
the shift from prehistory to history, and we have got very few indigenous written
sources that can give us information about the conversion from a Swedish perspective. However, the lack of documentary evidence is to some extent compensated
by an abundance of runestones that contain information about the contexts in
which they were erected, by virtue of the inscriptions they carry, their position
in the landscape and their ornamentation. Runes had been carved in Sweden long
before the conversion started. One of the earliest runestones in Sweden is the
Möjbro-stone. It is carved with 24-futhark runes and it was erected some time
around AD 500 (Jansson 1987:16). Inscriptions with this type of runes are often
very short and hard to decipher and only 50 inscriptions with this type of runes
have been found in present day Sweden (ibid.: 31). The majority of the Swedish
runestones (c.2500) are written in the 16-futhark runes that emerged around AD
800, and most of these runestones were erected during the eleventh century (ibid.:
31). The character of the texts on these later runestones differs very much from the
earlier ones since they are longer and usually rich in information. Apart from
presenting us with the name of the erectors of the runestone and the name of the
person(s) that is being commemorated, they often give us information of events
in the life of the deceased and sometimes contain a Christian prayer (Pl. 31.1).

It is also during the eleventh century that the characteristic ornamentation
on the runestones develops and about 50% of these runestones have inscribed
crosses (Pl. 31.1). The ornamentation on the runestones (the shape of the runic-
band) has proved to be very important for constructing the necessary chronological
framework for the runestones (Gräslund 1994). My own research is primarily
focused on the types of crosses used. Apart from the necessity of systematic

Plate 31.1 Inscribed rune-stone from Uppland; it reads *Gisl and Ingemund, good young men, had this stone raised in memory of Halvdan, their father, and Ödis, their mother. May God help her soul* (U 808)

analyses of the shapes of these crosses, it is apparent that they can also give us much information about the conversion of Sweden. It is fairly easy to establish that there has to have been a relationship between the crosses on the runestones and the crosses in other European material, since Christianity came to Scandinavia from the continent. By analysing cross-shapes on the runestones and how they relate to the cross-shapes in the European material it is possible to discern the level of accuracy in the imitation of the cross-shapes and also the impact of Christian influences from different areas of Europe (Lager, in press). The variety of different types of crosses on the runestones also points to geographical and chronological differences in the Swedish runestone material (and thus in the conversion) that can not as easily be seen through analyses of the rest of the ornamentation or the texts

(Lager 2000, 2002, in press). The runestones consequently contain crucial contemporary information about the first Christian centuries in Sweden both through their written words and through their ornamentation.

Even though not all runestones can be considered as objectively Christian through their texts or through the symbol of the cross, it is generally considered that the majority of the runestones from the eleventh century can be connected with the spread of the Christian faith in Sweden. In a sense the Christian runestones can be taken as a *terminus post quem* for the conversion – those who erected runestones had already converted. Studying the erection of runestones, both chronologically and geographically, should therefore give us information about the spread of Christianity in Sweden. However, there are a few other things that have to be taken into consideration. Even though runestones were erected in an area we should not take for granted that the whole population in that area had converted. It seems reasonable to assume that the erection of a runestone mostly reflects the faith of the family or the group of individuals that erected the runestone, and possibly also that of the deceased. On the other hand, even though we to some extent have to depend on the erection of runestones in order to study the spread of Christianity with any accuracy, it seems reasonable to assume that there were more converts in an area than the number of runestones implies. A large number of those who considered themselves to be Christian from the phase of infiltration and onwards did not erect runestones. In other words, the presence of runestones in an area indicates the presence of Christian individuals who had the ability to express their Christian faith in a monumental way during the conversion. At the same time the absence of runestones in an area does not necessarily mean that there was an absence of people who considered themselves to be Christians.

Runestone Production in Sweden during the Eleventh Century

In this study, chronology is crucial. Even though there have been several attempts by others to create chronological systems for the runestones, I find Gräslund's system the most reliable (for further discussions about chronological systems for runestones, see Gräslund 1991, 1994). Gräslund's system consists of seven different chronological phases that partially overlap each other; this makes it difficult to get an overview of the total number of runestones that were produced simultaneously. Since I felt the need for a generalised production-curve for the runestones in my research I started by dating all the Swedish runestones according to Gräslund's system. Then I divided the number of runestones produced within each chronological phase with the estimated number of years that each phase lasted. Since most of the phases overlap one or several other phases chronologically, I had to calculate the total amount of runestones produced during a specific year by adding the theoretical amount of runestones produced within each phase during that same year. This resulted in a diagram that displayed the estimated runestone production based on calculations for

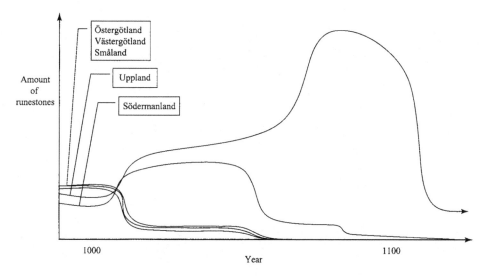

Figure 31.1 Schematised diagram showing the relative numbers of rune-stones produced in Östergötland, Västergötland, Småland, Uppland and Södermanland

every fifth year. Given the fact that these calculations are based on so many theoretical figures it cannot be emphasised enough that the exact number of rune-stones produced during a specific year should not be taken literally. Because of this I have chosen to present a schematised version of the tendencies in runestone production in this article (Fig. 31.1); the original diagram and more extensive discussions about it can be found in my thesis (Lager 2002).

The provinces that I have chosen to display in the diagram in this article are geographically spread from the border of Viking age Denmark and Norway into the eastern part of central Sweden, and this should give a good impression of the runestone tradition in Viking age Sweden (Fig. 31.2). Naturally the present day provinces did not exist exactly as they are now in the Viking age, but the areas of Väster- and Östergötland (also called Götaland) and the area of Svealand (approximately Södermanland and Uppland) were mentioned by Adam of Bremen (for example in book IV, chapter 14 and 23). The diagram that I present in this article is based on calculations of the total amount of runestones, that is the runestones with and without crosses. However, the same tendencies can be seen if one chooses to base the diagram only on the cross-incised rune-stones.

Looking at the diagram (Fig. 31.1), it is obvious that both the amount of rune-stones and the duration of the runestone production vary considerably between different areas. The majority of the Swedish runestones were produced in the province of Uppland (more than half of the total of about 2500 runestones), followed by the province of Södermanland. But if we take a chronological per-spective and look at the beginning of the runestone production in Sweden, we can see that the majority of the earliest runestones were produced in the provinces

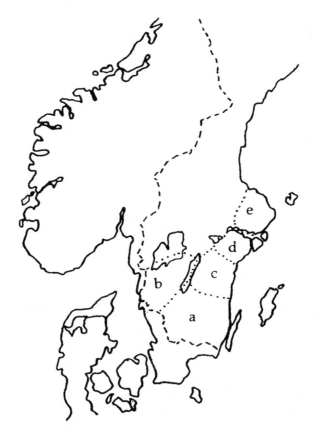

Figure 31.2 Location of Swedish provinces: (a) Småland; (b) Västergötland; (c) Östergötland; (d) Södermanland; (e) Uppland. The provinces of Västergötland and Östergötland together make up the area of Götaland and the provinces of Södermanland and Uppland make up the area of Svealand

of Östergötland, Västergötland and Småland. Even though the runestone production seems to have started at about the same time in all of the provinces represented in my diagram, the termination of the runestone tradition occurred at different times, giving runestone production different durations in different areas. It appears that we can see three successive series of runestone production where the first series consists of production, in Östergötland, Västergötland and Småland, the second in Södermanland and the third in Uppland (see also Herschend 1994). The spread of runestones to most parts seems to have ended in Östergötland, Västergötland and Småland by the middle of the eleventh century. At this time runestone production in Södermanland is still relatively high, though diminishing, and in Uppland the boom in runestone production is still to come. Since the erection of runestones during the eleventh century can be attributed to the first Christian generations in general, it seems reasonable to assume that the variations that can be seen in earlier runestone production represent real variations in the course that conversion took.

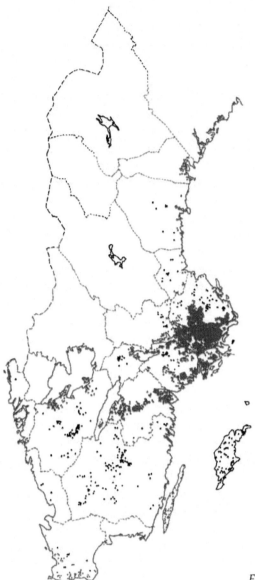

Figure 31.3 Distribution map of rune-stones

A Model of Conversion

It is impossible to say exactly when the first Christian influences reached Sweden and thus when the phase of infiltration in Sweden started. The whole of Scandinavia has always had intense contacts with the continent. From the time that Christianity became the state religion in the Roman Empire in the fourth century and onwards, contacts with Christians and a rudimentary knowledge of Christianity would not have been uncommon. It also seems reasonable to assume that there were Christian prisoners and slaves in Sweden quite early on – at least we know that there were Christian prisoners in Birka in 830 (Rimbert's *Vita Ansgarii*, chap. 11). We can therefore assume that there were individuals in Sweden who believed in the Christian God relatively early, even though their perception of Christianity and their way of being Christian might have differed quite radically from Christianity as it was practised in other parts of Europe at the time. Around the year 800 the interaction between people from Sweden and the Christian countries of Europe increased dramatically as the period known as the Viking age started. Even though the Scandinavians' respect for the religious aspects of Christianity can at times be said to have been moderate, the beginning of the Viking age coincides with our first documentary evidence that people in Sweden had started to convert. Christianity seems to have been a familiar and popular concept amongst some of the population in Birka by the time the Frankish missionary Ansgar arrived in 830.

According to Rimbert, Ansgar came to Birka at the request of king Björn on the behalf of those in Birka who wanted to convert to Christianity (*Vita Ansgarii*, chap. 9). A year after his visit to Birka a new archbishopric was established in Hamburg (later to become Hamburg-Bremen) by the Frankish emperor Louis the Pious with control over, and responsibility for, the conversion of the northern countries (*Vita Ansgarii*, chap. 12, 13). This started a long series of official missionary activities in Sweden by the Frankish church. But in spite of the efforts by the Frankish church and its missionaries, the progress of Christianity seems to have been slow. During Ansgar's second visit to Birka in 852 Christianity was still aggressively questioned (*Vita Ansgarii* chap. 26–28). The boom in runestone production did not occur until about 200 years after the mission by the Frankish church had started. This should imply either a boom in the number of converts, or at least that an increasing number of converts had made it socially acceptable to become Christian and to officially express this Christian faith. Since runestone production seems to have started at about the same time in all of the regions presented in my diagram (Fig. 31.1), all of these regions probably had people converting to Christianity by the end of the tenth century (albeit the number of converts initially might have been higher in the southernmost regions).

The first diocese was established in Skara in Västergötland in 1020, about 20 years after the boom in runestone production, indicating that the institutional phase is about to start. About 30 years after the establishment of the diocese in Skara runestone production in the southernmost regions ended. Even though the erection of runestones can be considered a Christian phenomenon in a Scandinavian context, the erection of this type of monument was not compatible with the mature Frankish Christian way of life, in which religious (and therefore also social) attention should be centred on the local church and its graveyard and not on monuments dispersed in the landscape. But the fact remains that the erection of runestones continued in Östergötland, Västergötland and Småland for about 30 years after the establishment of the diocese in Skara, indicating that the authority of the church remained rather modest until about 1050. In 1060, 40 years after the establishment of the diocese in Skara, a diocese is established in Sigtuna in Uppland. Södermanland seems to mirror the same tendencies as the southern provinces since the erection of runestones there also continued for about 40 years after the establishment of a diocese.

It is much more difficult to understand the relation of runestone production in Uppland to the establishment of a diocese in Sigtuna. Not only is the production in Uppland the largest in Sweden, it is also the latest; over 60% of runestone production in Uppland occurs after 1050. In other words, the establishment of a diocese in the region did not result in a decrease in runestone production, as it eventually seems to have done in the other regions, but instead runestone production increased. A possible reason for this can be found on the runestones themselves, in the shapes of the crosses which I have studied. While the more basic cross-shapes can be found on runestones in all regions of Sweden, most of the more complex crosses are concentrated in Svealand. In these more elaborate designs can be read evidence for external influence. Even though the designs of some of the more elaborate crosses are uniquely Scandinavian, I have traced most of the cross-shapes to an origin in the British Isles. Similarities can be found both in the cross-shapes on British coins brought to Sweden (see for example *Corpus Nummorum Saeculorum*) and in the shapes of stone crosses in the British Isles (*Corpus of Anglo-Saxon stone sculpture*). The apparent British influence in the shapes of these runestone crosses combined with linguistic evidence (Segelberg 1983: 48 ff. and Thors 1957: 631 ff.) suggests that there was a considerable British influence in Svealand during the conversion, in the form of British missionaries or Christians with a British background (Lager, in press). At about the same time as the runestones were being erected in Sweden, the areas on the British Isles that were most populated by Scandinavians saw the erection of stone-crosses with uniquely Scandinavian ornamental elements (see for example Kermode 1907, Collingwood 1927 and *Corpus of Anglo-Saxon stone sculpture* vol. 1–3). It seems reasonable to assume that the Christians who came to Sweden were aware of the Anglo-Scandinavian stone-crosses in the British Isles and that they recognised that the runestones were comparable with these as expressions of Christian faith. This in turn makes it reasonable to assume that these British Christians encouraged the erection of runestones and considered them an important aspect in the spread of Christianity (Lager, in press). The relative distance from areas under the dominance of the Frankish church combined with the strong British influence might have resulted in an especially strong runestone tradition in Uppland. The fact that the diocese of Sigtuna was not established until 1060 also means that Christian communities in Svealand were independent from ecclesiastical control for 40 years longer than the Christian communities in the southern provinces.

Years of relative ecclesiastical independence combined with partially different Christian influences makes it probable that the Christian communities in Uppland (and perhaps also in Södermanland) had developed their own Christian traditions. This in turn means that these communities might not have been overwhelmed with joy by the establishment of a diocese in Sigtuna run by a Frankish bishop. Actually, Adam of Bremen describes a heathen uprising in the area of Sigtuna in 1064 during which the bishop Adalvard the Younger was forced to leave the region (Adam of Bremen, book IV:E, scolion 136). This reaction took place in an area in which a lot of runestones had already been, and continuously were being erected, where there were several churches and a diocese. This area could therefore for several reasons 'objectively' be considered as formally Christian at the same time as the actions of at least a part of its population gives the opposite impression. Even though the area around Sigtuna probably was predominantly Christian at this time, it seems as if the area still was not ready, socially, politically and religiously, to be put under this type of ecclesiastical control. The phase of institution requires that the majority of the population is Christian, or at least that the majority of the population is willing to accept Christianity as the framework for the social and political structures that are developing. The heathen (or perhaps rather political) reaction against Adalvard the Younger indicates that this was not the case. And even though the establishment of a diocese would mean that the Christian population eventually would gain access to aspects of a Christian life that so far had been unobtainable to them, it would also mean that they would lose some of their religious independence. The phase of institution requires that the Christian population is ready to be subordinate to a stricter ecclesiastical framework and a more conventional Christian life. The increase in runestone production after the establishment of a diocese in Sigtuna might be the way that some of the Christians in Uppland chose to mark their desire not to participate in this religious development. The runestones erected in Uppland after 1050 are not only large in number, they also display an increasingly intricate Scandinavian ornamentation, an ornamentation that in many ways distinguish these expressions of Christian faith from the Romanesque style that was introduced by the church (Lager 2000 and Lager, in press). The erection of runestones in Uppland ceased in the beginning of the twelfth century, indicating that the ecclesiastical institution and its perception of a genuine Christian lifestyle had finally become imperative. Judging from the erection of runestones it seems reasonable to put the beginning of the institutional phase in Östergötland, Västergötland and Småland some time around 1050. In Uppland it would not have started until the end of the eleventh century, and Södermanland could be considered to have reached its institutional phase some time between that of the southern provinces and Uppland (see also Gräslund 1997). The first Swedish archbishopric is established in Uppsala in 1164, marking the status of Sweden as a Christian country in its own right.

Thus the conversion of Sweden stretched over several hundred years of infiltration followed by up to 250 years of mission and about a hundred years for the establishment of institutions. The conversion of Sweden was not only slow; it also had considerable geographical and chronological variations. While the southern parts of Sweden could be considered to be in the phase of institution Svealand was still in the phase of mission, in spite of the establishment of a diocese. The historical sources are also full of incidents from many parts of Sweden where the progress of Christianity had severe setbacks through heathen reactions, some of them caused by overzealous and ethnocentric missionaries. Areas that seem to have come quite far in the phase of mission were suddenly left without the spiritual guidance of missionaries and bishops. But in spite of the sometimes tumultuous character of the conversion, the number of generations that came and went during this process makes it obvious that the conversion as a whole did not constitute a sharp break in continuity. The Swedish population converted to Christianity voluntarily and Christianity slowly became a part of the Swedish culture.

References

Adam av Bremen, *Historien om Hamburgstiftet och dess biskopar*. Translated by Svenberg, E. Stockholm. 1984.

Birkeli, F. 1973. *Norske steinkors i tidlig middelalder*, et bidrag til belysning av overgangen fra norrøn religion til kristendom. Den Norske Videnskaps-Akademi i Oslo. II Hist.-filos. Klasse. Ny Serie no. 10. Oslo.

Collingwood, W. 1927. *Northumbrian Crosses of the Pre-Norman Age*. London.

Corpus Nummorum Saeculorum, qui in Suecia reperti sunt. (ed.) Malmer, B. Volumes 1–16, 1975–1982. Kungliga Vitterhets Historie och Antikvitets Akademien. Stockholm.

Corpus of Anglo-Saxon Stone Sculpture. (ed.) Cramp, R. Volumes I-V, 1984–1999. Oxford University Press.

Gräslund, A-S. 1991. Runstenar – om ornamentik och datering. Tor 23. Uppsala.

—— 1994. Runestones – On Ornamentation and chronology. In Birka Studies [3] *Developments Around the Baltic and the North Sea in the Viking Age*. (ed.) Ambrosiani, B. and Clarke, H. Stockholm: 117–31.

—— 1997. Religionsskiftet i Norden. In *Kyrka – Samhälle – Stat*. Från kristnande till etablerad kyrka. (ed.) Dahlbäck, G. Finska Historiska Samfundet. Helsingfors: 11–36.

Herschend, F. 1994. *The Recasting of a Symbolic Value* – Three Case Studies on Rune-Stones. Occasional Papers in Archaeology. Uppsala.

Jansson, S.B.F. 1987. *Runes in Sweden*. Royal Academy of Letters, History and Antiquities, Central Board of National Antiquities. Stockholm.

Kermode, P. 1907. *Manx Crosses*. The inscribed and sculptured monuments of the Isle of Man from about the end of the fifth to the beginning of the thirteenth century. London.

Lager, L. 2000. Art as a Reflection of Religious Change: The Process of Christianisation as Shown in the Ornamentation on Runestones. In (ed.) Puskowski, A. *Early Medieval Religion*. Archaeological Review from Cambridge, Volume 17:2. Cambridge: 117–32.

—— 2002. Den synliga tron, Runstenskors som en spegling av kristnandet av Sverige. (The Visible Faith. Runestone crosses as reflections of the Christianisation of Sweden). *Occasional Papers in Archaeology* 31, Uppsala.

—— in press. Art as a medium in defining 'us' and 'them' – the ornamentation on runestones in relation to the question of 'Europeanisation'. In: J. Staecker (ed.), *The European Frontier*. Symposium Lund 2000. CCC-papers. Lund Studies in Medieval Archaeology. Lund.

Rimbert, *Vita Ansgarii*. Translated by Odelman, E. Stockholm, 1986.

Segelberg, E. 1983. Missionshistoriska aspekter på runinskrifterna. *Kyrkohistorisk årsskrift 1983*. Uppsala: 45–57.

Thors, C. 1957. *Den kristna terminologien i fornsvenskan*. Helsingfors.

32

Christianity, Politics and Ethnicity in Early Medieval Jämtland, Mid Sweden

STIG WELINDER

Introduction: Peoples of Jämtland

The Christianization of the province of Jämtland (which together with the province of Härjedalen forms the present-day administrative area *Jämtlands län* in Mid Sweden), was a process which took about two centuries. During the tenth century only pagans of various kinds lived in the area. By the mid thirteenth century the province had been subdivided into parishes belonging to the Uppsala archdiocese. There were, however, still pagans living in the area: they were Saami (Zachrisson *et al.* 1997: 165–75, 185–8, 228–32). Christianization was part of a process that brought Jämtland into the Norwegian kingdom towards the end of the twelfth century. It was also a part of a process that formed the ethnicity of the Germanic and Saami peoples of the area. To become a Christian, or not to, was of political importance during the eleventh century.

I will discuss the process of Christianization with the stress on the archaeological monuments in Jämtland in the period AD 900–1200. My conclusions will differ from that of the Swedish national research project *Sveriges kristnande* (*The Christianization of Sweden*; Brinck 1996a; Nilsson 1996c, 1998), largely due to the use I have made of calibrated radiocarbon dates. I have also interpreted the stratigraphy of features underneath the altar of Frösö church in a less spectacular way (cf. Näsström 1996). The prime difference, however, is that I have tried to form a coherent overview of the full process of Christianization in a way that the research project did not, and perhaps did not intend to. The term 'Christianization' is itself problematic (cf. Kilbride 2000), and I use it here to denote the full process from the baptism of the first individuals in Jämtland to the final political and bureaucratic institution of the Christian church in the area.

Let's pull aside the curtain. The first act will show pagan society in the central agricultural part of Jämtland around Lake Storsjön during the Late Iron Age, where Saami and Germanic peoples lived together. The next shows the

Germanic people responding to the Christian project, first locally and then as part of a broader, ultimately an international community. The last shows the Saami stressing their difference to their newly converted neighbours.

Germanic Chieftains and Hov-manors (AD 800–1000)

The islands of Frösön and Norderön in Lake Storsjön bear the names of the pagan gods Frö and Njärd, respectively. These were fertility gods, one male and one female (Brink 1996b: 157). Thus, the Late Iron Age farms on the sunny slopes with calcareous soil along the shores of the lake, today visible as small groups of burial-mounds, were once situated in a landscape that was constructed according

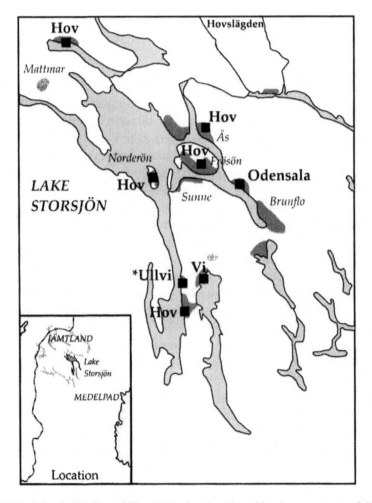

Figure 32.1 The islands Frösön and Norderön, farms with cultic place-names, and districts with Iron Age burial-mounds around Lake Storsjön in Jämtland, Mid Sweden (modified from Vikstrand 1996)

to sacred and fruitful intercourse. Among the farms there are five, possibly six, with the name *Hov*. Another three farms have the names *Odensala*, *Ullvi* and *Vi*. These are cultic place-names refering to the pagan gods *Oden* and *Ull*, and to places, *hov* and *vi*, where the pagan gods were worshipped. These eight or nine farms are spread all around Lake Storsjön in districts with Iron Age burial-mounds (Fig. 32.1).

The hov-farms and the other farms with cultic place-names were the seats of chieftains that formed the local élite, a Jämtlandic aristocracy (Vikstrand 1996: 88–91). In date, they began more recently than the earliest Iron Age burial-mounds in the fifth century, but before the introduction of Christianity during the eleventh century; and they lasted for centuries. Many of them today form the estates of Medieval churches (Vikstrand 1996: 90–92). It is a matter of discussion whether in the earlier period there was an overarching authority in Jämtland which had political power over the élite at the hov-farms. A royal manor and the site of a *thing* (Sw. *tingsplats*) common to all of Jämtland is known to have been situated at Fröson in the mid fourteenth century (Hemmendorff 1996: 52–3), near to the site of Jämtland's only hillfort, which was in use in about AD 400–700 (Hemmendorff 1996: 50–1; Pl. 32.1). The hillfort may have been the fortified seat of a paramount chief or a central place common to all of the local chieftains. There is no other evidence that Jämtland had a powerful individual leadership

Plate 32.1 View towards Lake Storsjön and the hillfort of Mjälleberget (centre) (Photo: Barbro Johnsen)

prior to the eleventh century, and possibly not even then (Vikstrand 1996: 94–7; cf. Hemmendorff 1996: 48–51).

The Jämtlandic élite who were the aristocratic owners of these farms had a double and intimately integrated position, with both social power and religious primacy. Nordic heathendom was not a religion, it was a way to organize society. It was a way of living. The words *hov* and *sal(a)* in the cultic place-names refer to the hall (Sw. *hall*) of the estate, which was the main building from a social point of view (Herschend 1997). In the halls, members of the élite confirmed their membership by drinking mead together. They formed alliances, possibly by intermarriage. The élite comprised a small number of interrelated families in which females were central (Pettersson 1997: 16–29). In the mid Iron Age gold-foils, women are depicted with drinking-horns in their hands, facing a man. These tiny artifacts are contextually related to the excavated halls. The couple is the female and the male representing the aristocratic hall-owners as well as the gods, e.g. Frö and Gerd, or Oden and Skade (Pettersson 1997: 2–3, 10–5; Hellqvist 1998: 22). The union between the female and the male secured the annual cycle of fertility and the cycle of the world on its way towards Ragnarök, the doomsday of Nordic heathendom (Hellqvist 1998: 14–8).

The hall was the site of the *blot*, which was the sacrifice of animals, and possibly humans (Patric 2000), but first of all it was a common meal. It was a meal together with the gods, and a meal for the chieftain and his retainers, especially the retinue of warriors (Sw. *hird*). To take part in the *blot* was to be accepted as a member of the group. To stay outside the group was to be god-forsaken and socially lost. The *blot* was based on gift-economy. The meal was a gift to the gods from the chieftain, and it was a gift from the chieftain to his retainers. In return the gods gave the cycle of fertility, and the retainers gave labour-force and products. Accordingly the chieftains had military power and merchandise at their disposal.

The farms in the central agricultural part of Jämtland around Lake Storsjön produced grain and cattle, but primarily they were centres for the exploitation of vast outlying areas in the forest, along the rivers, and in the high mountains. The farms had iron-furnaces, charcoal-stacks, pit-falls for elk, traps for fur-animals, water for fishing and so on. The chieftains seated at the most important farms had retainers not only at the small farms in the locality but also in the outlying areas. The latter, too, were parts of the gift-economy. It was a redistribution economy with the *blot* in the centre. At the times of the regular seasonal *blot* the retainers brought their goods to the chieftains' farms. Among the retainers and neighbours in the forest areas were the Saami (see below).

The hov-farms were the seats of an aristocracy which formed the governing element in pre-Christian society. The cyclical continuance of this society, year after year, was dependent on the gift-giving between the élite and the gods, and between the élite and its retainers in the agricultural area around Lake Storsjön as well as in the outlying areas. It was this élite that had to take a standpoint on Christianity when the time came.

The Last Pagan Burials around Storsjön (AD 1030–1040)

Small agglomerations of burial-mounds once formed a landscape of ancestors around the Iron Age farms along the shores of Lake Storsjön (Pl. 32.2). The first mounds were erected around AD 400. The last mounds to be erected contained the last generation of individuals that chose a pagan burial-rite for themselves, or rather for their family-members. The number of mounds was once considerably larger than what can be seen today, and only a small proportion of the known mounds have been excavated. Nevertheless there is a basis for statistical assessment (Grexing 1999: 20–32). The number of excavated mounds datable to the tenth century is 33 (Fig 32.2.A). They contain all in all 36 individuals, about twice as many men as women. From the eleventh century there are only four mounds with four individuals, two men and two women (Fig. 32.2B). It is reasonable to assume that approximately the same number of mounds were erected each century, or possibly an increasing number due to population growth, until the tradition changed in accordance with the introduction of the Christian burial-ritual. The erection of burial-mounds according to the pagan tradition ceased during the early part of the eleventh century in the central agricultural part of Jämtland around Lake Storsjön (Grexing 1999: 37–38). The latest known burial, organised according to the pagan ritual, may be the man buried with a sledge at Röstahammar, Ås parish, perhaps during the 1020s or 1030s. The two most recent coins in the grave were minted during the reigns of the English kings Ethelred

Plate 32.2 Late Iron Age mound in the churchyard of Frösö (Photo: Barbro Johnsen)

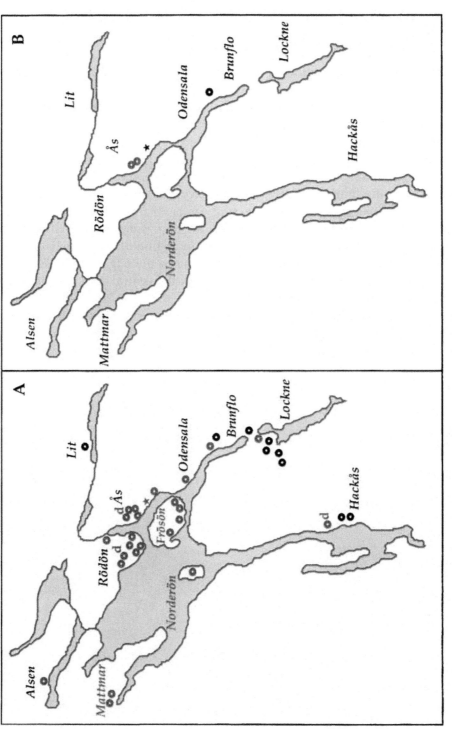

Figure 32.2 Excavated mounds from the tenth (A) and eleventh (B) centuries around Lake Storsjön in Jämtland. Double graves are not especially marked, and mounds of uncertain date are omitted (modified from Grexing 1999)

(978–1016) and Knut (1017–1023), respectively. The horse for the sledge was buried in a trench of its own. It had a bridle with cruciform pendants. The burial-rite and the pendants recall early continental practice (Gräslund 1996: 29–32).

These people probably spoke a Germanic language, possibly some kind of ancient Jämtlandic dialect, and looked at themselves as the peers of Germanic people to the west and south, whose houses, clothing, ornaments and burial-rites they emulated. After the 1030s, or not much later, all burials in the Lake Storsjön area were organised in accordance with the Christian burial-tradition.

Saami Burials (AD 200–1700)

A century or two before the erection of the first Iron Age burial-mounds in the central Lake Storsjön area, small round or square stone-settings were built on islands and headlands in lakes. That was the beginning of a burial-tradition which ran parallel to the Germanic burial-tradition in central Jämtland. The stone-setting burials included objects of the same kind as the Germanic burial-mounds, but the assemblages were often differently composed, and now and then they contain an object reminiscent of later Saami culture, or the remains of elk and reindeer which can be related to historically recorded Saami ritual (Sundström 1997: 21–4; Zachrisson 1997b: 189–90, 195–200). It is an attractive, if controversial possibility that the stone-settings, often denoted lake-burials (Sw. *insjögravar*) or forest-burials (Sw. *skogsgravar*), are the burials of early Saami groups.

The very idea of recognizing ethnic groups in prehistoric archaeology is controversial. According to some it should not be done at all (e.g. Bolin 1998), and to say the least, it is a delicate matter (Jones 1997). 'Ethnicity' is a form of social interaction between groups of people. The interaction may be friendly or hostile, but there are no isolated ethnic groups; ethnicity lies in the differences. Such differences may be expressed or emphasised through dress, ritual or other behavioural aspects (Odner 1983). It is not known whether the individuals that were buried in the forest-burials spoke a Saami language or even if they recognized themselves as another group than the Germanic individuals that were buried in the burial-mounds in the central Lake Storsjön area; but there were differences between them.

The latest in the series of forest-burials is a cremation-burial from the beginning of the thirteenth century (Sundström 1997: 23–24). Another, and so far unique, burial-tradition, was used at the Vivallen burial-ground in West Härjedalen (Zachrisson 1997a: 53–71) in the period AD 1000–1200. It is an inhumation burial-ground where the dead were wrapped in birch-bark and placed in narrow trenches. Some of them were richly dressed, ornamented with pendants and other objects not characteristic of Germanic dress. Remarkable is an old man buried in the late twelfth century with a dress suggesting him to have been a shaman. There is no doubt that the Vivallen burial-ground contains a Saami group of people.

Thus, there are at least two sites with non-Christian burials from the time AD 1100–1250 in Jämtland and Härjedalen (Grexing 1999: 39–40), and the burial

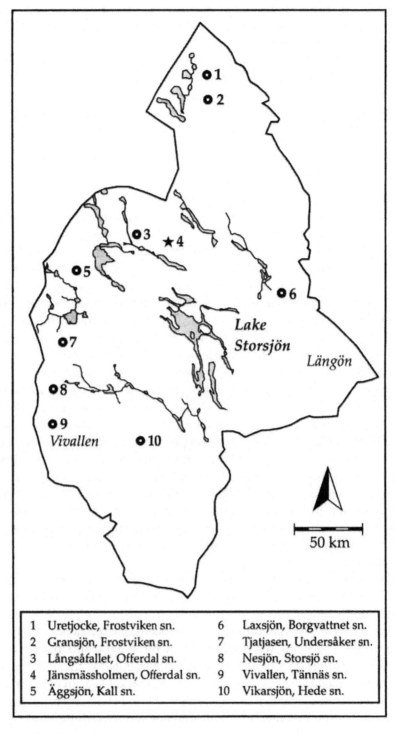

1	Uretjocke, Frostviken sn.	6	Laxsjön, Borgvattnet sn.
2	Gransjön, Frostviken sn.	7	Tjatjasen, Undersåker sn.
3	Långsåfallet, Offerdal sn.	8	Nesjön, Storsjö sn.
4	Jänsmässholmen, Offerdal sn.	9	Vivallen, Tännäs sn.
5	Äggsjön, Kall sn.	10	Vikarsjön, Hede sn.

Figure 32.3 Pagan and Saami burials from the period AD 1100–1700 in Jämtland and Härjedalen (from Grexing 1999)

ground at Långön is also significant for Saami culture (see below). At another eight sites there are burials organised according to the historically known Saami tradition (Fig. 32.3; Grexing 1999: 39–40). One of these burials has been dated to around AD 1500–1700. So not all people in Jämtland and Härjedalen turned Christian during the tenth and eleventh centuries. On the contrary, Christianization meant accentuation of the dividing-line between the Germanic chieftains and their households in the central Lake Storsjön area, on the one hand, and the small groups of people that built the forest-burials and used burial-grounds like Vivallen, on the other. If there was no dividing-line between Saami and Germanic groups previous to the eleventh century, from that century onwards there certainly was. Christianization was a part of the definition of Germanic and Saami ethnicity during Early Medieval times.

The Arrival of Churchyard Burial in Neighbouring Norway and Ångermanland (AD 900–1050)

No obviously Christian burials from prior to AD 1100 have been excavated in Jämtland, although Christian burials are difficult to detect when not situated in the churchyards of the early Medieval stone churches. Along the Norwegian west coast several early Christian churchyards are known (Solli 1995, 1996). Veøy in Romsdal began to be used in AD 900–950 (Solli 1996: 103–5), and Haug in Vesterålen began to be used AD 950–1000 (Solli 1995: 30). At the former site there is a Medieval stone church. At the latter one there are the archaeologically excavated remains of a turf church, which burnt in the eleventh century. The oldest burials at both the Clemens church in Olso and the Kaupanger wooden church in Sogn are from about AD 1000 (Solli 1995: 34). The churchyard at Björned in Ångermanland to the east of Jämtland is the oldest one in the northern half of Sweden. It was in continuous use in the period AD 1050–1250. In addition, one burial of a child has been radiocarbon dated to the tenth century. The burials were probably dug around a historically unknown wooden church indicated by an area empty of burials (Grundberg 1997: 39–40) and close to a few burial-mounds.

The argument is that burials built according to the pagan ritual turned rare towards the end of the tenth century (Skree 1996: 59–61) and at that time Christian churchyards began to be used. But in spite of two generations of efficient church archaeology no wooden churches older than AD 1050–1100 have been excavated in Norway. The priesthood was centralised at a few regional main churches (Nor. *fylkeskirker* or *hovedkirker*), and the numerous parish-churches were not built until the end of the eleventh century or the beginning of the twelfth (Skree 1996: 64–65).

From Hov to Church – Two Examples

Two excavations have produced evidence for halls, on the same sites as a later church. The church at Mære in Trøndelag, Mid Norway, has become a classic archaeological site (Lidén 1996). The present-day stone-church was built around

AD 1150–1200. It was preceded by a wooden church, roughly dated by coins to the eleventh century. This church superimposes Christian burials, thus indicating an older, although undated, wooden church (Lidén 1996: 63–64). The first church in its turn superimposes a cultural layer with four post-holes close to one another and nineteen gold-foils. The presence of a chieftain's farm or a farm with a cultic place-name is not historically known at Mære (Lidén 1996: 67–68), but these are the typical findings of the high-seat of a hall of a *hov* (Hellqvist 1998: 22). The gold-foils in the filling of the post-holes date the erection of the building to not later than the 9th century (Pettersson 1997: 3). The pagan ritual associated with the hall, that is the pre-Christian kind of society, seems to have come to an end at about the end of the tenth century at Mære not far from Jämtland.

The church at Frösön in Jämtland has in some respects yielded similar archaeological findings of a *hov*. The beautifully situated stone church at the top of Frösön was built around AD 1200. No wooden predecessors are known (Hildebrandt 1996: 153–154). Near the church is a late Iron Age burial mound (Pl. 32.2), and around the church, hearths and pits have been excavated and radiocarbon-dated to the time-span AD 200–1400 (Johansson 1996: 17–21), which belong to a farm of the type associated with a *hov*. Below the main altar of the church the *hov* itself has possibly been excavated. There was a birch-stump together with a layer of soot, charcoal, a few fire-cracked stones and lots of bones. Most of the bones, 60%, are from wild animals, notably bears but also elk, red deer, squirrel, fish and birds, some are domestic animals, cattle, sheep, pigs and possibly horse, dog and hens, and finally there are a few human bones (Iregren 1999: 1). A layer of fire-cracked stones is certainly older than the above findings (Hildebrandt 1996: 162–3). Of course these remarkable findings have caused a lot of writing about a pagan sacrificial grove, where the animals were hanged in the trees (Näsström 1996) and where dramas were performed displaying the red deer Eiktyrnir browsing from the Tree of the World, Yggdrasil, with the squirrel Ratatosk running up and down the trunk (Iregren 1999: 6–7).

The evidence that the tree and the bones form one and the same stratigraphic context is in my view not convincing (cf. Johansson 1996: 23). Charcoal from the layer with the bones is significantly older, AD cal. 1009+–136, than the birch-stump, AD cal. 1144+–69. The inherent age of the wood is not known for any of the two samples. Charcoal from the layer of fire-cracked stones is still older, AD 834+–85 (Hildebrandt 1996: 163 presents the uncalibrated dates). The *hov* at Frösön was not apparently used for *blot* after about the beginning of the eleventh century. The place was abandoned and overgrown by a birch grove, which was cut down at the building of the stone-church towards the end of the twelfth century. This is a less spectacular interpretation of the Frösö church site, although it still gives insight in the *blot* and notably its stress of the outlying landscape, where bears and elks roam. The hunting of bears, followed by ritual feasting and the painstaking burial of the remains was a Saami tradition (Näsström 1996: 74–7), as was the sacrifice of elk antlers at burial sites (Iregren 1999: 5–6). It is a matter of debate if the retainers of the Germanic chieftains in the outlying areas were Saami or not. It is a common view within Norwegian archaeological and early historical research that they were (Hansen 1990), but the real pattern could have been one of co-existence, before the conversion of the Germanic peoples forced a new relationship on the Saami.

The First Wooden Churches and Christian Grave-yards (AD 1100–1150)

The erection of churches was a part of the political competition between the emerging Norwegian kingdom and the aristocracy. Christianity, Christian burial-ritual, and churches were significant symbols and monuments that took part in the struggle for power. They displayed how the local élites chose factions and formed alliances (Røskaft 1996: 109–110). No later than AD 1050, possibly a generation before that, Norwegian society was Christian. The main part of the Norwegians were baptized and regularly performed Christian rites (Skree 1996: 62).

Only three archaeologically excavated sites in Jämtland have anything to say about the oldest wooden churches. All three correspond to Medieval stone churches, two of which are still in use. Mattmar stone-church is from about AD 1300. Inside the church the sill-stones, one central posthole, and possibly another one, and a few burials outline a wooden church with a nave and possibly a chancel. The church accidentally burnt down, or it was intentionally burnt down, prior to the erection of the stone church. The radiocarbon datings of wood from the outermost tree-rings and charcoal from the posts are surprisingly similar with central values in the timespan AD cal. 1138–1147. The charcoal from the pits of the sill-stone is older: AD cal. 1090+–93, 1122+–65, and a third hopelessly too old a sample (Sundström 1989a: 150–1). Reasonably the wooden church was built in the second half of the interval AD 1100–1150.

The stone church at Norderön is from about AD 1200. In the walls of the building wooden plugs have been found. They once belonged to the scaffolding that was used when the mason's work was done. The radiocarbon dates are fascinatingly early: AD cal. 1098+–87 and 1144+–71. The three oldest coins found in the church were minted during the reign of the Norwegian king Sverre (1177–1202). Thus, there was a church at the site from about the early half of the twelfth century (Sundström 1989b: 177–179). That is too early to have been the present-day stone church (cf. Bonnier 1996: 191–201). On the other hand, the dates are well in agreement with the samples from Mattmar. It is reasonable that a wooden church that preceded the stone church at Norderön was not burnt down, but its timber was used for scaffolding in the building of the stone church.

Thus, two wooden churches have been radiocarbon-dated to the interval AD 1100–1150. A third one is indicated by its adherent burials. The stone church at Västerhus was built around AD 1200 and the last remains of it were torn down in the 1950s after an archaeological excavation. The series of radiocarbon-dates from the hundreds of skeletons in the grave-yard of the church starts at AD 1100–1110 (Jonsson 1999: 13). This ought to be the date of the wooden church that is indicated by the outline of the burials in the grave-yard. A few burials are superimposed by the stone church (Jonsson 1999: 16).

The period AD 1100–1150, thus, was the time of the building of wooden churches in Jämtland. Possibly tens of churches were built within a few decades. Nothing is known about churches and Christian burials from the time prior to AD 1100. Christian activity during the period 1050–1100 is nevertheless implied by the documentary record including the famous inscription on the runestone at Fröson.

The Documentary Record

Christian buildings and ritual were of course known to Scandinavians already around AD 400. Travelling people brought objects and stories from the Roman empire, and no doubt also accounts of its religions (Skree 1996: 55–56). Missionaries are known to have visited and founded Christian congregations in Denmark and Sweden during the early ninth century. The same happened in Norway during the tenth century although the historical evidence is scanty. The Danish kingdom was Christian around the mid tenth century. There were Christian kings in Sweden in the beginning of the eleventh century. Also the kings that were the first seriously to claim to be kings of all Norwegians used Christianity as part of their politics, Olav Tryggvason (c. 995–1000) and Olav Haraldsson (1016–(1028)1030). Before them king Håkon Adalsteinsfostre (c. 945–960) had been a Christian, who sent for priests and bishops from England (Røskaft 1996: 102–104; Skree 1996: 59, 61–62).

The conversion of Mid Sweden is associated with the name of Olav Haraldsson who had to leave his kingdom in 1028 after a military defeat by the Danish king Knut and a part of the Norwegian aristocracy. In 1030 he marched through Sweden and Jämtland with a small military host once again to be defeated by the local aristocracy and he himself to be slain at Stiklestad in Trøndelag. The life and deeds of Olav Haraldsson form a main part of the sagas of the Norwegian kings written by the Icelandic chieftain Snorre Sturlason around AD 1230. The host of Olav Haraldsson was composed of both Christians and pagans. The latter were asked either to convert or to leave the host before the battle. Snorre Snurlason's saga retails Olav Haraldsson's conversations with some Jämtlandic men, foot-pads and others. They accepted Chistianity due to their admiration for the king and fought in the first line at Stiklestad (Snorre Sturlason's saga *Olav den helliges saga*, chapters 201, 215).

Snorre Sturlason's saga about Olav Haraldsson has, however, much of the characteristics of a hagiography. It is not even certain (though likely) that the host of Olav Haraldsson ever passed through Jämtland (Ahnlund 1948: 69–82). It has certainly little of value to tell us concerning the presence and distribution of Christianity in Jämtland in 1030. It is nevertheless of interest to note that the last pagan burial in the central part of Jämtland was erected around or soon after 1030, so the host of Olav Haraldsson probably marched through a province that already was more or less Christian. A short while after the interment of Olav Haraldsson miracles began to take place at his burial. His body was moved to a shrine, and Olav Haraldsson was turned into Saint Olav, the eternal Norwegian king, to whom all succeeding Norwegian kings have been vassals. Pilgrims arrived at Nidaros, that is Trondheim in Trøndelag, in the 1030s, and Saint Olav shrines were built all over Scandinavia. This is valid also for Jämtland, where local myths on Saint Olav are numerous and where the sites traditionally known as places where Saint Olav has rested or had a drink of water are numerous (Ahnlund 1948: 78–82). Olav Haraldsson did not convert Jämtland, but Saint Olav concluded the Chistianization of the province in the 1030s or soon thereafter (Sandnes 1996: 111–3).

The Runestone at Fröson and the Aristocracy (AD 1050–1080)

The runestone at Fröson (Pl. 32.3), the only one known in all of Jämtland, remains central to the question of Jämtland's conversion. Its text is indeed remarkable, and it has few counterparts (Williams 1996: 46). The inscription reads:

Plate 32.3 The runestone at Fröson dating from AD 1050–1080. The text refers to the Christianisation of Jämtland by Östman Gudfastson (Photo: Barbro Johnsen)

Östman Gudfasts son lät resa denna sten och göra denna bro, och han lät kristna Jämtland. Esbjörn gjorde bron. Tryn och Sten ristade dessa runor.

Östman, the son of Gudfast, had this stone erected and this bridge built, and he had Jämtland christianized. Esbjörn made the bridge. Tryn and Sten carved these runes.

According to the chronological system drawn up by Anne-Sofie Gräslund the runestone was made AD 1050–1080, which is slightly later than previous suggestions (Gräslund 1996: 22). There is nothing to suggest that the runestone was made later than the 1080s (Williams 1996: 50). Today the runestone overlooks the sound between Frösön and the mainland to the east at the place of the modern and a number of earlier bridges. This was also the site of the stone, when it was depicted and mapped for the first time in the seventeenth century. It is quite possible that the bridge ordered to be built by Östman spanned the length of 300 m above the 5 m deep sound. Similar wooden constructions and bridges are known from the eleventh century (Gräslund 1996: 24–5). An alternative is that the runestone has been moved to its present location from somewhere else, for example the *thing*, where there is a running brook which may have been bridged by Esbjörn (Williams 1996: 57–9). There is also a local myth which suggests that the runestone was moved from the site of the church at Frösön.

The original site of the runestone is perhaps of less interest than the text and its implications. Östman Gudfastsson, boasting to have christianized Jämtland, certainly belonged to the élite of the province during the second half of the eleventh century (Gräslund 1996: 26). The text of the stone gives the name of five men in total. In addition to hinting at a male-dominated society, at least in public, the names may tell something about the Jämtlandic élite.

'Östman' is 'the man from the east', which may indicate Jämtland in relation to Trøndelag or some part of Sweden in relation to Jämtland. *Gudfast* is a typical Swedish or Trøndelagian name. Esbjörn and Sten are common unlocalised names, while Tryn is an undoubtedly Jämtlandic name (Williams 1996: 52–6). Tryn was an experienced carver. The runestone at Frösön most probably was not the only one he ever made. He made that one in the style of the runestones of Central Sweden, the provinces around Stockholm, and he used a language of the same kind as the carvers in that area (Williams 1996: 49–59, 52). Several other stones may have been totally lost. It is even reasonable that he was only one of several carvers that made runestones for members of the aristocracy like Östman Gudfastsson (Williams 1996: 56).

The image is that of an aristocracy which could order craftsmen to construct bridges and carve runestones, and pay for their skill and work. One member of this aristocracy boasted to have christianized Jämtland. The name of his father, however, suggests that the province was Christian a generation before the erection of the runestone, which is well in agreement with my discussion of dating of the erection of the last pagan burials above.

Towards the mid eleventh century the Jämtlandic chieftains at the farms with cultic place-names were Christians that saw the Norwegian kingdom consolidated in Trøndelag around the city of Nidaros with the shrine of Saint Olav, a bishop at a royal manor and several churches. In the south the aristocracy in Central Sweden formed various alliances and periodically all followed the same king. The Jämtlandic chieftains had to negotiate with kings with growing power.

The runestone manifests the power of one man, not a *thing* decision by peers (Vikstrand 1996: 94–6). At the time Jämtland had already been Christian for decades, so the runestone actually tells something else. Östman was the head of a faction among the Jämtlandic élite with strong foreign, and (according to Snorre Snurlason's sagas) royal support, possibly from Central Sweden due to the style and language of his runestone. He did not Christianize Jämtland, but he organised the Christian church.

The Norwegian Kingdom and the Archiepiscopal See at Uppsala (AD 1178)

Snorre Sturlason tells in his saga of the sons of king Magnus that king Øystein Magnusson (1103–1123) exchanged gifts with the most wise and powerful men of the Jämtlandic aristocracy and made a treaty with them. Jämtland was to be a part of the Norwegian kingdom, and king Øystein was to help Jämtland in need, which the distant Swedish king was not able to do (Snorre Sturlason's saga *Magnussønnenes* saga, chapter 15). Snorre Sturlason's text has been variously assessed. The Swedish historian Nils Ahnlund has argued that the passage fairly correctly narrates how Jämtland was integrated in the Norwegian kingdom during a period when the Swedish kingdom was weak and occupied elsewhere (1948: 137–44; Lindkvist 1998: 296). The Norwegian historian Edvard Bull has argued, following standard historical source-criticism, that Jämtland was a part of no kingdom at all before the 1170s (1970 (1927): 15–8). The crucial discussion concerns the credibility in various sagas written some decades or a century after the events in question, and at various courts in various political situations.

The compromise seems to be that the Jämtlandic aristocracy exchanged gifts, which is about the same as paying taxes, with either the Norwegian or the Swedish king, and traded either to the west or to the south, in a pragmatic way depending on circumstances. This state of affairs changed in 1178. Much of the mid and late twelfth century in Norway was characterised by conflict and wars between several potential kings, usually sons of former kings. Sverre Sigurdsson, also, at least according to himself, descendant of a king, in the 1170s succeeded in creating a relatively stable kingdom. In the process he defeated the Jämtlandic aristocracy in a battle on the ice of Lake Storsjön in 1178, which is narrated as something of a comedy in king Sverre's saga: a small number of king Sverre's men defeated the entire Jämtlandic host, the members of the latter mainly slaying one another in the dark of night (Ahnlund 1948: 170). Both the above historians agree that from the late 1170s Jämtland was part of the Norwegian kingdom and paid taxes to the Norwegian king (Bull 1970 (1927): 9–15; Ahnlund 1948: 165–74). This was to remain so until 1645, when Jämtland was conquered by the Swedish state.

Given the above, it is remarkable that Jämtland, at the same time as it became a part of the Norwegian kingdom, was a part of the Swedish archiepiscopal see at Uppsala. The first document to demonstrate this is certainly not older than 1257 (Sandnes 1996: 112), but the link is reasonably much older. This anomaly may be due to Norwegian politics during the second half of the twelfth century. When Sverre Sigurdsson became king, he came into conflict with the archbishop seated in Nidaros since the 1150s. The archbishop, Øystein, was finally forced into exile. The Uppsala see on the other hand, founded in 1164, was an expanding one. Thus, there was no basis for a Norwegian bishop to contest the power of the Uppsala archbishop around the 1170s and 80s, when king Sverre consolidated the Norwegian kingdom (Hallencreutz 1996: 10–13). During the 1170s and 80s Jämtland became finally a part of the European kind of Early Medieval kingdoms.

The Stone Churches and Towers (AD 1180–1220)

The subservience of the Jämtlandic aristocracy and peasants to both the Norwegian kingdom and the Uppsala archiepiscopal see is visible in the landscape in a remarkable way. At the Brunflo and Sunne churches there are stone towers, one at each place. Both are fortifications with c. 2 m thick walls. The Brunflo tower, which is the best preserved one, is 16.5 m high (Ekroll 1995: 36–37). Both stone towers were built in the period AD 1150–1200. In fourteenth-century documents (there are none older) the Sunne tower is associated with taxes paid to the kingdom (Ekroll 1995: 37), and the Brunsflo tower with the Uppsala see (Vikstrand 1996: 99). It is hard to tell if matters were similar already at the end of the twelfth century. The Sunne tower was built close to the place acknowledged by the saga to be the site of the defeat of the Jämtlandic aristocracy by king Sverre in 1178. Possibly the stone tower was ordered to be built soon after the battle to function as the stronghold and symbol of the royal power. The Brunflo tower may have been built on ecclesiastical land (Vikstrand 1996: 93–4) as the archiepiscopal equivalent. It is notable that the province Härjedalen belonged both to the Norwegian kingdom and the Norwegian archiepiscopal see.

The first stone churches were built in the period AD 1150–1200 (Nilsson 1996c: 118–9) or around AD 1200 (Bonnier 1996: 191). They seem to have been ordered to be built by the aristocracy at the manors in the Lake Storsjön area. Many of them were built at the farms with the cultic place-names. The Västerhus stone-church is the only example of a stone church that succeeded a previous wooden church in the same place not to become a parish church in the thirteenth century (Nilsson 1996c: 130–44). Wooden churches that were not succeeded by stone churches are not known.

It is reasonable that the stone churches were built at about the time when the central part of Jämtland was organised into parishes. That was at about the same time as the Norwegian kingdom and the Uppsala archiepiscopal see got a firm grip of the province. The Christianization of the area had come to an end.

Economy, Power and Christianization (AD 1000–1100)

The material culture of the Germanic and Saami peoples shows that their trajectories diverged over the conversion period. Did one dominate the other or were they interdependent? How far could they choose their own religious paths? The forest-burials, attributed to Saami, contain small groups of individuals that exploited the richness of the forest area in terms of fishing-waters, iron-furnaces and pit-falls. These small groups may, or may not, have been the retainers of the Germanic chieftains, and they may, or may not, have taken part in the *blot* in the halls at the chieftains' manors. But I have suggested (above) that the composition of the animal-bones beneath the altar of the Frösön church suggests that they did. It is notable that the Röstahammar sword mentioned above has Saami ornaments on its hilt. My idea is that the people of the forest-burials and the Germanic chieftains were in close interaction as concerns the production of a surplus, which formed the economic basis of the life-style of the latter.

The economic trajectory of the region can be demonstrated by the radiocarbon dates for various productive activities (Fig 32.4). These show that the Late Iron Age was a period of expansion in Jämtland as concerns population growth and the clearance of new arable land. Examples of charcoal from clearance dated by radiocarbon peak in the eleventh and twelfth centuries (Bengtsson and Lindgren 1997, with additions). The number of radiocarbon-dated pitfalls for elk shows a steady increase from about AD 500, a long-term maximum in the period AD 800–1000, and the numbers remain high until about 1200 (Bengtsson 1997). This implies an expansion of production in the outlying forest land. New kinds of iron-furnaces were introduced around AD 1000, and at about the same time the number of radiocarbon-dated production sites increased (Magnusson 1986: 173–4). This increasing surplus was produced at new farms and production-sites in the forest. It was to be organised and exploited by the élite in order to uphold its position as a Germanic aristocracy. This required exchange with the Germanic élites of neighbouring areas, which in its turn required the formation of alliances. From the tenth century onwards this increasingly meant negotiations with Christian chieftains and kings.

The Germanic aristocracy of Jämtland itself had to convert to Christianity to be able to maintain its alliances and its exchange networks, for example the admission to the fairs on the Norwegian coast, possibly organised already during the Late Iron Age (Sandnes 1996: 111). The expanding trade in bulk-goods like iron-ingots and elk-hide around AD 1000–1100 is the reason why the Jämtlandic aristocracy accepted Christianity. Thus, the aristocracy was able to take part in the commercial networks, upon which it based its power and aristocratic life-style. Why did the Saami not follow in its footsteps?

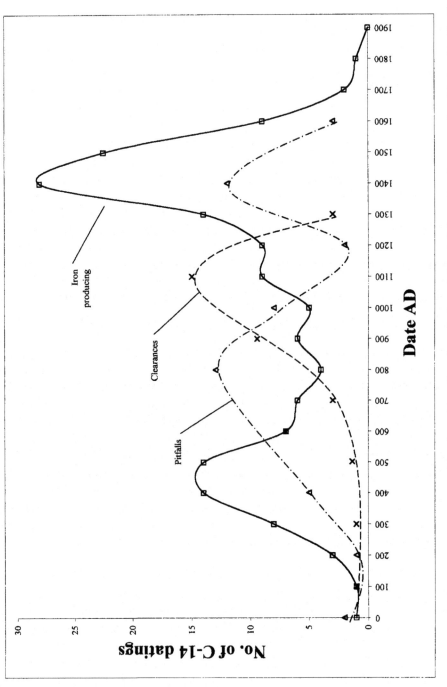

Figure 32.4 Composite graph showing radiocarbon data: (a) radiocarbon-dating of charcoal from the clearance of arable land in Jämtland and Härjedalen (from Bengtsson & Lindgren 1997 with additions); (b) the number of radiocarbon-dated pitfalls for elk in Jämtland and Härjedalen (from Bengtsson 1997); (c) the number of radiocarbon-dated iron-production sites in Jämtland and Härjedalen (from Magnusson 1986)

The Saami: To Be or Not to Be a Christian (AD 900–1200)

Some of the individuals buried in the Vivallen burial-ground, discussed above, were buried with obvious display objects (Gollwitzer 1997: 71–6; Zachrisson 1997b: 61–71, 1997c: 224–8). There are precious textiles, silver-coins, many of them Norwegian coins from the late eleventh century, tens of glass-beads, belt-fittings and a complete belt. These persons belonged to an élite among the Saami groups. At Långön is another burial-ground which provides endorsement of a Saami elite and of its close ties with its Germanic peers. Långön is a small group of burial-mounds of the Germanic kind situated at an island in a lake in the forest area in the easternmost part of Jämtlands län, but actually in the province Ångermanland. The sets of objects indicating the dress and roles of the buried persons suggest that the burial-ground was used, at least partly, by a Saami group in close interaction with Germanic people. The shores of the lake may have been a place where trade and exchange took place. This indicates the emergence of a Saami élite in the tenth and eleventh centuries, which was independent of the Germanic chieftains and the early Germanic kings.

Pagan society in the tenth century had a redistributive economy based on the social bond between the chieftains and their retainers. In the eleventh and twelfth centuries the social bonds inherent in the chieftains' holding of power and the *blot*-community broke down and a new economic order emerged which affected the distribution of the surplus-production in the outlying forest-areas. The social and economic bonds between Christian chieftains and those that had remained pagan, Germanic and Saami leaders, had to be forged in a new way. By choosing a Saami ethnicity during the time of political and social change and Christianization in the transition period between the Late Iron Age and the Early Medieval Age, they were able to form and uphold independent economic positions. Obviously this was to the advantage of both the Jämtlandic, i.e. Germanic, Christian aristocracy and the Saami elite. The growing surplus-production in the forest-area was enough for both.

The Germanic aristocracy invested its share of the surplus in its aristocratic life-style, and in the building of churches, while the Saami élite got display-objects and hoarded silver. The North Swedish metal hoards of Saami origin mainly were aquired during the very time-period in question here, AD 1000–1200 (Zachrisson 1984). The hoards were ritually sacrificed during the time AD 1000–1350 at lake-shores in Saami land. They contain lots of coins, pendants and other objects manufactured all over North and East Europe. The Saami élite were members of extensive exchange-networks during the Early Middle Ages. For them, there were advantages in not becoming Christian.

References

Ahnlund, N. 1948. *Jämtlands och Härjedalens historia. Först delen intill 1537*. P.A. Norstedt & Söners Förlag, Stockholm.

Bengtsson, P.G. 1997. *Fångstgroparnas konstruktion.* Seminar paper. Department of Humanities, Mid Sweden University, Östersund.

Bengtsson, C. and Lindgren, K. 1997. *Ödesbölen med järnåldersgravar.* Seminar paper. Department of Humanities, Mid Sweden University, Östersund.

Birkeli, F. 1973. *Norske steinkors i tidlig middelalder. Et bidrag til belysning av overgangen fra norrøn religion til kristendom.* Universitetsforlaget, Oslo.

Bolin, H. 1998. Ancient artifacts and ethnic archetypes. In: Andersson, A.-C. *et al.* (eds), *The kaleidoscopic past. Proceedings of the 5th Nordic TAG Conference, Göteborg, 2–5 April 1997.* Department of Archaeology, Gothenburg University, Göteborg (347–54).

Bonnier, A.C. 1996. Kyrkor, dopfuntar och gravmonument. In: Nilsson, B. (ed.), *Kristnandet i Sverige. Gamla källor och nya perspektiv.* Lunne Böcker, Uppsala (181–215).

Brink, S. (ed.) 1996a. *Jämtlands kristnande.* Lunne Böcker, Uppsala.

—— 1996b. Kristnande och kyrklig organisation i Jämtland. In: Brink, S. (ed.), *Jämtlands kristnande.* Lunne Böcker, Uppsala (155–188).

—— 1996c. Tidig kyrklig organisation i Norden. Aktörerna i sockenbildningen. In: Nilsson, B. (ed.), *Kristnandet i Sverige. Gamla källor och nya perspektiv.* Lunne Böcker, Uppsala (269–90).

Bull, E. 1970 (1927). *Jämtland og Norge.* Wisénska bokhandelns förlag, Östersund.

Ekroll, Ø. 1995. To kastell i Jämtland – og eitt i Trondheim? *Spor – fortidsnytt fra Midt-Norge* 2/10 (36–9).

Gollwitzer, M. 1997. Bältet i orientalisk stil. I: *Möten i gränsland. Samer och germaner i Mellanskandinavien.* Statens historiska museum, Stockholm (71–6).

Grexing, M. 1999. *Den siste hedningen. En undersökning av icke kristet gravskick i Jämtland och Härjedalen i ett kristet sammanhang.* Seminar paper. Department of Humanities, Mid Sweden University, Östersund.

Grundberg, L. 1997. Gravar, kyrkor och människor – aspekter på religionsskiftet i Mittnorden. Några exempel från pågående undersökningar i Ångermanland och Medelpad. In: Supphellen (ed.), *Kultursamanhengar i Midt-Norden. Tverrfagleg symposium for doktorgradsstudentar og forskarar. Førelesingar ved eit symposium i Levanger 1996.* Almqvist & Wiksell International, Stockholm (29–53).

Gräslund, A.-S. 1996. Kristna inslag i Jämtlands vikingatid. In: Brink, S. (ed.), *Jämtlands kristnande.* Lunne Böcker, Uppsala (21–44).

—— 2000. The conversion of Scandinavia: a sudden event or a gradual process? In: Pluskowski, A. (ed.), *Early Medieval religion.* Archaeological Review from Cambridge 17: 2 (83–98).

Hallencreutz, C.F. 1996. Jämtland i ett europeiskt perspektiv. In: Brink, S. (ed.), *Jämtlands kristnande.* Lunne Böcker, Uppsala (9–20).

Hansen, L.I. 1990. *Samisk fangstsamfunn og norsk høvdingeøkonomi.* Novus Forlag, Oslo.

Hellqvist, M.-L. 1998. *Hallen och maktens salar.* Seminar paper. Department of Archaeology and Ancient History, Uppsala University, Uppsala.

Hellström, J.A. 1996. *Vägar till Sveriges kristnande.* Atlantis, Stockholm.

Hemmendorff, O. 1996. Politiska och religiösa centra i Jämtland – före och efter Helig Olafs tåg genom landskapet. In: Walberg, Ø. (ed.), *Før og etter Stiklestad 1030. Religionsskifte, kulturforhold, politisk makt.* Stiklestad Nasjonale Kultursenter, Verdal (47–57).

Herschend, F. 1997. *Livet i hallen. Tre fallstudier i den yngre järnålderns aristokrati.* Occasional Papers in Archaeology 14.

Hildebrandt, M. 1989. Frösö kyrka på hednisk grund. In: Hemmendorff, O. (ed.), *Arkeologi i fjäll, skog och bygd. 2. Järnålder – medeltid*. Fornvårdaren 24 (153–66).

Iregren, E. 1999. Vi har hittat Yggdrasil – med Ratatosk och Eiktyrnir! *Artefact. Arkeologiska nyheter & fakta* (http://w1.403.telia.com/~u40305830/fastaknappar/forskning/forskning.html).

Johansson, M. 1996. *Ben, byggnader och begrepp. Ett försök att sammanföra arkeologisk praktik och teori vid Frösö kyrka*. Seminar paper. Department of Humanities, Mid Sweden University, Östersund.

Jones, S. 1997. *The archaeology of ethnicity. Constructing identities in the past and present*. Routledge, London.

Jonsson, K. 1999. Blandbarnaföderskor, spädbarn och 'vuxna barn' – social och religiös kontroll speglad i gravmaterialet från Västerhus. *META. Medeltidsarkeologisk tidskrift* 1999: 4 (12–35).

Kilbride, W. 2000. Why I feel cheated by the term Christianisation. In: Pluskowski, A. (ed.), *Early Medieval religion*. Archaeological Review from Cambridge 17: 2 (1–17).

Lidén, H.E. 1996. Utgravingen i Møre kirke. Hvordan skal funnene tolkes? In: Walberg, Ø. (ed.), *Før og etter Stiklestad 1030. Religionsskifte, kulturforhold, politisk makt*. Stiklestad Nasjonale Kultursenter, Verdal (59–68).

Lindkvist, Th. 1998. Bishops, kings and aristocrats in the making of a European society in Sweden 1100–1320. In: Blomkvist, N. (ed.), *Culture clash or compromise? The european-isation of the Baltic Sea Area 1100–1400 AD. Papers of the XIth Visby symposium held at Gotland Centre for Baltic Studies, Gotland University College, Visby. October 4th–9th, 1996*. Gotland Centre for Baltic Studies, Gotland University College, Visby (292–303).

Magnusson, G. 1986. *Lågteknisk järnhantering i Jämtlands län*. Jernkontorets Bergshistoriska Skriftserie 22.

Nilsson, B. (ed.) 1996a. *Kristnandet i Sverige. Gamla källor och nya perspektiv*. Lunne Böcker, Uppsala.

—— 1996b. Kristnandet i Sverige. Avslutande reflexioner. In: Nilsson, B. (ed.), *Kristnandet i Sverige. Gamla källor och nya perspektiv*. Lunne Böcker, Uppsala (419–41).

—— 1996c. Det tidigaste kyrkobyggandet i Jämtland. In: Brink, S. (ed.), *Jämtlands kristnande*. Lunne Böcker, Uppsala (117–53).

—— 1998. *Sveriges kyrkohistoria. I. Missionstid och tidig medeltid*. Verbum, Stockholm.

Näsström, B.-M. 1996. Offerlunden under Frösö kyrka. In: Brink, S. (ed.), *Jämtlands kristnande*. Lunne Böcker, Uppsala (65–85).

Odner, K. 1983. *Finner of Terfinner. Etniske prosesser i det nordlige Fenno-Skandinavia*. Oslo Occasional Papers in Social Anthropology 9.

Pettersson, J. 1997. *Guldbleck, gudar och kvinnor i hallens sfär*. Seminar paper. Department of Archaeology, Stockholm University, Stockholm.

Patric, Ph. 2000. Bloodlust, salvation or fertile imagination? Human sacrifice in Early Medieval Northern Europe. In: Pluskowski, A. (ed.), *Early Medieval religion*. Archaeological Review from Cambridge 17: 2 (19–54).

Røskaft, M. 1997. Religionsskiftet og lokale maktforhold i Trøndelag. In: Supphellen (ed.), *Kultursamanhengar i Midt-Norden. Tverrfagleg symposium for doktorgradsstudentar og forskarar. Førelesingar ved eit symposium i Levanger 1996*. Almqvist & Wiksell International, Stockholm (101–12).

Sandnes, J. 1996. Jämtene kristnet seg selv. Jämtlands kristning sett fra vest. In: Brink, S. (ed.), *Jämtlands kristnande*. Lunne Böcker, Uppsala (107–116).

530 FROM THE ALPS TO THE BALTIC

Skree, D. 1997. Misjonsvirksomhet i praksis – organisasjon og mål. In: Supphellen (ed.), *Kultursamanhengar i Midt-Norden. Tverrfagleg symposium for doktorgradsstudentar og forskarar. Førelesingar ved eit symposium i Levanger* 1996. Almqvist & Wiksell International, Stockholm (55–68).

Solli, B. 1995. Fra hedendom til kristendom. Religionsskiftet i Norge i arkeologisk belysning. *Viking* 1995 (23–48).

—— 1996. Narratives of encountering religions: on the christianization of the Norse around AD 900–1000. *Norwegian Archaeological Review* 29: 2 (89–114).

Sturlason, S. 1957 (c. 1230). *Kongesagaer* (transl. Holtsmark, A. and Arup Seip, D.). Gyldendal norsk forlag, Oslo.

Sundström, J. 1989a. Stavkyrka i Mattmar. In: Hemmendorff, O. (ed.), *Arkeologi i fjäll, skog och bygd. 2. Järnålder – medeltid.* Fornvårdaren 24 (145–52).

—— 1989b. Medeltidskyrka på Njords ö. In: Hemmendorff, O. (ed.), *Arkeologi i fjäll, skog och bygd. 2. Järnålder – medeltid.* Fornvårdaren 24 (175–82).

—— 1997. Järnålder i fångstlandet. I: Zachrisson, I. *et al.* 1997. *Möten i gränsland. Samer och germaner i Mellanskandinavien.* Statens historiska museum, Stockholm (21–7).

Vikstrand, P. 1996. Jämtland mellan Frö och Kristus. In: Brink, S. (ed.), *Jämtlands kristnande.* Lunne Böcker, Uppsala (87–106).

Williams, H. 1996. Runjämtskan på Frösöstenen och Östmans bro. In: Brink, S. (ed.), *Jämtlands kristnande.* Lunne Böcker, Uppsala (45–63).

Zachrisson, I. 1984. *De samiska metalldepåerna år 1000–1350 i ljuset av fyndet från Mörträsk, Lappland.* Archaeology and Environment 3.

—— 1997a. Varför samiskt? I: Zachrisson, I. *et al.* 1997. *Möten i gränsland. Samer och germaner i Mellanskandinavien.* Statens historiska museum, Stockholm (189–220).

—— 1997b. Svepta i näver. I: Zachrisson, I. *et al.* 1997. *Möten i gränsland. Samer och germaner i Mellanskandinavien.* Statens historiska museum, Stockholm (53–71).

—— 1997c. Möten mellan människor. I: *Möten i gränsland. Samer och germaner i Mellanskandinavien.* Statens historiska museum, Stockholm (221–34).

—— *et al.* 1997. *Möten i gränsland. Samer och germaner i Mellanskandinavien.* Statens historiska museum, Stockholm.

33

The Scandinavian Animal Styles in Response to Mediterranean and Christian Narrative Art

NANCY L. WICKER

Introduction

Conversion to Christianity in northern Europe was not just a shift to a different religion but also a transition to different modes of representation. In Scandinavia, artists at first adapted, then rejected, then adopted the figurative or narrative Mediterranean art associated with Christianity. Scandinavia was exposed to narrative Mediterranean art through Late Roman medallions which inspired Migration Period gold bracteates; however, the flowering of this initial phase of narrative art was short-lived. Instead, Scandinavian animal styles of the fifth through the eleventh centuries developed and continued specifically as a reaction to classically derived narrative art. In this chapter, I contend that the decorative animal styles were manipulated and advanced as a statement of 'otherness' from Mediterranean-based narrative Christian art, by which Scandinavians signalled their own agenda and expressed a specifically pagan mentality. This animal style persisted until narrative elements were finally incorporated into northern art – both Christian and pagan – as a result of institutional conversion in the tenth and eleventh centuries.

The Role of Narrative Art

The basic necessity of 'narrative' art is that it visually connotes a story that is recognizable to the target audience. Defining various types of narrative has been of great concern for classical art (e.g. Meyboom 1978). In his recent *Pictorial Narrative in Ancient Greek Art*, Mark Stansbury-O'Donnell (1999) divided narratives into different schemes including monoscenic, synoptic, simultaneous, progressive, unified, cyclical, continuous, episodic and serial. This is more detailed than necessary for the present consideration of Scandinavian art, but it is instructive to consider how Greek and Roman, as well as Early Christian art – which developed out of Late Roman Mediterranean styles – had strong historical or pedagogical intent expressed through narratives. By contrast, Scandinavian art tended toward the symbolic, with only minimal visual clues to indicate a story or theme.

Christianity is a religion of the Book and the Word. As Premysław Urbańczyk (Chapter 2 in this volume) has explained, pagan beliefs were 'naturally acquired in the informal process of gradual education', whereas Christianity is a 'religion of the book', and must be formally taught. The illiterate were often instructed in Christianity at least partly through visual sources, so visible narratives were very important to supplement the written account as promoted by Pope Gregory the Great in the seventh century (Diebold 2000, 18). However, visual representation in an oral culture may take a different form, with signifying elements that recall certain stories without illustrating or narrating them in a literal sense. If the story being 'told' (shown) is from a society that has not left written sources, it may be difficult for us to match specific narratives with their respective visual representations. In the absence of oral traditions, even recognizing a narrative from such a non-literate culture may be problematic. Whereas the Christian creed was taught formally or informally through doctrine, pagan beliefs may have been promulgated through enactment in the form of ritual (Rappaport 1999, 24–5).

Wilhelm Holmqvist (1977a, 197) stated quite simply that 'die ältere germanische Kunst ist arm an Figurendarstellungen'. Most Scandinavian art of the Early Medieval Period was non-figurative and even less was anthropomorphic and narrative. Nordic art is not the only largely non-narrative art during this period; Jane Hawkes (Chapter 22 in this volume) has pointed out that monuments with figural decoration were also rare for Anglo-Saxon England. Islamic art of the Medieval Period is also distinct because of its decorative rather than figural nature. Pre-Christian Scandinavian art had meaningful symbolism stressing form, decoration and symbolism over story-telling.

Scandinavian Migration Period Art

Even though Scandinavia was never invaded by the Romans, the region felt the impact of Rome and its anthropomorphic art. One of the major constructions of pan-European identity nowadays is to recognize that it includes all regions that were influenced by Rome, not only the parts of Europe that were invaded and conquered by the Romans; it is based on a culture 'emanating from a common Greco-Roman tradition' (Alibai 1989 in Shore 1996, 109; Webster and Brown 1997). Acknowledging that Scandinavia, too, was within the fold of this tradition has led to a change in attitudes toward the so-called Dark Ages that is finally contradicting the misconception that the northern area was a 'primitive and culturally deprived medieval world bereft of great art' (Hodges 1998, 61). The Nordic regions were affected by Mediterranean art at various times in prehistory and certainly absorbed influences from the Late Antique and Early Christian world.

I would like to trace the early impact of narrative art on Scandinavia as a model for the reception of foreign styles and ideology. The impact of Rome was felt especially through the arrival into the Nordic region of Late Imperial medallions, which were soon imitated within Scandinavia during the Migration Period in the fifth century AD. The originals were altered, sometimes out of all recognition. Was this a clumsiness of execution, a failure to understand the Roman iconography, or something more deliberate?

Migration Period Gold Bracteates

Late Roman Imperial medallions were gold coins minted to commemorate special occasions, with the emperor's portrait on the obverse and Imperial motifs on the reverse. A few of the actual medallions have been found in Scandinavia, but they were also imitated there, first as two-sided medallions and then on gold bracteates, carrying images derived from the Roman pieces, but made by a simpler technique and stamped on only one side. Over 900 bracteates of the fifth and first half of the sixth century have been found in Scandinavia, England and the Continent. On these objects, foreign style and ideology were acknowledged but then rejected and translated into a native equivalent. Latin inscriptions were replaced with Germanic runic inscriptions and the images, which still owed something to the Roman emperor portrait, were imbued with indigenous significance. Imagery on early examples emulates the emperor portrait on Roman medallions, but we are not certain who is portrayed. The hypothesis that the Germanic god Odin is represented has been accepted by many, though certainly not all, scholars of Germanic mythology and archaeology. On later bracteates, the emperor's portrait is transformed into a head more-or-less floating over – but usually not riding – a horse-like animal.

Previous research on bracteates has tended to be dominated (or perhaps ensnared by) one of two lines of inquiry: 1) attempts to classify them, as demonstrated by C. J. Thomsen (1855), Oscar Montelius (1869), Bernhard Salin (1895), and Mogens Mackeprang (1952), among others, and 2) efforts to interpret their subject matter, as exemplified by Karl Hauck (1985b, for bibliography). Here I concentrate on the subject matter to demonstrate a Scandinavian accommodation of Roman narrative and anthropomorphic content, followed by a movement away from purely foreign concepts toward a Scandinavian reinterpretation. All references to the medallion imitations as well as bracteates will be to the iconographic catalogue *Ikonographische Katalog* (= IK) by Karl Hauck and his team of scholars: Axboe *et al.* 1985–89; Hauck, 1985b, 1986, 1989)

On a medallion imitation from Tunalund in Sweden (IK 193, Pl. 33.1), folds of cloth at the neck of the Roman costume were re-configured by the Scandinavian artist as a bird-like figure with legs pointing upwards. Karl Hauck (1972c) has suggested that these forms display the human changing into a bird, expressing the shamanistic ability to shift from human to animal form. Alternatively, one can imagine this as a gross misunderstanding of the toga folds at the neck, an extrapolation by artisans who did not know how to read the stylised though illusionistic Late Antique style. We should remember, as William Diebold (2000,

Plate 33.1 Medallion imitation (IK193) from
Tunalund, Uppland, Sweden. Statens
historiska museum, Stockholm
(Photo: N. Wicker)

Plate 33.2 Bracteate (IK 190) from
Trollhättan, Västergötland, Sweden.
Statens historiska museum, Stockholm
(Photo: N. Wicker)

Plate 33.3 Bracteate (IK 215) from Aversi,
Sjælland, Denmark. Nationalmuseum,
Copenhagen (Photo: N. Wicker)

Plate 33.4 Bracteate (IK 269.2) from
Grumpan, Västergötland, Sweden.
Statens historiska museum, Stockholm
(Photo: N. Wicker)

Plate 33.5 Bracteate (IK 510.1) from Skodborg, Jutland, Denmark. Nationalmuseum, Copenhagen (Photo: N. Wicker)

19–20) has cautioned, that 'anthropologists, psychologists, and art historians are still debating whether the illusionistic representational schemes used in the Mediterranean are naturally comprehensible or if the ability to read them is culturally determined'. In either case, images on both the obverse and the reverse of medallion imitations were transformed from Roman iconography into something that expressed Germanic mythological concepts. Adaptation to Scandinavian needs and tastes was paramount, and there apparently was no reason to copy Roman art slavishly.

Interpreting particular bracteate images as Odin, Thor, Tyr and other Nordic deities in the light of post-Viking Age Eddic literature of the thirteenth century may be appropriate in certain cases. One such instance, originally recognized by Axel Oxenstierna (1956, 36, 78), is the bracteate from Trollhättan (IK 190, Pl. 33.2), which portrays the god Tyr being tricked into allowing the wolf Fenrir to bite off his hand, as described in the introduction to the Eddic poem *Locasenna* (Neckel and Kühn 1962, 96; Terry 1990, 72). This is a key example that Hauck uses to bolster his contextual iconographic interpretations. I agree that this is a convincing example of narrative art in which we can identify a specific incident that is illustrated, just as we recognize Greek and Roman mythological tales painted on Greek pottery or Roman frescoes. However, such explicit examples in Nordic art are extremely rare, and most bracteate motifs cannot be interpreted as a one-to-one correspondence of tale and depiction. Many motifs may be more emblematic, symbolic or even archetypal (Beck 1964, 16–9, 40–5) than specifically identifiable as particular incidents involving the Germanic gods.

Two other identifications of later Germanic subject matter on bracteates by Hauck are less persuasive. The first is his interpretation of the bent animal's leg seen on several bracteates (e.g. Aversi, IK 215, Pl. 33.3) as a representation of the injured leg of the god Balder's horse. He interpreted this motif from the so-called second Merseburg charm in a ninth-century manuscript in Old High German that deals with Odin healing Balder's horse (DuBois 1999, 107–8; Hauck 1972a, 1972b). The second motif is that of the man's mouth touching the horse's ear or neck on numerous bracteates (e.g. Grumpan, IK 269.2, Pl. 33.4). Hauck (1977, 499–501) argues that this depicts Odin blowing onto the horse's neck to heal the lame animal, as documented in Late Antique veterinary techniques. Often, the man (perhaps Odin?) breathes directly into the horse's ear, an action that Hauck (1983, 522) relates to a Christian practice of healing a horse by whispering into its ear. However, these stories of healing lameness are not extant in Nordic literature, and we are on insecure ground to match them with bracteate imagery.

I am sceptical that either the bent animal's leg or the man's mouth touching the horse's ear specifically represents Odin healing Balder's lame horse. I believe that exigency of design should also be considered as a reason for these features. A simpler explanation gives some credit to the capabilities of the artisan, who has been left out of the academic discussion. Patrons, who were sometimes runic-literate, may have controlled the overall iconographic scheme and also the degree of artefact enrichment through their wealth or amount of gold provided. However, the final appearance of the bracteate was dependent upon design and technical decisions made by goldsmiths who understood their medium better than the elite patrons or runemasters who chose the iconography. Patrons' desires must have been balanced with artisans' capabilities. The leg bent upwards underneath the body is a viable design solution for a restricted circular space to be filled with an awkwardly shaped animal. Similarly, the ear at the mouth, or 'horse-whisperer' looks very elegant and also uses the limited space economically. Hauck interprets the placement of the man's mouth near the ear, head, neck, or shoulder of the horse as a narrative of healing; however, it is difficult to imagine how the face of the man could be positioned so that it would not be in that general area of the horse. Even if a design explanation may be less satisfying than the 'horse-whisperer' to historians of religion, specific examples of pagan Nordic narrative art are the exception rather than the rule in the Migration Period and I would like to emphasise the role of the jewellers who made the pieces.

Animal Style Ornamentation on Bracteates

Narrative interest thus mostly died out after a false start, either because of rejection of outside influences or because representative, literal art was not particularly relevant and not as necessary to pagan beliefs as it was to the promulgation of the Christian religion. Instead, the abstract animal style became the norm in Scandinavia throughout the rest of the Iron Age. On later gold bracteates of the sixth century (e.g. Skodborg, IK 510.1, Pl. 33.5), the horse-like animal became successively stylized until it was transformed into an unrecognizable animal of the Nordic animal style, called Salin's Style I, after the 1904 study by Bernhard Salin, *Die Altgermanische Thierornamentik*. Lennart Karlsson has itemised some hundred variations of these stylised animals, and pointed out that Scandinavian artists seem to have had no compunction about biological coherence, so that we cannot identify what kind of animal is represented (1983, 23). The abstract form does not suggest any phenomenon of nature, and it is far removed from anthropomorphic, narrative classically based art. Sir David Wilson (1970, 69) has characterised Scandinavian animal styles as 'distorted and degenerate' and also referred to the human head on bracteates as 'grotesque'. Wilhelm Holmqvist wrote of the 'brutal and ruthless tearing apart of the forms' in Migration Period art (1977b, 35, my trans.), and Nils Åberg (1925, 92, my trans.) who described this art as 'disintegrated and degenerate', also commented upon its violence and the barbaric nature by which animal and sometimes human parts are torn apart. Rather than use these derogatory labels, it might be more profitable to consider why animals were displayed in such a manner.

Gregory of Tours (Thorpe, ed., 1974), writing in the sixth century, recounted in Book Six of *The History of the Franks* that Emperor Tiberius II had given medallions to the Frankish king Chilperic. Such pieces were apparently distributed to so-called 'barbarian' chieftains to allot in turn to their warriors. Lotte Hedeager (1992a, 250–4; 1992b) has proposed that a new élite was gaining control in Scandinavia from the Late Roman Iron Age into the Migration Period. High status members of society may have retained goldsmiths to fashion precious metalwork such as bracteates as displays of ethnicity, social status, gender and religion, and for gift-giving to strengthen bonds of loyalty between warriors and the political aristocracy (see also Axboe 1991). Though gifts of bracteates might reflect warrior bonds, burial evidence from the peripheral areas of their distribution – from Norway to England to Hungary – indicates that women were the ultimate consumers, that is, the wearers, of Scandinavian bracteates. Most bracteates found in inhumation burials have been found near the neck (for four exceptions, see Lamm and Axboe 1989). One bracteate from Sievern (IK 157) in Schleswig was found with a braided leather hanging cord, material that rarely is preserved (Schröter and Gummel 1957, 113). In addition, the suspension loops of many (e.g. Sletner, IK 170) are extremely worn, demonstrating that bracteates were worn in life as well as death. As an explanation of how women obtained these artifacts, Birgit Arrhenius (1992) has proposed that bracteates were part of a bride-price. Thus, distant marriage alliances may explain the presence of this Nordic type of jewellery in areas far away from the Scandinavian homeland, especially in areas of political conflict such as Kent and Pannonia, where Anders Andrén (1991, 253–4) has posited that women might wear bracteates as emblems of Nordic ethnic and religious identity. Arne Johansen (1981, 121) also stressed that 'in times of crisis, differentiation becomes increasingly important'. I agree that bracteate iconography and style may have been self-conscious Germanic expressions of difference from Christian early medieval culture on the Continent and in Anglo-Saxon England, and animal-style art was a way for Scandinavian women to signal their heritage.

Some of the pendants worn by these women had runic inscriptions. Many are difficult to interpret, but a few are quite clear. Two Danish pieces from Køge (IK

98) on the island of Zealand are inscribed with 'I bring luck', which is crucial for the interpretation of bracteates as amulets (cf. Gladigow 1992). Other words on bracteates may also be understood as amuletic, including *alu* perhaps meaning either 'ale' (Høst Heyerdahl 1980, 45) or 'magic', *lathu* for 'invitation', and *laukar* for 'leek', which was a plant of fertility significance (Düwel 1983, 38). However, as is often the case with pendent objects (Hansmann and Kriss-Rettenbeck 1977, 40), the amuletic and ornamental function of bracteates may not have been clearly differentiated. Bracteates may have had several functions, but they rarely seem to have had a narrative pedagogical intent.

Bracteates thus demonstrate one way that an exotic art and ideology can be accommodated, then rejected. Salin's Style 1 was also developed and used on objects other than gold bracteates, especially metalwork such as weapon-mounts and jewellery. On all these objects, the non-identifiable animal is characterised by intense stylisation, dislocation of parts that are arbitrarily isolated from the whole, and transformation of details that is not consistent with classically based art. Conscious distortion certainly did not begin with Picasso in the twentieth century, and the abstract Style I animal art of the Migration Period is antithethical to Late Roman sensibilities.

Functions of Animals in Animal-style Art

Andrén (2000, 11) has rightly noted that the attitude of most scholars 'has been to regard animal art as decoration without any deeper meaning'. Anna Hed Jakobsson (1999, 41) posits that 'the art lack[s] any claims of being realistic representations, which makes it difficult to find the images meaningful'. However the animals must have had meaning, and we should not avoid asking what it was.

Many scholars, in particular Hallvard Lie (1952, 3), have pointed out that the Nordic animal style with its stylized forms is analogous to Old Norse skaldic poetry in its use of the poetic metaphor called a kenning (Andrén 2000). A kenning is an implied simile composed of two words that together mean something that the isolated components by themselves do not express. A simple example is 'the storm of the spear' for 'battle'. To understand a kenning, the listener must be able to assemble the parts in a particular way that builds on perceived connections between the words. Lee Hollander (1945, 15) called kennings 'mere gaudy building blocks, put in for showy effect, but entirely stereotyped, or unmeaning'. Although in skaldic poetry 'virtually nothing is mentioned by its own name' (Hollander 1945, 15), a kenning does designate something that could have been expressed more simply. Just as kennings may signify something by a circumlocution without naming it directly, animal art as 'pictorial kenning' may elicit the idea of an animal without showing any particular species. Evocative, non-representational art was the norm in pre-Christian Nordic art, so when we see a clearly recognizable scene, such as the bracteate from Trollhättan with Tyr's hand being bitten off by Fenrir the wolf, the depiction seems oddly non-Nordic.

Siv Kristoffersen (1995, 12) has discussed the efficacy of animals and animal representations in rituals, citing Maurice Bloch's (1992) recognition of the dualism of animals that 'they are at the same time like and unlike human beings'. Birgitta Johansen (1997,153) has stressed that the snake-like forms prevalent in Nordic art are liminal creatures that are particularly appropriate to transformational ritual because they appear at the borders between this world and the underworld. Jakobsson (1999, 42) has carried these ideas further, comparing transformations from human to animal in art to shape-shifting indicative of shamanism in the mythological literature. While some scholars have expended much effort on identifying specific animals with specific gods (Werner 1963), others have perceived the animal forms as metaphoric (Müller 1968) and as an 'alter ego' distinctive to shamanistic rituals (Roth 1986). I believe the fact that some of the animals are not biologically identifiable, as demonstrated by Helmut Roth (1986, 24), reinforces the sense that they were symbolic rather than specifically narrative.

Art of the Vendel Period

Animal ornamentation of the Vendel (or Merovingian) Period of the late sixth through eighth centuries, such as on harness mounts from Vendel in Sweden, is characterised by increasing stylisation (Wilson and Klindt-Jensen, 1980, 30–3). Salin's Style II ribbon animal is gracefully and symmetrically interlaced, more coherent, decorative and rhythmic than the violently broken-up animal of Style I (Pl. 33.6). In some ways the style would seem more Scandinavian and thus less Mediterranean, but this is the period when the animal style becomes a nearly pan-European mode (Høilund Nielsen 1998), contributing to the development of contemporary European styles such as Frankish, Lombard and Anglo-Saxon. The ribbon animal is so generalised that it is difficult to search for attributes of particular Germanic gods or to distinguish a particular species of animal. There is no real possibility to recognise distinct narratives in Style II animal art with this lack of specificity.

However, there is also figural art dating to the Vendel Period. One type consists of the so-called 'guldgubber' or gold foils (Pl. 33.7), which probably began in the Migration Period and continued into the Viking Age (Watt 1992, 220). Over 2,300 have been found at Sorte Muld on the Baltic island of Bornholm. The images are unquestionably anthropomorphic, but it is difficult to identify specific figures, at least partly because of their size – most are smaller than a fingernail. Hauck (1993) has derived the images from votive offerings of Roman cults and has identified them as representations of the Nordic gods. However, I maintain that they are too generalised to recognise as specific gods, just as the animal ornamentation of the period is often too imprecise to classify to species. Although fewer in number than these foils, helmet panels and stamps for impressing them constitute another important group of figural images of this period (Pl. 33.8). Helmets with such impressions include ones from Anglo-Saxon Sutton Hoo (Bruce-Mitford 1978) as well as Swedish Vendel (Stolpe and Arne 1912, 1927) and Valsgärde (Arwidsson

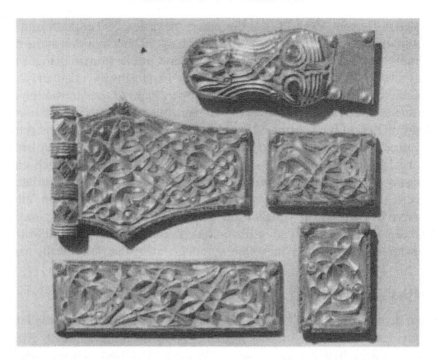

Plate 33.6 Gilt bronze harness mounts from Vendel, Sweden. Statens historiska museum, Stockholm (Photo: ATA, Stockholm)

Plate 33.7 Gold foil plaques (*guldgubber*) from Helgö, Sweden. Statens historiska museum, Stockholm (Photo: ATA, Stockholm)

Plate 33.8 Bronze matrix from Torslunda, Öland, Sweden. Statens historiska museum, Stockholm (Photo: ATA, Stockholm)

1942, 1954, 1977), and stamps for imprinting such panels were found at Torslunda on the Swedish island of Öland (Beck 1968). While Hauck (1978) has tried to distinguish Germanic gods among these representations, Heinrich Beck (1964, 1968) has identified them as archetypal images rather than specific gods. Even when anthropomorphic images occur in the Vendel Period, as on both these groups of images – the gold foils and the helmet panels – they cannot be construed as telling a narrative, pagan or otherwise. The scenes are too terse to tell elaborate stories; once again, they seem to be symbolic rather than narrative.

Art of the Viking Age

Nordic art of the ninth through eleventh centuries AD – the Viking Age – is characterised by continuing development of the animal style of the previous Migration and Vendel periods, and also increasing exposure to Christian iconography. We begin to see the tentative reintroduction of figural and narrative art, along with the first evidence of Christianisation, marked in particular by the Frankish monk Ansgar's failed mission to Birka in the 830s and 850s (Rimbert in

Plate 33.9 The Jelling stone. Depiction of Christ, Jelling, Denmark (Photo: Nationalmuseum, Copenhagen)

Waitz, ed. 1884; Sawyer *et al.* 1987, 10) and the stone that Harald Bluetooth erected in memory of his parents at Jelling in Denmark *c*.983–985 (Wilson and Klindt-Jensen 1980, 120) (Pl. 33.9). As Christianity was introduced, the animal style was still used in addition to Christian symbols, for instance, on the Jelling stone which simultaneously displays Nordic style animal art next to the crucified Christ. The cross was the first and most commonplace emblem of Christian art that was introduced into Scandinavia (Staecker, Chapter 29 in this volume), but truly narrative Christian art appears only in isolated cases, such as on an early eleventh-century Norwegian runestone from Dynna which displays the Journey and Adoration of the Magi (Fuglesang 1980, 87–9, 174–6; see Chapter 30, Pl. 30.7). Here, as on the tenth-century Danish Jelling stone, animal-style art appears side-by-side with Christian motifs.

The animal style during the Viking Age assumed many different forms, culminating in the interlaced dragon of the Urnes style, which was displayed on Upplandic runestones (Lager, Staecker, Gräslund, Welinder, Chapters 31, 29, 30 and 32 in this volume) and named after eleventh-century fragments preserved on the twelfth-century Norwegian Urnes stave church (Wilson and Klindt-Jensen 1980, 147; Pl. 33.10). The elegant panels from a portal on the north side of the church reflect Germanic animal style, but the combat motif of a highly stylised lion fighting dragons and snakes has been interpreted alternatively as the Lion of Judah (Anker 1970, 415–6), a symbol of Christ's victory over forces of evil, or as Ragnarök, the end of the world of the Viking gods equated with the Last Judgment of Christ at the Apocalypse (DuBois 1999, 91, 150). Although sometimes incorporating Christian iconography, the Urnes style of the late Viking Age follows in a direct line of development from the fifth century Migration Period style – eight centuries of the Nordic animal style.

There are some curious instances of pagan Scandinavian art displaying principles of Mediterranean-based narrative art, most exceptionally picture stones from the Baltic island of Gotland (Lindqvist 1941–1942, Nylén and Lamm 1988; see Chapter 30, Pl. 30.1). As Andrén (1993, 33) has exclaimed, 'Gotlandic picture stones are unique! Their well-known wealth of images is a challenge to

Plate 33.10 Urnes stave church, Norway. North wall (Photo: Oldsaksamling, Oslo)

all students of Gotland.' There have indeed been countless 'students of Gotland', and many of them have conjectured about outside influences – Roman, Carolingian, insular Celtic, and even Pictish art – to explain the extreme degree of narrativity and lack of comparable Scandinavian material (Nylén and Lamm 1988, 17–8). Although these stones apparently depict specific stories of Nordic mythology familiar from later written sources, scholars who study the scenes on the stones easily recognize the non-Scandinavian, classically derived narrative mode of representation.

By the late Viking Age, the influence of classically based Christian *narrativity* had become internalised and less foreign in Scandinavia. The Vikings perpetuated the animal style to reflect their culture and ideology, but they also developed their own pagan narrative art. Pagan myths can be traced on isolated monuments that are not as coherent an assemblage as the Gotlandic picture stones. For example, the story of Thor fishing for the World Serpent is attested on two Viking Age runestones, one English from Gosforth, Cumbria (Kendrick 1949, Pl. XC), and the other Swedish from Altuna church in Uppland (Jansson 1987, 150). The incident is mentioned in the Eddic poem *Hymiskviða* (Neckel and Kühn 1962, 92; Terry 1990, 69). The depiction of Thor raising his hammer Mjölnir, holding a fishing line with an ox-head as bait, and pushing his foot through the bottom of the boat to catch the all-powerful World Serpent is too specific not to be recognised as a narrative from Eddic literature.

Other popular stories that were depicted include cycles about Sigurd and the dragon, especially as on a carved outcropping of stone at Ramsund in Sweden (Pl. 33.11). The tale is known from thirteenth-century sources including *Fáfnismál* in the *Poetic Edda* (Neckel and Kühn 1962; Terry 1990) and Snorri Sturluson's *Prose Edda* (Faulkes 1987), as well as *Völsunga Saga* (Byock 1990). Briefly, the scenes displayed on the rock face (which include only part of the entire story) include Sigurd killing the dragon Fafnir with a sword forged by Regin the smith, roasting its heart and licking the blood on his fingers. Sigurd is then able to understand the birds depicted in the tree, who warn him that Regin will betray him. The result is the next two scenes, which show Sigurd slaying Regin and taking Fafnir's treasure away on his horse Grani. The runic inscription on the carving at Ramsund does not serve as a caption to the picture of the pagan incidents but instead reflects a Christian context. It is inscribed, 'Sigrid, Alrik's mother, Orm's daughter, made this bridge for the soul of her husband Holmger, Sigröd's father' (Brate 1924 Sö101, my trans.). As described by Anne-Sofie Gräslund (Chapter 30 in this volume and 2000, 88), building a bridge or causeway to facilitate communication was a pious act in this period of Christianisation. The Ramsund carving adapts Mediterranean narrativity to an indigenous pagan story that is contained within a ribbon band of animal-style ornament that in turn holds a Christian inscription, typifying the complex interrelationships between pagan and Christian cultures during the period of conversion.

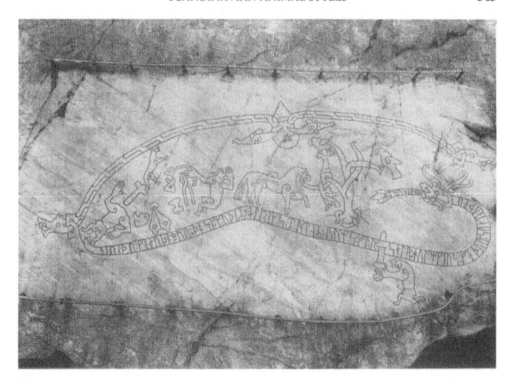

Plate 33.11 Rock engraving and runic inscription at Ramsund, Södermanland, Sweden (Photo: ATA, Stockholm)

Syncretism and Accommodation during the Transition to Christianity

During the transition from paganism to Christianity, old and new, and indigenous and foreign overlapped, and there was a slow infiltration of the new faith, with syncretic manifestations of paganism and Christianity co-existing (Urbańczyk, Chapter 2 in this volume). Even the supposedly pagan concept of Ragnarök probably reflects Christian influence (DuBois 1999, 150). In addition, the very notion of Valhalla, the place where dead warriors arose daily to fight again and be served mead by valkyries, appears only during the later Viking Age when Scandinavia was strongly influenced by Christianity (Sawyer and Sawyer 1993, 104). Similarly, the cross as a symbol seems to have provided the impetus for development of the Thor's hammer as a pagan symbol that only came to be used during the introduction of Christianity into Scandinavia (Staecker 1999, 234; Chapter 29 in this volume). DuBois (1999, 159–61) has suggested that the popularity of Thor's hammers may reflect a 'tendency to match attractive aspects of Christianity', an amulet for pagan Scandinavians to wear as a symbol of their religion analogous to the cross as a symbol for Christians.

Sometimes the introduction of a Christian prototype seems to have motivated the adaptive development in Scandinavia of a new direction in art. The appearance of pagan narrative art on the Gotlandic picture stones and some runestones implies a knowledge of other classically derived, probably Christian, narrative art. Mediterranean pictorial narration was here transformed into indigenous visual imagery, and the animal style was simultaneously perpetuated. A melding and accommodation of ideas could also occur. The practice of raising runestones, though pagan in origin, was particularly popular during the period of conversion and reflects the changes taking place in art and religion (Lager, Chapter 31 in this volume). Similarly, pagan Scandinavians sometimes received Christian baptism upon their deathbed, as documented on several rune-stones (Jansson 1987, 112–3), perhaps using traditional animal-style art along with a Christian message reflected a hope to harness the power of animals while also acknowledging the possibility of Christian salvation, thus embracing elements from both religions.

Conclusion

Although figural and narrative art had been introduced into the North with Late Roman medallions in the fifth century AD, it was initially rejected. The north was not well-prepared for narrative art nor for Christianity in the fifth century. A Migration Period reaction to Roman art was to reinterpret or transform unfamiliar stories into meaningful indigenous-symbolic images. Attempts at producing narratives depicting the pagan religion were soon replaced by animal-style art. When Scandinavians clung to animal art as a conscious choice, it was a signal that they looked to animal art as legitimisation and to identify themselves as the 'other', different from Christians and thus from much of Europe. Abstract animal art was not merely of decorative interest; its function probably was to allow access to the power of animals through allusion rather than by representing specific animals or incidents. The use of animal-style art throughout the whole Early Medieval Period from the fifth through eleventh centuries confirms that it continued to hold important meaning (Jakobsson 1999, 41).

The way was finally paved for the full-fledged incorporation of narration into Scandinavian art during the Viking Age. Scandinavians embraced the idea of narrative art only after a second infusion of Mediterranean-based texts and images through the acceptance of Christianity. In some communities, such as the producers of the Gotlandic picture stones, the new facility was applied to pagan themes. Elsewhere, Christian iconography began to appear as the Scandinavian church became institutionalised.

ACKNOWLEDGEMENTS

As always, I would like to thank Dr. Matthew L. Murray for reading and commenting upon my manuscript. He has helped me think through many issues more clearly and raised some points that I will have to save for future papers.

References

Åberg, N. 1925. *Förhistorisk Nordisk Ornamentik* (Uppsala: Lindblads Förlag).

Andrén, A. 1991. 'Guld och makt – en tolkning av de skandinaviska guldbrakteaternas funktion', in C. Fabech and J. Ringtved (eds), *Samfundsorganisation og Regional Variation*. Jysk Arkæologisk Selskabs Skrifter, 27 (Århus: Aarhus Universitetsforlag), 245–56.

Andrén, A. 1993. 'Doors to other worlds: Scandinavian death rituals in Gotlandic perspectives', *Journal of European Archaeology*, 1, 33–56.

Andrén, A. 2000. 'Re-reading embodied texts – an interpretation of rune-stones,' *Current Swedish Archaeology*, 8, 7–32.

Anker, P. 1970. *The Art of Scandinavia*, 2 (London: Paul Hamlyn).

Arrhenius, B. 1992. 'Smycken som diplomati', in *Föremål som Vittnesbörd. En festskrift till Gertrud Grenander Nyberg* (Stockholm: Nordiska Museet), 18–25.

Arwidsson, G. 1942. *Valsgärde 6. Die Gräberfunde von Valsgärde I* (Uppsala: Almqvist and Wiksell).

—— 1954. *Valsgärde 8. Die Gräberfunde von Valsgärde II* (Uppsala: Almqvist and Wiksell).

—— 1977. *Valsgärde 7. Die Gräberfunde von Valsgärde III* (Uppsala: Uppsala Universitets Museum för nordiska Fornsaker).

Axboe, M. 1991. 'Guld og guder i folkevandringstiden. Brakteaterne som kilde til politisk/religiøse forhold', in C. Fabech and J. Ringtved (eds), *Samfundsorganisation og Regional Variation*. Jysk Arkeologisk Selskabs Skrifter, 27 (Århus: Aarhus Universitetsforlag), 187–202.

Axboe, M., U. Clavadetscher, K. Düwel, K. Hauck, and L. von Padberg 1985. *Die Goldbrakteaten der Völkerwanderungszeit. 1,2 Ikonographischer Katalog 1, Text.* Münstersche Mittelalter-Schriften 24/1,2 (Munich: Wilhelm Fink).

Axboe, M., K. Düwel, K. Hauck, L. von Padberg, and C. Wypior 1986. *Die Goldbrakteaten der Völkerwanderungszeit. 2,1, Ikonographischer Katalog 2, Text.* Münstersche Mittelalter-Schriften 24/2,1 (Munich: Wilhelm Fink).

Axboe, M., K. Düwel, K. Hauck, L. von Padberg, and H. Rulffs 1989. *Die Goldbrakteaten der Völkerwanderungszeit. 3,1, Ikonographischer Katalog 3, Text.* Münstersche Mittelalter-Schriften 24/3,1 (Munich: Wilhelm Fink).

Beck, H. 1964. *Einige vendelzeitliche Bilddenkmäler und die literarische Überlieferung.* Bayerische Akademie der Wissenschaften, Philosophisch-historische Klasse, Sitzungsberichte, 6 (Munich: Beck).

—— 1968. 'Die Stanzen von Torslunda und die literarische Überlieferung', *Frühmittelalterliche Studien*, 2, 237–50.

Bloch, M. 1992. *Prey into Hunter: The Politics of Religious Experience* (Cambridge: Cambridge University Press).

Brate, E. 1924. Södermanlands Runinskrifter 1. *Sveriges Runinskrifter 3* (Stockholm: Wahlström & Widstrand)

Bruce-Mitford, R. 1978. *The Sutton Hoo Ship-Burial*, 2 (London: British Museum Publications).

Byock, J. 1990. *The Saga of the Volsungs* (Berkeley: University of California Press).

Diebold, W. 2000. *Word and Image: An Introduction to Early Medieval Art* (Boulder, Colorado: Westview Press).

DuBois, T. 1999. *Nordic Religions in the Viking Age* (Philadelphia: University of Pennsylvania Press).

Düwel, K. 1983. *Runenkunde*, 2nd edn (Stuttgart: Metzler).

Faulkes, A. (trans.) 1987. *Snorri Sturluson: Edda* (London: Dent).

Fuglesang, S.H. 1980. *Some Aspects of the Ringerike Style* (Odense: Odense University Press).

Gladigow, B. 1992. 'Schutz durch Bilder. Bildmotive und Verwendungsweisen antiker Amulette', in K. Hauck (ed.), *Der historische Horizont der Götterbild-Amulette aus der Übergangsepoche von der Spätantike zum Frühmittelalter. Abhandlungen der Akademie der Wissenschaften in Göttingen*, Philologisch-historische Klasse, Dritte Folge, 200 (Göttingen: Vandenhoeck & Ruprecht), 12–31.

Gräslund, A.-S. 2000. 'The conversion of Scandinavia – a sudden event or a gradual process?', in A. Pluskowski (ed.), *Early Medieval Religion. Archaeological Review from Cambridge*, 17:2, 83–98.

Gregory of Tours (L. Thorpe, trans.) 1974. *The History of the Franks* (New York: Penguin Books).

Hansmann, L., and L. Kriss-Rettenbeck 1977. *Amulett und Talisman. Erscheinungsform und Geschichte*, 2nd edn (Munich: Georg D. W. Callwey).

Hauck, K. 1972a. 'Neue Windgott-Amulette' (Zur Ikonologie der Goldbrakteaten, 1), in *Festschrift für Herman Heimpel*. Veröffentlichungen des Max-Planck-Institutes für Geschichte, 36:3 (Göttingen: Max Planck Institut), 627–60.

—— 1972b. 'Die missionsgeschichtliche Bedeutung des zweiten Merseburger Spruchs und seiner völkerwanderungszeitlichen Bildentsprechungen' (Zur Ikonologie der Goldbrakteaten, 2), *Praehistorische Zeitschrift*, 46:2 (1971), 139–42.

—— 1972c. 'Metamorphosen Odins nach dem Wissen von Snorri und von Amulettmeistern der Völkerwanderungszeit' (Zur Ikonologie der Goldbrakteaten 4), in O. Bandle, H. Klingenberg and F. Maurer (eds), *Festschrift für Siegfried Guttenbrunner* (Heidelberg: Winter) 47–70.

—— 1977. 'Die Spannung zwischen Zauber- und Erfahrungsmedizin, erhellt an rezepten aus zwei Jahrtausenden' (Zur Ikonologie der Goldbrakteaten, 14), *Frühmittelalterliche Studien* 11, 414–510.

—— 1978. 'Bildforschung als historische Sachforschung. Zur vorchristlichen Ikonographie der figuralen Helmprogramme der Vendelzeit', in K. Hauck and H. Mordek (eds), *Geschichtsschreibung und geistiges Leben im Mittelalter* (Cologne: Böhlau Verlag), 22–70.

—— 1983. 'Text und Bild in einer oralen Kultur' (Zur Ikonologie der Goldbrakteaten, 25), *Frühmittelalterliche Studien*, 17, 510–99.

—— 1985a. *Die Goldbrakteaten der Völkerwanderungszeit. 1,1 Einleitung*. Münstersche Mittelalter-Schriften 24/1,1 (Munich: Wilhelm Fink).

—— (ed.). 1985b. *Die Goldbrakteaten der Völkerwanderungszeit. 1,3 Ikonographischer Katalog, 1, Tafeln*. Münstersche Mittelalter-Schriften 24/1,3 (Munich: Wilhelm Fink).

—— (ed.) 1986. *Die Goldbrakteaten der Völkerwanderungszeit. 2,2 Ikonographischer Katalog, 2 Tafeln*. Münstersche Mittelalter-Schriften 24/2,2 (Munich: Wilhelm Fink).

—— (ed.) 1989. *Die Goldbrakteaten der Völkerwanderungszeit. 3,2, Ikonographischer Katalog, 3, Tafeln*. Münstersche Mittelalter-Schriften 24/3,2 (Munich: Wilhelm Fink).

—— 1993. 'Die bremische Überlieferung zur Götter-Dreiheit Altuppsalas und die bornholmischen Goldfolien aus Sorte Muld' (Zur Ikonologie der Goldbrakteaten, 52), *Frühmittelalterliche Studien*, 27, 409–78.

Hedeager, L. 1992a. *Iron-Age Societies* (Oxford: Blackwell).

—— 1992b. 'Kingdoms, ethnicity and material culture: Denmark in a European perspective,' in M.O.H. Carver (ed.), *The Age of Sutton Hoo* (Woodbridge: Boydell), 279–300.

Hodges, R. 1998. 'The Not-So-Dark Ages', *Archaeology*, 51(5), 61–5.

Høilund Nielsen, K. 1998. 'Animal Style – A symbol of might and myth. Salin's Style II in a European context', *Acta Archaeologica*, 69, 1–52.

Høst Heyerdahl, G. 1980. 'Tryllerordet alu', *Det norske Videnskaps-Akademies Årbok*, 35–49.

Hollander, L. 1945. *The Skalds* (Ann Arbor: University of Michigan Press).

Holmqvist, W. 1977a. 'Figürliche Darstellungen aus frühgeschichtlicher Zeit', in H.-J. Hässler (ed.), *Studien zur Sachsenforschung*, 1 (Hildesheim: Lax), 197–214.

Holmqvist, W. 1977b. *Vår Tidiga Konst* (Stockholm: L.T.s Förlag).

Jakobsson, A.H. 1999. 'Towns, plots, crafts and fertility', *Current Swedish Archaeology*, 7, 37–53.

Jansson, S.B.F. 1987. *Runes in Sweden* (Stockholm: Gidlunds).

Johansen, A.B. 1981. 'Nordic animal style – background and origin', *Norwegian Archaeological Review*, 14, 118–22.

Johansen, B. 1997. *Ormalur. Aspekter av tillvaro och landskap*. Stockholm Studies in Archaeology 14. (Stockholm: Arkeologiska Institutionen, Stockholms Universitet).

Karlsson, L. 1983. *Nordisk Form om Djurornamentik* (Stockholm: Statens Historiska Museum).

Kendrick, T.D. 1949. *Late Saxon and Viking Art* (London: Methuen).

Kristoffersen, S. 1995. 'Transformation in Migration Period animal art', *Norwegian Archaeological Review*, 28, 1–17.

Lamm, J.P. and M. Axboe 1989. 'Neues zu Brakteaten und Anhängern in Schweden', *Fornvännen* 23, 453–77.

Lie, H. 1952. 'Skaldestilstudier', *Maal og Minne*, 1–92.

Lindqvist, S. 1941–1942. *Gotlands Bildsteine I–II* (Stockholm: Wahlström & Widstrand).

Mackeprang, M. 1952. *De Nordiske Guldbrakteater*. Jysk Arkeologisk Selskabs Skrifter, 2 (Aarhus: Aarhus Universitetsforlaget).

Meyboom, P. 1978. 'Some observations on narration in Greek art', *Medelingen van het Nederlands Historisch Instituut te Rome*, 40, 55–82.

Montelius, O. 1869. *Från jernåldern* (Stockholm: Ivar Heggström).

Müller, G. 1968. 'Germanische Tiersymbolik und Namengebung', *Frühmittelalterliche Studien*, 2, 202–17.

Neckel, G., and H. Kühn 1962. *Edda. Die Lieder des Codex Regius nebst verwandten Denkmälern, 1. Text* (Heidelberg: Winter).

Nylén, E. and J. P. Lamm 1988. *Stones, Ships and Symbols. The Picture Stones of Gotland from the Viking Age and Before*, 2nd edn (Stockholm: Gidlunds).

Oxenstierna, E. 1956. *Die Goldhörner von Gallehus* (Lidingö).

Rappaport, R. 1999. *Ritual and Religion in the Making of Humanity* (Cambridge: Cambridge University Press).

Rimbert (G. Waitz, ed.) 1977 (rpt.), 1884 (edn) *Vita Anskarii* (Hannover: Hahnsche Buchhandlung). English trans., C.H. Robinson. 1921. *Anskar, the Apostle of the North* (London: Society for the Propagation of the Gospel in Foreign Parts).

Roth, H. 1986. 'Einführung in die Problematik, Rückblick und Ausblick', in H. Roth (ed.), *Zum Problem der Deutung frühmittelaltericher Bildinhalte*. Veröffentlichungen des Vorgeschichtlichen Seminars der Philipps-Universität Marburg a. d. Lahn (Sigmaringen: Jan Thorbecke), 9–24.

Salin, B. 1895. 'De nordiska guldbrakteaterna', *Antiqvarisk tidskrift för Sverige*, 14:2, 1–111.

—— 1904. *Die Altgermanische Thierornamentik* (Stockholm: Beckman).

Sawyer, B., P. Sawyer, and I. Wood (eds) 1987. *The Christianization of Scandinavia* (Alingsås: Viktoria Bokförlag).

Sawyer, B. and P. Sawyer 1993. *Medieval Scandinavia* (Minneapolis: University of Minnesota Press).

Schröter, T. and H. Gummel 1957. 'Der Goldbrakteatenfund von Sievern', *Die Kunde* 8, 112–29.

Selling, D. 1951. 'Probelm kring vikingatida keramikkannor', *Fornvännen*, 46, 275–97.

Shore, C. 1996. 'Imagining the new Europe: Identity and heritage in European Community discourse', in P. Graves-Brown, S. Jones, and C. Gamble (eds), *Cultural Identity and Archaeology* (London: Routledge), 96–115.

Staecker, J. 1999. *Rex regum et dominus dominorum. Die wikingerzeitlichen Kreuz- und Kruzifixanhänger als Ausdruck der Mission in Altdänemark und Schweden* (Stockholm: Almqvist & Wiksell International).

Stansbury-O'Donnell, M. 1999. *Pictorial Narrative in Ancient Greek Art* (Cambridge: Cambridge University Press).

Stolpe, H. and T.J. Arne 1912. Graffältet vid Vendel (Stockholm: K. L. Beckman).

—— 1927. *La nécropole de Vendel* (Stockholm: Akademiens Förlag).

Terry, P. (trans.) 1990. *Poems of the Elder Edda* (Philadelphia: University of Pennsylvania Press).

Thomsen, C.J. 1855. 'Om guldbracteaterne', *Annaler for Nordisk Oldkyndighed og Historie*, 265–347.

Watt, M. 1992. 'Die Goldblechfiguren ('guldgubber') aus Sorte Muld, Bornholm', in K. Hauck (ed.), *Der historische Horizont der Götterbild-Amulette aus der Übergangsepoche von der Spätantike zum Frühmittelalter. Abhandlungen der Akademie der Wissenschaften in Göttingen*, Philologisch-Historische Klass, Dritte Folge, 200 (Göttingen: Vandenhoeck & Ruprecht), 195–227.

Webster, L. and M. Brown (eds) 1997. *The Transformation of the Roman World, AD 400–900* (Berkeley: University of California Press).

Werner, J. 1963. 'Tiergestaltige Heilsbilder und germanische Personennamen', *Deutsche Vierteljahrsschrift für Literaturwissenschaft und Geistesgeschichte*, 37, 377–83.

Wilson, D. 1970. *The Vikings and Their Origins* (London: Thames and Hudson).

Wilson, D. and O. Klindt-Jensen 1980. *Viking Art*, 2nd edn (London: George Allen and Unwin).

34

The Role of Secular Rulers in
the Conversion of Sweden

ALEXANDRA SANMARK

The scarcity of written source material is a constant problem for scholars of the Christianisation of Sweden. In order to overcome this problem, at least to some extent, comparisons with Christianisation in other geographical areas can be useful. In this way similarities and differences between the areas can be identified. It may also be possible to illuminate the meagre and at times confusing source material, and to find indications of what questions could be asked. The purpose of this chapter is to investigate the role played by secular rulers in the conversion of Sweden. Background information has been derived from the better documented conversions of Anglo-Saxon England, Frisia and Saxony. The emphasis will be placed on the role of secular rulers in the early stages of conversion, that is England, in the seventh century, Frisia and Saxony during the seventh and eighth centuries and Sweden between the ninth and early twelfth centuries. Despite the obvious differences in time and geography, it is evident that important parallels can be found.

From the study of Anglo-Saxon England, Frisia and Saxony, it clearly emerged that a converted ruler was necessary, although not sufficient, for widespread conversion. Missionaries who worked without the support of a Christian ruler could gain a few converts. They were however not able to turn a non-Christian society into a Christian one. Evidence suggests that rulers aided conversion by certain means, many of which were common for all geographical areas. These will now be discussed in order to illuminate how secular rulers in Sweden may have helped the spread of Christianity. The following issues will be discussed: the rulers' use of bonds of loyalty in society, secular legislation in support of Christianity, together with royal protection and material aid given to missionaries and converts.

Christianity in Anglo-Saxon England seems to have spread between the various kingdoms via the power of the overkings. It is unlikely that underkings were forced to accept Christianity, and there is no evidence that armies were actively employed in the name of conversion. Instead, overkings made use of the strong bonds of loyalty that tied the underkings to their overlordship. Christianity was then spread to the aristocracy and further down in society via the pre-feudal hierarchical structure within the Anglo-Saxon kingdoms. The way in which an overking influenced conversion can be demonstrated by the example of King Ethelbert of Kent. He had been converted by Augustine in c.597 and acted as overlord of the Southumbrian kingdoms. Around 604, King Sabert of Essex was baptised by the Roman missionary Mellitus, who most likely had been sent there by the Kentish king. After this event, Ethelbert built a church in London and appointed Mellitus as its bishop. Some years later, another subject king, Raedwald of East Anglia, also converted to Christianity and received baptism in Kent.[1] The importance of the bonds of loyalty between the king and his aristocracy for the conversion of a kingdom can also be clearly seen. During his lifetime, King Penda of Mercia had allowed missionaries to preach in his territory, although he himself had refused to accept Christianity. According to Bede, Penda also stated that he 'hated and despised any whom he knew to be insincere in their practice of Christianity once they had accepted it'.[2] If these were the circumstances under which missionaries had to work, it is not surprising that they were unable to persuade the king's followers to be baptised.

In Frisia and Saxony, the Franks enforced the observance of Christianity through their military conquest. The Frankish armies were accompanied by bishops and missionaries, who settled in the newly won areas. The local population was then forced to accept Christianity as part of Frankish lordship. Before this time, missionaries such as Wilfrid and Wihtbert, had evangelised in Frisia without secular support. Such missionaries did not manage to convert either the Frisian rulers or any larger parts of the population. When Willibrord arrived on the Continent he decided to follow a different strategy and turned to King Pepin for help. It was from this time that the strong link between Frankish military power and conversion began to be established, and Christianity started to seriously gain ground. A similar pattern can be observed in Saxony. Missionaries in this area were unable to convert a significant number of the population until Charlemagne had begun his conquest.[3]

[1] Bede, *The Ecclesiastical History of the English People* (hereafter HE), eds, J. McClure and R. Collins (Oxford 1994), II.3 and II.15; Henry Mayr-Harting, *The Coming of Christianity to Anglo-Saxon England*, third edition (London 1991), pp. 64–5 and 99–100; Carole M. Cusack, *Conversion among the Germanic Peoples*. Cassell Religious Studies (London and New York 1998), pp. 101–8; Nicholas Brooks, *The Early History of the Church of Canterbury. Christ Church from 597 to 1066. Studies in the early history of Britain* (Leicester 1984), pp. 63–4.

[2] HE III.21.

[3] HE V.9–11 and 19; Alcuin, 'The Life of St. Willibrord', *The Anglo-Saxon Missionaries in Germany. Being the Lives of SS. Willibrord, Boniface, Sturm, Leoba and Lebuin, together with the Hodoeporicon of St. Willibald and a selection from the correspondence of St. Boniface*, ed. and tr., C.H. Talbot (London 1954), pp. 3–24, esp. pp. 7–9; Heinrich Büttner, 'Mission und Kirchenorganisation des Frankerreiches bis zum Tode Karls des Grossen', *Karl der Grosse. Lebenswerk und Nachleben*, vol. 1, *Persönlichkeit und Geschichte*, ed., Helmut Beumann (Düsseldorf 1965), pp. 454–87, esp. 462; Franz Flaskamp, *Die Anfänge friesischen und Sächsischen Christentums* (Hildesheim 1929); Franz Flaskamp, *Willibrord/Clemens und Wynfrith/Bonifatius*. Sonderdruck aus St Bonifatius (Fulda 1954); Richard

The first documented missions to Sweden took place during the ninth century, when missionaries began to arrive at Birka. These missions were at first organised by Louis the Pious,[4] and later jointly by the emperor and the archbishopric of Hamburg-Bremen.[5] There is no indication that the Swedes were put under strong pressure or force to accept Christianity, and the population does not seem to have been strongly opposed to missionary activity. According to the Life of Ansgar, the local *things* gave missionaries permission to preach and to build churches. It was also permitted for anyone to adopt the new religion. The missionaries seem to have gained some converts, including Birka's *praefectus* Hergeir. They did not however manage to convert either King Björn or the later King Olof.[6] Christianity did not begin to spread on a wider scale across Sweden until the baptism of King Olof Erikson Skötkonung in *c*.1000. It thus seems that also here, missionaries needed the support of a Christian ruler in order to convert substantial parts of the population. The religion appears to have spread in a similar way as it did in England, that is from the secular ruler to the aristocracy and then further down in society. The rulers promoted Christianity via the bonds of loyalty in society, and do not seem to have employed military force.[7]

Secular rulers used material rewards in conjunction with their lordship in order to further evangelisation. A central element of the old religion seems to have been to gain material benefits from the gods. Non-Christians might therefore have been particularly susceptible to such offerings. Rulers offered advantages that

---

Fletcher, *The Conversion of Europe. From Paganism to Christianity 371–1386 AD* (London 1997), pp. 199–200 and 213–5; Heinz Löwe, 'Pirmin, Willibrord und Bonifatius. Ihre Bedeutung für die Missionsgeschichte ihrer Zeit', *Die Kirche des früheren Mittelalters*, vol. 2, *Kirchengeschichte als Missionsgeschichte*, ed., Knut Schäferdiek (Munich 1978), pp. 192–226, esp. pp. 202–3; *Lexikon des Mittelalters* (München and Zürich 1977–1998), vol. 9, col. 213; *Reallexikon der Germanischen Altertumskunde. Zweite, völlig neu bearbeitete und stark erweiterte Auflage unter Mitwirkung zahlreicher Fachgelehrter*, ed., Heinrich Beck *et al.* (Berlin and New York 1973–2001), vol. 2, pp. 185–6; J.M. Wallace-Hadrill, *The Frankish Church* (Oxford 1983), pp. 144–5 and 183–4; Ian Wood, *The Merovingian Kingdoms 450–751* (London and New York 1994), p. 317; Rosamund McKitterick, *The Frankish Kingdoms under the Carolingians 751–987* (London and New York 1983), pp. 61–3. Willibrord was not the first missionary to receive secular support. This case can be compared to King Dagobert I's support of Amandus. Fletcher, *The Conversion of Europe*, p. 200.

4   According to the Life of Ansgar, King Björn had asked Louis the Pious to send missionaries to Birka. Rimbert, 'Ansgars liv' (hereafter VA), *Boken om Ansgar*, tr., Eva Odelman (Stockholm 1986), pp. 13–77, chapter 9.

5   The bishopric of Hamburg was founded by Louis the Pious. In 847–8 Louis the German amalgamated the sees of Hamburg and Bremen and gave the new see archiepiscopal status. VA 12–14 and 22–3; Carl Fredrik Hallencreutz, *När Sverige blev europeiskt. Till frågan om Sveriges kristnande* (Stockholm 1993), p. 20.

6   VA 11 and 26–8.

7   Thomas Lindkvist, 'Kungamakt, kristnande, statsbildning', *Kristnandet i Sverige. Gamla källor och nya perspektiv*, ed., Bertil Nilsson, Projektet Sveriges kristnande, publikationer 5 (Uppsala 1996), pp. 217–42, esp. pp. 219–21; Anne-Sofie Gräslund has pointed out that the archaeological evidence suggests that Christianity continued to be present in Sweden in the period between the missions to Birka and the conversion of Olof Skötkonung. Anne-Sofie Gräslund, *Ideologi och Mentalitet. Om religionsskiftet i Skandinavien från en arkeologisk horisont*, Occasional Papers in Archaeology (Uppsala 2001), p. 130.

were not directly connected with the Christian teachings, and may thus have given Christianity added attraction, in a way that missionaries were unable to. In this manner a favourable climate for missionary work was created. According to Bede, King Ethelbert showed special favour to those who converted. This presumably happened also in other Anglo-Saxon kingdoms. On the Continent, the Franks offered native leaders who accepted Frankish lordship, and thus also Christianity, positions of power and wealth. According to one source, when Hessi, chieftain of the Ostphalians, 'along with many others' surrendered to the Franks, Charlemagne gave them 'countships and rewarded them with great honors'.[8]

Since the rulers at Birka were not Christian, it is unlikely that they offered any rewards to those who converted. However, the evidence suggests that converted rulers in Sweden used rewards in the same way as other Christian kings. This can be demonstrated by the example of the kings at Sigtuna. This town must have been planned and built as a royal base of power, rather than as a commercial centre. The majority of excavated buildings from the earliest phase were dwelling houses. There were not sufficient means within the town to support all the inhabitants, and supplies must have been delivered from the surrounding countryside. Sigtuna thus seems to have functioned as a meeting-place, from which the king arranged alliances with other powerful men. Scholars have argued that the king exercised his control not by military means, but instead by exerting his influence over the people. The giving of gifts must be seen as an important means of power at this time. A runic inscription from Siguna dated to the early twelfth century reads: 'The king is the most hospitable. He gave the most, he is the most popular'. Snorri Sturluson tells us that when Olav Haraldsson rebuilt Trondheim he distributed plots of land to farmers and merchants that he liked and who wanted to build in the town. It has been argued that Olof Skötkonung used the plots in Sigtuna in the same way in order to secure the loyalty of powerful local nobility. Sigtuna with its c.1,000 inhabitants was a large town at this time. It was something out of the ordinary in the otherwise agrarian society. It must thus have been a place in which it was prestigious to own property. The gift of a piece of land in the town may therefore have strengthened the nobility's loyalty to their king.[9]

Secular rulers often introduced legislation in support of Christianity. Ethelbert introduced penalties against theft from the Church and clergy. The laws of King Eorcenberht of Kent (c.640) seem to have included more detailed regulations. According to Bede, all idols were to be destroyed and 40 days of fast were to be observed at Lent. Offenders against these laws were to be punished.[10]

[8] HE I.26; Richard E. Sullivan, 'The Carolingian Missionary and the Pagan', Speculum 28 (1953), pp. 705–40, esp. pp. 722–3. This article is also published in *Christian missionary activity in the early Middle Ages* (Aldershot 1994). Bede also stated that Pepin of Herstal 'bestowed many favours on those who were willing to receive the faith'. HE V.10.

[9] Brita Malmer, Jonas Ros, and Sten Tesch, eds., *Kung Olofs mynthus i kvarteret Urmakaren, Sigtuna*, Sigtuna museers skriftserie 3 (Stockholm 1991), pp. 5–6; Sten Tesch, 'Det sakrala stadsrummet – den medeltida kyrkotopografin i Sigtuna', *Meta* 2000:1, pp. 3–26, esp. pp. 4–6.

[10] Aethelberht c. 1; F.L. Attenborough, ed. and tr., *The Laws of the Earliest English Kings* (Cambridge 1922), pp. 4–5; HE III. 8.

In Frisia, the Frankish rulers outlawed the practice of 'paganism'. Carloman confirmed a law, previously issued by Charles Martel, which made the performance of 'pagan practices' illegal and subject to a penalty of 15 solidi. In 744, Pepin III issued a law that required bishops to ensure that no acts of 'paganism' were carried out in their dioceses.[11] Charlemagne's First Saxon Capitulary (*Capitulatio de partibus Saxoniae*) outlawed practices regarded as 'pagan', such as human sacrifice, cremations, and making offerings to springs or groves. It is difficult to establish to what extent such laws were beneficial to missionaries, since the sources provide very information about their enforcement in practice.[12]

There is no evidence of any formal legislation from the missionary period in Sweden. However, judging from the examples given above, it could be expected that at least some kind of publicly stated prohibitions or restrictions of 'pagan practices' appeared from the time of Olof Skötkonung. It is also likely that attempts were made to enforce the observance of some Christian practices. This is further supported by several pieces of evidence, which suggest that Olof and his successors wished to be seen as Christian kings. Around the time of his baptism, Olof began to issue coins at Sigtuna. These were the first coins minted in Sweden. For this task, Olof employed Anglo-Saxon moneyers. The coins were decorated with Christian crosses together with the picture of Olof. Some bore the words *OLAF REX SVEVORUM* and others *OLAF REX AN SITUN*. The majority of the coins were very similar to those issued by Olof's contemporary King Ethelred II of England.[13] Further evidence is provided by the late eleventh or early twelfth-century church at Husaby (Västergötland). The oldest part of the church consists of two tall towers and a royal balcony. These features are likely to have been modelled on Frankish royal churches, such as St. Denis and the imperial chapel at Aachen. Such features are also found at the monastery of Corvey, which was established during the reign of Louis the Pious as centre for evangelisation

---

[11] Löwe, 'Pirmin, Willibrord und Bonifatius', pp. 223–4; Sullivan, 'The Carolingian Missionary and the Pagan', p. 731; McKitterick, *The Frankish Kingdoms*, p. 55. Carloman's law was issued in 743. *Decrevimus quoque, quod et pater meus ante praecipiebat, ut qui paganas observationes in aliqua re fecerit, multetur et damnetur quindecim solidis. Monumenta Germaniae Historica* (hereafter MGH), *Leges*, vol. I (Hanover 1885), p. 18; *Pippini principis capitulare suessionense* (744), c. 6: *Et omnino, decrevimus, ut unusquisque episcopus in usa parrochia sollicitudinem habeat, ut populus christianus paganus non fiant [paganismum non faciant]. Et per omnes civitates legitimus forus et mensuras faciat, secundum habundantia temporis.* No penalty for guilty parties was stated. MGH *Leges*, vol. I, pp. 20–2.

[12] P.D. King, *Charlemagne: Translated Sources* (Lancaster 1987), pp. 205–7.

[13] At a slightly later date, coins with the inscription +*OLFAF ON SIDEI* were also produced. Many scholars have interpreted this as 'God's Sigtuna', and it could thus be one of the clearest pieces of evidence of Sigtuna's role as a missionary centre. However, this particular interpretation cannot be relied on, as the text can be read in several different ways. Brita Malmer, 'Sigtunamyntningen som källa till Sveriges kristnande', *Kristnandet i Sverige. Gamla källor och nya perspektiv*, ed., Bertil Nilsson, Projektet Sveriges kristnande, publikationer 5 (Uppsala 1996), pp. 85–113, esp. pp. 100–3 and 108–10; Malmer *et al.*, *Kung Olofs mynthus*, pp. 11, 14, 34, and 42; Brita Malmer, 'Kort orientering om myntningen i Sigtuna ca 995–1030', *Avstamp – för en ny Sigtunaforskning. 18 forskare om Sigtuna heldagsseminarium kring Sigtunaforskning den 26 november 1987 Gröna Ladan, Sigtuna*, ed., Sten Tesch, Kommittén för Sigtunaforskning (Sigtuna 1989), pp. 74–5.

in Scandinavia.[14] The evidence from Sigtuna and Husaby thus strongly suggests that Olof Skötkonung and his successors had knowledge of the activities of Christian rulers, and that they wished to portray themselves as such. It was presumably the examples of these men who gave kings in Sweden the impetus to accept Christianity. It was demonstrated above that legislation in support of Christianity was a part of Christian kingship that Swedish kings may well have adopted. The observance of Christian practices is moreover likely to have been included in the nobility's loyalty to their ruler.

The Carolingians used legislation to put missionaries under royal protection. Missionaries enjoyed the usual protection of all clergy that was included in Frankish law. As well as this, missionaries could receive specific proof of protection. In 690, Pepin II prohibited anyone to interfere in Willibrord's preaching, and in 753 the Saxons were obliged to permit Christian missionaries to enter their country. Charlemagne's legislation also protected clergy through heavy penalties against violators.[15] There is no evidence in England of any special protection of missionaries. This may not have been necessary, firstly because Christianity was not violently enforced, as it was in Frisia and Saxony. Secondly, many of the missionaries seem to have been working very closely with the kings and may thus have been more or less automatically under royal protection.

Rimbert, the author of the Life of Ansgar, reported that the missionary Nithard was killed by 'pagans' at Birka, and that all the other missionaries were exiled. The guilty parties do not seem to have received any punishment from the king. It thus seems that even though the missionaries and their work had been approved by thing, they were not under the king's protection. It was presumably for this reason that Ansgar, during his second mission, specifically asked the king to help and protect the missionaries.[16] According to Adam of Bremen, when Bishops Adalvard and Egino wished to destroy the (alleged) 'temple' at Gamla Uppsala, they were convinced by King Stenkil not to go. The king told them that they would be facing certain death. The bishops are instead said to have preached in Götaland where they also destroyed idols. There are no reports of violent reactions in response to their activities.[17] It thus seems that missionaries enjoyed royal protection in the areas that were under Christian rule.

---

[14] It should also be noted that Ansgar was a monk at Corvey. Ann Catherine Bonnier, 'Kyrkor, dopfuntar och gravmonument', Kristnandet i Sverige. Gamla källor och nya perspektiv, ed., Bertil Nilsson, Projektet Sveriges kristnande, publikationer 5 (Uppsala 1996), pp. 181–214, esp., p. 200; Sven Ulric Palme, Kristendomens genombrott i Sverige (Stockholm 1959), pp. 49–50 and 115–20; Lindkvist, 'Kungamakt, kristnande, statsbildning', p. 223.

[15] Sullivan, 'The Carolingian Missionary and the Pagan', p. 730; HE V.10; Löwe, 'Pirmin, Willibrord und Bonifatius', p. 213; The First Saxon Capitulary c. 5; King, Charlemagne: Translated Sources, p. 205. The later Capitulare Saxonium made theft from clergy or hostility towards them punishable by heavy fines. King, Charlemagne: Translated Sources, pp. 230–2.

[16] VA 17 and 28.

[17] Adam of Bremen, 'Historien om Hamburgstiftet och dess biskopar', Adam av Bremen. Historien om Hamburgstiftets och dess biskopar, tr., Emmanuel Svenberg, eds., C. F. Hallencreutz,. K. Johannesson, T. Nyberg and A. Piltz, Skrifter utg. av Samfundet Pro Fide et Christianisimo 6 (Stockholm 1984), pp. 13–292, chapter IV:30.

Secular rulers gave economic support to evangelisation. When missionaries arrived in a new area they needed living quarters, and land from which they could support themselves. Moreover, as Christianity spread, funds were required for the erection and upkeep of churches and monasteries to accommodate the needs of converts.[18] The sources provide us with plenty of examples of rulers who fulfilled such needs. King Ethelbert gave Augustine lodgings and later erected the church of SS. Peter and Paul in Canterbury. Other kings, such as Sigbert of East Anglia and Oswald of Northumbria, supplied monasteries and episcopal sees with land and gifts.[19] Pepin, Carloman and Charlemagne all gave endowments and thus enabled the foundation of important monastic houses such as Echternach, Fulda, Kitzingen and Ohrdruf. The First Saxon Capitulary required the Saxons to pay tithe and provide land for churches.[20]

Missionaries in Sweden also received economic support from secular rulers. The missionaries in Birka received initial support from Louis the Pious. He is reported to have provided Ansgar with gifts for the people at Birka. Some time later, when Gautbert was preparing to leave for Sweden he was 'generously' rewarded with 'what was needed' in order to carry out the Christian service together with 'the necessary economic resources', jointly from the emperor and Bishop Ebo of Reims. This was necessary for the missionaries as the king at Birka was not Christian. According to Rimbert, the first church in Birka was built by Hergeir on his own land.[21] Since the king had not converted, he may not have been as motivated as a Christian ruler to provide missionaries with land for a church. During Ansgar's second visit, the king gave the missionaries a piece of land in Birka where they could erect a church. However, the unconverted king does not seem to have been as generous as for example King Ethelbert, for it is stated that the missionaries had to buy a house in order to find a place to live.[22] It must be pointed out that no archaeological evidence of a church has yet been found in Birka, although several possible locations have been put forward. Evidence suggests that also in Sweden, convert kings erected churches in the early stages of the conversion. According to Adam of Bremen, Olof Skötkonung built a church at Skara and made this the first episcopal see.[23] It is also possible that Olof erected a wooden church at his stronghold in Husaby. On the site of

---

[18] Hermann Lau, *Die Angelsächsische Missionsweise im Zeitalter des Bonifaz* (Preetz 1909), pp. 62–3.

[19] HE I.25–6, III.19, I.33, and III.3; Cuthbert John Godfrey, *The Church in Anglo-Saxon England* (Cambridge 1962), p. 99; Richard P. Abels, *Lordship and Military Obligation in Anglo-Saxon England* (Berkeley 1988), pp. 30–2 and 43–5; Ben Whitwell, 'Flixborough', *Current Archaeology* 126 (1991), pp. 244–7.

[20] Löwe, 'Pirmin, Willibrord und Bonifatius', p. 204; McKitterick, *The Frankish Kingdoms*, pp. 56–7 and 60; Roger Collins, *Charlemagne* (London 1998), p. 53; Friederich Prinz, 'Schenkungen und Privilegien Karls des Grossen', *Karl der Grosse. Lebenswerk und Nachleben*, vol. 1, *Persönlichkeit und Geschichte*, ed., Helmut Beumann (Düsseldorf 1965), pp. 455–6; Josef Semmler, 'Pippin III. und die Fränkischen Klöster', *Francia* 3 (1975), pp. 90–146.

[21] VA 10–11 and 14.

[22] VA 28.

[23] Adam of Bremen, 'Historien om Hamburgstiftet och dess biskopar', II:58.

the presumed royal manor in Sigtuna, a church appears to have been erected in the second quarter of the twelfth century. It is surrounded by older graves, which strongly suggests the existence of an older, wooden, church.[24]

In this chapter the role of secular rulers in the conversion in Sweden has been discussed in relation to the comparative material from Anglo-Saxon England, Frisia and Saxony. By using this method it has been possible to consider the involvement of Swedish rulers also in areas that are partly hidden by the lack of extant source material. It is important to remember that this method must be used with great caution in order to avoid over-interpretations. The available evidence from Sweden has therefore at every stage been taken into careful consideration. It does, however, seem clear that when comparative studies are applied in a correct manner they can contribute to our existing knowledge of events. They can also be used to indicate areas that may prove to be fruitful in future research.

[24] Bonnier, 'Kyrkor, dopfuntar och gravmonument', pp. 192–3 and 201.

35

Byzantine Influence in the Conversion of the Baltic Region?

PER BESKOW

Scandinavia is situated between two seas, the North Sea and the Baltic. Norway and Iceland have North Sea coastlines, whereas Finland's coastline is entirely Baltic. Denmark and Sweden have the best of both worlds and face in both directions. This geographical situation is of importance when we consider the routes taken by Christianity and European culture to the Northern countries.

The main trade route from the Baltic to the Continent went via Hedeby in southern Denmark and from the coast southwest inwards to Frisian Dorestad and from there to France and Spain. There was, however, an important route leading eastwards: from the ninth century or even earlier, there was constant traffic between the Baltic region and the Byzantine Empire. Swedish and Danish tradesmen and Vikings crossed over the Baltic and the Gulf of Finland, and travelled further inland along the Russian rivers, to Staraja Ladoga and Bulgaria, which were important centres of commerce. The main products exported were fur and amber, and in exchange the Northern traders acquired Arabic silver coins in great number. Impressive hoards of these coins are still discovered, especially on the island of Gotland. The Arabic traveller Ibn Fadlan has written a vivid account of his encounter with these wild and exotic visitors. Many of the travellers went on as far as Constantinople, where some of them were recruited to the Emperor's Varangian guard. In Hagia Sophia there is still a memento from this time. In the balustrade of one of the galleries, a Scandinavian visitor has carved a line of runes, which, unfortunately, are no longer readable.

The Scandinavians played a vital role in the formation of Russia. The *Nestor Chronicle*, written by a monk at the Cave Monastery of Kiev around 1100, introduces the story that a dynasty from Sweden was invited to take power in the kingdom of Kiev around 860, because of the political chaos there. A Swedish chieftain named Rurik thus became the forefather of the ruling dynasty in Kiev. The name of *Rus'* for the kingdom of Kiev – later on transformed into the name of Russia – has been interpreted as coming from *Roslagen*, the name of the Swedish coast-line north of the Mälar lake. This name is related to the English verb to *row*, thus 'ros lagen' implying a team of oarsmen. This so-called Norman theory has often been vividly disputed by Russian historians but cannot be entirely dismissed.

However, it is obvious that such a Scandinavian connection existed. Vladimir the Great, the first Christian ruler in Kiev, baptized in 988, belonged to a half-Scandinavian dynasty, which is evident from the many personal names of Northern origin in the family. The Slavonic name of Vladimir accordingly spread to Scandinavia in the form of Valdemar, the name of several of the Danish kings. The Norwegian king Harold the Hardruler is said to have spent part of his youth in Kiev. Vladimir's son, Jaroslav the Wise, married Ingegerd, the daughter of the first Christian king of Sweden, Olof Eriksson. She was finally venerated as a saint in the Russian Church, Saint Anna of Novgorod.

With such facts in mind, it is reasonable to ask the question: was there a corresponding traffic from Byzantium and Russia to the Baltic region in the eleventh and twelfth centuries, and if so, are there any traces left? In Scandinavia, this question has been much debated. Some Swedish scholars in particular have been eager to provide evidence of a Russian mission, and many arguments for such a mission have been put forward.

There is certainly a great number of Byzantine objects which have been found in Scandinavia and especially along the Swedish east coast, notably in Sigtuna by the Mälar lake. There is a considerable number of pendent crosses of precious metal or bronze, often in the form of *encolpia*, portable reliquaries. Glazed ceramic eggs from the principality of Kiev – of a possible religious significance – have also been found in tombs. A steatite relief of the Mother of God with Greek letters also found its way to Gotland. Other objects such as pewter spoons and ivory combs are sometimes believed to have pertained to the Byzantine liturgy, but for no good reason. All these objects are signs of an on-going trade with the East but offer no evidence for any political or religious influence. A sign of warning for these farfetched theories is a bronze figure of the Buddha from the seventh century, which was found on an island in the Mälar lake, not far from its commercial centre in Birka. This is of course not an indication of Buddhist influence in this area.

Of far more interest are the intriguing remains of wall-paintings in the twelfth century churches of Källunge and Garda on Gotland, and possibly in some other churches on the island. They have obviously been done by Russian artists and are dated to the end of the twelfth century. In particular, two figures of saints in Byzantine style in the church of Garda (possibly the martyr princes Boris and Gleb) have been well preserved. From the fifteenth century there is some evidence of Russian churches on the island, and a ruin of one of these has been partly preserved in the city of Visby. These churches were obviously used by Russian tradesmen. There has thus been a certain presence of Russians on Gotland, but there is no sign of a Russian mission or of a more profound cultural influence.

Christianity and European culture reached Scandinavia via Hamburg and Bremen, originating in the ninth century with the mission of St. Ansgar. Denmark,

Norway and Iceland were the first countries to be reached by Christianity, followed by Sweden (including Finland). During the period of Danish hegemony in England (under the reign of Svein Forkbeard and Canute the Great) there was a strong English mission in the North, which has also left traces in Scandinavian liturgy and art. There was, however, no corresponding Eastern influence in the same region during this period.

Some of the Swedish runic inscriptions mention Scandinavian expeditions to the East. Quite a number of these refer to a certain Ingvar, who was the leader of such an expedition, which may have penetrated as far as Georgia. On the other hand, there is no evidence of a Byzantine influence in the Scandinavian runic inscriptions. Some formulas have been believed to be of Eastern origin, but I think I have myself demonstrated convincingly that these formulas are by no means Byzantine but are reminiscent of the Latin liturgy for the dead, and are thus connected with the Western mission. The references to 'light and paradise' thus refer to the formulas *lux perpetua luceat eis*, at the beginning of the requiem Mass, and *in paradisum deducant te angeli* at the end of the liturgy. As far as I can judge, this view has been accepted by most Swedish scholars. The expression 'Mother of God' in some inscriptions is not an exclusively Byzantine title, but is known from England and Frisia as a translation of Latin *Dei Genetrix*. There are no written texts, runic or Latin, which refer to Byzantine Christianity. Some crosses on rune-stones may have been inspired by Byzantine pendant crosses, which must have existed in great numbers.

There are some obvious Byzantine elements in Scandinavian art during the period of Christianisation, especially on baptismal fonts. One of the font-masters has even been given the modern name of Byzantius. But these influences have not reached Scandinavia over the Baltic. From about the year 1000 there was a strong Byzantine influence in the German Empire, due to the Empress Theophanou, the Greek consort of the Emperor Otto II. These impulses spread northward and are to be seen also in Scandinavian art.

But the question of Byzantine influence remains, especially when we turn to the east coast of the Baltic, to Finland, Estonia and Latvia. (Lithuania was always strongly connected with Poland.) Already in the Viking age, a Swedish-speaking population was established in the south-west of Finland and had strong connections with Sweden. Danish and Swedish Vikings used to ravage the Baltic coast, enterprises which were renamed as crusades, as Christianity prevailed. Thus Finland was incorporated into Sweden, and Estonia became a Danish province.

Let us also keep in mind that the southern shore of the Baltic was not in the hands of the Germans in the eleventh century. South-east of the Danish border was a little tip of Saxony, delimited by the *Limes Saxoniae*, the border of the Slavonic lands. The coast further east was populated by Slavonic and Baltic tribes (to which also the Old Prussians belonged). There was a constant German pressure towards the Baltic, which had its first success when Count Henry the Lion re-founded Lübeck in 1159. Later on the German knights penetrated along the coast all the way up to Latvia, and finally even Estonia came under German rule.

Thus this whole area received Western European culture and was connected to the Western Church.

All the problems I have mentioned here were the subject of a conference in Kiel in 1994 with scholars from the entire Baltic region. It resulted in two substantial volumes in German and English with the title *Rom und Byzanz im Norden*, edited by Professor Michael Müller-Wille. The question of Western and Byzantine influence is discussed in all its aspects – archaeological, epigraphical and historical, including such matters as burial customs. The two volumes are now the current reference work on this subject and should be studied by any one with an interest in the Christianisation of the North.

Some of the suggested proofs of a Byzantine influence in fact dissolved into thin air. One of these is the case of Bishop Osmund. According to Adam of Bremen, Osmund was an Englishman, who came to Norway and then to Sweden as a missionary. After studies in Bremen he went to Rome in order to be consecrated bishop but failed. Instead he turned to 'a Polanian archbishop', in all likelihood the Polish archbishop of Gniezno, who consecrated him. For some time he was bishop at the court of Emund, the third Christian king of Sweden, but without the consent of Bremen and therefore frowned upon by Adam. According to the *Liber Eliensis*, a collection of privileges from the Abbey of Ely, he returned to England and stayed at the court of Edward the Confessor. There is a monument to him in Ely Cathedral. Osmund's life-story gives a good impression of the mobile and sometimes chaotic life of the missionaries during the eleventh century but seems to have taken place entirely within the Western Church. It is true that the population around Kiev were also called Polanians ('plainsfolk'), but the Metropolitan of Kiev Rus' would hardly have been mentioned in such terms, and the idea that Osmund had been consecrated by him is most unlikely. His adventure in Gniezno rather reminds us of the importance of Poland in the Baltic region, which tends to be generally overlooked.

For the same reason the hypothesis of an Eastern influence as far west as Iceland is equally suspect. In Ari Thorgilsson's *Islendingabók*, some of the bishops mentioned are said to have been *ermsker*, and these are also mentioned in the old Icelandic law-book, the *Grágás*. Already in 1874 the theory was put forward that these bishops may have been Armenians, and this fairly wild guess sometimes appears also in modern literature. More reasonable is the opinion that they came from Ermland on the Pomeranian coast, which had many contacts with Scandinavia. Also these bishops seem to have belonged to the Western, not to the Eastern Church.

A third hypothesis, that the Swedish rune-master Öpir should be identified with a certain priest Upir in Novgorod is too weak to need discussion. It would only make sense if we really knew anything about Russian activity in Sweden at that time, which is not the case.

Far more interesting is the undeniable presence of some Russian loan-words in early Finnish and Estonian. They are words such as Finnish *raamattu*, 'Bible', from Russian *gramota* (= Greek *grammata*), *risti*, 'cross' from Old Russian *krestu*, and *pappi*, 'priest', from Old Russian *popu*. Is this an indication of an Eastern influence, perhaps of a Russian mission around the Gulf of Finland? Impressive as this idea may seem, there might be a different explanation for these loan-words. The Estonian scholar Enn Tarve has studied the evidence and has come to the conclusion that these words may be given various explanations. They have partly been transmitted by Germans and thus point to the West rather than the East. In any case they are not the result of a Russian mission, although there were of course contacts with the Russian Church. The rulers in Novgorod subdued some Finnish and Baltic tribes and took tributes from them, but they showed no interest in converting them to Christianity. The Russian empire was in its period of formation, with Novgorod as its new centre in the north, and they had no time for cultural or religious expansion into other areas than their own.

The schism of 1054 between Rome and Constantinople, however, seems to have been of little importance in the North. It is not mentioned even in the *Nestor Chronicle*, which was written in Kiev and was far more closely related to the Byzantine Empire. There is no reason to believe in a power struggle here between the Eastern and the Western Church, as the latter was always in full control of the mission, and the former played no active role. Byzantine saints in the churches of Gotland may have looked unfamiliar but were by no means unacceptable.

The outcome of this survey thus seems fairly negative. Byzantine and Russian contacts with the Baltic seem to have been entirely connected with warriors and trade. Only in the post-Reformation period was there a more vivid encounter between East and West in the Baltic region.

References

RUBIN = Michael Müller-Wille (ed.), *Rom und Byzanz im Norden: Mission und Glaubenswechsel im Ostseeraum während des 8.-14. Jahrhunderts* 1-2, Mainz & Stuttgart 1997–98.

Beskow, Per, 'Runor och liturgi', Per Beskow and Reinhart Staats, *Nordens kristnande i europeiskt perspektiv*, Skara 1994, pp. 16–36.

—— 'Runes, Liturgy and Eschatology', Ingmar Brohed (ed.), *Church and People in Britain and Scandinavia*, Lund 1996, pp. 77–89.

Cutler, Anthony, 'Garda, Källunge and the Byzantine tradition of Gotland', *Art Bulletin* 51 (1969), pp. 257–66.

Duczko, Wladyslaw, 'Byzantine Presence in Viking Age Sweden', *RUBIN* 1, pp. 291–311.

Gustafsson, Berndt, 'Osmundus episcopus a Suedia', *Kyrkohistorisk Årsskrift* 50 (1959), pp. 138–45.

Horn Fuglesang, Signe, 'A Critical Survey on Theories on Byzantine Influence in Scandinavia', *RUBIN* 1, pp. 35–58.

Lárusson, M. Már, 'On the so-called Armenian bishops', *Studia Islandica* 18 (1960), pp. 23–38.

Müller-Wille, Michael, 'Relations between Byzantium and the North in the Light of Archaeology', *RUBIN* 1, pp. 405–22.

Roslund, Mats, 'Brosamen vom Tisch der Reichen: Byzantinische Funden aus Lund und Sigtuna (ca 980–1250)', *RUBIN* 2, pp. 325–88.

Tarvel, Enn, 'Mission und Glaubenswechsel in Estland und Livland im 11.-13. Jahrhundert aufgrund sprachlicher Quellen', *RUBIN* 2, pp. 57–67.

36

St Botulph: An English
Saint in Scandinavia

JOHN TOY

Many English saints were commemorated in Scandinavia, but one – St Botulph from East Anglia – stands out. He survives in the liturgy and dedications of three countries, Norway, Sweden and Denmark, and during the Middle Ages was as well known there as in his homeland. Even after the reformation Botulph remained in the Scandinavian folk memory. In this chapter I summarise the evidence and ask what was significant about this link with England for the conversion period further north (see also Lager, Chapter 31 in this volume).

Botulph appears in history as the founder of a monastery in East Anglia in AD 654, at Icanhoe, now generally agreed as identifiable with Iken near Aldeburgh in Suffolk. Recent archaeological work there has suggested a seventh century use of the site, and part of a late ninth/early tenth-century cross-shaft was discovered built into the base of the church tower (Fig. 36.1). The monastery perished in the Viking invasions but by the tenth century Botulph relics were preserved at Thorney, Bury St Edmunds and Westminster. In the eleventh century his life was written by Folcard.[1] Botulph was thus a seventh-century saint who was enjoying a revival in the tenth–eleventh century.

During the Middle Ages 64 churches were under his patronage, most, apart from some overspill to the south-east, in just those parts of England most influenced by Viking settlement. His feast day, 17 June, was observed in many places in Medieval England, but with high grades only in East Anglia. The observance died out when it was excluded from the Sarum tradition which came to dominate the liturgy in later medieval England.

Details of the cult of St Botulph in the Nordic lands are summarised in Oloph Odenius' article in the the *Kulturhistoriskt Lexicon för Nordisk Medeltid*.[2]

---

[1] *Historia Abbatum Auctore Anonymo* (ed. C. Plummer), 4, 372. The Anglo-Saxon Chronicle gives the date 654 for the foundation. For the archaeology, S.E. West, N. Scarfe and R. Cramp 'Iken, St Botulph and the coming of East Anglian Christianity' *Proc. of the Suffolk Inst of Archaeology* 35 (1984) (iv), 279–301; summary in P. Warner *The Origins of Suffolk* (Manchester University Press), 114–15, 142.

[2] *KHLNM* II, cols 190–192.

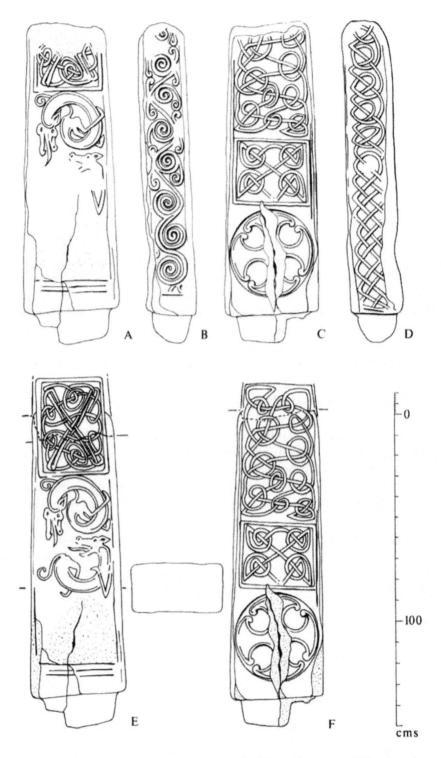

Figure 36.1 Late ninth-/early tenth-century cross shaft from the tower of Iken church

Twelve churches are known to have been under his patronage: in Denmark, these are Alborg, Viborg, Roskilde, Lund, Tirstrup, Tømmerby, Ängelholm (Luntertun) and Bodilisker on Bornholm; in Norway, Slagn and Ignabakke; and in Sweden Kråkerum and Gränna. Two bell inscriptions (one using a text from the Proper Office, see below), a Botulph Guild, Botulf fairs and market days are also known. There seem to have been relics in Broddetorp, since the golden altar has an inscription about the relics of three saints, the third being Botulph. The inscription is now illegible to the naked eye, although it could be recovered under infra-red light. There are representations of Botulph in all three countries, the earliest being the painting from Ardal, Sogn. The personal name of 'Botulf' appears from the thirteenth century in Norway, Sweden and Gotland.

Many thousands of medieval manuscript fragments are preserved in Oslo, Copenhagen, Stockholm and Helsinki. The majority are in the Riksarkivet in Stockholm, an estimated 20,000. Since cataloguing is still in progress what follows can only be an interim report, yet the evidence already available is impressive. Virtually all the known **kalendars** that have a June page show Botulph on 17 June. Sixty-nine examples are known already, 26 of which give him a high grade, at dates all through the Middle Ages up to the Reformation. All the Nordic dioceses are represented. Five fragments date to the twelfth century[3] and sixteen from the thirteenth century. Two other kalendars of twelfth-century date, including the well-known Vallentuna Kalendar of 1198, have Botulph added in the fourteenth century, showing a desire to commemorate him even when he is not in the kalendar the community has inherited.[4] The remaining kalendars featuring Botulph are later medieval and he appears in all the printed kalendars on the eve of the reformation except at Åbo, where 17 June was reserved for the consecration feast of the cathedral. The printed kalendars with high grades are those for Lund, Copenhagen, Roskilde, Aarhus, Odense, Slesvig, Uppsala, Linköping, Skara and Strängnäs; only Viborg, Nidaros and Vesterås have him as a simple feast.

The available **litanies** mostly show Botulph among the confessors. When we turn to the **missals**, we are faced with a large number of fragments from Sweden and few from Denmark and Norway. Forty-six fragments contain Botulph masses, only one of which is Danish, and none is Norwegian, although a Botulph mass is given in the *Ordo* as reconstructed by Lilli Gjerløw.[5] Many variants of the Collects, Secret and Postcommunion prayers are represented and the majority have the usual English one which almost certainly originated in East Anglia where the Botulph cult began.[6] All the printed missals have Botulph masses,

---

[3] KB Copenhagen, Thott 143 2° ; RA Oslo Kal 12; RA Stockholm CF Kal 14, CF Seq 88; UB Lund med ms 6.

[4] Toni Schmid *Liber Ecclesiae Vallentunensis* Stockholm 1945, Plate XLVI; Staffan Helmfrid (ed.) *Valentuna Anno Domini* 1198 (Valentuna, 1998) plate f 29v.

[5] Lilli Gjerløw *Ordo Nidrosiensis Ecclesiae* Oslo 1968, 351ff.

[6] The collect beginning *Deus omnium regnorum gubernator et rector* . . . ; the Secret beginning *Munus tibi a devotis oblatum* . . . ; and the Postcommunion beginning *Celestibus pasti dapibus.* . . .

except those of Åbo and Odense, but the omission at Odense is probably an error, since the Odense Breviary has an office for him.

It is the **Breviary** material which is the most abundant and indeed the most important; Scandinavia provides the only witness to a Proper Office of Botulph (unknown in Britain) and to some previously unknown hymns and antiphons with their musical notation. This signals the importance of this evidence for the study of the medieval liturgy in general. The normal English *Vita*[7] used for lections in Botulph's office is represented in sixteen out of 40 fragments and in seven out of eleven printed breviaries. We know from English sources that this *Vita* was issued, if not written, by Folcard, Abbot of Thorney in 1070, and its text copied there and at Bury St Edmunds.[8]

An interesting feature of many of the Scandinavian fragments is that their texts omit reference to St Adulph or Jermin (Germin) whose relics were with St Botulph's from the eleventh century at St Edmundsbury (Bury St Edmunds). Folcard may therefore have inserted Adulph into an earlier text he was editing, as was suggested by D.F. Wilkinson in 1961.[9] This might imply that an earlier Life of Botulph was known at least in Scandinavia.

Another *Vita* was until recently only known from the printed Schleswig Breviary whence it was reproduced by the Bollandists.[10] Wilkinson and F.S. Stevenson have both suggested it was composed in Denmark,[11] but examples have already turned up in five earlier Scandinavian fragments and a fourteenth-century Breviary, probably from the Augustinian house at Ebelholt in North Zealand.[12] Here, following a Collect taken from the Common, we have four of the six lections identical to that of the Schleswig Breviary. Of the other four manuscript fragments, two are from Sweden, one now in Helsinki (so possibly also Swedish) and the other now in Copenhagen.[13] The other printed breviaries that have this *Vita* are Aarhus, Uppsala and Linköping. This means that although the theory that this *Vita* was composed in Scandinavia still holds, there is no longer evidence to fix it to Denmark.

Still more interesting for liturgical scholars are three manuscripts, one of which contains a hitherto unknown Proper Office for St Botulph and two early Antiphonaries with musical notation. We start with the complete text as known from a Lund breviary of 1470 called *Hans Svenssen's Breviary*, now in Uppsala.[14]

---

[7] AASS [*Acta Sanctorum*] June III, 402ff.

[8] See note 1 above.

[9] D.F. Wilkinson 'The Life of Botulph' *Studia Patristica* IV, Berlin, 1961. Mabillon thought the Life in AASS June III, 402 was earlier than the tenth-century translation of Botulph's relics, which it does not mention (Plummer, *op. cit.* 372).

[10] AASS June III, 404ff.

[11] Wilkinson, *ibid.*; F.S. Stevenson 'St Botulph and Iken' *Proc. of the Suffolk Institute of Archaeology* 18.1 (1922), 29–52.

[12] Manchester Public Libraries Ms F 091 F9.

[13] KB Copenhagen NKS 54 8° ; UB Helsinki Lec III frag 51; KB Stockholm A 50; UB Uppsala C 507.

[14] UB Uppsala C 447.

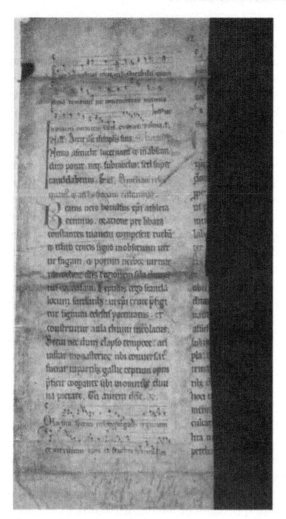

Plate 36.1 Part of an office of St Botulph showing two hitherto unknown antiphons with musical notation. In a twelfth-century breviary from Sweden (BL Add. Ms. 34388 f 52r) (By permission of the British Library)

Included here are six antiphons followed by the Collect, an Invitorium and then three antiphons for the first nocturn, three lections from Folcard's *Vita* with their versicles and responses. The second text is the early twelfth-century Antiphonary from Sweden in which the Office begins with the Responsorium *O claritas gremina* and continues with only the last antiphon of the full office as known later, the Antiphon beginning *Germinaverunt campi heremi*, and then the Invitorium *Sanctorum domino jubilem*. This is followed by all the antiphons for the first nocturn, at which point it ends.[15]

Of an equally early date is a twelfth-century breviary from Sweden now in the British Library[16] (Pl. 36.1). The fragment begins with an antiphon at the beginning

---

[15] RA Stockholm CF Ant 86. Published by Toni Schmid in 'Problemata' *Fornvännen* 58 (1963): 182–4
[16] BL London Add ms 34388.

of the third nocturn *Erat hec vastitas*, and continues with a gospel passage from Luke 11:33, the second lection from Folcard, the antiphon *Quesitas species*, the eighth lection and continuing fragmentarily on the other side with some antiphons and the ninth lection. These three witnesses to the complete Proper Office of Botulph are crucially important, and the early date of the two Swedish fragments shows that the texts came over with a first flush of English influence near the time of the institutional conversion (see Lager, Chapter 31 and Welinder, Chapter 32 in this volume).

How then do we explain the virtually universal cult in Scandinavia of this only moderately known Anglo-Saxon saint and his continuing commemoration? I suggest there are four factors at work here. The first must be a close connection with the conversions that were taking place in Scandinavia in the tenth–eleventh century. The implication is that missals and breviaries, and possibly clerics, were brought from Eastern England, and East Anglia in particular, and spread to every part of Scandinavia in the eleventh–twelfth century.

Subsequently the popularity of Botulph may have been maintained or developed due to his association with seafaring, and thus with traders who plied their trade over the North Sea. Several churches dedicated to St Botulph are located in market places and on quay-sides.[17] Yet this could not be the whole explanation as other Botulph churches do not have such locations.

In the later middle ages, Botulph might have found favour in Scandinavia due to the season in which his feast day fell. The approach of mid-summer was an appropriate time for planting root crops, and in parts of Sweden Botulph was known as *rov grubben* 'the turnip chap'.[18] These factors will surely help to explain the occurrence long after the Reformation of the boy's name and the Botulph Fairs that took place in several towns until the eighteenth century.[19] These commemorations were no longer cultic since they had a social, not a liturgical function. But the phenomenon of St Botulph in Scandinavia is one of the most enduring signs of the English role in the Christianising process in the Nordic lands.

[17] Richard Morris *Churches in the Landscape* London 1989; 217–19.
[18] G. Lindberg *Kyrkans Heliga År* Stockholm 1937, 313.
[19] N. Staf *Marknad och Möten* Stockholm 1935.

37

Christianisation in Estonia:
A Process of Dual-Faith
and Syncretism

HEIKI VALK

Introduction: Historical Background

When compared with centres of innovation and their surroundings, cultural processes have a slower course and longer duration in peripheries. This general rule is valid also for the Eastern Baltic: Estonia, Latvia and Lithuania, the eastern peripheral region of Western Christianity on the border of the Orthodox world. Even as late as at the turn of the twelfth and thirteenth centuries the lands east of the Baltic Sea formed a pagan area between the Catholic West and the Orthodox East. Apart from the Saamis in Northern Fennoscandia and the Finno-Ugric peoples within Russia, the Eastern Baltic territories formed the last pagan region of Europe.

Estonia was Christianised by German and Danish crusaders in course of the violent conquest in 1208–1227, described in the Chronicle of Livonia, written by the missionary priest Henry/Henricus (*HCL*). Orthodox cross-pendants, certain changes in burial customs such as transition to west- orientation and the appearance of graves with no major grave goods indicate that there was some infiltration of Christian ideas and beliefs into Estonia before this time (Selirand 1979). But Christian structures, common for Western Europe, and a Christian society, arrived only after the conquest.

The Christianisation of Estonia meant introducing the ecclesiastical and political structures of Medieval Europe and caused great changes in society. As a result of the conquest the local elite lost its position. The historical landscape of Medieval and Post-medieval Estonia is characterised by a strong ethnosocial polarisation of society (Johansen 1963): on the one hand, the native, Estonian-speaking lower strata, and on the other, the German-speaking upper classes, including the clergy. The social status of a person was directly determined by their language: serfdom and labour-duty on manor fields were clearly connected with the native, 'non-German' ethnic background, while a precondition for belonging to the higher social strata was being 'German'. This system of apartheid and ethnosocial segregation lasted until the early nineteenth century when serfdom was abolished. The conservative social system of medieval origin also caused the preservation of the medieval way of life and mentality. Only the great innovations of the nineteenth century – replacing serfdom by private farming and market economy, school education, newspapers in the local languages and the national awakening of the mid-nineteenth century – caused changes in thinking and mentality, designating a transition from 'the long Middle Ages' to modern society.

Against such historical background, what was the religious situation in medieval and post-medieval Estonia? How far and in which way was Christianity accepted and which were the main features of conversion? Although the power of the God, first perceived as the god of the Christians (*HCL* XIV: 11; XXIII: 9), was recognised, the acceptance of Christianity did not necessarily mean neglecting former beliefs. The largest study of Estonian popular religion (Loorits 1949, 1951, 1957) goes so far as to describe religious practice in the Christian Period as *predominantly* of pre-Christian character, with only some influences of Christian origin. Thus, formal Christianisation did not bring individual intellectual conversion but the beginning of a long period of dual-faith and syncretism. As the medieval mind endured as a result of the long existence of the medieval social system partly until the time of folklore-collecting in the late nineteenth century, the study of popular mentality of the Christian period is favoured by rich source material in Estonia. Folkloric information on the nineteenth and the twentieth centuries can be combined with archaeological data – excavation results and sites of religious meaning in the landscape.

Sacred and Sacrificial Sites

The syncretism and dual-faith of medieval and post-medieval times is reflected in different contexts. Most clearly it is expressed in the co-existence of a large number of holy sites of different character, some ostensibly Christian, some not, some semi-Christian, over which religious activities were spread. As a result of Christianisation, Estonia became covered with a network of parish **churches** and consecrated cemeteries. The churches served as religious centres at parish level. According to written data, big popular meetings and offerings at churches occurred on holidays (*LUB* VII, 690:19; Westrén-Doll 1926; Kõpp 1959, 217–31).

Beside churches an important role in popular religion belonged to numerous local **chapels**. Data about them exist from 1428: the decisions of the Provincial Council of Riga complain about popular superstitious offerings at chapels with the statues of St Anthony and other saints. It is mentioned that chapels built without ecclesiastical permission must be destroyed within one year (*LUB* VII, 690: 29). According to archaeological data, coin offerings at chapels begin in the late fourteenth century. Their number increased after the mid-fifteenth century and most of the finds come from the second half of the sixteenth and seventeenth centuries. Popular cults connected with chapels at saints' days, far from real

Christian ceremonies, lasted, in spite of the Lutheranisation of the country and violent activities of the Lutheran Church against chapels, until the late seventeenth and even in the eighteenth centuries (Kõpp 1959, 217–231; Westrén-Doll 1926). Evidently, the chapels and related cult activities represent a syncretic mixture of popular Catholicism and pre-Christian beliefs.

Parallel to churches and chapels there co-existed also a third group of holy sites – **sacred natural sites** of non-Christian character. These sites preserved their importance as offering and healing places until the nineteenth century. Due to the lateness of the great mentality change, holy sites in nature and attached beliefs are well remembered in oral tradition. Holy groves and trees connected with offering are reflected in folkloric data all over Estonia. In northern and western Estonia a sacred grove, known as a *hiis*, which often included a holy stone or spring, was located at many of the medieval villages. The *hiis*-sites were sanctuaries with a communal background. Concerning these sites there sometimes exist faint memories of ritual dancing and collective cult practices in folklore collections. In southern Estonia predominantly single-standing holy trees were worshipped.

The number of holy or offering stones is a little more than 400 in Estonia (Tvauri 1999, 53). They are situated in settled areas, not far from farms and villages. Most of the holy, healing or offering stones are natural granite boulders without any specific features referring to their special meaning. Only a small number of the offering stones have big man-made cup-marks with a diameter of 15–20 cm. In northern and western Estonia also some 10% of the stones with small cup-marks (diameter 5–8 cm) from the Pre-Roman or Roman Iron Age – such is the Estonian dating for cup-marks (Tvauri 1997, 38–41) – were used for offerings. However, it is likely that medieval practice was not based on continuity of tradition from the Iron Age but is of secondary origin.

Holy springs, mostly used for healing eye and skin diseases, are also represented with no fewer than 416 sites (Tamla 1985). While trees, groves and stones are often related with offering of a higher level, i.e. for more general purposes, springs are mostly connected with healing. Especially in southern Estonia (Mulgimaa district) there existed at older farms offering gardens – small holy areas surrounded with a fence, without any visibly specific characteristics (Loorits 1935). These sites were taboo areas which were visited only for offering purposes. Offering small items, e.g. money, food, clothing and ribbons to the holy sites in nature is repeatedly remembered in oral tradition. Often 'the new' or 'the first' is mentioned as a gift.

Among the sacred sites it is possible to distinguish two subgroups with different purposes. The first group has a general meaning both at communal (farm, village, area) and individual level: they can grant luck, success and welfare, as well as protection against misfortune. Such functions of holy places, especially those of communal background (e.g. *hiis*-places) are still reflected in the oral tradition rather weakly and mostly in general terms. Holy sites of general meaning might also have a healing function. Several *hiis*-sites are known in oral tradition only as healing places: evidently, the lowest of their former several functions has survived for a longer time.

The second group of sites includes those used only for personal healing purposes. Such sites – trees, stones and springs – are numerous in western Estonia. While there exist only faint memories of offering-places of communal and general character, healing is more strongly reflected in the oral tradition. The healing objects – stones, groves, springs and trees – provided help mostly against skin diseases, abscesses, scabs or aching. As method of healing, often transfer magic was used: the aching place was pressed against the healing object, or items which had been in contact with it were offered. Spring water was used either by drinking or washing. Healing was connected with making a small gift: a means for creating the connection between man and the supernatural. Healing at holy natural objects persisted longer than cult activities of a more general character. In western Estonia corresponding practices lasted widely into the 1920s and 1930s. Evidently, the higher cult was expelled much earlier by the Church and Christianity than that practised at the lowest, personal level.

Popular relations with sacred sites of the higher and the lower status seem to have differed greatly. High-status sacred sites were subject to agreements detailing mutual responsibilities; making offerings was a duty and neglecting the site might bring about supernatural punishment. Local healing sites were less demanding; oral tradition expresses no need for permanent contact or communication. These sites were visited in cases of emergency and there are no indications that there were penalties for neglecting them. Holy sites of higher level seem to be more subject to taboos and the consequences of destroying or damaging them were supposed to be accidents, diseases and even death. Cautionary tales of this character survive from the nineteenth century when some people still worshipped the sacred sites and others no longer did.

A big difference seems to exist also in the meaning of holy sites of different religious background. Non-Christian sites, i.e. holy natural objects, are reflected in oral tradition much more vividly than the chapel sites; their perceived sacredness is reflected in stories of taboos and sacrilege. The sacredness of the chapel sites, although high according to the written data in the Late Catholic Period, is not reflected in folkloric data. Although in 1627 each peasant in the whole district of Tartu is mentioned as having a private chapel for worshipping his saint (Kõpp 1959, 86), most of the chapels seem to have been totally forgotten by the time folklore was collected. In oral tradition, the sites of former chapels are mostly known only at the level of toponyms. If narrative information exists, it is merely of historical character (popular dating; causes or method of disappearance). Thus sites of older origin and longer use show a greater resistance to time, while sites taken into use more recently tended to disappear more quickly. It must also be noted that in Estonia sacred natural sites, i.e. boulders, springs and trees, are almost never coincident with Christian sites. Nor are they associated with saint's legends, saints' names or toponyms referring to chapels. The situation is, however, somewhat different in the Orthodox Setomaa region in the south-eastern corner of Estonia: there contamination of sacred sites by the Christian cult can be observed.

Cemeteries and Burial Customs

Beside offering places, religious syncretism of the Christian period is also expressed in cemeteries and burial customs. In this field, as a specific feature of Medieval and Post-Medieval Period, the tradition of **village cemeteries** is important. In Estonia (also Latvia and Lithuania) as well as churchyards there existed numerous local burial grounds of semi-Christian character (Valk 2001). These cemeteries lie usually at a distance of 4–10 km from each other. Parish churches, towns and manors did not influence the density of their network. The village cemeteries were extensively used in parallel to churchyards until the late seventeenth – early eighteenth centuries.

In the Catholic period, the village cemeteries were often associated with small chapels and many of them probably had a semi-legal or legal status (Valk 1995). In the Lutheran Period burying there was prohibited: in North Estonia in the late sixteenth century, in southern Estonia from the 1630s. In spite of that their usage still lasted a further three or four more generations. For example, in Rõuge parish, southern Estonia, in 1660–1696 only 27–32% of the dead were buried in churchyards (Palli 1973, 82). Estonian oral tradition reflects the holiness of all burial grounds – both churchyards and newer Christian parish cemeteries, as well as the village cemeteries. According to folkloric data their sacredness does not arise from consecration but from the dead buried there.

Pre-Christian traditions also continued in Estonia in the Christian Period in **burial customs** (Valk 2001, 60–86). Christianisation in the thirteenth century caused big changes in rural burial traditions: cremation graves almost disappeared and graves with large grave goods (weapons, tools and clay vessels) were generally superseded by poorly furnished west-oriented graves. But such changes were not universal. Cremation continued locally in southern Estonia until the sixteenth century. Small grave goods (coins, knives, needles) were preserved and the dead were not buried naked, wrapped in a shroud, but in a burial costume furnished with some ornaments (brooches, rings, necklaces). This syncretist practice endured from Christianisation in the thirteenth century until the nineteenth century. The custom of grave goods in peripheral rural regions in Estonia has survived even today: the dead are provided with coins, a needle or vodka; sometimes with explanations that these will be needed in the other world.

Syncretism in Beliefs and Ritual Communication

Syncretism is reflected also in the way that people attempted ritual communication with deities. First, the parallel worship of **spiritual beings of different religious background** can be observed. Evidently, the authority and power of God in the Christian sense was accepted soon after the conquest. Data from chapels and coin finds give evidence about the cult of saints since the fifteenth century. According to written sources the cult of saints was deeply rooted in popular religion in the Late Catholic Period and the seventeenth century (Kõpp 1959; Westrén-Doll 1926). In addition, however, trust in powers of non-Christian origin persisted. Thunder was worshipped by the peasants in the Middle Ages and there exist data of a Thunder priest even from the 1644. Folkloric data also give evidence of the cult of a god in some way related to Scandinavian Tor (*taara, tooru, toari, tuuri* etc.). The same is also reflected in the holiness of Thursday. Work on Thursday evenings was locally prohibited in Estonian villages even in the early twentieth century.

Most of the higher pre-Christian deities had been forgotten by the time of folklore-collecting – an exception is the fertility and welfare god Peko in the Orthodox Setomaa region in south-east Estonia, whose collective mysterium-like sermons were held until the early 1930s (Loorits 1951, 100–6; Hagu 1975). But lower deities and fertility spirits had a great importance in popular religion until the second half of the nineteenth century. The luck of a household was connected with local spirits – these were worshipped in the form of dolls and images – and house snakes; both were provided with small gifts and offerings, mainly food. In addition, nature spirits inhabiting forests, wilderness and water bodies – creatures almost untouched by Christian influences – existed.

Contact was also kept with **the dead and the ancestors**. Communication with the dead occurred through ritual meals on the graves which took place at funerals, certain anniversaries after the death and on holidays. In Orthodox Setomaa eating on the graves has been preserved until the present time: on church holidays the cemeteries are filled with people who eat the best food and actively communicate on the graves (Fig. 37.1). These cemetery feasts are not connected with puritanical mourning and commemoration: a positive holiday spirit and even merriment predominate. According to written data from 1428 (*LUB* VII, 690: 19) and folkloric data, eating on the graves also occurred earlier in formerly Catholic, later Lutheran parts of Estonia.

In Estonian tradition the ancestors were also believed to visit their homes at Souls' Visiting Time between September and December: then the souls were given food and sauna was heated for them (Hiiemäe 1995). It was possible to meet the dead either as home-wanderers or in the form of insects or small animals – moths, bees, butterflies, flies, birds or frogs. The deceased may appear in dreams, predict the future and can even influence the life of the living. These beliefs have a common background: the dead are not dead in the real sense but continue their life in the other world, open for contacts under certain circumstances. The ancient concept of the cemetery differs from the modern one: it is not only a site for remembering or commemorating the dead but, first and foremost, their dwelling site and a place where communication is possible. Such ideas applied to not only the local village cemeteries but also the central Christian burial grounds.

Plate 37.1 Food on the grave. Obinitsa, Setomaa, 2001

Conclusions and Discussion

In Estonian popular religion, since the Christianisation of the thirteenth century three different belief systems and ideologies co-existed: Christian, local non-Christian and semi-Christian of mixed character. Their parallelism exists not only within the same communities and congregations but also at the level of the individual: it is possible to believe simultaneously in things and spiritual beings of different religious background. In fact, the same congregation members who visited churches on Sundays made offerings to holy stones and house spirits. In the parallelism of different beliefs the practical and pragmatic nature of popular religion, free from 'ideological ' limitations is expressed: help is help, no matter from which sources it came. The folkloric data of Estonia give evidence of a long preservation of pre-Christian beliefs within the framework of a syncretist ideology.

Syncretist mixture of beliefs was characteristic for Estonia not only throughout the Middle Ages but also much later. Religious changes within Christianity, expressed in the Reformation, did not cause changes in popular beliefs and mentality. Remains of the world view characteristic for the Catholic Period still existed 150–200 years after the Reformation: it was only the movement of the Moravian brothers from the 1720s–1730s which gave a strong impetus for a more profound conversion of Estonia and for the transition from a syncretist to a predominantly Christian system of beliefs. A continuity of traditions could be observed from pre-Christian times until the nineteenth–twentieth centuries and in peripheral rural regions ancient beliefs have even nowadays not totally disappeared. Especially strong is the persistence of old traditions in Orthodox Setomaa in the south-eastern corner of Estonia where a medieval way of life and mentality existed as a whole until the 1920s (Valk 1996).

Within the beliefs of non-Christian origin, the fall of higher deities can be noted as the most important change during the Middle Ages. Evidently, after Christianisation just the higher deities lost their position and abandoned it to God and the saints. Nevertheless, offering to lower deities and spirits occurred until the second half of the nineteenth century and healing at natural places lasted even longer. It is possible to speak of the spatial expansion of non-Christian cult sites in the Christian Period: holy stones, trees and groves also exist in villages of medieval or post-medieval origin. Burial customs have, however, preserved a conservative character the longest: when comparing archaeological data with folkloric ones, no major changes from the thirteenth century until the nineteenth century can be observed.

Ancient attitudes, beliefs and concepts also exist among modern populations and in some cases a continuous connection with pre-Christian traditions can be observed. Animistic approaches to things, using nature as a source of energy, and belief in contacts with the dead are still realities for many people, both in town and the countryside. The situation seems to reflect a general principle which was also expressed in the greater persistence of sacred natural sites as compared with Catholic chapels: archaic layers of beliefs and attitudes tend to survive longer than Christian ones of later origin.

ACKNOWLEDGEMENT

The research reported here was carried out with the assistance of a grant from the Estonian Science Foundation (No 4633).

References

HCL = *The Chronicle of Henry of Livonia*. A Translation with Introduction and Notes by James A. Brundage. Madison, 1961.

Hagu, P., 1975. Setu viljakusjumal Peko. *Keel ja Kirjandus*, 1975, 166–73.

Hiiemäe, M. 1995. Soul's Visiting Time in the Estonian Folk calendar. *Folk Belief Today*. Ed. by Mare Kõiva and Kai Vassiljeva. (Tartu), 124–9.

Johansen, P. 1963. Nationale Vorurteile und Minderwertigkeitsgefühl als sozialer Faktor im mittelalterlichen Livland. *Alteuropa und die moderne Gesellschaft. Festschrift für Otto Brunner*. Göttingen, 87–114.

Kõpp, J. 1959. *Kirik ja rahvas. Sugemeid eesti rahva vaimse palge kujunemise teelt*. Lund

Loorits O. 1935. Mulgimaa ohvrikohad. *Kaleviste mailt*. Õpetatud Eesti Seltsi Kirjad, III. Tartu, 225–300.

—— 1949, 1951, 1957 = O. Loorits, *Grundzüge des estnischen Volksglaubens*. Skrifter utgivna av kungl. Gustav Adolfs Akademien för folklivsforskning 18. Uppsala–Köpenhamn.

LUB = Liv-, Ehst- und Curländisches Urkundenbuch. Bd. VII. Riga, Moskau, 1881.

Palli, H. 1973. Rõuge rahvas XVII sajandi teisel poolel. – Ajaloolise demograafia probleeme Eestis. Tallinn, 63–131.

Selirand, J. 1979. Von der Verbreitung der ersten Elementen des Christentums bei den Esten. *Rapports du IIIe Congres International d'Archéologie Slave, Bratislava, 7–14 septembre 1975* (Bratislava 1979), 713–19.

Tamla, T. 1985. Kultuslikud allikad Eestis. Rahvasuust kirjapanekuni. Uurimusi rahvaluule proosaloomingust ja kogumisloost. Emakeele Seltsi Toimetised, 17. Tallinn, 122–46.

Tvauri, A. 1997. Eesti lohukivid. *Arheoloogilisi uurimusi*, 1. Tartu Ülikooli arheoloogia kabineti toimetised, 9. Tartu, 11–53.

—— 1999. Ohvrikividest. *Mäetagused*, 11. Hüperajakiri. Tartu, 34–57.

Valk, H., 1995. The Estonian Village Burial Grounds – Some Aspects of their Sanctification in the Catholic Period. *En Norrlandsbygd möter yttervärlden. Styresholmsprojektets medeltidssymposium på Hola Folkhögskola 2–28 juni 1992*. Härnösand, 1995, 55–61.

—— 1996. About the Field-Work in Setomaa. Results, Context and Background. *Palve, vanapatt ja pihlakas. Setomaa 1994. a kogumisretke tulemusi*. Vanavaravedaja, 4. Tartu, 289–92.

—— 2001. *Rural Cemeteries of Southern Estonia 1225–1800 AD*. 2nd edition. CCC Papers, 3. Visby–Tartu.

—— 2002. *The interrelations of Christian and non-Christian Holy Sites in medieval Estonia: a Reflection of ecclesiastical Attitudes towards Popular Religion*. CCC Papers, 9. Ed. J. Staecker. Lund. In print.

Westrén-Doll, A., 1926. Abgötterey zu Ausgang der schwedischen und Beginn der Russischen Zeit. *Sitzungsberichte der Gelehrten Estnischen Gesellschaft 1925*. Tartu (Dorpat), 7–25.

Index

Lightning Source UK Ltd.
Milton Keynes UK
UKOW07f1517170217

294680UK00003B/3/P